CHILTON'S
REPAIR & TUNE-UP GUIDE
MUSTANG   CAPRI
MERKUR
1979-85

All U.S. and Canadian models of FORD Mustang •
MERCURY Capri, Merkur

President LAWRENCE A. FORNASIERI
Vice President and General Manager JOHN P. KUSHNERICK
Executive Editor KERRY A. FREEMAN, S.A.E.
Senior Editor RICHARD J. RIVELE, S.A.E.

CHILTON BOOK COMPANY
Radnor, Pennsylvania
19089

TL
215
.M8
C49
1985

SAFETY NOTICE

Proper service and repair procedures are vital to the safe, reliable operation of all motor vehicles, as well as the personal safety of those performing repairs. This book outlines procedures for servicing and repairing vehicles using safe, effective methods. The procedures contain many NOTES, CAUTIONS and WARNINGS which should be followed along with standard safety procedures to eliminate the possibility of personal injury or improper service which could damage the vehicle or compromise its safety.

It is important to note that repair procedures and techniques, tools and parts for servicing motor vehicles, as well as the skill and experience of the individual performing the work vary widely. It is not possible to anticipate all of the conceivable ways or conditions under which vehicles may be serviced, or to provide cautions as to all of the possible hazards that may result. Standard and accepted safety precautions and equipment should be used when handling toxic or flammable fluids, and safety goggles or other protection should be used during cutting, grinding, chiseling, prying, or any other process that can cause material removal or projectiles.

Some procedures require the use of tools specially designed for a specific purpose. Before substituting another tool or procedure, you must be completely satisfied that neither your personal safety, nor the performance of the vehicle will be endangered.

Although information in this guide is based on industry sources and is as complete as possible at the time of publication, the possibility exists that the manufacturer made later changes which could not be included here. While striving for total accuracy, Chilton Book Company cannot assume responsibility for any errors, changes, or omissions that may occur in the compilation of this data.

PART NUMBERS

Part numbers listed in this reference are not recommendations by Chilton for any product by brand name. They are references that can be used with interchange manuals and aftermarket supplier catalogs to locate each brand supplier's discrete part number.

SPECIAL TOOLS

Special tools are recommended by the vehicle manufacturer to perform their specific job. Use has been kept to a minimum, but where absolutely necessary, they are referred to in the text by the part number of the tool manufacturer. These tools can be purchased, under the appropriate part number, from Owatonna Tool Company, Owatonna, MN 55060 or an equivalent tool can be purchased locally from a tool supplier or parts outlet. Before substituting any tool for the one recommended, read the SAFETY NOTICE at the top of this page.

ACKNOWLEDGMENTS

The Chilton Book Company expresses its appreciation to the Ford Motor Company, Dearborn, Michigan for their generous assistance.

Copyright © 1985 by Chilton Book Company
All Rights Reserved
Published in Radnor, Pennsylvania 19089 by Chilton Book Company

Manufactured in the United States of America
  234567890   432109876

Chilton's Repair & Tune-Up Guide: Mustang/Capri/Merkur 1979–85
ISBN 0-8019-7585-9 pbk.
Library of Congress Catalog Card No. 84-45470

CONTENTS

1 General Information and Maintenance
- **1** How to Use this Book
- **2** Tools and Equipment
- **7** Routine Maintenance and Lubrication

2 Tune-Up and Performance Maintenance
- **31** Tune-Up Procedures
- **32** Tune-Up Specifications

3 Engine and Engine Rebuilding
- **48** Engine Electrical System
- **53** Engine Service and Specifications

4 Emission Controls and Fuel System
- **102** Emission Control System and Service
- **110** Fuel System

5 Chassis Electrical
- **148** Heater and Accessory Service
- **161** Instrument Panel Service
- **163** Lights, Fuses and Flashers

6 Clutch and Transmission
- **167** Manual Transmission
- **170** Clutch
- **174** Automatic Transmission

7 Drive Train
- **179** Driveshaft and U-Joints
- **182** Rear Axle

8 Suspension and Steering
- **186** Front Suspension
- **192** Rear Suspension
- **196** Steering

9 Brakes
- **203** Brake Specifications
- **206** Front Brakes
- **211** Rear Brakes

10 Troubleshooting
- **224** Problem Diagnosis

258 Mechanic's Data
260 Index

124 Chilton's Fuel Economy and Tune-Up Tips

236 Chilton's Body Repair Tips

Quick Reference Specifications For Your Vehicle

Fill in this chart with the most commonly used specifications for your vehicle. Specifications can be found in Chapters 1 through 3 or on the tune-up decal under the hood of the vehicle.

Tune-Up

Firing Order_____

Spark Plugs:

  Type_____

  Gap (in.)_____

Point Gap (in.)_____

Dwell Angle (°)_____

Ignition Timing (°)_____

  Vacuum (Connected/Disconnected)_____

Valve Clearance (in.)

  Intake_____ Exhaust_____

Capacities

Engine Oil (qts)

  With Filter Change_____

  Without Filter Change_____

Cooling System (qts)_____

Manual Transmission (pts)_____

  Type_____

Automatic Transmission (pts)_____

  Type_____

Front Differential (pts)_____

  Type_____

Rear Differential (pts)_____

  Type_____

Transfer Case (pts)_____

  Type_____

FREQUENTLY REPLACED PARTS

Use these spaces to record the part numbers of frequently replaced parts.

PCV VALVE	OIL FILTER	AIR FILTER
Manufacturer_____	Manufacturer_____	Manufacturer_____
Part No._____	Part No._____	Part No._____

General Information and Maintenance

HOW TO USE THIS BOOK

Chilton's Repair & Tune-Up Guide is intended to help you learn more about the inner workings of your vehicle and save you money on its upkeep and operation.

The first two chapters will be the most used, since they contain maintenance and tune-up information and procedures. Studies have shown that a properly tuned and maintained car can get at least 10% better gas mileage than an out-of-tune car. The other chapters deal with the more complex systems of your car. Operating systems from engine through brakes are covered to the extent that the average do-it-yourselfer becomes mechanically involved. This book will not explain such things as rebuilding the differential for the simple reason that the expertise required and the investment in special tools make this task uneconomical. It will give you detailed instructions to help you change your own brake pads and shoes, replace plugs, and do many more jobs that will save you money, give you personal satisfaction, and help you avoid expensive problems.

A secondary purpose of this book is a reference for owners who want to understand their car and/or their mechanics better. In this case, no tools at all are required.

Before removing any bolts, read through the entire procedure. This will give you the overall view of what tools and supplies will be required. There is nothing more frustrating than having to walk to the bus stop on Monday morning because you were short one bolt on Sunday afternoon. So read ahead and plan ahead. Each operation should be approached logically and all procedures thoroughly understood before attempting any work.

All chapters contain adjustments, maintenance, removal and installation procedures, and repair or overhaul procedures. When repair is not considered practical, we tell you how to remove the part and then how to install the new or rebuilt replacement. In this way, you at least save the labor costs. Backyard repair of such components as the alternator is just not practical.

Two basic mechanic's rules should be mentioned here. One, whenever the left side of the car or engine is referred to, it is meant to specify the driver's side of the car. Conversely, right side of the car means the passenger's side. Secondly, most screws and bolts are removed by turning counterclockwise, and tightened by turning clockwise.

Safety is always the most important rule. Constantly be aware of the dangers involved in working on an automobile and take the proper precautions. (See the section in this chapter "Servicing Your Vehicle Safely" and the SAFETY NOTICE on the acknowledgement page.)

Pay attention to the instructions provided. There are 3 common mistakes in mechanical work:

1. Incorrect order of assembly, disassembly or adjustment. When taking something apart or putting it together, doing things in the wrong order usually just costs you extra time; however, it CAN break something. Read the entire procedure before beginning disassembly. Do everything in the order in which the instructions say you should do it, even if you can't immediately see a reason for it. When you're taking apart something that is very intricate (for example, a carburetor), you might want to draw a picture of how it looks when assembled at one point in order to make sure you get everything back in its proper position. (We will supply exploded view whenever possible.) When making adjustments, especially tune-up adjustments, do them in order; often, one adjustment affects another, and you cannot expect

2 GENERAL INFORMATION AND MAINTENANCE

even satisfactory results unless each adjustment is made only when it cannot be changed by any other.

2. Overtorquing (or undertorquing). While it is more common for overtorquing to cause damage, undertorquing can cause a fastener to vibrate loose, causing serious damage. Especially when dealing with aluminum parts, pay attention to torque specifications and utilize a torque wrench in assembly. If a torque figure is not available, remember that if you are using the right tool to do the job, you will probably not have to strain yourself to get a fastener tight enough. The pitch of most threads is so slight that the tension you put on the wrench will be multiplied many, many times in actual force on what you are tightening. A good example of how critical torque is can be seen in the case of spark plug installation, especially when you are putting the plug into an aluminum cylinder head. Too little torque can fail to crush the gasket, causing leakage of combustion gases and consequent overheating of the plug and engine parts. Too much torque can damage the threads, or distort the plug. which changes the spark gap.

There are many commercial products available for ensuring that fasteners won't come loose, even if they are not torqued just right (a very common brand is "Loctite®"). If you're worried about getting something together tight enough to hold, but loose enough to avoid mechanical damage during assembly, one of these products might offer substantial insurance. Read the label on the package and make sure the product is compatible with the materials, fluids, etc. involved before choosing one.

3. Crossthreading. This occurs when a part such as a bolt is screwed into a nut or casting at the wrong angle and forced. Cross threading is more likely to occur if access is difficult. It helps to clean and lubricate fasteners, and to start threading with the part to be installed going straight in. Then, start the bolt, spark plug, etc. with your fingers. If you encounter resistance, unscrew the part and start over again at a different angle until it can be inserted and turned several turns without much effort. Keep in mind that many parts, especially spark plugs, use tapered threads so that gentle turning will automatically bring the part you're threading to the proper angle if you don't force it or resist a change in angle. Don't put a wrench on the part until it's been turned a couple of turns by hand. If you suddenly encounter resistance, and the part has not seated fully, don't force it. Pull it back out and make sure it's clean and threading properly.

Always take your time and be patient; once you have some experience, working on your car will become an enjoyable hobby.

TOOLS AND EQUIPMENT

Naturally, without the proper tools and equipment it is impossible to properly service your vehicle. It would be impossible to catalog each tool that you would need to perform each or any operation in this book. It would also be unwise for the amateur to rush out and buy an expensive set of tools on the theory that he may need one or more of them at some time.

The best approach is to proceed slowly, gathering together a good quality set of those tools that are used most frequently. Don't be misled by the low cost of bargain tools. It is far better to spend a little more for better quality. Forged wrenches, 10 or 12 point sockets and fine tooth ratchets are by far preferable to their less expensive counterparts. As any good mechanic can tell you, there are few worse experiences than trying to work on a car or truck with bad tools. Your monetary savings will be far outweighed by frustration and mangled knuckles.

Begin accumulating those tools that are used most frequently: those associated with routine maintenance and tune-up.

In addition to the normal assortment of screwdrivers and pliers you should have the following tools for routine maintenance jobs:

1. SAE (or Metric) or SAE/Metric wrenches—sockets and combination open end/box end wrenches in sizes from ⅛ in. (3 mm) to ¾ in. (19 mm) and a spark plug socket (13/16 or ⅝ in. depending on plug type).

If possible, buy various length socket drive extensions. One break in this department is that the metric sockets available in the U.S. will all fit the ratchet handles and extensions you may already have (¼, ⅜, and ½ in. drive).

2. Jackstands—for support;
3. Oil filter wrench;
4. Oil filler spout—for pouring oil;
5. Grease gun—for chassis lubrication;
6. Hydrometer—for checking the battery;
7. A container for draining oil;
8. Many rags for wiping up the inevitable mess.

In addition to the above items there are several others that are not absolutely necessary, but handy to have around. These include oil dry, a transmission funnel and the usual supply of lubricants, antifreeze and fluids, although these can be purchased as needed. This is a basic list for routine maintenance, but only your personal needs and desire can accurately determine your list of tools.

The second list of tools is for tune-ups. While the tools involved here are slightly more sophisticated, they need not be outrageously expensive. There are several inexpensive

GENERAL INFORMATION AND MAINTENANCE 3

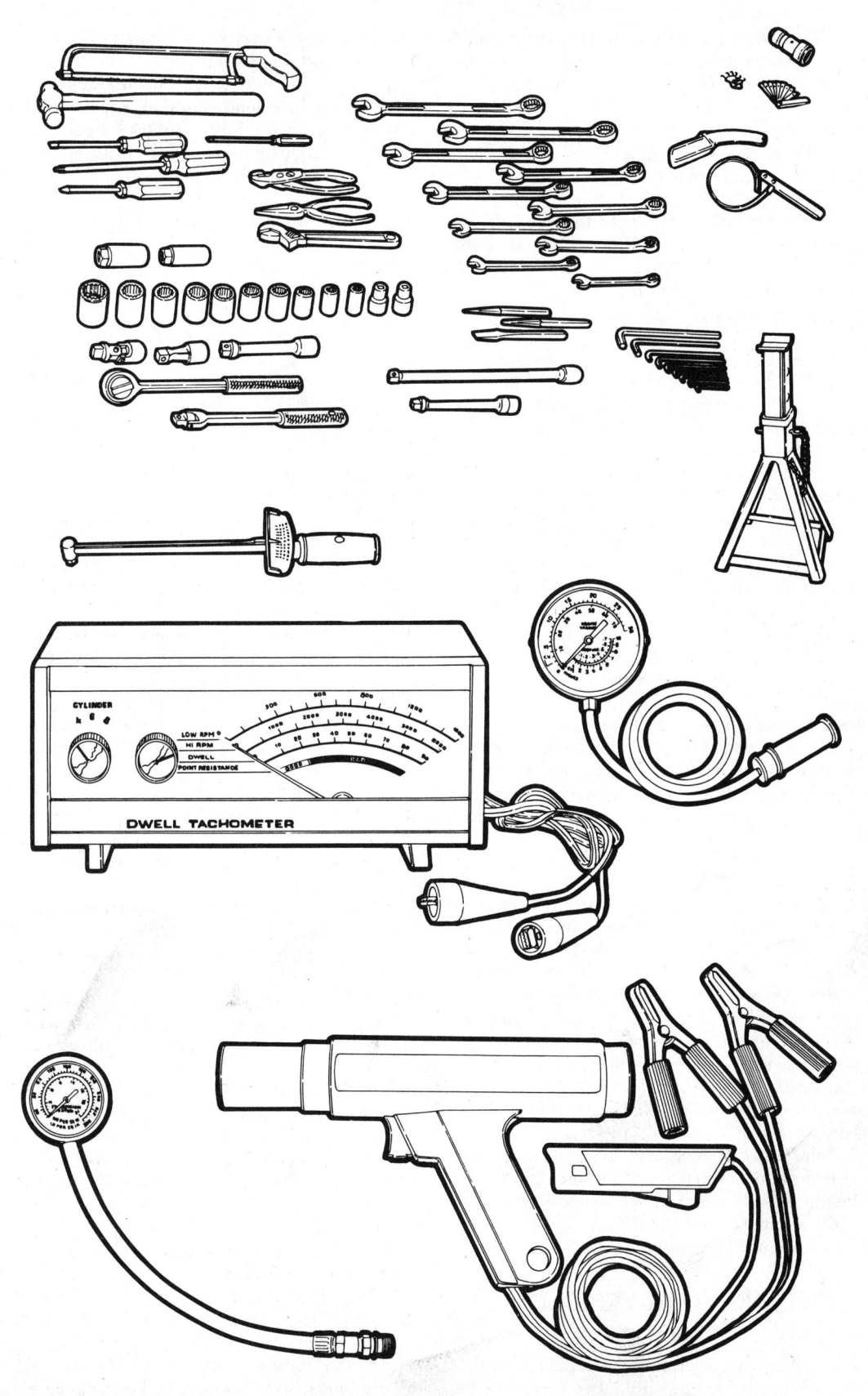

The tools and equipment shown here will handle the majority of the maintenance on a car

GENERAL INFORMATION AND MAINTENANCE

tach/dwell meters on the market that are every bit as good for the average mechanic as a $100.00 professional model. Just be sure that it goes to at least 1,200–1,500 rpm on the tach scale and that it works on 4, 6 or 8 cylinder engines. A basic list of tune-up equipment could include:

1. Tach-dwell meter;
2. Spark plug wrench;
3. Timing light (a DC light that works from the car's battery is best, although an AC light that plugs into 110V house current will suffice at some sacrifice in brightness);
4. Wire spark plug gauge/adjusting tools;
5. Set of feeler blades.

Here again, be guided by your own needs. A feeler blade will set the points as easily as a dwell meter will read well, but slightly less accurately. And since you will need a tachometer anyway . . . well, make your own decision.

In addition to these basic tools, there are several other tools and gauges you may find useful. These include:

1. A compression gauge. The screw-in type is slower to use, but eliminates the possibility of a faulty reading due to escaping pressure;
2. A manifold vacuum gauge;
3. A test light;
4. An induction meter. This is used for determining whether or not there is current in a wire. These are handy for use if a wire is broken somewhere in a wiring harness.

As a final note, you will probably find a torque wrench necessary for all but the most basic work. The beam type models are perfectly adequate, although the newer click type are more precise.

Special Tools

Normally, the use of special factory tools is avoided for repair procedures, since these are not readily available for the do-it-yourself mechanic. When it is possible to perform the job with more commonly available tools, it will be pointed out, but occasionally, a special tool was designed to perform a specific function and should be used. Before substituting another tool, you should be convinced that neither your safety nor the performance of the vehicle will be compromised.

Some special tools are available commercially from major tool manufacturers. Others can be purchased from your car dealer or from:

Owatonna Tool Company
Owatonna, Minnesota 55060

SERVICING YOUR VEHICLE SAFELY

It is virtually impossible to anticipate all of the hazards involved with automotive maintenance and service but care and common sense will prevent most accidents.

The rules of safety for mechanics range from "don't smoke around gasoline," to "use the proper tool for the job." The trick to avoiding injuries is to develop safe work habits and take every possible precaution.

Do's

• DO keep a fire extinguisher and first aid kit within easy reach.
• DO wear safety glasses or goggles when cutting, drilling, grinding or prying, even if you have 20–20 vision. If you wear glasses for the sake of vision, then they should be made of hardened glass that can serve also as safety glasses, or wear safety goggles over your regular glasses.
• DO shield your eyes whenever you work around the battery. Batteries contain sulphuric acid; in case of contact with the eyes or skin, flush the area with water or a mixture of water and baking soda and get medical attention immediately.
• DO use safety stands for any undercar service. Jacks are for raising vehicles; safety stands are for making sure the vehicle stays raised until you want it to come down. Whenever the vehicle is raised, block the wheels remaining on the ground and set the parking brake.
• DO use adequate ventilation when working with any chemicals. Like carbon monoxide, the asbestos dust resulting from brake lining wear can be poisonous in sufficient quantities.
• DO disconnect the negative battery cable when working on the electrical system. The primary ignition system can contain up to 40,000 volts.
• DO follow manufacturer's directions whenever working with potentially hazardous materials. Both brake fluid and antifreeze are poisonous if taken internally.
• DO properly maintain your tools. Loose hammerheads, mushroomed punches and chisels, frayed or poorly grounded electrical cords, excessively worn screwdrivers, spread wrenches (open end), cracked sockets, slipping ratchets, or faulty droplight sockets can cause accidents.
• DO use the proper size and type of tool for the job being done.
• DO when possible, pull on a wrench handle rather than push on it, and adjust your stance to prevent a fall.
• DO be sure that adjustable wrenches are tightly adjusted on the nut or bolt and pulled

GENERAL INFORMATION AND MAINTENANCE

so that the face is on the side of the fixed jaw.
- DO select a wrench or socket that fits the nut or bolt. The wrench or socket should sit straight, not cocked.
- DO strike squarely with a hammer—avoid glancing blows.
- DO set the parking brake and block the drive wheels if the work requires that the engine be running.

Don'ts

- DON'T run an engine in a garage or anywhere else without proper ventilation—EVER! Carbon monoxide is poisonous; it takes a long time to leave the human body and you can build up a deadly supply of it in your system by simply breathing in a little every day. You may not realize you are slowly poisoning yourself. Always use power vents, windows, fans, or open the garage doors.
- DON'T work around moving parts while wearing a necktie or other loose clothing. Short sleeves are much safer than long, loose sleeves and hard-toed shoes with neoprene soles protect your toes and give a better grip on slippery surfaces. Jewelry such as watches, fancy belt buckles, beads or body adornment of any kind is not safe working around a car. Long hair should be hidden under a hat or cap.
- DON'T use pockets for toolboxes. A fall or bump can drive a screwdriver deep into your body. Even a wiping cloth hanging from the back pocket can wrap around a spinning shaft or fan.
- DON'T smoke when working around gasoline, cleaning solvent, or other flammable material.
- DON'T smoke when working around the battery. When the battery is being charged, it gives off explosive hydrogen gas.
- DON'T use gasoline to wash your hands; there are excellent soaps available. Gasoline may contain lead, and lead can enter the body through a cut, accumulating in the body until you are very ill. Gasoline also removes all the natural oils from the skin so that bone dry hands will suck up oil and grease.
- DON'T service the air conditioning system unless you are equipped with the necessary tools and training. The refrigerant, 12, is extremely cold and when exposed to the air, will instantly freeze any surface it comes in contact with, including your eyes. Although the refrigerant is normally nontoxic, R-12 becomes a deadly poisonous gas in the presence of an open flame. One good whiff of the vapors from burning refrigerant can be fatal.

F 9S63H100001 F

Vehicle identification number through 1980

1FABP34D9CB100001

Vehicle Identification Number, 1981-82

MODEL AND SERIAL NUMBER IDENTIFICATION

Vehicle Identification Number (VIN)

Mustang and Capri

The (VIN) Vehicle Identification Number for title and registration purposes is stamped on a metal tab attached to the instrument panel close to the windshield and is visible from the outside. The first number indicates the model year. The letter following the model year number indicates the manufacturing assembly plant. The next two numbers designate the body serial code followed by a letter expressing the Engine Code. The last six digits indicate the Consecutive Unit Number of each unit built at each assembly plant.

Merkur

An official Vehicle Identification Number (VIN) for title and registration purposes is stamped on a metal tab that is fastened to the instrument panel close to the windshield on the driver's side of the vehicle and is visible from the outside of the vehicle. The eighth number or letter of the VIN indicates installed engine. The tenth indicates model year. For instance; if the eighth number or letter was a W, that would indicate a 2.3L (140 cid) Turbo equipped engine. If the tenth letter was an F, that would indicate the vehicle was a 1985 model. Model years will be indicated by following the alphabet. G would be a 1986 model, F would be 1987 etc.

Vehicle Certification Label

The Vehicle Certification Label is attached to the left front door lock face panel or door pillar. The Vehicle Identification Number (VIN) also appears on this label.

Engine Identification

Identification of the engine can be made by finding the letter code in the Vehicle Identification Number, then referring to the engine identification chart to determine the engine type

6 GENERAL INFORMATION AND MAINTENANCE

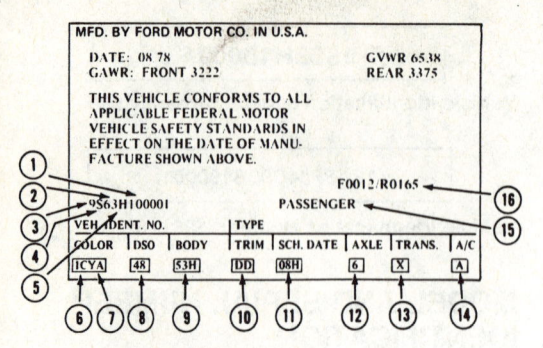

① Consecutive unit no.
② Body serial code
③ Model year code
④ Assembly plant code
⑤ Engine code
⑥ Body color code
⑦ Vinyl roof type/color
⑧ District—special equipment
⑨ Body type code
⑩ Trim code (First letter = Type of trim; Second letter = color of trim)
⑪ Scheduled build date
⑫ Rear axle code
⑬ Transmission code
⑭ Air conditioning
⑮ Vehicle type
⑯ Accessory reserve load

Vehicle certification label (United States)

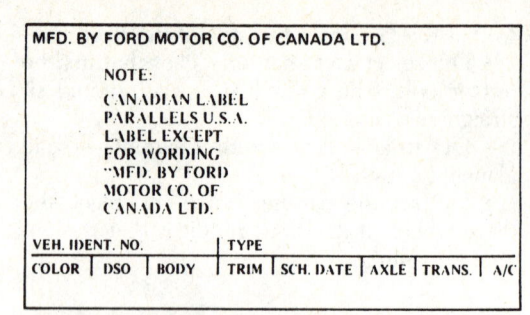

Vehicle certification label (Canada)

and size. An engine identification label is also attached to the engine, usually to the valve cover. The symbol codes on the identification tag not only identifies the engine but are used for determining parts usage. The codes are shown in the dealers master parts catalog to designate unique parts.

Transmission Identification

The transmission can be identified by finding the transmission code which appears on the bottom right side of the Vehicle Certification Label and referring to the transmission identification chart. There is also a transmission identification tag attached to the transmission.

Engine Codes

Year	Model	Code	Number of Cylinders	Litres	Cu. in.	Carb. Barrels
1979	Mustang, Capri	Y	4	2.3	140	2
		W	4	2.3	140	2-Turbo
		Z	6	2.8	170	2
		F	8	5.0	302	2
1980	Mustang, Capri	A	4	2.3	140	2
		T	4	2.3	140	2-Turbo
		B	6	3.3	200	1
		D	8	4.2	255	2
1981	Mustang, Capri	A	4	2.3	140	2
		T	4	2.3	140	2-Turbo
		B	6	3.3	200	1
		D	8	4.2	255	2
1982	Mustang, Capri	A	4	2.3	140	2
		T	4	2.3	140	2-Turbo ①
		B	6	3.3	200	1
		D	8	4.2	255	2
		F	8	5.0	302	2
1983–85	Mustang, Capri Merkur	A	4	2.3	140	2
		W	4	2.3	140	Turbo
		B	6	3.3	200	1
		3	V6	3.8	232	CFI
		F	V8	5.0	302	CFI
		M	V8	5.0	302HO	②

① Canada Only
② 4 bbl or CFI
CFI—Fuel Injection

GENERAL INFORMATION AND MAINTENANCE

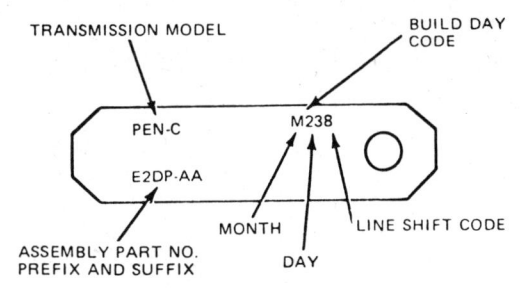

Identification tag—C-5 automatic. Under lower intermediate servo cover

Transmission Codes

1.	Three speed
2.	Five speed overdrive
4.	Four speed overdrive (SROD)
5.	Five speed
5.	Five speed overdrive (RAP)
6.	Four speed (Borg Warner)
7.	Four speed overdrive (RUG)
7.	Four speed (ET) (Hummer)
C.	C5 automatic
S.	JATCO automatic
T.	AOD (automatic overdrive)
U.	C6 automatic
V.	C3 automatic
W.	C4 automatic
X.	FMX automatic
Y.	Borg Warner automatic
Z.	C6 police automatic

Refer to the vehicle certification plate on the driver's door frame for transmission identification code.

ROUTINE MAINTENANCE

Air Cleaner Element

All engines are equipped with a dry type, replaceable air filter element. The element should be replaced at the recommended intervals shown on the Maintenance Chart in this Chapter. If your vehicle is operated under severely dusty conditions or severe operating conditions, more frequent changes are necessary. Inspect the element at least twice a year. Early spring and at the beginning of fall are good times for the inspection. Remove the element and check for holes in the filter. Check the cleaner housing for signs of dirt or dust that has leaked through the filter element. Place a light on the inside of the element and look through the filter at the light. If no glow of light can be seen through the element material, replace the filter. If holes in the filter are apparent or signs of dirt leakage through the filter are noticed, replace the filter.

REMOVAL AND INSTALLATION

Air Cleaner Assembly

1. Disconnect all hoses, ducts and vacuum tubes from the air cleaner assembly.
2. Remove the top cover wing nut and grommet (if equipped). Remove any side bracket mount retaining bolts (if equipped). Remove the air cleaner assembly from the top of the carburetor or intake assembly.
3. Remove the cover and the element, wipe

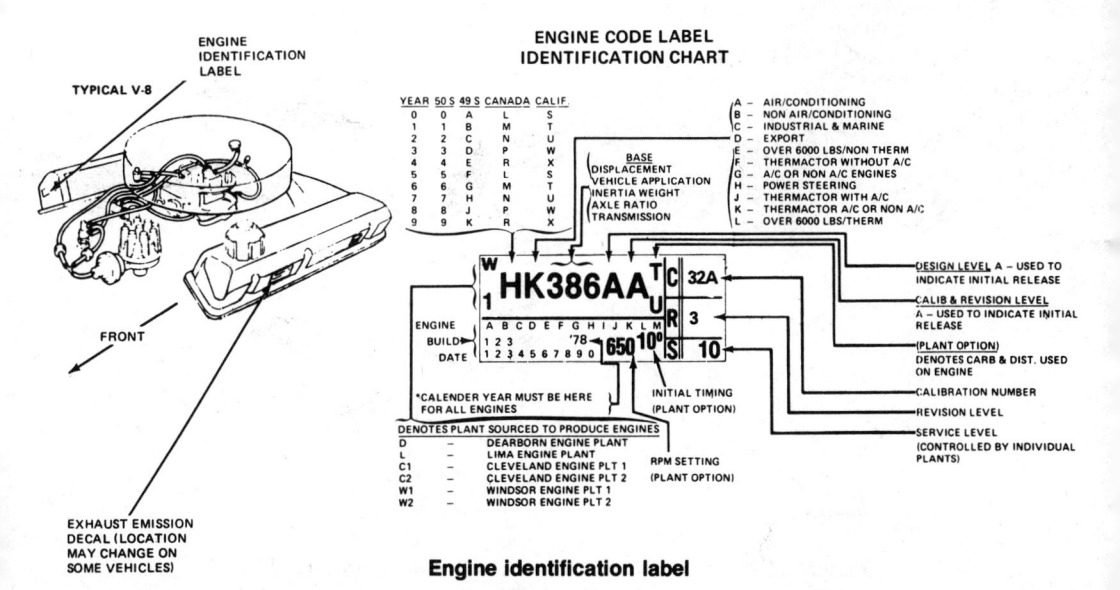

Engine identification label

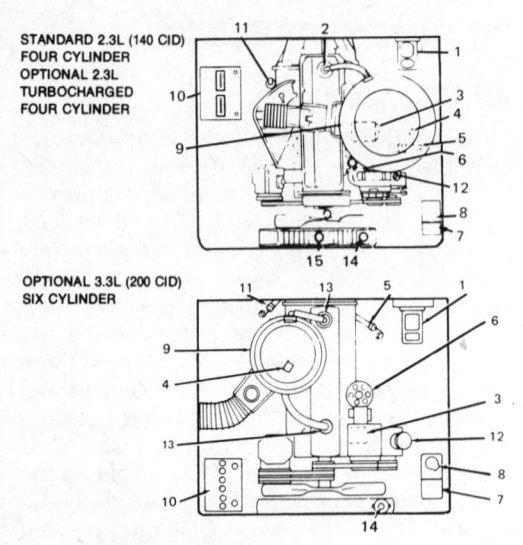

8 GENERAL INFORMATION AND MAINTENANCE

STANDARD 2.3L (140 CID) FOUR CYLINDER
OPTIONAL 2.3L TURBOCHARGED FOUR CYLINDER

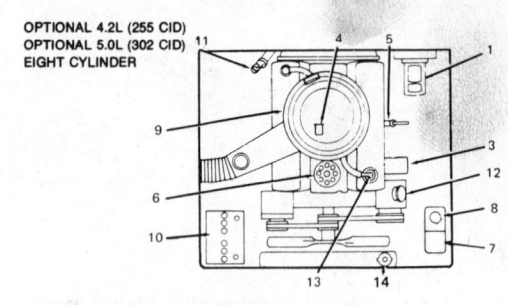

OPTIONAL 3.3L (200 CID) SIX CYLINDER

OPTIONAL 4.2L (255 CID)
OPTIONAL 5.0L (302 CID) EIGHT CYLINDER

1. Brake master cylinder
2. Engine oil filler cap & PCV filter (2.3L)
3. Engine oil filter
4. Fuel filter (on carburetor)
5. Engine oil dipstick
6. Distributor
7. Coolant expansion bottle
8. Windshield washer reservoir
9. Air cleaner assembly
10. Battery
11. Automatic transmission dipstick
12. Power steering reservoir dipstick
13. PCV valve & grommet & oil filler cap (3.3L & 4.2L)
14. Radiator cap (all except 2.3L non-A/C)
15. Radiator cap (2.3L non-A/C)

Vehicle service points

clean all inside surfaces of the air cleaner housing and cover. Check the condition of the mounting gasket (cleaner base to carburetor). Replace the mounting gasket if it is worn or broken.

4. Reposition the cleaner assembly, element and cover on the carburetor or intake assembly.

5. Reconnect all hoses, duct and vacuum hoses removed. Tighten the wing nut finger tight.

Element

The element can, in most cases, be replaced by removing the wing nut and cleaner assembly cover. If the inside of the housing is dirty, however, remove the assembly for cleaning to prevent dirt from entering the carburetor.

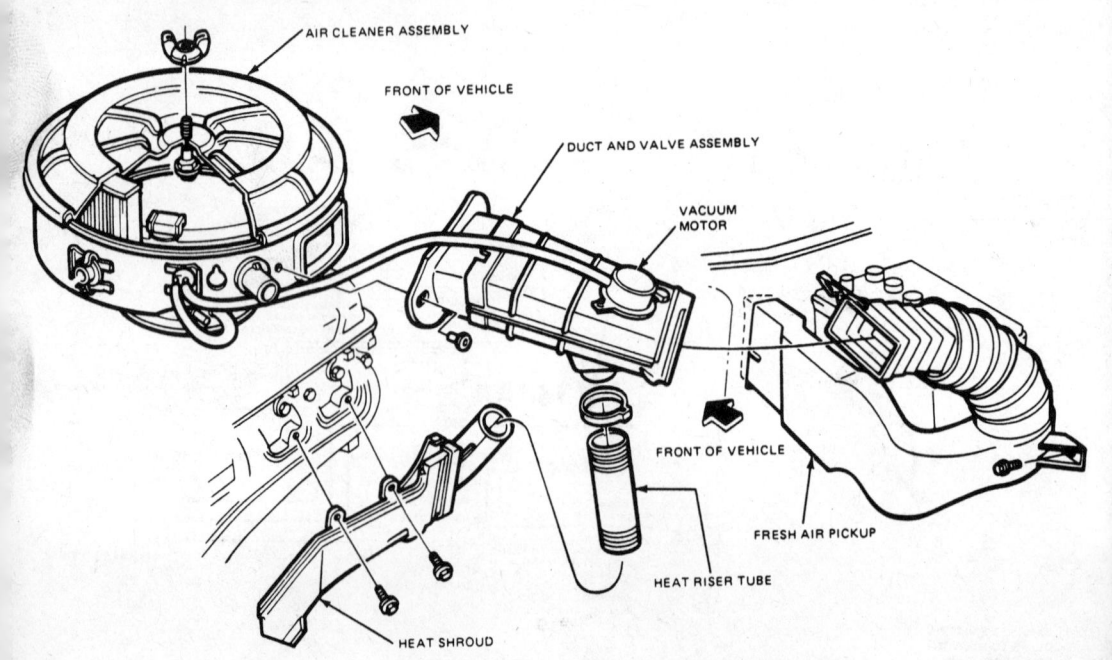

Typical air cleaner and duct system—V8 shown, V6 similar

GENERAL INFORMATION AND MAINTENANCE

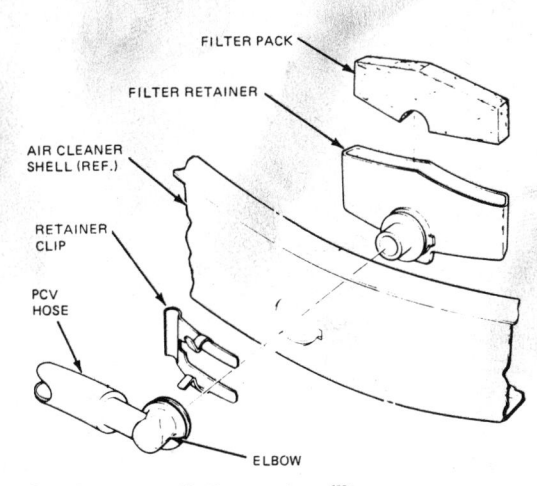

Crankcase ventilation system filter

CRANKCASE VENTILATION FILTER-IN AIR CLEANER

Replace or inspect cleaner mounted crankcase ventilation filter (on models equipped) at the same time the air cleaner filter element is serviced. To replace the filter, simply remove the air cleaner top cover and pull the filter from its housing. Push a new filter into the housing and install the air cleaner cover. If the filter and plastic holder need replacement, remove the clip mounting the feed tube to the air cleaner housing (hose already removed) and remove the assembly from the air cleaner. Install in reverse order.

PCV Valve

Most models use a closed ventilation system with a sealed breather cap connected to the air cleaner by a rubber hose. The PCV valve is usually mounted in the valve cover and connected to the intake manifold by a rubber hose. Its task is to regulate the amount of crankcase (blow-by) gases which are recycled.

Since the PCV valve works under severe load it is very important that it be replaced at the interval specified in the maintenance chart. Replacement involves removing the valve from the grommet in the rocker arm cover disconnecting the hose(s) and installing a new valve. Do not attempt to clean a used valve.

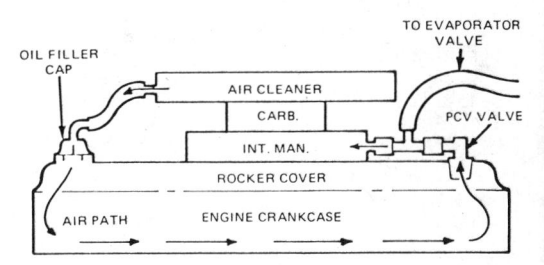

Typical PCV system

Evaporative Emissions Canister

The canister functions to cycle the fuel vapor from the fuel tank and carburetor float chamber into the intake manifold and eventually into the cylinders for combustion. The activated charcoal element within the canister acts as a storage device for the fuel vapor at times when the engine operating condition will not permit fuel vapor to burn efficiently.

The only required service for the evaporative emissions canister is inspection at the interval specified in the maintenance chart. If the

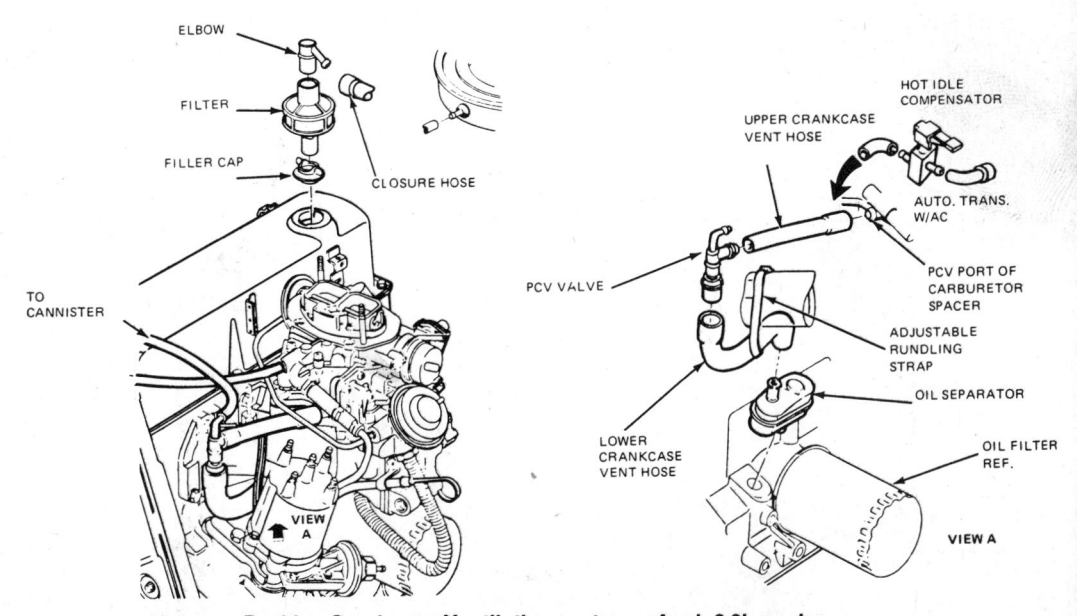

Positive Crankcase Ventilation system—4 cyl. 2.3L engine

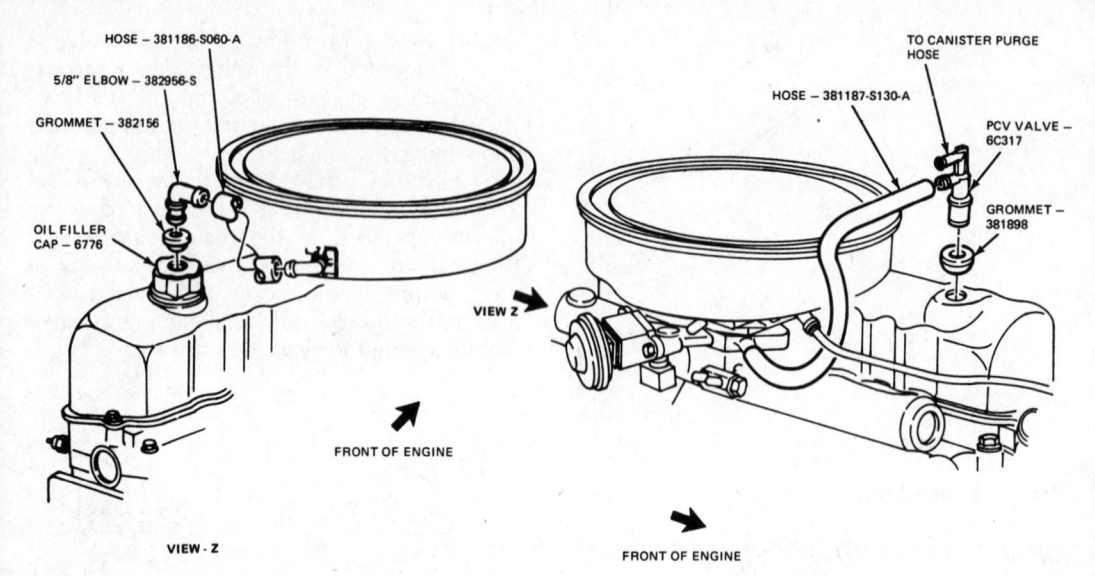

10 GENERAL INFORMATION AND MAINTENANCE

Positive Crankcase Ventilation system—6 cyl. 3.3L engine

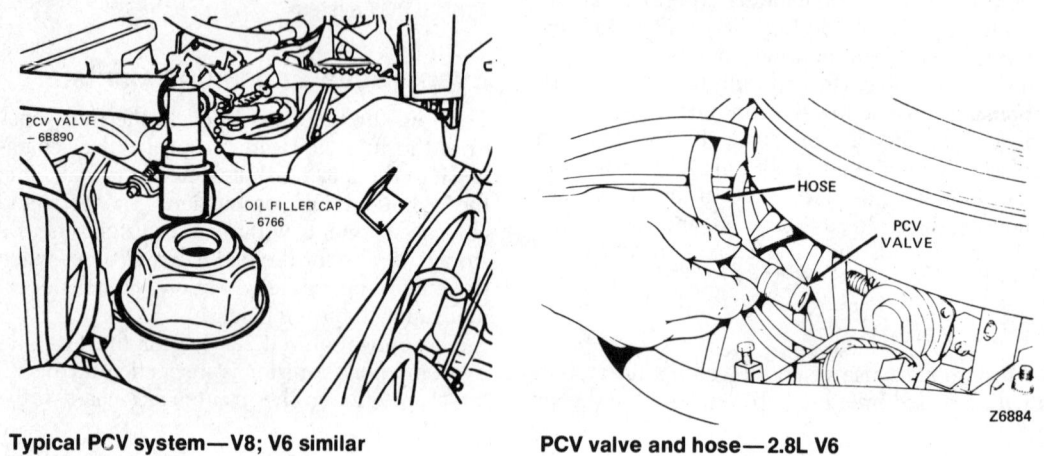

Typical PCV system—V8; V6 similar

PCV valve and hose—2.8L V6

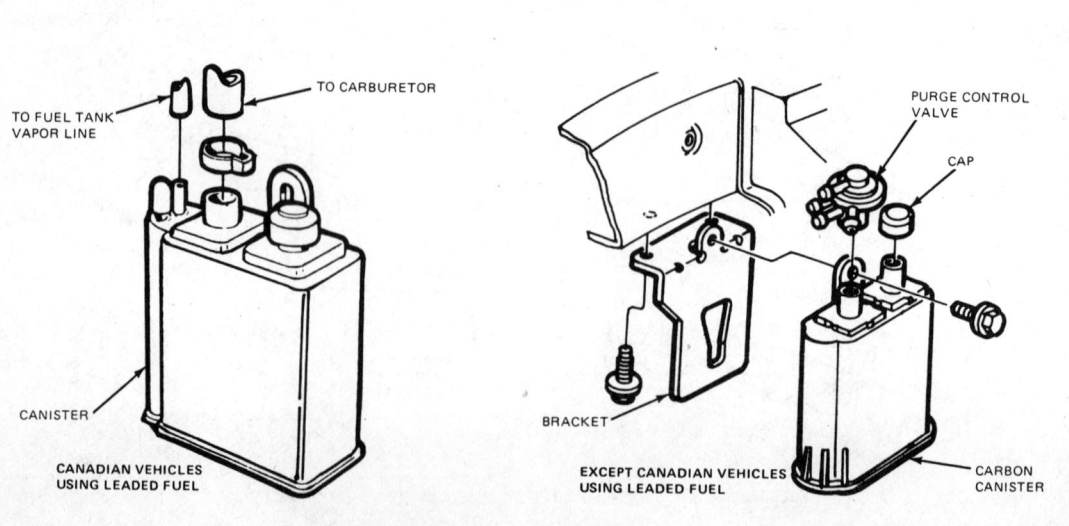

Evaporator canister—typical

charcoal element is gummed up the entire canister should be replaced. Disconnect the canister purge hose(s); loosen the canister retaining bracket; lift out the canister. Installation is the reverse of removal.

Battery

FLUID LEVEL (EXCEPT "MAINTENANCE FREE" BATTERIES)

Check the battery electrolyte level at least once a month, or more often in hot weather or during periods of extended car operation. The level can be checked through the case on translucent polypropylene batteries; the cell caps must be removed on other models. The electrolyte level in each cell should be kept filled to the split ring inside, or the line marked on the outside of the case.

If the level is low, add only distilled water, or colorless, odorless drinking water, through the opening until the level is correct. Each cell is completely separate from the others, so each must be checked and filled individually.

If water is added in freezing weather, the car should be driven several miles to allow the water to mix with the electrolyte. Otherwise, the battery could freeze.

SPECIFIC GRAVITY (EXCEPT "MAINTENANCE FREE" BATTERIES)

At least once a year, check the specific gravity of the battery. It should be between 1.20 and 1.26 at room temperature.

The specific gravity can be checked with the use of an hydrometer, an inexpensive instrument available from many sources, including auto parts stores. The hydrometer has a squeeze bulb at one end and a nozzle at the other. Battery electrolyte is sucked into the hydrometer until the float is lifted from its seat. The specific gravity is then read by noting the position of the float. Generally, if after charging, the specific gravity between any two cells varies more than 50 points (.50), the battery is bad and should be replaced.

It is not possible to check the specific gravity in this manner on sealed ("maintenance free") batteries. Instead, the indicator built into the top of the case must be relied on to display any signs of battery deterioration. If the indicator is dark, the battery can be assumed to be OK. If the indicator is light, the specific gravity is low, and the battery should be charged or replaced.

CABLES AND CLAMPS

Once a year, the battery terminals and the cable clamps should be cleaned. Loosen the clamps and remove the cables, negative cable first. On batteries with posts on top, the use of a puller specially made for the purpose is recommended. These are inexpensive, and available in auto parts stores. Side terminal battery cables are secured with a bolt.

Clean the cable clamps and the battery terminal with a wire brush, until all corrosion, grease, etc. is removed and the metal is shiny. It is especially important to clean the inside of the clamp thoroughly, since a small deposit of foreign material or oxidation there will prevent a sound electrical connection and inhibit either starting or charging. Special tools are available for cleaning these parts, one type for conventional batteries and another type for side terminal batteries.

Before installing the cables, loosen the battery hold-down clamp or strap, remove the battery and check the battery tray. Clear it of any debris, and check it for soundness. Rust should be wire brushed away, and the metal given a coat of anti-rust paint. Replace the battery and tighten the hold-down clamp or strap securely, but be careful not to overtighten, which will crack the battery case.

After the clamps and terminals are clean, reinstall the cables, negative cable last; do not hammer on the clamps to install. Tighten the clamps securely, but do not distort them. Give the clamps and terminals a thin external coat of grease after installation, to retard corrosion.

Check the cables at the same time that the terminals are cleaned. If the cable insulation is cracked or broken, or if the ends are frayed, the cable should be replaced with a new cable of the same length and gauge.

CAUTION: *Keep flame or sparks away from the battery; it gives off explosive hydrogen gas. Battery electrolyte contains sulphuric acid. If you should splash any on your skin or in your eyes, flush the affected area with plenty of clear water; if it lands in your eyes, get medical help immediately.*

Belts

Once a year or at 12,000 mile intervals, the tension (and condition) of the alternator, power steering (if so equipped), air conditioning (if so equipped), and Thermactor air pump drive belts should be checked, and, if necessary, adjusted. Loose accessory drive belts can lead to poor engine cooling and diminish alternator, power steering pump, air conditioning compressor or Thermactor air pump output. A belt that is too tight places a severe strain on the water pump, alternator, power steering pump, compressor or air pump bearings.

Replace any belt that is so glazed, worn or

12 GENERAL INFORMATION AND MAINTENANCE

HOW TO SPOT WORN V-BELTS

V-Belts are vital to efficient engine operation—they drive the fan, water pump and other accessories. They require little maintenance (occasional tightening) but they will not last forever. Slipping or failure of the V-belt will lead to overheating. If your V-belt looks like any of these, it should be replaced.

This belt has deep cracks, which cause it to flex. Too much flexing leads to heat build-up and premature failure. These cracks can be caused by using the belt on a pulley that is too small. Notched belts are available for small diameter pulleys.

Cracking or weathering

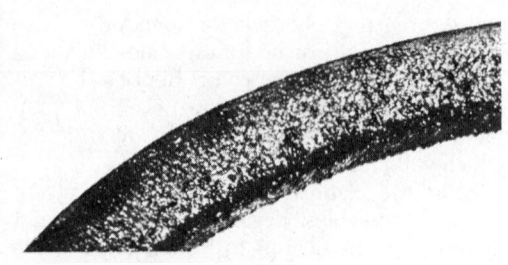

Oil and grease on a belt can cause the belt's rubber compounds to soften and separate from the reinforcing cords that hold the belt together. The belt will first slip, then finally fail altogether.

Softening (grease and oil)

Glazing is caused by a belt that is slipping. A slipping belt can cause a run-down battery, erratic power steering, overheating or poor accessory performance. The more the belt slips, the more glazing will be built up on the surface of the belt. The more the belt is glazed, the more it will slip. If the glazing is light, tighten the belt.

Glazing

The cover of this belt is worn off and is peeling away. The reinforcing cords will begin to wear and the belt will shortly break. When the belt cover wears in spots or has a rough jagged appearance, check the pulley grooves for roughness.

Worn cover

This belt is on the verge of breaking and leaving you stranded. The layers of the belt are separating and the reinforcing cords are exposed. It's just a matter of time before it breaks completely.

Separation

GENERAL INFORMATION AND MAINTENANCE

HOW TO SPOT BAD HOSES

Both the upper and lower radiator hoses are called upon to perform difficult jobs in an inhospitable environment. They are subject to nearly 18 psi at under hood temperatures often over 280°F., and must circulate nearly 7500 gallons of coolant an hour—3 good reasons to have good hoses.

A good test for any hose is to feel it for soft or spongy spots. Frequently these will appear as swollen areas of the hose. The most likely cause is oil soaking. This hose could burst at any time, when hot or under pressure.

Swollen hose

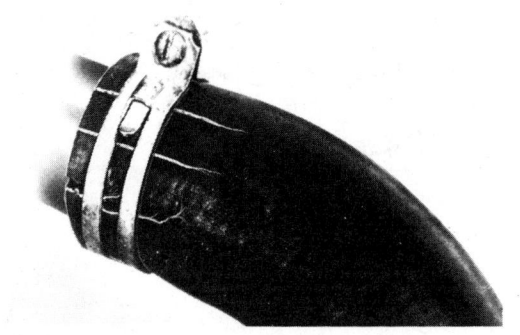

Cracked hoses can usually be seen but feel the hoses to be sure they have not hardened; a prime cause of cracking. This hose has cracked down to the reinforcing cords and could split at any of the cracks.

Cracked hose

Weakened clamps frequently are the cause of hose and cooling system failure. The connection between the pipe and hose has deteriorated enough to allow coolant to escape when the engine is hot.

Frayed hose end (due to weak clamp)

Debris, rust and scale in the cooling system can cause the inside of a hose to weaken. This can usually be felt on the outside of the hose as soft or thinner areas.

Debris in cooling system

14 GENERAL INFORMATION AND MAINTENANCE

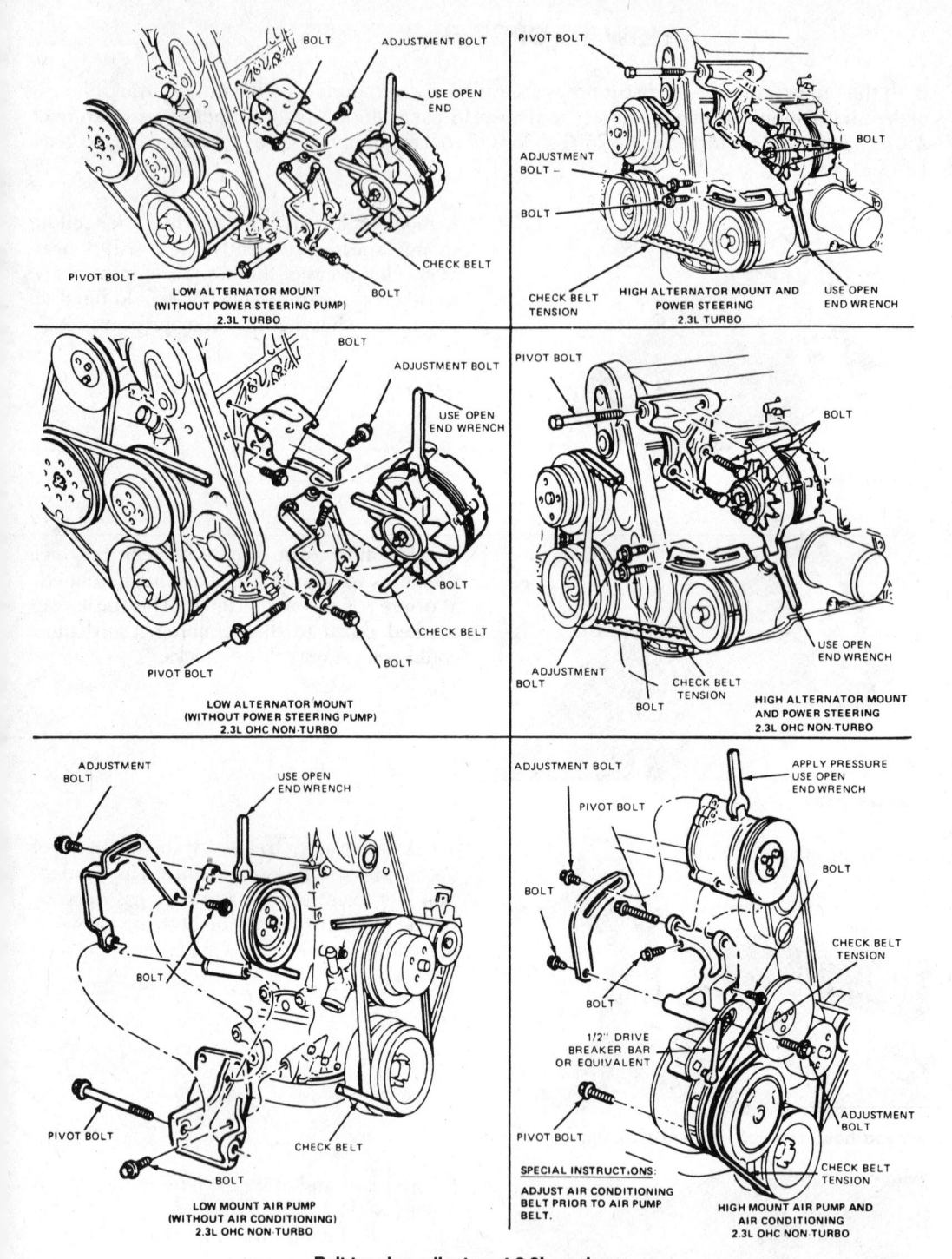

Belt tension adjustment 2.3L engines

stretched that it cannot be tightened sufficiently.

NOTE: *The material used in late model drive belts is such that the belts do not show wear. Replace belts at least every three years.*

On vehicles with matched belts, replace both belts. New belts are to be adjusted to a tension of 140 lbs (½ in., ⅜ in., and 15/32 in. wide belts) or 80 lbs (¼ in. wide belts) measured on a belt tension gauge. Any belt that has been operating for a minimum of 10 minutes, the belt should stretch to its maximum extent. After 10 minutes, stop the engine and recheck the belt tension. Belt tension for a used belt should be

GENERAL INFORMATION AND MAINTENANCE

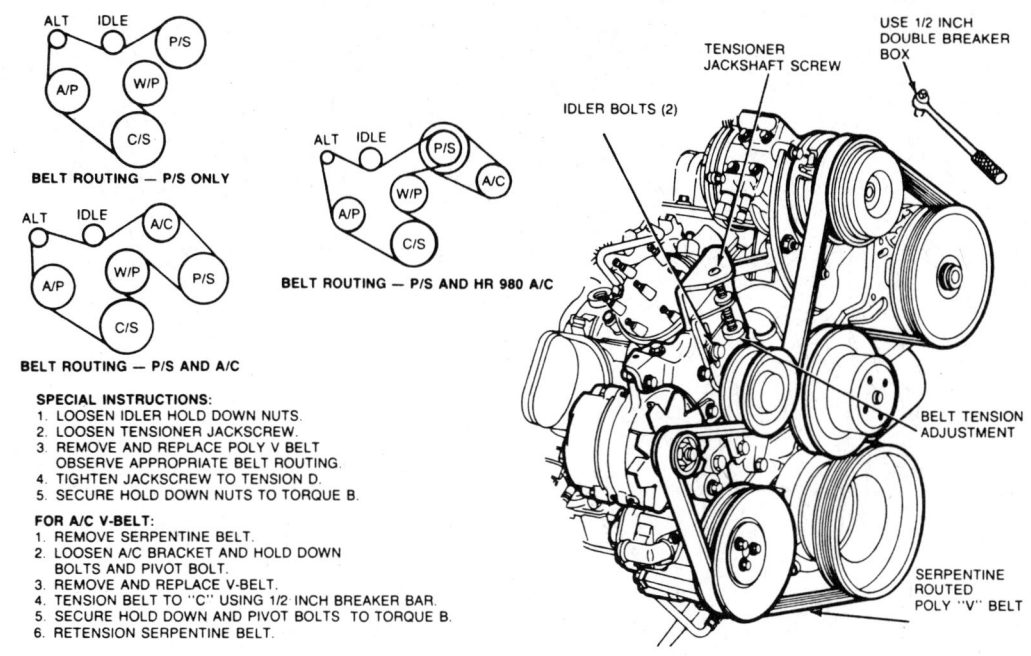

SPECIAL INSTRUCTIONS:
1. LOOSEN IDLER HOLD DOWN NUTS.
2. LOOSEN TENSIONER JACKSCREW.
3. REMOVE AND REPLACE POLY V BELT OBSERVE APPROPRIATE BELT ROUTING.
4. TIGHTEN JACKSCREW TO TENSION D.
5. SECURE HOLD DOWN NUTS TO TORQUE B.

FOR A/C V-BELT:
1. REMOVE SERPENTINE BELT.
2. LOOSEN A/C BRACKET AND HOLD DOWN BOLTS AND PIVOT BOLT.
3. REMOVE AND REPLACE V-BELT.
4. TENSION BELT TO "C" USING 1/2 INCH BREAKER BAR.
5. SECURE HOLD DOWN AND PIVOT BOLTS TO TORQUE B.
6. RETENSION SERPENTINE BELT.

Belt tension adjustment 3.8L engine

maintained at 110 lbs (all except ¼ in. wide belts) or 60 lbs (¼ in. wide belts). If a belt tension gauge is not available, the following procedures may be used.

ADJUSTMENTS

CAUTION: *On models equipped with an electric cooling fan, disconnect the negative battery cable or fan motor wiring harness connector before replacing or adjusting drive belts. The fan may come on, under certain circumstances, even though the ignition is off.*

Alternator (Fan Drive) Belt

ALL EXCEPT "SERPENTINE" (SINGLE) BELT

1. Position a ruler perpendicular to the drive belt at its longest run. Test the tightness of the belt by pressing it firmly with your thumb. The deflection should not exceed ¼ in.
2. If the deflection exceeds ¼ in., loosen the alternator mounting and adjusting arm bolts.
3a. On 1971–72 V8 and 6 cylinder models, use a pry bar or broom handle to move the alternator toward or away from the engine until the proper tension is reached.

CAUTION: *Apply tension to the front of the alternator only. Positioning the pry bar against the rear end housing will damage the alternator.*

3b. On 1973 and later models, place a 1 in. open-end or adjustable wrench on the adjusting ridge cast on the body, and pull on the wrench until the proper tension is achieved.
4. Holding the alternator in place to maintain tension, tighten the adjusting arm bolt. Recheck the belt tension. When the belt is properly tensioned, tighten the alternator mounting bolt.

Power Steering Drive Belt

1. Position a ruler perpendicular to the drive belt at its longest run. Test the tightness of the belt by pressing it firmly with your thumb. The deflection should be about ¼ in.
2. To adjust the belt tension, loosen the three bolts in the three elongated adjusting slots at the power steering pump attaching bracket.
3. Turn the steering pump drive belt adjusting nut as required until the proper deflection is obtained. Turning the adjusting nut clockwise will increase tension and decrease deflection; counterclockwise will decrease tension and increase deflection.
4. Without disturbing the pump, tighten the three attaching bolts.

Air Conditioning Compressor Drive Belt (Except Single Drive Belt)

1. Position a ruler perpendicular to the drive belt at its longest run. Test the tightness of the belt by pressing it firmly with your thumb. The deflection should not exceed ¼ in.
2. If the engine is equipped with an idler pulley, loosen the idler pulley adjusting bolt, insert a pry bar between the pulley and the engine (or in the idler pulley adjusting slot), and adjust the tension accordingly. If the engine is not equipped with an idler pulley, the

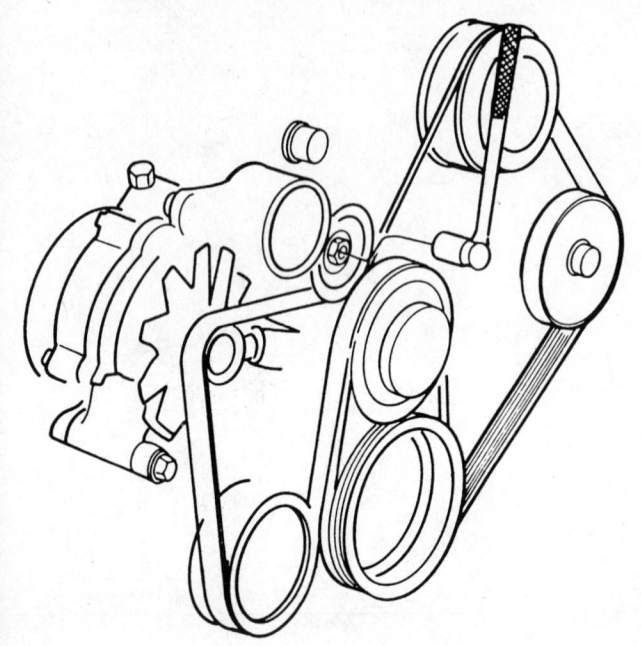

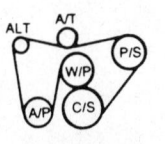

16 GENERAL INFORMATION AND MAINTENANCE

BELT ROUTING P/S ONLY

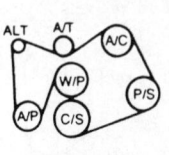

BELT ROUTING P/S & A/C

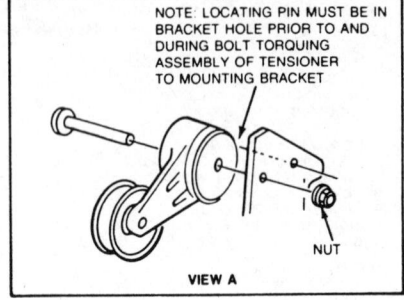

NOTE: LOCATING PIN MUST BE IN BRACKET HOLE PRIOR TO AND DURING BOLT TORQUING ASSEMBLY OF TENSIONER TO MOUNTING BRACKET

VIEW A

NOTE:
THE SINGLE BELT, SERPENTINE DRIVE ARRANGEMENT OF THE 5.0L ENGINE USES AN AUTOMATIC BELT TENSIONER. NO BELT TENSION ADJUSTMENT IS REQUIRED.

SPECIAL INSTRUCTIONS:
1. LIFT AUTO TENSIONER PULLEY BY APPLYING TORQUE TO IDLER PULLEY PIVOT BOLT WITH WRENCH & SOCKET
2. INSTALL DRIVE BELT OVER PULLEYS PER APPROPRIATE BELT ROUTING
3. CHECK BELT TENSION. REFERENCE TENSION CODE E (MUST/CAPRI, MARK/CONTI, LTD/MARQUIS) OR F (LTD POLICE)
4. IF TENSION IS NOT WITHIN SPECIFICATION INSTALL A NEW AUTOMATIC TENSIONER. LOCATE TANG AS SHOWN IN VIEW A.

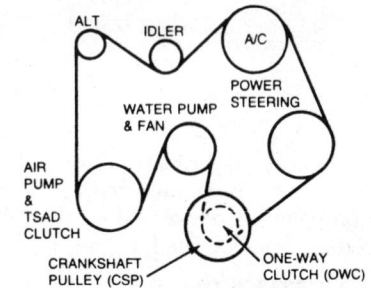

FOR MUSTANG/CAPRI 5.0L WITH MANUAL T5AD TRANSMISSION

Belt tension adjustment 5.0L engine

REPLACEMENT INSTRUCTIONS FOR THE SERPENTINE DRIVE BELT ARE COMMON WITH THE OTHER 5.0L SERPENTINE BELTS. BECAUSE OF THE ROUTING IT IS POSSIBLE TO REMOVE AND REPLACE THE REARWARD SHEAVE SERPENTINE BELT WITHOUT DISTURBING THE FOREWARD SHEAVE JACKSHAFT BELT.

TO INSTALL A NEW JACKSHAFT BELT LOOSEN THE THREE CLUTCH HOLD DOWN BOLTS. THEN LOOSEN THE JACKSCREW NUT TO PERMIT BELT REMOVAL AND REPLACEMENT. ADJUST JACKSCREW NUT   SECURE HOLD DOWN BOLTS

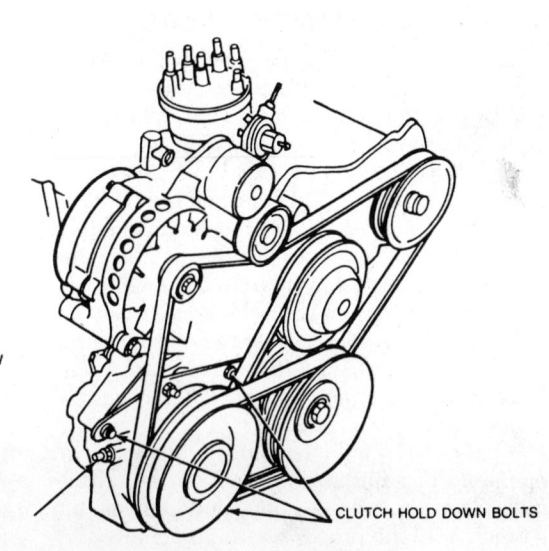

JACKSCREW TENSION ADJUSTMENT NUT

CLUTCH HOLD DOWN BOLTS

Belt tension adjustment 5.0L engine with two speed accessory drive

GENERAL INFORMATION AND MAINTENANCE

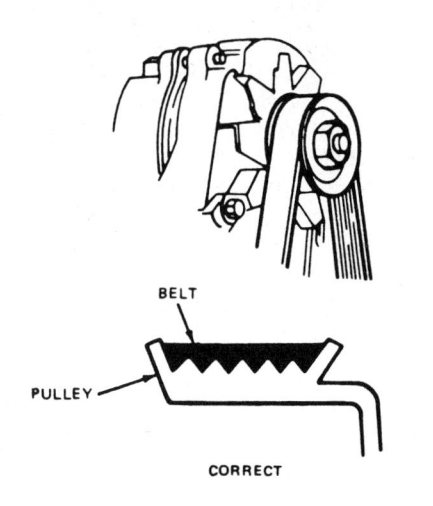

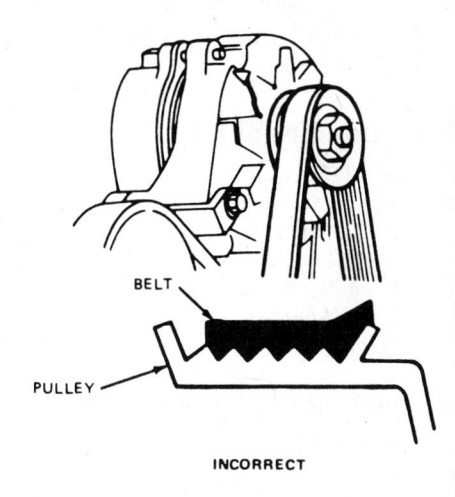

Ribbed belt alignment

alternator must be moved to accomplish this adjustment, as outlined under "Alternator (Fan Drive) Belt."

3. When the proper tension is reached, tighten the idler pulley adjusting bolt (if so equipped) or the alternator adjusting and mounting bolts.

Thermactor Air Pump Drive Belt

1. Position a ruler perpendicular to the drive belt at its longest run. Test the tightness of the belt by pressing it firmly with your thumb. The deflection should be about ¼ in.

2. To adjust the belt tension, loosen the adjusting arm bolt slightly. If necessary, also loosen the mounting belt slightly.

3. Using a pry bar or broom handle, pry against the pump rear cover to move the pump toward or away from the engine as necessary.

CAUTION: *Do not pry against the pump housing itself, as damage to the housing may result.*

4. Holding the pump in place, tighten the adjusting arm bolt and recheck the tension. When the belt is properly tensioned, tighten the mounting bolt.

Single Drive Belt Models

(SERPENTINE DRIVE BELT)

Most late models (starting in 1979) feature a single, wide, ribbed V-belt that drives the water pump, alternator, and (on some models) the air conditioner compressor. To install a new belt, loosen the bracket lock bolt; retract the belt tensioner with a pry bar and slide the old belt off of the pulleys. Slip on a new belt and release the tensioner and tighten the lock bolt. The spring powered tensioner eliminates the need for periodic adjustments.

NOTE: *Check to make sure that the V-ribbed belt is located properly in all drive pulleys before applying tensioner pressure.*

Hoses

CAUTION: *On models equipped with an electric cooling fan, disconnect the negative battery cable, or fan motor wiring harness connector before replacing any radiator/heater hose. The fan may come on, under certain circumstances, even though the ignition is Off.*

REPLACEMENT

Inspect the condition of the radiator and heater hoses periodically. Early spring and at the beginning of the fall or winter, when you are performing other maintenance, are good times. Make sure the engine and cooling system are cold. Visually inspect for cracking, rotting or collapsed hoses, replace as necessary. Run your hand along the length of the hose. If a weak or swollen spot is noted when squeezing the hose wall, replace the hose.

Drain the cooling system into a suitable container (if the coolant is to be reused). Loosen the hose clamps at each end of the hose that requires replacement. Twist, pull and slide the hose off of the radiator, water pump, thermostat or heater connection. Clean the hose mounting connections. Position the hose clamps on the new hose. Coat the connection surfaces with a water resistant sealer and slide the hose into position. Make sure the hose clamps are located beyond the raised head of the connector (if equipped) and centered in the clamping area of the connection. Tighten the clamps to between 20–30 inch lbs. Do not overtighten. Fill the cooling system. Start the engine and

18 GENERAL INFORMATION AND MAINTENANCE

allow to reach normal operating temperature. Check for leaks.

Air Conditioning

CAUTION: *Do not loosen any lines or fittings on the air conditioning system. Refrigerant, when exposed to air, will instantly freeze anything it comes in contact with. When exposed to flame, it becomes highly toxic. Have repair work done by a professional.*

CHECKING REFRIGERANT LEVEL

Sight Glass Equipped

First, wipe the sight glass clean with a cloth wrapped around the eraser end of a pencil. Connect a tachometer to the engine with the positive line connected to the distributor side of the ignition coil and the negative line connected to a good ground, such as the steering box. Have a friend operate the air conditioner controls while you look at the sight glass. Have your friend set the dash panel control to maximum cooling. Start the engine and idle at 1,500 rpm. While looking at the sight glass, signal your friend to turn the blower switch to the High position. If a few bubbles appear immediately after the blower is turned on and then disappear, the system is sufficiently charged with refrigerant. If, on the other hand, a large amount of bubbles, foam or froth continue after the blower has operated for a few seconds, then the system is in need of additional refrigerant.

If no bubbles appear at all, then there is either sufficient refrigerant in the system or it is bone dry. To make a determination follow the procedure given below for models without a sight glass.

Models Without a Sight Glass

To determine if the refrigerant is at the proper level of charge, turn on the engine and run the air conditioner for a few minutes. Feel the temperature of the hose running from the receiver/dryer and of the hose running to the condensor. They should both be cold and approximately the same temperature. If they are both warm the system probably has no refrigerant. If they are different temperatures there is a malfunction in the system.

CAUTION: *Do not attempt to work on the air conditioning system yourself. Consult a professional garage with the proper testing equipment.*

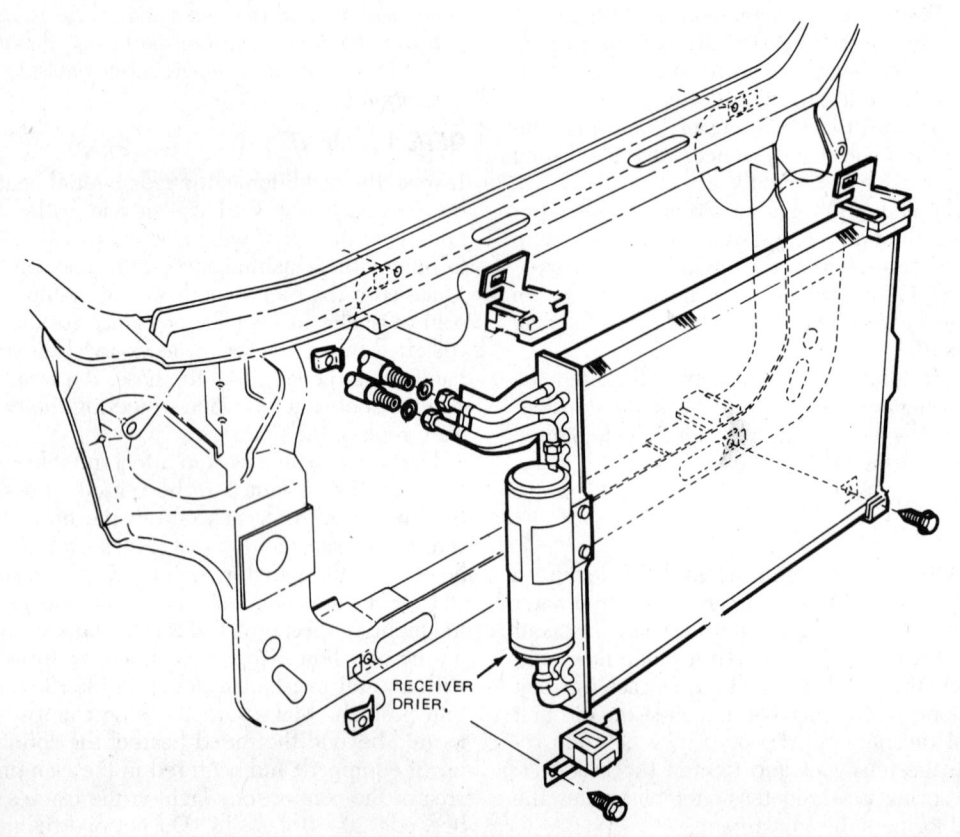

The receiver—drier assembly is mounted to the side of the condenser

GENERAL INFORMATION AND MAINTENANCE

Windshield Wipers

For maximum effectiveness and longest element life, the windshield and wiper blades should be kept clean. Dirt, tree sap, road tar and so on will cause streaking, smearing and blade deterioration if left on the glass. It is advisable to wash the windshield carefully with a commercial glass cleaner at least once a month. Wipe off the rubber blades with the wet rag afterwards. Do not attempt to move the wipers by hand; damage to the motor and drive mechanism will result.

If the blades are found to be cracked, broken or torn, they should be replaced immediately. Replacement intervals will vary with usage, although ozone deterioration usually limits blade life to about one year. If the wiper pattern is smeared or streaked, or if the blade chatters across the glass, the elements should be replaced. It is easiest and most sensible to replace the elements in pairs.

There are basically three different types of refills, which differ in their method of replacement. One type has two release buttons, approximately one-third of the way up from the ends of the blade frame. Pushing the buttons down releases a lock and allows the rubber filler to be removed from the frame. The new filler slides back into the frame and locks in place.

The second type of refill has two metal tabs which are unlocked by squeezing them to-

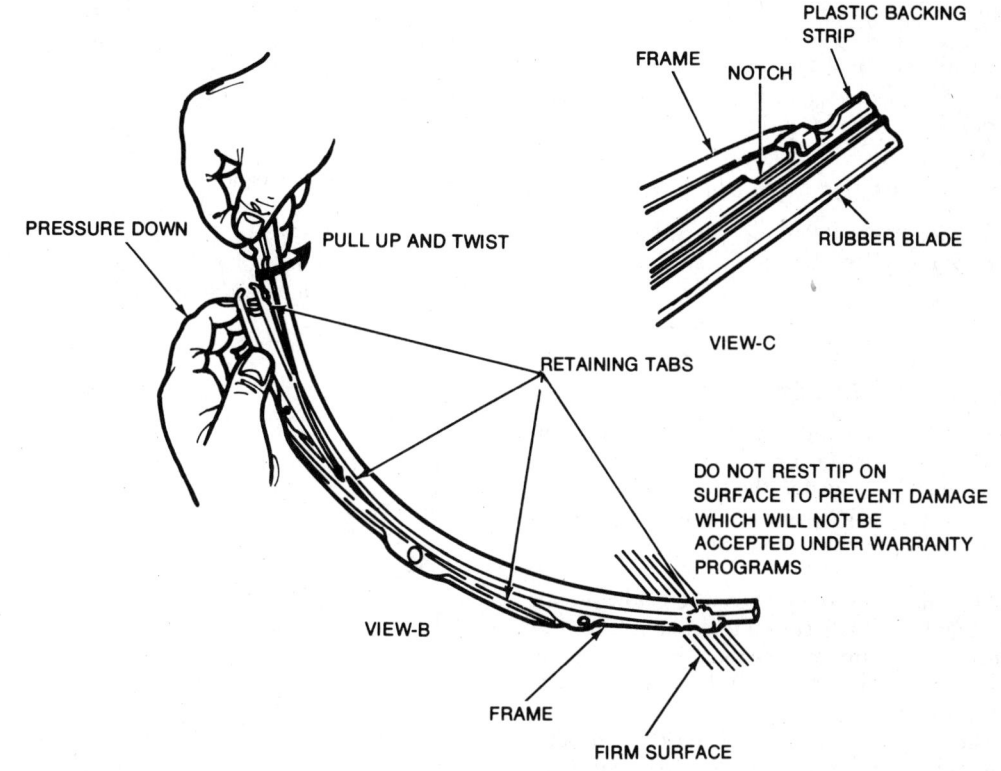

Tridon wiper blades—refill replacement

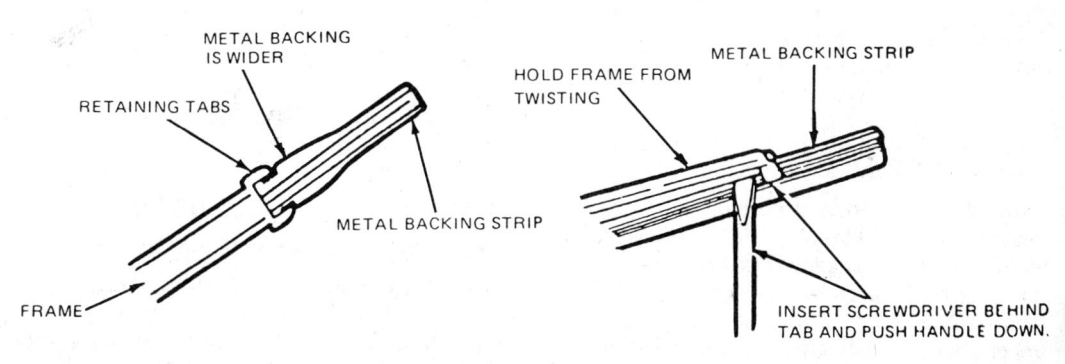

Trico wiper blades refill replacement

GENERAL INFORMATION AND MAINTENANCE

gether. The rubber filler can then be withdrawn from the frame jaws. A new refill is installed by inserting the refill into the front frame jaws and sliding it rearward to engage the remaining frame jaws. There are usually four jaws; be certain when installing that the refill is engaged in all of them. At the end of its travel, the tabs will lock into place on the front jaws of the wiper blade frame.

The third type is a refill made from polycarbonate. The refill has a simple locking device at one end which flexes downward out of the groove into which the jaws of the holder fit allowing easy release. By sliding the new refill through all the jaws and pushing through the slight resistance when it reaches the end of its travel, the refill will lock into position.

Regardless of the type of refill used, make sure that all of the frame jaws are engaged as the refill is pushed into place and locked. The metal blade holder and frame will scratch the glass if allowed to touch it.

ARM AND BLADE REPLACEMENT

A detailed description and procedures for replacing the wiper arm and blade is found in Chapter 5.

Tires and Wheels

Inspect the tires regularly for wear and damage. Remove stones or other foreign particles which may be lodged in the tread. If tread wear is excessive or irregular it could be a sign of front end problems, or simply improper inflation.

The inflation should be checked at least once per month and adjusted if necessary. The tires must be cold (driven less than one mile) or an inaccurate reading will result. Do not forget to check the spare.

The correct inflation pressure for your vehicle can be found on a decal mounted to the car. Depending upon model and year, the decal can be located at the driver's door, the passenger's door or the glove box. If you cannot find the decal a local automobile tire dealer can furnish you with the information.

TIRE ROTATION

Tires should be rotated periodically to get the maximum tread life available. A good time to do this is when changing over from regular tires to snow tires, or about once per year. If front end problems are suspected have them corrected before rotating the tires. Torque the lug nuts to 70–115 ft. lbs.

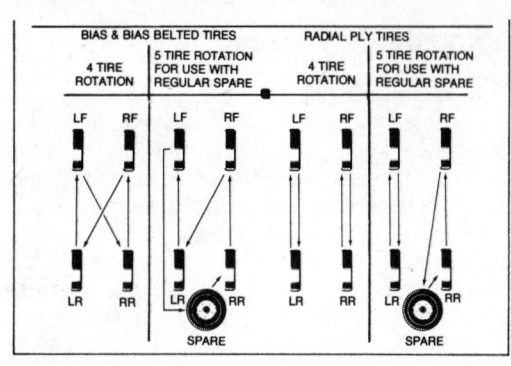

Tire rotation diagram

Fuel Filter

Engines are equipped with a carburetor mounted gas filter. Externally mounted filters are of one piece construction and cannot be cleaned. Model 2700/7200VV carburetors use a replaceable filter located behind the carburetor inlet fitting. Replace the fuel filter at the same time the air cleaner element is changed. Replace the filter immediately if it becomes clogged or restricted. The diesel engine is equipped with a fuel filter/water separator. The filter is of spin-on cartridge-type design.

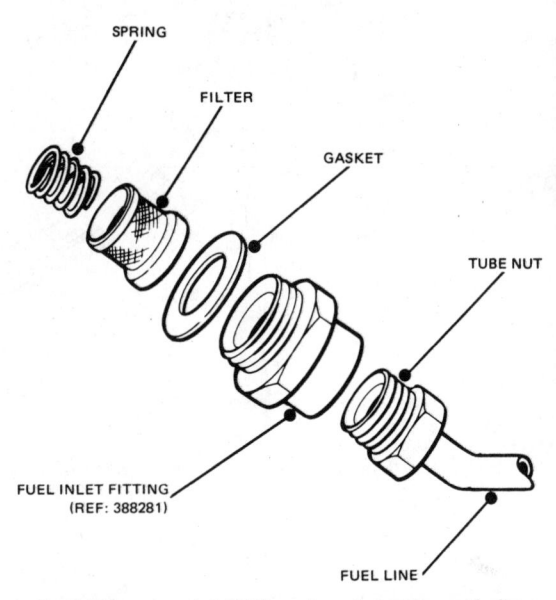

Fuel filter—model 2700 carburetor; others similar

REPLACEMENT—GASOLINE ENGINES
Externally Mounted-Steel Line Connected

1. Remove the air cleaner assembly.
2. Place an 11/16 or suitable size open-end wrench on the filter hex nut to prevent the filter from turning, when loosening the fuel line.

GENERAL INFORMATION AND MAINTENANCE

3. Loosen the fuel line fitting nut with a proper size wrench (½ or ⅝ inch).
4. Remove the fuel line from the filter.
5. Remove the fuel filter from the carburetor by rotating it counterclockwise.
6. Apply one drop of Loctite Hydraulic Sealant No. 069 to the external threads of the new filter and install the filter. Tighten to 5–6 ft. lbs.
7. Apply a drop of oil to the threads of the fuel line fitting. Start the fuel line fitting into the filter by hand.
8. Hold the fuel filter with a suitable wrench and tighten the fuel line fitting to 15–18 ft. lbs.
9. Start the engine and check for fuel leaks. Shut off the engine and install the air cleaner assembly.

Externally Mounted-Hose Connected

1. Remove the air cleaner assembly.
2. Remove or slide the hose clamps from the rubber hose. Remove the hose connector from the fuel filter.
3. Unscrew the fuel filter from the carburetor.
4. Discard the fuel filter, hose and clamps.
5. Apply one drop of Loctite Hydraulic Sealant No. 069 on the external threads of the new fuel filter.
6. Hand star the filter into the carburetor inlet fitting, tighten the filter to 80–100 inch lbs.
7. Position the retaining clamps in the center of the connecting hose.
8. Slide the hose over the inlet fitting of the fuel filter, and over the steel gas line.
9. Slide the clamps into their proper position. Both the filter and steel supply line are equipped with a ridge, position the clamp behind the ridge and tighten the clamp (if worm drive).
10. Start the engine and check for fuel leaks. Shut off the engine and install the air cleaner.

Internally Mounted—2700/7200 VV Carburetors

1. Remove the air cleaner assembly.
2. Hold the carburetor inlet fitting with the proper size flare wrench. Loosen and remove the steel fuel supply line from the carburetor.
3. Unscrew the fuel inlet fitting from the carburetor.
4. Remove the fitting, gasket, filter and spring.
5. Install the spring, new filter, gasket and inlet fitting. Tighten the fitting to 90–125 inch lbs.
6. Lubricate the steel line fitting with a drop of light oil. Hand start the fitting into the carburetor inlet.

7. Hold the carburetor inlet fitting with the proper size flare wrench and tighten the steel line fitting to 15–18 ft. lbs.
8. Start the engine and check for fuel leaks. Shut off the engine and install the air cleaner assembly.

REPLACEMENT-FUEL INJECTED ENGINES

The in-line fuel filter is located on a bracket under the vehicle near the right rear wheel well. The filter usually shares a common mounting bracket with the electric fuel pump.

CAUTION: *Always depressurize the fuel system, on fuel injected vehicles, before disconnecting any fuel lines.*

See Chapter 4 for instructions.

1. Depressurize the fuel system using Tool T80L9974A or the equivalent.
2. Raise the rear of the vehicle and support safely on jackstands.
3. Disconnect the quick connect fitting at both ends of the fuel filter. See Chapter 4 for fuel fitting disconnect instructions.
4. Remove the fuel filter and retainer from the mounting bracket.
5. Remove the filter and insulating (rubber) ring from the retainer. Note that the direction of the flow arrow points to the open end of the retainer. Discard the old filter.
6. Place the new filter into the retainer with the flow arrow pointing in the proper direction. (Toward the open end of the retainer).
7. Install the rubber insulating. If the filter moves freely in the retainer after installing the rubber insulating rings, replace the insulators.
8. Install the retainer on to the bracket. Tighten the mounting bolts to 51–60 inch lbs.
9. Push the quick connect fuel fittings onto the filter ends.
10. Start the engine and check for fuel leaks. Shut off the engine and lower the vehicle to the ground.

FLUIDS AND LUBRICANTS

Fuel

RECOMMENDATIONS

It is important to use fuel of the proper octane rating in your car. Octane rating is based on the quantity of anti-knock compounds added to the fuel and it determines the speed at which the gas will burn. The lower the octane rating, the faster it burns. The higher the octane, the slower the fuel will burn and a greater percentage of compounds in the fuel prevent spark ping (knock), detonation and preignition (dieseling).

22 GENERAL INFORMATION AND MAINTENANCE

Capacities

Year	Engine No. Cyl. Displacement (Cu. In.)	Engine Crankcase Add 1 Qt For New Filter	Transmission Pts to Refill After Draining — Manual 3-Speed	Manual 4/5-Speed	Automatic (Total Capacity) ⑮	Drive Axle (pts)	Gasoline Tank (gals)	Cooling System (qts) With Heater	With A/C
'79–'82 Mustang, Capri	4-140	4	—	2.8	②③	①	11.5 ⑤	8.6 ⑦	10 ⑨
	4-140T	4.5	—	3.5	②③	①	11.5 ⑤	8.6 ⑧	10.2 ⑧
	6-170	4.5	—	4.5	②③	①	12.5	9.2	9.2
	6-200	4	—	4.5	12 ②④	①	16 ⑤⑥	9 ⑩	9 ⑩
	8-255	4	—	4.5	19 ④	①	12.5 ⑥	13.4 ⑪	13.7 ⑫
	8-302	4	—	4.5	19	①	12.5 ⑥	13.9	14.2
'83–'85 Mustang/Capri	4-140	4 ⑬	—	2.8 ⑭	16	①	15.4	8.6	9.4
	6-232	4	—	—	22	①	15.4	8.4	8.4
	8-302	4	—	4.5	—	①	15.4	13.1	13.4
'85 Merkur	4-140T	4	—	2.64	16	3.2	15	10.5	10.5

① 6.75 in.—2.5 pts
   7.50 in.—3.5 pts
   Traction-Lok—3.55 pts
② C3—16 pts; C4—14 pts
③ '81—C4—13.25 pts; 19 pts w/V8
④ '82—C5—22 pts
⑤ '82—15.4 gal
⑥ '80–'81—12.5 gal
⑦ '82—10.2 qts
⑧ '80–'81—9.2 qts
⑨ '80–'81—9.0 qts; '82—10.2 qts
⑩ '80–'82—8.1 qts
⑪ '82—14.7 qts
⑫ '82—15 qts
⑬ 4.5 Turbo/add .5 w/filter
⑭ 5 speed—4.75 pts
⑮ Capacity when totally dry. When changing pan contents, add 2 qts, run engine and check with dipstick. Add fluid as necessary to correct level.

As the temperature of the engine increases, the air-fuel mixture exhibits a tendency to ignite before the spark plug is fired. If fuel of an octane rating too low for the engine is used, this will allow combustion to occur before the piston has completed its compression stroke, thereby creating a very high pressure very rapidly.

Fuel of the proper octane rating, for the compression ratio and ignition timing of your car, will slow the combustion process sufficiently to allow the spark plug enough time to ignite the mixture completely and smoothly. Many non-catalyst models are designed to run on regular fuel. The use of some "super-premium" fuel is no substitution for a properly tuned and maintained engine. Chances are that if your engine exhibits any signs of spark ping, detonation or preignition when using regular fuel, the ignition timing should be checked against specifications or the cylinder head should be removed for decarbonizing.

Vehicles equipped with catalytic converters must use UNLEADED GASOLINE ONLY. Use of unleaded fuel shortens the life of spark plugs, exhaust systems and EGR valves and can damage the catalytic converter. Most converter equipped models are designed to operate using unleaded gasoline with a minimum rating of 87 octane. Use of unleaded gas with octane ratings lower than 87 can cause persistent spark knock which could lead to engine damage.

Light spark knock may be noticed when accelerating or driving up hills. The slight knocking may be considered normal (with 87 octane) because the maximum fuel economy is obtained under condition of occasional light spark knock. Gasoline with an octane rating higher than 87 may be used, but it is not necessary (in most cases) for proper operation.

If spark knock is constant, when using 87 octane, at cruising speeds on level ground, ignition timing adjustment may be required.

Engine

OIL RECOMMENDATION

When adding the oil to the crankcase or changing the oil or filter, it is important that oil of an equal quality to original be used in your car. The use of inferior oils may void your warranty. Generally speaking, oil that has been rated "SE"; "SF" for 1980 and later models;

ADD 2 | ADD 1 | SAFE

V8 and six cylinder dipstick; four cylinder similar

Oil Viscosity—Temperature Chart

When Outside Temperature is Consistently	Use SAE Viscosity Number
SINGLE GRADE OILS	
−10°F to 32°F	10W
10°F to 60°F	20W-20
32°F to 90°F	30
Above 60°F	40
MULTIGRADE OILS	
Below 32°F	5W-30*
−10°F to 90°F	10W-30
Above—10°F	10W-40
Above 10°F	20W-40
Above 20°F	20W-50

*When sustained high-speed operation is anticipated, use the next higher grade.

heavy-duty detergent" by the American Petroleum Institute will prove satisfactory.

Oil of the SE/SF variety performs a multitude of functions in addition to its basic job of reducing friction of the engine's moving parts. Through a balanced formula of polymeric dispersants and metallic detergents, the oil prevents high temperature and low temperature deposits and also keeps sludge and dirt particles in suspension. Acids, particularly sulphuric acid, as well as other products of combustion of sulphur fuels, are neutralized by the oil. These acids, if permitted to concentrate, may cause corrosion and rapid wear of the internal parts of the engine.

It is important to choose an oil of the proper viscosity for climatic and operational conditions. Viscosity in an index of the oil's thickness at different temperatures. A thicker oil (higher numerical rating) is needed for high temperature operation, whereas thinner oil (lower numerical rating) is required for cold weather operation. Due to the need for an oil that embodies both these characteristics in parts of the country where there is wide temperature variation within a small period of time, multigrade oils have been developed. Basically a multigrade oil is thinner at low temperatures and thicker at high temperatures. For example, a 10W–40 oil exhibits the characteristics of a 10 weight oil when the car is first started and the oil is cold. Its lighter weight allows it to travel to the lubricating surfaces quicker and offer less resistance to starter motor cranking than, let's say, a straight 30 weight oil. But after the engine reaches operating temperature, the 10W–40 oil begins acting like a straight 40 weight oil, its heavier weight providing greater lubricating protection and less susceptibility to foaming than a straight 30 weight oil. Whatever your driving needs, the oil viscosity-temperature chart should prove useful in selecting the proper grade. The SAE viscosity rating is printed or stamped on the top of every oil container.

OIL LEVEL CHECK

The engine oil level should be checked frequently; for instance, at each refueling stop. Be sure that the vehicle is parked on a level surface with the engine off. Also, allow a few minutes after turning off the engine for the oil to drain into the pan or an inaccurate reading will result.

1. Open the hood and remove the engine oil dipstick.
2. Wipe the dipstick with a clean, lint-free rag and reinsert it. Be sure to insert it all the way.
3. Pull out the dipstick and note the oil level. It should be between the SAFE (MAX) mark and the ADD (MIN) mark.
4. If the level is below the lower mark, replace the dipstick and add fresh oil to bring the level within the proper range. Do not overfill.
5. Recheck the oil level and close the hood.

NOTE: *Use a multi-grade oil with API classification SE, or SF*

OIL AND FILTER CHANGE

The engine oil and oil filter should be changed at the recommended intervals on the maintenance schedule chart. After the engine has reached operating temperature, shut it off, firmly apply the parking brake, block the wheels, place a drip pan beneath the oil pan and remove the drain plug. Allow the engine to drain thoroughly before replacing the drain plug.

NOTE: *On some V8 engines a dual sump oil pan was used. When changing the oil both drain plugs (front and side)) must be removed. Failure to remove both plugs can lead to an incorrect oil level reading.*

Place the drip pan beneath the oil filter. To remove the filter, turn it counterclockwise using a strap wrench. Wipe the contact surface of the new filter clean of all dirt and coat the rubber gasket with clean engine oil. Clean the mating surface of the adapter on the block. To install, hand turn the new filter clockwise until the gasket just contacts the cylinder block. Do not use a strap wrench to install. Then hand-turn the filter ½ additional turn. Unscrew the filler cap on the valve cover and fill the crankcase to the proper level on the dipstick with the recommended grade of oil. Install the cap, start the engine and operate at fast idle. Check the oil filter contact area and then drain plug for leaks.

Shut off the engine and allow enough time for the oil to drain back into the oil pan. Recheck the oil level with the dipstick. Add oil as necessary to proper level indicated by the dipstick.

Certain operating conditions may warrant more frequent oil changes. If the vehicle is used for short trips, where the engine does not have a chance to fully warm-up before it is shut off, water condensation and low temperature deposits may make it necessary to change the oil sooner. If the vehicle is used mostly in stop-and-go traffic, corrosive acids and high temperature deposits may necessitate shorter oil changing intervals. The shorter intervals also apply to industrial or rural areas where high concentrations of dust and other airborne particulate matter contaminate the oil. Finally, if the car is used for towing trailers, a severe load is placed on the engine causing the oil to "thin-out" sooner, making necessary the shorter oil changing intervals.

Transmission
LEVEL CHECK
Automatic Transmissions

It is very important to maintain the proper fluid level in an automatic transmission. If the level is either too high or too low, poor shifting operation and internal damage are likely to occur. For this reason a regular check of the fluid level is essential.

1. Drive the vehicle for 15–20 minutes to allow the transmission to reach operating temperature.
2. Park the car on a level surface, apply the parking brake and leave the engine idling. Shift the transmission and engage each gear, then place the gear selector in P (PARK).
3. Wipe away any dirt in the area of the transmission dipstick to prevent it from falling into the filler tube. Withdraw the dipstick, wipe it with a clean, lint-free rag and reinsert it until it seats.
4. Withdraw the dipstick and note the fluid level. It should be between the upper (FULL) mark and the lower (ADD) mark.
5. If the level is below the lower mark, use a funnel and add fluid in small quantities through the dipstick filler neck. Keep the engine running while adding fluid and check the level after each small amount. Do not overfill.

Manual Transmission

The fluid level should be checked every 6 months/6,000 miles, whichever comes first.

1. Park the car on a level surface, turn off the engine, apply the parking brake and block the wheels.
2. Remove the filler plug from the side of the transmission case with a proper size wrench. The fluid level should be even with the bottom of the filler hole.
3. If additional fluid is necessary, add it through the filler hole using a syphon pump or squeeze bottle.
4. Replace the filler plug; do not overtighten.

DRAIN AND REFILL
Automatic Transmission

Refer to Chapter 6 for fluid change procedures.

Manual Transmission

Place a suitable drain pan under the transmission. Remove the drain plug and allow the gear lube to drain out. Replace the drain plug, remove the filler plug and fill the transmission to the proper level with the required fluid. Reinstall the filler plug.

Rear Axle (Differential)
FLUID LEVEL CHECK

Like the manual transmission, the rear axle fluid should be checked every six months/6,000 miles. A filler plug is provided near the center of the rear cover or on the upper (driveshaft) side of the gear case. Remove the plug and check to ensure that the fluid level is even with the bottom of the filler hole. Add SAE 85W/90/95 gear lube as required. If the vehicle is equipped with a limited slip rear axle, add the required special fluid. Install the filler plug but do not overtighten.

DRAIN AND REFILL

Normal maintenance does not require changing the rear axle fluid. However, to do so, re-

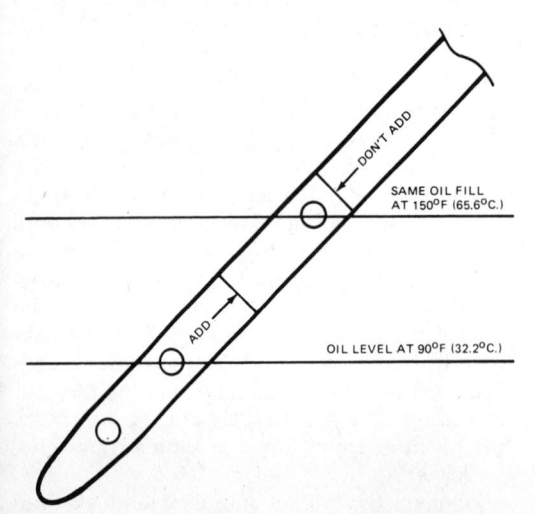

Typical fluid expansion during automatic transmission warm-up

GENERAL INFORMATION AND MAINTENANCE

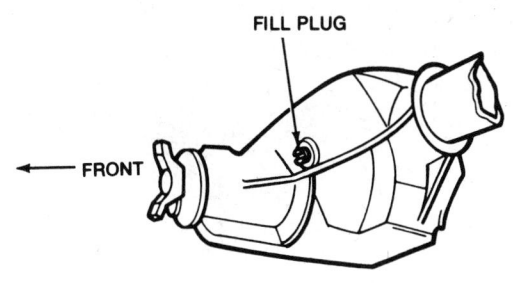

Rear axle fill plug

move the rear drain plug (models equipped), the lower two cover bolts, or the cover. Catch the drained fluid in a suitable container. If the rear cover was removed, clean the mounting surfaces of the cover and rear housing. Install a new gasket (early models) or (on late models) apply a continuous bead of Silicone Rubber Sealant (D6AZ19562A/B or the equivalent) around the rear housing face inside the circle of bolt holes. Install the cover and tighten the bolts. Parts must be assembled within a half hour after the sealant is applied. If the fluid was drained by removing the two lower cover bolts, apply sealant to the bolts before reinstallation. Fill the rear axle through the filler hole with the proper lube. Add friction modifier to limited slip models if required.

Coolant

FLUID RECOMMENDATIONS

When additional coolant is required to maintain the proper level, always added a 50/50 mix of anti-freeze/coolant and water.

LEVEL CHECK

> CAUTION: *Exercise extreme care when removing the cap from a hot radiator. Wait a few minutes until the engine has time to cool somewhat, then wrap a thick towel around the radiator cap and slowly turn it counterclockwise to the first stop. Step back and allow the pressure to release from the cooling system. Then, when the steam has stopped venting, press down on the cap, turn it one more stop counterclockwise and remove the cap.*

The coolant level in the radiator should be checked on a monthly basis, preferably when the engine is cold. On a cold engine, the coolant level should be maintained at one inch below the filler neck on vertical flow radiators, and 2½ in. below the filler neck at the "COLD FILL" mark on crossflow radiators. On cars equipped with the Coolant Recovery System, the level is maintained at the "COLD LEVEL" mark in the translucent plastic expansion bottle. Top up as necessary with a mixture of 50%

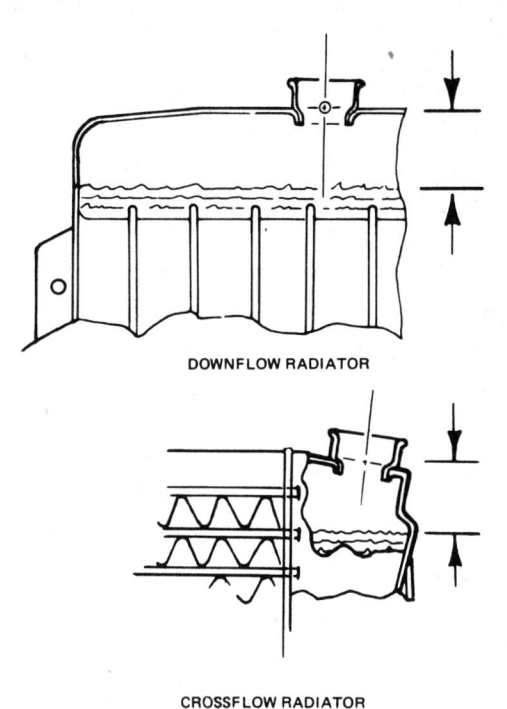

Fill level—crossflow and downflow radiator

water and 50% ethylene glycol antifreeze, to ensure proper rust, freezing and boiling protection. If you have to add coolant more often than once a month or if you have to add more than one quart at a time, check the cooling system for leaks. Also check for water in the crankcase oil, indicating a blown cylinder head gasket.

DRAIN AND REFILL

Completely draining and refilling the cooling system every two years at least will remove accumulated rust, scale and other deposits.

> NOTE: *Use a good quality antifreeze with water pump lubricants, rust inhibitors and other corrosion inhibitors along with acid neutralizers.*

Use a permanent type coolant that meets specification ESE-M97B44A or the equivalent.

1. Drain the existing antifreeze and coolant. Open the radiator and engine drain petcocks (models equipped), or disconnect the bottom radiator hose, at the radiator outlet. Set heater temperature controls to the full HOT position.

> NOTE: *Before opening the radiator petcock, spray it with some penetrating lubricant.*

2. Close the petcock or re-connect the lower hose and fill the system with water.

3. Add a can of quality radiator flush. If equipped with a V6 or diesel engine, be sure flush is safe to use in engines having aluminum components.

26 GENERAL INFORMATION AND MAINTENANCE

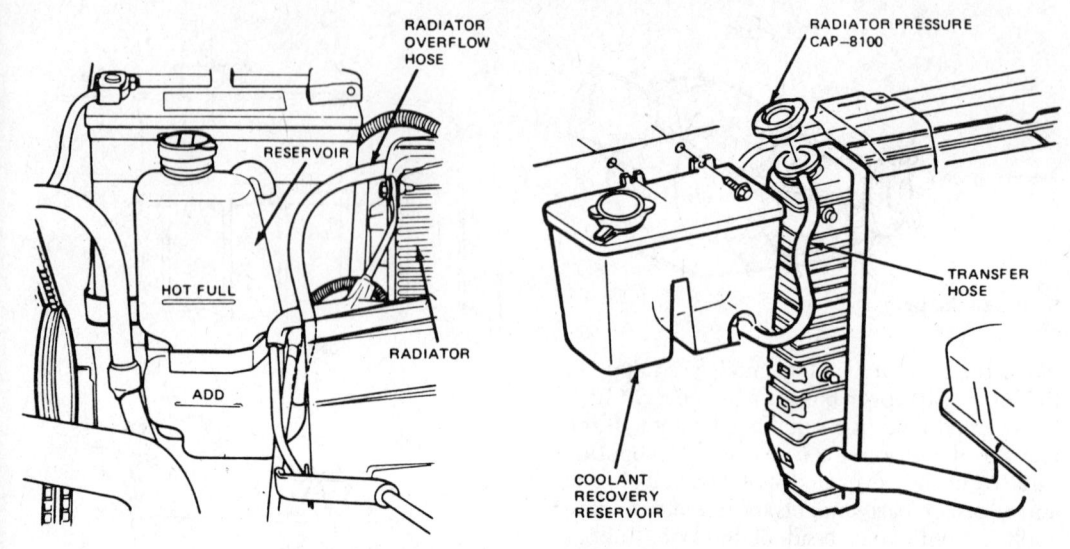

Coolant recovery system variations

4. Idle the engine until the upper radiator hose gets hot.
5. Drain the system again.
6. Repeat this process until the drained water is clear and free of scale.
7. Close all petcocks and connect all the hoses.
8. If equipped with a coolant recovery system, flush the reservoir with water and leave empty.
9. Determine the capacity of your cooling system (see capacities specifications). Add a 50/50 mix of quality antifreeze (ethylene glycol) and water to provide the desired protection.

SYSTEM INSPECTION

Most permanent anti-freeze/coolant have a colored dye added which makes the solution an excellent leak detector. When servicing the cooling system, check for leakage at:
- All hoses and hose connections
- Radiator seams, radiator core, and radiator draincock
- All engine block and cylinder head freeze (core) plugs, and drain plugs
- Edges of all cooling system gaskets (head gaskets, thermostat gasket)
- Transmission fluid cooler
- Heating system components, water pump
- Check the engine oil dipstick for signs of coolant in the engine oil
- Check the coolant in the radiator for signs of oil in the coolant

Investigate and correct any indication of coolant leakage.

Check the Radiator Cap

While you are checking the coolant level, check the radiator cap for a worn or cracked gasket. If the cap doesn't seal properly, fluid will be lost and the engine will overheat.

Worn caps should be replaced with a new one.

Clean Radiator of Debris

Periodically clean any debris—leaves, paper, insects, etc.—from the radiator fins. Pick the large piece off by hand. The smaller pieces can be washed away with water pressure from a hose.

Carefully straighten any bent radiator fins with a pair of needle nose pliers. Be careful—the fins are very soft, Don't wiggle the fins back and forth too much. Straighten them once and try not to move them again.

CHECKING SYSTEM PROTECTION

A 50/50 mix of coolant concentrate and water will usually provide protection to −35°F. Freeze protection may be checked by using a cooling system hydrometer. Inexpensive hydrometers (floating ball types) may be obtained from a local dept. store (automotive section) or an auto supply store. Follow the directions packaged with the coolant hydrometer when checking protection.

Master Cylinder
LEVEL CHECK

The brake fluid in the master cylinder should be checked every 6 months/6,000 miles.

Cast Iron Reservoir

1. Park the vehicle on a level surface and open the hood.
2. Pry the retaining spring bar holding the cover onto the master cylinder to one side.

GENERAL INFORMATION AND MAINTENANCE

3. Clean any dirt from the sides and top of the cover before removal. Remove the master cylinder cover and gasket.
4. Add fluid, if necessary, to within ⅜ths of an inch of the top of the reservoir, or to the full level indicator (on models equipped).
5. Push the gasket bellows back into the cover. Reinstall the gasket and cover and position the retainer spring bar.

Plastic Reservoir

Check fluid level on side of reservoir. If fluid is required, remove the screw on filler cap and gasket from the master cylinder. Fill the reservoir to the full line in the reservoir. Install the filler cap, making sure the gasket is properly seated in the cap.

FLUID RECOMMENDATION

Use only Heavy Duty Brake Fluid meeting DOT 3 specifications.

Power Steering

LEVEL CHECK

Check the power steering fluid level every 6 months/6,000 miles.
1. Park the vehicle on a level surface. Run the engine until normal operating temperature is reached.
2. Turn the steering all the way to the left and then all the way to the right several times. Center the steering wheel and shut off the engine.
3. Open the hood and check the power steering reservoir fluid level.
4. Remove the filler cap and wipe the dipstick attached clean.
5. Reinsert the dipstick and tighten the cap. Remove the dipstick and note the fluid level indicated on the dipstick.
6. The level should be at any point below the Full mark, but not below the Add mark.
7. Add fluid if necessary. Do not overfill.

FLUID RECOMMENDATION

Add Type F automatic transmission fluid, do not overfill the reservoir.

Chassis Greasing

BALL JOINTS

1. Park the vehicle on a level surface, set the parking brake, block the rear wheels, raise the front end and support it with jack stands.
2. Wipe away any dirt from the ball joint lubrication plugs.
3. Pull out the plugs and install grease fittings.
4. Using a hand-operated grease gun con-

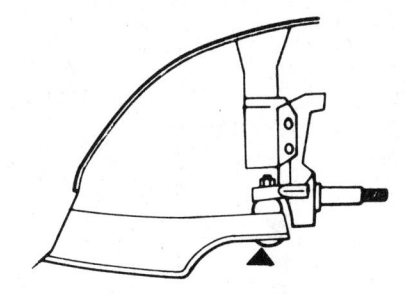

Lower ball joint lubrication points

taining multi-purpose grease, force lubricant into the joint until the joint boot swells.
5. Remove the grease fitting and push in the lubrication plug.
6. Lower the vehicle.

STEERING ARM STOPS

The steering arm stops are attached to the lower control arm. They are located between each steering arm and the upturned end of the front suspension strut.
1. Park the vehicle on a level surface, set the parking brake, block the rear wheels, raise the front end and support it with jack stands.
2. Clean the friction points and apply multipurpose grease.
3. Lower the vehicle.

MANUAL TRANSMISSION AND CLUTCH LINKAGE

On models so equipped, apply a small amount of chassis grease to the pivot points of the transmission and clutch linkage as per the chassis lubrication diagram.

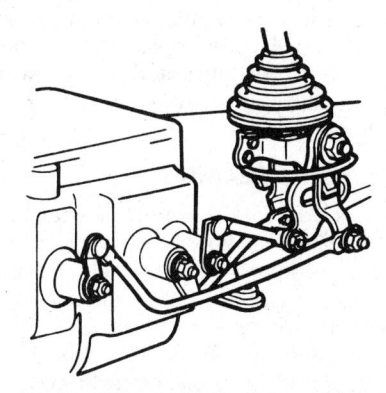

Typical manual transmission linkage lube points

AUTOMATIC TRANSMISSION LINKAGE

On models so equipped, apply a small amount of 10W engine oil to the kickdown and shift linkage at the pivot points.

28 GENERAL INFORMATION AND MAINTENANCE

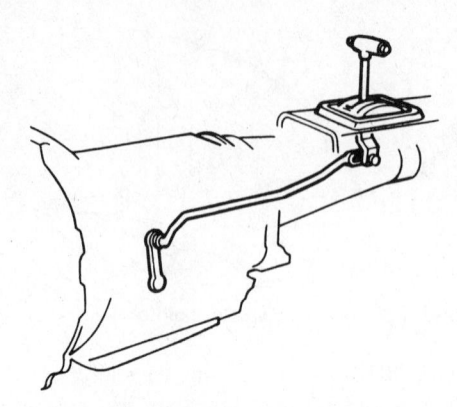

Automatic transmission linkage lube points

PARKING BRAKE LINKAGE

At yearly intervals or whenever binding is noticeable in the parking brake linkage, lubricate the cable guides, levers and linkages with a suitable chassis grease.

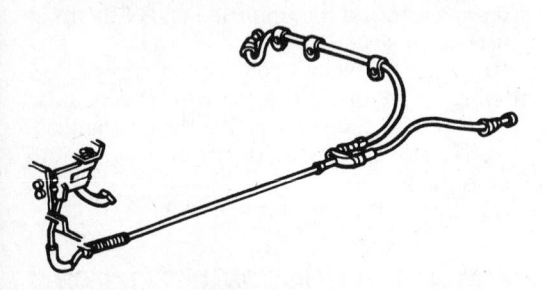

Typical parking brake lube points

BODY LUBRICATION

At the intervals recommended in the maintenance schedule, door, hood and trunk hinges, checks and latches should be greased with a white grease such as Lubriplate®. Also, the lock cylinders should be lubricated with a few drops of graphite lubricant.

DRAIN HOLE CLEANING

The doors and rocker panels of your car are equipped with drain holes to allow water to drain out of the inside of the body panels. If the drain holes become clogged with dirt, leaves, pine needles, etc., the water will remain inside the panels, causing rust. To prevent this, open the drain holes with a screwdriver. If your car is equipped with rubber dust valves instead, simply open the dust valve with your finger.

Front Wheel Bearings

Refer to Chapter 9, "Brakes" for procedure.

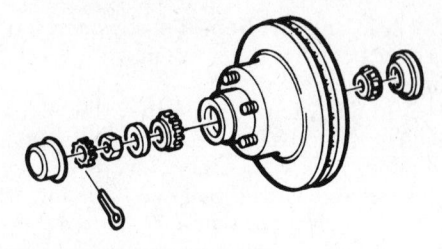

Front wheel bearings

PUSHING AND TOWING

To push start your manual transmission equipped car (automatic transmission models cannot be push started), make sure of bumper alignment. If the bumper of the car pushing does not match with your car's bumper, it would be wise to tie an old tire either on the back of your car, or on the front of the pushing car. Switch the ignition to "ON" and depress the clutch pedal. Shift the transmission to third gear and hold the accelerator pedal about halfway down. Signal the push car to proceed, when the car speed reaches about 10 mph, gradually release the clutch pedal. The car engine should start, if not have the car towed.

NOTE: *Push starting is not recommended for cars equipped with a catalytic converter. Raw gas collecting in the converter may cause damage. Jump starting is recommended.*

If the transmission and rear axle are in proper working order, the car can be towed with the rear wheels on the ground for distances under 15 miles at speeds no greater than 30 mph. If the transmission or rear is known to be damaged or if the car has to be towed over 15 miles or over 30 mph the car must be dollied or towed with the rear wheels raised and the steering wheel secured so that the front wheels remain in the straight-ahead position. Never use the key controlled steering wheel lock to hold the front wheels in position. The steering wheel must be clamped with a special clamping device designed for towing service. If the key

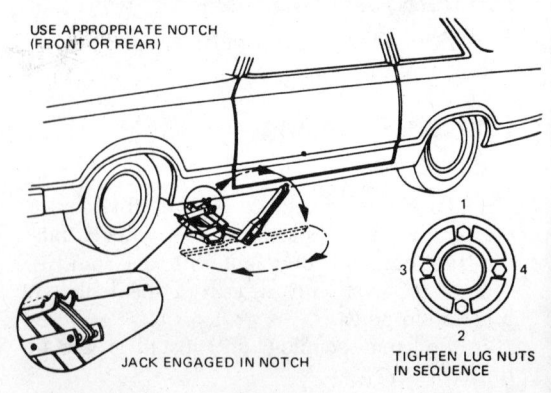

Positioning of scissors jack

GENERAL INFORMATION AND MAINTENANCE

JUMP STARTING A DEAD BATTERY

The chemical reaction in a battery produces explosive hydrogen gas. This is the safe way to jump start a dead battery, reducing the chances of an accidental spark that could cause an explosion.

Jump Starting Precautions

1. Be sure both batteries are of the same voltage.
2. Be sure both batteries are of the same polarity (have the same grounded terminal).
3. Be sure the vehicles are not touching.
4. Be sure the vent cap holes are not obstructed.
5. Do not smoke or allow sparks around the battery.
6. In cold weather, check for frozen electrolyte in the battery. Do not jump start a frozen battery.
7. Do not allow electrolyte on your skin or clothing.
8. Be sure the electrolyte is not frozen.

CAUTION: *Make certain that the ignition key, in the vehicle with the dead battery, is in the OFF position. Connecting cables to vehicles with on-board computers will result in computer destruction if the key is not in the OFF position.*

Jump Starting Procedure

1. Determine voltages of the two batteries; they must be the same.
2. Bring the starting vehicle close (they must not touch) so that the batteries can be reached easily.
3. Turn off all accessories and both engines. Put both cars in Neutral or Park and set the handbrake.
4. Cover the cell caps with a rag—do not cover terminals.
5. If the terminals on the run-down battery are heavily corroded, clean them.
6. Identify the positive and negative posts on both batteries and connect the cables in the order shown.
7. Start the engine of the starting vehicle and run it at fast idle. Try to start the car with the dead battery. Crank it for no more than 10 seconds at a time and let it cool off for 20 seconds in between tries.
8. If it doesn't start in 3 tries, there is something else wrong.
9. Disconnect the cables in the reverse order.
10. Replace the cell covers and dispose of the rags.

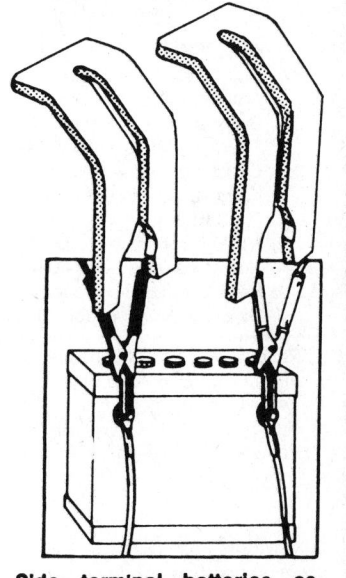

Side terminal batteries occasionally pose a problem when connecting jumper cables. There frequently isn't enough room to clamp the cables without touching sheet metal. Side terminal adaptors are available to alleviate this problem and should be removed after use.

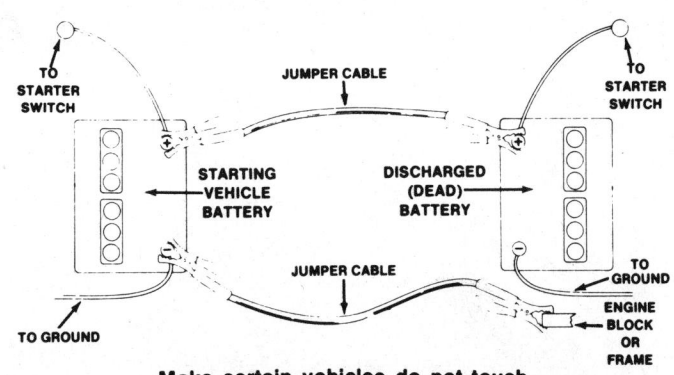

Make certain vehicles do not touch
This hook-up for negative ground cars only

30 GENERAL INFORMATION AND MAINTENANCE

Maintenance Interval Chart
(Intervals in months or miles in thousands whichever occurs first)

Operation	Miles/Months	See Chapter
ENGINE		
Air cleaner element replacement	24	1
Carburetor Idle speed and mixture	22.5	1
Cooling system check	12	1
Coolant replacement; system draining and flushing	24	1
Crankcase breather filter replacement (in air cleaner)	24	1
Drive belts check and adjust	10	1
Evaporator control system check; inspect carbon canister	30	1
Exhaust gas recirculation system (EGR) check	15	4
Fuel filter replacement	12	1
Ignition timing adjustment	①	2
Oil change	7.5 ②	1
Oil filter replacement	②,③	1
PCV valve replacement	20	1
Spark plug replacement	20	2
CHASSIS		
Automatic transmission band adjustment	④	6
Automatic transmission fluid level check	20	1
Brake system inspection, lining replacement	30	9
Brake master cylinder reservoir fluid level check	30	1
Clutch pedal free play adjustment	10	6
Front suspension ball joints and steering linkage lubrication	30	1
Front wheel bearings cleaning, adjusting and repacking	30	9
Manual transmission fluid level check	⑤	1
Power steering pump fluid level check	15	1
Rear axle fluid level check	15	1
Steering arm stop lubrication; steering linkage inspection	15	1

① Periodic adjustment unnecessary
② All 4 cyl. turbocharged vehicles require an oil and oil filter change at 3,000 mile intervals
③ Every oil change
④ Normal service—12,000 miles, Severe (fleet) service—6,000/18,000/30,000 miles
⑤ Periodic fluid level check is unnecessary

controlled lock is used damage to the lock and steering column may occur.

JACKING

Your car is equipped with a scissors type jack. The scissor-type jack is placed under the side of the car so that it fits into the notch in the vertical rocker panel flange nearest the wheel to be changed. These jacking notches are located approximately 8 inches from the wheel opening on the rocker panel flanges.

When raising the car with a jack follow these precautions: Park the car on a level spot, put the selector in P (PARK) with an automatic transmission or in reverse if your car has a manual transmission, apply the parking brake and block the front and the back of the wheel that is diagonally opposite the wheel being changed. These jacks are fine for changing a tire, but never crawl under the car when it is supported only by the scissors or bumper jack.

CAUTION: *If you're going to work beneath the vehicle, always support it on jackstands.*

Tune-Up and Performance Maintenance

TUNE/UP PROCEDURES

The tune-up is a routine maintenance operation which is essential for the efficient and economical operation, as well as the long life of your car's engine. The interval between tune-ups is a variable factor which depends upon the way you drive your car, the conditions under which you drive it (weather, road type, etc.), and the type of engine installed in your car. It is generally correct to say that no car should be driven more than 12,000 miles between tune-ups, especially in this age of emission controls and fuel shortages. If you plan to drive your car extremely hard or under severe weather conditons, the tune-ups should be performed at closer intervals. High performance engines (turbocharged four cylinder and 5.0L V8) require more frequent tuning than other engines, regardless of weather or driving conditions.

Four-cylinder engines are much more sensitive to "state-of-tune" than are six-cylinder or V8 engines, because each cylinder is responsible for 25% of the engine's power output. A misfiring or fouled spark plug in a "four" cuts engine power by *one quarter*, and affects engine efficiency and mileage the same way. The problem *doubles* when two cylinders are not running properly. An out-of-tune six or V8 may not be as noticeable as an out-of-tune four, as there are more cylinders to "take up the slack," but this does not mean that these larger engines should be neglected. Rather, you should adhere to the recommended tune-up schedule for *all* engines.

The replaceable parts involved in a tune-up include the spark plugs, air filter, distributor cap, rotor, and spark plug wires. In addition to these parts and the adjustments involved in properly adapting them to your engine, there are several adjustments of other parts involved in completing the job. These include carburetor idle speed and air/fuel mixture, ignition timing, and valve clearance adjustments.

This chapter gives specific procedures on how to tune-up your car and is intended to be as complete and basic as possible. There is another more generalized section for tune-ups in Chapter 10, which includes trouble-shooting diagnosis for the more experienced weekend mechanic.

CAUTION: *When working with a running engine, make sure that there is proper ventilation. Also make sure that the transmission is in Neutral (unless otherwise specified) and the parking brake is fully applied. Always keep hands, clothing and tools well clear of the hot exhaust manifold(s) and radiator. Remove any wrist or long neck jewelry, or ties before beginning any job, and tuck long hair under a cap. Use EXTREME caution when working around spinning fan blades or belts. When the engine is running, do not grasp the ignition wires, distributor cap, or coil wire, as a shock in excess of 20,000 volts may result. Whenever working around the distributor, even if the engine is not running, make sure that the ignition is switched off.*

Spark Plugs

A typical spark plug consists of a metal shell surrounding a ceramic insulator. A metal electrode extends downward through the center of the insulator and protrudes a small distance. Located at the end of the plug and attached to the side of the outer metal shell is the side electrode. The side electrode bends in at a 90° angle so that its tip is even with, and parallel to, the tip of the center electrode. The distance between these two electrodes (measured in thousandths of an inch) is called the spark plug gap. The spark plug in no way produces a spark but merely provides a gap across which the

32 TUNE-UP AND PERFORMANCE MAINTENANCE

Tune-Up Specifications

Year	Engine No. Cyl Displacement (cu. in.)	Spark Plugs Orig Type	Gap (in.)	Distributor	Ignition Timing (deg)▲ Man	Auto	Intake Valve Opens (deg)	Fuel Pump Pressure (psi)	Idle Speed (rpm)▲ Man	Auto
1979	4-140	AWSF-42	.034	Electronic	6B	20B	22	5.5–6.5	850	850(750)
	4-140 (Turbo)	AWSF-32	.034	Electronic	2B	—	22	6.5–7.5	900	—
	6-170	AWSF-42	.034	Electronic	—	9(6)B	28	3.5–5.8	—	650(600)
	8-302	ASF-52	.050	Electronic	12B	6B	16	5.5–6.5	800	600
	8-302 (Calif.)	ASF-52-6	.060	Electronic	12B	6B	16	5.5–6.5	800	600
1980	4-140	AWSF-42	.035	Electronic	6B	20(12)B	22	5.5–6.5	850	750
	4-140 (Turbo)	AWSF-32	.050	Electronic	6(2)B	8(2)B	22	6.5–7.5	900	800
	6-200	BSF-82	.050	Electronic	10B	10B	20	5.5–6.5	700①	550(600)②
	8-255	ASF-42	.050	Electronic	8B	8B	16	4.0–6.0	500	550(500)
1981	4-140	AWSF-42	.034	Electronic	6B	20(12)B	22	5.5–6.5	850	750
	4-140 (Turbo)	AWSF-42	.034	Electronic	6(2)B	—	22	5.5–6.5	900	800(600)
	6-200	BSF-92	.050	Electronic	10B	10B	20	5.5–6.5	700①	550④
	8-255	ASF-52	.050	Electronic	8B	8B	16	5.5–6.5	—	550
1982	4-140	AWSF-42	.034	Electronic	6B	20(12)B	22	5.5–6.5	850	750
	4-140 (Turbo)③	AWSF-42	.034	Electronic	6B	—	22	6.5–7.5	900	—
	6-200	BSF-92	.050	Electronic	10B	10B	20	6.0–8.0	—	700
	8-255	ASF-52	.050	Electronic	—	10B	16	6.0–8.0	—	500
	8-302	ASF-42	.044	Electronic	12B	—	15	6.5–8.0	800	—
1983–85	4-140	AWSF-44	.044	Electronic	⑤	⑤	22	5½–6½	850	800
	4-140 (Turbo)	AWSF-32C	.034	Electronic	⑤	⑤	—	—	⑤	⑤
	6-200	BSF-92	.050	Electronic	⑤	⑤	20	6–8	—	550
	6-232	AWSF-52	.044	Electronic	⑤	⑤	13	6–8⑦	—	700
	8-302	ASF-42⑥	.044	Electronic	⑤	⑤	16	6–8⑧	700	550

NOTE: The underhood specifications sticker often reflects tune-up specification changes made in production. Sticker figures must be used if they disagree with those in the chart.
① 900 with air conditioning
② 700 with air conditioning
③ Canada only
④ 49 states; 700 w/A/C, 600 Calif. and 700 Calif. w/A/C
⑤ Refers to emission sticker
⑥ 1985–ASF52/HO-ASF42
⑦ In tank pump—40–45
⑧ CFI—39 psi
▲ Figures in parentheses are for California; automatic figures taken w/transmission in "Drive"

current can arc. The coil produces anywhere from 20,000 to 40,000 volts which travels to the distributor where it is distributed through the spark plug wires to the spark plugs. The current passes along the center electrode and jumps the gap to the side electrode, and, in so doing, ignites the air/fuel mixture in the combustion chamber.

SPARK PLUG HEAT RANGE

Spark plug heat range is the ability of the plug to dissipate heat. The longer the insulator (or the farther it extends into the engine), the hotter the plug will operate; the shorter the insulator the cooler it will operate. A plug that absorbs little heat and remains too cool will quickly accumulate deposits of oil and carbon since it is not hot enough to burn them off. This leads to plug fouling and consequently to misfiring. A plug that absorbs too much heat will have no deposits, but, due to the excessive heat, the electrodes will burn away quickly and in some instances, preignition may result. Preignition takes place when plug tips get so hot that they

TUNE-UP AND PERFORMANCE MAINTENANCE 33

glow sufficiently to ignite the fuel/air mixture before the actual spark occurs. This early ignition will usually cause a pinging during low speeds and heavy loads.

The general rule of thumb for choosing the correct heat range when picking a spark plug is: if most of your driving is long distance, high speed travel, use a colder plug; if most of your driving is stop and go, use a hotter plug. Original equipment plugs are compromise plugs, but most people never have occasion to change their plugs from the factory-recommended heat range.

REPLACING SPARK PLUGS

A set of spark plugs usually requires replacement after about 10,000 miles on cars with conventional ignition systems and after about 20,000 to 30,000 miles on cars with electronic ignition, depending on your style of driving. In normal operation, plug gap increases about 0.001 in. for every 1,000–2,500 miles. As the gap increases, the plug's voltage requirement also increases. It requires a greater voltage to jump the wider gap and about two to three times as much voltage to fire a plug at high speeds than at idle.

When you're removing spark plugs, you should work on one at a time. Don't start by removing the plug wires all at once, because unless you number them, they may become mixed up. Take a minute before you begin and number the wires with tape. The best location for numbering is near where the wires come out of the cap.

1. Twist the spark plug boot and remove the boot and wire from the plug. Do not pull on the wire itself as this will ruin the wire.
2. If possible, use a brush or rag to clean the area around the spark plug. Make sure that all the dirt is removed so that none will enter the cylinder after the plug is removed.
3. Remove the spark plug using the proper size socket. (Use a 13/16 in. for BRF plugs or 5/8 in. for AWSF and ASF plugs.) Turn the socket counterclockwise to remove the plug. Be sure to hold the socket straight on the plug to avoid breaking the plug, or rounding off the hex on the plug.
4. Once the plug is out, check it against the plugs shown in the "Color" section of this book to determine engine condition. This is crucial since plug readings are vital signs of engine condition.
5. Use a round wire feeler gauge to check the plug gap. The correct size gauge should pass through the electrode gap with a slight drag. If you're in doubt, try one size smaller and one larger. The smaller gauge should go through easily while the larger one shouldn't go through

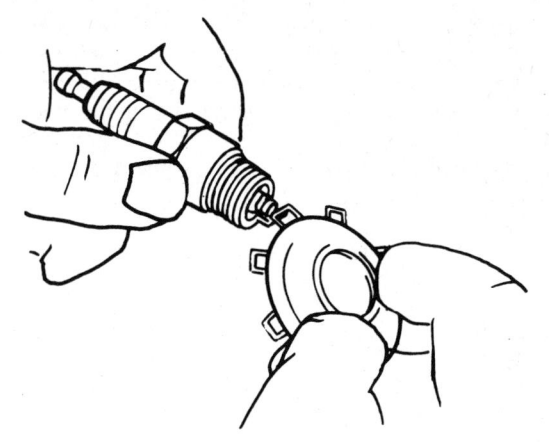

Checking spark plug gap

at all. If the gap is incorrect, use the electrode bending tool on the end of the gauge to adjust the gap. When adjusting the gap, always bend the side electrode. The center electrode is non-adjustable.

6. Squirt a drop of penetrating oil on the threads of the new plug and install it. Don't oil the threads too heavily. Turn the plug in clockwise by hand until it is snug.
7. When the plug is finger tight, tighten it with a wrench. Torque to 10–15 ft. lbs.
8. Install the plug boot firmly over the plug. Proceed to the next plug.

NOTE: *Coat the inside of each spark plug boot with silicone grease (Motorcraft WA-10-D7AZ-19A331A, Dow Corning No. 111 or General Electric G627 are acceptable.) Failure to do so could result in a misfired plug.*

CHECKING AND REPLACING SPARK PLUG CABLES

Visually inspect the spark plug cables for burns, cuts, or breaks in the insulation. Check the spark plug boots and the nipples on the distributor cap and coil. Replace any damaged wiring. If no physical damage is obvious, the wires can be checked with an ohmmeter for excessive resistance. See the "Troubleshooting" chapter.

When installing a new set of spark plug cables, replace the cables one at a time so there will be no mixup. Start by replacing the longest cable first. Install the boot firmly over the spark plug. Route the wire exactly the same as the original. Insert the nipple firmly into the tower on the distributor cap. Repeat the process for each cable.

Ford Solid State Ignition System

All cars are equipped with a solid state igniton system. This system requires no distributor

TUNE-UP AND PERFORMANCE MAINTENANCE

maintenance other than checking the condition of the cap and wires. There are no points to wear out or adjust. Due to the sensitive nature of the system and the complexity of the test procedures, it is recommended that you refer to your dealer if you suspect a problem.

DISTRIBUTOR AND ROTOR CHECK

1. Turn off ignition switch. Inspect distributor components as in distributor exploded illustration to see that all snap rings are in place, and that the electronic pickup assembly moves freely on the fixed base.
2. Blow assembly clean with a bicycle tire pump or other air if available. Make sure no filings or metal chips adhere to the magnetic pickup face.
3. Inspect the cap for cracks, burned contacts, broken carbon button, carbon tracks, or dirt or corrosion in the sockets. Replace the cap if at all damaged.
4. Inspect the rotor for breaks, cracks, carbon tracks, or burns. Replace the rotor if at all corroded or damaged.
5. Install distributor cap, make sure all spark plug wires are tight on their plugs and on the distributor, and start the engine.

NOTE: *When it is necessary to remove a distributor cap or rotor for cleaning and inspection, or when a new rotor is being installed, silicone grease must be applied $1/16$ in. thick to all sides of the brass rotor blade, outboard of the plastic.*

CAUTION: *Do not reapply or attempt to remove any silicone coating from the distributor cap electrodes. As this compound ages, it has the appearance of being a contaminant of the rotor and cap electrodes. This condition is normal and causes no performance loss. Distributor caps and rotors containing silicone grease MUST NOT be cleaned with solvent or mineral spirits. The inside of the cap may be wiped with a soft, dry cloth.*

Dura Spark (Solid State) Ignition

Basically, four electronic ignition systems have been used in Ford Motor Company vehicles.

1. Dura Spark I
2. Dura Spark II
3. Dura Spark III
4. Universal Distributor-TFI (EECIV)

In 1977, the Dura Spark systems, were introduced. Dura Spark I and Dura Spark II systems are nearly identical in operation, and virtually identical in appearance. The Dura Spark I uses a special control module which senses current flow through the ignition coil and adjust the dwell, or coil "on" time for maximum spark intensity. If the Dura Spark I module

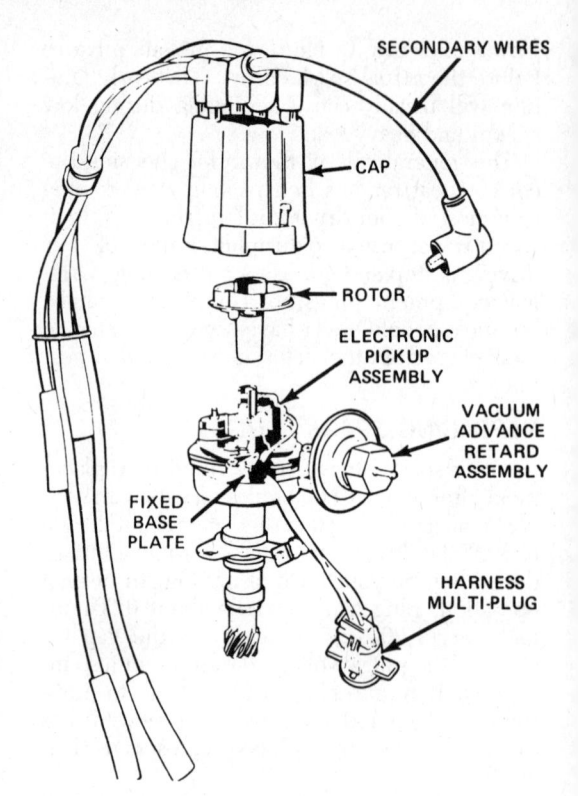

Dura Spark II distributor, disassembled

senses that the ignition is ON, but the distributr shaft is not turning, the current to the coil is turned OFF by the module. The Dura Spark II system does not have this feature—the coil is energized for the full amount of time that the ignition switch is ON. Keep this in mind when servicing the Dura Spark II system, as the ignition system could inadvertently "fire" while performing ignition system services (such as distributor cap removal) while the ignition is ON. All Dura Spark II systems are easily identified by having a two-piece, flat topped distributor cap.

In 1980, the new Dura Spark III system was introduced. This version is based on the previous systems, but the input signal is controlled by the EEC system, rather than as a function of engine timing and distributor armature position. The distributor, rotor, cap, and control module are unique to this system; the spark plugs and plug wires are the same as those used with the Dura Spark II system. Although the Dura Spark II and III control modules are similar in appearance, they cannot be interchanged between systems.

The Versailles with the modified Dura Spark II system, uses a special control module designed to function with the vehicles EEC system.

Some 1978 and later engines use a special

TUNE-UP AND PERFORMANCE MAINTENANCE

Dura Spark Dual Mode ignition control module. The module is equipped with an altitude sensor, an economy modulator, or pressure switches (turbocharged engines only). This module, when combined with the additional switches and sensor, varies the base engine timing according to altitude and engine load conditions. Dura Spark Dual Mode ignition control modules have three wiring harness from the module.

1980–81 49-state and 1982 Canadian 2.3 liter engines with automatic transmissions have Dual Mode Crank Retard ignition module, which has the same function as the Dura Spark II module plus an ignition timing retard function which is operational during engine cranking. The spark timing retard feature eases engine starting, but allows normal timing advance as soon as the engine is running. This module can be identified by the presence of a white connector shell on the four-pin connector at the module.

Some 1981 and later Dura Spark II systems used with some 255 and 302 cu. in. engines are equipped with a Universal Ignition Module (UIM) which includes a run-retard function. The operation of the module is basically the same as the Dura Spark Dual Mode module.

The Universal Distributor (EEC-IV) has a diecast base which incorporates an externally mounted TFI-IV ignition module, and contains a "Hall-Effect" vane switch stator assembly and provision for fixed octane adjustment. No distributor calibration is required and initial timing adjustment is normally not required. The primary function of the EEC-IV Universal Distributor system is to direct high secondary voltage to the spark plugs. In addition, the distributor supplies crankshaft position and frequency information to a computer using a Profile Ignition Pickup. The "Hall-Effect" switch in the distributor consists of a Hall Effect device on one side and a magnet on the other side. A rotary cup which has windows and tabs rotates and passes through the space between the device and the magnet. When a window is between the sides of the switch the magnetic path is not completed and the switch is Off, sending no signal. When a tab passes between the switch the magnetic path is completed and the Hall Effect Device is turned On and a signal is sent. The voltage pulse (signal) is used by is EEC-IV system for sensing crankshaft position and computing the desired spark advance based on engine demand and calibration.

TROUBLESHOOTING DURA SPARK I

The following Dura Spark II troubleshooting procedures may be used on Dura Spark I systems with a few variations. The Dura Spark I module has internal connections which shut off the primary circuit in the run mode when the engine stalls. To perform the above troubleshooting procedures, it is necessary to by-pass these connections. However, with these connections by-passed, the current flow in the primary becomes so great that it will damage both the ignition coil and module unless a ballast resistor is installed in series with the primary circuit at the BAT terminal of the ignition coil. Such a resistor is available from Ford (Motorcraft part number DY-36). A 1.3 ohm, 100 watt wire-wound power resistor can also be used.

To install the resistor, proceed as follows.

NOTE: *The resistor will become very hot during testing.*

1. Release the BAT terminal lead from the coil by inserting a paper clip through the hole in the rear of the horseshoe coil connector and manipulating it against the locking tab in the connector until the lead comes free.

2. Insert a paper clip in the BAT terminal of the connector on the coil. Using jumper leads, connect the ballast resistor as shown.

3. Using a straight pin, pierce both the red and white leads of the module to short these two together. This will by-pass the internal connections of the module which turn off the ignition circuit when the engine is not running.

CAUTION: *Pierce the wires only AFTER the ballast resistor is in place or you could damage the ignition coil and module.*

4. With the ballast resistor and by-pass in place, proceed with the Dura Spark II troubleshooting procedures.

TROUBLESHOOTING DURA SPARK II

The following procedures can be used to determine whether the ignition system is working or not. If these procedures fail to correct the problem, a full troubleshooting procedure should be performed.

Preliminary Checks

1. Check the battery's state of charge and connections.

2. Inspect all wires and connections for breaks, cuts, abrasions, or burn spots. Repair as necessary.

3. Unplug all connectors one at a time and inspect for corroded or burned contacts. Repair and plug connectors back together. DO NOT remove the Lubriplate® compound in the connectors.

4. Check for loose or damaged spark plug or coil wires. A wire resistance check is given at the end of this section. If the boots or nipples are removed on 8mm ignition wires, reline the inside of each with new silicone di-electric compound (Motorcraft WA 10).

TUNE-UP AND PERFORMANCE MAINTENANCE

Special Tools

To perform the following tests, two special tools are needed; the ignition test jumper and a modified spark plug. The test jumper must be used when performing the following tests. The modified spark plug is basically a spark plug with the side electrode removed. Ford makes a special tool called a Spark Tester for this purpose, which besides not having a side electrode is equipped with a spring clip so that it can be grounded to engine metal. It is recommended that the Spark Tester be used as there is less chance of being shocked.

Run Mode Spark Test

NOTE: *The wire colors given here are the main colors of the wires, not the dots or hashmarks.*

STEP 1

1. Remove the distributor cap and rotor from the distributor.
2. With the ignition off, turn the engine over by hand until one of the teeth on the distributor armature aligns with the magnet in the pickup coil.
3. Remove the coil wire from the distributor cap. On 1978 and later models, install the modified spark plug (see Special Tools, above) in the coil wire terminal and using heavy gloves and insulated pliers, hold the spark plug shell against the engine block.
4. Turn the ignition to RUN (not START) and tap the distributor body with a screwdriver handle. There should be a spark at the modified spark plug or at the coil wire terminal.
5. If a good spark is evident, the primary circuit is OK: perform Start Mode Spark Test. If there is no spark, proceed to Step 2.

STEP 2

1. Unplug the module connector(s) which contain(s) the green and black module leads.
2. In the harness side of the connector(s), connect the special test jumper (see Special Tools, above) between the leads which connect to the green and black leads of the module pig tails. Use paper clips on connector socket holes to make contact. Do not allow clips to ground.
3. Turn the ignition switch to RUN (not START) and close the test jumper switch. Leave closed for about 1 second, then open. Repeat several times. There should be a spark each time the switch is opened. On Dura Spark I systems, close the test switch for 10 seconds on the first cycle. After that, 1 second is adequate.
4. If there is no spark, the problem is probably in the primary circuit through the ignition switch, the coil, the green lead or the black lead, or the ground connection in the distributor: perform Step 3. If there is a spark, the primary circuit wiring and coil are probably OK. The problem is probably in the distributor pickup, the module red wire, or the module: perform Step 6.

STEP 3

1. Disconnect the test jumper lead from the black lead and connect it to a good ground. Turn the test jumper switch on and off several times as in Step 2.
2. If there is no spark, the problem is probably in the green lead, the coil, or the coil feed circuit: perform Step 5.
3. If there is spark, the problem is probably in the black lead or the distributor ground connection: perform Step 4.

STEP 4

1. Connect an ohmmeter between the black lead and ground. With the meter on its lowest scale, there should be no measureable resistance in the circuit. If there is resistance, check the distributor ground connection and the black lead from the module. Repair as necessary, remove the ohmmeter, plug in all connections and repeat step 1.
If there is no resistance, the primary ground wiring is OK: perform Step 6.

STEP 5

1. Disconnect the test jumper from the green lead and ground and connect it between the TACH-TEST terminal of the coil and a good ground on the engine.
2. With the ignition switch in the RUN position, turn the jumper switch on. Hold it on for about 1 second then turn it off as in Step 2. Repeat several times. There should be a spark each time the switch is turned off. If there is no spark, the problem is probably in the primary circuit running through the ignition switch to the coil BAT terminal, or in the coil itself. Check coil resistance (test given later in this section), and check the coil for internal shorts or opens. Check the coil feed circuit for opens, shorts or high resistance. Repair as necessary, reconnect all connectors and repeat Step 1. If there is spark, the coil and its feed circuit are OK. The problem could be in the green lead between the coil and the module. Check for open or short, repair as necessary, reconnect all connectors and repeat Step 1.

STEP 6

To perform this step, a voltmeter which is not combined with a dwell meter is needed. The

TUNE-UP AND PERFORMANCE MAINTENANCE

slight needle oscillations (½ V) you'll be looking for may not be detectable on the combined voltmeter/dwell meter unit.

1. Connect a voltmeter between the orange and purple leads on the harness side of the module connectors.

CAUTION: *On catalytic converter equipped cars, disconnect the air supply line between the Thermactor by-pass valve and the manifold before cranking the engine with the ignition off. This will prevent damage to the catalytic converter. After testing, run the engine for at least 3 minutes before reconnecting the by-pass valve, to clear excess fuel from the exhaust system.*

2. Set the voltmeter on its lowest scale and crank the engine. The meter needle should oscillate slightly (about ½ volt). If the meter does not oscillate, check the circuit through the magnetic pick-up in the distributor for open, shorts, shorts to ground and resistance. Resistance between the orange and purple leads should be 400–1000 ohms, and between each lead and ground should be more than 70,000 ohms. Repair as necessary, reconnect all connectors and repeat Step 1.

If the meter oscillates, the problem is probably in the power feed to the module (red wire) or in the module itself: proceed to Step 7.

STEP 7

1. Remove all meters and jumpers and plug in all connectors.

2. Turn the ignition switch to the RUN position and measure voltage between the battery positive terminal and engine ground. It should be 12 volts.

3. Next, measure voltage between the red lead of the module and engine ground. To make this measurement, it will be necessary to pierce the red wire with a straight pin and connect the voltmeter to the straight pin and to ground. DO NOT ALLOW THE STRAIGHT PIN TO GROUND ITSELF.

4. The two readings should be within one volt of each other. If not within one volt, the problem is in the power feed to the red lead. Check for shorts, open, or high resistance and correct as necessary. After repairs, repeat Step 1.

If the readings are within one volt, the problem is probably in the module. Replace with a good module and repeat Step 1. If this corrects the problem, reconnect the old module and repeat Step 1. If problem returns, permanently install the new module.

Start Mode Spark Test

NOTE: *The wire colors given here are the main colors of the wires, not the dots or hashmarks.*

1. Remove the coil wire from the distributor cap. Install the modified spark plug mentioned under "Special Tools," above, in the coil wire and ground it to engine metal either by its spring clip (Spark Tester) or by holding the spark plug shell against the engine block with insulated pliers.

NOTE: *See "CAUTION" under Step 6 of "Run Mode Spark Test," above.*

2. Have an assistant crank the engine using the ignition switch and check for spark. If there is good spark, the problem is probably in the distributor cap, rotor, ignition cables or spark plugs. If there is no spark, proceed to Step 3.

3. Measure the battery voltage. Next, measure the voltage at the white wire of the module while cranking the engine. To make this measurement, it will be necessary to pierce the white wire with a straight pin and connect the voltmeter to the straight pin and to ground. DO NOT ALLOW THE STRAIGHT PIN TO GROUND ITSELF. The battery voltage and the voltage at the white wire should be within 1 volt of each other. If the readings are not within 1 volt of each other, check and repair the feed through the ignition switch to the white wire. Recheck for spark (Step 1). If the readings are within 1 volt of each other, or if there is still no spark after power feed to white wire is repaired, proceed to Step 4.

4. Measure the coil BAT terminal voltage while cranking the engine. The reading should be within 1 volt of battery voltage. If the readings are not within 1 volt of each other, check and repair the feed through the ignition switch to the coil. If the readings are within 1 volt of each other, the problem is probably in the ignition module. Substitute another module and repeat test for spark (Step 1).

TFI SYSTEM TESTING EXCEPT MERKUR

NOTE: *If the engine operates but has no power, the problem could be in the EEC system. Check the initial timing, if the engine is operating at a fixed 10° BTDC the system is in fail-safe mode. Have the EEC system checked with necessary diagnostic equipment.*

NOTE: *After performing any test which requires piercing a wire with a straight pin, remove the straight pin and seal the holes in the wire with silicone sealer.*

Ignition Coil Secondary Voltage

1. Disconnect the secondary (high voltage) coil wire from the distributor cap and install a spark tester (see Special Tools, located with the Dura Spark Troubleshooting) between the coil wire and ground.

2. Crank the engine—a good, strong spark

should be noted at the spark tester. If spark is noted, but the engine will not start, check the spark plugs, spark plug wiring, and fuel system. If there is no spark at the tester:

 a. Check the ignition coil secondary wire resistance; it should be no more than 5000 ohms per inch.
 b. Inspect the ignition coil for damage and/or carbon tracking.
 c. With the distributor cap removed, verify that the distributor shaft turns with the engine; if it does not, repair the engine as required.
 d. If the fault was not found in a, b, or c, proceed to the next test.

Ignition Coil Primary Circuit Switching

1. Insert a small straight pin in the wire which runs from the coil negative (−) terminal to the TFI module, about one inch from the module.
 CAUTION: *The pin must not touch ground.*
2. Connect a 12VDC test lamp between the straight pin and an engine ground.
3. Crank the engine, noting the operation of the test lamp. If the test lamp flashes, proceed to the next test. If the test lamp lights but does not flash, proceed to the Wiring Harness test. If the test lamp does not light at all, proceed to the Primary Circuit Continuity test.

Ignition Coil Resistance

Replace the ignition coil if the resistance is out of the specification range.

Wiring Harness

1. Disconnect the wiring harness connector from the TFI module; the connector tabs must be PUSHED to disengage the connector. Inspect the connector for damage, dirt, and corrosion.
2. Attach the negative lead of a voltmeter to the base of the distributor. Attach the other voltmeter lead to a small straight pin.
 a. With the ignition switch in the RUN position, insert the straight pin into the No. 1 terminal of the TFI module connector. Note the voltage reading and proceed to b.
 b. With the ignition switch in the RUN position, move the straight pin to the No. 2 connector terminal. Again, note the voltage reading, then proceed to c.
 c. Move the straight pin to the No. 3 connector terminal, then turn the ignition switch to the START position. Note the voltage reading then turn the ignition OFF.
3. The voltage readings from a, b, and c should all be at least 90% of the available battery voltage. If the readings are okay, proceed to the Stator Assembly and Module test. If any reading is less than 90% of the battery voltage, inspect the wiring, connectors, and/or ignition switch for defects. If the voltage is low only at the No. 1 terminal, proceed to the ignition coil primary voltage test.

Stator Assembly and Module

1. Remove the distributor from the engine.
2. Remove the TFI module from the distributor.
3. Inspect the distributor terminals, ground screw, and stator wiring for damage. Repair as necessary.
4. Measure the resistance of the stator assembly, using an ohmmeter. If the ohmmeter reading is 800–975 ohms; the stator is okay, but the TFI module must be replaced. If the ohmmeter reading is less than 800 ohms or more than 975 ohms; the TFI module is okay, but the stator assembly must be replaced.
5. Reinstall the TFI module and the distributor.

Primary Circuit Continuity

This test is performed in the same manner as the previous Wiring Harness test, but only the No. 1 terminal conductor is tested (ignition switch in RUN position). If the voltage is less than 90% of the available battery voltage, proceed to the next test.

Ignition Coil Primary Voltage

1. Attach the negative lead of a voltmeter to the distributor base.
2. Turn the ignition switch ON and connect the positive voltmeter lead to the negative (−) ignition coil terminal. Note the voltage reading and turn the ignition OFF. If the voltmeter reading is less than 90% of the available battery voltage, inspect the wiring between the ignition module and the negative (−) coil terminal, then proceed to the last test, which follows.

Ignition Coil Supply Voltage

1. Attach the negative lead of a voltmeter to the distributor base.
2. Turn the ignition switch ON and connect the positive voltmeter lead to the positive (+) ignition coil terminal.
 NOTE: *Note the voltage reading then turn the ignition OFF.*
 If the voltage reading is at least 90% of the battery voltage, yet the engine will still not run: check the ignition coil connector and terminals for corrosion, dirt, and/or damage. Replace the ignition switch if the connectors and terminals are okay.
3. Connect any remaining wiring.

TUNE-UP AND PERFORMANCE MAINTENANCE

TFI MODULE—MERKUR

REMOVAL AND INSTALLATION

1. Disconnect the negative battery cable.
2. Remove the distributor cap with the spark plug wires attached, and position the assembly out of the way.
3. Disconnect the wiring harness from the TFI module.
4. Remove the distributor from the engine. (See distributor removal and installation procedures).
5. Place the distributor on a work bench and remove the two screws that retain the module to the distributor body.
6. Slide the right side of the module down slightly toward the gear end of the gear end of the distributor. Then slide the left end down slightly. Carefully alternate side to side until the module connector pins are free from the distributor.

CAUTION: *Do not attempt to lift the module from the distributor without following Step 6 or the connector pins will be broken.*

7. Coat the metal base of the module uniformly with silicone dielectric compound, approximately 1/32 inch thick.
8. Carefully install the module in the reverse order of removal. Install the two mounting screws and tighten them to 20–30 inch lbs.
9. Install the distributor. Check and adjust the engine ignition timing as required.

Octane Rod—Merkur

REMOVAL AND INSTALLATION

CAUTION: *Changing the timing by using different octane rods will affect emissions calibration.*

1. Remove the distributor cap and rotor.
2. Locate the octane rod adjustment boss and remove the retaining screw.
3. Slide the rod away from the boss slightly until the stator assembly can move freely. Carefully lift the rod over the stator post and remove the rod and grommet. Save the grommet for use with the new rod.
4. Install the grommet on the new rod and reinstall on the distributor. Make sure to "capture" the stator post with the hole in the octane rod.
5. Install and tighten the retaining screw, tighten to 20–30 inch lbs.
6. Reinstall the rotor and distributor cap.

TFI-IV Troubleshooting—Merkur

PRELIMINARY CHECKS

Visually inspect the engine compartment to insure all vacuum hoses and spark plug wires are properly routed and securely connected. Examine all wiring harnesses and connectors for insulation damage, burned, overheated, loose, or broken connections. Check that the TFI module is securely fastened to the distributor base. Make sure that the battery is fully charged and the terminals are clean and tight.

SPARK TEST

1. Connect a spark plug tester (a spark plug with the ground electrode cut off and a grounding clip attach to the hex drive, can be purchased or made from an old spark plug) between the ignition coil wire and good engine ground.
2. Crank the engine. If spark, but the engine will not start; inspect the distributor cap and rotor for damage, carbon tracking or cracks.
3. If no spark; measure the resistance of the ignition coil wire. Replace the wire if the resistance is greater than 5,000 ohms per foot. Inspect the ignition coil for damage or carbon tracking. Crank the engine to verify distributor rotation.
4. Still no spark; proceed to Primary Circuit Switching Test.

PRIMARY CIRCUIT SWITCHING TEST

1. Disconnect the wiring harness from the ignition module and inspect for dirt, corrosion and damage. Reconnect the harness.
2. Attach a 12V DC test light between the coil TACH TEST terminal and engine ground. Crank the engine. If the light flashes or lights without flashing go to the Primary Resistance Test.
3. If the test light does not light or produces a very dim light go to the Primary Circuit Continuity Test.

PRIMARY RESISTANCE TEST

1. Make sure the ignition switch is turned Off. Disconnect the ignition coil connector and inspect for dirt, corrosion and damage.
2. Measure the resistance from the positive (+) to negative (−) terminal of the ignition coil.
3. If resistance is between 0.3–1.0 ohms, resistance is correct. Go to the Secondary Resistance Test.
4. If the resistance measures less than 0.3 or more than 1.0 ohms, replace the ignition coil.

SECONDARY RESISTANCE TEST

1. Measure the resistance between the negative (−) terminal to the high voltage terminal of the ignition coil. If the resistance measures between 8,000–11,500 ohms, resistance is correct. Go to the Wiring Harness Test.
2. If the resistance measures less than 8,000 or greater than 11,500 ohms, replace the ignition coil.

TUNE-UP AND PERFORMANCE MAINTENANCE

WIRING HARNESS TEST

1. Disconnect the wiring harness connector from the ignition module. Inspect for dirt, corrosion and damage.
2. Disconnect the "S" terminal of the starter relay. Attach the negative (−) lead of the VOM to the distributor base. Measure the battery voltage. If the battery voltage measures 90 percent, inspect for damage in the wiring harness and connectors. Check the ignition switch and replace if necessary.
4. Check the circuits of the connectors as follows;
CAUTION: *During the testing, do not allow the straight pin to contact an electrical ground point.*
5. Connect the VOM with the negative (−) lead to the distributor base for ground and the positive (+) lead to a straight pin inserted in the module connector terminal.

Connector Terminal	Wire Circuit	Ign Switch Position
Term 2	To ign coil neg (−) term	Run
Term 3	Run circuit	Run & Start
Term 4	Start circuit	Start

6. Turn the ignition switch Off. Repair circuit as required. Remove the straight pin. Reconnect the "S" terminal of the starter relay.

EEC-IV/TFI-IV TEST

1. Disconnect the ignition module wiring harness and check for dirt, corrosion and damage. Reconnect harness.
2. Disconnect the single wire connector near the distributor and perform a spark test. Check IMS wire for continuity if there is spark. If OK go to EEC Testing Quick Checks.
3. If there is no spark perform Distributor/Module Test.

DISTRIBUTOR/MODULE TEST

1. Remove the distributor from the engine.
2. Install a new module on the distributor. Connect the harness to the module and ground the distributor with a jumper wire. Make a good ground connection.
3. Connect a test spark plug and perform a spark test by rotating the distributor by hand. If spark occurs, install the distributor with the new module.
4. If there is no spark, install the old module on a new distributor and retest. If there is spark, install the new distributor with the old module.

PRIMARY CIRCUIT CONTINUITY

1. Disconnect the harness from the module. Inspect for dirt, corrosion and damage. Connect the negative (−) lead of the VOM to the distributor base. Measure battery voltage.
2. Attach the VOM to a small straight pin inserted in connector terminal No. 2.
CAUTION: *Do not allow the straight pin to be grounded.*
3. Turn the ignition switch to the Run position and measure voltage.
4. Turn the ignition switch Off and remove the straight pin.
5. If the battery is 90 percent of minimum voltage perform the Wiring Harness Test.
6. If the battery voltage is less than 90 percent go to the Primary Voltage Test.

PRIMARY VOLTAGE TEST

1. Attach the negative (−) lead of the VOM to the distributor base for ground.
2. Measure the battery voltage.
3. Turn the ignition switch to the Run position.
4. Measure the voltage at the negative (−) terminal of the igniton coil.
5. Turn the ignition switch Off.
6. If the battery voltage is 90 percent of minimum voltage, check the wiring harness between the ignition module and the coil negative (−) terminal.
7. If the battery voltage is less than 90 percent, perform the Coil Supply Voltage Test.

COIL VOLTAGE SUPPLY TEST

1. Remove the coil connector. Attach the negative (−) lead of the VOM to the distributor base for ground.
2. Measure the battery voltage.
3. Turn the ignition switch to the Run position.
4. Measure the voltage at the positive (+) terminal of the coil.
5. Turn the ignition switch Off. Reconnect the ignition module.
6. If 90 percent of minimum battery voltage is measured, inspect the ignition coil connector for dirt, corrosion and damage. Inspect the coil terminals for dirt corrosion or damage. Replace the ignition coil.
7. If less than 90 percent battery voltage, inspect and service the wiring between the ignition coil and ignition switch. Repair as necessary. Check and replace the ignition switch if necessary.

TUNE-UP AND PERFORMANCE MAINTENANCE

GENERAL TESTING—ALL SYSTEMS

Ignition Coil Test

The ignition coil must be diagnosed separately from the rest of the ignition system.

1. Primary resistance is measured between the two primary (low voltage) coil terminals, with the coil connector disconnected and the ignition switch off. Primary resistance must be 0.71–0.77 ohms for Dura Spark I. For Dura Spark II, it must be 1.13–1.23 ohms. For TFI systems, the primary resistance should be 0.3–1.0 ohms.

2. On Dura Spark ignitions, the secondary resistance is measured between the BATT and high voltage (secondary) terminals of the ignition coil with the ignition off, and the wiring from the coil disconnected. Secondary resistance must be 7350–8250 ohms on Dura Spark I systems. Dura Spark II figure is 7700–9300 ohms. For TFI systems, the primary resistance should be 8000–11,500 ohms.

3. If resistance tests are alright, but the coil is still suspected, test the coil on a coil tester by following the test equipment manufacturer's instructions for a standard coil. If the reading differs from the original test, check for a defective harness.

Resistance Wire Test

Replace the resistance wire if it doesn't show a resistance of 1.05–1.15 for Dura Spark II. The resistance wire isn't used on Dura Spark I or TFI systems.

Spark Plug Wire Resistance

Resistance on these wires must not exceed 5,000 ohms per inch. To properly measure this, remove the wires from the plugs, and remove the distributor cap. Measure the resistance through the distributor cap at that end. Do not pierce any ignition wire for any reason. Measure only from the two ends.

NOTE: *Silicone grease must be reapplied to the spark plug wires whenever they are removed:*

When removing the wires from the spark plugs, a special tool such as the one pictured should be used. Do not pull on the wires. Grasp and twist the boot to remove the wire.

Whenever the high tension wires are removed from the plugs, coil, or distributor, silicone grease must be applied to the boot before reconnection. Use a clean small screwdriver blade to coat the entire interior surface with Ford silicone grease D7AZ-19A331-A, Dow Corning #111, or General Electric G-627.

Adjustments

The air gap between the armature and magnetic pick-up coil in the distributor is not adjustable, nor are there any adjustments for the amplifier module. Inoperative components are simply replaced. Any attempt to connect components outside the vehicle may result in component failure.

Ignition Timing

Ignition timing is the measurement, in degrees of crankshaft rotation, of the point at which the spark plugs fire in each of the cylinders. It is measured in degrees before or after Top Dead Center (TDC) of the compression stroke. Ignition timing is controlled by turning the distributor body in the engine.

Ideally, the air/fuel mixture in the cylinder will be ignited by the spark plug just as the piston passes TDC of the compression stroke. If this happens, the piston will be beginning the power stroke just as the compressed and ignited air/fuel mixture starts to expand. The expansion of the air/fuel mixture then forces the piston down on the power stroke and turns the crankshaft.

Because it takes a fraction of a second for the spark plug to ignite the mixture in the cylinder, the spark plug must fire a little before the piston reaches TDC. Otherwise, the mixture will not be completely ignited as the piston passes TDC and the full power of the explosion will not be used by the engine.

The timing measurement is given in degrees of crankshaft rotation before the piston reaches TDC (BTDC). If the setting for the ignition timing is 5° BTDC, each spark plug must fire 5° before each piston reaches TDC. This only holds true, however, when the engine is at idle speed.

As the engine speed increases, the pistons go faster. The spark plugs have to ignite the fuel even sooner if it is to be completely ignited when the piston reaches TDC. To do this, the distributor has a means to advance the timing

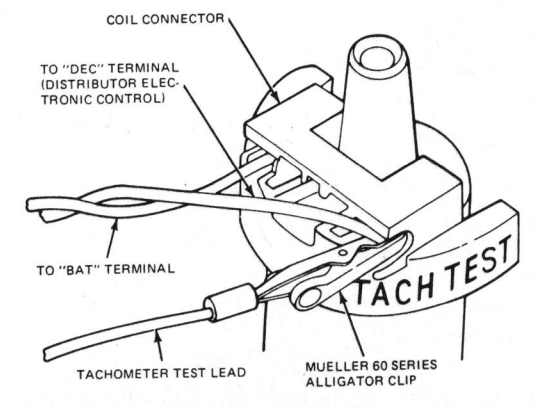

Attaching tachometer lead to coil connector

TUNE-UP AND PERFORMANCE MAINTENANCE

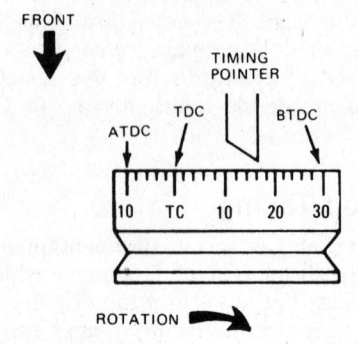

Crankshaft timing marks—4 cyl. 140 engine

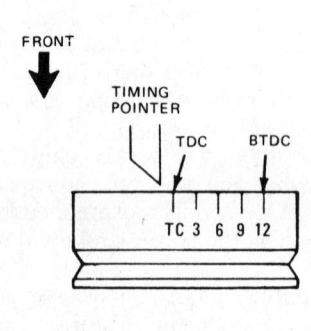

Crankshaft timing marks V6 170 engine

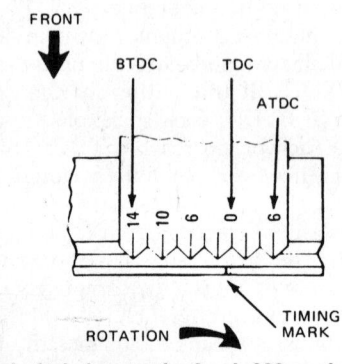

Crankshaft timing marks 6 cyl. 200 engine

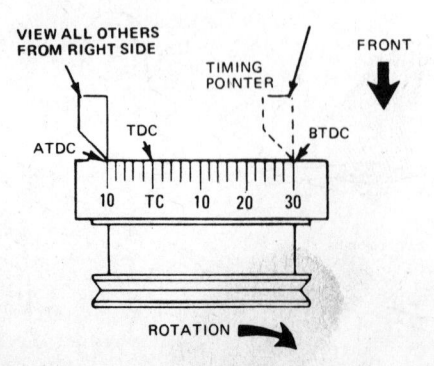

Crankshaft timing marks V6 232 and V8 255, 302 engines

of the spark as the engine speed increases. This is accomplished by centrifugal weights within the distributor and a vacuum diaphragm mounted on the side of the distributor. It is necessary to disconnect the vacuum lines from the diaphragm when the ignition timing is being set.

If the ignition is set too far advanced (BTDC), the ignition and expansion of the fuel in the cylinder will occur too soon and tend to force the piston down while it is still traveling up. This causes engine ping. If the ignition spark is set too far retarded after TDC (ATDC), the piston will have already passed TDC and started on its way down when the fuel is ignited. This will cause the piston to be forced down for only a portion of its travel. This will result in poor engine performance and lack of power.

The timing is best checked with a timing light. This device is usually connected in series with the No. 1 spark plug. The current that fires the spark plug also causes the timing light to flash.

There is a notch on the crankshaft pulley on in-line 6 cyl. engines. A scale of degrees of crankshaft rotation is attached to the engine block in such a position that the notch will pass close by the scale. On the V6 and V8 engines, the scale is located on the crankshaft pulley and a pointer is attached to the engine block so that the scale will pass close by. When the engine is running, the timing light is aimed at the mark on the crankshaft pulley and the scale.

ADJUSTMENT

NOTE: *Some engines have monolithic timing set at the factory. The monolithic system uses a timing receptacle on the front of the engine which can be connected to digital readout equipment, which electronically determines timing. Timing can also be adjusted in the conventional way. Many 1980 and later models are equipped with EEC engine controls. All ignition timing is controlled by the EEC module. Initial ignition timing is not adjustable and no attempt at adjustment should be made on EECIII models, or models equipped with an indexed distributor base. For a description of EEC systems, refer to the Unit Repair sections on "Electronic Ignition Systems" and on "Engine Controls."*

NOTE: *Requirements vary from model to model. Always refer to the "Emissions Specification Sticker" for exact timing procedures.*

1. Locate the timing marks and pointer on the lower engine pulley and engine's front cover.
2. Clean the marks and apply chalk or bright-colored paint to the pointer.
3. On 1981 and later models, if the ignition module has (-12A244-) as a basic part number,

TUNE-UP AND PERFORMANCE MAINTENANCE 43

disconnect the two wire connector (yellow and black wires). On engines equipped with the EECIV system, disconnect the single white (black on some models) wire connector near the distributor.

4. Attach a timing light and tachometer according to manufacturer's specifications.

5. Disconnect the plug all vacuum lines leading to the distributor.

6. Start the engine, allow it to warm to normal operating temperature, then set the idle to the specifications given on the underhood sticker (for timing).

7. On 1981 and later models equipped with the module mentioned in Step 3, jumper the pins in the module connector for the yellow and black wires.

8. Aim the timing light at the timing mark and pointer on the front of the engine. If the marks align when the timing light flashes, remove the timing light, set the idle to its proper specification, and connect the vacuum lines at the distributor. If the marks do not align when the light flashes, turn the engine off and loosen the distributor holddown clamp slightly.

9. Start the engine again, and observe the alignment of the timing marks. To advance the timing, turn the distributor counterclockwise, on six cylinder engines except the 232 (3.8L) V6, or clockwise, for the 232 (3.8L) V6 and V8 engines. When altering the timing, it is wise to tap the distributor lightly with a wooden hammer handle to move it in the desired direction. Grasping the distributor with your hand may result in a painful electric shock. When the timing marks are aligned, turn the engine off and tighten the distributor hold-down clamp. Remove the test equipment, reconnect the vacuum hoses and white (black) single wire connector (EECIV).

10. On 1981 and later models equipped with the module mentioned in Step 3, remove the jumper connected in Step 7 and reconnect the two wire connector. Test the module operation as follows:

   a. Disconnect and plug the vacuum source hose to the ignition timing vacuum switch.

   b. Using an external vacuum source, apply vacuum greater than 12 in. Hg to the switch, and compare the ignition timing with the requirements below:
   - 4 cylinder—per specifications less 32°–40°
   - 6 cylinder—per specifications less 21°–27°
   - 8 cylinder—per specifications less 16°–20°

TACHOMETER CONNECTION

The coil connector used with DuraSpark is provided with a cavity for connection of a tachometer, so that the connector doesn't have to be removed to check engine rpm.

Install a tach lead with an alligator clip on its end into the cavity marked TACH TEST and connect the other lead to a good ground.

If the coil connector must be removed, pull it out horizontally until it is disengaged from the coil terminal.

FIRING ORDERS

To avoid confusion, replace spark plug wires one at a time.

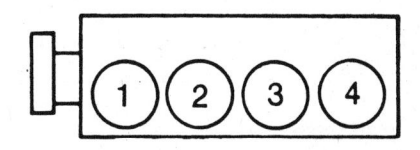

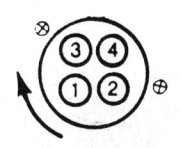

FORD MOTOR CO. 2300 cc 4-cyl.
Engine firing order: 1-3-4-2
Distributor rotation: clockwise

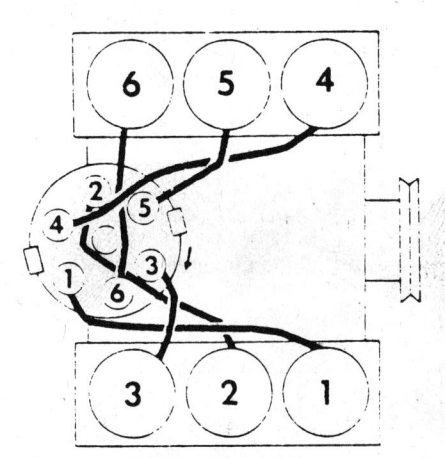

FORD MOTOR CO, 2800cc V6
Engine firing order: 1-4-2-5-3-6
Distributor rotation: Clockwise

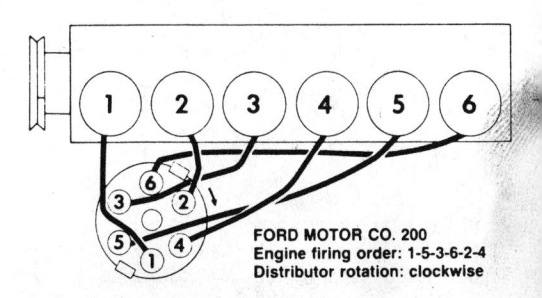

FORD MOTOR CO. 200
Engine firing order: 1-5-3-6-2-4
Distributor rotation: clockwise

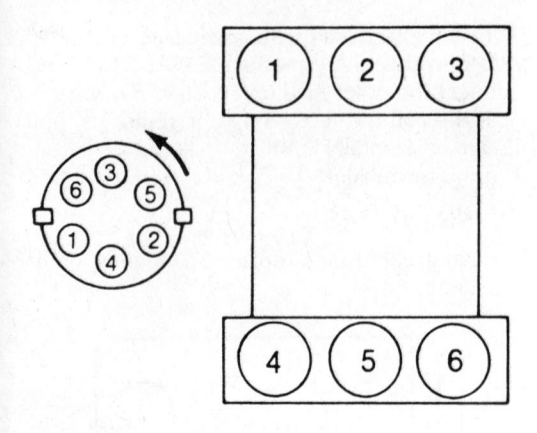

44 TUNE-UP AND PERFORMANCE MAINTENANCE

FORD MOTOR CO. 232 V6
Engine firing order: 1-4-2-5-3-6
Distributor rotation: counterclockwise

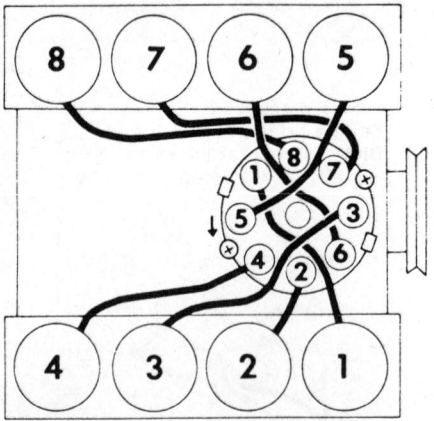

FORD MOTOR CO. 255,302 (exc. HO)
V8 Engine firing order: 1-5-4-2-6-3-7-8
Distributor rotation: counterclockwise

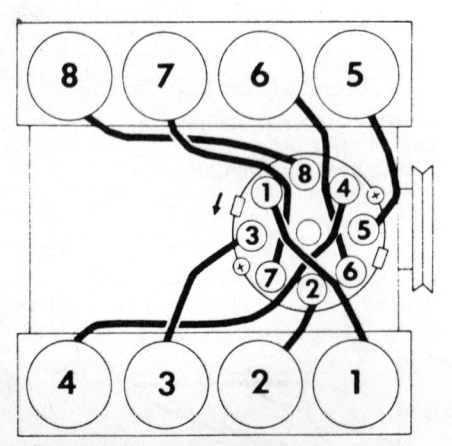

FORD MOTOR CO. 302HO
Engine firing order: 1-3-7-2-6-5-4-8
Distributor rotation: counterclockwise

Carburetor Adjustments

This section contains only carburetor adjustments as they normally apply to engine tuneup. Descriptions of the carburetor and complete adjustment procedures can be found in Chapter 4, under "Fuel System."

IDLE SPEED AND MIXTURE ADJUSTMENTS

NOTE: *Since the design of the 2700 VV and 7200 VV carburetor is different from all other Motorcraft carburetors in many respects, the adjusting procedures are necessarily different as well. Although the idle speed adjustment alone is identical, there is further information you will need to know in order to adjust the 2700 VV and 7200 VV properly. Refer to Chapter 4 for an explanation.*

NOTE: *In order to limit exhaust emissions, plastic caps have been installed in the idle fuel mixture screw(s), which prevent the carburetor from being adjusted to an overly rich idle fuel mixture. Under no circumstances should these limiters be modified or removed. A satisfactory idle should be obtained within the range of the limiter(s).*

1. Start the engine and run it at idle until it reaches operating temperature (about 10–20 minutes, depending on outside temperatures). Stop the engine.

2. Check the ignition timing as outlined earlier in this chapter.

3. Remove the air cleaner, taking note of the hose locations, and check that the choke plate is in the open position (plate in vertical position). Check the accompanying illustrations to see where the carburetor adjustment locations are. If you cannot reach them with the air cleaner installed, leave it off temporarily. Otherwise, reinstall the air cleaner assembly including all the hose connections.

NOTE: *Leaving the air cleaner removed will affect the idle speed; therefore, adjust the curb idle speed to a setting 50–100 rpm higher than specified, if the air cleaner is off. When the air cleaner is reinstalled the idle speed should be to specifications.*

4. Attach a tachometer to the engine, with the positive wire connected to the distributor side of the ignition coil, and the negative wire connected to a good ground, such as an engine bolt.

NOTE: *In order to attach an alligator clip to the distributor side (terminal) of the coil (primary connection), it will be necessary to lift off the connector and slide a female loop type connector (commercially available) down over the terminal threads. Then push down the rubber connector over the loop connec-*

TUNE-UP AND PERFORMANCE MAINTENANCE

tor and connect the alligator clip of your tachometer. *On late models a "tach" connector is provided.*

5. All idle speed adjustments are made with the headlights off (unless otherwise specified on the engine decal), with the air conditioning off (if so equipped), with all vacuum hoses connected, with the throttle solenoid positioner activated (connected, if so equipped), and with the air cleaner on. (See Note after Step 3.) Finally, all idle speed adjustments are made in Neutral on cars with manual transmission, and in Drive on cars equipped with automatic transmission.

CAUTION: *Whenever performing these adjustments, block all four wheels and set the parking brake.*

6a. On cars not equipped with a throttle solenoid positioner, the idle speed is adjusted with the curb idle speed adjusting screw. Start the engine. Turn the curb idle speed adjusting screw inward or outward until the correct idle speed (see "Tune-Up Specifications" chart) is reached, remembering to make the 50–100 rpm allowance if the air cleaner is removed.

6b. On cars equipped with a throttle solenoid positioner, the idle speed is adjusted with solenoid adjusting screw (nut), in two stages. Start the engine. The higher speed is adjusted with the solenoid connected. Turn the solenoid adjusting screw (nut) on 1 or 4 barrel carburetors, or the entire bracket on 2 barrel carburetors inward or outward until the correct higher idle speed (see "Turn-Up Specifications" chart) is reached, remembering to make the 50–100 rpm allowance if the air cleaner is removed. After making this adjustment on cars equipped with 2 barrel carburetors, tighten the solenoid adjusting locknut. The lower idle speed is adjusted with the solenoid lead wire disconnected near the harness (not at the carburetor). Place automatic transmission equipped cars in Neutral for this adjustment. Using the curb idle speed adjusting screw on the carburetor, turn the idle speed adjusting screw inward or outward until the correct lower idle speed (see "Tune-Up Specifications" chart) is reached, remembering again to make the 50–100 rpm allowance if the air cleaner is removed. Finally, reconnect the solenoid, slightly depress the throttle lever and allow the solenoid plunger to fully extend.

7. If removed, install the air cleaner. Recheck the idle speed. If it is not correct, Step 6 will have to be repeated and the approximate corrections made.

8. To adjust the idle mixture, turn the idle mixture screw(s) inward to obtain the smoothest idle possible within the range of the limiter(s).

9. Turn off the engine and disconnect the tachometer.

NOTE: *If any doubt exists as to the proper idle mixture setting for your car, have the exhaust emission level checked at a diagnostic center or garage with an exhaust (HC/CO) analyzer or an air/fuel ratio meter.*

Fuel Injection

NOTE: *Prior to adjusting the curb idle speed, set the parking brake and block all four wheels. Make all adjustments with the engine at normal operating temperature. Have all accessories turned off. If the underhood "Emissions Sticker" gives different specs and procedures than those following, always follow the sticker as it will reflect production changes and calibration differences.*

V6-CENTRAL FUEL INJECTION (CFI)

NOTE: *The EEC-IV system and an idle speed motor control the curb idle speed on models equipped with the V6 engine. The idle speed is not adjustable except for minimum and maximum throttle stop adjustment screw clearance. Too little clearance will prevent the throttle from closing as required thus causing a faster than normal idle speed. Any other problems with the system must be checked by EEC-IV system diagnosis.*

Minimum/Maximum Limit Adjustment

NOTE: *Exact sequence must be followed when checking the adjustment.*

1. Adjust is checked with the idle speed motor plunger fully retracted. Run the engine until normal operating temperature is reached, shut the engine off. Remove the air cleaner.

2. Locate the self test connector and self test input connector. Both are under the hood by the driver's side strut tower.

3. Connect a jumper wire between the single input connector and the signal return pin of the self test connector. The signal return pin is on the upper right of the plug when the plug is held straight on with the four prongs on the bottom facing you.

4. The motor plunger should retract when the jumper wire is connected and the ignition key turned to the Run position. If not, the EEC-IV system requires testing and service.

5. Wait about ten seconds until the plunger is fully retracted. Turn the key Off and remove the jumper.

6. If the idle speed was too high, remove the throttle stop adjusting screw and install a new one. With the throttle plates completely closed, turn the throttle stop adjusting screw in until a gap of .005 inch is present between the screw

tip and the throttle lever contact surface. Turn the screw in an additional 1½ turns to complete the adjustment.

7. If the idle speed was too low, remove the dust cover from the motor tip. Push the tip back toward the motor to remove any play. Measure the clearance between the motor tip and throttle lever by passing a 9/32 inch drill bit in between, a slight drag is required.

8. If adjustment is required, turn the motor bracket adjusting screw until proper clearance is obtained. Tighten the lock and install the dust cover.

V8-CENTRAL FUEL INJECTION (CFI)

1. Connect a tachometer, start the engine and allow to reach normal operating temperature.
2. Shut the engine Off and restart. Run at about 2000 rpm for a minute. Allow the engine to return to idle and stabilize for about 30 seconds. Place the gear selector in Reverse (Parking brake on and all four wheels blocked).
3. Adjust the curb idle as required using the saddle bracket adjusting screw.
4. If the rpms are too low, turn off the engine and turn the adjusting screw one full turn. If the speed is too high, turn off the engine and turn the screw counterclockwise.
5. Repeat Steps 2 and 4 until correct idle speed is obtained.

4 CYLINDER EFI TURBO

NOTE: *Idle speed is controlled by the EEC-IV system and a air by-pass valve. If the following procedure does not correct idle rpm, EEC-IV system diagnosis is required.*

1. Run the engine until normal operating temperature is reached. Turn off all accessories.
2. Turn off the engine. Disconnect the power lead to the idle speed by-pass control valve. Connect a tachometer to the engine.
3. Start the engine and run at 2000 rpm for two minutes. If the electric cooling fan comes on, disconnect the wiring harness connector.
4. Let the engine return to normal idling rpm and check speed on the tachometer.
5. Adjust rpm if necessary with the throttle plate stop screw.
6. Turn the engine off and reconnect the by-pass valve lead and cooling fan harness.
7. Restart the engine and check idle speed.

Valve Adjustment

All of the Mustang and Capri engines use hydraulic valve lifters except the V6 170 cu in. engine. Valve systems with hydraulic valve lifters operate with zero clearance in the valve train, and because of this the rocker arms are non-adjustable. The V6 170 cu in. engine however, is equipped with mechanical lifters and should be adjusted at the recommended interval.

NOTE: *While all valve adjustments must be as accurate as possible, it is better to have the valve adjustment slightly loose than slightly tight, as burnt valves may result from overly tight adjustments.*

V6 170 CU IN. ENGINE

1. Remove the air cleaner assembly and disconnect the negative battery cable.
2. Remove the Thermactor air by-pass valve and its mounting bracket.
3. Remove the two engine lifting eyes; remove the alternator drive belt, loosen the alternator mounting bolts and wing the alternator outward toward the fender.
4. Remove the plug wires and remove the rocker covers.
5. When removing the rocker covers, remove or reposition any wires or hoses which might block the removal of the rocker covers.
6. Torque the rocker arm support bolts to 46 ft. lbs.
7. Reconnect the battery cable, place the transmission in Neutral (manual) or Park (automatic), and apply the parking brake.
8. Place a finger on the adjusting screw of the intake valve rocker arm for cylinder No. 5. Cylinder numbering is shown under Firing Order at the start of the section. Valve arrangement, from front to rear, on the left bank is I-E-E-I-E-I; on the right it is I-E-I-E-E-I. You will be able to feel the rocker arm begin to move.
9. Use a remote starter switch to turn the engine over until you can just feel the valve begin to open. Now the cam is in position to adjust the intake and exhaust valves on the No. 1 cylinder.

Adjusting valve lash, 2.8L V6

Valve Clearance Adjustment
V6 170 Cu. In. Engine

Intake Valve Just Opening for Cyl.:	Adjust Both Valves For This Cylinder (Intake—0.016 in.; Exhaust—0.018 in.)
5	1
3	4
6	2
1	5
4	3
2	6

10. Adjust the No. 1 intake valve so that a 0.016 in. feeler gauge has a slight drag, while a 0.017 in. feeler gauge is a tight fit. To decrease lash, turn the adjusting screw clockwise; to increase lash, turn the adjusting screw counterclockwise. There are no lockbolts to tighten as the adjusting screws are self-tightening.

CAUTION: *Do not use a step-type "go-no go" feeler gauge. When checking lash, you must insert the feeler gauge and move it parallel with the crankshaft. Do not move it in and out perpendicular with the crankshaft as this will give an erroneous feel which will result in overtightened valves.*

11. Adjust the exhaust valve the same way so that an 0.018 in. feeler gauge has a slight drag, while a 0.019 in. gauge is a tight fit.

12. The rest of the valves are adjusted in the same way, in their firing order (1-4-2-5-3-6), by positioning the cam according to the following chart:

13. Remove all the old gasket material from the cylinder heads and rocker cover gasket surfaces, and disconnect the negative cable from the battery.

14. Remove the spark plug wires and reinstall the rocker arm covers.

15. Reinstall any hoses and wires which were removed previously.

16. Reinstall the spark plug wires, the alternator drive belt, and the Termactor air bypass valve and its mounting bracket.

17. Reconnect the battery cable, replace the air cleaner assembly, start the engine, and check for leaks.

Engine and Engine Rebuilding

3

ENGINE ELECTRICAL

Distributor

REMOVAL

1. Remove the air cleaner on the V6 and V8 engines.
2. On the 4-cylinder and 6-cylinder in-line engines, remove one thermactor pump mounting bolt, and the drive belt; then swing the pump to one side to allow access to the distributor. If necessary disconnect the thermactor air filter and lines.
3. Disconnect the distributor wiring connector from the vehicle wiring harness.
4. Disconnect the vacuum lines from the distributor.
5. Remove the distributor cap and wires and lay to one side. Remove the rotor and adapter then reinstall the rotor.
6. Scribe a mark on the distributor body and the cylinder block indicating the position of the rotor in the distributor and the distributor in the block. These marks will be used as guides during installation of the distributor.
7. Remove the distributor hold down bolt and clamp and lift the distributor out of the block.

NOTE: *Do not rotate the engine while the distributor is out of the block, or it will be necessary to time the engine.*

INSTALLATION

1a. If the engine was cranked (disturbed) with the distributor removed, it will now be necessary to retime the engine. If the distributor has been installed incorrectly and the engine will not start, remove the distributor from the engine and start over again. Hold the distributor close to the engine and install the cap on the distributor in its normal position. Locate the No. 1 spark plug tower on the distributor cap. Scribe a mark on the body of the distributor

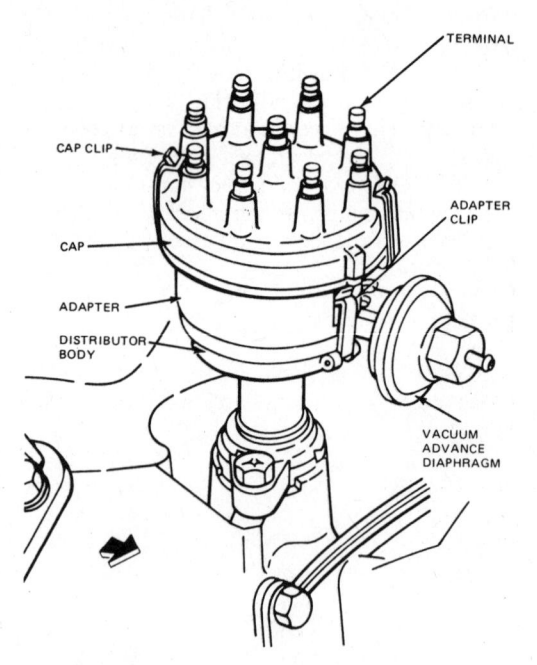

Typical distributor assembly

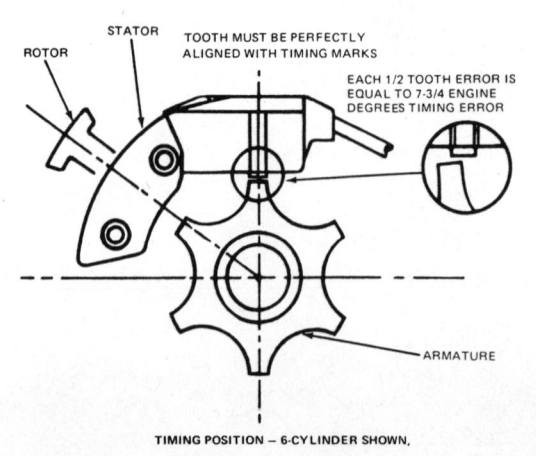

Static timing position, six cylinder shown, four cylinder very similar

ENGINE AND ENGINE REBUILDING

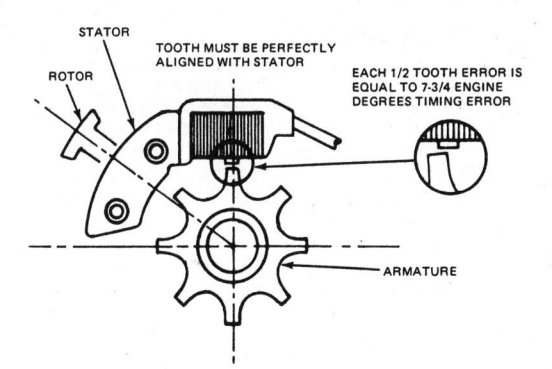

Static timing position, V8 engine; V6 similar

directly below the No. 1 spark plug wire tower on the distributor cap. Remove the distributor cap from the distributor and move the distributor and cap to one side. Remove the No. 1 spark plug and crank the engine over until the No. 1 cylinder is on its compression stroke. To accomplish this, place a wrench on the lower engine pulley and turn the engine slowly in a clockwise (4 & 6 cylinder) or counterclockwise (V8) direction until the TDC mark on the crankshaft damper aligns with the timing pointer. If you place your finger in the No. 1 spark plug hole, you will feel air escaping as the piston rises in the combustion chamber. One of the armature segments must be aligned with the stator as shown in the accompanying illustration to install the distributor. Make sure that the oil pump intermediate shaft properly engages the distributor shaft. It may be necessary to crank the engine with the starter, after the distributor drive gear is partially engaged, in order to engage the oil pump intermediate shaft. Install, but do not tighten the retaining clamp and bolt. Rotate the distributor to advance the timing to a point where the armature tooth is aligned properly. Tighten the clamp.

1b. If the engine was not cranked (disturbed) when the distributor was removed, position the distributor in the block with the rotor aligned with the mark previously scribed on the distributor body and the marks on the distributor body and cylinder block in alignment. Install the distributor hold-down bolt and clamp fingertight.

2. Install the vacuum hoses and connect the ignition wire to the wiring harness.
3. Install the rotor adapter and distributor cap.
4. Install the thermactor pump and belt on the four and in-line six cylinder engines. Adjust the belt tension so that there is a ¼ inch deflection at its longest point.
5. Connect the thermactor hoses and the filter.
6. Install the air cleaner if removed and check the ignition timing.

Alternator

ALTERNATOR PRECAUTIONS

To prevent damage to the alternator and regulator, the following precautions should be taken when working with the electrical system.
1. Never reverse the battery connections.
2. Booster batteries for starting must be connected properly—positive-to-positive and negative-to-negative.
3. Disconnect the battery cables before using a fast charger; the charger has a tendency to force current through the diodes in the opposite direction for which they were designed. This burns out the diodes.
4. Never use a fast charger as a booster for starting the vehicle.
5. Never disconnect the voltage regulator while the engine is running.
6. Avoid long soldering times when replacing diodes or transistors. Prolonged heat is damaging to AC generators.
7. Do not use test lamps of more than 12 volts (V) for checking diode continuity.
8. Do not short across or ground any of the terminals on the AC generator.
9. The polarity of the battery, generator, and regulator must be matched and considered before making any electrical connections within the system.
10. Never operate the alternator on an open circuit. Make sure that all connections within the circuit are clean and tight.
11. Disconnect the battery terminals when performing any service on the electrical system. This will eliminate the possibility of accidental reversal of polarity.
12. Disconnect the battery ground cable if arc welding is to be done on any part of the car.

SIDE TERMINAL ALTERNATOR
Removal

1. Disconnect the ground cable at the battery.
2. Loosen the alternator attaching bolt and remove the adjustment arm attaching bolt. Remove the drive bolt from the pulley.
3. Remove the electrical connectors from the alternator. To remove the stator and field connectors depress the lock tab and pull the connector straight off the terminals.
4. Remove the alternator attaching bolt and remove the alternator.

ENGINE AND ENGINE REBUILDING

Charging System Diagnosis

Condition	Possible Cause	Resolution
Battery does not stay charged—engine starts OK	1. Battery 2. Loose or worn alternator belt 3. Defective wiring or cables 4. Alternator 5. Regulator 6. Other vehicle electrical systems	1. Test battery, replace if necessary 2. Adjust or replace belt 3. Service as required 4. Test and/or replace components as required 5. Test, replace if necessary 6. Check other systems for current draw. Service as required
Alternator noisy	1. Loose or worn alternator belt 2. Bent pulley flanges 3. Alternator	1. Adjust or replace belt 2. Replace pulley 3. Service or replace alternator
Battery uses excessive water—lights and/or fuses burn out frequently	1. Defective wiring 2. Alternator regulator 3. Battery	1. Service as required 2. Replace if necessary 3. Test, replace if necessary
Charge indicator light stays on after engine starts	1. Loose or worn alternator belt 2. Alternator 3. Regulator	1. Adjust or replace 2. Service or replace 3. Replace
Charge indicator lights flickers while vehicle is being driven	1. Loose or worn alternator belt 2. Loose or improper wiring connections 3. Alternator 4. Regulator	1. Adjust or replace belt 2. Service as required 3. Service or replace 4. Service or replace
Charge indicator gauge shows discharge. (If constant high reading, see "Battery uses excessive water").	1. Loose or worn alternator belt 2. Defective wiring (Battery to alternator for ground or open) 3. Alternator 4. Regulator 5. Charge indicator gauge wiring and connections 6. Defective gauge 7. Other vehicle electrical systems malfunction	1. Adjust or replace belt 2. Service or replace wiring 3. Service or replace 4. Replace 5. Service as required 6. Replace gauge 7. Service as required

Installation

1. Position the alternator to the engine, and install the spacer (if used) and the alternator attaching bolt. Tighten the bolt to a snug position.
2. Install the adjustment arm attaching bolt.
3. Install the drive belt on the pulley and adjust the belt tension. Apply pressure on the alternator front housing adjusting ear and tighten the adjusting arm bolt and the alternator mounting bolt. Test the tightness of the belt by pressing it firmly with your thumb at its longest run. The deflection should be about a 1/4 inch.
4. Connect the electrical connectors to the alternator.
5. Connect the battery ground cable.

REAR TERMINAL ALTERNATOR

Removal

1. Disconnect the ground cable from the battery.
2. Loosen the alternator pivot bolt and adjuster bolt and remove the drive belt.
3. Disconnect the wiring terminals from the back of the alternator. The push on type terminals should be pulled straight off the terminal to prevent damage to the terminal.
4. Remove the alternator adjuster bolt and pivot bolt and remove the alternator.

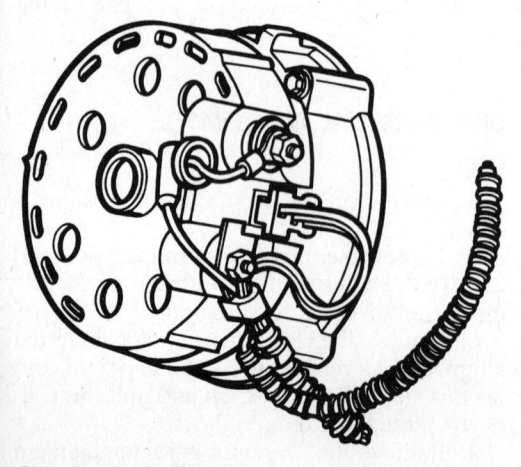

Side terminal alternator

ENGINE AND ENGINE REBUILDING 51

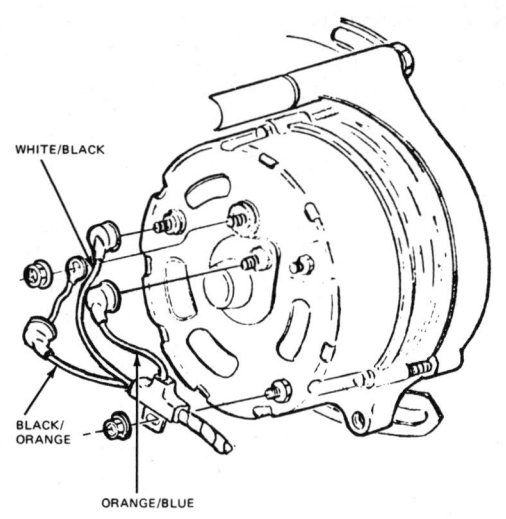

Rear terminal alternator

Installation

1. Position the alternator on the engine and install the pivot bolt and the adjuster bolt and tighten until snug.
2. Connect the wiring terminals to the back of the alternator.
3. Install the drive belt and tighten the tension until there is a ¼ inch deflection at its longest span. Apply pressure on the front housing only.
4. Tighten the adjuster bolt and connect the ground cable to the battery.

Regulator
Except Merkur

The electronic regulators used on the Mustang and Capri are 100 percent solid stage, consisting of transistors, diodes, and resistors. The Merkur uses a solid state regulator "built-into" the rear of the alternator. The regulators are preset and calibrated by the manufacturer. No readjustment is required or possible on these units.

REMOVAL AND INSTALLATION

1. Remove the battery ground cable.
2. Disconnect the regulator from the wiring harness.
  NOTE: *Always disconnect the connector plug from the regulator before removing the regulator mounting screws. Removing the connector from an ungrounded regulator with the ignition switch on will destroy the regulator.*
3. Remove the regulator mounting screws and remove the regulator.
4. Installation is the reverse of removal.

Starter

For starting system troubleshooting refer to the Troubleshooting chapter.

The function of the starting system is to crank the engine at a speed fast enough to permit the engine to start. Heavy-duty cables, connectors, and switches are used in the starting system because of the large current required by the starter while it is cranking the engine. It is critical that the amount of resistance in the starting system be kept to a minimum to provide maximum current for starter operation. A discharged or damaged battery, loose or corroded connections or partially broken cables will result in slower than normal cranking speeds, and may even prevent the starter from cranking the engine.

The starting system consists of a positive engagement drive starter, battery, a remote control starter switch (part of the ignition switch), the neutral-start switch (automatic transmission with floor shift only), the starter relay, and the heavy circuit wiring.

When the ignition swtich is turned to the start position it actuates the starter relay, through the starter control circuit. The starter relay then connects the battery to the starter.

REMOVAL AND INSTALLATION
1979–80
ALL ENGINES

1. Disconnect the ground cable from the battery.
2. Jack up the front end of the car and safely support it with jackstands. Firmly apply the parking brake and block the rear wheels.
3. Remove the four bolts retaining the crossmember under the bellhousing.
4. Remove the flex coupling clamping screw at the attachment point to the steering gear.
5. Remove the three nuts and bolts that attach the steering gear to the crossmember.
6. Disengage the steering gear from the flex coupling and pull the steering gear down to provide access to the starter motor.
7. Disconnect the starter cable from the motor.
8. Remove the starter motor attaching bolts and remove the motor.
9. Installation is the reverse of removal.

1981 and Later Models
2.3L 4-CYLINDER ENGINE

1. Disconnect negative battery cable.
2. Jack up the front of the car and safely support it with jackstands. Firmly apply the parking brake and block the rear wheels.

52 ENGINE AND ENGINE REBUILDING

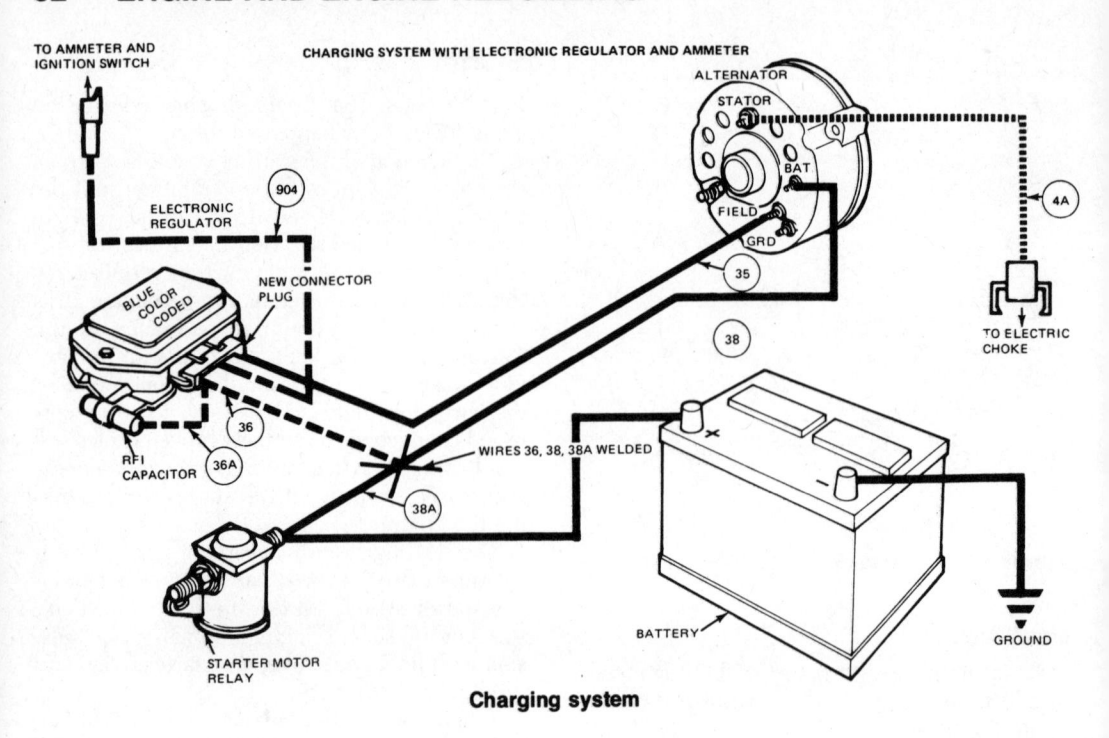

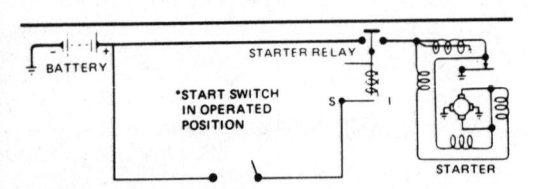

Charging system

3. Remove the two bolts retaining the starter heat shield.
4. Disconnect starter cable from motor.
5. Remove starter attaching bolts and carefully slide starter out and clear of engine.
6. Installation is the reverse of removal.

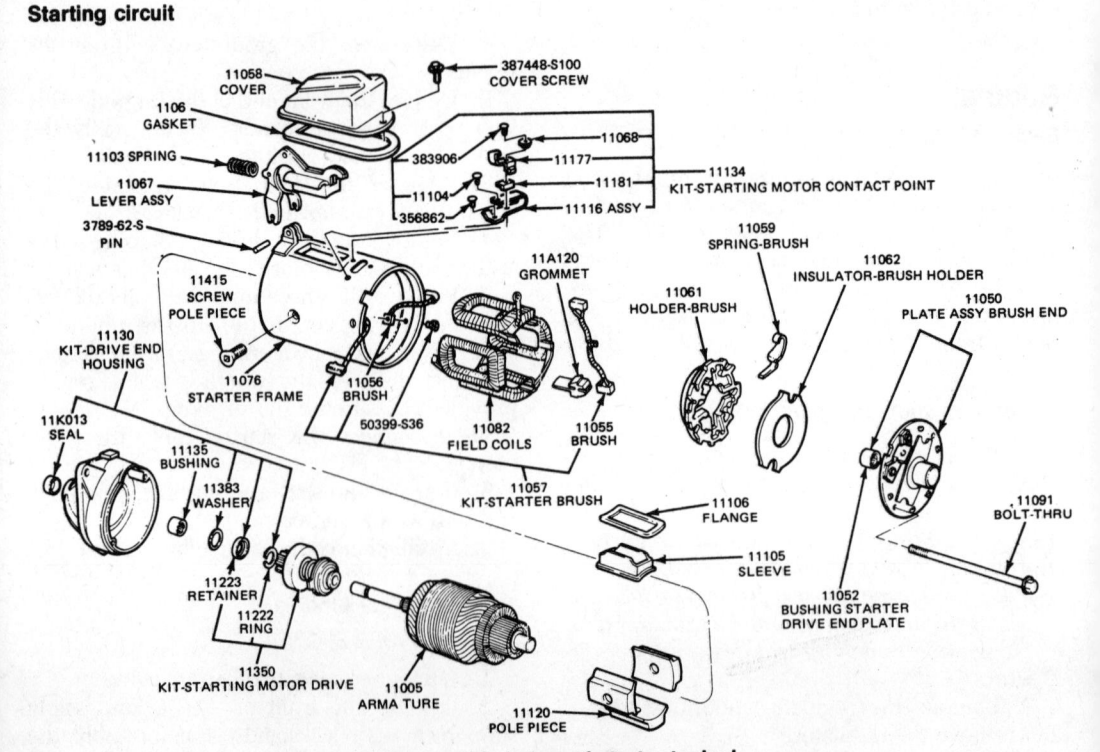

Starting circuit

Disassembled view of starter typical

ENGINE AND ENGINE REBUILDING

3.3L 6-CYLINDER ENGINE

1. Disconnect negative battery cable.
2. Jack up the front of the car and safely support it with jackstands. Firmly apply the parking brake and block the rear wheels.
3. Remove the top starter bolt.
4. Remove starter heat shield by loosening the bottom starter bolt, and removing the nut from the stud.
5. Disconnect starter cable from motor.
6. Remove the bottom starter mounting bolt.
7. Carefully slide starter out and clear of engine.
8. Installation is the reverse of removal.

4.2L AND 5.0L V8 ENGINES

1. Disconnect the negative battery cable.
2. Jack up the front end of the car and safely support it with jackstands. Firmly apply the parking brake and block the rear wheels.
3. Remove the wishbone brace.
4. Disconnect the starter cable from motor.
5. Remove starter attaching bolts and remove starter assembly.
6. Installation is reverse of removal.

STARTER BRUSH REPLACEMENT

Rebuilt starters for all Mustang and Capri models are available at most auto parts stores. The relative low cost of these starters, compared with the time and cost of starter brush replacement, makes brush replacement impractical.

STARTER DRIVE REPLACEMENT

1. Remove the starter from the engine.
2. Remove the brush cover band.
3. Remove the starter drive plunger lever cover.
4. Loosen the thru-bolts just enough to allow removal of the drive end housing and the starter drive plunger lever return spring.
5. Remove the pivot pin which attaches the starter drive plunger lever to the starter frame and remove the lever.
6. Remove the stop ring retainer and stopring from the armature shaft.
7. Remove the starter drive from the armature shaft.
8. Inspect the teeth on the starter drive. If they are excessively worn, inspect the teeth on the ring gear of the flywheel. If the teeth on the flywheel are excessively worn, the flywheel ring gear should be replaced.
9. Apply a thin coat of white grease to the armature shaft, in the area in which the starter drive operates.
10. Install the starter drive on the armature shaft and install a new stop-ring.
11. Position the starter drive plunger lever on the starter frame and install the pivot pin. *Make sure the plunger lever is properly engaged with the starter drive.*
12. Install a new stop ring retainer on the armature shaft.
13. Fill the drive end housing bearing bore ¼ full with grease.
14. Position the starter drive plunger lever return spring and the drive end housing to the starter frame.
15. Tighten the starter thru-bolts to 65 in. lbs.
16. Install the starter drive plunger lever cover and the brush cover band on the starter.
17. Install the starter.

Battery

REMOVAL AND INSTALLATION

1. Loosen the battery cable bolts and spread the ends of the battery cable terminals using a small pry lever.
2. Disconnect the negative battery cable first, then the positive cable, using pliers or slip-joint pliers. If the cables seem stuck on the terminal posts, twist the clamps on the posts gently in both directions until they turn freely.
3. Remove the battery hold-down.
4. Wearing work gloves, remove the battery from under the hood. *Be careful not to tip the battery and spill acid on yourself or the car during removal.*
5. Before installation, follow all recommended steps in the "Battery Maintenance" section of this book.
6. Place the battery in its holder, wearing work gloves to protect your hands from any acid that may be present.
7. Install the positive battery cable first, then install the negative cable.
8. Apply a light coating of grease or petroleum jelly to the battery cables once connected. This will help retard corrosion on the terminals.

ENGINE MECHANICAL

Engine Removal and Installation

NOTE: *Disconnect the negative battery cable before beginning any work. Always label all disconnected hoses, vacuum lines and wires, to prevent incorrect reassembly. Do not disconnect any air conditioning lines unless you are thoroughly familiar with A/C systems and the hazards involved; escaping refrigerant (freon) will freeze any surface it contacts, including skin and eyes. Have the*

54 ENGINE AND ENGINE REBUILDING

General Engine Specifications

Year	Engine Displacement Cu. In.	Carburetor Type	Horsepower (@ rpm)	Torque @ rpm (ft. lbs.)	Bore x Stroke (in.)	Compression Ratio	Oil Pressure @ rpm (psi)
1979	4-140	2 bbl.	88 @ 4800	118 @ 2800	3.781 x 3.126	9.0:1	50 @ 2000
	4-140 (Turbo)	2 bbl.	—	—	3.781 x 3.126	9.0:1	55 @ 2000
	6-170	2 bbl.	109 @ 4800	142 @ 2800	3.66 x 2.70	8.7:1	40–55 @ 1500
	8-302	2 bbl.	140 @ 3600	250 @ 1800	4.00 x 3.00	8.4:1	40–60 @ 2000
	8-302 (Calif.)	2 bbl.	143 @ 3600	243 @ 2200	4.00 x 3.00	8.1:1	40–60 @ 2000
1980–81	4-140	2 bbl.	88 @ 4600	119 @ 2600	3.781 x 3.126	9.0:1	50 @ 2000
	4-140 (Calif.)	2 bbl.	89 @ 4800	122 @ 2600	3.781 x 3.126	9.0:1	50 @ 2000
	4-140 (Turbo)	2 bbl.	—	—	3.781 x 3.126	9.0:1	55 @ 2000
	6-200	2 bbl.	90 @ 3800	160 @ 1600	3.68 x 3.126	8.6:1	30–50 @ 2000
	8-255	VV	118 @ 3800	193 @ 2200	3.68 x 3.00	8.8:1	40–60 @ 2000
1982	4-140	2 bbl.	88 @ 4600	118 @ 2600	3.781 x 3.126	9.0:1	50 @ 2000
	4-140 (Turbo) ①	2 bbl.	—	—	3.781 x 3.126	9.0:1	55 @ 2000
	6-200	1 bbl.	88 @ 3800	158 @ 1400	3.68 x 3.126	8.6:1	30–50 @ 2000
	8-255	2 bbl.	111 @ 3400	205 @ 2600	3.68 @ 3.00	8.2:1	40–60 @ 2000
	8-302	2 bbl.	155 @ 4200	235 @ 2400	4.00 x 3.00	8.4:1	40–60 @ 2000
1983	4-140	1 bbl.	88 @ 4600	118 @ 2800	3.781 x 3.126	9.0:1	40–60 @ 2000
	6-200	1 bbl.	87 @ 3800	154 @ 1400	3.680 x 3.130	8.6:1	30–50 @ 2000
	6-232	CFI	112 @ 4000	175 @ 2600	3.810 x 3.390	8.7:1	40–60 @ 2000
	8-302	4 bbl.	140 @ 3400	265 @ 2000	4.000 x 3.000	8.4:1	40–60 @ 2000
'84–'85	4-140	1 bbl.	88 @ 4600	118 @ 2800	3.781 x 3.126	9.0:1	40–60 @ 2000
	4-140	EFI ①	145 @ 3800	180 @ 3600	3.781 x 3.126	8.0:1	40–60 @ 2000
	6-232	CFI	—	—	3.810 x 3.390	8.6:1	40–60 @ 2000
	8-302	2 bbl.	155 @ 3600	265 @ 2000	4.000 x 3.000	8.4:1	40–60 @ 2000
	8-302	CFI	140 @ 3200	250 @ 1600	4.000 x 3.000	8.4:1	40–60 @ 2000
	8-302	4 bbl	175 @ 4000	245 @ 2200	4.000 x 3.000	8.3:1	40–60 @ 2000

■ Horsepower and torque are SAE net figures. They are measured at the rear of the transmission with all accessories installed and operating. Since the figures vary when a given engine is installed in different models, some are representative rather than
① Merkur w/manual trans: HP-175 @ 5000 Torque—200 @ 3000

---

system discharged professionally before required repairs are started.

1. Scribe the hood hinge outline on the under-hood, disconnect the hood and remove.
2. Drain the entire cooling system and crankcase.
3. Remove the air cleaner, disconnect the battery at the cylinder head. On automatic transmission equipped cars, disconnect the fluid cooler lines at the radiator. On the four cylinder, remove the exhaust manifold shroud.
4. Remove the upper and lower radiator hoses and remove the radiator. If equipped with air conditioning, unbolt the compressor and position compressor out of way with refrigerant lines intact. Unbolt and lay the refrigerant condenser forward without disconnecting refrigerant lines.

NOTES: *If there is not enough slack in the refrigerant lines to position the compressor out of the way, the refrigerant in the system must be evacuated (using proper safety precautions) before the lines can be disconnected from the compressor.*

5. Remove the fan, fan belt and upper pulley. On models equipped with an electric cooling fan, disconnect the power lead and remove the fan and shroud as an assembly.
6. Disconnect the heater hoses from the engine. On four cylinder engines, disconnect

ENGINE AND ENGINE REBUILDING

Valve Specifications

Year	Engine Displacement cu. in.	Seat Angle (deg.)	Face Angle (deg.)	Spring Test Pressure (lbs. @ in.)	Spring Installed Height (in.)	Stem to Guide Clearance (in.) Intake	Stem to Guide Clearance (in.) Exhaust	Stem Diameter (in.) Intake	Stem Diameter (in.) Exhaust
1979	4-140	45	45	159–175 @ 1.16	1 9/16	.0010–.0027	.0015–.0032	.3420	.3415
	V6-170	45	45	138–149 @ 1.22	1 19/32	.0008–.0025	.0018–.0035	.3163	.3153
	8-302	45	45	①	②	.0010–.0027	.0015–.0032	.3420	.3429
1980–85	4-140	45	44	⑥	1 9/16	.0010–.0027	.0015–.0032	.3420	.3415
	6-200	45	44	148–156 @ 1.21	1 19/32	.0008–.0025	.0010–.0027	.3104	.3104
	8-255	45	44	200 @ 1.30	④	.0010–.0027	.0015–.0032	.3400	.3415
	8-302	45	44	⑤	②	.0010–.0027	.0015–.0032	.3420	.3415
	6-232	45	44	215 @ 1.79	1 3/4	.0010–.0027	.0015–.0032	.3420	.3415

① Intake: 200 @ 1.31
   Exhaust: 200 @ 1.20
② Intake: 1 11/16
   Exhaust: 1 5/8
③ Intake: 200 @ 1.30
   Exhaust: 200 @ 1.20
④ Intake: 1 44/64
   Exhaust: 1 38/64
⑤ 194–214 @ 1.36
   Exhaust: 190–210 @ 1.20
⑥ 1979–81: Intake 71–79 @ 1.56
   Exhaust: 159–175 @ 1.16
   1982: 167 @ 1.16
   1983: 149 @ 1.12
   1984/85: 154 @ 1.12
   1985 Merkur—71–79 @ 1.52

the heater hose from the water pump and choke fittings.

7. Disconnect the alternator wires at the alternator, the starter cable at the starter, the accelerator rod at the carburetor.

8. Disconnect and plug the fuel tank line at the fuel pump on models equipped with fuel injection, de-pressurize the fuel system.

9. Disconnect the coil primary wire harness. Disconnect wires at the oil pressure and water temperature sending units. Disconnect the brake booster vacuum line, if so equipped.

10. Remove the starter and dust seal.

11. With manual transmission, remove the clutch retracting spring. Disconnect the clutch equalizer shaft and arm bracket at the under-

Torque Specifications
All readings in ft. lbs.

Year	Engine Displacement cu. in. (cc)	Cylinder Head Bolts	Rod Bearing Bolts	Main Bearing Bolts	Crankshaft Pulley Bolt	Flywheel-to-Crankshaft Bolts	Manifolds
1979	4-140	80–90	30–36	80–90	100–120	54–64	①
	V6-170	65–80	21–25	65–75	92–103	47–51	②
	8-302	65–72	19–24	60–70	70–90	75–85	19–27
1980–85	4-140	80–90 ⑤	30–36	80–90	100–120	54–64	①
	6-200	70–75	19–24	60–70	85–100	75–85	—
	6-232	⑥	⑦⑧	85–100	75–85	18.4	15–22
	8-255	65–72 ④	19–24	60–70	70–90	75–85	19–27 ③
	8-302	65–72 ④	19–24	60–70	70–90	75–85	19–27 ③

① Two steps: 5–7, then 14–21
② Four steps: 3–6, 6–11, 11–15, 15–18
③ After assembly retorque with engine hot
④ Torque in 2 steps:
   First step 55–62 ft. lbs.
   Second step 65–72 ft. lbs.
⑤ Torque in two steps: First 50–60. Second 80–90
⑥ Soak bolts in oil, torque in sequence to 68–81 ft. lbs. Loosen two turns then retorque to 65–81 ft. lbs.
⑦ Soak nuts in oil, torque to 30–36 ft. lbs. Loosen two turns then retorque to 30–36 ft. lbs.
⑧ Soak bolts in oil, torque to 62–81 ft. lbs. Loosen two turns then retorque to 62–81 ft. lbs.

ENGINE AND ENGINE REBUILDING

Crankshaft and Connecting Rod Specifications
All measurements are given in inches

Year	Engine No. Cyl. Displacement (cu. in.)	Main Brg. Journal Dia	Main Brg. Oil Clearance	Shaft End-Play	Thrust on No.	Journal Diameter	Oil Clearance	Side Clearance
'78–'85	6-200	2.2482–2.2490	.0005–.0022 ①	.004–.008	5	2.1232–2.1240	.0008–.0015	.0035–.0105
	8-255, 302	2.2482–2.2490	.0005–.0015 ②	.004–.008	3	2.1228–2.1236	.0008–.0026 ③	.010–.020
'79–'85	4-140	2.3990–2.3982	.0008–.0015	.004–.008	3	2.0464–2.0472	.0008–.0015	.0035–.0105
'78–'79	V6-170	2.2433–2.2441	.0008–.0015	.004–.008	3	2.1252–2.1260	.0006–.0015	.004–.011
'82–'85	V6-232	2.5190	.0001–.001	.004–.008	3	2.3103–2.3111	.0008–.0026	.0047–.0114

① .0008–.0015 in. in 1977–81
② .0001–.0015 No. 1 bearing only
③ .0008–.0015 in. thru 81

ENGINE AND ENGINE REBUILDING

Piston and Ring Specifications
(All measurements in inches)

Engine Displacement (cu. in)	Piston Clearance	Ring Gap Top Compression	Ring Gap Bottom Compression	Ring Gap Oil ① Control	Ring Side Clearance Top Compression	Ring Side Clearance Bottom Compression	Ring Side Clearance Oil Control	Wear Limit
4-140 (2.3L)	0.0014–0.0022	.010–.020	.010–.020	.015–.055	.002–.004	.002–.004	Snug	.006
4-140 (2.3L) ('79–'82 Turbo)	0.0034–0.0042	.010–.020	.010–.020	.015–.055	.002–.004	.002–.004	Snug	.006
4-140 (2.3L) ('83–'85 Turbo)	0.0030–0.0038	.010–.020	.010–.020	.015–.055	.002–.004	.002–.004	Snug	.006
6-170 (2.8L)	0.0011–0.0019	.015–.023	.015–.023	.015–.055	.002–.0033	.002–.0033	Snug	.006
6-200 (3.3L)	0.0013–0.0021	.008–.016	.008–.016	.015–.055	.002–.004	.002–.004	Snug	.006
6-232 (3.8L)	0.0014–0.0028	.010–.020	.010–.020	0.15–.055	.002–.004	.002–.004	Snug	.006
8-255 (4.2L) 302 (5.0L)	0.0018–0.0026	.010–.020	.010–.020	.015–.055	.002–.004	.002–.004	Snug	.006

① Steel rails

Camshaft Specifications
(All measurements in inches)

Engine	Journal Diameter 1	2	3	4	5	Bearing Clearance	Lobe Lift Intake	Lobe Lift Exhaust	Endplay
4-140 (2.3L)	1.7713–1.7720	1.7713–1.7720	1.7713–1.7720	1.7713–1.7720	—	.001–.003	.2437 ①	.2437 ①	.001–.007
6-200 (3.3L)	1.8095–1.8105	1.8095–1.8105	1.8095–1.8105	1.8095–1.8105	—	.001–.003	.245	.245	.001–.007
6-232 (3.8L)	2.0505–2.0515	2.0505–2.0515	2.0505–2.0515	2.0505–2.0515	—	.001–.003	.240	.241	②
8-255 (4.2L)	2.0805–2.0815	2.0655–2.0665	2.0505–2.0515	2.0355–2.0365	2.0205–2.0215	.001–.003	.2375	.2375	.001–.007
8-302 (5.0L)	2.0805–2.0815	2.0655–2.0665	2.0505–2.0515	2.0355–2.0365	2.0205–2.0215	.001–.003	.2375 ③	.2474 ③	.001–.003

① '84 and later: .2381
② Endplay controlled by button and spring on camshaft end.
③ HO engine: Intake—.2600; Exhaust—.2780

body rail and remove the arm bracket and equalizer shaft.

12. Raise the car and safely support on jackstands. Remove the flywheel or converter housing upper retaining bolts.

13. Disconnect the exhaust pipe or pipes at the exhaust manifold. Disconnect the right and left motor mount at the underbody bracket. Remove the flywheel or converter housing cover. On models equipped, disconnect the engine roll dampener on the left front of the engine to frame.

14. On manual shift, remove the lower wheel housing bolts.

15. On automatic transmission, disconnect throttle valve vacuum line at the intake manifold and disconnect the converter from the flywheel. Remove the converter housing lower retaining bolts. On power steering, disconnect power steering pump from cylinder head. Remove the drive belt and wire steering pump out of the way. Do not disconnect the hoses.

16. Lower the car. Support the transmission and flywheel or converter housing with a jack.

17. Attach an engine lifting hook. Lift the engine up and out of the compartment and onto workstand.

Engine Weights*
1979 and Later

Engine	Weight (lbs.)
2.3L 4-cylinder	341 (308) ①
2.3L Turbo	370 (337) ①
2.8L V6	433 (390) ①
3.3L 6-cylinder	397 (348) ①
4.2L V8	431 ①
5.0L V8	550

*Weights are "dry", without oil or water
① Automatic transmission

18. Place a new gasket on exhaust pipe flange.
19. Attach engine sling and lifting device. Lift engine from workstand.
20. Lower the engine into the engine compartment. Be sure the exhaust manifold/s is in proper alignment with the muffler inlet pipe/s, and the dowels in the block engage the holes in the flywheel housing.
On a car with automatic transmission, start the converter pilot into the crankshaft; make sure converter studs align with flexplate holes.
On manual transmission, start the transmission main drive gear into the clutch disc. If the engine hangs up after the shaft enters, rotate the crankshaft slowly (with transmission in gear) until the shaft and clutch disc splines mesh. Rotate 4 cyl. engines clockwise only, when viewed from the front.
21. Install the flywheel or converter housing upper bolts.
22. Install the engine support insulator to bracket retaining nuts. Disconnect the engine lifting sling and remove lifting brackets.
23. Raise the front of car. Connect the exhaust line/s and tighten attachments.
24. Install the starter.
25. On manual transmission, install remaining flywheel housing-to-engine bolts. Connect clutch release rod. Position the clutch equalizer bar and bracket, and install retaining bolts. Install clutch pedal retracting spring.
26. On automatic transmission, remove the retainer holding the converter in the housing. Attach the converter to the flywheel. Install the converter housing inspection cover and the remaining converter housing retaining bolts.
27. Remove the support from the transmission and lower the car.
28. Connect the engine ground strap and coil primary wire.
29. Connect the water temperature gauge wire and the heater hose at coolant outlet housing. Connect the accelerator rod at the bellcrank.
30. On automatic transmission, connect the transmission filler tube bracket. Connect the throttle valve vacuum line.
31. On power steering, install the drive belt and power steering pump bracket. Install the bracket retaining bolts. Adjust the drive belt to proper tension.
32. Remove the plug from the fuel tank line. Connect the flexible fuel line and the oil pressure sending unit wire.
33. Install the pulley, belt, spacer, and fan. Adjust belt tension.
34. Tighten the alternator adjusting bolts. Connect the wires and the battery ground cable. On the four cylinder, install the exhaust manifold shroud.
35. Install the radiator. Connect radiator hoses. On air conditioned cars, install the compressor and condensor.
36. On automatic transmission, connect fluid cooler lines. On cars with power brakes, connect the brake booster line.
37. Install oil filter. Connect heater hose at water pump and carburetor choke (4 cyl.).
38. Bring the crankcase to level with correct grade of oil. Run the engine at fast idle and check for leaks. Install the air cleaner and make final engine adjustments.
39. Install and adjust hood.

Valve Rocker Arm Cover
REMOVAL AND INSTALLATION
2.3L 4 Cylinder Engine
6 Cylinder In-Line Engines

1. Remove the air cleaner assembly and mounting brackets.
2. Label for identification and remove all wires and vacuum hoses interfering with valve cover removal. Remove the PCV valve with hose. Remove the accelerator control cable bracket if necessary.
NOTE: *4 Cylinder Turbocharged models require removal of the air intake tube and air throttle body. Refer to the "Fuel Injection" section of Chapter 4 for procedures.*
3. Remove the valve cover retaining bolts. On four cylinder models, the front bolts equipped with rubber sealing washers must be installed in the same location to prevent oil leakage.
4. Remove the valve cover. Clean all old gasket material from the valve cover and cylinder head gasket surfaces.
5. Install in reverse order of removal. Use oil resistant sealing compound and a new valve cover gasket. When installing the valve cover gasket, make sure all the gasket locating tangs are engaged into the cover notches provided.

ENGINE AND ENGINE REBUILDING

V6 and V8 Engines

NOTE: *When disconnecting wires and vacuum lines, label them for reinstallation identification.*

1. Remove the air cleaner assembly.
2. On the right side:
    a. Disconnect the automatic choke heat chamber hose from the inlet tube near the right valve cover if equipped.
    b. Remove the automatic choke heat tube if equipped and remove the PCV valve and hose from the valve cover. Disconnect EGR valve hoses.
    c. Remove the thermactor bypass valve and air supply hoses as necessary to gain clearance.
    d. Disconnect the spark plug wires from the plugs with a twisting, pulling motion; twist and pull on the boots only, never on the wire; position the wires and mounting bracket out of the way.
    e. Remove the valve cover mounting bolts; remove the valve cover.
3. On the left side:
    a. Remove the spark plug wires and bracket.
    b. Remove the wiring harness and any vacuum hoses from the bracket.
    c. Remove the valve cover mounting bolts and valve cover.
4. Clean all old gasket material from the valve cover and cylinder head mounting surfaces.

NOTE: *Some V6 engines do not use valve cover gaskets in product. Scrap away old RTV sealant and clean covers. Spread an even bead 3/16" wide of RTV sealant on the valve covers and reinstall, or install with gaskets.*

5. Installation is in reverse order of removal. Use oil resistant sealing compound and a new valve cover gasket. When installing the valve cover gasket, make sure all the gasket tangs are engaged into the cover notches provided.

Rocker Arm (Cam Follower) and Hydraulic Lash Adjuster
REMOVAL AND INSTALLATION

Four Cylinder 140 Cu In. Engine

NOTE: *A special tool is required to compress the lash adjuster.*

1. Remove the valve cover and associated parts as required.
2. Rotate the camshaft so that the base circle of the cam is against the cam follower you intend to remove.
3. Remove the retaining spring from the cam follower, if so equipped.
4. Using special tool T74P-6565-B or a valve spring compressor tool, collapse the lash adjuster and/or depress the valve spring, as necessary, and slide the cam follower over the lash adjuster and out from under the camshaft.
5. Install the cam follower in the reverse order of removal. Make sure that the lash adjuster is collapsed and released before rotating the camshaft.

Rocker Arm Shaft/Rocker Arms
REMOVAL AND INSTALLATION

6 Cylinder In-Line and V6 170 Engines

1. Remove the rocker arm (valve) cover (see previous section).
2. Remove the rocker arm shaft mounting bolts, two turns at a time for each bolt. Start at the ends of the rocker shaft and work toward the middle.
3. Lift the rocker arm shaft assembly from the engine. Remove the pin and washer from each end of the shaft. Slide the rocker arms, springs and supports off the shaft. Keep all parts in order or label them for position.
4. Clean and inspect all parts, replace as necessary.
5. Assemble the rocker shaft parts in reverse order of removal. Be sure the oil holes in the shaft are pointed downward. Reinstall the rocker shaft assembly on the engine.

NOTE: *Lubricate all parts with motor oil before installation.*

V6 and V8 Engines

1. Right side
    a. disconnect the automatic choke heat chamber air inlet hose.
    b. remove the air cleaner and duct.
    c. remove the automatic choke heat tube (232, 302).
    d. remove the PCV fresh air tube from the rocker cover, and disconnect the EGR vacuum amplifier hoses.
2. Remove the Thermactor by-pass valve and air supply hoses.
3. Disconnect the spark plug wires.
4. On the left side:
    a. remove the wiring harness from the clips.
    b. remove the rocker arm cover.
5. Remove the rocker arm stud nut or bolt, fulcrum seat and rocker arm.
6. Lubricate all parts with heavy SE oil before installation. When installing, rotate the crankshaft until the lifter is on the base of the cam circle (all the way down) and assemble the rocker arm. Torque the nut or bolt to 17–23 ft. lb.

NOTE: *Some later engines are using RTV sealant instead of valve cover gaskets.*

60 ENGINE AND ENGINE REBUILDING

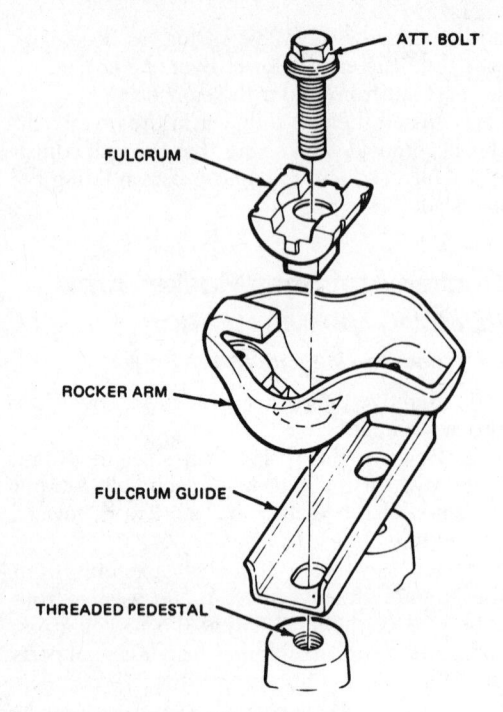

Valve rocker arms—V8 engines

Intake Manifold

REMOVAL AND INSTALLATION

Four Cylinder 140 Cu In. Engine

NOTE: *If fuel-injected model, refer to the illustration provided.*

1. Drain the cooling system.
2. Remove the air cleaner and disconnect the throttle linkage from the carburetor.
3. Disconnect the fuel and vacuum lines from the carburetor.
4. Disconnect the carburetor solenoid wire at the quick-disconnect.
5. Remove the choke water housing and thermostatic spring from the carburetor.
6. Disconnect the water outlet and crankcase ventilation hoses from the intake manifold.
7. Disconnect the deceleration valve-to-carburetor hose (if equipped) at the carburetor.
8. Start from each end; work toward the middle; remove the intake manifold attaching bolts and remove the manifold.
9. Clean all old gasket material from the manifold and cylinder head.
10. Apply water-resistant sealer to the intake manifold gasket and position it on the cylinder head.
11. Install the intake manifold attaching nuts. Follow the sequence given in the illustrations.
12. Connect the water and crankcase ventilation hoses to the intake manifold.
13. Connect the deceleration valve-to-carburetor hose to the carburetor.
14. Position the choke water housing and thermostatic spring on the carburetor and engage the end of the spring coil in the slot and the choke adjusting lever. Align the tab on the spring housing. Tighten the choke water housing attaching screws.
15. Connect the carburetor solenoid wire.
16. Connect the fuel and vacuum lines to the carburetor.
17. Connect the throttle linkage to the carburetor.
18. Install the air cleaner and fill the cooling system.

Six Cylinder In-Line Engines

On six cylinder in-line engines, the intake manifold is integral with the cylinder head and cannot be removed.

V6 and V8 Engines

1. Drain the cooling system and disconnect the negative battery cable. Remove the air cleaner assembly.
2. Disconnect the upper radiator hose and water pump by-pass hose from the thermostat

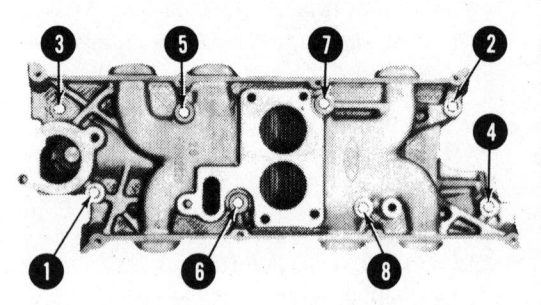

Intake manifold torque sequence—V6 170 engine

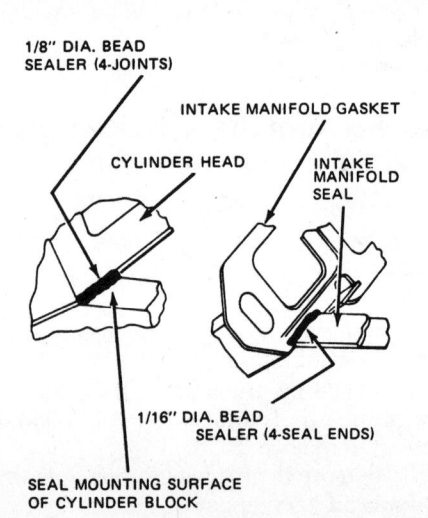

Applying a non-hardening sealer to the intake manifold

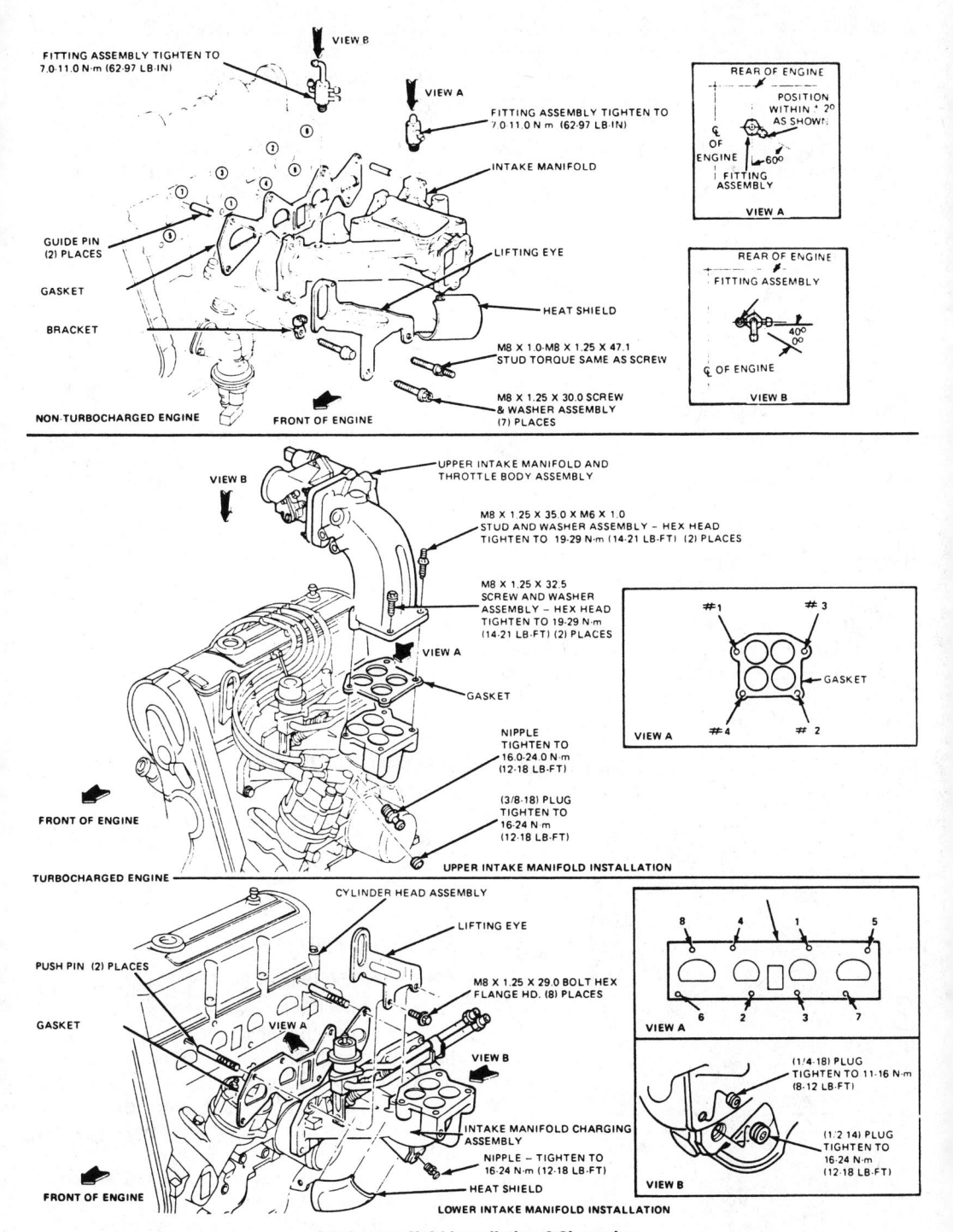

ENGINE AND ENGINE REBUILDING 61

Intake manifold installation 2.3L engine

housing and/or intake manifold. Disconnect the temperature sending unit wire connector. Remove the heater hose from the choke housing bracket and disconnect the hose from the intake manifold.

3. Disconnect the automatic choke heat chamber air inlet tube and electric wiring connector from the carburetor. Remove the crankcase ventilation hose, vacuum hoses and EGR hose and coolant lines (if equipped). Label the various hoses and wiring for reinstallation identification.

4. Disconnect the Thermactor air supply hose at the check valve. Loosen the hose clamp

62 ENGINE AND ENGINE REBUILDING

at the check valve bracket and remove the air by-pass valve from the bracket and position to one side.

CAUTION: *On CFI (fuel injected) engines. System pressure must be released before disconnecting fuel lines. See Chapter 4 for pressure release and fuel line procedures.*

5. Remove all carburetor and automatic transmission linkage attached to the carburetor or intake manifold. Remove the speed control servo and bracket, if equipped. Disconnect the fuel line and any remaining vacuum hoses or wiring from the carburetor, CFI unit, solenoids, sensors, or intake manifold.

6. On V8 engines, disconnect the distributor vacuum hoses from the distributor. Remove the distributor cap and mark the relative position of the rotor on the distributor housing. Disconnect the spark plug wires at the spark plugs and the wiring connector at the distributor. Remove the distributor hold-down bolt and remove the distributor. (See "Distributor Removal and Installation").

NOTE: *Distributor removal is not necessary on V6 engines.*

7. If your car is equipped with air conditioning and the compressor or mounting brackets interfere with manifold removal, remove the brackets and compressor and position out of the way. Do not disconnect any compressor lines.

8. Remove the intake manifold mounting bolts. Lift off the intake manifold and carburetor or CFI unit as an assembly.

NOTE: *The manifold on V6 engines is sealed at each end with an RTV type sealer. If prying at the front of the manifold is necessary to break the seal, take care not to damage the machined surfaces.*

9. Clean all gasket mounting surfaces. V6 engines have aluminum cylinder heads and intake manifold; exercise care when cleaning the old gasket material or RTV sealant from the machined surfaces.

10. Installation is in the reverse order of removal.

11. End seals are not used on V6 engines. Apply a 1/8 inch bead of RTV sealant at each end of the engine where the intake manifold seats. Install the intake gaskets and the manifold.

12. On V8 engines, make sure the intake gaskets interlock with the end seals. Use silicone rubber sealer (RTV) on the end seals.

13. After installing the intake manifold, run a finger along the manifold ends to spread the RTV sealer and to make sure the end seals have not slipped out of place.

14. Torque the manifold mounting bolts to the required specifications in the proper sequence. Recheck the torque after the engine has reached normal operating temperature.

Exhaust Manifold

NOTE: *Although, in most cases, the engine does not have exhaust manifold gaskets installed by the factory, aftermarket gaskets are available from parts stores.*

REMOVAL AND INSTALLATION

Four Cylinder 140 Cu In. Engine

1. Remove the air cleaner.
2. Remove the heat shroud from the exhaust manifold. On turbocharged models, remove the turbocharger.
3. Place a block of wood under the exhaust pipe and disconnect the exhaust pipe from the exhaust manifold.
4. Remove the exhaust manifold attaching nuts and remove the manifold.
5. Install a light coat of graphite grease on the exhaust manifold mating surface and position the manifold on the cylinder head.
6. Install the exhaust manifold attaching nuts and tighten them in the sequence shown in the illustration to 12–15 ft. lbs.
7. Connect the exhaust pipe to the exhaust manifold and remove the wood support from under the pipe.
8. Install the air cleaner.

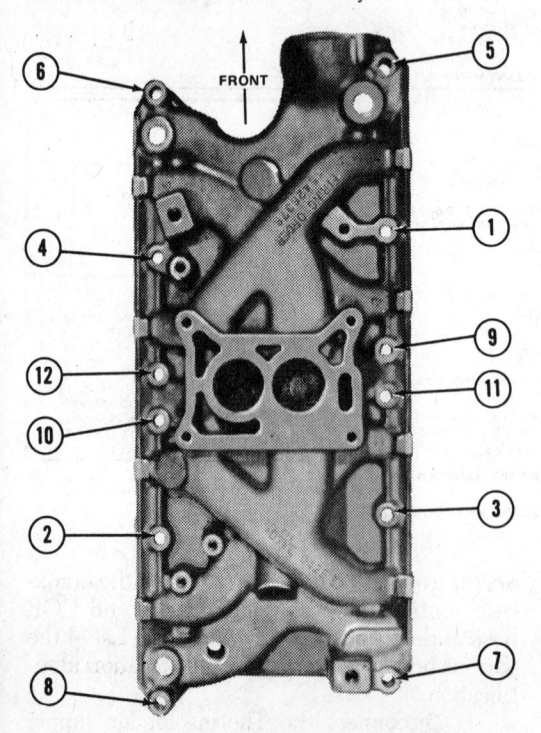

Intake manifold torque sequence—V8 engines

ENGINE AND ENGINE REBUILDING 63

INSTRUCTIONS:
INSTALL 3/8-16 STUD & WASHER ASSEMBLY – HOLES NUMBERED 4 & 5 TIGHTEN TO SPECIFICATIONS.
3/8-16 X 2.62 BOLT – HOLES 3-6-7-8 TIGHTEN TO SPECIFICATIONS.
3/8-16 X 1.12 BOLT – HOLES 1-2-9-10-11 TIGHTEN TO SPECIFICATIONS.

Exhaust manifold torque sequence—6 cyl. 200 engine

Six Cylinder In-Line Engines

1. Remove the air cleaner and heat duct body.
2. Disconnect the muffler inlet pipe and remove the choke hot air tube from the manifold.
3. Remove the EGR tube and any other emission components which will interfere with manifold removal.
4. Bend the exhaust manifold attaching bolt lock tabs back, remove the bolts and the manifold.
5. Clean all manifold mating surfaces and place a new gasket on the muffler inlet pipe.
6. Reinstall manifold by reversing the procedure. Torque attaching bolts in sequence shown. After installation, warm the engine to operating temperature and re-torque to specifications.

V6, V8 Engines

1. If removing the right side exhaust manifold, remove the air cleaner and related parts and the heat stove, if so equipped.
2. On some models dipstick any tube removal may be required. Remove and speed control brackets that interfere.
3. Disconnect the exhaust manifold(s) from the muffler (or converter) inlet pipe(s).

NOTE: *On certain vehicles with automatic transmission and column shift it may be necessary to disconnect the selector lever cross shaft for clearance.*

4. Disconnect the spark plug wires and remove the spark plugs and heat shields. Disconnect the EGO sensor (models equipped), and heat control valve vacuum line (models equipped).

NOTE: *On some engines the spark plug wire heat shields are removed with the manifold. Transmission dipstick tube and thermactor air tube removal may be required on certain models. Air tube removal is possible by cutting the tube clamp at the converter.*

5. Remove the exhaust manifold attaching bolts and washers, and remove the manifold(s).
6. Inspect the manifold(s) for damaged gasket surfaces, cracks, or other defects.
7. Clean the mating surfaces of the manifold(s), cylinder head and muffler inlet pipe(s).
8. Install the manifold(s) in reverse order of removal. Torque the mounting bolts to the value listed in the "Torque Specifications" chart. Start with the centermost bolt and work outward in both directions.

NOTE: *Slight warpage may occur on V6 manifolds. Elongate the holes in the manifold as necessary. Do not, however, elongate the lower front No. 5 cylinder hole on the left side, nor the lower rear No. 2 cylinder hole on the right side. These holes are used as alignment pilots.*

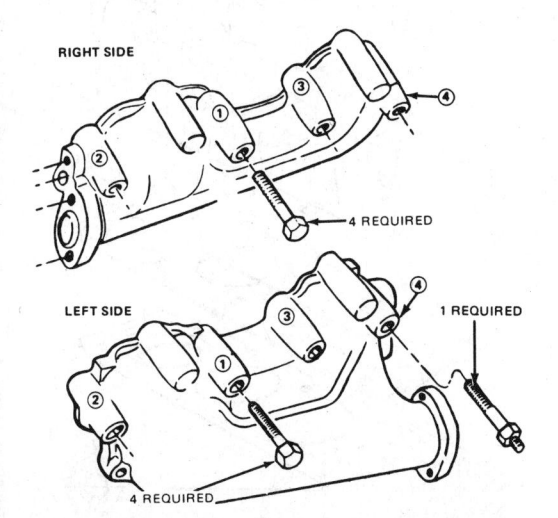

Typical V6 engine exhaust manifold showing torque sequence

Turbocharger

NOTE: *The turbocharger is serviced by replacement only.*

REMOVAL AND INSTALLATION

NOTE: *Before starting removal/service procedures, clean the area around the turbocharger with a non-caustic solution. Cover the openings of component connections to prevent entry of dirt and foreign materials. Exercise care when handling the turbocharger not to nick, bend or in any way damage the compressor wheel blades.*

1. Disconnect the negative battery cable.
2. Drain the cooling system.
3. Loosen the upper clamp on the turbocharger inlet hose. Remove the two bolts mounting the throttle body discharge tube to the turbo.
4. Label for identification and location all

64 ENGINE AND ENGINE REBUILDING

vacuum hoses and tubes to the turbo and disconnect them.

5. Disconnect the PCV tube from the turbo air inlet elbow. Remove the throttle body discharge tube and hose as an assembly.

6. Disconnect the ground wire from the air inlet elbow. Remove (disconnect) the water outlet connection (and fitting if a new turbo unit is to be installed) from the turbo center housing.

7. Remove the turbo oil supply feed line. Disconnect the oxygen sensor connector at the turbocharger.

8. Raise and support the front of the vehicle on jackstands. Disconnect the exhaust pipe from the turbocharger.

9. Disconnect the oil return line from the bottom of the turbocharger. Take care not to damage or kink the line.

10. Disconnect the water inlet tube at the turbo center housing.

11. Remove the lower turbo mounting bracket to engine bolt. Lower the vehicle from the stands.

12. Remove the lower front mounting nut. Remove the three remaining mounting nuts evenly while sliding the turbocharger away from mounting.

13. Position a new turbocharger mounting gasket in position with the bead side facing outward. Install the turbocharger in position over the four mounting studs.

14. Position the lower mounting bracket over the two bottom studs. Using new nuts, start the two lower then the two upper mountings. Do not tighten completely at this time, allow for slight turbo movement.

15. Raise and support the front of the vehicle on jackstands.

16. Install and tighten the lower bracket to engine mounting bolt to 28–40 ft. lbs.

17. Position a new oil return line gasket and connect the return line. Tighten the mounting bolts to 14–21 ft. lbs.

18. Connect the water inlet tube assembly. Install the exhaust pipe to turbo. Tighten the mounting nuts to 25–35 ft. lbs.

19. Lower the vehicle. Tighten the turbo mounting nuts to 28–40 ft. lbs.

20. Connect the water outlet assembly to the turbocharger, tighten to 11–14 ft. lbs. Hold the fitting with a wrench when tightening the line.

21. Install the air inlet tube to the turbo inlet elbow (15–22 ft. lbs.). Tighten the clamp.

22. Connect the PCV tube and all vacuum lines.

23. Connect the oxygen sensor and other wiring and lines.

24. Connect the oil supply line. Connect the intake tube. Fill the cooling system.

25. Connect the negative battery cable. Start the engine and check for coolant leaks. Check vehicle operation.

NOTE: *When installing the turbocharger, or after an oil and filter change, disconnect the distributor feed harness and crank the engine with the starter motor until the oil pressure light on the dash goes out. Oil pressure must be up before starting the engine.*

Cylinder Head

REMOVAL AND INSTALLATION

NOTE: *On cars with air conditioning, remove the mounting bolts and the drive belt, and position the compressor out of the way. Remove the compressor upper mounting bracket from the cylinder head.*

CAUTION: *If the compressor refrigerant lines do not have enough slack to permit repositioning of the compressor without first disconnecting the refrigerant lines, the air conditioning system will have to be evacuated by a trained air conditioning serviceman. Under no circumstances should an untrained person attempt to disconnect the air conditioning refrigerant lines.*

4 Cylinder 140 Engine

NOTE: *Set the engine to TDC position for No. 1 piston, if possible prior to head removal.*

1. Drain the cooling system.

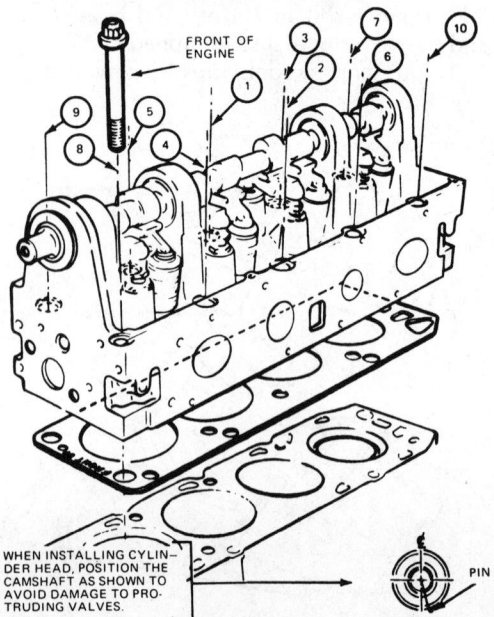

Cylinder head installation—4 cyl. 140 engine

ENGINE AND ENGINE REBUILDING 65

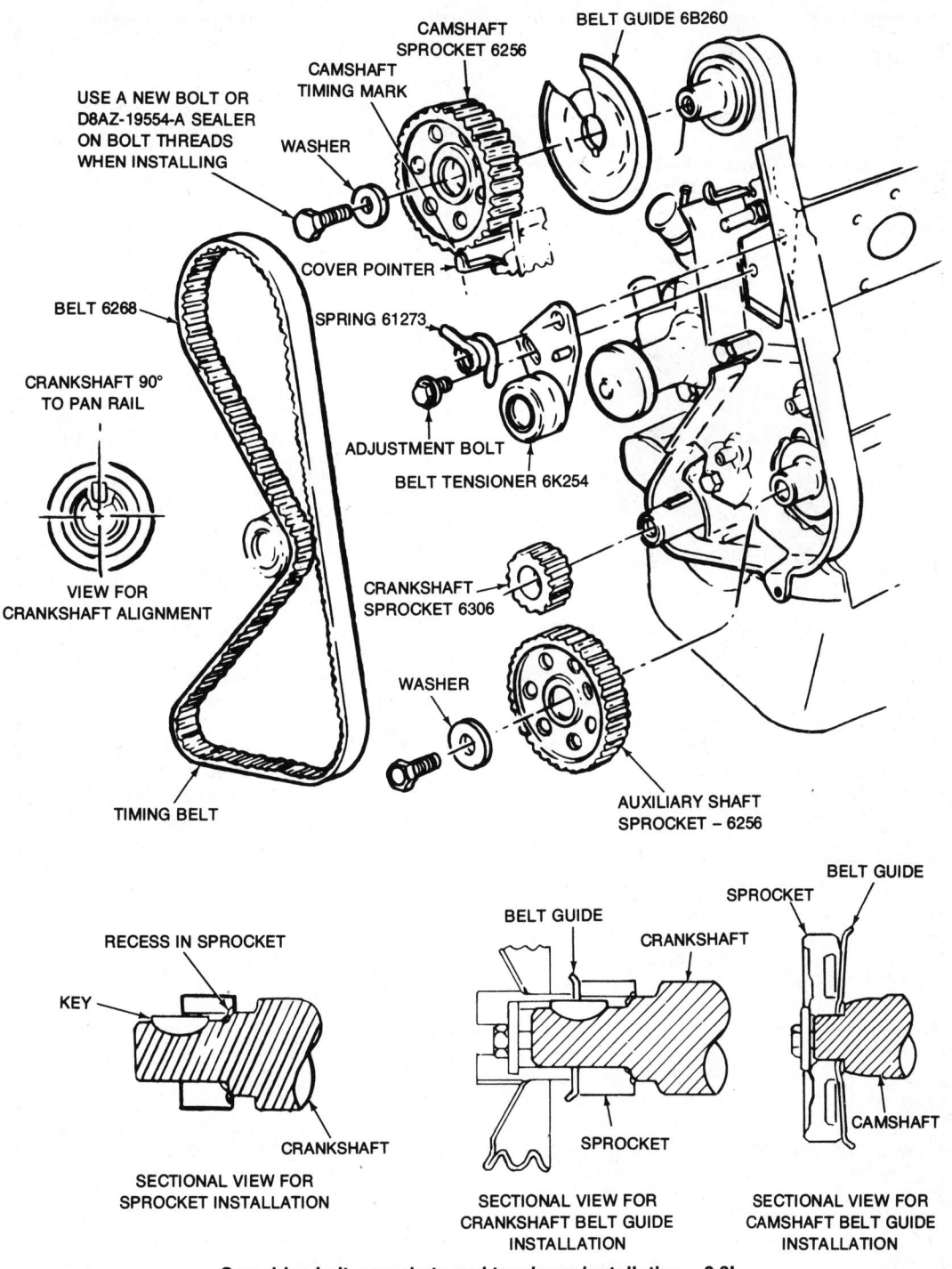

Cam drive belt, sprockets and tensioner installation—2.3L

2. Remove the air cleaner. Disconnect the negative battery cable.

3. Remove the valve cover. Note the location of the valve cover attaching screws that have rubber grommets.

4. Remove the intake and exhaust manifolds from the head. See the procedures for intake manifold, exhaust manifold, and turbocharger removal.

5. Remove the camshaft drive belt cover. Note the location of the belt cover attaching screws that have rubber grommets.

6. Loosen the drive belt tensioner and remove the belt.

ENGINE AND ENGINE REBUILDING

ENGINE OVERHAUL

Most engine overhaul procedures are fairly standard. In addition to specific parts replacement procedures and complete specifications for your individual engine, this chapter also is a guide to accepted rebuilding procedures. Examples of standard rebuilding practice are shown and should be used along with specific details concerning your particular engine.

Competent and accurate machine shop services will ensure maximum performance, reliability and engine life. Procedures marked with the symbol shown above should be performed by a competent machine shop, and are provided so that you will be familiar with the procedures necessary to a successful overhaul.

In most instances it is more profitable for the do-it-yourself mechanic to remove, clean and inspect the component, buy the necessary parts and deliver these to a shop for actual machine work.

On the other hand, much of the rebuilding work (crankshaft, block, bearings, pistons, rods, and other components) is well within the scope of the do-it-yourself mechanic.

Tools

The tools required for an engine overhaul or parts replacement will depend on the depth of your involvement. With a few exceptions, they will be the tools found in a mechanic's tool kit (see Chapter 1). More in-depth work will require any or all of the following:
 • a dial indicator (reading in thousandths) mounted on a universal base
  • micrometers and telescope gauges
  • jaw and screw-type pullers
  • scraper
  • valve spring compressor
  • ring groove cleaner
  • piston ring expander and compressor
  • ridge reamer
  • cylinder hone or glaze breaker
 • Plastigage®
 • engine stand

Use of most of these tools is illustrated in this chapter. Many can be rented for a one-time use from a local parts jobber or tool supply house specializing in automotive work.

Occasionally, the use of special tools is called for. See the information on Special Tools and the Safety Notice in the front of this book before substituting another tool.

Inspection Techniques

Procedures and specifications are given in this chapter for inspecting, cleaning and assessing the wear limits of most major components. Other procedures such as Magnaflux and Zyglo can be used to locate material flaws and stress cracks. Magnaflux is a magnetic process applicable only to ferrous materials. The Zyglo process coats the material with a flourescent dye penetrant and can be used on any material. Check for suspected surface cracks can be more readily made using spot check dye. The dye is sprayed onto the suspected area, wiped off and the area sprayed with a developer. Cracks will show up brightly.

Overhaul Tips

Aluminum has become extremely popular for use in engines, due to its low weight. Observe the following precautions when handling aluminum parts:
 • Never hot tank aluminum parts (the caustic hot-tank solution will eat the aluminum)
 • Remove all aluminum parts (identification tag, etc.) from engine parts prior to hot-tanking.
 • Always coat threads lightly with engine oil or anti-seize compounds before installation, to prevent seizure.
 • Never over-torque bolts or spark plugs, especially in aluminum threads.

Stripped threads in any component can be repaired using any of several commercial repair kits (Heli-Coil, Microdot, Keenserts, etc.).

When assembling the engine, any parts that will be in frictional contact must be pre-lubed to provide lubrication at initial start-up. Any product specifically formulated for this purpose can be used, but engine oil is not recommended as a pre-lube.

When semi-permanent (locked, but removable) installation of bolts or nuts is desired, threads should be cleaned and coated with Loctite® or other similar, commercial non-hardening sealant.

ENGINE AND ENGINE REBUILDING

Repairing Damaged Threads

Several methods of repairing damaged threads are available. Heli-Coil® (shown here), Keenserts® and Microdot® are among the most widely used. All involve basically the same principle—drilling out stripped threads, tapping the hole and installing a prewound insert—making welding, plugging and oversize fasteners unnecessary.

Two types of thread repair inserts are usually supplied—a standard type for most Inch Coarse, Inch Fine, Metric Coarse and Metric Fine thread sizes and a spark plug type to fit most spark plug port sizes. Consult the individual manufacturer's catalog to determine exact applications. Typical thread repair kits will contain a selection of prewound threaded inserts, a tap (corresponding to the outside diameter threads of the insert) and an installation tool. Spark plug inserts usually differ because they require a tap equipped with pilot threads and a combined reamer/tap section. Most manufacturers also supply blister-packed thread repair inserts separately in addition to a master kit containing a variety of taps and inserts plus installation tools.

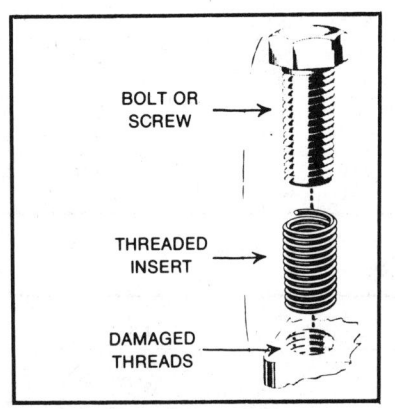

Before effecting a repair to a threaded hole, remove any snapped, broken or damaged bolts or studs. Penetrating oil can be used to free frozen threads; the offending item can be removed with locking pliers or with a screw or stud extractor. After the hole is clear, the thread can be repaired, as follows:

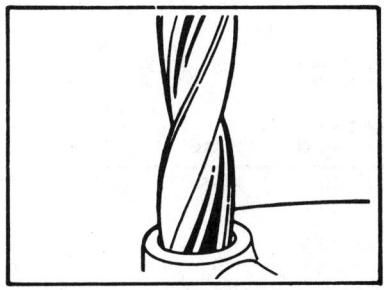

Drill out the damaged threads with specified drill. Drill completely through the hole or to the bottom of a blind hole

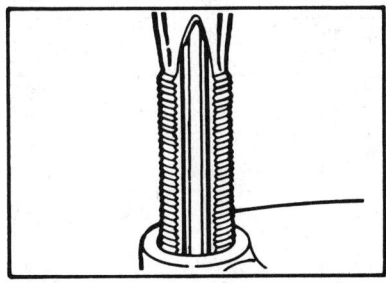

With the tap supplied, tap the hole to receive the thread insert. Keep the tap well oiled and back it out frequently to avoid clogging the threads

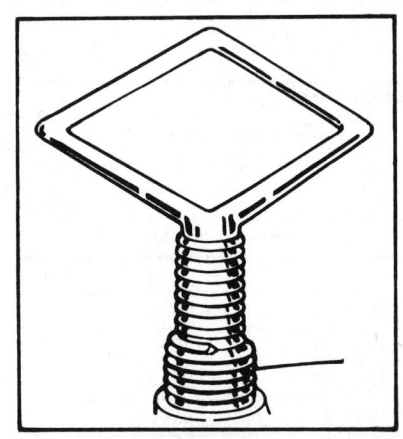

Damaged bolt holes can be repaired with thread repair inserts

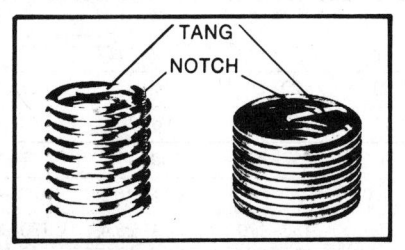

Standard thread repair insert (left) and spark plug thread insert (right)

Screw the threaded insert onto the installation tool until the tang engages the slot. Screw the insert into the tapped hole until it is ¼–½ turn below the top surface. After installation break off the tang with a hammer and punch

Standard Torque Specifications and Fastener Markings

In the absence of specific torques, the following chart can be used as a guide to the maximum safe torque of a particular size/grade of fastener.
- There is no torque difference for fine or coarse threads.
- Torque values are based on clean, dry threads. Reduce the value by 10% if threads are oiled prior to assembly.
- The torque required for aluminum components or fasteners is considerably less.

U.S. Bolts

SAE Grade Number: 1 or 2, 5, 6 or 7

Number of lines always 2 less than the grade number.

Bolt Size (Inches)—(Thread)	1 or 2 Ft./Lbs.	1 or 2 Kgm	1 or 2 Nm	5 Ft./Lbs.	5 Kgm	5 Nm	6 or 7 Ft./Lbs.	6 or 7 Kgm	6 or 7 Nm
¼—20	5	0.7	6.8	8	1.1	10.8	10	1.4	13.5
—28	6	0.8	8.1	10	1.4	13.6			
5/16—18	11	1.5	14.9	17	2.3	23.0	19	2.6	25.8
—24	13	1.8	17.6	19	2.6	25.7			
⅜—16	18	2.5	24.4	31	4.3	42.0	34	4.7	46.0
—24	20	2.75	27.1	35	4.8	47.5			
7/16—14	28	3.8	37.0	49	6.8	66.4	55	7.6	74.5
—20	30	4.2	40.7	55	7.6	74.5			
½—13	39	5.4	52.8	75	10.4	101.7	85	11.75	115.2
—20	41	5.7	55.6	85	11.7	115.2			
9/16—12	51	7.0	69.2	110	15.2	149.1	120	16.6	162.7
—18	55	7.6	74.5	120	16.6	162.7			
⅝—11	83	11.5	112.5	150	20.7	203.3	167	23.0	226.5
—18	95	13.1	128.8	170	23.5	230.5			
¾—10	105	14.5	142.3	270	37.3	366.0	280	38.7	379.6
—16	115	15.9	155.9	295	40.8	400.0			
⅞—9	160	22.1	216.9	395	54.6	535.5	440	60.9	596.5
—14	175	24.2	237.2	435	60.1	589.7			
1—8	236	32.5	318.6	590	81.6	799.9	660	91.3	894.8
—14	250	34.6	338.9	660	91.3	849.8			

Metric Bolts

Relative Strength Marking: 4.6, 4.8 ; 8.8

Bolt Size Thread Size x Pitch (mm)	4.6, 4.8 Ft./Lbs.	4.6, 4.8 Kgm	4.6, 4.8 Nm	8.8 Ft./Lbs.	8.8 Kgm	8.8 Nm
6 x 1.0	2–3	.2–.4	3–4	3–6	.4–.8	5–8
8 x 1.25	6–8	.8–1	8–12	9–14	1.2–1.9	13–19
10 x 1.25	12–17	1.5–2.3	16–23	20–29	2.7–4.0	27–39
12 x 1.25	21–32	2.9–4.4	29–43	35–53	4.8–7.3	47–72
14 x 1.5	35–52	4.8–7.1	48–70	57–85	7.8–11.7	77–110
16 x 1.5	51–77	7.0–10.6	67–100	90–120	12.4–16.5	130–160
18 x 1.5	74–110	10.2–15.1	100–150	130–170	17.9–23.4	180–230
20 x 1.5	110–140	15.1–19.3	150–190	190–240	26.2–46.9	160–320
22 x 1.5	150–190	22.0–26.2	200–260	250–320	34.5–44.1	340–430
24 x 1.5	190–240	26.2–46.9	260–320	310–410	42.7–56.5	420–550

CHECKING ENGINE COMPRESSION

A noticeable lack of engine power, excessive oil consumption and/or poor fuel mileage measured over an extended period are all indicators of internal engine wear. Worn piston rings, scored or worn cylinder bores, blown head gaskets, sticking or burnt valves and worn valve seats are all possible culprits here. A check of each cylinder's compression will help you locate the problems.

As mentioned in the "Tools and Equipment" section of Chapter 1, a screw-in type compression gauge is more accurate than the type you simply hold against the spark plug hole, although it takes slightly longer to use. It's worth it to obtain a more accurate reading. Follow the procedures below for gasoline and diesel-engined cars.

Gasoline Engines

1. Warm up the engine to normal operating temperature.
2. Remove all spark plugs.

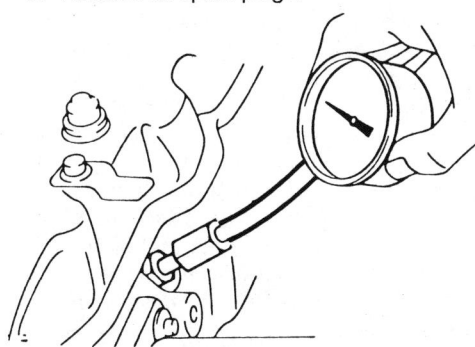

The screw-in type compression gauge is more accurate

3. Disconnect the high-tension lead from the ignition coil.
4. On carbureted cars, fully open the throttle either by operating the carburetor throttle linkage by hand or by having an assistant "floor" the accelerator pedal. On fuel-injected cars, disconnect the cold start valve and all injector connections.
5. Screw the compression gauge into the No. 1 spark plug hole until the fitting is snug.
   NOTE: *Be careful not to crossthread the plug hole. On aluminum cylinder heads use extra care, as the threads in these heads are easily ruined.*
6. Ask an assistant to depress the accelerator pedal fully on both carbureted and fuel-injected cars. Then, while you read the compression gauge, ask the assistant to crank the engine two or three times in short bursts using the ignition switch.

7. Read the compression gauge at the end of each series of cranks, and record the highest of these readings. Repeat this procedure for each of the engine's cylinders. Compare the highest reading of each cylinder to the compression pressure specifications in the "Tune-Up Specifications" chart in Chapter 2. The specs in this chart are maximum values.

A cylinder's compression pressure is usually acceptable if it is not less than 80% of maximum. The difference between each cylinder should be no more than 12–14 pounds.

8. If a cylinder is unusually low, pour a tablespoon of clean engine oil into the cylinder through the spark plug hole and repeat the compression test. If the compression comes up after adding the oil, it appears that that cylinder's piston rings or bore are damaged or worn. If the pressure remains low, the valves may not be seating properly (a valve job is needed), or the head gasket may be blown near that cylinder. If compression in any two adjacent cylinders is low, and if the addition of oil doesn't help the compression, there is leakage past the head gasket. Oil and coolant water in the combustion chamber can result from this problem. There may be evidence of water droplets on the engine dipstick when a head gasket has blown.

Diesel Engines

Checking cylinder compression on diesel engines is basically the same procedure as on gasoline engines except for the following:

1. A special compression gauge adaptor suitable for diesel engines (because these engines have much greater compression pressures) must be used.
2. Remove the injector tubes and remove the injectors from each cylinder.
   NOTE: *Don't forget to remove the washer underneath each injector; otherwise, it may get lost when the engine is cranked.*

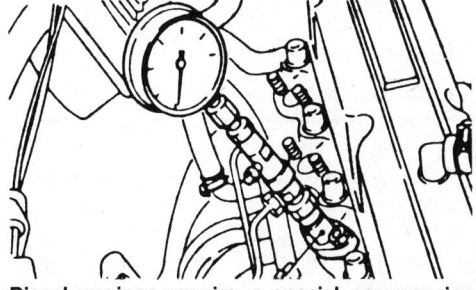

Diesel engines require a special compression gauge adaptor

3. When fitting the compression gauge adaptor to the cylinder head, make sure the bleeder of the gauge (if equipped) is closed.
4. When reinstalling the injector assemblies, install new washers underneath each injector.

70 ENGINE AND ENGINE REBUILDING

7. Remove the water outlet elbow from the cylinder head with the hose attached.
8. Remove the cylinder head attaching bolts.
9. Remove the cylinder head from the engine.
10. Clean all gasket material and carbon from the top of the cylinder block and pistons and from the bottom of the cylinder head.
11. Position a new cylinder head gasket on the engine. Rotate the camshaft so that the gear locating pin is at the five o'clock position to avoid damage to the valves and pistons.

NOTE: *If you encounter difficulty in positioning the cylinder head on the engine block, it may be necessary to install guide studs in the block to correctly align the head and the block. To fabricate guide studs, obtain two new cylinder head bolts and cut their heads off with a hack saw. Install the bolts in the holes in the engine block which correspond with cylinder head bolt holes Nos. 3 and 4, as identified in the cylinder head bolt tightening sequence illustration. Then, install the head gasket and head over the bolts. Install the cylinder head attaching bolts, replacing the studs with the original head bolts.*

12. Using a torque wrench, tighten the head bolts in the sequence shown in the illustration.
13. Install the camshaft drive belt. See "Camshaft Drive Belt Installation."
14. Install the camshaft drive belt cover and its attaching bolts. Make sure the rubber grommets are installed on the bolts. Tighten the bolts to 6–13 ft. lbs.
15. Install the water outlet elbow and a new gasket on the engine and tighten the attaching bolts to 12–15 ft. lbs.
16. Install the intake and exhaust manifolds. See the procedures for intake and exhaust manifold installation.
17. Install the air cleaner and the valve cover.
18. Fill the cooling system.

6 Cylinder In-Line Engines

1. Drain cooling system, remove the air cleaner and disconnect the negative battery cable.

NOTE: *On cars with air conditioning, remove the mounting bolts and the drive belt, and position the compressor out of the way of the left cylinder head. Remove the compressor upper mounting bracket from the cylinder head.*
CAUTION: *If the compressor refrigerant lines do not have enough slack to permit repositioning of the compressor without first disconnecting the refrigerant lines, the air conditioning system will have to be evacuated by a trained air conditioning serviceman. Under no circumstances should an untrained person attempt to disconnect the air conditioning refrigerant lines.*

2. Disconnect exhaust pipe at the manifold end, spring the exhaust pipe down and remove the flange gasket.
3. Disconnect the fuel and vacuum lines from the carburetor. Disconnect the intake manifold line at the intake manifold.
4. Disconnect the accelerator and retracting spring at the carburetor. Disconnect the transmission kick-down linkage, if equipped.
5. Disconnect the carburetor spacer outlet line at the spacer. Disconnect the radiator upper hose and the heater hose at the water outlet elbow. Disconnect the radiator lower hose and the heater hose at the water pump.
6. Disconnect the distributor vacuum control line at the distributor. Disconnect the gas filter line on the inlet side of the filter.
7. Disconnect and label the spark plug wires and remove the plugs. Disconnect the temperature sending unit wire.
8. Remove the rocker arm cover.
9. Remove the rocker arm shaft attaching bolts and the rocker arm and shaft assembly. Remove the valve pushrods; keep them in order for installation in their original positions.
10. Remove the remaining cylinder head bolts and lift off the cylinder head. Do not pry under the cylinder head as damage to the mating surfaces can easily occur.

To help in installation of cylinder head, two 6 in. x 7/16–14 bolts with heads cut off and the head end slightly tapered and slotted, for installation and removal with a screwdriver, will reduce the possibility of damage during head replacement.

11. Clean the cylinder head and block surfaces. Be sure of flatness and no surface damage.
12. Apply cylinder head gasket sealer to both sides of the new gasket and slide the gasket down over the two guide studs in the cylinder block.

NOTE: *Apply gasket sealer only to steel shim head gaskets. Steel/asbestos composite head gaskets are to be installed without any sealer.*

13. Carefully lower the cylinder head over the guide studs. Place the exhaust pipe flange on the manifold studs (new gasket).
14. Coat the threads of the end bolts for the right side of the cylinder head with a small

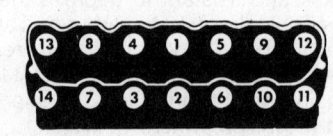

Cylinder head torque sequence—6 cyl. 200 engine

amount of water-resistant sealer. Install, but do not tighten, two head bolts at opposite ends to hold the head gasket in place. Remove the guide studs and install the remaining bolts.

15. Cylinder head torquing should proceed in three steps and in prescribed order. Tighten to 55 ft. lbs., then give them a second tightening to 65 ft. lbs. The final step is to 75 ft. lbs., at which they should remain undisturbed.

16. Lubricate both ends of the pushrods and install them in their original locations.

17. Apply lubricant to the rocker arm pads and the valve stem tips and position the rocker arm shaft assembly on the head. Be sure the oil holes in the shaft are in a down position.

18. Tighten all the rocker shaft retaining bolts to 30–35 ft. lbs. and do a preliminary valve adjustment (make sure there are no tight valve adjustments).

19. Hook up the exhaust pipe.

20. Reconnect the heater and radiator hoses.

21. Reposition the distributor vacuum line, the carburetor gas line and the intake manifold vacuum line on the engine. Hook them up to their respective connections and reconnect the battery cable to the cylinder head.

22. Connect the accelerator rod and retracting spring. Connect the choke control cable and adjust the choke. Connect the transmission kickdown linkage.

23. Reconnect the vacuum line at the distributor. Connect the fuel inlet line at the fuel filter and the intake manifold vacuum line at the vacuum pump.

24. Lightly lubricate the spark plug threads and install them. Connect spark plug wires and be sure the wires are all the way down in their sockets. Connect the temperature sending unit wire.

25. Fill the cooling system. Run the engine to stabilize all engine part temperatures.

26. Adjust engine idle speed and idle fuel-air adjustment.

27. Coat one side of a new rocker cover gasket with oil-resistant sealer. Lay the treated side of the gasket on the cover and install the cover. Be sure the gasket seals evenly all around the cylinder head.

V6 170 Cu. In. Engine

1. Remove the air cleaner assembly and disconnect the battery and accelerator linkage. Drain the cooling system.

2. Remove the distributor cap with the spark plug wires attached. Remove the distributor vacuum line and distributor. Remove the hose from the water pump to the water outlet which is on the carburetor.

3. Remove the valve covers, fuel line and filter, carburetor, and the intake manifold.

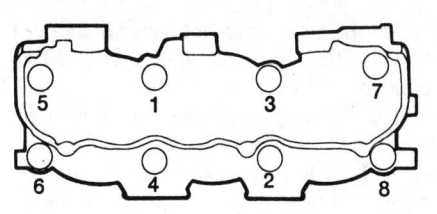

Cylinder head bolt torque sequence—V6 170 engine

4. Remove the rocker arm shaft and oil baffles. Remove the pushrods, keeping them in the proper sequence for installation.

5. Remove the exhaust manifold, referring to the appropriate procedures.

6. Remove the cylinder head retaining bolts and remove the cylinder heads and gaskets.

7. Remove all gasket material and carbon from the engine block and cylinder heads.

8. Place the head gaskets on the engine block.

NOTE: *The left and right gaskets are not interchangeable.*

9. Install guide studs in the engine block. Install the cylinder head assemblies on the engine block one at a time. Tighten the cylinder head bolts in sequence, and in steps, 65–80 lbs.

10. Install the intake and exhaust manifolds.

11. Install the pushrods in the proper sequence. Install the oil baffles and the rocker arm shaft assemblies. Adjust the valve clearances.

12. Install the valve covers with new gaskets.

13. Install the distributor and set the ignition timing.

14. Install the carburetor and the distributor cap with the spark plug wires.

15. Connect the accelerator linkage, fuel line, with fuel filter installed, and distributor vacuum line to the carburetor. Fill the cooling system.

V6 Engine (Except V6-170)

1. Drain the cooling system.

2. Disconnect the cable from the battery negative terminal.

3. Remove the air cleaner assembly including air intake duct and heat tube.

4. Loosen the accessory drive belt idler. Remove the drive belt.

5. If the left cylinder head is being removed:

   a. If equipped with power steering, remove the pump mounting brackets' attaching bolts, leaving the hoses connected, place the pump/bracket assembly aside in a position to prevent the fluid from leaking out.

   b. If equipped with air conditioning, re-

ENGINE AND ENGINE REBUILDING

move the mounting brackets' attaching bolts, leaving the hoses connected, position the compressor aside.

6. If the right cylinder head is being removed:

   a. Disconnect the thermactor diverter valve and hose assembly at the by-pass valve and downstream air tube.
   b. Remove the assembly.
   c. Remove the accessory drive idler.
   d. Remove the alternator.
   e. Remove the thermactor pump pulley. Remove the thermactor pump.
   f. Remove the alternator bracket.
   g. Remove the PCV valve.

7. Remove the intake manifold.

8. Remove the valve rocker arm cover attaching screws. Loosen the silicone rubber gasketing material by inserting a putty knife under the cover flange. Work the cover loose and remove. The plastic rocker arm covers will break if excessive prying is applied.

9. Remove the exhaust manifold(s).

10. Loosen the rocker arm fulcrum attaching bolts enough to allow the rocker arm to be lifted off the pushrod and rotated to one side.

11. Remove the pushrods. Label the pushrods; they should be installed in the original position during assembly.

12. Remove the cylinder head attaching bolts. Remove the cylinder head(s).

13. Remove and discard the old cylinder head gasket(s). Discard the cylinder head bolts.

14. Lightly oil all bolt and stud bolt threads before installation except those specifying special sealant.

15. Clean the cylinder head, intake manifold, valve rocker arm cover and cylinder head gasket surfaces. If the cylinder head was removed for a cylinder head gasket replacement, check the flatness of the cylinder head and block gasket surfaces.

16. Position new head gasket(s) on the cylinder block using the dowels for alignment.

17. Position the cylinder heads to the block.

18. Apply a thin coating of pipe sealant or equivalent to the threads of the short cylinder head bolts (nearest to the exhaust manifold). Do not apply sealant to the long bolts. Lightly oil the cylinder head bolt flat washers. Install the flat washers and cylinder head bolts (Eight each side).

CAUTION: *Always use new cylinder head bolts to assure a leak tight assembly. Torque retention with used bolts can vary, which may result in coolant or compression leakage at the cylinder head mating surface area.*

19. Tighten the attaching bolts in sequence. Back-off the attaching bolts 2–3 turns. Repeat tightening sequence.

NOTE: *When the cylinder head attaching bolts have been tightened using the above sequential procedure, it is not necessary to retighten the bolts after extended engine operation. However, the bolts can be checked for tightness if desired.*

20. Dip each pushrod end in heavy engine oil. Install the push rods in their original position. For each valve rotate the crankshaft until the tappet rests on the heel (base circle) of the camshaft lobe.

21. Position the rocker arms over the push rods, install the fulcrums, and tighten the fulcrum attaching bolts to 61–132 in. lbs.

CAUTION: *Fulcrums must be fully seated in cylinder head and pushrods must be seated in rocker arm sockets prior to final tightening.*

22. Lubricate all rocker arm assemblies with heavy engine oil. Finally tighten the fulcrum bolts to 19–25 ft. lbs. For final tightening, the camshaft may be in any position.

NOTE: *If the original valve train components are being installed, a valve clearance check is not required. If a component has been replaced, perform a valve clearance check.*

23. Install the exhaust manifold(s).

24. Apply a 1/8–3/16 inch bead of RTV silicone sealant to the rocker arm cover flange. Make sure the sealer fills the channel in the cover flange. The rocker arm cover must be installed within 15 minutes after the silicone sealer application. After this time, the sealer may start to set-up, and its sealing effectiveness may be reduced.

25. Position the cover on the cylinder head and install the attaching bolts. Note the location of the wiring harness routing clips and spark plug wire routing clip stud bolts. Tighten the attaching bolts to 36–60 in. lbs. torque.

26. Install the intake manifold.

27. Install the spark plugs, if necessary.

28. Connect the secondary wires to the spark plugs.

29. Install the oil fill cap. If equipped with air conditioning, install the compressor mounting and support brackets.

30. On the right cylinder head:

    a. Install the PCV valve.
    b. Install the alternator bracket. Tighten attaching nuts to 30–40 ft. lbs.
    c. Install the thermactor pump and pump pulley.
    d. Install the alternator.
    e. Install the accessory drive idler.
    f. Install the thermactor diverter valve and hose assembly. Tighten the clamps securely.

31. Install the accessory drive belt and tighten to the specified tension.

ENGINE AND ENGINE REBUILDING

32. Connect the cable to the battery negative terminal.
33. Fill the cooling system with the specified coolant.
CAUTION: *This engine has an aluminum cylinder head and requires a special unique corrosion inhibited coolant formulation to avoid radiator damage.*
34. Start the engine and check for coolant, fuel, and oil leaks.
35. Check and, if necessary, adjust the curb idle speed.
36. Install the air cleaner assembly including the air intake duct and heat tube.

V8 Engines

1. Drain the cooling system.
2. Remove the intake manifold and the carburetor or CFI unit as an assembly.
3. Disconnect the spark plug wires, marking them as to placement. Position them out of the way of the cylinder head. Remove the spark plugs.
4. Disconnect the exhaust pipes at the manifolds.
5. Remove the rocker arm covers.
6. On cars with air conditioning, remove the mounting bolts and the drive belt, and position the compressor out of the way of the left cylinder head. Remove the compressor upper mounting bracket from the cylinder head.
NOTE: *If the compressor refrigerant lines do not have enough slack to permit repositioning of the compressor without first disconnecting the refrigerant lines, the air conditioning system will have to be evacuated by a trained air conditioning serviceman. Under no circumstances should an untrained person attempt to disconnect the air conditioning refrigerant lines.*
7. In order to remove the left cylinder head, on cars equipped with power steering, it may be necessary to remove the steering pump and bracket, remove the drive belt, and wire or tie the pump out of the way, but in such a way as to prevent the loss of its fluid.
8. In order to remove the right head it may be necessary to remove the alternator mounting bracket bolt and spacer, the ignition coil, and the air cleaner inlet duct from the right cylinder head.
9. In order to remove the left cylinder head on a car equipped with a Thermactor air pump system, disconnect the hose from the air manifold on the left cylinder head.
10. If the right cylinder head is to be removed on a car equipped with a Thermactor air pump system, remove the Thermactor air pump and its mounting bracket. Disconnect the hose from the air manifold on the right cylinder head.

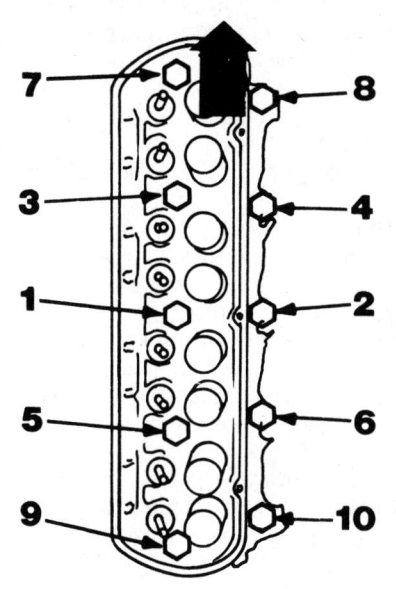

Cylinder head torque sequence—V8 engine. Arrow points to front

11. Loosen the rocker arm stud nuts enough to rotate the rocker arms to the side, in order to facilitate the removal of the pushrods. Remove the pushrods in sequence, so that they may be installed in their original positions. Remove the exhaust valve stem caps, if equipped.
12. Remove the cylinder head attaching bolts, noting their positions. Lift the cylinder head off the block. Remove and discard the old cylinder head gasket. Clean all mounting surfaces.
13. Installation is as follows: Position the new cylinder head gasket over the dowels on the block. Position new gaskets on the muffler inlet pipes at the exhaust manifold flange.
1. Position the cylinder head to the block, and install the head bolts, each in its original position. On engines on which the exhaust manifold has been removed from the head to facilitate removal, it is necessary to properly guide the exhaust manifold studs into the muffler inlet pipe flange when installing the head.
2. Step-torque the cylinder head retaining bolts first to 50 ft. lbs. then to 60 ft. lbs., and finally to the torque specification listed in the "Torque Specifications" chart. Tighten the exhaust manifold to cylinder head attaching bolts to specifications.
3. Tighten the nuts on the exhaust manifold studs at the muffler inlet flanges to 18 ft. lbs.
4. Clean and inspect the pushrods one at a time. Clean the oil passage within each pushrod with solvent and blow the passage out with compressed air. Check the ends of the pushrods for nicks, grooves, roughness, or excessive wear. Visually inspect the pushrods for

straightness, and replace any bent ones. Do not attempt to straighten pushrods.

5. Install the pushrods in their original positions. Apply Lubriplate® or a similar product to the valve stem tips and to the pushrod guides in the cylinder head. Install the exhaust valve stem caps.

6. Apply Lubriplate® or a similar product to the fulcrum seats and sockets. Turn the rocker arms to their proper position and tighten the stud nuts enough to hold the rocker arms in position. Make sure that the lower ends of the pushrods have remained properly seated in the valve lifters. Tighten the stud nuts 17–23 ft. lbs. in the order given under the preliminary valve adjustment.

7. Install the valve covers.

8. Install the intake manifold and carburetor, following the procedure under "Intake Manifold Installation."

9. Reinstall all other items removed.

PRELIMINARY VALVE ADJUSTMENT
V6 and V8 Engines Only

This adjustment is actually part of the installation procedure for the individually mounted rocker arms found on the V-type engine, and is necessary to achieve an accurate torque value for each rocker arm nut.

By its nature, an hydraulic valve lifter will expand when it is not under load. Thus, when the rocker arms are removed and the pressure via the pushrod is taken off the lifter, the lifter expands to its maximum. If the lifter happens to be at the top of the camshaft lobe when the rocker arm is being reinstalled, a large amount of torque would be necessary when tightening the rocker arm nut just to overcome the pressure of the expanded lifter. This makes it very difficult to get an accurate torque setting with individually mounted rocker arms. For this reason, the rocker arms are installed in a certain sequence which corresponds to the low points of the camshaft lobes.

1. Turn the engine until No. 1 cylinder is at TDC of the compression stroke and the timing pointer is aligned with the mark on the crankshaft damper.

2. Scribe a mark on the damper at this point.

3. Scribe two additional marks on the damper if V8, single line if V6. (see illustration).

4. With the timing pointer aligned with Mark 1 on the damper, tighten the following valves to the specified torque:
- V6-232 No. 1 intake and exhaust; No. 3 intake and exhaust; No. 4 exhaust and No. 6 intake.
- 255, 302 (EXC. H.O) No. 1, 7 and 8 Intake; No. 1, 5, and 4 Exhaust.

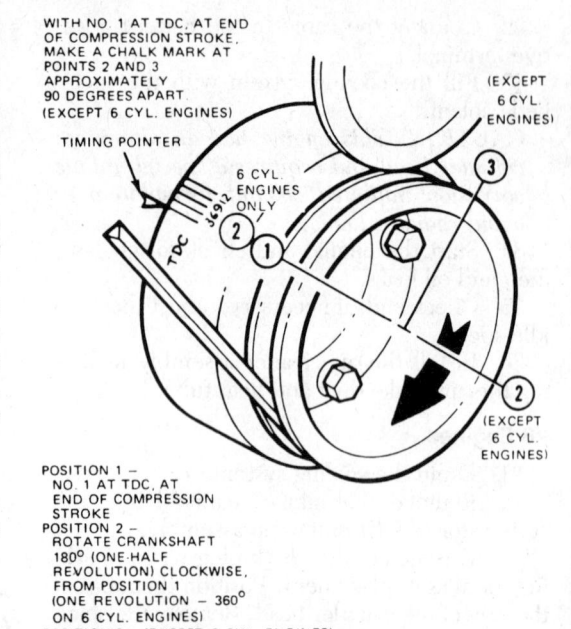

Crankshaft pulley marking for preliminary valve adjustment

- H.O. 302, No. 1, 4, and 8 Intake; No. 1, 3 and 7 Exhaust.

5. Rotate the crankshaft 180° to point 2 and tighten the following valves:
- V6-232 No. 2 intake; No. 3 exhaust; No. 4 intake; No. 5 intake and exhaust; No. 6 exhaust.
- 255, 302 (EXC. H.O) No. 5 and 4 Intake; No. 2 and 6 Exhaust
- H.O. 302 No. 3 and 7 Intake; No. 2 and 6 Exhaust

6. Rotate the crankshaft 270° to point 3 and tighten the following valves:
- 302 (EXC. H.O) No. 2, 3, and 6 Intake; No. 7, 3 and 8 Exhaust
- H.O. 302 No. 2, 5 and 6 Intake; No. 4, 5 and 8 Exhaust

7. Rocker arm tighten specifications are: 232, 255, 302—tighten nut until it contacts the rocker shoulder, then torque to 18–20 ft. lbs.; 351C and 400—tighten to bolt to 18–25 ft. lbs.; 429 and 460—tighten nut until it contacts rocker shoulder, then torque to 18–22 ft. lbs.

CYLINDER HEAD OVERHAUL

1. Remove the cylinder head(s) from the car engine (see Cylinder Head Removal and Installation). Place the head(s) on a workbench and remove any manifolds that are still connected. Remove all rocker arm retaining parts and the rocker arms, if still installed. On four

ENGINE AND ENGINE REBUILDING 75

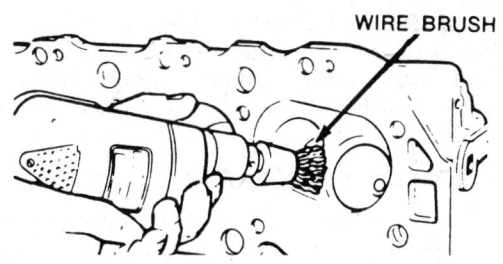

Remove the carbon from the cylinder head with a wire brush and electric drill

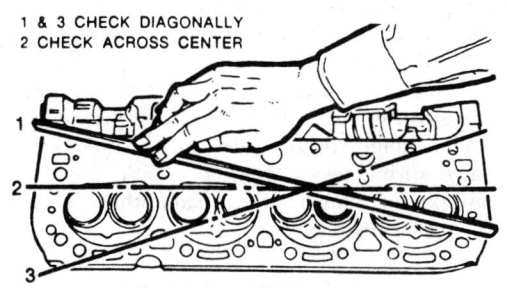

Check the cylinder head for warpage

cylinder engines, remove the camshaft (see Camshaft Removal).

2. Turn the cylinder head over so that the mounting surface is facing up and support evenly on wooden blocks.

CAUTION: *V6 engines use aluminum cylinder heads, exercise care when cleaning.*

3. Use a scraper and remove all of the gasket material stuck to the head mounting surface. Mount a wire carbon removal brush in an electric drill and clean away the carbon on the valves and head combustion chambers.

CAUTION: *When scraping or decarbonizing the cylinder head take care not to damage or nick the gasket mounting surface.*

4. Number the valve heads with a permanent felt-tip marker for cylinder location.

Resurfacing

If the cylinder head is warped resurfacing by a machine shop is required. Place a straightedge across the gasket surface of the head. Using feeler gauges, determine the clearance at the center and along the length between the head and straight-edge. Measure clearance at the center and along the lengths of both diagonals. If warpage exceeds .003 inches in a six inch span, or .006 inches over the total length the cylinder head must be resurfaced.

Valves and Springs
REMOVAL AND INSTALLATION

1. Block the head on its side, or install a pair of head-holding brackets made especially for valve removal.

2. Use a socket slightly larger than the valve stem and keepers, place the socket over the valve stem and gently hit the socket with a plastic hammer to break loose any varnish buildup.

3. Remove the valve keepers, retainer, spring shield and valve spring using a valve spring compressor (the locking C-clamp type is the easiest kind to use).

4. Put the parts in a separate container numbered for the cylinder being worked on; do not mix them with other parts removed.

5. Remove and discard the valve stem oil seal, a new seal will be used at assembly time.

6. Remove the valve from the cylinder head and place, in order, through numbered holes punched in a stiff piece of cardboard or wooden valve holding stick.

NOTE: *The exhaust valve stems, on some engines, are equipped with small metal caps. Take care not to lose the caps. Make sure to reinstall them at assembly time. Replace any caps that are worn.*

7. Use an electric drill and rotary wire brush to clean the intake and exhaust valve ports, combustion chamber and valve seats. In some cases, the carbon will need to be chipped away. Use a blunt pointed drift for carbon chipping, be careful around the valve seat areas.

8. Use a wire valve guide cleaning brush and safe solvent to clean the valve guides.

9. Clean the valves with a revolving wire brush. Heavy carbon deposits may be removed with the blunt drift.

NOTE: *When using a wire brush to clean carbon on the valve ports, valves etc., be sure that the deposits are actually removed, rather than burnished.*

10. Wash and clean all valve springs, keepers, retaining caps etc., in safe solvent.

11. Clean the head with a brush and some safe solvent and wipe dry.

12. Check the head for cracks. Cracks in the cylinder head usually start around an exhaust valve seat because it is the hottest part of the combustion chamber. If a crack is suspected but cannot be detected visually have the area checked with dye penetrant or other method by the machine shop.

13. After all cylinder head parts are reasonably clean check the valve stem-to-guide clearance. If a dial indicator is not on hand, a visual inspection can give you a fairly good idea if the guide, valve stem or both are worn.

14. Insert the valve into the guide until slightly away from the valve seat. Wiggle the valve sideways. A small amount of wobble is normal, excessive wobble means a worn guide or valve stem. If a dial indicator is on hand, mount the indicator so that the stem of the valve

ENGINE AND ENGINE REBUILDING

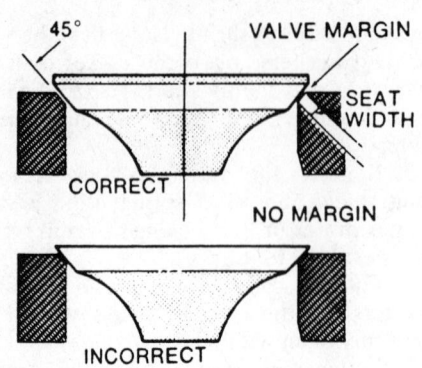

Valve seat width and centering

is at 90° to the valve stem, as close to the valve guide as possible. Move the valve off the seat, and measure the valve guide-to-stem clearance by rocking the stem back and forth to actuate the dial indicator. Measure the valve stem using a micrometer and compare to specifications to determine whether stem or guide wear is causing excessive clearance.

15. The valve guide, if worn, must be repaired before the valve seats can be resurfaced. Ford supplies valves with oversize stems to fit valve guides that are reamed to oversize for repair. The machine shop will be able to handle the guide reaming for you. In some cases, if the guide is not too badly worn, knurling may be all that is required.

16. Reface, or have the valves and valve seats refaced. The valve seats should be a true 45° angle. Remove only enough material to clean up any pits or grooves. Be sure the valve seat is not too wide or narrow. Use a 60° grinding wheel to remove material from the bottom of the seat for raising and a 30° grinding wheel to remove material from the top of the seat to narrow.

17. After the valves are refaced by machine, hand lap them to the valve seat. Clean the grinding compound off and check the position of face-to-seat contact. Contact should be close to the center of the valve face. If contact is close to the top edge of the valve narrow the seat; if too close to the bottom edge, raise the seat.

18. Valves should be refaced to a true angle of 44°. Remove only enough metal to clean up the valve face or to correct runout. If the edge of a valve head, after machining, is 1/32 inch or less replace the valve. The tip of the valve stem should also be dressed on the valve grinding machine; however, do not remove more than .010 inch.

19. After all valve and valve seats have been machined, check the remaining valve train parts (springs, retainers, keepers, etc.) for wear. Check the valve springs for straightness and tension.

20. Reassemble the head in the reverse order of disassembly using new valve guide seals and lubricating the valve stems. Check the valve spring installed height, shim or replace as necessary.

CHECKING VALVE SPRINGS

Place the valve spring on a flat surface next to a carpenters square. Measure the height of the spring, and rotate the spring against the edge of the square to measure distortion. If the spring height varies (by comparison) by more than 1/16 inch or if the distortion exceeds 1/16 inch, replace the spring.

Have the valve springs tested for spring pressure at the installed and compressed (installed height minus valve lift) height using a valve spring tester. Springs should be within one pound, plus or minus each other. Replace springs as necessary.

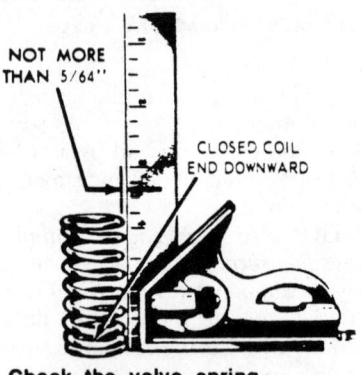

Check the valve spring free length and squareness

VALVE SPRING INSTALLED HEIGHT

After installing the valve spring, measure the distance between the spring mounting pad and the lower edge of the spring retainer. Compare the measurement to specifications. If the installed height is incorrect, add shim washers between the spring mounting pad and the spring. Use only washers designed for valve springs; available at most parts houses.

VALVE STEM OIL SEALS

Umbrella type oil seals fitting on the valve stem over the top of the valve guide are used on the in-line six and eight cylinder engines. The four cylinder and V6 engine uses a positive valve stem seal using a Teflon insert. Teflon seals are available for other engines but usually require valve guide machining, consult your automotive machine shop for advice on having positive valve stem oil seals installed.

When installing valve stem oil seals, ensure that a small amount of oil is able to pass the

ENGINE AND ENGINE REBUILDING 77

Measure the valve spring installed height (A) with a modified steel rule

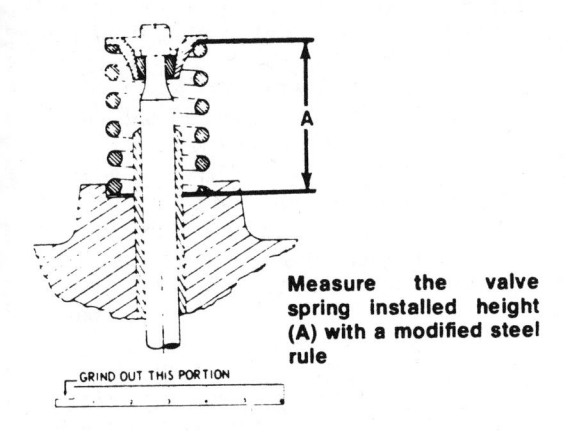

GRIND OUT THIS PORTION

seal to lubricate the valve stems and guide walls; otherwise, excessive wear will occur.

VALVE SEATS

If a valve seat is damaged or burnt and cannot be serviced by refacing, it may be possible to have the seat machined and an insert installed. Consult the automotive machine shop for their advice.

NOTE: *The aluminum heads on V6 engines are equipped with inserts.*

VALVE GUIDES

Worn valve guides can, in most cases, be reamed to accept a valve with an oversized stem. Valve guides that are not excessively worn or distorted may, in some cases, be knurled rather than reamed. However, if the valve stem is worn reaming for an oversized valve stem is the answer since a new valve would be required.

Knurling is a process in which metal is displaced and raised, thereby reducing clearance. Knurling also produces excellent oil control. The possibility of knurling instead of reaming the valve guides should be discussed with a machinist.

HYDRAULIC VALVE CLEARANCE

Hydraulic valve lifters operate with zero clearance in the valve train, and because of this the rocker arms are nonadjustable. The only means by which valve system clearances can be altered is by installing over or undersize pushrods; but, because of the hydraulic lifter's natural ability to compensate for slack in the valve train, all components of all the valve system should be checked for wear if there is excessive play in the system.

When a valve in the engine is in the closed position, the valve lifter is resting on the base circle of the camshaft lobe and the pushrod is in its lowest position. To remove this additional clearance from the valve train, the valve lifter expands to maintain zero clearance in the valve system. When a rocker arm is loosened or removed from the engine, the lifter expands to its fullest travel. When the rocker arm is reinstalled on the engine, the proper valve setting is obtained by tightening the rocker arm to a specified limit. But with the lifter fully expanded, if the camshaft lobe is on a high point it will require excessive torque to compress the lifter and obtain the proper setting. Because of this, when any component of the valve system has been removed, a preliminary valve adjustment procedure must be followed to ensure that when the rocker arm is reinstalled on the engine and tightened, the camshaft lobe for that cylinder is in the low position.

To determine whether a shorter or longer push rod is necessary, make the following check:

Mark the crankshaft pulley as described under "Preliminary Valve Adjustment" procedure. Follow each step in the procedure. As each valve is positioned, mount a suitable hydraulic lifter compressor tool on the rocker arm. Slowly apply pressure to bleed down the lifter until the plunger is completely bottomed. Take care to avoid excessive pressure that might bend the pushrod. Hold the lifter in bottom position and check the available clearance between the rocker arm and the valve stem tip with a feeler gauge. If the clearance is less than specified, install an under-sized pushrod. If the clearance is greater than specified, install an over-sized pushrod. When compressing the valve spring to remove the pushrods, be sure the piston in the individual cylinder is below TDC to avoid contact between the valve and the piston. To replace a pushrod, it will be necessary to remove the valve rocker arm shaft assembly on in-line engines. Upon replacement of a valve push rod, valve rocker arm shaft assembly or hydraulic valve lifter, the engine should not be cranked or rotated until the hydraulic lifters have had an opportunity to leak down to their normal operation position. The leak down rate can be accelerated by using the tool shown on the valve rocker arm and applying pressure in a direction to collapse the lifter.

Collapsed tappet gap:

IN-LINE ENGINES

- Allowable—.085–.209
- Desired—.110–.184

V6 ENGINES

- Allowable—.088–.189

V8 ENGINES (255 CU IN.)

- Allowable—.098–.198
- Desired—.123–.173

- Allowable—.–.193
- Desired—.096–.163

VALVE CLEARANCE—HYDRAULIC VALVE LASH ADJUSTERS

NOTE: *Refer to Chapter 2 for valve clearance adjustment on the V6-170 engine.*

Four Cylinder 140 Cu In. Engine

Hydraulic valve lash adjusters are used in the valve train. These units are placed at the fulcrum point of the cam followers (or rocker arms). Their action is similar to the hydraulic tappets used in push rod engines.

1. Position the camshaft so that the base circle of the lobe is facing the cam follower of the valve to be checked.
2. Using the tool shown in the illustration, slowly apply pressure to the cam follower until the lash adjuster is completely collapsed. Hold the follower in this position and insert 0.045 in. feeler gauge between the base circle of the cam and the follower.

NOTE: *The minimum gap is 0.035 in. and the maximum is 0.055 in. The desire gap is between 0.040 in. and 0.050 in.*

3. If the clearance is excessive, remove the cam follower and inspect it for damage.
4. If the cam follower seems OK measure the valve spring assembled height to be sure the valve is not sticking. See the Valve Specifications chart in this chapter.
5. If the valve spring assembled height is OK check the dimensions of the camshaft.
6. If the camshaft dimensions are OK the lash adjuster should be cleaned and tested.
7. Replace any worn parts as necessary.

NOTE: *For any repair that includes removal of the camshaft follower (rocker arm), each affected hydraulic lash adjuster must be collapsed after reinstallation of the camshaft follower, and then released. This step must be taken prior to any rotation of the camshaft.*

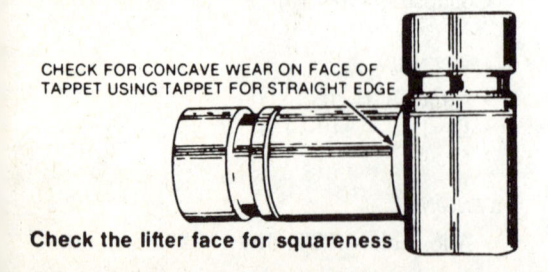

CHECK FOR CONCAVE WEAR ON FACE OF TAPPET USING TAPPET FOR STRAIGHT EDGE

Check the lifter face for squareness

HYDRAULIC VALVE LIFTER INSPECTION

Remove the lifters from their bores and remove any gum and varnish with safe solvent. Check the lifters for concave wear. If the bottom of the lifter is worn concave or flat, replace the lifter. Lifters are built with a convex bottom, flatness indicates wear. If a worn lifter is detected, carefully check the camshaft for wear.

CAUTION: *Mark lifters for cylinder and position location: Lifter must be reinstalled in the same bore they were removed from.*

To test lifter leak down, submerge the lifter in a container of kerosene. Chuck a used pushrod or its equivalent into a drill press. Position the container of kerosene so the pushrod acts on the lifter plunger. Pump the lifter with the drill press until resistance increases. Pump several more times to bleed any air from the lifter. Apply very firm, constant pressure to the lifter and observe the rate which fluid bleeds out of the lifter. If the lifter bleeds down very quickly (less than 15 seconds), the lifter should be replaced. If the time exceeds 60 seconds, the lifter is sticking and should be cleaned or replaced. If the lifter is operating properly (leak down time 15–60 seconds) and not worn, lubricate and reinstall in engine.

REMOVAL AND INSTALLATION

1. Remove the intake manifold and related parts.
2. Remove the crankcase ventilation hoses, PCV valve and elbows from the valve rocker arm covers.
3. Remove the valve rocker arm covers. Loosen the valve rocker arm fulcrum bolts and rotate the rocker arms to the side.
4. Remove the valve pushrods and identify them so that they can be installed in their original positions.

NOTE: *On 5.0L engines with roller tappets, the pushrods have a collar at the upper end and can only be installed one way. This is necessary because the balls at each end are not the same.*

5. Remove the tappet guide retainer bolts.
6. Remove the retainer and tappet guide plates. Identify the guide plates so they may be installed in their original positions.
7. Using a magnet, remove the tappets and place them in a rack so that they can be installed in their original bores.

NOTE: *For roller tappets, note their original orientation so that when reinstalled the roller rotates in the same direction. If the tappets cannot be removed from their bores due to excessive varnish, etc., it may be necessary to use a plier-type Tool T70L-6500-A or equivalent or a claw type tool to remove them. Rotate the tappet back and forth to loosen it from the gum or varnish that may have formed on the tappet. Tappets and bores*

ENGINE AND ENGINE REBUILDING 79

are to be lubricated with engine oil SF before installation.

1. Clean outside of tappets and install in the bores from which they were removed. Install roller tappets as they were originally oriented so that they rotate in the same direction. If a new tappet is being installed, check the new tappet for a free fit in the bore in which it is to be installed. Lubricate the tappet and bore with engine oil SF before inserting it in the bore.
2. Install tappet guide plates in their original positions, then install guide plate retainer.
3. Install the pushrods in their original position. Install roller tappet pushrods with with collar up. Apply Ford Polyethylene Grease D0AZ-19584-A, or equivalent to the valve stem tips and the push rod ends.
4. Lubricate the rocker arms and fulcrum seats with engine oil SF. Position the rocker arms over the pushrods and install fulcrum bolts. Perform a valve clearance adjustment.
5. Install the valve rocker arm covers with a new service gasket or RTV sealant or equivalent where specified. Install the PCV valve or elbow in the valve rocker arm cover.
6. Install the intake manifold and related parts.
7. Run the engine and check for leaks. Check engine idle speed and adjust as necessary.

Timing Cover and Chain
REMOVAL AND INSTALLATION
In-Line Six Cylinder Engines

1. Drain the cooling system and crankcase.
2. Disconnect the upper radiator hose from the intake manifold and the lower hose from the water pump. On cars with automatic transmission, disconnect the cooler lines from the radiator.
3. Remove the radiator, fan and pulley, and engine-drive belts. On the models with air conditioning, remove the condenser retaining bolts and position the condenser forward. *Do not disconnect the refrigerant lines.*
4. Remove the cylinder front cover retaining bolts and front oil pan bolts and gently pry the cover away from the block.
5. Remove the crankshaft pulley bolt and use a puller to remove the vibration damper.
6. With a socket wrench of the proper size on the crankshaft pulley bolt, gently rotate the crankshaft in a clockwise direction until all slack is removed from the lift side of the timing chain. Scribe a mark on the engine block parallel to the present position on the left side of the chain. Next, turn the crankshaft in a counterclockwise direction to remove all the slack from the right side of the chain. Force the left side of the chain outward with the fingers and measure the distance between the reference point and the present position of the chain. If the distance exceeds ½ inch, replace the chain and sprockets.
7. Crank the engine until the timing marks are aligned as shown in the illustration. Remove the bolt, slide sprocket and chain forward and remove as an assembly.
8. Position the sprockets and chain on the engine, making sure that the timing marks are aligned, dot to dot.
9. Reinstall the front cover, applying oil resistant sealer to the new gasket.

NOTE: *On 6-200 engines. Trim away the exposed portion of the old oil pan gasket flush with front of the engine block. Cut and position the required portion of a new gasket to the oil pan, applying sealer to both sides of it.*

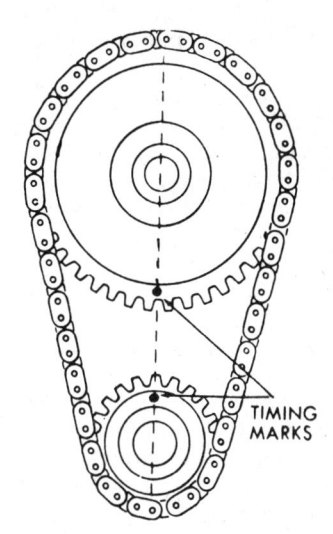

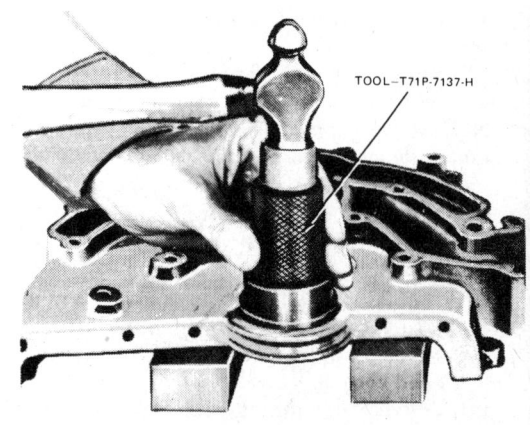

Timing mark alignment—6 cyl. 200 eng., all V8 engines

Installing front cover oil seal; a large socket can be used in place of tool shown

ENGINE AND ENGINE REBUILDING

10. Install the fan, pulley and belts. Adjust belt tension.
11. Install the radiator, connect the radiator hoses and transmission cooling lines. If equipped with air conditioning, install the condenser.
12. Fill the crankcase and cooling system. Start the engine and check for leaks.

V6 Engine (Except V6-170)

1. Disconnect the negative battery cable from the battery. Drain the cooling system.
2. Remove the air cleaner and air duct assemblies.
3. Remove the radiator fan shroud and position back over the water pump. Remove the fan clutch assembly and shroud.
4. Remove all drive belts. If equipped with power steering, remove the pump with hoses attached and position out of the way. Be sure to keep the pump upright to prevent fluid leakage.
5. If your car is equipped with air conditioning, remove the front compressor mounting bracket. If is not necessary to remove the compressor.
6. Disconnect the coolant by-pass hose and the heater hose at the water pump.
7. Disconnect the upper radiator hose at the thermostat housing. Remove the distributor.
8. If your car is equipped with a tripminder, remove the flow meter support bracket and allow the meter to be supported by the hoses.
9. Raise the front of the car and support on jackstands.
10. Remove the crankshaft pulley using a suitable puller. Remove the fuel pump shield.
11. Disconnect the fuel line from the carburetor at the fuel pump. Remove the mounting bolts and the fuel pump. Position pump out of the way with tank line still attached.
12. Drain the engine oil and remove the oil filter.
13. Disconnect the lower radiator hose at the water pump.
14. Remove the oil pan mounting bolts and lower the oil pan.
NOTE: *The front cover cannot be removed unless the oil pan is lowered.*
15. Lower the car from the jackstands.
16. Remove the front cover mounting bolts.
NOTE: *Water pump removal is not necessary.*
CAUTION: *A front cover mounting bolt is located behind the oil filter adapter. If the bolt is not removed and the cover is pried upon breakage will occur.*
17. Remove the timing indicator. Remove the front cover and water pump assembly.
18. Remove the camshaft thrust button and spring from the end of the camshaft. Remove the camshaft sprocket attaching bolts.
19. Remove the camshaft sprocket, crankshaft sprocket and timing chain by pulling forward evenly on both sprockets. If the crankshaft sprocket is difficult to remove, position two small prybars, one on each side, behind the sprocket and pry forward.
20. Clean all gasket surfaces on the front cover, cylinder block, fuel pump and oil pan.
21. Install a new front cover oil seal. If a new front cover is to be installed: Install the oil pump, oil filter adapter and intermediate shaft from the old cover. Remove the water pump from the old cover. clean the mounting surface, install a new mounting gasket and the pump on the new front cover. Pump attaching bolt torque is 13–22 ft. lbs.
22. Rotate the crankshaft, if necessary, to bring No. 1 piston to TDC with the crankshaft keyway at the 12 o'clock position.
23. Lubricate the timing chain with motor oil. Install the chain over the two gears making sure the marks on both gears are positioned across from each other. Install the gears and chain on the cam and crankshaft. Install the camshaft mounting bolts. Tighten the bolts to 15–22 ft. lbs.
24. Install the camshaft thrust button and spring. Lubricate the thrust button with Polyethylene grease before installation.
NOTE: *The thrust button and spring must be bottomed in the camshaft seat and must not be allowed to fall out during front cover installation.*
25. Position a new cover gasket on the front of the engine and install the cover and water pump assemblies. Install the timing indicator. Torque the front cover bolts to 15–22 ft. lbs.
26. The remaining steps of installation are in the reverse order of removal.
CAUTION: *When installing the fuel pump, turn the crankshaft 180 degrees to position the fuel pump drive eccentric away from the fuel pump arm. Failure to turn the drive eccentric away from the pump arm can cause stress on the pump mounting threads and strip them out when installing the pump.*

V6 170 Cu In. Engine—Front Cover

1. Remove the oil pan as described later in this chapter.
2. Drain the coolant and remove the radiator and any other parts to provide the necessary clearance.
3. If equipped with air conditioning remove the compressor and bracket.
4. Remove the alternator, thermactor pump and drive belts.
5. Remove the water pump and fan.

ENGINE AND ENGINE REBUILDING

6. Remove the drive pulley from the crankshaft.
7. Remove the front cover retaining bolts. It might be necessary to tap the cover lightly with a plastic hammer to break the gasket seal. Remove the front cover. If necessary remove the two screws and cover plate for replacement of the cover plate gasket.
8. If necessary, remove the guide sleeves from the cylinder block.
9. To install reverse the removal procedures, cleaning all surfaces of gasket material and installing new gaskets and sealing compound.

SEAL REMOVAL AND INSTALLATION WITH FRONT COVER REMOVED

1. Support the front cover to prevent damage while driving out the seal.
2. Drive out the seal from the front cover.
3. Support the front cover to prevent damage while installing the seal.
4. Coat the new front cover oil seal with a light grease. Install the new seal in the front cover.

WITH FRONT COVER INSTALLED

1. Drain the coolant.
2. Remove the radiator and crankshaft pulley and water pump drive belt.
3. Using a puller, remove the front seal.
4. Coat the new seal with Lubriplate® or equivalent then slide the tool and the seal onto the crankshaft.
5. Drive the oil seal in until the tool butts against the front cover.
6. Replace the crankshaft pulleys and bolt and torque to specifications. (Damper bolt—95 ft. lbs., Crankshaft pulley-to-damper—20 ft. lbs.)
7. Replace the radiator and drive belt.
8. Fill the cooling system, run the engine at the fast idle and check for leaks.

V6 170 Cu In. Engine—Camshaft and Gears

1. Drain the coolant and remove the radiator, fan, spacer, water pump pulley and the drive belt.
2. Remove the distributor cap with spark plug wires as an assembly. Remove the distributor vacuum line, distributor, alternator, Thermactor, rocker arm covers, fuel line and filter, carburetor, EGR tube, and intake manifold. Remove the spark plug wire boots.
3. Drain the crankcase. Remove the rocker arm and the shaft assemblies. Lift out the pushrods and place in a marked rack so they can be reinstalled in the same location.
4. Remove the oil pan.
5. Remove the drive sprocket attaching bolt and slide the sprocket off the end of the shaft.

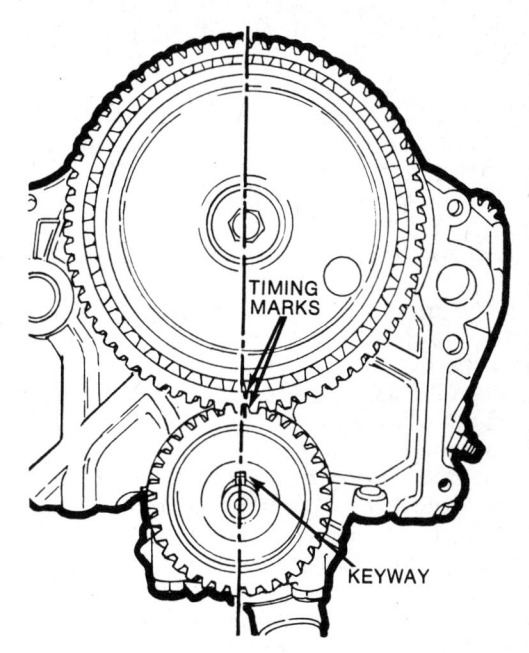

V6 timing gear alignment

6. Remove the engine front cover and water pump as an assembly.
7. Remove the camshaft gear retaining bolt and slide the gear off the camshaft.
8. Remove the camshaft thrust plate and the screws.
9. Using a magnet, remove the valve lifters.
10. Carefully pull the camshaft from the block, avoiding any damage to the camshaft bearings. Remove the camshaft gear key and spacer ring.
11. Oil the camshaft journals with gear oil or assembly lube and apply it to the cam lobes.
12. Install the camshaft in the block, carefully avoiding damage to the bearing surfaces.
13. Install the spacer ring with the chamfered side toward the camshaft. Insert the camshaft key and install the thrust plate so that it covers the main oil gallery. Torque the attaching screws to specifications.
14. Check the camshaft for the specified end-play. The spacer ring and thrust plate are available in two thicknesses to permit adjusting the end-play.
15. Turn the camshaft and the crankshaft as necessary to align the timing marks and install the camshaft gear. Install the retaining washer and bolt and tighten to 34 ft. lbs.
16. Install the valve lifters to their original locations.
17. Install the engine front cover and water pump as an assembly.
18. Install the belt drive pulley and secure

82 ENGINE AND ENGINE REBUILDING

with washer and retaining bolt. Tighten the bolt to specifications.

19. Install the oil pan.
20. Apply a light grease to both ends of the pushrods. Install the valve pushrods in their original locations.
21. Install the intake manifold.
22. Install the oil baffles and the rocker arm and shaft assemblies. Tighten the rocker arm stand bolts to 45 ft. lb. Adjust the valves.
23. Install the water pump pulley, fan spacer, fan, and the drive belt. Adjust the belt tension to specifications. Install the carburetor, EGR tube, fuel line and filter, alternator, Thermactor, distributor, distributor vacuum line, and distributor cap and wires. Install the radiator. Fill the cooling system to the proper level with the specified coolant. Adjust the timing.
24. Install the rocker arm covers.
25. Run the engine and check the idle speed.
26. Run the engine at fast idle speed and check for coolant and oil leaks.

V8 Engines

1. Drain cooling system, remove air cleaner and disconnect the battery.
2. Disconnect the transmission cooler lines and radiator hoses and remove the radiator.
3. Disconnect heater hose at water pump. Slide water pump by-pass hose clamp toward the pump.
4. Loosen alternator mounting bolts at the alternator. Remove the alternator support bolt at the water pump. Remove Thermactor pump on all engines so equipped. If equipped with power steering or air conditioning, unbolt the component, remove the belt, and lay the pump aside with the lines attached.
5. Remove the fan, spacer, pulley, and drive belt.
6. Drain the crankcase.
7. Remove the pulley from crankshaft pulley adapter. Remove cap screw and washer from front end of crankshaft. Remove crankshaft pulley adapter with a puller.
8. Disconnect fuel pump outlet line at the pump. Remove fuel pump retaining bolts and lay the pump to the side. Remove the engine oil dipstick.
9. Remove the front cover attaching bolts.
10. Remove the crankshaft oil slinger if so equipped.
11. Check timing chain deflection, using the procedure outlined in Step 6 of the in-line six cylinder cover and chain removal.
12. Rotate the engine until sprocket timing marks are aligned as shown in valve timing illustration.
13. Remove crankshaft sprocket cap screw, washers, and fuel pump eccentric. Slide both sprockets and chain forward and off as an assembly.
14. Position sprockets and chain on the camshaft and crankshaft with both timing marks dot to dot on a centerline. Install fuel pump eccentric, washers and sprocket attaching bolt. Torque the sprocket attaching bolt to 40–45 ft. lbs.
15. Install crankshaft front oil slinger.
16. Clean front cover and mating surfaces of old gasket material. Install a new oil seal in the cover. Use a seal driver too, if available.
17. Coat a new cover gasket with sealer and position it on the block.

NOTE: *Trim away the exposed portion of the oil pan gasket flush with the cylinder block. Cut and position the required portion of a new gasket to the oil pan, applying sealer to both sides of it.*

18. Install front cover, using a crank-shaft-to-cover alignment tool. Coat the threads of the attaching bolts with sealer. Torque attaching bolts to 12–15 ft. lbs.
19. Install fuel pump, connect fuel pump outlet tube.
20. Install crankshaft pulley adapter and torque attaching bolt. Install crankshaft pulley.
21. Install water pump pulley, drive belt, spacer and fan.
22. Install alternator support bolt at the water pump. Tighten alternator mounting bolts. Adjust drive belt tension. Install Thermactor pump if so equipped.
23. Install radiator and connect all coolant and heater hoses. Connect battery cables.
24. Refill cooling system and the crankcase. Install the dipstick.
25. Start engine and operate at fast idle.
26. Check for leaks, install air cleaner. Adjust ignition timing and make all final adjustments.

Front Cover Oil Seal

REMOVAL AND INSTALLATION
Except 4-140

It is recommended to replace the cover seal any time the front cover is removed.

NOTE: *On V6 engines, the seal may be removed, after the crank pulley is off without removing the cover.*

1. With the cover removed from the car, drive the old seal from the rear of cover with a pinpunch. Clean out the recess in the cover.
2. Coat the new seal with grease and drive it into the cover until it is fully seated. Check the seal after installation to be sure the spring is properly positioned in the seal.

ENGINE AND ENGINE REBUILDING 83

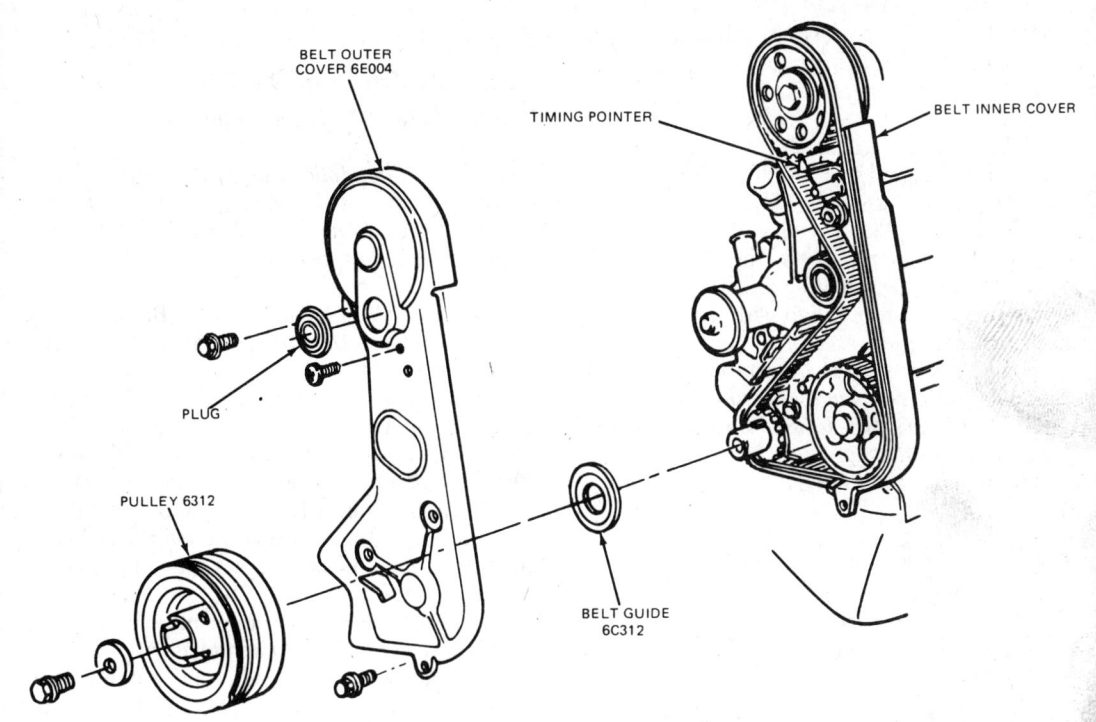

Timing belt outer cover, crankshaft belt guide and pulley installation—4 cyl. engine

Camshaft Drive Belt and Cover

Four Cylinder 140 Cu In. Engine

The correct installation and adjustment of the camshaft drive belt is mandatory if the engine is to run properly. The camshaft controls the opening of the camshaft and the crankshaft. When any given piston is on the intake stroke the corresponding intake valve must be open to admit air/fuel mixture into the cylinder. When the same piston is on the compression and power strokes, both valves in that cylinder must be closed. When the piston is on the exhaust stroke, the exhaust valve for that cylinder must be open. If the opening and closing of the valves is not coordinated with the movements of the pistons, the engine will run very poorly, if at all.

The camshaft drive belt also turns the engine auxiliary shaft. The distributor is driven by the engine auxiliary shaft. Since the distributor controls ignition timing, the auxiliary shaft must be coordinated witht the camshaft and the crankshaft, since both valves in any given cylinder must be closed and the piston in that cylinder near the top of the compression stroke when the spark plug fires.

Due to this complex interrelationship between the camshaft, the crankshaft and the auxiliary shaft, the cogged pulleys on each component must be aligned when the camshaft drive belt is installed.

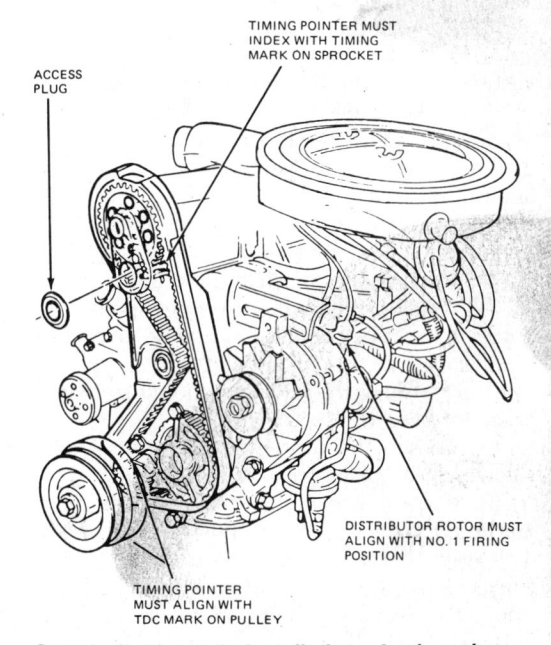

Camshaft drive train installation—4 cyl. engine

TROUBLESHOOTING

Should the camshaft drive belt jump timing by a tooth or two, the engine could still run; but very poorly. To visually check for correct timing of the crankshaft, auxiliary shaft, and the camshaft follow this procedure:

ENGINE AND ENGINE REBUILDING

NOTE: *There is an access plug provided in the cam drive belt cover so that the camshaft timing can be checked without moving the drive belt cover.*

1. Remove the access plug.
2. Turn the crankshaft until the timing marks on the crankshaft indicate TDC.
3. Make sure that the timing mark on the camshaft drive sprocket is aligned with the pointer on the inner belt cover. Also, the rotor of the distributor must align with the No. 1 cylinder firing position.

NOTE: *Never turn the crankshaft of any of the overhead cam engines in the opposite direction of normal rotation. Back rotation of the crankshaft may cause the timing belt to slip and alter the timing.*

REMOVAL AND INSTALLATION

1. Set the engine to TDC as described in the troubleshooting section. The crankshaft and camshaft timing marks should align with their respective pointers and the distributor rotor should point to the No. 1 plug tower.
2. Loosen the adjustment bolts on the alternator and accessories and remove the drive belts. To provide clearance for removing the camshaft belt, remove the fan and pulley.
3. Remove the belt outer cover.
4. Remove the distributor cap from the distributor and position it out of the way.
5. Loosen the belt tensioner adjustment and pivot bolts. Lever the tensioner away from the belt and retighten the adjustment bolt to hold it away.
6. Remove the crankshaft bolt and pulley. Remove the belt guide behind the pulley.
7. Remove the camshaft drive belt.
8. Install the new belt over the crankshaft pulley first, then counter-clockwise over the auxiliary shaft sprocket and the camshaft sprocket. Adjust the belt fore and aft so that it is centered on the sprockets.
9. Loosen the tensioner adjustment bolt, allowing it to spring back against the belt.
10. Rotate the crankshaft two complete turns in the normal rotation direction to remove any belt slack. Turn the crankshaft until the timing check marks are lined up. If the timing has slipped, remove the belt and repeat the procedure.
11. Tighten the tensioner adjustment bolt to 14–21 ft. lbs., and the pivot bolt to 28–40 ft. lbs.
12. Replace the belt guide and crankshaft pulley, distributor cap, belt outer cover, fan and pulley, drive belts and accessories. Adjust the accessory drive belt tension. Start the engine and check the ignition timing.

Camshaft

REMOVAL AND INSTALLATION
Four Cylinder 140 cu in. Engine

NOTE: *The following procedure covers camshaft removal and installation with the cylinder head on or off the engine. If the cylinder head has been removed start at Step 9.*

1. Drain the cooling system. Remove the air cleaner assembly and disconnect the negative battery cable.
2. Remove the spark plug wires from the plugs, disconnect the retainer from the valve cover and position the wires out of the way. Disconnect rubber vacuum lines as necessary.
3. Remove all drive belts. Remove the alternator mounting bracket-to-cylinder head mounting bolts, position bracket and alternator out of the way.
4. Disconnect and remove the upper radiator hose. Disconnect the radiator shroud.
5. Remove the fan blades and water pump pulley and fan shroud. Remove cam belt and valve covers.
6. Align engine timing marks at TDC. Remove cam drive belt.
7. Jack up the front of the car and support on jackstands. Remove the front motor mount bolts. Disconnect the lower radiator hose from the radiator. Disconnect and plug the automatic transmission cooler lines.
8. Position a piece of wood on a floor jack and raise the engine carefully as far as it will go. Place blocks of wood between the engine mounts and crossmember pedestals.
9. Remove the rocker arms as described earlier in this chapter.
10. Remove the camshaft drive gear and belt guide using a suitable puller. Remove the front oil seal with a sheet metal screw and slide hammer.
11. Remove the camshaft retainer located on the rear mounting stand by unbolting the two bolts.
12. Remove the camshaft by carefully withdrawing toward the front of the engine. Caution should be used to prevent damage to cam bearings, lobes and journals.
13. Check the camshaft journals and lobes for wear. Inspect the cam bearings, if worn (unless the proper bearing installing tool is on hand), the cylinder head must be removed for new bearings to be installed by a machine shop.
14. Cam installation is in the reverse order of removal. See following notes.

NOTE: *Coat the camshaft with heavy SF oil before sliding it into the cylinder head. Install a new front seal. Apply a coat of sealer*

ENGINE AND ENGINE REBUILDING 85

Camshaft installation—4 cyl. engine

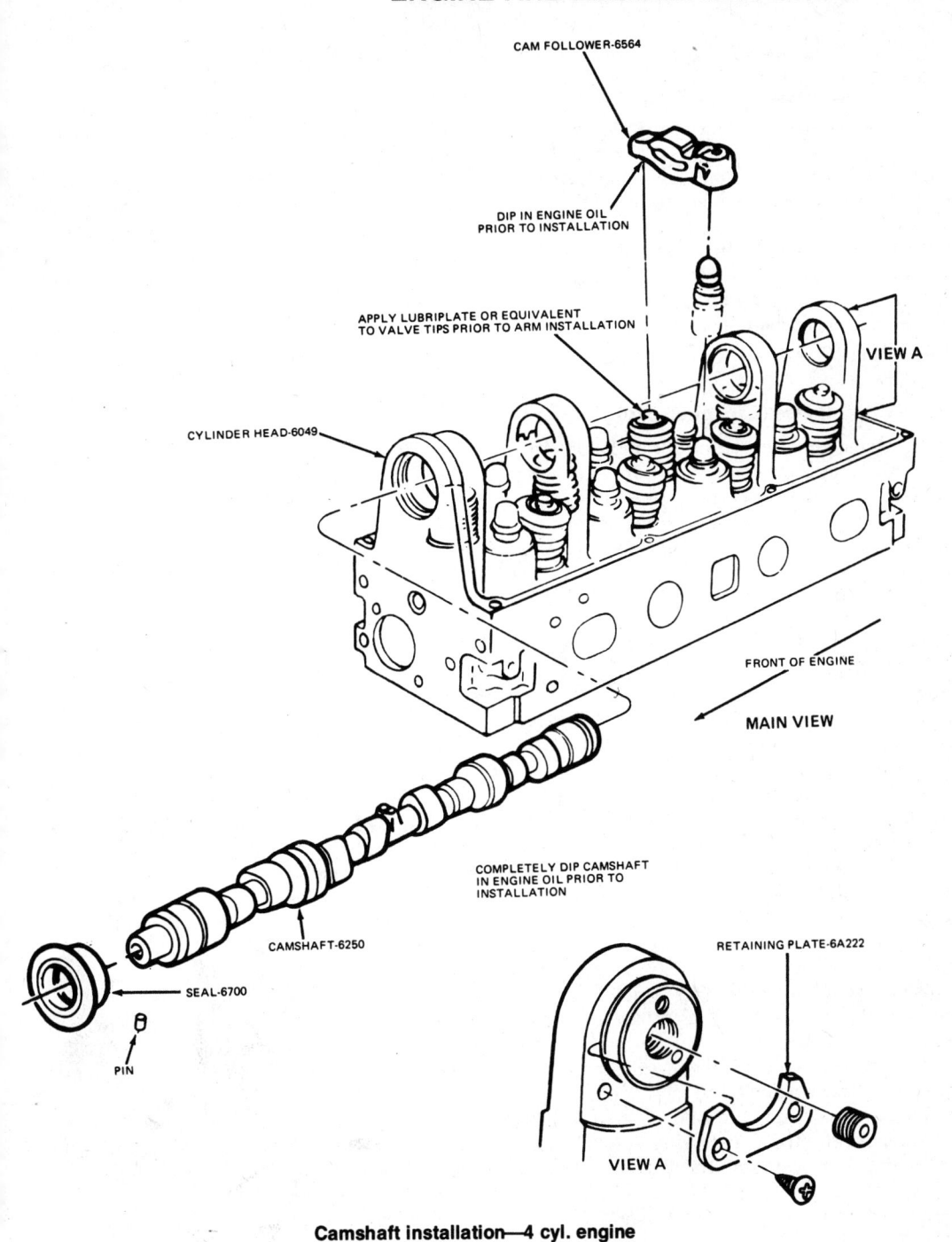

or teflon tape to the cam drive gear bolt before installation.
NOTE: *After any procedure requiring removal of the rocker arms, each lash adjuster must be fully collapsed after assembly, then released. This must be done before the camshaft is turned. See Valve Clearance-Hydraulic Valve Lash Adjusters.*

In-Line Six Cylinder Engines

1. Remove the cylinder head.
2. Remove the cylinder front cover, timing chain and sprockets as outlined in the proceding section.
3. Disconnect and remove the radiator, condenser and grille. Remove the gravel deflector.

ENGINE AND ENGINE REBUILDING

4. Using a magnet, remove the valve lifters and keep them in order so that they can be installed in their original positions.

5. Remove the camshaft thrust plate and remove the camshaft by pulling it from the front of the engine. Use care not to damage the camshaft lobes or journals while removing the cam from the engine.

6. Before installing the camshaft, coat the lobes with engine assembly lubricant and the journals and all valve parts with heavy oil. Clean the oil passage at the rear of the cylinder block with compressed air.

V6 and V8 Engines (Except V6-170)

1. Remove or reposition the radiator. A/C condenser and grille components are necessary to provide clearance to remove the camshaft.

2. Remove the cylinder front cover and timing chain as previously described in this chapter.

3. Remove the intake manifold and related parts described earlier in this chapter.

4. Remove the crankcase ventilation valve and tubes from the valve rocker covers. Remove the EGB cooler, if so equipped.

5. Remove the rocker arm covers and loosen the valve rocker arm fulcrum bolts and rotate the rocker arms to the side.

6. Remove the valve push rods and identify them so that they can be installed in their original positions.

7. Remove the valve lifters and place them in a rack so that they can be installed in their original bores.

8. Remove the camshaft thrust plate or button and spring and carefully remove the camshaft by pulling toward the front of the engine. Be careful not to damage the camshaft bearings.

9. Before installing, oil the camshaft journals with heavy engine oil SF and apply Lubriplate® or equivalent to the lobes. Carefully slide the camshaft through the bearings.

10. Install the camshaft thrust plate with the groove towards the cylinder block.

11. Lubricate the lifters with heavy SF engine oil and install in their original bores.

12. Apply Lubriplate® or equivalent to the valve stem tips and each end of the push rods. Install the push rods in their original position.

13. Lubricate the rocker arms and fulcrum seats with heavy SF engine oil and position the rocker arms over the push rods.

14. Install all other parts previously removed.

15. Fill the crankcase and cooling system and adjust the timing.

V6 170 cu in. Engine

1. Drain the coolant and remove the radiator, fan, spacer, water pump pulley and the drive belt.

2. Remove the distributor cap with spark plug wires as an assembly. Remove the distributor vacuum line, distributor, alternator, Thermactor, rocker arm covers, fuel line and filter, carburetor, EGR tube, and intake manifold. Remove the spark plug wire boots.

3. Drain the crankcase. Remove the rocker arm and the shaft assemblies. Lift out the pushrods and place in a marked rack so they can be reinstalled in the same location.

4. Remove the oil pan.

5. Remove the drive sprocket attaching bolt and slide the sprocket off the end of the shaft.

6. Remove the engine front cover and water pump as an assembly.

7. Remove the camshaft gear retaining bolt and slide the gear off the camshaft.

8. Remove the camshaft thrust plate and the screws.

9. Using a magnet, remove the valve lifters.

10. Carefully pull the camshaft from the block, avoiding any damage to the camshaft bearings. Remove the camshaft gear key and spacer ring.

11. Oil the camshaft journals with gear oil or assembly lube and apply it to the cam lobes.

12. Install the camshaft in the block, carefully avoiding damage to the bearing surfaces.

13. Install the spacer ring with the chamfered side toward the camshaft. Insert the camshaft key and install the thrust plate so that if covers the main oil gallery. Torque the attaching screws to specifications.

14. Check the camshaft for the specified end-play. The spacer ring and thrust plate are available in two thicknesses to permit adjusting the end-play.

15. Turn the camshaft and the crankshaft as necessary to align the timing marks and install the camshaft gear. Install the retaining washer and bolt and tighten to 34 ft. lbs.

16. Install the valve lifters to their original locations.

17. Install the engine front cover and water pump as an assembly.

18. Install the belt drive pulley and secure with washer and retaining bolt. Tighten the bolt to specifications.

19. Install the oil pan.

20. Apply a light grease to both ends of the pushrods. Install the valve pushrods in their original locations.

21. Install the intake manifold.

22. Install the oil baffles and the rocker arm

ENGINE AND ENGINE REBUILDING

and shaft assemblies. Tighten the rocker arm stand bolts to 45 ft. lb. Adjust the valves to .014 intake—.016 Exhaust.

23. Install the water pump pulley, fan spacer, fan, and the drive belt. Adjust the belt tension to specifications. Install the carburetor. EGR tube, fuel line and filter, alternator, Thermactor, distributor, distributor vacuum line, and distributor cap and wires. Install the radiator. Fill the cooling system to the proper level with the specified coolant. Adjust the timing.

24. Install the rocker arm covers.
25. Run the engine and check the idle speed.
26. Run the engine at fast idle speed and check for coolant and oil leaks.

CHECKING CAMSHAFT

Degrease the camshaft using safe solvent, clean all oil grooves. Visually inspect the cam lobes and bearing journals for excessive wear. If a lobe is questionable, check all lobes and journals with a micrometer.

Measure the lobes from nose to base and again at 90°. The lift is determined by subtracting the second measurement from the first. If all exhaust lobes and all intake lobes are not identical, the camshaft must be reground or replaced. Measure the bearing journals and compare to specifications. If a journal is worn there is a good chance that the cam bearings are worn too, requiring replacement.

If the lobes and journals appear intact, place the front and rear cam journals in V-blocks and rest a dial indicator on the center journal. Rotate the camshaft to check for straightness, if deviation exceeds .001 inch, replace the camshaft.

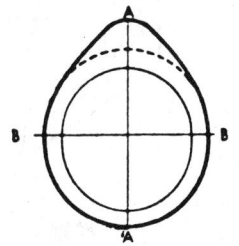

Camshaft lobe measurement

Auxillary Shaft

REMOVAL AND INSTALLATION

Four Cylinder 140 cu in. Engine

1. Remove the camshaft drive belt cover.
2. Remove the drive belt. Remove the auxiliary shaft sprocket. A puller may be necessary to remove the sprocket.
3. Remove the distributor and fuel pump.
4. Remove the auxiliary shaft cover and thrust plate.

5. Withdraw the auxiliary shaft from the block.

NOTE: *The distributor drive gear and the fuel pump eccentric on the auxiliary shaft must not be allowed to touch the auxiliary shaft bearings during removal and installation. Completely coat the shaft with oil before sliding it into place.*

6. Slide the auxiliary shaft into the housing and insert the thrust plate to hold the shaft.
7. Install a new gasket and auxiliary shaft cover.

NOTE: *The auxiliary shaft cover and cylinder front cover share a gasket. Cut off the old gasket around the cylinder cover and use half of the new gasket on the auxiliary shaft cover.*

8. Fit a new gasket into the fuel pump and install the pump.
9. Insert the distributor and install the auxiliary shaft sprocket.
10. Allign the timing marks and install the drive belt.
11. Install the drive belt cover.
12. Check the ignition timing.

Pistons and Connection Rods

REMOVAL AND INSTALLATION

NOTE: *Although, in most cases, the pistons and connecting rods can be removed from the engine (after the cylinder head and oil pan are removed) while the engine is still in the car; it is far easier to remove the engine from the car. If removing pistons with the engine still installed, disconnect the radiator hoses, automatic transmission cooler lines and radiator shroud. Unbolt front mounts before jacking up the engine. Block the engine in position with wooden blocks between the mounts.*

1. Remove the engine from the car. Remove cylinder head(s), oil pan and front cover (if necessary).
2. Because the top piston ring does not travel to the very top of the cylinder bore, a ridge is built up between the end of the travel and the top of the cylinder. Pushing the piston and connecting rod assembly past the ridge is difficult and may cause damage to the piston. If new rings are installed and the ridge has not been removed, ring breakage and piston damage can occur when the ridge is encountered at engine speed.
3. Turn the crankshaft to position the piston at the bottom of the cylinder bore. Cover the top of the piston with a rag. Install a ridge reamer in the bore and follow the manufacturer's instructions to remove the ridge. Use cau-

88 ENGINE AND ENGINE REBUILDING

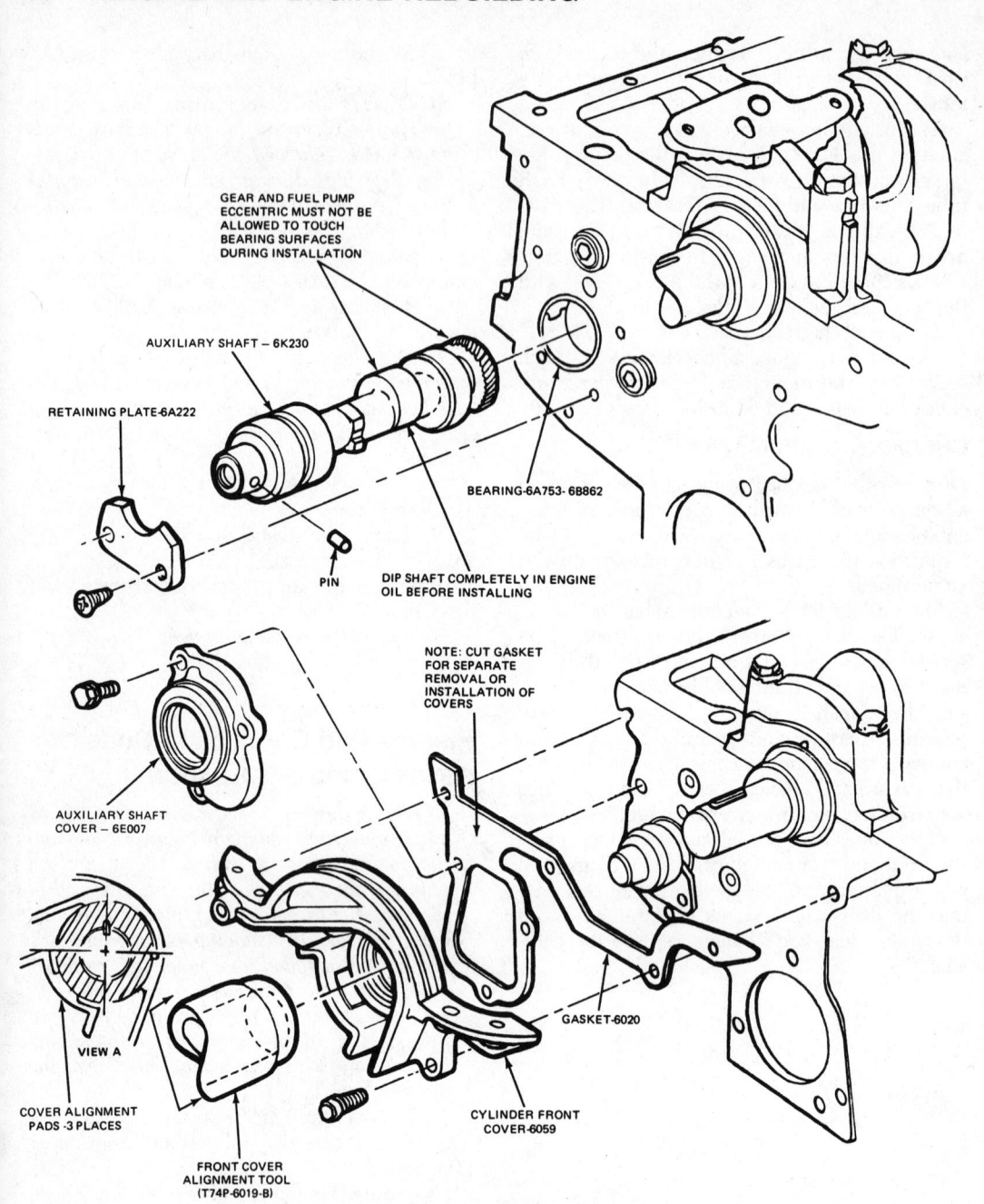

Auxiliary shaft installation—4 cyl. engine

tion; avoid cutting too deeply or into the ring travel area. Remove the rag and cuttings from the top of the piston. Remove the ridge from all cylinders.

4. Check the edges of the connecting rod and bearing cap for numbers or matchmarks, if none are present mark the rod and cap numerically and in sequence from front to back of engine. The numbers or marks not only tell from which cylinder the piston came from but also ensures that the rod caps are installed in the correct matching position.

5. Turn the crankshaft until the connecting rod is at the bottom of travel. Remove the two attaching nuts and the bearing cap. Take two pieces of rubber tubing and cover the rod bolts to prevent crank or cylinder scoring. Use a wooden hammer handle to help push the piston and rod up and out of the cylinder. Reinstall the rod cap in proper position. Remove all pistons and connecting rods. Inspect cylinder walls and deglaze or hone as necessary.

6. Installation is in the reverse order of removal. Lubricate each piston, rod bearing and

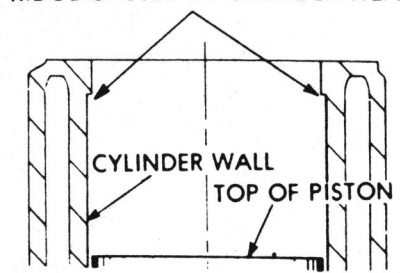

ENGINE AND ENGINE REBUILDING 89

Cylinder bore ridge

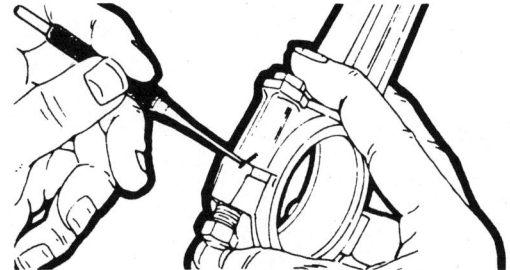

Match the connecting rod and cap with scribe marks

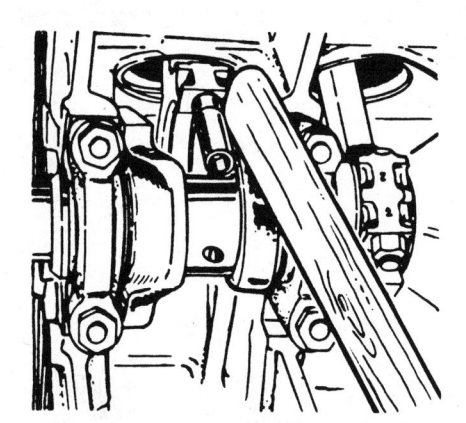

Push the piston out with a hammer handle

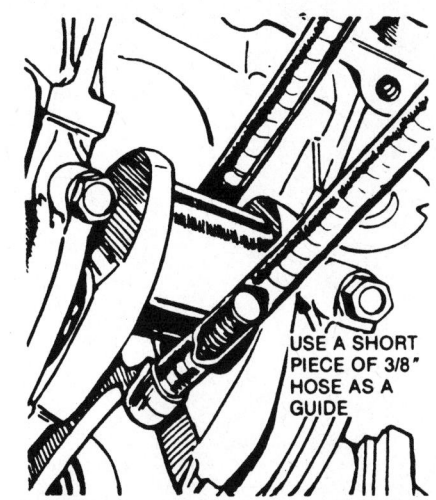

Use lengths of vacuum hose or rubber tubing to protect the crankshaft journals and cylinder walls during piston installation

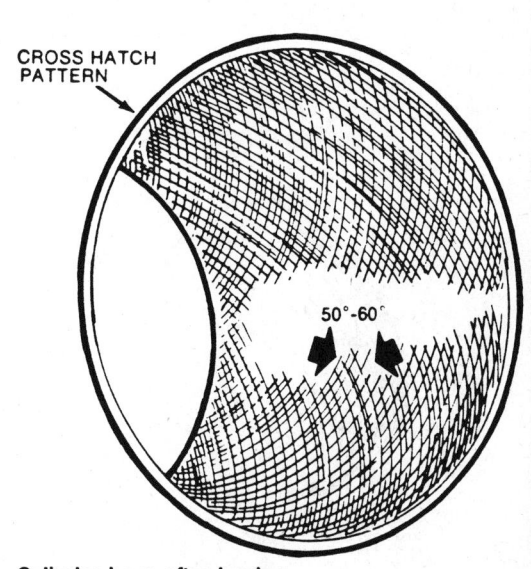

Cylinder bore after honing

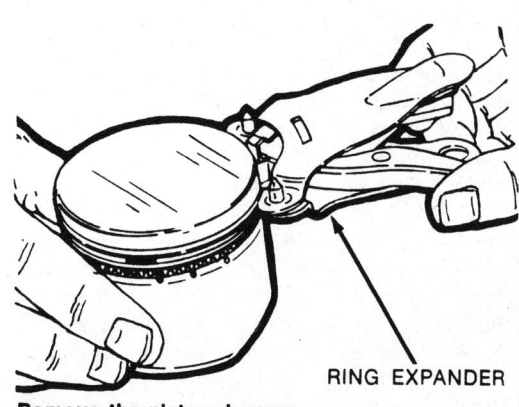

Remove the piston rings

cylinder wall. Install a ring compressor over the piston, position piston with mark toward front of engine and carefully install. Position connecting rod with bearing insert installed over the crank journal. Install the rod cap with bearing in proper position. Secure with rod nuts and torque to proper specifications. Install all rod and piston assemblies.

CLEANING AND INSPECTION

1. Use a piston ring expander and remove the rings from the piston.
2. Clean the ring grooves using an appropriate cleaning tool, exercise care to avoid cutting too deeply.
3. Clean all varnish and carbon from the

ENGINE AND ENGINE REBUILDING

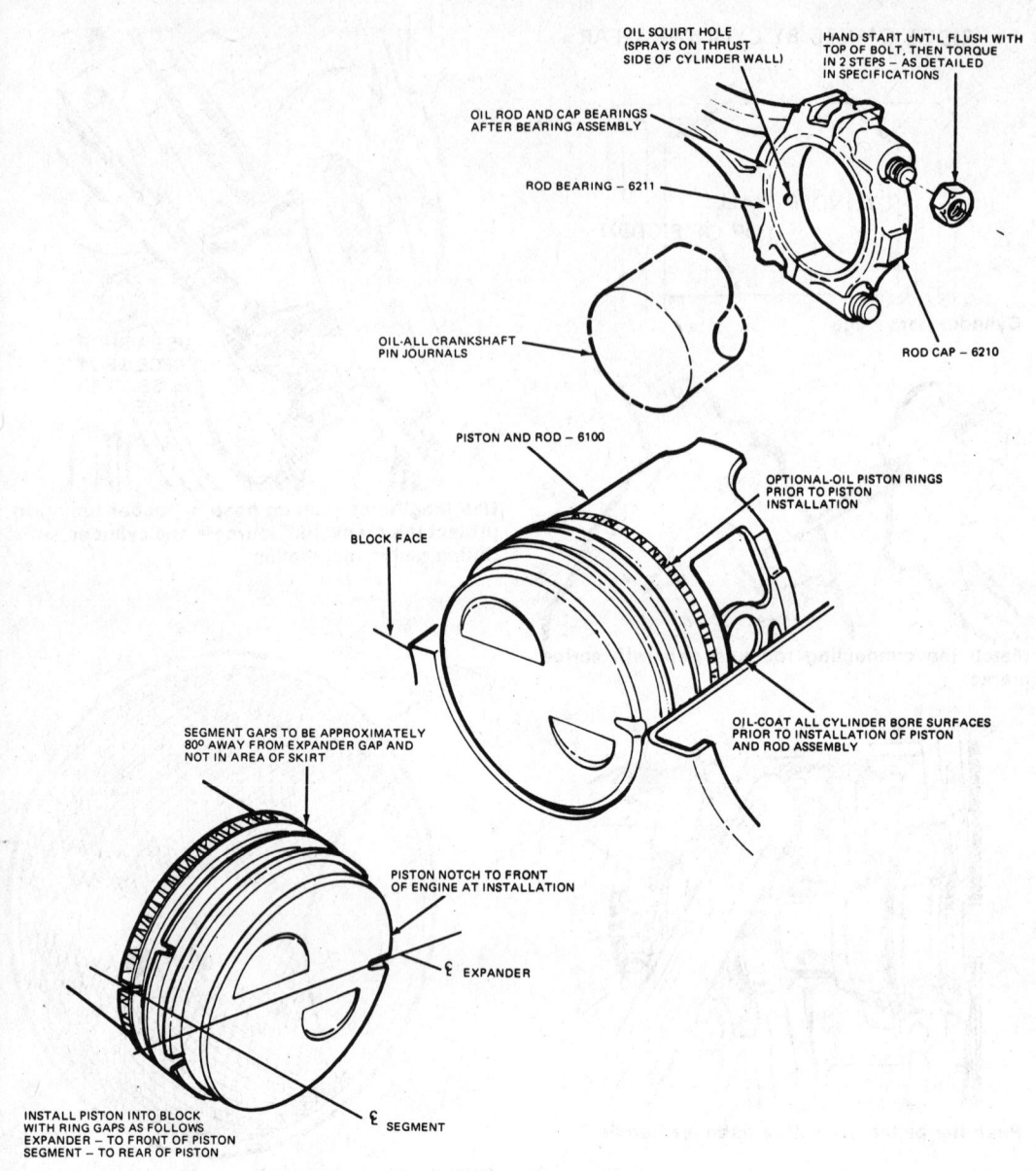

Pistons, rings and connecting rods—4 cyl. engine

piston with a safe solvent. Do not use a wire brush or caustic solution on the pistons.

4. Inspect the pistons for scuffing, scoring, cracks, pitting or excessive ring groove wear. If wear is evident, the piston must be replaced.

5. Have the piston and connecting rod assembly checked by a machine shop for correct alignment, piston pin wear and piston diameter. If the piston has "collapsed" it will have to be replaced or knurled to restore original diameter. Connecting rod bushing replacement, piston pin fitting and piston changing can be handled by the machine shop.

CYLINDER BORE

1. Check the cylinder bore for wear using a telescope gauge and a micrometer, measure the cylinder bore diameter perpendicular to the piston pin at a point 2½ inches below the top of the engine block. Measure the piston skirt perpendicular to the piston pin. The difference between the two measurements is the piston clearance. If the clearance is within specifications, finish honing or glaze breaking is all that is required. If clearance is excessive a slightly oversize piston may be required. If greatly

ENGINE AND ENGINE REBUILDING 91

oversize, the engine will have to be bored and .010 inch or larger oversized pistons installed.

FITTING AND POSITIONING PISTON RINGS

1. Take the new piston rings and compress them, one at a time into the cylinder that they will be used in. Press the ring about one inch below the top of the cylinder block using an inverted piston.

2. Use a feeler gauge and measure the distance between the ends of the ring; this is called measuring the ring end-gap. Compare the reading to the one called for in the specifications table. File the ends of the ring with a fine file to obtain necessary clearance.

NOTE: *If inadequate ring end-gap is utilized, ring breakage will result.*

3. Inspect the ring grooves on the piston for excessive wear or taper. If necessary have the grooves recut for use with a standard ring and spacer. The machine shop can handle the job for you.

4. Check the ring grooves by rolling the new piston ring around the groove to check for burrs or carbon deposits. If any are found, remove with a fine file. Hold the ring in the groove and measure side clearance with a feeler gauge. If clearance is excessive, spacer(s) will have to be added.

NOTE: *Always add spacers above the piston ring.*

5. Install the rings on the piston, lower oil ring first. Use a ring installing tool on the compression rings. Consult the instruction sheet that comes with the rings to be sure they are installed with the correct side up. A mark on the ring usually faces upward.

6. When installing oil rings; first, install the expanding ring in the groove. Hold the ends of the ring butted together (they must not overlap) and install the bottom rail (scraper) with the end about one inch away from the butted end of the control ring. Install the top rail about an inch away from the butted end of the control but on the opposite side from the lower rail.

7. Install the two compression rings.

8. Consult the illustration for ring position-

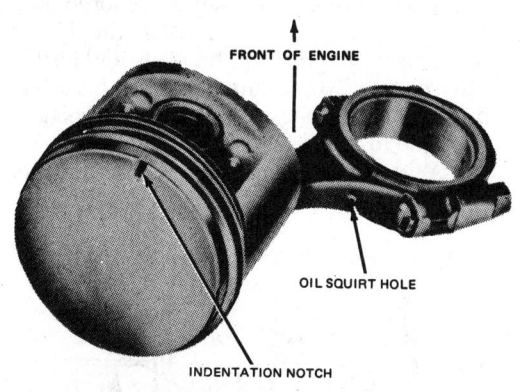

Piston and connecting rod positioning (notch to the front of the engine)—6 cyl. 200 engine

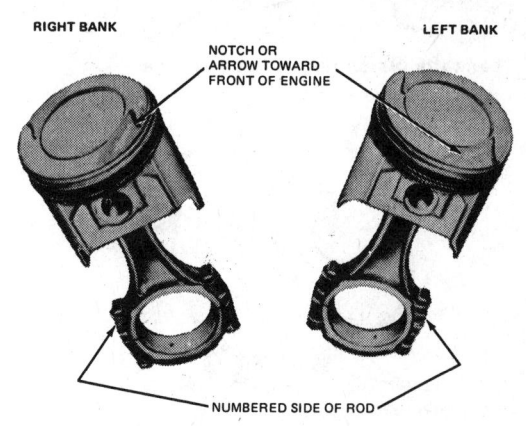

Piston and connecting rod positioning—V6 engine

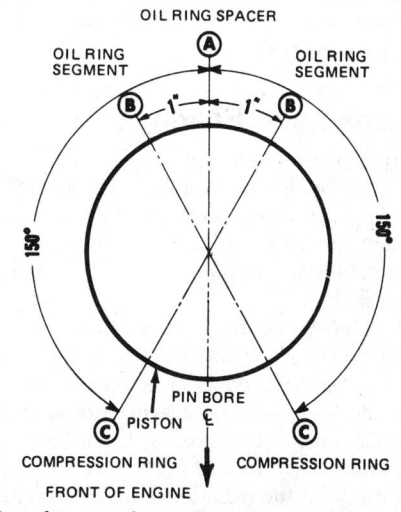

Piston and connecting rod positioning—V8 engines

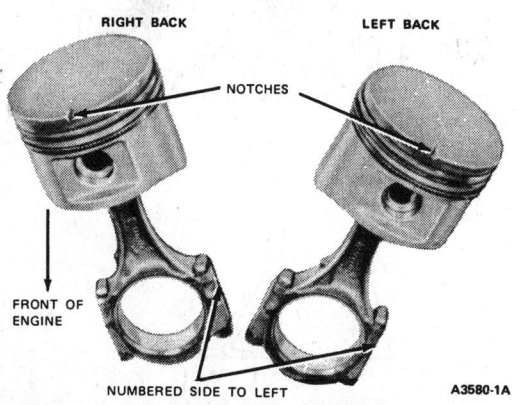

Piston ring spacing—all engines

ENGINE AND ENGINE REBUILDING

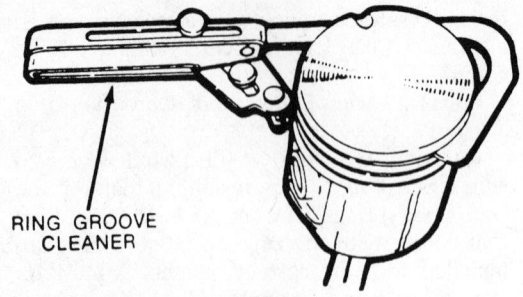

Clean the piston ring grooves

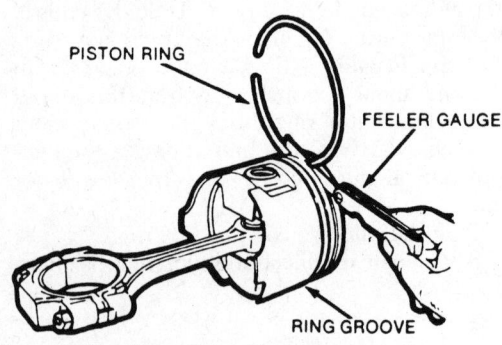

Check the piston ring side clearance

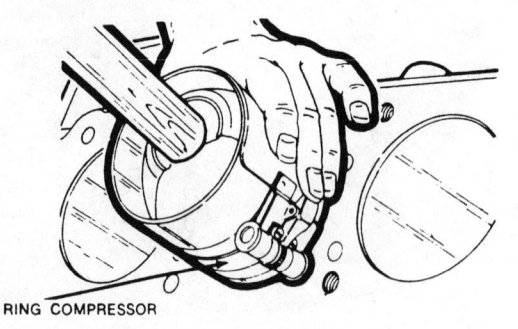

Install the piston using a ring compressor

care not to push the rod assembly up too far or the top ring will engage the cylinder ridge or come out of the cylinder and require head removal for reinstallation.

3. Clean the rod journal, the connecting rod end and the bearing cap after removing the old bearing inserts. Install the new inserts in the rod and bearing cap, lubricate them with oil. Position the rod over the crankshaft journal and install the rod cap. Make sure the cap and rod numbers match, torque the rod nuts to specifications.

4. Main bearings may be replaced while the engine is still in the car by "rolling" them out and in.

5. Special roll out pins are available from automotive parts houses or can be fabricated from a cotter pin. The roll out pin fits in the oil hole of the main bearing journal. When the crankshaft is rotated opposite the direction of the bearing lock tab, the pin engages the end of the bearing and "rolls" out the insert.

6. Remove main bearing cap and roll out upper bearing insert. Remove insert from main bearing cap. Clean the inside of the bearing cap and crankshaft journal.

7. Lubricate and roll upper insert into position, make sure the lock tab is anchored and the insert is not "cocked." Install the lower bearing insert into the cap, lubricate and install on the engine. Make sure the main beaaring cap is installed facing in the correct direction and torque to specifications.

8. With the engine out of the car, remove the intake manifold, cylinder heads, front cover,

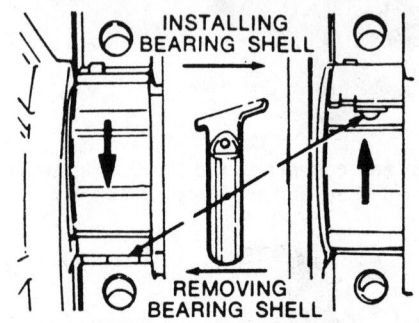

Remove or install the upper bearing insert using a roll-out pin

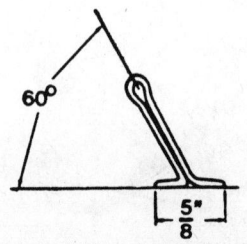

Home-made bearing roll-out pin

ing, arrange the rings as shown, install a ring compressor and insert the piston and rod assembly into the engine.

Crankshaft and Bearings

1. Rod bearings can be installed when the pistons have been removed for servicing (rings etc.) or, in most cases, while the engine is still in the car. Bearing replacement, however, is far easier with the engine out of the car and disassembled.

2. For in car service, remove the oil pan, spark plugs and front cover if necessary. Turn the engine until the connecting rod to be serviced is at the bottom of travel. Remove the bearing cap, place two pieces of rubber hose over the rod cap bolts and push the piston and rod assembly up the cylinder bore until enough room is gained for bearing insert removal. Take

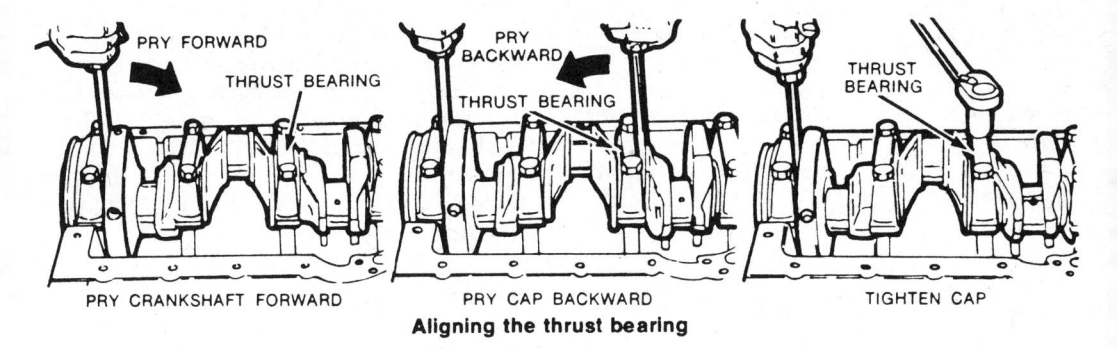

ENGINE AND ENGINE REBUILDING

Aligning the thrust bearing

timing gears and/or chain, oil pan, oil pump and flywheel.

9. Remove the piston and rod assemblies. Remove the main bearing caps after marking them for position and direction.

10. Remove the crankshaft, bearing inserts and rear main oil seal. Clean the engine block and cap bearing saddles. Clean the crankshaft and inspect for wear. Check the bearing journals with a micrometer for out-of-round condition and to determine what size rod and main bearing inserts to install.

11. Install the main bearing upper inserts and rear main oil seal half into the engine block.

12. Lubricate the bearing inserts and the crankshaft journals. Slowly and carefully lower the crankshaft into position.

13. Install the bearing inserts and rear main seal into the bearing caps, install the caps working from the middle out. Torque cap bolts to specifications in stages, rotate the crankshaft after each torque state. Note the illustration for thrust bearing alignment.

14. Remove bearing caps, one at a time and check the oil clearance with Plastigage®. Reinstall if clearance is within specifications. Check the crankshaft end-play; if within specifications install connecting rod and piston assemblies with new rod bearing inserts. Check connecting rod bearing oil clearance and side play; if correct assemble the rest of the engine.

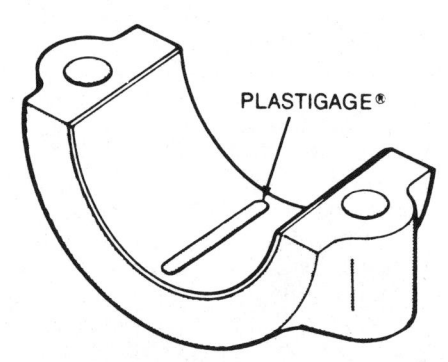

BEARING OIL CLEARANCE

Remove cap from the bearing to be checked. Using a clean, dry rag, thoroughly clean all oil from crankshaft journal and bearing insert.

NOTE: *Plastigage® is soluble in oil; therefore, oil on the journal or bearing could result in erroneous readings.*

Place a piece of Plastigage® along the full width of the bearing insert, reinstall cap, and torque to specifications.

NOTE: *Specifications are given in the engine specifications earlier in this chapter.*

Remove bearing cap, and determine bearing clearance by comparing width of Plastigage® to the scale on Plastigage® envelope. Journal taper is determined by comparing width of the bearing insert, reinstall cap, and torque to specifications.

NOTE: *Do not rotate crankshaft with Plastigage® installed. If bearing insert and journal appear intact, and are within tolerances, no further main bearing service is required. If bearing or journal appear defective, cause of failure should be determined before replacement.*

CRANKSHAFT END-PLAY/CONNECTING ROD SIDE PLAY

Place a pry bar between a main bearing cap and crankshaft casting taking care not to damage any journals. Pry backward and forward, measure the distance between the thrust bearing and crankshaft with a feeler gauge. Com-

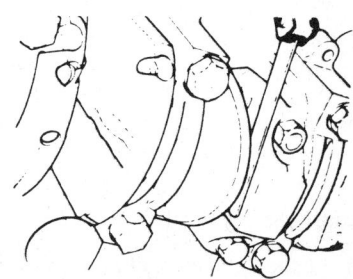

Plastigage® installed on the lower bearing shell

Check the connecting rod side clearance with a feeler gauge

94 ENGINE AND ENGINE REBUILDING

pare reading with specifications. If too great a clearance is determined, a main bearing with a larger thrust surface or crank machining may be required. Check with an automotive machine shop for their advice.

Connecting rod clearance between the rod and crankthrow casting can be checked with a feeler gauge. Pry the rod carefully to one side as far as possible and measure the distance on the other side of the rod.

CRANKSHAFT REPAIRS

If a journal is damaged on the crankshaft, repair is possible by having the crankshaft machined to a standard undersize.

In most cases, however, since the engine must be removed from the car and disassembled, some thought should be given to replacing the damaged crankshaft with a reground shaft kit. A reground crankshaft kit contains the necessary main and rod bearings for installation. The shaft has been ground and polished to undersize specifications and will usually hold up well if installed correctly.

COMPLETING THE REBUILDING PROCESS

Complete the rebuilding process as follows:

Fill the oil pump with oil, to prevent cavitating (sucking air) on initial engine start up. Install the oil pump and the pickup tube on the engine. Coat the oil pan gasket as necessary, and install the gasket and the oil pan. Mount the flywheel and the crankshaft vibration damper or pulley on the crankshaft.

NOTE: *Always use new bolts when installing the flywheel. Inspect the clutch shaft pilot bushing in the crankshaft. If the bushing is excessively worn, remove it with an expanding puller and a slide hammer, and tap a new bushing into place.*

Position the engine, cylinder head side up. Lubricate the lifters, and install them into their bores. Install the cylinder head, and torque it as specified. Insert the pushrods (where applicable), and install the rocker shaft(s) (if so equipped) or position the rocker.

Install the intake and exhaust manifolds, the carburetor(s), the distributor and spark plugs. Mount all accessories and install the engine in the car. Fill the radiator with coolant, and the crankcase with high quality engine oil.

BREAK-IN PROCEDURE

Start the engine, and allow it to run at low speed for a few minutes, while checking for leaks. Stop the engine, check the oil level, and fill as necessary. Restart the engine, and fill the cooling system to capacity. Check and adjust the ignition timing. Run the engine at low to medium speed (800–2500 rpm) for approximately ½ hour. Road test the car, and check again for leaks.

Follow the manufacturer's recommended engine break-in procedure and maintenance schedule for new engines.

ENGINE LUBRICATION

Oil Pan

REMOVAL AND INSTALLATION
All Engines Except V6-232

1. Remove the oil dipstick. Disconnect the two cooler lines at the radiator, if equipped.
2. On the four cyl. and inline six cyl., remove the two radiator top support bolts.
3. On the V6 only, drain the cooling system and disconnect the upper and lower radiator hoses at the radiator.
4. Remove the fan shroud bolts and position the shroud over the fan.
5. Raise the car and drain the oil.
6. Remove the sway bar attaching bolts and allow it to hang down.
7. Remove the steering gear to crossmember attaching bolts and allow the steering gear to rest on the frame away from the pan.
8. Disconnect the battery lead and remove the starter except on V8s.
9. Remove the engine mount bolts.
10. Raise the engine and place a 1¼ in. wooden block between the mount and chassis on each side. Use a 2 x 4 in. wood block on each side with the V8. Remove the K braces.
11. On the four and inline six only, place a jack under the transmission and raise it slightly.
12. Remove the oil pan bolts and lower the pan to the crossmember. Move the transmission cooler lines out of the way, if necessary, and remove the oil pan, rotating the crankshaft for clearance if required.
13. Clean the mounting surfaces thoroughly before installation. Coat the block and pan gasket surfaces with sealer. On the four cyl. only, the front and rear seal tabs go under the pan (side) gaskets. On all other engines, place the pan gaskets on the block first; the seal tabs go over the pan gaskets on these engines.
14. Install the pan mounting bolts. Torque the bolts from the center outwards on inline sixes and V8s. Use the torque sequences illustrated. The rest of installation is the reverse of removal.

ENGINE AND ENGINE REBUILDING 95

Engine oil pan torque sequence—V6 engine

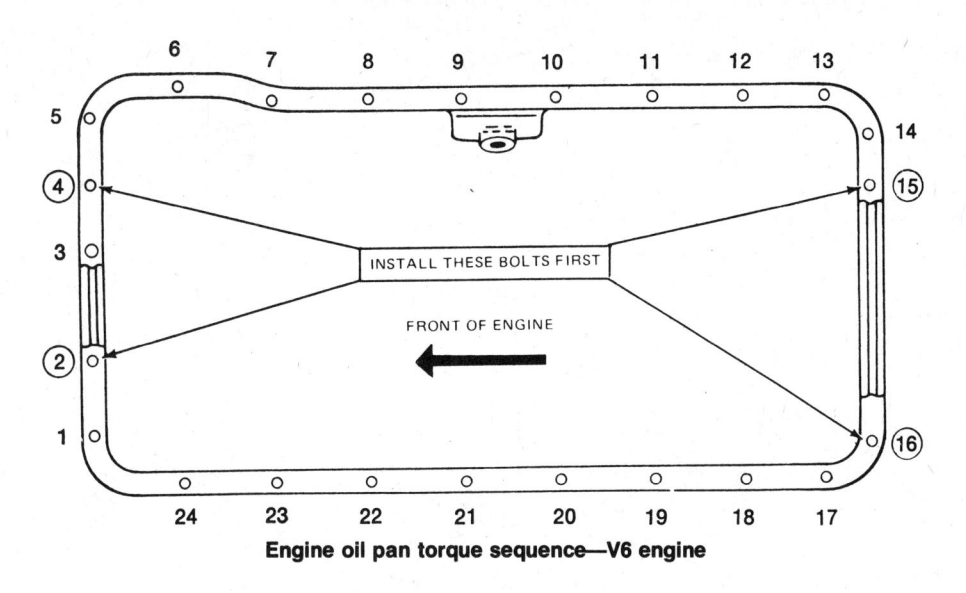

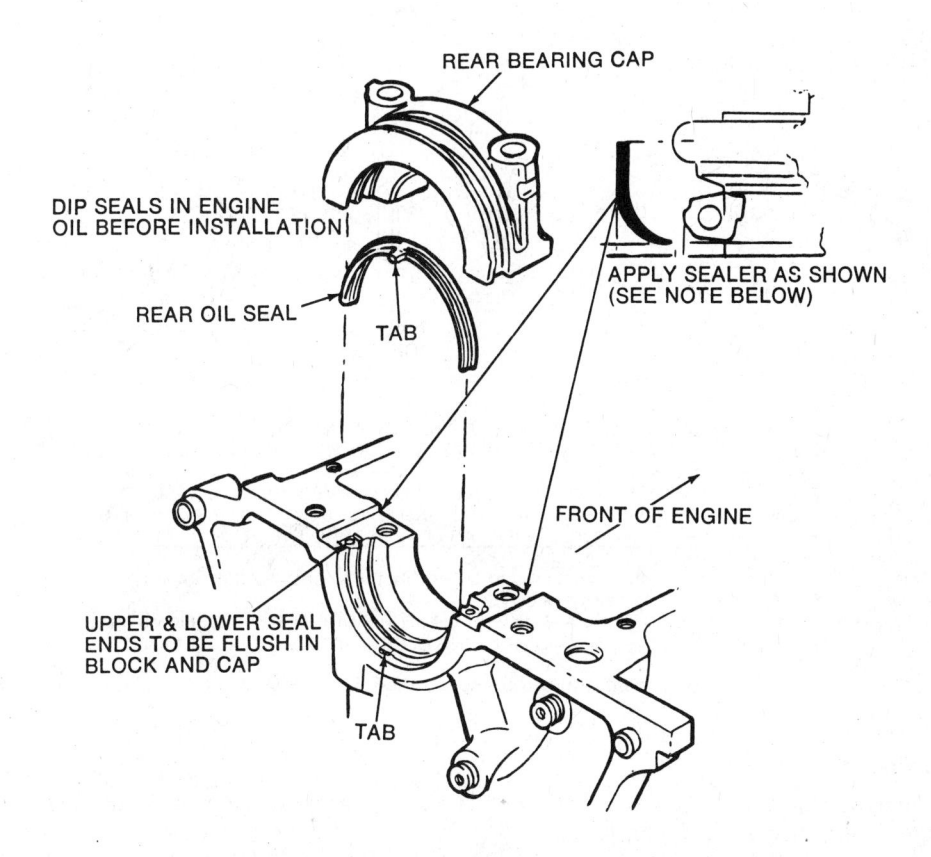

NOTE: CLEAN THE AREA WHERE SEALER IS TO BE APPLIED BEFORE INSTALLING THE SEALS. AFTER THE SEALS ARE IN PLACE, APPLY A 1/16 INCH BEAD OF SEALER AS SHOWN. *SEALER MUST NOT TOUCH SEALS*

Replacement of the crankcase rear main oil seal—4 cyl. engine

96 ENGINE AND ENGINE REBUILDING

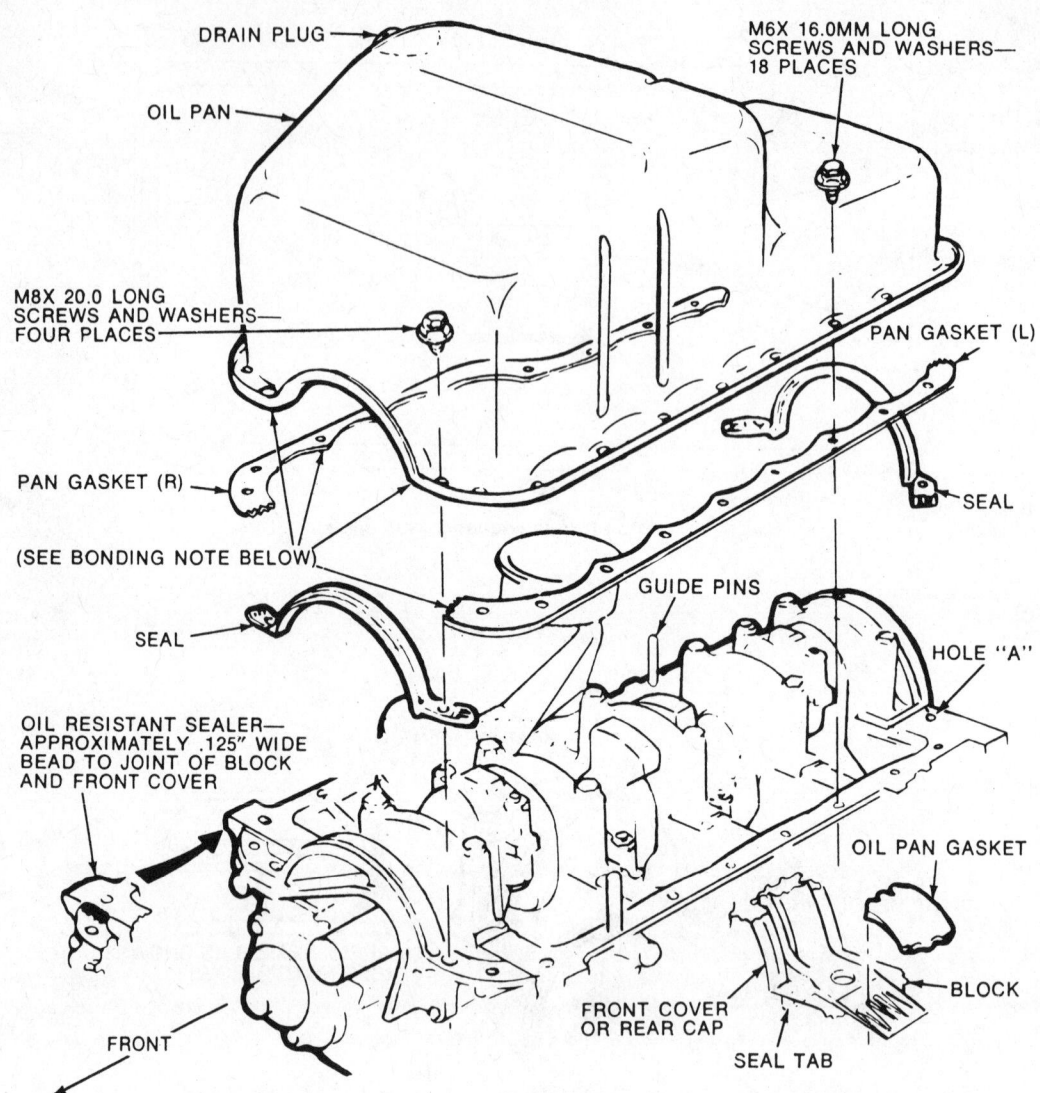

1. APPLY GASKET ADHESIVE EVENLY TO OIL PAN FLANGE AND TO PAN SIDE GASKETS. ALLOW ADHESIVE TO DRY PAST WET STAGE, THEN INSTALL GASKETS TO OIL PAN.
2. APPLY SEALER TO JOINT OF BLOCK AND FRONT COVER. INSTALL SEALS TO FRONT COVER AND REAR BEARING CAP AND PRESS SEAL TABS FIRMLY INTO BLOCK. BE SURE TO INSTALL THE REAR SEAL BEFORE THE REAR MAIN BEARING CAP SEALER HAS CURED.
3. POSITION 2 GUIDE PINS AND INSTALL THE OIL PAN. SECURE THE PAN WITH THE FOUR M8 BOLTS SHOWN ABOVE.
4. REMOVE THE GUIDE PINS AND INSTALL AND TORQUE THE EIGHTEEN M6 BOLTS, BEGINNING AT HOLE "A" AND WORKING CLOCKWISE AROUND THE PAN.

Engine oil pan torque sequence—4 cyl. engine

V6-232 Engine

1. Remove the air cleaner assembly including the air intake duct. Drain the cooling system.
2. Remove the fan shroud attaching bolts and position the shroud back over the fan.
3. Remove the oil level dipstick.
4. Remove the screws attaching the vacuum solenoids to the dash panel. Lay the solenoids on the engine without disconnecting the vacuum hoses or electrical connectors.
5. Remove the exhaust manifold to exhaust pipe attaching nuts. Disconnect the radiator hoses from the radiator.
6. Drain the crankcase.
7. Remove the oil filter.
8. Remove the bolts attaching the shift linkage bracket to the transmission bell hous-

ENGINE AND ENGINE REBUILDING

ing. Remove the starter motor for more clearance if necessary.

9. Disconnect the transmission cooler lines at the radiator. Remove power steering hose retaining clamp from frame.

10. Remove the converter cover.

11. Remove the engine damper to No. 2 crossmember bracket attaching bolt. The damper must be disconnected from the crossmember. Disconnect steering flex coupling. Remove two bolts attaching steering gear to main crossmember and let steering gear rest on the frame away from oil pan.

12. Remove the nut and washer assembly attaching the front engine insulator to the chassis.

13. Raise the engine 2–3 in. or higher on some models and insert wood blocks between the engine mounts and the vehicle frame.

CAUTION: *Watch the clearance between the transmission dipstick tube and the thermactor downstream air tube. If the tubes contact before adequate pan-to-crossmember clearance is provided, lower the engine and remove the transmission dipstick tube and the downstream air tube.*

14. Remove the oil pan attaching bolts. Work the oil pan loose and remove.

15. Lower the oil pan onto the crossmember. Remove the oil pickup tube attaching nut. Lower the pickup tube/screen assembly into the pan and remove the oil pan through the front of the vehicle.

16. Remove the oil pan seal from the main bearing cap.

17. Clean the gasket surfaces on the cylinder block, oil pan and oil pick-up tube.

18. Apply 1/8 in. bead of RTV sealer to all matching surfaces of oil pan and engine front cover.

19. Install the oil pan.

NOTE: *On models with limited clearance place the oil pick-up tube/screen assembly in the oil pan.*

20. Install all other components removed.

21. Fill the crankcase to the correct level with the oil.

22. Start the engine and check the fluid levels in the transmission.

23. Check for engine oil, and transmission fluid leaks.

Rear Main Oil Seal

REMOVAL AND INSTALLATION

NOTE: *Refer to the "build" dates listed below to determine if the engine is equipped with a split-type or one piece rear main oil seal. Engines after the date indicated have a one-piece oil seal. 2.3 (140) OHC: after 9/28/81; 232 V6: after 4/1/83; 302 V8: after 12/1/82; 351W-V8: after 7/11/83. Engines prior to the date indicated are equipped with a split type seal. V6 170 engine use a one piece seal.*

Split-Type Seal

NOTE: *The rear oil seal installed in these engines is a rubber type (split-Lip) seal.*

1. Remove the oil pan, and, if required, the oil pump.

2. Loosen all main bearing caps allowing the crankshaft to lower slightly.

NOTE: *The crankshaft should not be allowed to drop more than 1/32 in.*

3. Remove the rear main bearing cap and

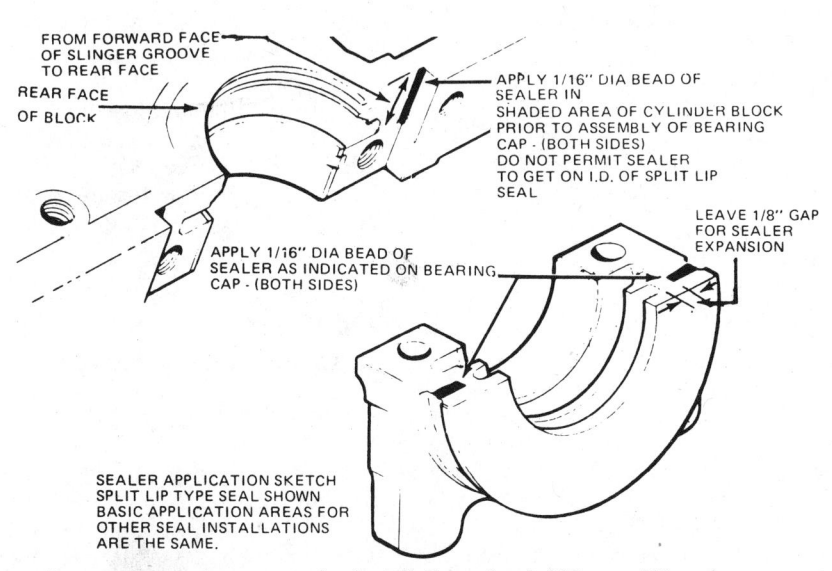

Rear main bearing cap sealer installation—6 cyl. 200 eng., V8 engines

ENGINE AND ENGINE REBUILDING

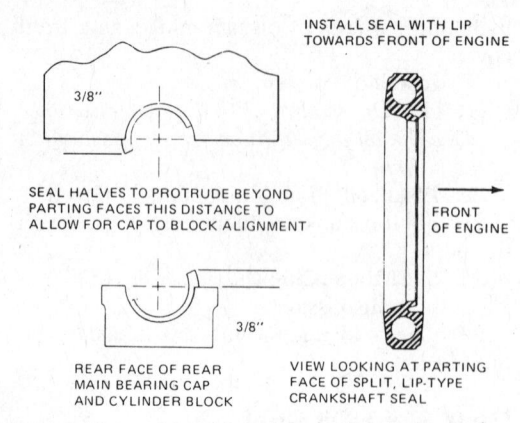

Rear main seal installation—except 4 cyl. and V6 engines

One piece rear main oil seal installation

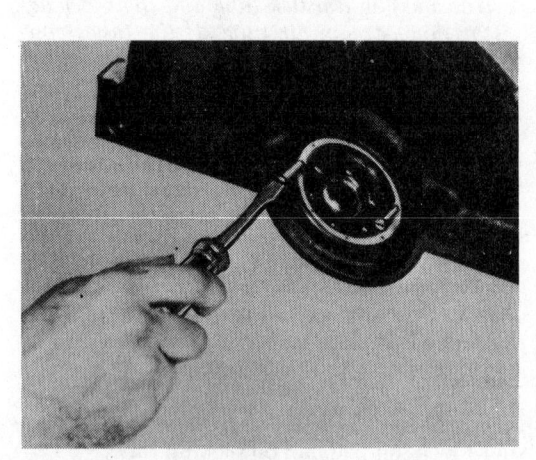

Removing crankshaft rear oil seal, 1979 V6

remove the seal from the cap and block. Be very careful not to scratch the sealing surface. Remove the old seal retaining pin from the cap, if equipped. It is not used with the replacement seal.

4. Carefully clean the seal grooves in the cap and block with solvent.
5. Soak the new seal halves in clean engine oil.
6. Install the upper half of the seal in the block with the undercut side of the seal toward the front of the engine. Slide the seal around the crankshaft journal until ⅜ in. protrudes beyong the base of the block.
7. Tighten all the main bearing caps (except the rear main bearing) to specifications.
8. Install the lower seal into the rear cap, with the undercut side facing the front of the engine. Allow ⅜ in. of the seal to protrude above the surface, at the opposite end from the block seal.
9. Squeeze a ¹⁄₁₆ in. bead of silicone sealant onto the areas shown.
10. Install the rear cap and torque to specifications.
11. Install the oil pump and pan. Fill the crankcase with oil, start the engine, and check for leaks.

One-Piece Seal

1. Remove the transmission, clutch and flywheel or driveplate after refering to the appropriate section for instructions.
2. Punch two holes in the crankshaft rear oil seal on opposite sides of the crankshaft just above the bearing cap to cylinder block split line. Install a sheet metal screw in each of the holes or use a small slide hammer, and pry the crankshaft rear main oil seal from the block.
   NOTE: *Use extreme caution not to scratch the crankshaft oil seal surface.*

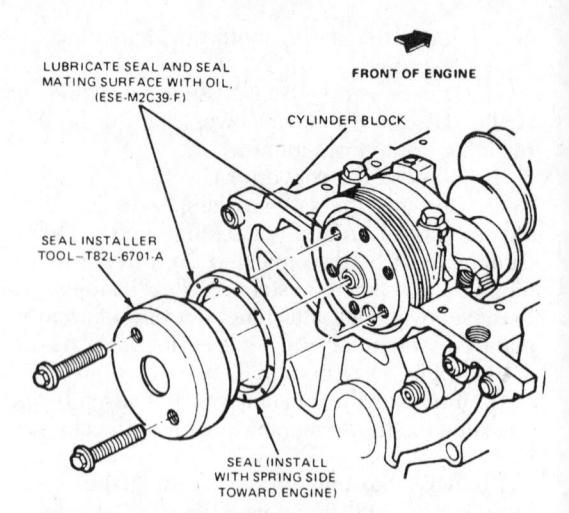

3. Clean the oil seal recess in the cylinder block and main bearing cap.
4. Coat the seal and all of the seal mounting surfaces with oil and install the seal in the recess, driving it in place with an oil seat installation tool or a large socket.
5. Install the driveplate or flywheel and clutch and transmission in the reverse order of removal.

Oil Pump

REMOVAL AND INSTALLATION

Except V6 232

1. Remove oil pan.
2. Remove oil pump inlet tube and screen assembly.
3. Remove oil pump attaching bolts and remove oil pump gasket and intermediate shaft.
4. Prime oil pump by filling inlet and outlet

ENGINE AND ENGINE REBUILDING 99

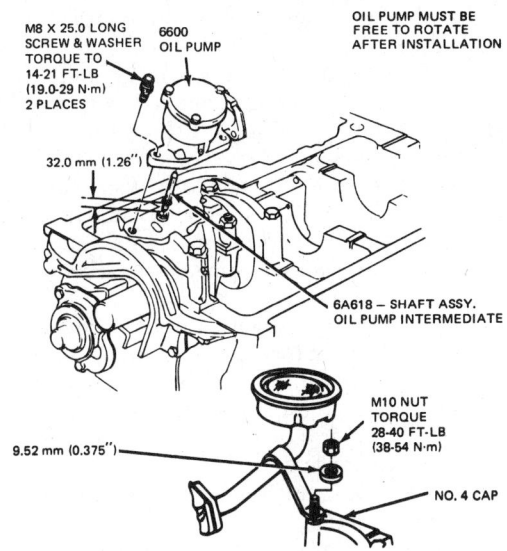

Oil pump installation—4 cyl. engine; others similar location

port with engine oil and rotating shaft of pump to distribute it.

5. Position intermediate drive shaft into distributor socket.

6. Position new gasket on pump body and insert intermediate drive shaft into pump body.

7. Install pump and intermediate shaft as an assembly.

NOTE: *Do not force pump if it does not seat readily. The drive shaft may be misaligned with the distributor shaft. To align rotate intermediate drive shaft into a new position.*

8. Install and torque oil pump attaching screws to 14–21 ft. lb.

9. Install oil pan.

V6 232 Engine

NOTE: *The oil pump is mounted in the front cover assembly.*

NOTE: *Oil pan removal is necessary for pickup tube/screen replacement or service.*

1. Raise and safely support the vehicle on jackstands.

2. Remove the oil filter.

3. Remove the cover/filter mount assembly.

4. Lift the two pump gears from their mounting pocket in the front cover.

5. Clean all gasket mounting surfaces.

6. Inspect the mounting pocket for wear. If excessive wear is present, complete timing cover assembly replacement is necessary.

7. Inspect the cover/filter mount gasket to timing cover surface for flatness. Place a straight edge across the flat and check clearance with a feeler gauge. If the measured clearance exceeds .004 inch, replace the cover/filter mount.

8. Replace the pump gears if wear is excessive.

9. Remove the plug from the end of the pressure relief valve passage using a small drill and slide hammer. Use caution when drilling.

10. Remove the spring and valve from the bore. Clean all dirt, gum and metal chips from the bore and valve. Inspect all parts for wear. Replace as necessary.

11. Install the valve and spring after lubricating them with engine oil. Install a new plug flush with machined surface.

12. Install the pump gears and fill the pocket with petroleum jelly. Install cover/filter mount using a new mounting gasket. Tighten the mounting bolts to 18–22 ft. lbs. Install the oil filter, add necessary oil for correct level.

COOLING SYSTEM

Radiator

REMOVAL AND INSTALLATION

All Models

1. Drain cooling system.

2. Disconnect upper and lower hoses at the radiator.

3. On automatic transmission-equipped cars, disconnect oil cooler lines at radiator.

4. On vehicles equipped with a fan shroud, remove the shroud retaining screws and position the shroud out of the way.

5. Remove radiator attaching bolts and lift out the radiator.

6. If a new radiator is to be installed, transfer the petcock from the old radiator to the new one. On cars equipped with automatic transmissions, transfer the fluid cooler line fittings from the old radiator to the new one.

7. Position the radiator and install, but do not tighten, the radiator support bolts. On cars equipped with automatic transmissions, connect the fluid cooler lines. Then tighten the radiator support bolts.

8. On vehicles equipped with a fan shroud, reinstall the shroud.

9. Connect the radiator hoses. Close the radiator petcock. Then fill and bleed the cooling system.

10. Start the engine and bring to operating temperature. Check for leaks.

11. On cars equipped with automatic transmissions, check the cooler lines for leaks and interference. Check transmission fluid level.

ENGINE AND ENGINE REBUILDING

Water Pump

REMOVAL AND INSTALLATION

Four Cylinder 140 Cu In. Engine

1. Drain the cooling system.
2. Disconnect the lower radiator hose and heater hose from the water pump.
3. Loosen the alternator retaining and adjusting bolt, and remove the drive belt.
4. Remove the fan shroud, fan and water pump pulley. On 2300 cc engines, remove the camshaft drive belt cover first. It is not necessary to remove the cam belt or inner cover.
5. Remove the water pump retaining bolts and remove the pump from the engine.
6. Clean all mating surfaces and install the pump with a new gasket coated with sealer. If a new pump is being installed, transfer the heater hose fitting from the old pump.
7. Reverse the removal steps to install the pump. Refill the cooling system.

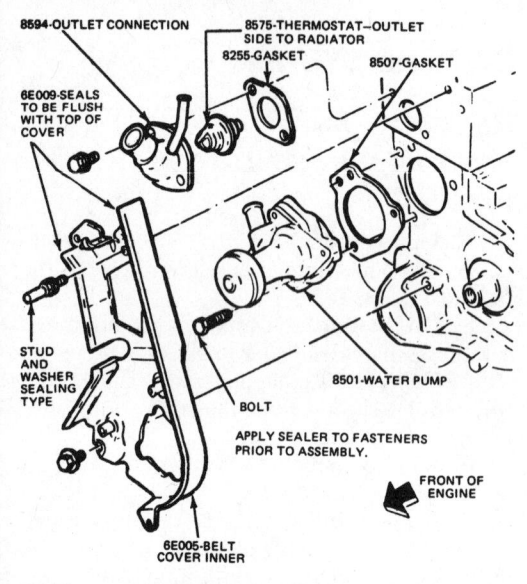

Water pump, thermostat, and inner timing belt installation—4 cyl. engine

All Except Four Cylinder Engine

1. Drain cooling system.
2. Disconnect the negative battery cable.
3. On cars with power steering, remove the drive belt.
4. If the vehicle is equipped with air conditioning, remove the idler pulley bracket and air conditioner drive belt.
5. On engines with Thermactor, remove the belt.
6. Disconnect the lower radiator hose and heater hose from the water pump.
7. On cars equipped with a fan shroud, remove the retaining screws and position the shroud rearward.
8. Remove the fan and spacer from the engine, and if the car is equipped with a fan shroud, remove the fan and shroud from the engine as an assembly.
9. On cars equipped with water pump mounted alternators, loosen alternator mounting bolts, remove the alternator belt and remove the alternator adjusting arm bracket from the water pump.
10. Loosen bypass hose at water pump.
11. Remove water pump retaining screws and remove pump from engine. On V6s, the two bolts through the thermostat housing must also be removed; they retain the lower portion of the pump housing.
12. Clean any gasket material from the pump mounting surface.

NOTE: *The 6-200 engine originally uses a one-piece gasket for the cylinder front cover and water pump. Trim away the old gasket at the edge of the cylinder cover and replace with service gasket. Replace the thermostat housing gasket on V6s.*

13. Remove the heater hose fitting from the old pump and install it on the new pump.
14. Coat both sides of the new gasket with a water-resistant sealer, then install the pump reversing the procedure.

Thermostat

REMOVAL AND INSTALLATION

All Engines

1. Open the drain cock and drain the radiator so the coolant level is below the coolant outlet elbow which houses the thermostat.
2. Remove the outlet elbow retaining bolts and position the elbow sufficiently clear of the intake manifold or cylinder head to provide access to the thermostat. The V6 thermostat is located on the lower water pump housing, under the lower radiator hose inlet. See the Bobcat section for an illustration.
3. Remove the thermostat and the gasket. On the V6, also remove the O-ring.

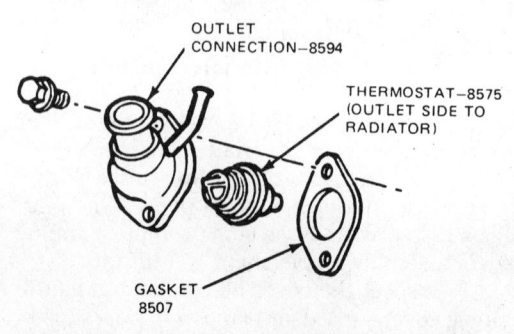

Engine thermostat and housing—4 cyl. engine

ENGINE AND ENGINE REBUILDING 101

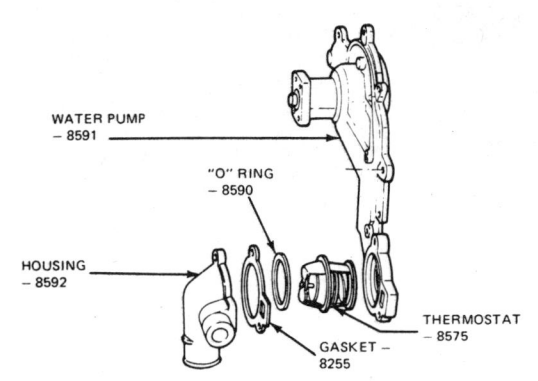

Engine thermostat and housing—V6 engine; water pumps on other engines similar

4. Clean the mating surfaces of the outlet elbow and the engine to remove all old gasket material and sealer. Coat the new gasket with water-resistant sealer and install it on the engine. Install the thermostat in the outlet elbow. The thermostat must be rotated clockwise to lock it in position. On V6s, the thermostat must be installed into the pump housing first, then the O-ring, and finally the gasket and inlet elbow.

5. Install the outlet elbow and retaining bolts in the engine. Torque the bolts to 12–15 ft. lbs.

6. Refill the radiator. Run the engine at operating temperature and check for leaks. Recheck the coolant level.

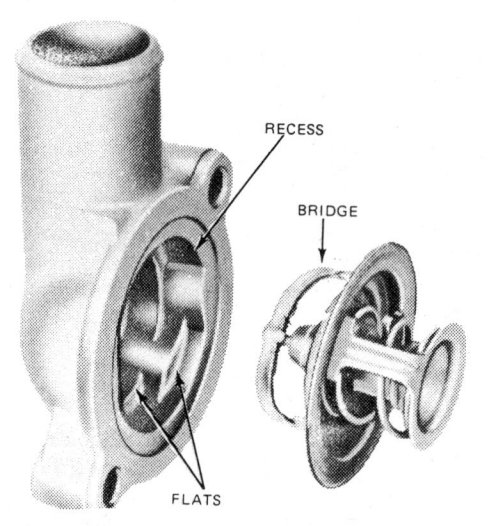

Engine thermostat and housing—6 cyl. 200, V8 engines

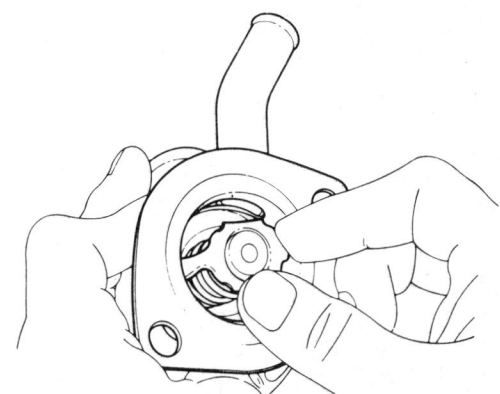

On all engines, turn thermostat clockwise to lock it into position on the flats in the outlet elbow

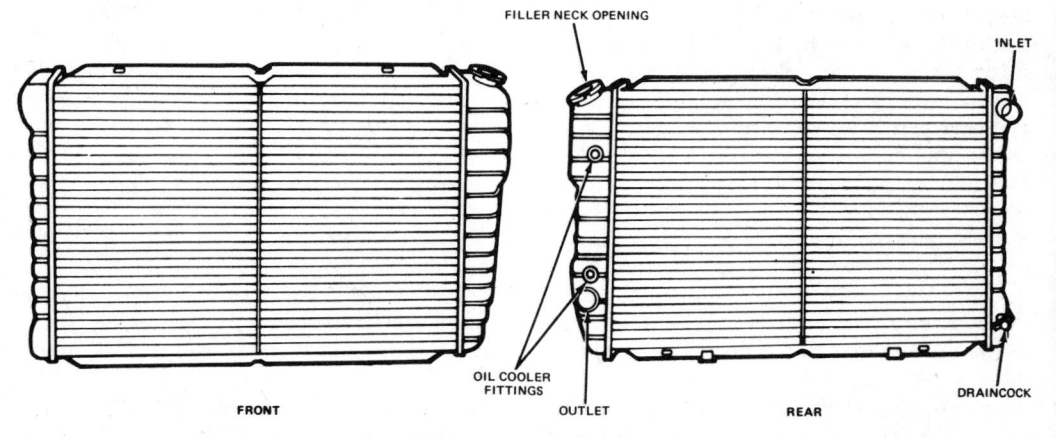

Typical crossflow radiator

Emission Controls and Fuel System 4

EMISSION CONTROLS

Automotive pollutants fall into three categories: crankcase fumes, terminal exhaust gases, and gasoline evaporation. Automotive manufacturers have developed ways to limit environmental pollutants that come from each of these sources and the equipment they use to obtain this end is commonly referred to as emission control equipment.

Crankcase Emission Controls

Crankcase emission control equipment consists of an oil separator, mounted on the side of the engine block, a positive crankcase ventilation (PCV) valve, mounted on the top of the oil separator, a closed oil filler cap, and the hoses that connect this equipment.

When the engine is running, a small portion of the gases which are formed in the combustion chamber leak by the piston rings and enter the crankcase. Since these gases are under pressure, they tend to escape from the crankcase and enter the atmosphere. If these gases are allowed to remain in the crankcase for any period of time, they contaminate the engine oil and cause sludge to build up in the crankcase. If the gases are allowed to escape into the atmosphere, they pollute the air, with unburned hydrocarbons. The job of the crankcase emission control equipment is to recycle these gases back into the engine combustion chamber where they are reburned.

The crankcase gases are recycled in the following way: as the engine is running, clean, filtered air is drawn through the air filter and the oil filler cap and into the crankcase. As the air passes through the crankcase, it picks up the combustion gases and carries them out of the crankcase, through the oil separator, through the PCV valve, and into the intake manifold. As they enter the intake manifold, they are drawn into the combustion chamber where they are reburned.

The most critical component in the system is the PCV valve. This valve controls the amount of gases which are recycled into the combustion chamber. At low engine speeds, the valve is partially closed, limiting the flow of the gases into the intake manifold. As engine speed increases, the valve opens to admit greater quantities of the gases into the intake manifold. If the valve should become blocked or plugged, the gases will be prevented from escaping from the crankcase by the normal route. Since these gases are under pressure, they will find their own way out of the crankcase. This alternate route is usually a weak oil seal or gasket in the engine. As the gas escapes by the gasket, it also creates an oil leak. Besides causing oil leaks, a clogged PCV valve also allows these gases to remain in the crankcase for an extended period of time, promoting the formation of sludge in the engine.

Exhaust Emission Controls

Aside from internal engine modifications, there are three areas automobile manufacturers have concentrated on in the quest to reduce emission: ignition system controls, fuel system controls, and exhaust system controls. As these systems become more sophisticated, the number of components that can be effectively owner-serviced in each system decreases. Most of the ignition system computer modules, or "black boxes" as they are known, require electronic diagnostic equipment for service. Indeed, much of the entire emissions network on your car can only be examined and repaired by experienced emissions mechanics. Systems which can be serviced by the owner/mechanic are covered here.

EMISSION CONTROLS AND FUEL SYSTEM

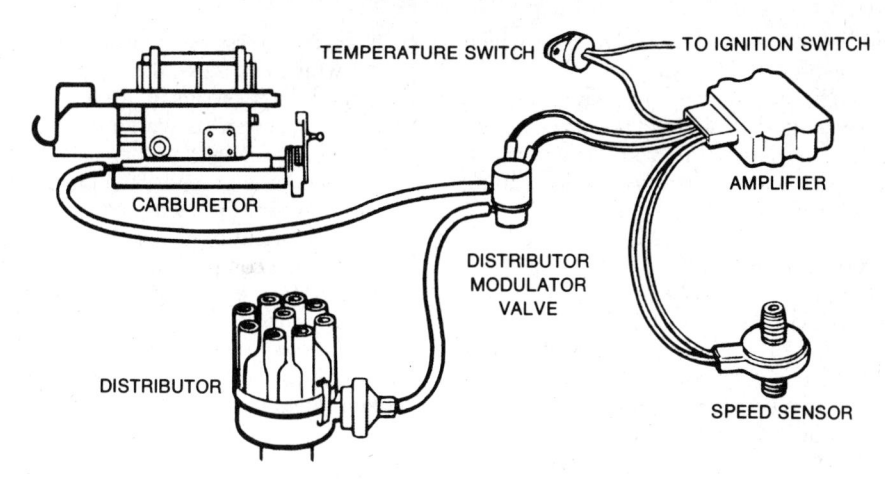

Electronic spark control system

SPARK DELAY VALVE (SDV)

The spark delay valve is a plastic, spring-loaded, color coded valve used to permit closer control of vacuum operated emission equipment. The valve is installed in the vacuum line to the distributor advance diaphragm on most models.

Under heavy throttle application, the valve will close, blocking normal carburetor vacuum to the distributor. After the designated "closed" time, the valve opens, restoring the carburetor vacuum to the distributor. The following chart outlines the spark relay applications:

Valve Color	ID #	Time Delay (seconds) Min.	Max.
Black/Gray	1	1	4
Black/Brown	2	2	5
Black/White	5	4	12
Black/Yellow	10	5.8	14
Black/Blue	15	7	16
Black/Green	20	9	20
Black/Orange	30	13	24
Black/Red	40	15	28
White/Brown*	2	2	5
White/Green*	20	9	20

*Dual delay, all others are single delay

NOTE: *The black side of the valve always faces the vacuum source—the carburetor.*

Troubleshooting

DUAL DIAPHRAGM DISTRIBUTOR

1. Connect a timing light and start the engine.
2. Disconnect the vacuum hose from the outer distributor diaphragm. Plug the line with a golf tee or pencil.
3. Shine the timing light on the lower engine pulley and observe the position of the ignition timing marks.
4. Disconnect the vacuum hose from the rear vacuum diaphragm on the distributor and hold your finger over the line.
5. Again check the ignition timing. It should be advanced beyond the reading obtained in step three. If it is not, the rear diaphragm on the distributor is defective or the vacuum hose from the intake manifold is broken.

DISTRIBUTOR VACUUM CONTROL VALVE

1. Attach a tachometer and start the engine.
2. Observe the reading on the tachometer.
3. Disconnect the hose from the intake manifold to the control valve and plug it with a golf tee or pencil.
4. Observe the reading again on the tachometer. If it has not changed, the control valve does not have an internal vacuum leak. If it does change, replace the valve.
5. Reconnect the intake manifold hose to the vacuum valve.
6. Block the front of the radiator with cardboard, warming up the engine, and have an assistant watch the warning light on the instrument panel.
7. As soon as the red warning light comes on, again observe the reading on the tachometer. It should be at least 100 rpm higher than the reading obtained in step two. If it is not, replace the vacuum control valve.
8. Remove the cardboard in front of the radiator and allow the engine to cool off before stopping the engine.

SPARK DELAY VALVE

1. Disconnect the vacuum hose that runs from the spark delay valve to the distributor at the spark delay valve. Connect a vacuum gauge

104 EMISSION CONTROLS AND FUEL SYSTEM

to the end of the spark delay valve from which you just disconnected the vacuum hose.

2. Start the engine and quickly raise the speed of the engine to about 2000 rpm with the transmission in Neutral. As soon as you accelerate the engine, the vacuum gauge reading should drop to zero.

3. With the engine speed held steady at about 2000 rpm, observe the time in seconds required until the vacuum gauge reading moves up to at least 6 in. Hg.

4. If the time required is less than two seconds, the valve is defective.

6. If the time required is more than 20 seconds, disconnect the vacuum gauge from the spark delay valve. Remove the carburetor-to-spark delay valve hose from the spark delay valve and connect the vacuum gauge to it.

Start the engine and raise the speed of the engine to about 2000 rpm. The vacuum gauge should show a reading of about 10–16 in. Hg. If it does not, there is a blockage in the carburetor vacuum port or the vacuum hose from the carburetor to the spark delay valve is plugged or broken.

Electronic Spark Control

SYSTEM OPERATION CHECK

1. Raise the rear of the car until the rear wheels are clear of the ground by at least 4 inches. Safely support the rear of the car with jackstands.

> CAUTION: *The rear of the car must be safely supported during this test; the emergency brake must be firmly applied and both front wheels blocked. Use care not to rock the car when climbing in to start the engine. If one of the rear wheels should come in contact with the ground while it is turning, the car will jump forward rapidly and unexpectedly, damaging or injuring (or both) whatever or whomever is in the way.*

2. Disconnect the vacuum hose from the distributor vacuum advance chamber (this is the outer hose on cars with the dual diaphragm distributor).

3. Connect a vacuum gauge to the hose you just disconnected from the distributor.

4. If the air temperature is below 65°F, pour hot water on the temperature sensor to ensure that its temperature is at least 65°F (the sensor is located on the right door pillar).

5. Start the engine, apply the emergency brake, and shift the transmission into low (1st) gear (or "Drive" with an automatic transmission).

6. Slowly release the hand brake and shift the transmission into high gear (4th or 5th), depending on transmission or "high" on the automatic (you'll feel it shift twice).

7. Have an assistant observe the vacuum gauge while you raise the engine speed until the speedometer reads 35 mph.

8. If the system is working properly, there should be no reading on the vacuum gauge until the speedometer reads 35 mph, at which time the gauge should show a reading.

9. If the vacuum gauge shows a reading *below* 35 mph, a component in the electronic spark control system is defective. If the gauge does not show a reading, even at 35 mph, there is either a defective component in the electronic spark control system, or there is a clogged or broken vacuum passage or hose between the carburetor and distributor.

VACUUM PASSAGES CHECK

1. Disconnect the vacuum hose that runs from the carburetor to the distributor modulator vacuum valve at the vacuum valve. Connect the end of the hose that was just disconnected to a vacuum gauge. Start the engine and keep the transmission selector lever in either the Park or Neutral position. Raise the speed of the engine to about 1500 rpm and observe the reading on the vacuum gauge. If the vacuum gauge shows a reading, this section of the system is OK. If the vacuum gauge does not show a reading, either the vacuum port in the carburetor is plugged or the vacuum hose out of the carburetor is plugged or broken.

2. Reconnect the vacuum hose that was disconnected in step one. Disconnect the vacuum hose coming out of the distributor modulator vacuum valve and connect it to a vacuum gauge. Disconnect the lead wires that run to the distributor modulator. Connect a tachometer to the engine and raise the engine speed to 1500 rpm. If the vacuum gauge does not show a reading, the distributor modulator vacuum valve is defective.

3. On cars with air conditioning, reconnect the vacuum hose to the modulator valve but leave the wires to the valve disconnected. Disconnect the vacuum hose coming out of the second nipple on the distributor control valve. Start the engine and raise the speed of the engine to about 1500 rpm. If the vacuum gauge does not show a reading, the distributor control valve is defective or the hose leading to the valve is plugged or broken. Replace as necessary.

4. Reconnect all vacuum lines but leave the lead wires to the distributor modulator vacuum valve disconnected. Disconnect the vacuum hose to the distributor vacuum advance chamber. Connect this hose to a vacuum hose. Start the engine and raise the speed of the engine to about 1500 rpm. Observe the reading on the vacuum gauge. If the gauge does not show a

EMISSION CONTROLS AND FUEL SYSTEM

reading, the hose to the distributor vacuum advance chamber is plugged or broken.

Distributor Controls
REPLACEMENT
Distributor Dual Diaphragm

1. Tag the two vacuum hoses that attach to the diaphragm (for later assembly) and disconnect them.
2. Remove the cap, rotor, and adaptor.
3. Remove the C-clip that secures the diaphragm rod to the movable advance plate.
4. Remove the diaphragm unit attaching screws and identification tag. Carefully remove the diaphragm by tilting downward to disengage the diaphragm rod from the post on the movable advance plate.
5. Install the C-clip that retains the arm on the plate.
6. Position the diaphragm unit attaching screws on the distributor and hook the diaphragm rod in position.
7. Install the C-clip that secures the diaphragm rod to the movable advance plate. Install the diaphragm unit attaching screws and identification tag.
8. Install the rotor, adapter, and distributor cap. Connect the vacuum lines.

NOTE: *When a new diaphragm is installed on a distributor, it must be calibrated. The approved procedure for calibrating a diaphragm is included in the carton with the new diaphragm.*

NOTE: *Be sure the new diaphragm is the correct part number.*

Spark Delay Valve

1. Locate the spark delay valve in the distributor vacuum line and disconnect it from the line.
2. Install a new spark delay valve in the line, making sure the black end of the valve is connected to the line from the carburetor and the red end is connected to the line from the spark delay valve to the distributor.

Fuel System Controls

Fuel system modifications for the purpose of exhaust emission control consist of leaner carburetor mixtures, idle mixture limiter caps, a deceleration valve, heated intake air cleaner, and a EGR valve.

Carburetor Mixtures

All carburetors have been calibrated for leaner mixtures to decrease the amount of unburned hydrocarbons contained in the vehicle exhaust. Also, plastic limiter caps have been installed on the idle mixture adjusting screws. These caps limit the travel of the idle mixture screws, preventing them from being adjusted in such a way that the air/fuel mixture at idle would be excessively rich.

Exhaust Gas Recirculation

1979 and later vehicles utilize an Exhaust Gas Recirculation system (EGR) to control nitrous oxides (NOx). The system is designed to re-introduce small amounts of exhaust gas into the combustion cycle, thus reducing the output of NOx. The amount of gas re-introduced and the timing of the cycle are controlled by various factors such as engine vacuum, exhaust system backpressure and engine coolant temperature.

EGR valves appear at different locations on different engines. On the 1979 V6 engines, exhaust gases travel through the exhaust gas crossover passage in the intake manifold. A portion of these gases are diverted into a spacer which is mounted under the carburetor. The EGR control valve, which is attached to the rear of the spacer (as on all V8 engines), consists of a vacuum diaphragm with an attached plunger which normally blocks off exhaust gases from entering the intake manifold. On 4-cylinder engines, an external tube carries exhaust manifold gases to the carburetor spacer. The EGR valve is controlled by a vacuum line from the carburetor.

The vacuum diaphragm opens the EGR valve, permitting exhaust gases to flow through the carburetor spacer and enter the intake manifold where they combine with the fuel mixture and enter the combustion chamber. The re-circulated exhaust gases are relatively oxygen-free, and tend to dilute the combustion charge, lowering peak combustion temperature and reducing oxides of nitrogen.

EGR-CSC SYSTEM

For 1979 and later models, the exhaust gas recirculation (EGR) system has been connected to the coolant spark control system (CSC). There are now two vacuum sources available to the distributor to aid driveability with either a hot or cold engine.

When the engine is cold the PVS valve gives the distributor vacuum which is normally routed to the EGR valve. When coolant temperature rises above 95°F, the EGR valve receives its normal vacuum from the carburetor and the distributor receives vacuum through the other PVS valve and the SDV valve.

EGR Valve Service

Valves which are riveted cannot be disassembled. Valves which can be disassembled should

EMISSION CONTROLS AND FUEL SYSTEM

be thoroughly cleaned and reassembled with extreme care not to enlarge orifices or bend any parts. Rebuilding is not recommended. Defective valves should be replaced.

Amplifier and other components are limited to replacement if defective.

EGR Valve Cleaning

Remove the EGR valve for cleaning. Do not pry on the diaphragm supports or strike the diaphragm housing, as this may damage the valve operating mechanism and/or change the valve calibration. Check the orifice hole in the EGR valve body for deposits. A small drill bit of *no more than* 0.060 in. diameter may be used to clean the hole if plugged. Compressed air is better, if available. *Extreme care* must be taken to avoid enlarging the hole or damaging the surface of the orifice plate.

VALVES WHICH CAN BE DISASSEMBLED

Separate the diaphragm section from the main mounting body. Clean the valve plates, stem, and the mounting plate, using a small power driven rotary type wire brush. Take care not to damage the parts. Remove deposits between stem and valve disc by using a steel blade or shim approximately 0.028 inch thick in a sawing motion around the stem shoulder at both sides of the disc.

The poppet must wobble and move axially before re-assembly.

Clean the cavity and passages in the main body of the valve with a power driven rotary wire brush. If the orifice plate has a hole less than 0.450 in., it must be removed for cleaning. Remove all loosened debris using shop compressed air. Reassemble the diaphragm section on the main body using a new gasket between them. Tighten the attaching screws. Clean the orifice plate and the counterbore in the valve body. Re-install the orifice plate using a small amount of contact cement to retain the plate in placing during assembly of the valve to the carburetor spacer. Apply cement only to outer edges of the orifice plate to avoid restriction of the orifice.

EGR Supply Passages and Carburetor Spacer Cleaning

Remove the carburetor and carburetor spacer on engines so equipped. Clean the supply tube with a small power driven rotary type wire brush or blast cleaning equipment. Clean the exhaust gas passages in the spacer using a suitable wire brush and/or scraper. The machined holes in the spacer can be cleaned by using a suitable round wire brush. Hard encrusted material should be probed loose first, then brushed out.

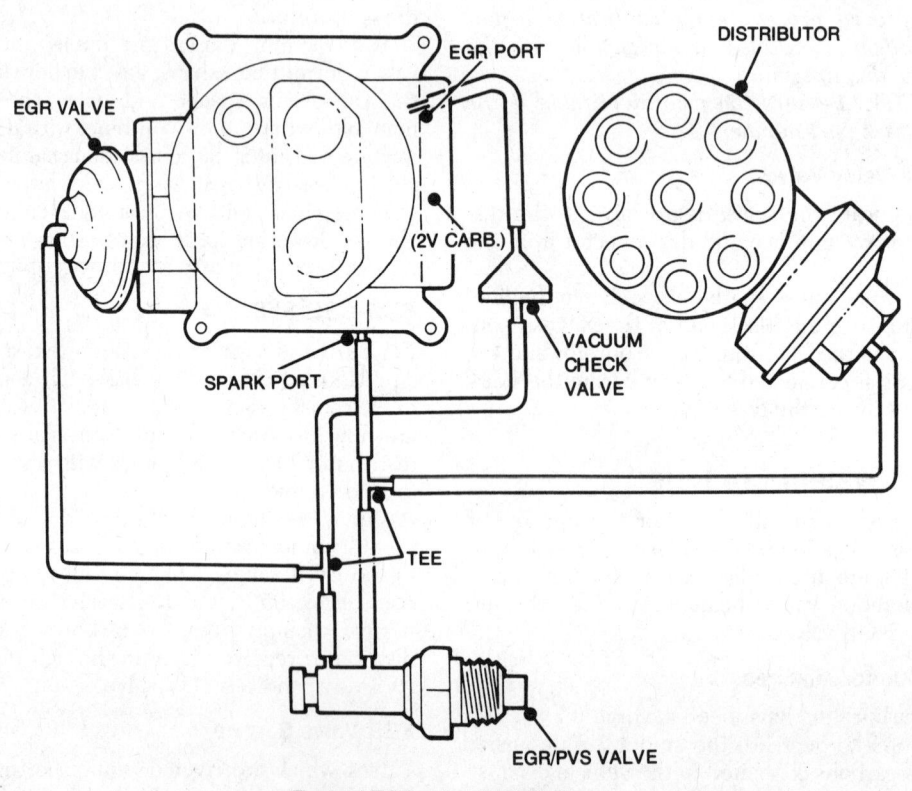

Typical EGR valve installation

EMISSION CONTROLS AND FUEL SYSTEM

EGR Exhaust Gas Channel Cleaning

Clean the exhaust gas channel, where applicable, in the intake manifold, using a suitable carbon scraper. Clean the exhaust gas entry port in the intake manifold by hand passing a suitable drill bit thru the holes to auger out the deposits. Do not use a wire brush. The manifold riser bore(s) should be plugged during the above action to prevent any of the residue from entering the induction system.

Exhaust Systems Controls

THERMACTOR (AIR PUMP)

The "Thermactor" air injection system reduces carbon monoxide and hydrocarbon content of exhaust gases, by injecting fresh air into the exhaust gas stream as it leaves the combustion chamber. A belt-driven pump supplies air to the exhaust port near the exhaust valve, by either an external manifold or internal drilled passages. The oxygen in the fresh air plus the heat of the exhaust gases causes burning which converts exhaust gases to carbon dioxide and water vapor.

Testing and Troubleshooting the System

Prior to testing the system, a test gauge adapter must be made. This can easily be done as follows, with the help of your local hardware or plumbing supply store.

Obtain:
1. ½ in. pipe "tee"
2. ½ in. (O.D.) pipe, 2 in. long, threaded at one end

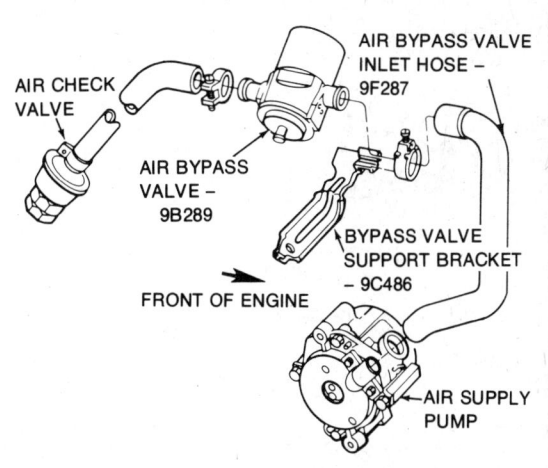

Typical Thermactor (air pump) system

3. ½ in. pipe plug
4. ½ in. reducer bushing

Apply pipe sealer to all threaded portions, thread plug and pipe into opposite ends of the "tee" and the reducer into the perpendicular orifice of the "tee."

Drill an $^{11}/_{32}$ in. hole through the center of the plug. Attach a pressure gauge with ¼ psi increments to the bushing or adapter.

PRELIMINARY THERMACTOR SYSTEM CHECK

1. Check the belt for tension, remove the air cleaner, and check all components for wear.
2. With automatic transmissions in Park or manual transmissions in Neutral and the parking brake on, start the engine and warm it.
3. Stop the engine and connect a tach-

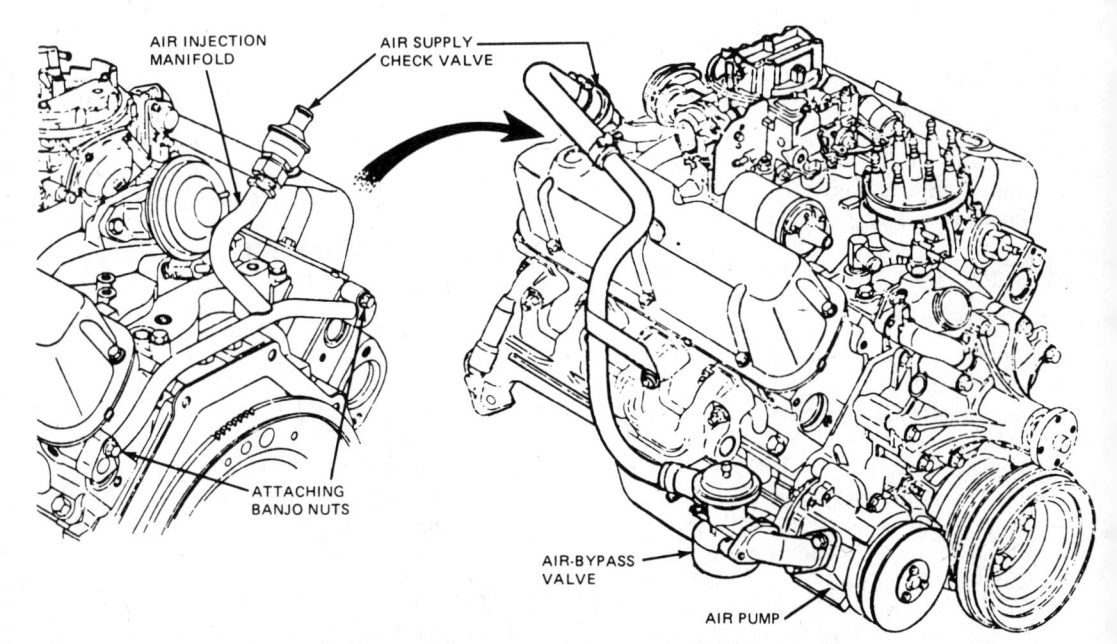

Thermactor installation on 5.0L Mustangs and Capris

108 EMISSION CONTROLS AND FUEL SYSTEM

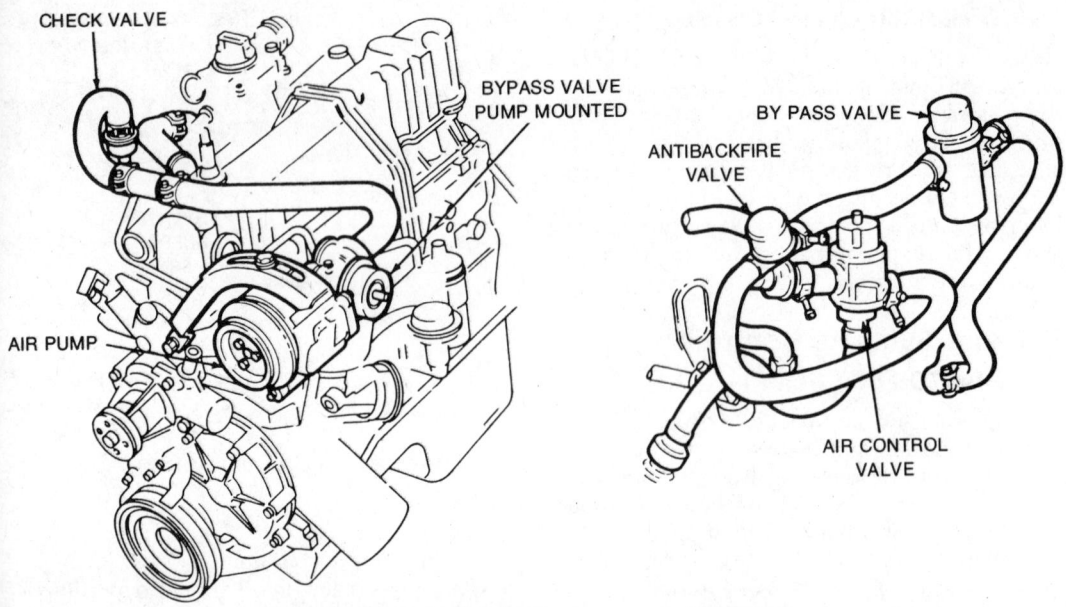

3.3L six cylinder showing Thermactor and installation

ometer. Remove the air supply hose at the check valve (if there are two supply hoses, remove both).

4. Start and run the engine at 1,500 rpm. Place your hand over the open hose. If you don't feel any air, perform the "Pump Test."

PUMP TEST (AIR SUPPLY)

1. Operate engine at normal operating temperature. Inspect hoses and connections for leaks. Correct if necessary.
2. Check and adjust pump drive belt tension.
3. Disconnect air supply hose at check valve. With more than one hose, plug one.
4. Insert adapter with gauge into the open air supply hose and clamp securely.
5. Connect a tachometer to the engine.
6. Start engine and operate at 1000 rpm.
7. Pressure reading should be at least 2¼ psi.

If 2¼ psi. is not attained, replace the pump.

CHECK VALVE TEST

1. Operate engine until normal temperature is reached.
2. Disconnect air supply hose at the check valve.
3. Visually make certain that the valve plate is lightly seated and away from the manifolds.
4. Depress the valve plate with some kind of probe and release. It should return freely to its original position.
5. With the hose still connected, start and run the engine at 1,500 rpm and check for leakage at the check valve.

BY-PASS VALVE TEST

1. Remove the hose connecting the by-pass valve to the check valve at the by-pass valve.
2. Place transmission in Neutral, apply the parking brake, start the engine and operate at normal idle speed.
3. Pinch off the vacuum line to the by-pass valve for 5–8 seconds, then release. Air flow should diminish or stop for a short time.
4. Remove the vacuum supply to the by-pass valve at the by-pass valve.
5. Insert a tee connection in the supply hose. Connect a gauge and a three inch hose to the remaining connections.
6. Plug the open end of the short hose. Start the engine and note the reading.
7. Unplug and connect the short hose. The reading should correspond to the first reading within 60 seconds. If not, replace the valve.

THERMACTOR II SYSTEM

Pulsed Air Type

Some 4 cylinder engines are equipped with an air injection system called pulse air or Thermactor II. The system does not use an air pump; instead it uses the natural pulses present in the exhaust system to pull air into the exhaust manifold through pulsed air valves. The pulse air valve is connected to the exhaust manifold with a long tube and to the air cleaner with a hose.

TROUBLESHOOTING

1. Check that air can flow freely through the air cleaner to the check valve.

EMISSION CONTROLS AND FUEL SYSTEM 109

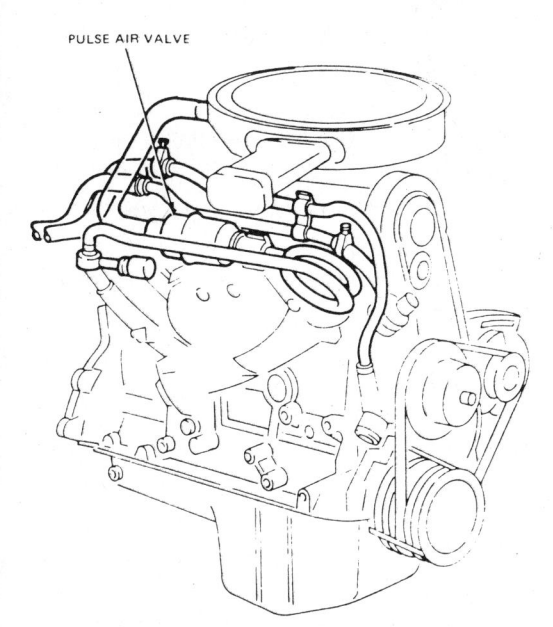

Typical Thermactor II system on 2.3L engine

2. Blow through the check valve, toward the manifold, then attempt to suck back through the valve. The valve should flow freely in the direction of the exhaust manifold only. If it doesn't replace the valve.

SERVICE

Repairs to the Thermactor system are limited to drive belt replacement and check valve and hose replacement. All other service should be performed by professionals.

Catalytic Converter

All models are equipped with catalytic converters. The function of the catalytic converter is to reduce hydrocarbon and carbon monoxide emission levels, converting a certain amount of these pollutants to water vapor and carbon dioxide. Lead-free gasoline *must* be used in all cars equipped with the catalytic converter. Do not park the car on top of dry leaves or long dry grass. The catalytic converter gets hot very quickly and remains so for a long time; it is possible that the car could ignite leaves or dry material if contact is made with the converter.

REMOVAL AND INSTALLATION

2.3L Four and 3.3L Six-Cylinder Engines

NOTE: *Make sure catalytic converter is cold before proceeding.*

1. Jack up the car and safely support it with jackstands.
2. Remove the upper and lower heat shields attached to the converter.
3. Remove the front and rear converter flange fasteners. On six-cylinder cars, loosen the support bracket attaching screws at the muffler and tailpipe and remove.
4. Separate the catalytic converter inlet and outlet flanges and remove the converter.
5. Installation is the reverse of removal.

2.8L V6 and All V8 Engines

SINGLE CONVERTER

1. Jack up the vehicle and support it with jackstands.
2. Remove the exhaust shield(s) attached to the converter.
3. Remove the bolts attaching the Y pipe to the converter inlet flange. Remove the nuts attaching the muffler inlet pipe to the converter outlet flange, and separate the flange connections.
4. Remove the converter.
5. Installation is the reverse of removal, except: Replace all gaskets, and do not fully tighten any bolts until the entire system is aligned. Tighten all bolts.

DOUBLE CONVERTER SYSTEM

1. Jack up the car and safely support it with jackstands, and remove the exhaust shield(s) from the converters.
2. Support the Y using wire, and remove the bolts attaching the converters to the Y pipe flanges.
3. Remove the flange nuts attaching the converters to the exhaust manifolds.
4. Slide the inlet pipe rearward until the catalytic converters can be removed. It may be necessary to remove the muffler support bracket attaching screw to obtain sufficient clearance to separate the converter at the manifold connection(s).
5. Installation is the reverse of removal, except: Alternately tighten the converter to inlet pipe flange attaching nuts to 20–30 ft. lbs.; align the entire exhaust system to proper clearance, then alternately tighten the manifold nuts to 16–24 ft. lbs.

NOTE: *Alternate tightening of joint fasteners is required to provide uniform clamping and to prevent joint distortion, a major cause of system leaks and the misalignment.*

Fuel Evaporation Controls

When liquid gasoline is subjected to heat, it expands and vaporizes. If this expansion and vaporization takes place in a conventional automobile gas tank, the fuel vapor escapes and pollutes the atmosphere once it has left the fuel tank. All models are equipped with an evaporative emission control system to prevent gasoline vapors from entering the atmosphere.

EMISSION CONTROLS AND FUEL SYSTEM

The major components of this system are an expansion area in the gas tank, a foam-filled vapor separator which is mounted on the fuel tank, a carbon canister which stores fuel vapors, and hoses which connect this equipment.

As the gasoline in the fuel tank of a parked vehicle begins to expand due to heat, the vapor that forms moves to the top of the fuel tank. It leaves the fuel tank through the vapor separator. The separator permits fuel vapors to leave the gas tank but prevents liquid gasoline from escaping. The fuel vapor enters the vapor separator outlet hose and passes through the hose to the carbon canister, which is mounted in the engine compartment. The vapor enters the canister, passes through a charcoal filter, and then exits from the canister through its grated bottom. As the vapor passes through the carbon, it is cleansed of hydrocarbons, so that the air that passes out of the bottom of the canister is free of atmospheric pollutants.

When the engine is started, vacuum from the carburetor draws fresh air into the carbon canister. As the entering air passes through the carbon in the canister, it picks up the hydrocarbons that were deposited there. This gas mixture is then carried through a hose to the air cleaner. In the carburetor it combines with the incoming air/fuel mixture and enters the combustion chambers of the engine where it is burned.

SERVICING

The canisters do not have to be replaced unless they are leaking or damaged.

Electronic Engine Controls
EEC-IV

The center of the EEC system is a microprocessor called an Electronic Control Assembly (ECA). The ECA receives data from a number of sensors, and other electronic components (switches, relays, etc.). Based on the information received and information programmed in the ECA's memory, output signals are generated to control various relays, solenoids and other actuators thereby setting specific calibrations for optimizing emissions, fuel economy and driveability.

The EEC-IV system can be divided into three subsystems. Fuel, Air, and Electronic Engine Control.

Fuel-Subsystem

The fuel subsection consists of a high pressure electric fuel pump, a fuel filter, a fuel charging manifold, a fuel pressure regulator and solid and flexible fuel supply and return lines. Refer to the Fuel Injection section.

Air Subsystem

The air subsystem consists of an air cleaner, an air cleaner valve assembly, vane meter, a throttle air bypass valve, a turbocharger and associated air tubes. Refer to the Fuel Injection section.

Electronic Engine Control Subsystem

The electronic engine control subsystem consists of the ECA and the various sensors and actuators.

In order for the ECA to properly control engine operations, it must first receive current status reports on various operating conditions. These include; crankshaft position, throttle plate position, engine coolant temperature, exhaust gas oxygen level, air intake volume/temperature, A/C on-off, and others.

The operating conditions are monitored by; Profile Ignition Pickup (PIP), Throttle Position Sensor (TPS), Engine Coolant Temperature Sensor (ECT), Exhaust Gas Oxygen Sensor (EGO), Vane Airflow (VAF) and Vane Temperature Sensor (VAT), A/C Clutch Compressor Signal (ACC), Barometric Pressure (BPS) and others.

When the ECA receives an input signal that indicates a change in one or more of the operating conditions, the change(s) must be evaluated to determine whether or not an output signal should be provided to control one or more of the following; air/fuel ratio, engine idle speed, EGR/CAN-on/off status, fuel pump-on/off status, engine cooling fan-on/off status, spark output signal and boost control.

System outputs control; EGR shut-off solenoid, canister purge valve, backpressure variable transducer EGR valve control, A/C and fan controller module, TFI-IV ignition module, fuel injectors and fuel pump relay and others.

A keep-alive memory is featured with the EEC-IV system. The ECA retains any intermittent trouble codes stored within the last 20 re-starts. The memory is not erased when the key is shut off. The trouble codes retained are a tremendous aid when servicing by professionals using the required test equipment.

FUEL SYSTEM

Mechanical Fuel Pump

The fuel pump is bolted to the left side of the front timing cover. It is operated mechanically by an eccentric bolted to the end of the camshaft. The pump rocker arm riding against the eccentric provides the diaphragm up and down

EMISSION CONTROLS AND FUEL SYSTEM

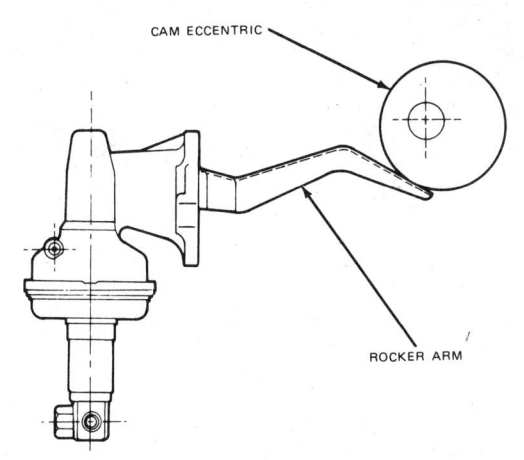

Mechanical fuel pump; all except V6 and turbo automatic

pumping motion. The fuel pump is not repairable and must be replaced if defective.

2.8L V6 Engines (1979)

The V6 fuel pump is mounted to the lower left side of the cylinder block. It is mechanically operated by a separate lobe ground into the camshaft. A pushrod riding against the lobe provides the diaphragm in and out pumping motion. The pump is not repairable and must be replaced if defective.

TROUBLESHOOTING

The fuel pump can fail in two ways; it can fail to provide a sufficient volume of gasoline under the proper amount of pressure to the carburetor, or it can develop an internal or external leak. An external leak will be very evident; not so with an internal leak. A quick check for an internal leak is to remove the oil dipstick and examine the oil on it. A fuel pump with an internal leak will leak fuel into the engine oil pan. If the oil on the dipstick is very thin and smells of gasoline, a defective fuel pump could be the cause.

PRESSURE TEST

Disconnect the fuel line from the carburetor and attach a pressure tester to the end of the line. Crank the engine over and note the reading on the tester. The pressures are listed in the Tune-Up Specifications Chart in Chapter 2.

VOLUME TEST

Disconnect the fuel line from the carburetor and insert it into a one quart container and crank the engines to the specifications listed below:
- 4 cyl. eng., one pint in 25 sec. @ idle
- 6 cyl. eng., one pint in 30 sec. @ idle
- V6 eng., one pint in 25 sec. @ idle
- V8 eng., one pint in 20 sec. @ idle

REPLACEMENT

NOTE: *Before removing the pump, rotate the engine so that the low point of the cam lobe is against the pump arm. This can be determined by rotating the engine with the fuel pump mounting bolts loosened slightly; when tension (resistance) is removed from the arm, proceed.*

1. Disconnect the fuel lines from the fuel pump and plug the inlet line from the gas tank to prevent gas leakage.
2. Remove the fuel pump retaining screws and remove the pump.
3. Remove the fuel pump actuating rod, if so equipped.
4. Clean all gasket mounting surfaces.
5. Install the fuel pump actuating rod, if so equipped.
6. Apply oil-resistant sealer to the fuel pump, position the pump on the engine and install the retaining screws.
7. Connect the fuel lines to the fuel pump, start the engine and check for leaks.

Electric Fuel Pump

1980–83

An electric fuel pump, located in the fuel tank, is used on all 1980 and later Mustangs and Capris equipped with automatic transmissions (manual shift cars have the mechanical pump). The circuit provides an interlock system that provides power to the fuel pump during starting through a contact of the starter relay, and provides reduced operating voltage during normal operation. In addition should the engine's oil pressure be lost during operation, the fuel pump is automatically disconnected from the electrical circuit.

Troubleshooting

1. Check for an adequate fuel supply in the gas tank.
2. Check that the inertia switch has not been tripped.
3. Check for fuel pump operation by removing the fuel line from the filter, disconnecting the lead from the oil pressure switch and turning the ignition switch to the ON position. If fuel is pumped from the line, check the oil pressure switch. If there is no fuel pumped from the line, check for a blown fuse (in-line type). If no fuel with the ignition switch ON, and the oil pressure lead disconnected, check for current at the relay feed and output terminals.
   A. If current is OK at the feed, but not at the output terminal, replace the relay.

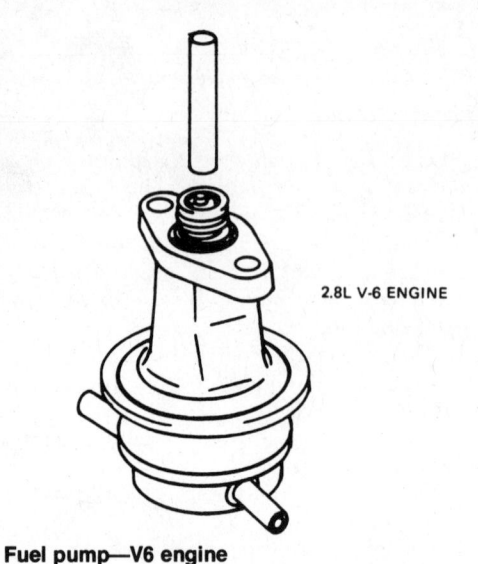

EMISSION CONTROLS AND FUEL SYSTEM

Fuel pump—V6 engine

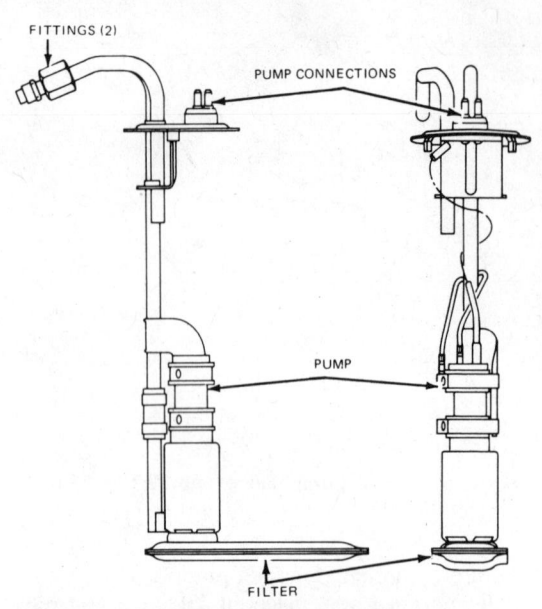

Electric fuel pump, "in tank" location

B. If there is no current at the feed, trace the current back at the source.

C. If current is present at both the feed and output terminals, trace the circuit back to the pump. If there is current at the pump and no fuel flow, remove the tank and change the fuel, fuel pump and bracket assembly.

Removal

1. Disconnect the negative battery cable.
2. Jack up the car and safely support it with jackstands.
3. Disconnect the fuel outlet and return line at the fuel pump.
4. Make sure the fuel level is below the fuel pump level by removing fuel from the tank as necessary.

NOTE: *Most automotive supply stores and parts houses have available a small, manually operated pump for removing fuel from the fuel tank. These pumps are generally inexpensive, and eliminate the need to siphon fuel—which can be hazardous to your health, let alone be very nauseating.*

5. Clean the area around the fuel pump at-

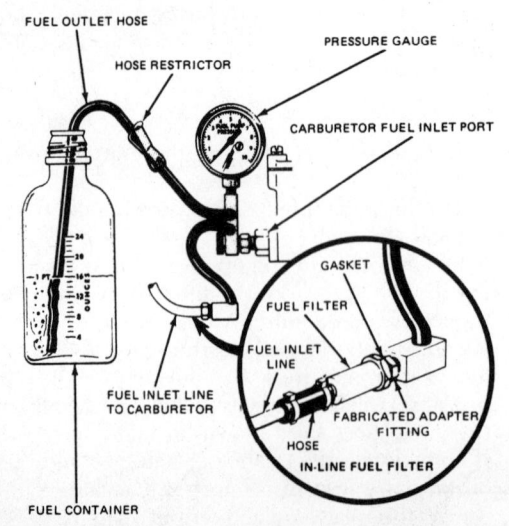

Typical fuel pump pressure and capacity test equipment

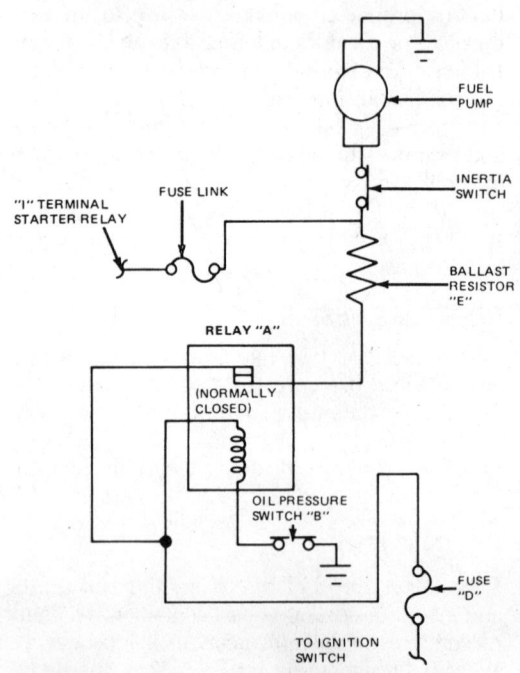

Electric fuel pump wiring diagram

EMISSION CONTROLS AND FUEL SYSTEM 113

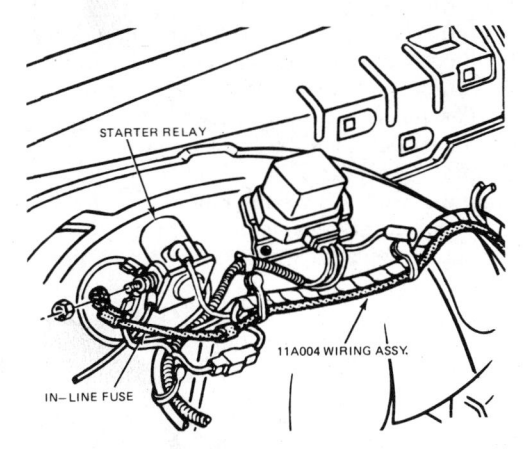

In-line-fuse—electric fuel pump

Relay "A" location identified in the wiring diagram

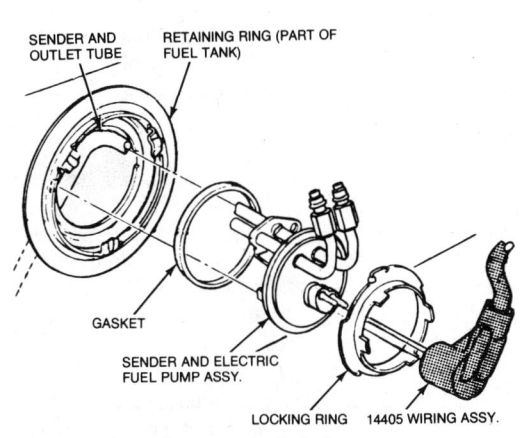

Electric fuel pump, exploded view

taching flange so that dirt will not enter the fuel tank during removal and installation.

6. Turn the fuel tank pump locking ring counterclockwise and remove the locking ring, mounting gasket and fuel pump.

Installation

1. Clean the fuel pump mounting flange at the fuel tank. Position a new gasket on the mounting flange.

NOTE: *Place a light coating of heavy grease on the gasket to hold it in place during assembly.*

2. Insert the pump into the fuel tank and twist and feed the free end of the filter into the fuel tank hole.
3. Position and rotate the locking ring against the stop to secure the fuel pump unit.
4. Connect the fuel lines to the pump and install the wiring connector to the fuel pump/sender unit.
5. Lower the vehicle and connect the battery cable.
6. Replace the fuel in the tank, start the engine and carefully check for fuel leaks.

1984 AND LATER

Removal and Installation

NOTE: *1984 and later models equipped with a high output injected or turbocharged injected engine are equipped with two electric pumps. A low-pressure pump is mounted in the tank and a high pressure pump is externally mounted.*

CAUTION: *Before servicing any part of the fuel injection it is necessary to depressurize the system. A special tool is available for testing and bleeding the system.*

IN-TANK PUMP

1. Disconnect the negative battery cable.
2. Depressurize the system and drain as much gas from the tank by pumping out through the filler neck.
3. Raise the back of the car and safely support on jackstands.
4. Disconnect the fuel supply, return and vent lines at the right and left side of the frame.
5. Disconnect the wiring to the fuel pump.
6. Support the gas tank, loosen and remove the mounting straps. Remove the gas tank.
7. Disconnect the lines and harness at the pump flange.
8. Clean the outside of the mounting flange and retaining ring. Turn the fuel pump lock ring counterclockwise and remove.
9. Remove the fuel pump.
10. Clean the mounting surfaces. Put a light coat of grease on the mounting surfaces and on the new sealing ring. Install the new fuel pump.
11. Installation is in the reverse order of removal. If single high pressure pump system, fill the tank with at least 10 gals. of gas. Turn the ignition key ON for three seconds. Repeat

6 or 7 times until the fuel system is pressurized. Check for any fitting leaks. Start the engine and check for leaks.

EXTERNAL PUMP

1. Disconnect the negative battery cable.
2. Depressurize the fuel system.
3. Raise and support the rear of the vehicle on jackstands.
4. Disconnect the inlet and outlet fuel lines.
5. Bend down the retaining tab and remove the pump from the mounting bracket ring.
6. Install in reverse order, make sure the pump is indexed correctly in the mounting bracket insulator.

"Quick-Connect" Fuel Line Fittings

REMOVAL AND INSTALLATION

NOTE: *"Quick-Connect" (push) type fuel fittings are used on most models equipped with a pressurized fuel system. The fittings must be disconnected using proper procedures or the fitting may be damaged. Two types of retainers are used on the push connect fittings. Line sizes of 3/8 in. and 5/16 in. use a "hairpin" clip retainer, 1/4 in. line connectors use a "duck bill" clip retainer.*

Hairpin Clip

1. Clean all dirt and/or grease from the fitting. Spread the two clip legs about an 1/8 inch each to disengage from the fitting and pull the clip outward from the fitting. Use finger pressure only, do not use any tools.
2. Grasp the fitting and hose assembly and pull away from the steel line. Twist the fitting and hose assembly slightly while pulling, if necessary, when a sticking condition exists.
3. Inspect the hairpin clip for damage, replace the clip if necessary. Reinstall the clip in position on the fitting.
4. Inspect the fitting and inside of the connector to insure freedom of dirt or obstruction. Install fitting into the connector and push together. A click will be heard when the hairpin clip snaps into proper connection. Pull on the line to insure full engagement.

Duck Bill Clip

1. A special tool is available from Ford for removing the retaining clips (Ford Tool No. T82L-9500-AH). If the tool is not on hand see Step 2. Align the slot on the push connector disconnect tool with either tab on the retaining clip. Insert the tool to disengage the clip. Pull the line from the connector.
2. If the special clip tool is not available, use a pair of narrow 6 in. channel lock pliers with a jaw width of 0.2 in. or less. Align the jaws of the pliers with the openings of the fitting case and compress the part of the retaining clip that engages the case. Compressing the retaining clip will release the fitting which may be pulled from the connector. Both sides of the clip must be compressed at the same time to disengage.
3. Inspect the retaining clip, fitting end and connector. Replace clip if any damage is apparent.
4. Push the line into the steel connector until a click is heard, indicating clip is in place. Pull on line to check engagement.

Electric Choke

The choke is powered from the center tap of the alternator, so that current is constantly applied to the temperature sensing disc. The system is grounded through the carburetor body. At temperatures below approximately 60°F, the switch is open and no current is supplied to the ceramic heater, thereby resulting in normal unassisted thermostatic spring choke action. When the temperature rises above about 60°F, the temperature sensing disc closes and current is supplied to the heater, which in turn, acts on the thermostatic spring. Once the heater starts, it causes the thermostatic spring to pull the choke plate(s) open within 1½ minutes, which is sooner than it would open if non-assisted.

OPERATIONAL TEST

1. Detach the electrical lead from the choke cap.
2. Use a jumper lead to connect the terminal on the choke cap and the wire terminal, so that the electrical circuit is still completed.
3. Start the engine.
4. Hook up a test light between the connector on the choke lead and ground.
5. The test light should glow. If it does not, current is not being supplied to the electrically-assisted choke.
6. Connect the test light between the terminal on the alternator and the terminal on the choke cap. If the light now glows, replace the lead, since it is not passing current to the choke assist.

CAUTION: *Do not ground the terminal on the alternator while performing Step 6.*

7. If the light still does not glow, the fault lies somewhere in the electrical system. Check the system out.

If the electrically-assisted choke receives power but still does not appear to be functioning properly, reconnect the choke lead and proceed with the rest of the test.

8. Tape the bulb end of the thermometer

EMISSION CONTROLS AND FUEL SYSTEM 115

to the metallic portion of the choke housing.

9. If the electrically-assisted choke operates below 55°F, it is defective and must be replaced.

10. Allow the engine to warm up to between 80 and 100°F; at these temperatures the choke should operate for about 1½ minutes.

11. If it does not operate for this length of time, check the bimetallic spring to see if it is connected to the tang on the choke lever.

12. If the spring is connected and the choke is not operating properly, replace the cap assembly.

THROTTLE SOLENOID (ANTI-DIESELING SOLENOID) TEST

1. Turn the ignition key on and open the throttle. The solenoid plunger should extend (solenoid energize).

2. Turn the ingition off. The plunger should retract, allowing the throttle to close.

NOTE: *With the antidieseling de-energized, the carburetor idle speed adjusting screw must make contact with the throttle shaft to prevent the throttle plates from jamming in the throttle bore when the engine is turned off.*

3. If the solenoid if functioning properly and the engine is still dieseling, check for one of the following:
   a. High idle or engine shut off speed;
   b. Engine timing not set to specification;
   c. Binding throttle linkage;
   d. Too low an octane fuel being used.

Correct any of these problems as necessary.

4. If the solenoid fails to function as outlined in Steps 1–2, disconnect the solenoid leads; the solenoid should de-energize. If it does not, it is jammed and must be replaced.

5. Connect the solenoid to a 12 V power source and to ground. Open the throttle so that the plunger can extend. If it does not, the solenoid is defective.

6. If the solenoid is functioning correctly and no other source of trouble can be found, the fault probably lies in the wiring between the solenoid and the ignition switch or in the ignition switch itself. Remember to reconnect the solenoid when finished testing.

NOTE: *On some 1971 models, dieseling may occur when the engine is turned off because of feedback through the alternator warning light circuit. A diode kit is available from Ford to cure this problem.*

REMOVAL AND INSTALLATION

1. Remove the air cleaner.
2. Remove the throttle cable from the throttle lever.
3. Disconnect all vacuum lines, emission hoses, the fuel line, electrical connection and the choke heat tube at the carburetor.

4. Remove the carburetor retaining nuts and remove the carburetor.

5. Remove the carburetor mounting gasket, spacer (if equipped) and lower gasket from the intake manifold.

6. Clean all gasket mounting surfaces and place the spacer between two new gaskets and position the spacer and gaskets on the intake manifold.

7. Position the carburetor on the spacer and gasket.

8. Position and connect the choke heat tube.

9. Install the spark and EGR vacuum lines (if so equipped) before bolting the carburetor in place.

10. Install the carburetor attaching nuts to a snug position, then tighten in a criss-cross pattern.

11. Connect the fuel line, throttle cable and vacuum lines. The vacuum lines and connections on the carburetor are color coded.

OVERHAUL

Efficient carburetion depends greatly on careful cleaning and inspection during overhaul, since dirt, gum, water, or varnish in or on the carburetor parts are often responsible for poor performance.

NOTE: *The following is a general overhaul procedure for all carburetors except the Motorcraft Variable Venturi 2700 VV Carburetor. Since the design of this carburetor differs considerably from the other carburetors the overhaul procedures are different. Refer to the Motorcraft Variable Venturi 2700 VV Carburetor section.*

Overhaul your carburetor in a clean, uncluttered dust-free area. Make sure there is ample light available. Disassemble the carburetor, when possible, in sections to eliminate the chance of losing the many small clips, springs, screws, O-rings and pins. Keep all similar and look alike parts segregated during the disassembly and cleaning to avoid accidental interchange of parts during assembly. Make a note of all jet sizes, which are marked on the jet bodies.

NOTE: *Before removing any jets or mixture screws from the carburetor body, it is necessary to check the setting of each as a reference for later assembly and tuning. Slowly turn each jet into its seat, until it is just snug, and note the number of turns until each jet begins to seat. DO NOT screw the jets down tight, as this will severely damage the tip and seat of each jet. When you have noted the number of turns of each, remove and mark the jets for later assembly. During assembly, barely snug the jets again and back each one out until the former setting is attained.*

When the carburetor is disassembled, clean all parts (except diaphragms, electric choke units, pump plunger and any other plastic, leather, fiber, or rubber parts) in clean carburetor solvent. If the air horn with choke plate(s) and main body show a large accumulation of dirt and deposits, they can be soaked overnight in a solvent can. These cans have a metal basket inside to hold the parts, which are lowered into the solvent for soaking. Solvent cans are available in sizes at most auto supply houses, and come in very handy for cleaning many different small metal parts.

Do not leave parts in the solvent any longer than is necessary to sufficiently loosen the deposits. Excessive cleaning may remove the special finish from the float bowl and choke valve bodies, leaving these parts unfit for service. Rinse all parts in clean solvent and blow them dry with compressed air or allow them to air dry. Wipe clean all cork, rubber, plastic, leather and fiber parts with a clean, lint-free cloth.

Blow out all passages and jets with compressed air and make sure there are no restrictions or blockages. *Never* use wire or similar metal tools to clean jets, fuel passages, or air bleeds. Clean all jets and valves separately to avoid accidental parts interchange.

Check all parts for wear or damage. If wear or damage is found, replace the defective parts. Especially check the following:

1. Check the float needle and seat for wear. If wear is found, replace the complete assembly.
2. Check the float hinge pin for wear and the float(s) for dents or distortion. Replace the float if fuel has leaked into it.
3. Check the throttle and choke shaft bores for wear or an out-of-round condition. Damage or wear to the throttle arm, shaft, or shaft bore will often require replacement of the throttle body. These parts require a close tolerance of fit; wear may allow air leakage, which could affect starting and idling.

NOTE: *Throttle shafts and bushings are not included in overhaul kits. They can be purchased separately.*

4. Inspect the idle mixture adjusting needles for burrs or grooves. Any such condition requires replacement of the needle, since you will not be able to obtain a satisfactory idle.
5. Test the accelerator pump check valves. They should pass air one way but not the other. Test for proper seating by blowing and sucking on the valve. Replace the valve if necessary. If the valve is satisfactory, wash the valve again to remove breath moisture.
6. Check the bowl cover for warped surfaces with a straightedge.
7. Closely inspect the valves and seats for wear and damage, replacing as necessary.
8. After the carburetor is assembled, check the choke valve for freedom of operation.

Carburetor overhaul kits are a must for each overhaul. These kits are usually very complete and include all gaskets, O-rings and new parts to replace those which deteriorate most rapidly. Failure to replace all parts supplied with the kit—especially gaskets—can result in poor performance and a leaky carburetor later.

Some carburetor manufacturers supply overhaul kits of three basic types: minor repair; major repair; and gasket kits. Basically, they contain the following:

Minor Repair Kits:
- All gaskets
- Float needle valve
- Volume control screw
- All diaphragms
- Spring for the pump diaphragm

Major Repair Kits:
- All jets and gaskets
- All diaphragms
- Float needle valve
- Volume control screw
- Pump ball valve
- Float
- Complete intermediate rod
- Intermediate pump lever
- Some cover hold-down screws and washers

Gasket Kits:
- All gaskets

After cleaning and checking all components, reassemble the carburetor, using new parts and referring to the exploded view. When reassembling, make sure that all screw and jets are tight in their seats, but *do not overtighten* as the tips will be distorted. Tighten all screws gradually, in rotation. Do not tighten needle valves into their seats; uneven jetting will result. Always use new gaskets. Be sure to adjust the float level when reassembling.

Holley Model 1946-C Carburetor Adjustments

FAST IDLE CAM ADJUSTMENT

Fast idle cam position adjustment is necessary to make sure the fast idle screw contacts the various steps of the fast idle cam at the proper time during engine warm-up. This adjustment can be made with the carburetor on the engine (with the engine off) or with the carburetor removed from the engine.

EMISSION CONTROLS AND FUEL SYSTEM

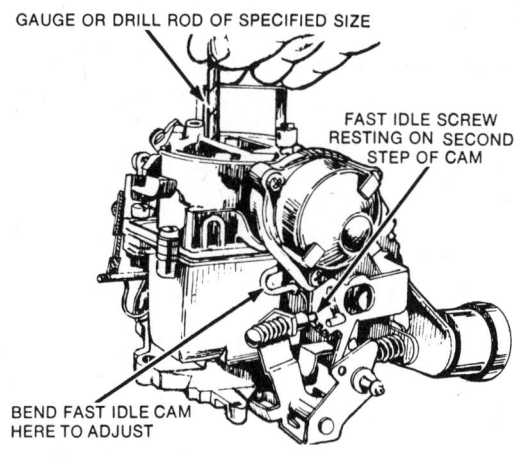

Fast idle cam position adjustment—Model 1946-C

1. With the fast idle speed adjusting screw contacting the second highest step of the fast idle cam (kickdown step), move the choke plate toward the closed position with light pressure on the choke lever or choke plate.
2. Check the fast idle cam setting using the specified size gauge or drill bit between the upper edge of the choke plate and the wall of the air horn.
3. Bend the fast idle cam link to achieve the specified setting.

NOTE: *To make a convenient bending tool, file a slot in the blade of a flat screwdriver just wide enough to slip over the 1/8 in. fast idle cam link. The tool can also be used in other applications where bending a similar small rod for adjustment is required.*

ACCELERATOR PUMP STROKE ADJUSTMENT

The accelerator pump stroke is pre-set at the factory and should not be adjusted.

DECHOKE CLEARANCE ADJUSTMENT

The dechoke feature provides a means of partially opening the choke plate during cold engine starts, even though the choke bimetal spring is holding it closed. By depressing the accelerator pedal fully, engines that may have become 'flooded' or that have stalled due to excessive choke action can be cleared. To adjust the dechoke clearance, proceed as follows:
1. With the engine off, hold the throttle in the wide open position.
2. Insert a No. 25 drill bit between the upper edge of the choke plate and the inner wall of the air horn.
3. With light pressure against the choke shaft lever, a slight drag should be felt as the gauge or drill bit is withdrawn.
4. To adjust, bend the tang on the throttle

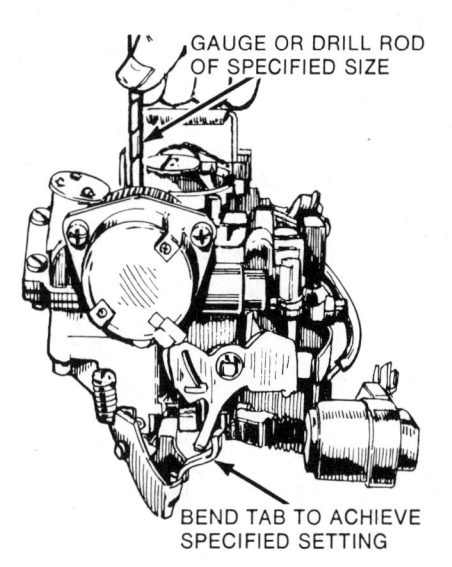

Dechoke clearance adjustment—Model 1946-C

lever until the correct opening is obtained. The tab can be bent with a pair of pliers or other suitable bending tool. Bending the tab upward will increase the dechoke clearance.

CHOKE PULLDOWN ADJUSTMENT

Adjust choke pulldown by bending the choke pulldown diaphragm connecting link. Use a gauge or drill bit of the specified diameter to check the clearance between the top of the choke plate and the air horn (Carburetors with suffixes EOZE-DA, EA, GA use a No. 35 bit; suffixes EOBE-ZA, AAA use a No. 32 bit; suffixes EOBE-AA, CA use a No. 39 bit; and suffix EOZE-BBA uses a No. 31 bit).

EXTERNAL FUEL BOWL VENT ADJUSTMENT

Adjust the external fuel bowl vent with the carburetor installed on the engine and the ignition OFF, after having first adjusted the curb idle speed.
1. Remove the air cleaner assembly.
2. Disconnect the canister vent hose from the bowl vent tube on the air horn.
3. Using a straight edge, check the position of the floats as shown in the illustration.
   • For all exc. California carburetors:
   The straight edge should just touch the lowest point on the float (toe) when held as pictured.
   • For California carburetors:
   The straight edge should just contact the step (or heel) of the float.
4. Once the adjustment is correct, turn the main body right side up and check the float alignment. The float should move freely

EMISSION CONTROLS AND FUEL SYSTEM

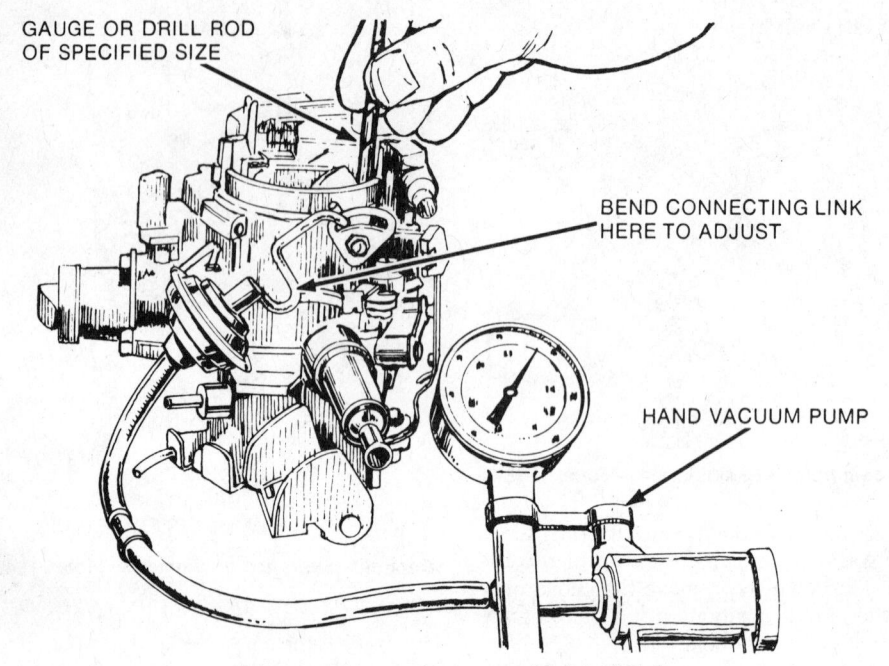

Choke pulldown adjustment—Model 1946-C

throughout its range without contacting the fuel bowl walls. If the float pontoons are misaligned, straighten by bending the float arms. Recheck the float level adjustment.

3. Attach a hand operated vacuum pump (Rotunda 21-0014 or equivalent) to the bowl vent tube, using a 3/8 inch adaptor.

4. Remove the three bowl vent cover screws located on the top of the air horn.

5. Remove the bowl vent cover gasket and spring.

6. Turn the vent adjusting screw (located on the nylon vent arm) clockwise until no more than 1/8 inch of the adjustment screw threads is visible above the vent arm.

7. While operating the hand vacuum pump, gradually turn the adjusting screw counterclockwise 1/8 turn at a time until vacuum is in-

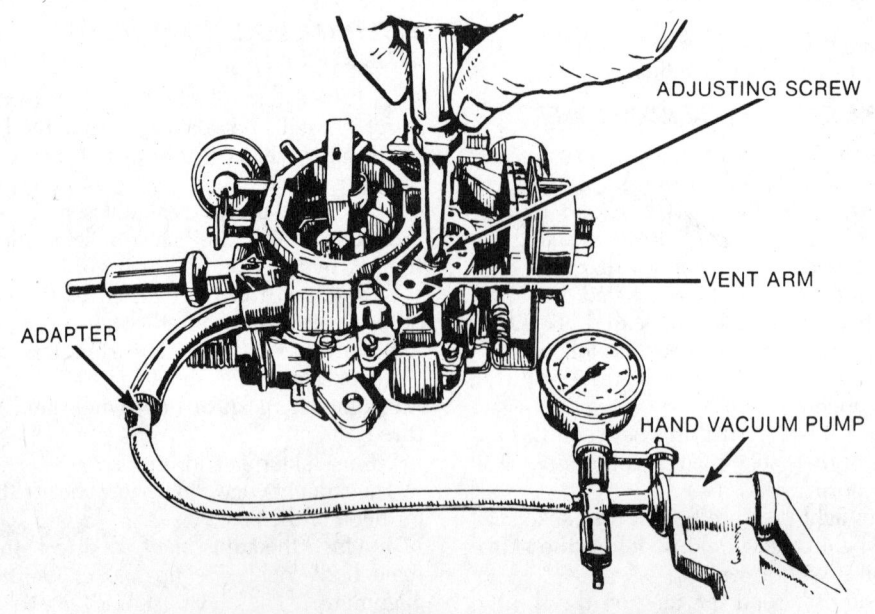

External fuel bowl vent adjustment—Model 1946-C

EMISSION CONTROLS AND FUEL SYSTEM

dicated on the gauge, showing that the valve is closed. Release the vacuum and turn the adjusting screw ½ turn clockwise. Disconnect the hand vacuum pump and adaptor from the vent hose.

8. Reconnect the canister vent hose and install the air cleaner assembly.

FLOAT ADJUSTMENT

1. Remove the carburetor upper body (air horn) assembly.
2. With the upper body assembly removed, place a finger over the float hinge pin retainer and invert the main body. Catch the accelerator pump check ball and weight as they drop from the pump channel.
3. Using a straight edge, check the position of the floats (see illustration). If adjustment is required, bend the float tabs to raise or lower the float level. Both tabs must be bent the exact same distance for proper operation.
- For California carburetors:

The straight edge should just contact the step (or heel) of the float.

4. Once the adjustment is correct, turn the body right side up and check the float alignment. The float should move freely throughout its range without contacting the fuel bowl walls. If the float pontoons are misaligned, straighten by bending the float arms. Recheck the float level adjustment.
5. During assembly, insert the check ball first and then the weight.

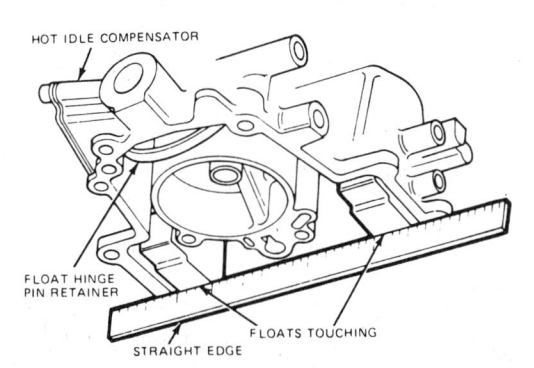

Float adjustment—Model 1946-C

5200 Carburetor Adjustment
FLOAT LEVEL ADJUSTMENT

1. Remove the air cleaner.
2. Disconnect the fuel and deceleration valve hoses from the carburetor.
3. Remove the small clip that attaches the choke rod to the choke plate shaft and disconnect the rod from the shaft.
4. Remove the screws that attach the upper body of the carburetor to the main body of the carburetor and carefully lift the upper body off the main body. Be careful not to tear the upper body gasket.
5. Turn the carburetor upper body upside down and measure the clearance with the float tang resting lightly on the spring loaded fuel inlet needle. Measure the clearance between the bottom of each float and the bottom of the carburetor upper body. The clearance should be 0.420 in., which equals the width of a No. 58 drill bit.
6. If the clearance is incorrect, bend the float level adjusting tang to adjust the level. Do not scratch or damage the tang.

NOTE: *Both floats must be adjusted to the same clearance.*

7. Position the upper body and gasket of the main body of the carburetor and connect the choke rod to the choke plate level. Install the choke rod attaching clip in the hole in the rod. Install the upper body attaching screws.
8. The remaining assembly steps are in the reverse order of removal.

FAST IDLE CAM ADJUSTMENT

1. Insert a 5/32 in. (no. 22) drill bit between the lower edge of the choke plate and the air horn wall.
2. Hold the fast idle screw on the bottom step of the fast idle cam. Measure the clearance between the tang of the choke lever and the arm of the fast idle cam (see illustration). The tang and arm should be in light contact. Bend the choke lever tang up or down as required.

CHOKE PLATE VACUUM PULLDOWN

1. Remove the choke thermostatic spring cover.
2. Pull the water cover and the thermostatic spring cover assembly out of the way.
3. Remove the choke electric assist assembly.
4. Set the fast idle cam on the second step.
5. Using a screwdriver, push the diaphragm stem against its stop and insert the proper gauge rod or drill bit between the lower edge of the choke plate and the air horn wall (for 2.3L use a No. 9 drill, for 2.3L Turbo use a letter "I" drill).
6. Remove the slack from the choke linkage by applying sufficient pressure to the upper edge of the choke valve. Slack can also be removed by attaching a rubber band to the choke operating lever as shown in the illustration.
7. To adjust the choke plate-to-air horn clearance, turn the vacuum diaphragm adjusting screw in or out as required.

120 EMISSION CONTROLS AND FUEL SYSTEM

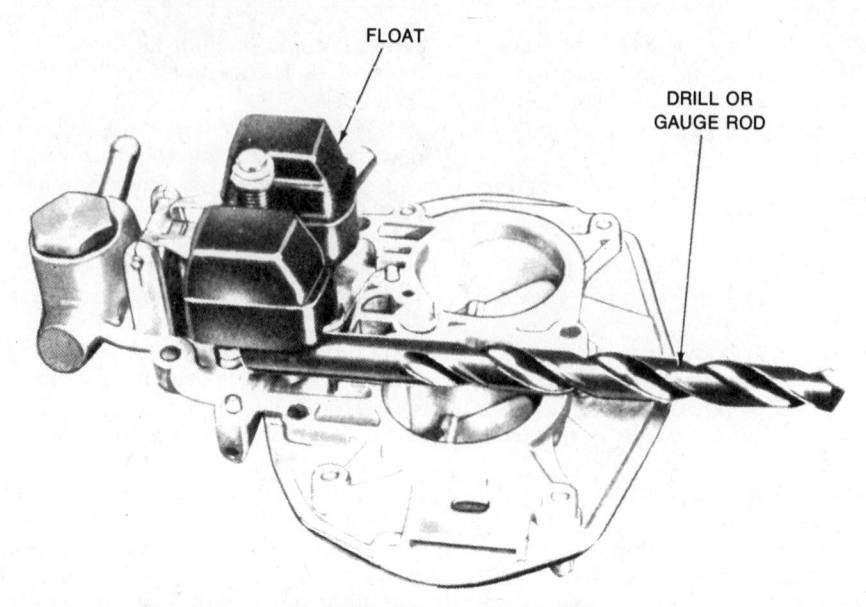

Float level check—Model 5200

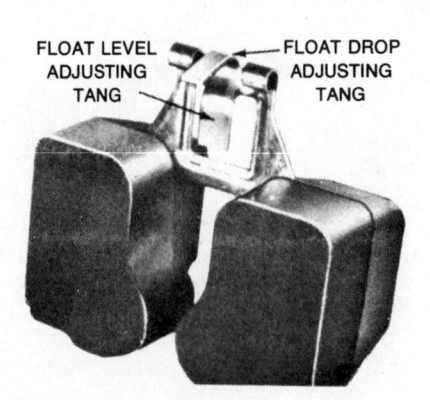

Float adjustment—Model 5200

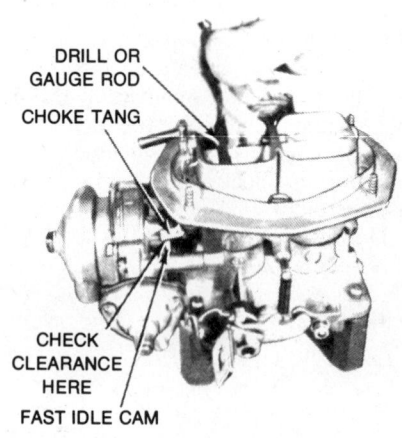

Fast idle cam clearance—Model 5200

SECONDARY THROTTLE STOP SCREW

1. Back off (turn counterclockwise) the secondary throttle stop screw until the secondary throttle plate seats in its bore.
2. Turn the screw clockwise (in) until it touches the tab on the secondary throttle lever, then add ¼ turn.

ELECTRIC CHOKE ADJUSTMENT

For electric choke procedures refer to the 2150 carburetor section.

FAST IDLE SPEED ADJUSTMENT

1. Remove the air cleaner assembly and plug the vacuum line at the source of the vacuum.
2. Set the parking brake and block the wheels.
3. Connect a tachometer to the engine. Start the engine and warm up to normal operating temperature.
4. Make sure all distributor vacuum lines are in place. Check the ignition timing.
5. Remove the EGR vacuum line at the valve and plug the line with a pencil or golf tee.
6. If applicable, remove the spark delay valve and route the primary distributor advance vacuum signal directly to the primary distributor diaphragm (advance side). If the distributor has a secondary (retard) side diaphragm, leave the vacuum connection intact.
7. Disconnect and plug the fuel deceleration valve hose (if equipped) at the carburetor connection.
8. The air conditioner, if equipped, must be "off".

EMISSION CONTROLS AND FUEL SYSTEM 121

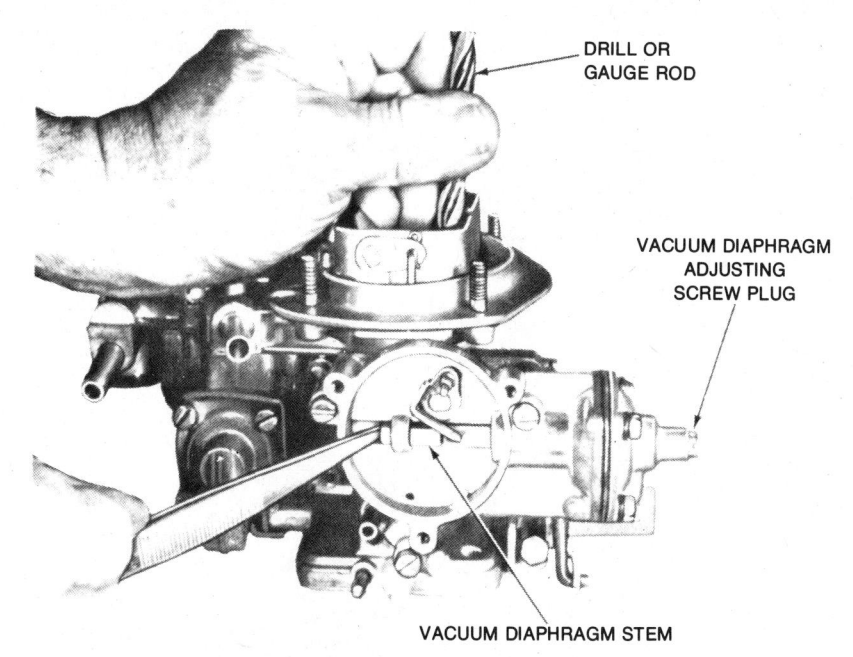

Choke vacuum pulldown adjustment—Model 5200

Measuring choke plate pulldown, 5200

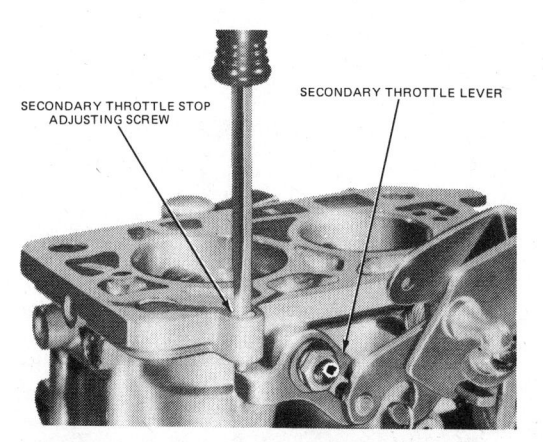

Secondary throttle stop adjustment, 5200 carburetor

9. With the engine running at normal operating temperature and the choke plate fully opened (automatic transmission in Park and manual trans in Neutral) set the throttle so that the fast idle adjustment screw contacts the kickdown step of the choke cam and adjust the fast idle adjusting screw to obtain the specified rpm according to specifications listed in the Tune Up section of this book.

10. Set the throttle to the high step of the choke cam and allow the engine to run approximately 5 seconds.

11. Rotate the choke cam until the fast idle adjustment screw touches the kickdown step of the choke cam. After allowing the rpm to stabilize, recheck the fast idle rpm and readjust if necessary by repeating steps 9–11 until the specified fast idle speed is obtained and can be repeated.

12. Stop the engine and install all vacuum lines and the air cleaner assembly.

2150 2V Carburetor Adjustments
FLOAT LEVEL ADJUSTMENT—DRY
(CARBURETOR OFF ENGINE)

The dry float adjustment is a preliminary fuel level adjustment only, "setting up" the float level (after a carburetor rebuild, etc.) until the final "wet" adjustment is made with the carburetor mounted on the engine.

1. With the air horn removed, the air float raised and the inlet needle seated, check the distance between the top surface of the main

122 EMISSION CONTROLS AND FUEL SYSTEM

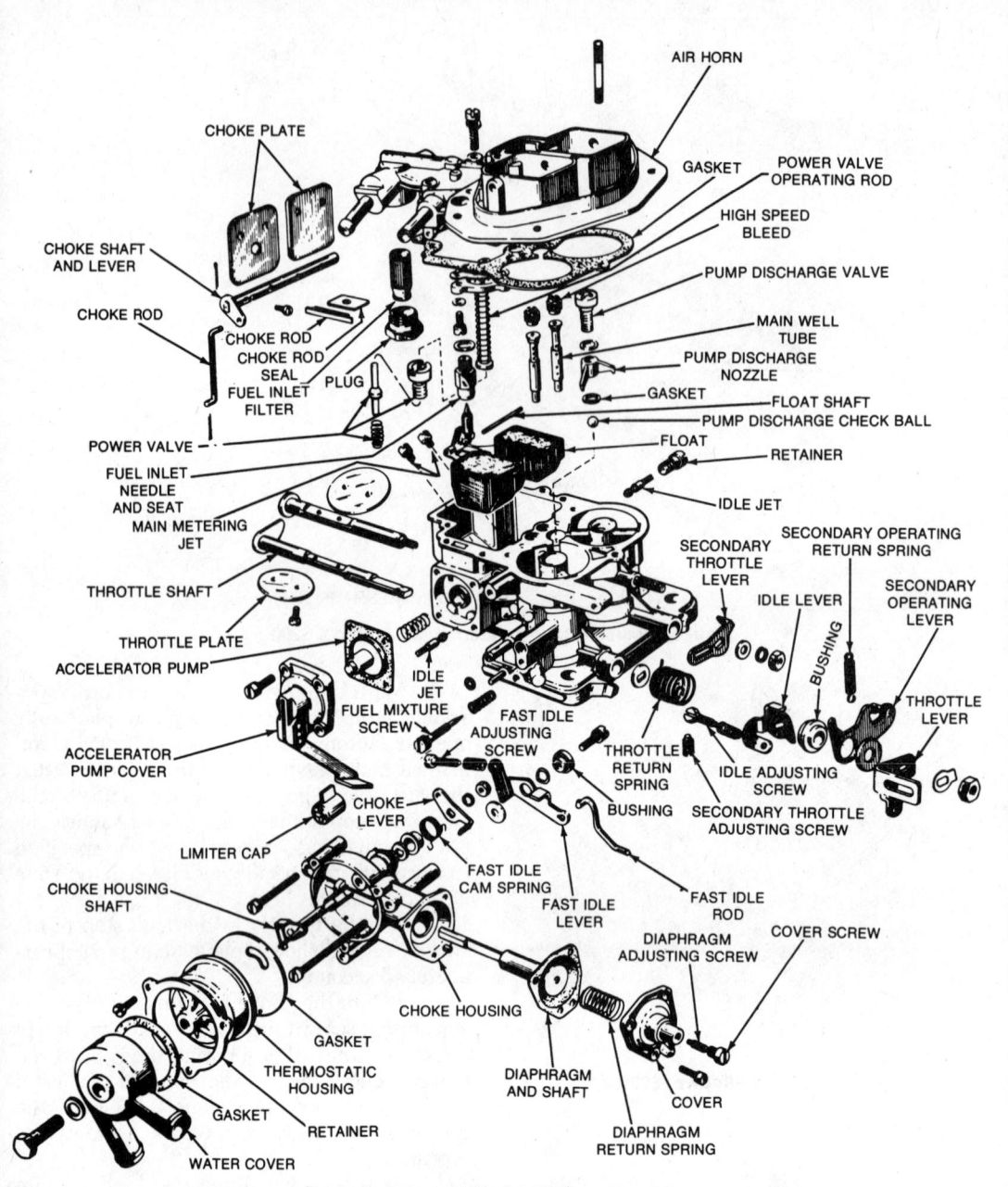

Exploded view of Model 5200 carburetor

body (gasket removed) and the surface of the float.

a. Depress the float tab to seat the fuel inlet needle.

CAUTION: *Excessive pressure can cause damage to the Vikton tip on the needle.*

b. Measure near the center of the float around 1/8 in. from the free end.

c. To adjust, bend the tab on the float to bring the setting to within the proper specified limits (7/16 in.). This should give a good preliminary fuel level setting before going to the final "wet" adjustment.

FLOAT LEVEL ADJUSTMENT—WET

1. Make sure the car is parked on a level surface with the parking brake set firmly. Run the engine up to normal operating temperature and stop the engine.

2. Remove the air cleaner assembly.

3. Remove the air horn attaching screws and the carburetor identification tag. Leave the air horn and gasket in position on the carburetor main body and start the engine. Let the engine idle a few minutes, then remove the air cleaner stud and the air horn and gasket to provide access to the float assembly.

EMISSION CONTROLS AND FUEL SYSTEM

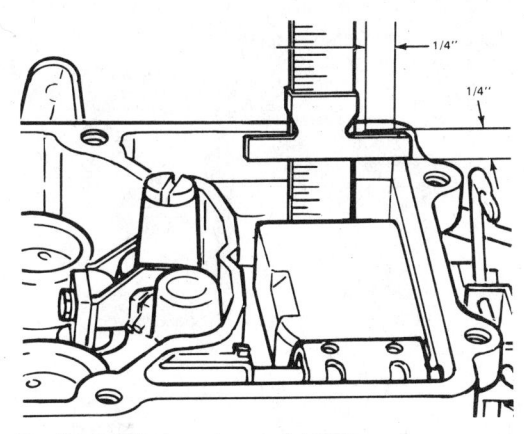

Dry float adjustment—model 2150

Model 2150 float adjustment—wet

4. While the engine is idling use a standard depth scale to measure the vertical distance from the top machined surface of the carburetor main body to the level of the fuel in the fuel bowl. The measurement must be made at least a ¼ inch away from any vertical surface to assure an accurate reading. The fuel level should be measured at the point of contact of the float with the fuel. To raise the fuel level bend the flat tab contacting the fuel inlet valve upward and downward to lower it.

5. Install a new air horn gasket and install the air horn assembly.

6. Install the air cleaner anchor stud and install the air cleaner.

ELECTRIC CHOKE

Linkage Check

1. With the engine off, remove the air cleaner assembly. Check that the A/C housing (if equipped) is not interfering with choke plate operation.

2. Make sure all vacuum hoses, solenoid, and electrical choke wires are properly connected.

3. Check the engine throttle system, choke plate, linkage and fast idle cam for freedom of operation.

Electrical Test

1. Disconnect the choke lead wire from the choke cap and connect a jumper wire between the choke cap terminal and the wire terminal. Start the engine.

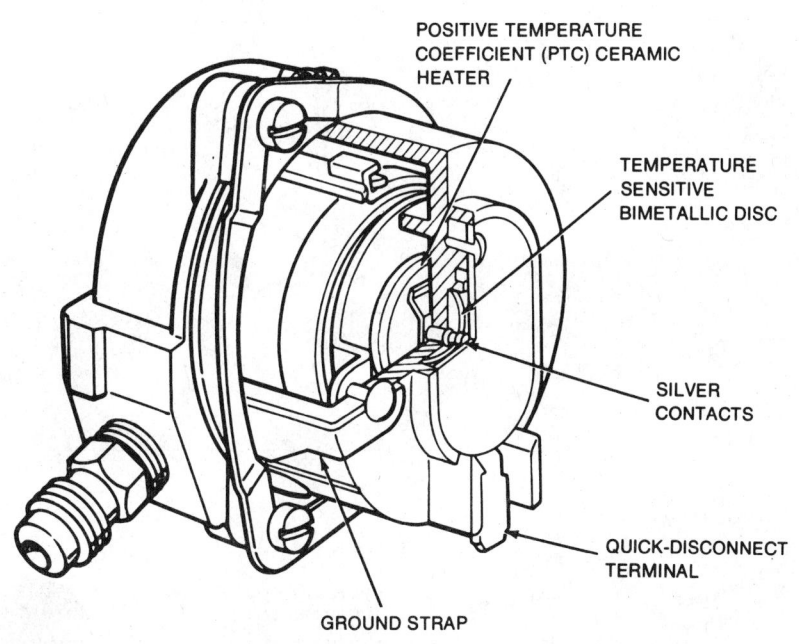

Electric assist choke—Model 2150

124 EMISSION CONTROLS AND FUEL SYSTEM

2. Connect a test light between the connector of the choke lead wire and ground. If the light glows, current is available to the choke cap. The choke cap should be replaced. If the light does not glow, connect the test light between the alternator stator and the choke lead wire. If the light glows, replace the lead wire. If the light does not glow, the problem lies in the engine electrical circuit.

Automatic Choke Adjustment

The automatic choke has an adjustment to control its reaction to engine temperature.
1. Remove the air cleaner assembly.
2. Remove the heater hose from the bracket (if so equipped).
3. Loosen the thermostatic spring housing clamp retaining screws.
4. Set the spring housing to the specified index mark and tighten the clamp attaching screws.
5. Replace the heater hose and air cleaner assembly.

CHOKE PLATE PULLDOWN AND FAST IDLE CAM

The Model 2150 2V carburetor is equipped with a choke pulldown diaphragm assembly. Vacuum is metered to the diaphragm through internal passages in the carburetor, through a connecting external tube. As the vacuum bleeds through the orifices in the carburetor, the choke diaphragm pulls the choke plate to the pulldown position.

Choke Pulldown Check

1. Set the throttle on the fast idle cam top step.
2. Note the index position of the choke bi-

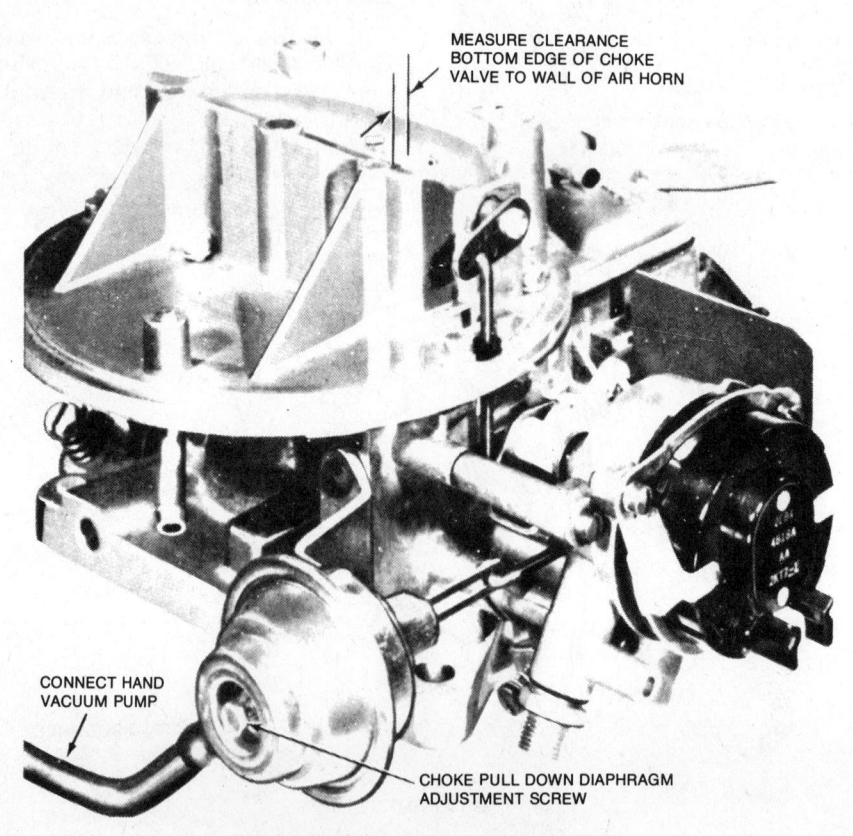

Automatic choke thermostatic spring housing adjustment—Model 2150

Adjusting plate pulldown—Model 2150

CHILTON'S
FUEL ECONOMY & TUNE-UP TIPS

55 WAYS TO IMPROVE FUEL ECONOMY

Tune-up • Spark Plug Diagnosis • Emission Controls

Fuel System • Cooling System • Tires and Wheels

General Maintenance

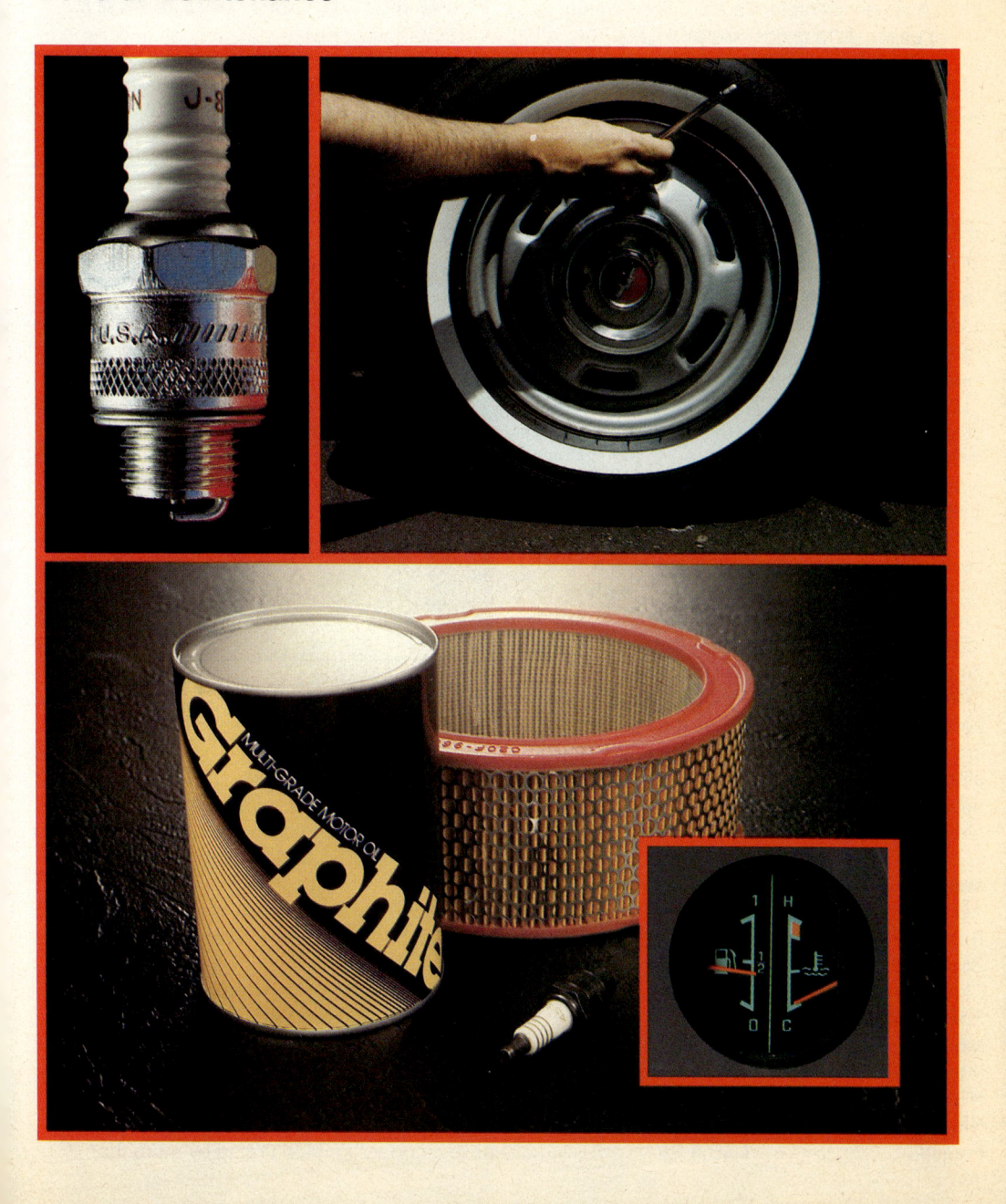

CHILTON'S FUEL ECONOMY & TUNE-UP TIPS

Fuel economy is important to everyone, no matter what kind of vehicle you drive. The maintenance-minded motorist can save both money and fuel using these tips and the periodic maintenance and tune-up procedures in this Repair and Tune-Up Guide.

There are more than 130,000,000 cars and trucks registered for private use in the United States. Each travels an average of 10-12,000 miles per year, and, and in total they consume close to 70 billion gallons of fuel each year. This represents nearly ⅔ of the oil imported by the United States each year. The Federal government's goal is to reduce consumption 10% by 1985. A variety of methods are either already in use or under serious consideration, and they all affect you driving and the cars you will drive. In addition to "down-sizing", the auto industry is using or investigating the use of electronic fuel delivery, electronic engine controls and alternative engines for use in smaller and lighter vehicles, among other alternatives to meet the federally mandated Corporate Average Fuel Economy (CAFE) of 27.5 mpg by 1985. The government, for its part, is considering rationing, mandatory driving curtailments and tax increases on motor vehicle fuel in an effort to reduce consumption. The government's goal of a 10% reduction could be realized — and further government regulation avoided — if every private vehicle could use just 1 less gallon of fuel per week.

How Much Can You Save?

Tests have proven that almost anyone can make at least a 10% reduction in fuel consumption through regular maintenance and tune-ups. When a major manufacturer of spark plugs sur-

---

TUNE-UP

1. Check the cylinder compression to be sure the engine will really benefit from a tune-up and that it is capable of producing good fuel economy. A tune-up will be wasted on an engine in poor mechanical condition.
2. Replace spark plugs regularly. New spark plugs alone can increase fuel economy 3%.
3. Be sure the spark plugs are the correct type (heat range) for your vehicle. See the Tune-Up Specifications.

Heat range refers to the spark plug's ability to conduct heat away from the firing end. It must conduct the heat away in an even pattern to avoid becoming a source of pre-ignition, yet it must also operate hot enough to burn off conductive deposits that could cause misfiring.

The heat range is usually indicated by a number on the spark plug, part of the manufacturer's designation for each individual spark plug. The numbers in bold-face indicate the heat range in each manufacturer's identification system.

Manufacturer	Typical Designation
AC	R **45** TS
Bosch (old)	WA **145** T30
Bosch (new)	HR **8** Y
Champion	RBL **15** Y
Fram/Autolite	4**15**
Mopar	P-**62** PR
Motorcraft	BRF-**4**2
NGK	BP **5** ES-15
Nippondenso	W **16** EP
Prestolite	14GR **5** 2A

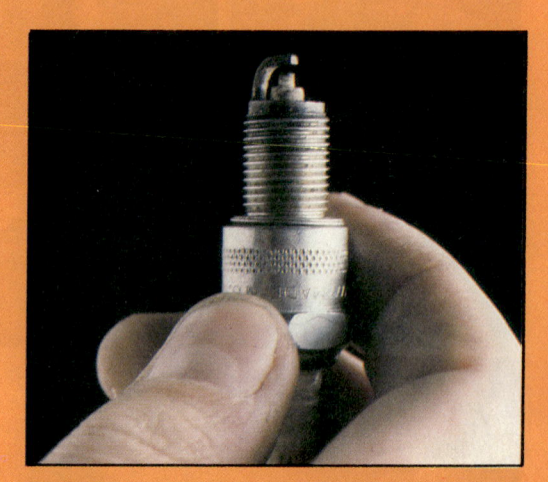

Periodically, check the spark plugs to be sure they are firing efficiently. They are excellent indicators of the internal condition of your engine.

On AC, Bosch (new), Champion, Fram/Autolite, Mopar, Motorcraft and Prestolite, a higher number indicates a hotter plug. On Bosch (old), NGK and Nippondenso, a higher number indicates a colder plug.

4. Make sure the spark plugs are properly gapped. See the Tune-Up Specifications in this book.
5. Be sure the spark plugs are firing efficiently. The illustrations on the next 2 pages show you how to "read" the firing end of the spark plug.
6. Check the ignition timing and set it to specifications. Tests show that almost all cars have incorrect ignition timing by more than 2°.

veyed over 6,000 cars nationwide, they found that a tune-up, on cars that needed one, increased fuel economy over 11%. Replacing worn plugs alone, accounted for a 3% increase. The same test also revealed that 8 out of every 10 vehicles will have some maintenance deficiency that will directly affect fuel economy, emissions or performance. Most of this mileage-robbing neglect could be prevented with regular maintenance.

Modern engines require that all of the functioning systems operate properly for maximum efficiency. A malfunction anywhere wastes fuel. You can keep your vehicle running as efficiently and economically as possible, by being aware of your vehicle's operating and performance characteristics. If your vehicle suddenly develops performance or fuel economy problems it could be due to one or more of the following:

PROBLEM	POSSIBLE CAUSE
Engine Idles Rough	Ignition timing, idle mixture, vacuum leak or something amiss in the emission control system.
Hesitates on Acceleration	Dirty carburetor or fuel filter, improper accelerator pump setting, ignition timing or fouled spark plugs.
Starts Hard or Fails to Start	Worn spark plugs, improperly set automatic choke, ice (or water) in fuel system.
Stalls Frequently	Automatic choke improperly adjusted and possible dirty air filter or fuel filter.
Performs Sluggishly	Worn spark plugs, dirty fuel or air filter, ignition timing or automatic choke out of adjustment.

Check spark plug wires on conventional point type ignition for cracks by bending them in a loop around your finger.

Be sure that spark plug wires leading to adjacent cylinders do not run too close together. (Photo courtesy Champion Spark Plug Co.)

7. If your vehicle does not have electronic ignition, check the points, rotor and cap as specified.

8. Check the spark plug wires (used with conventional point-type ignitions) for cracks and burned or broken insulation by bending them in a loop around your finger. Cracked wires decrease fuel efficiency by failing to deliver full voltage to the spark plugs. One misfiring spark plug can cost you as much as 2 mpg.

9. Check the routing of the plug wires. Misfiring can be the result of spark plug leads to adjacent cylinders running parallel to each other and too close together. One wire tends to pick up voltage from the other causing it to fire "out of time".

10. Check all electrical and ignition circuits for voltage drop and resistance.

11. Check the distributor mechanical and/or vacuum advance mechanisms for proper functioning. The vacuum advance can be checked by twisting the distributor plate in the opposite direction of rotation. It should spring back when released.

12. Check and adjust the valve clearance on engines with mechanical lifters. The clearance should be slightly loose rather than too tight.

SPARK PLUG DIAGNOSIS

Normal

APPEARANCE: This plug is typical of one operating normally. The insulator nose varies from a light tan to grayish color with slight electrode wear. The presence of slight deposits is normal on used plugs and will have no adverse effect on engine performance. The spark plug heat range is correct for the engine and the engine is running normally.
CAUSE: Properly running engine.
RECOMMENDATION: Before reinstalling this plug, the electrodes should be cleaned and filed square. Set the gap to specifications. If the plug has been in service for more than 10-12,000 miles, the entire set should probably be replaced with a fresh set of the same heat range.

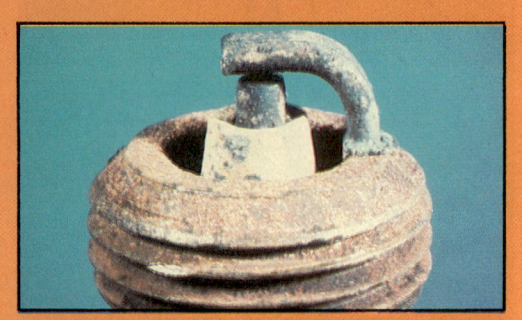

Oil Deposits

APPEARANCE: The firing end of the plug is covered with a wet, oily coating.
CAUSE: The problem is poor oil control. On high mileage engines, oil is leaking past the rings or valve guides into the combustion chamber. A common cause is also a plugged PCV valve, and a ruptured fuel pump diaphragm can also cause this condition. Oil fouled plugs such as these are often found in new or recently overhauled engines, before normal oil control is achieved, and can be cleaned and reinstalled.
RECOMMENDATION: A hotter spark plug may temporarily relieve the problem, but the engine is probably in need of work.

Incorrect Heat Range

APPEARANCE: The effects of high temperature on a spark plug are indicated by clean white, often blistered insulator. This can also be accompanied by excessive wear of the electrode, and the absence of deposits.
CAUSE: Check for the correct spark plug heat range. A plug which is too hot for the engine can result in overheating. A car operated mostly at high speeds can require a colder plug. Also check ignition timing, cooling system level, fuel mixture and leaking intake manifold.
RECOMMENDATION: If all ignition and engine adjustments are known to be correct, and no other malfunction exists, install spark plugs one heat range colder.

Carbon Deposits

APPEARANCE: Carbon fouling is easily identified by the presence of dry, soft, black, sooty deposits.
CAUSE: Changing the heat range can often lead to carbon fouling, as can prolonged slow, stop-and-start driving. If the heat range is correct, carbon fouling can be attributed to a rich fuel mixture, sticking choke, clogged air cleaner, worn breaker points, retarded timing or low compression. If only one or two plugs are carbon fouled, check for corroded or cracked wires on the affected plugs. Also look for cracks in the distributor cap between the towers of affected cylinders.
RECOMMENDATION: After the problem is corrected, these plugs can be cleaned and reinstalled if not worn severely.

Photos Courtesy Fram Corporation

MMT Fouled

APPEARANCE: Spark plugs fouled by MMT (Methycyclopentadienyl Maganese Tricarbonyl) have reddish, rusty appearance on the insulator and side electrode.
CAUSE: MMT is an anti-knock additive in gasoline used to replace lead. During the combustion process, the MMT leaves a reddish deposit on the insulator and side electrode.
RECOMMENDATION: No engine malfunction is indicated and the deposits will not affect plug performance any more than lead deposits (see Ash Deposits). MMT fouled plugs can be cleaned, regapped and reinstalled.

High Speed Glazing

APPEARANCE: Glazing appears as shiny coating on the plug, either yellow or tan in color.
CAUSE: During hard, fast acceleration, plug temperatures rise suddenly. Deposits from normal combustion have no chance to fluff-off; instead, they melt on the insulator forming an electrically conductive coating which causes misfiring.
RECOMMENDATION: Glazed plugs are not easily cleaned. They should be replaced with a fresh set of plugs of the correct heat range. If the condition recurs, using plugs with a heat range one step colder may cure the problem.

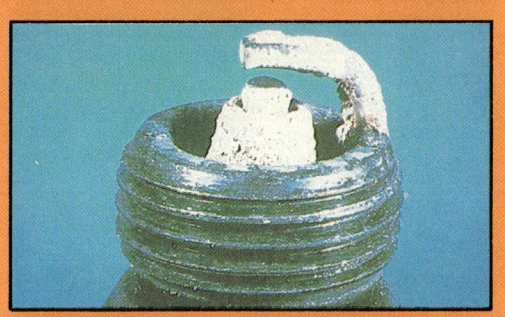

Ash (Lead) Deposits

APPEARANCE: Ash deposits are characterized by light brown or white colored deposits crusted on the side or center electrodes. In some cases it may give the plug a rusty appearance.
CAUSE: Ash deposits are normally derived from oil or fuel additives burned during normal combustion. Normally they are harmless, though excessive amounts can cause misfiring. If deposits are excessive in short mileage, the valve guides may be worn.
RECOMMENDATION: Ash-fouled plugs can be cleaned, gapped and reinstalled.

Detonation

APPEARANCE: Detonation is usually characterized by a broken plug insulator.
CAUSE: A portion of the fuel charge will begin to burn spontaneously, from the increased heat following ignition. The explosion that results applies extreme pressure to engine components, frequently damaging spark plugs and pistons.

Detonation can result by over-advanced ignition timing, inferior gasoline (low octane) lean air/fuel mixture, poor carburetion, engine lugging or an increase in compression ratio due to combustion chamber deposits or engine modification.
RECOMMENDATION: Replace the plugs after correcting the problem.

Photos Courtesy Champion Spark Plug Co.

EMISSION CONTROLS

13. Be aware of the general condition of the emission control system. It contributes to reduced pollution and should be serviced regularly to maintain efficient engine operation.

14. Check all vacuum lines for dried, cracked or brittle conditions. Something as simple as a leaking vacuum hose can cause poor performance and loss of economy.

15. Avoid tampering with the emission control system. Attempting to improve fuel econ-

FUEL SYSTEM

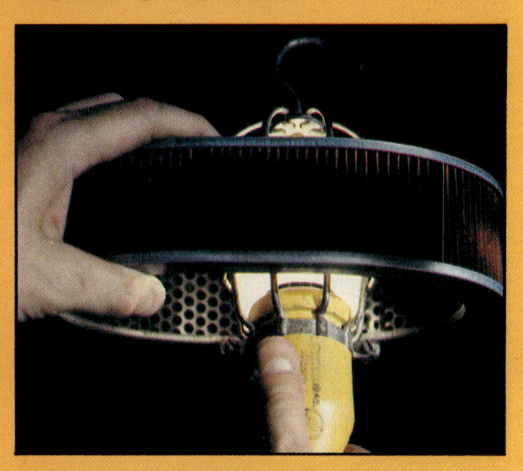

Check the air filter with a light behind it. If you can see light through the filter it can be reused.

Extremely clogged filters should be discarded and replaced with a new one.

18. Replace the air filter regularly. A dirty air filter richens the air/fuel mixture and can increase fuel consumption as much as 10%. Tests show that ⅓ of all vehicles have air filters in need of replacement.

19. Replace the fuel filter at least as often as recommended.

20. Set the idle speed and carburetor mixture to specifications.

21. Check the automatic choke. A sticking or malfunctioning choke wastes gas.

22. During the summer months, adjust the automatic choke for a leaner mixture which will produce faster engine warm-ups.

COOLING SYSTEM

29. Be sure all accessory drive belts are in good condition. Check for cracks or wear.

30. Adjust all accessory drive belts to proper tension.

31. Check all hoses for swollen areas, worn spots, or loose clamps.

32. Check coolant level in the radiator or expansion tank.

33. Be sure the thermostat is operating properly. A stuck thermostat delays engine warm-up and a cold engine uses nearly twice as much fuel as a warm engine.

34. Drain and replace the engine coolant at least as often as recommended. Rust and scale

TIRES & WHEELS

38. Check the tire pressure often with a pencil type gauge. Tests by a major tire manufacturer show that 90% of all vehicles have at least 1 tire improperly inflated. Better mileage can be achieved by over-inflating tires, but never exceed the maximum inflation pressure on the side of the tire.

39. If possible, install radial tires. Radial tires deliver as much as ½ mpg more than bias belted tires.

40. Avoid installing super-wide tires. They only create extra rolling resistance and decrease fuel mileage. Stick to the manufacturer's recommendations.

41. Have the wheels properly balanced.

omy by tampering with emission controls is more likely to worsen fuel economy than improve it. Emission control changes on modern engines are not readily reversible.

16. Clean (or replace) the EGR valve and lines as recommended.

17. Be sure that all vacuum lines and hoses are reconnected properly after working under the hood. An unconnected or misrouted vacuum line can wreak havoc with engine performance.

23. Check for fuel leaks at the carburetor, fuel pump, fuel lines and fuel tank. Be sure all lines and connections are tight.

24. Periodically check the tightness of the carburetor and intake manifold attaching nuts and bolts. These are a common place for vacuum leaks to occur.

25. Clean the carburetor periodically and lubricate the linkage.

26. The condition of the tailpipe can be an excellent indicator of proper engine combustion. After a long drive at highway speeds, the inside of the tailpipe should be a light grey in color. Black or soot on the insides indicates an overly rich mixture.

27. Check the fuel pump pressure. The fuel pump may be supplying more fuel than the engine needs.

28. Use the proper grade of gasoline for your engine. Don't try to compensate for knocking or "pinging" by advancing the ignition timing. This practice will only increase plug temperature and the chances of detonation or pre-ignition with relatively little performance gain.

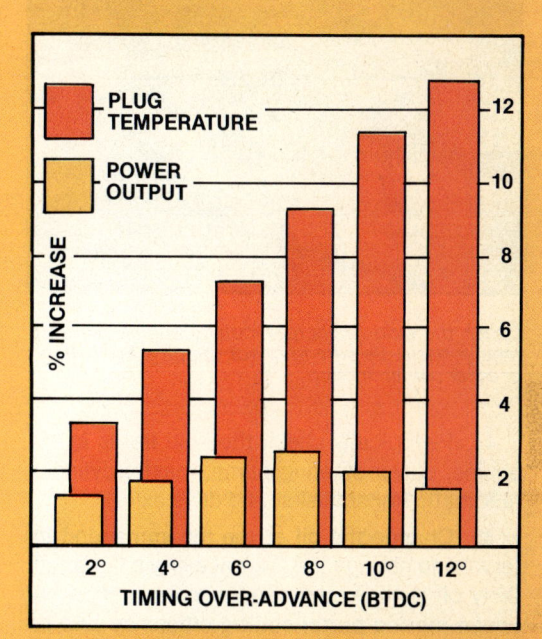

Increasing ignition timing past the specified setting results in a drastic increase in spark plug temperature with increased chance of detonation or preignition. Performance increase is considerably less. (Photo courtesy Champion Spark Plug Co.)

that form in the engine should be flushed out to allow the engine to operate at peak efficiency.

35. Clean the radiator of debris that can decrease cooling efficiency.

36. Install a flex-type or electric cooling fan, if you don't have a clutch type fan. Flex fans use curved plastic blades to push more air at low speeds when more cooling is needed; at high speeds the blades flatten out for less resistance. Electric fans only run when the engine temperature reaches a predetermined level.

37. Check the radiator cap for a worn or cracked gasket. If the cap does not seal properly, the cooling system will not function properly.

42. Be sure the front end is correctly aligned. A misaligned front end actually has wheels going in differed directions. The increased drag can reduce fuel economy by .3 mpg.

43. Correctly adjust the wheel bearings. Wheel bearings that are adjusted too tight increase rolling resistance.

Check tire pressures regularly with a reliable pocket type gauge. Be sure to check the pressure on a cold tire.

GENERAL MAINTENANCE

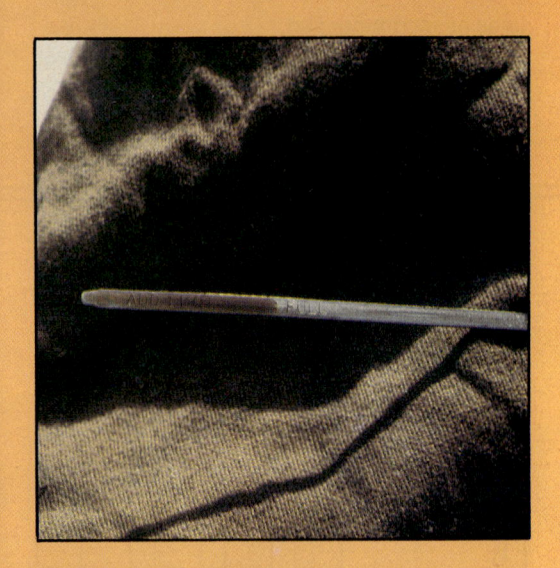

Check the fluid levels (particularly engine oil) on a regular basis. Be sure to check the oil for grit, water or other contamination.

A vacuum gauge is another excellent indicator of internal engine condition and can also be installed in the dash as a mileage indicator.

44. Periodically check the fluid levels in the engine, power steering pump, master cylinder, automatic transmission and drive axle.

45. Change the oil at the recommended interval and change the filter at every oil change. Dirty oil is thick and causes extra friction between moving parts, cutting efficiency and increasing wear. A worn engine requires more frequent tune-ups and gets progressively worse fuel economy. In general, use the lightest viscosity oil for the driving conditions you will encounter.

46. Use the recommended viscosity fluids in the transmission and axle.

47. Be sure the battery is fully charged for fast starts. A slow starting engine wastes fuel.

48. Be sure battery terminals are clean and tight.

49. Check the battery electrolyte level and add distilled water if necessary.

50. Check the exhaust system for crushed pipes, blockages and leaks.

51. Adjust the brakes. Dragging brakes or brakes that are not releasing create increased drag on the engine.

52. Install a vacuum gauge or miles-per-gallon gauge. These gauges visually indicate engine vacuum in the intake manifold. High vacuum = good mileage and low vacuum = poorer mileage. The gauge can also be an excellent indicator of internal engine conditions.

53. Be sure the clutch is properly adjusted. A slipping clutch wastes fuel.

54. Check and periodically lubricate the heat control valve in the exhaust manifold. A sticking or inoperative valve prevents engine warm-up and wastes gas.

55. Keep accurate records to check fuel economy over a period of time. A sudden drop in fuel economy may signal a need for tune-up or other maintenance.

© 1980 Chilton Book Company, Radnor, PA 19089

EMISSION CONTROLS AND FUEL SYSTEM

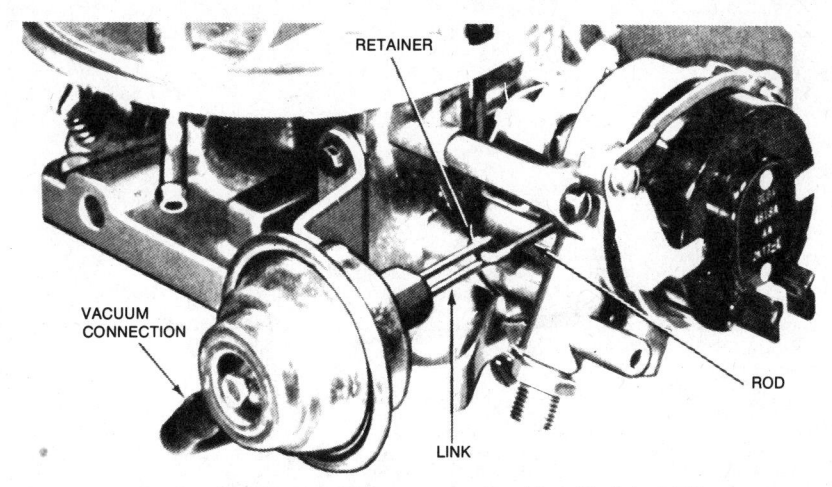

Choke pulldown diaphragm assembly—Model 2150

metallic cap. Loosen the retaining screws and rotate the cap 90 degrees in the rich (closing) direction.

3. Manually force the pulldown control diaphragm link in the direction of the applied vacuum or apply vacuum to the external vacuum tube to activate the pulldown motor.

4. Measure the vertical hard gauge clearance between the choke plate and the center of the carburetor air horn wall nearest the fuel bowl. Adjust the choke plate pulldown to .125 in. by adjusting the diaphragm stop on the end of the choke pulldown diaphragm.

5. Set the choke bimetallic cap to specification.

Fast Idle Speed Adjustment

1. Remove the EGR vacuum line and air cleaner and plug both vacuum lines.
2. Check the ignition timing.
3. Place the transmission in Neutral and engage the parking brake.
4. Start the engine and run it up to normal operating temperature.
5. Remove the spark delay valve (if so equipped) and route part of the throttle vacuum signal directly to the advance side of the distributor. If the distributor is a dual diaphragm model, leave the manifold vacuum line connected to the retard side of the distributor.

6. Set the throttle to the kickdown step on the choke cam (choke plate will be open) and make sure the adjusting screw is up against the shoulder of the kickdown step.

ACCELERATOR PUMP STROKE ADJUSTMENT

The accelerator pump stroke has been preset at the factory for each particular engine and should not be readjusted.

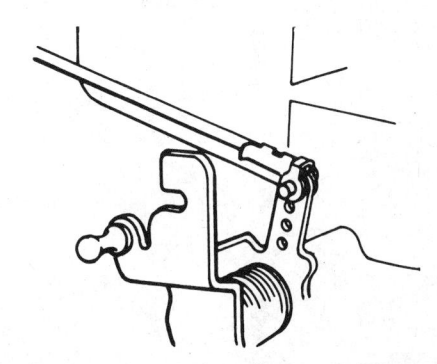

Accelerator pump stroke adjustment—Model 2150

Motorcraft Variable Venturi 2700VV

In 1979, Ford made their new variable venturi 2700VV carburetor available on California Mustangs and Capris equipped with the 2.8L V6 and the 5.0L V8. The only similarity between this carburetor and conventional units is that both have a normal float and fuel bowl system. However, in place of the conventional choke plate and fixed area venturis, the 2700VV has castings that slide across the top of the car-

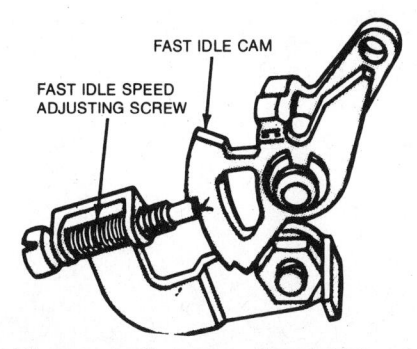

Fast idle speed adjustment—Model 2150

126 EMISSION CONTROLS AND FUEL SYSTEM

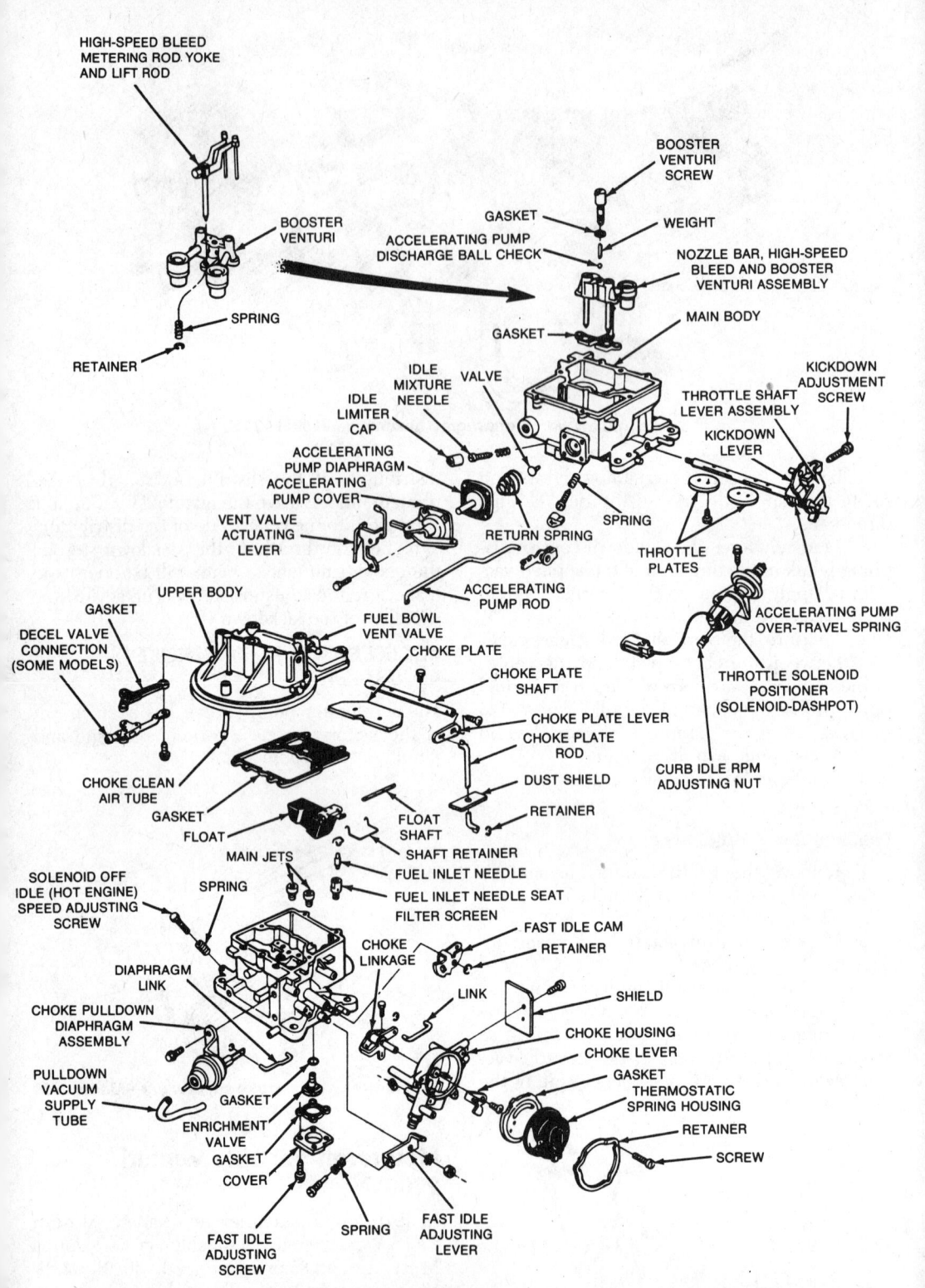

Exploded view of Model 2150 carburetor

EMISSION CONTROLS AND FUEL SYSTEM

buretor in response to fuel-air demands and is controlled by vacuum. Fuel metering rods are attached to the venturis, and, as the venturus open or close in response to air demand, the fuel needed to maintain the proper mixture increases or decreases as the metering rods slide in the jets. This system provides much more precise fuel-air metering compared to a fixed venturi carburetor, because there are fewer fuel metering systems and fuel passages.

NOTE: *Most service and adjustment procedures on the 2700VV require special tools and experience. Do not attempt any operations other than those included below.*

Before making any adjustments with the engine running, set the parking brake and block the wheels. Make sure the engine is at normal operating temperature and that any power accessories are turned off.

CURB IDLE SPEED

Adjust the curb idle speed as you would on a conventional carburetor. Check the emission control decal under the hood for the proper idle speed, or see the specs in the Tune Up section.

INTERNAL VENT ADJUSTMENT

This adjustment must be checked whenever the curb idle speed is adjusted. After you have set the curb idle, place an .010 feeler gauge between the accelerator pump stem and the pump operating link. Turn the adjusting nut until there is just a slight drag when the gauge is removed.

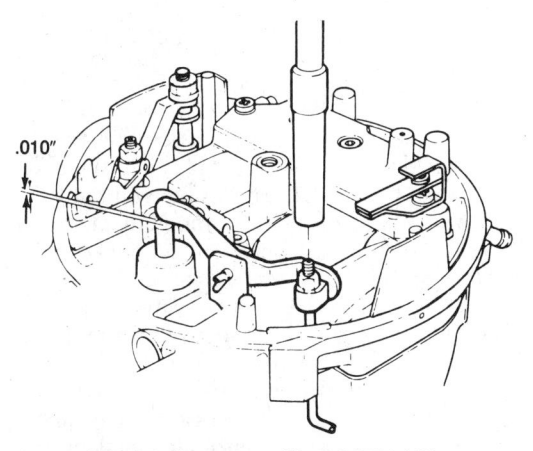

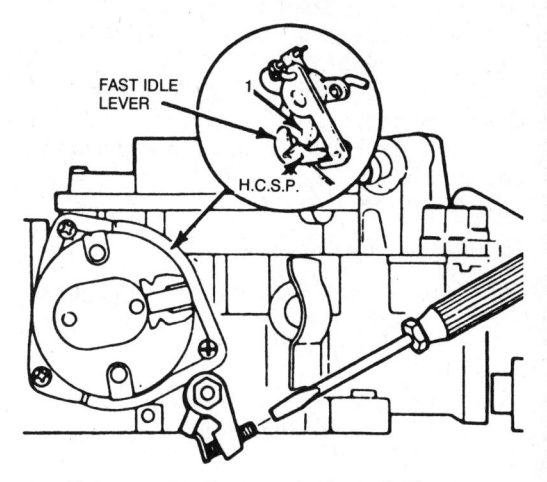

Fast idle speed adjustment—Model 2700 VV

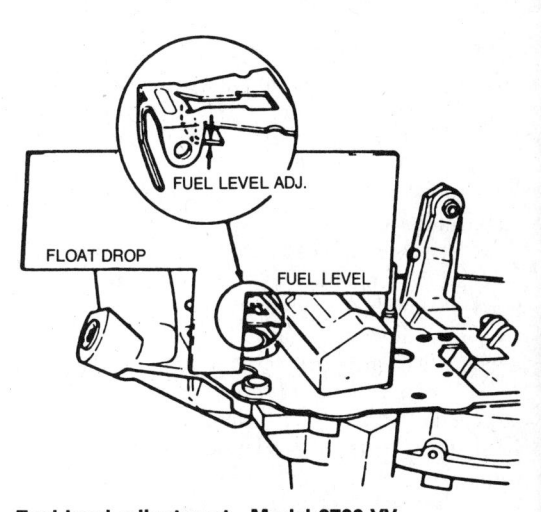

Fuel level adjustment—Model 2700 VV

Internal vent adjustment—Model 2700 VV

FAST IDLE SPEED

With the engine idling, EGR valve disconnected and the vacuum line plugged, make sure the fast idle lever is on the second step of the fast idle cam. Turn the fast idle adjusting screw clockwise to increase speed and counterclockwise to decrease speed.

YFA Carburetor Adjustments

CHOKE ADJUSTMENT

Piston Type Choke

NOTE: *This adjustment requires that the thermostatic spring housing and gasket (choke cap) are removed. Refer to the "Choke Cap" removal procedure below.*

1. Remove the air cleaner assembly, then the choke cap.
2. Bend a 0.026 in. diameter wire gauge at a 90 degree angle approximately ⅛ in. from one end. Insert the bent end of the gauge between the choke piston slot and the right hand slot in the choke housing. Rotate the choke piston lever counterclockwise until the gauge is shut in the piston slot.
3. Apply light pressure on the choke piston lever to hold the gauge in place. Then measure

EMISSION CONTROLS AND FUEL SYSTEM

the clearance between the lower edge of the choke plate and the carburetor bore using a drill with the diameter equal to the specified pulldown clearance.

4. Bend the choke piston lever to obtain the proper clearance.
5. Install the choke cap.

Diaphragm Type Choke

1. Activate the pulldown motor by applying an external vacuum source.
2. Close the choke plate as far as possible without forcing it.
3. Using a drill of the specified size, measure the clearance between the lower edge of the choke plate and the air horn wall.
4. If adjustment is necessary, bend the choke diaphragm link as required.

Choke Cap Removal

NOTE: *The automatic choke has two rivets and a screw, retaining the choke cap in place. There is a locking and indexing plate to prevent misadjustment.*

1. Remove the air cleaner assembly from the carburetor.
2. Check choke cap retaining ring rivets to determine if mandrel is well below the rivet head. If mandrel appears to be at or within the rivet head thickness, drive it down or out with a 1/16 inch diameter punch.
3. Use a 1/8 inch diameter of No. 32 drill. (.128 inch diameter) for drilling the rivet heads. Drill into the rivet head until the rivet head comes loose from the rivet body.
4. After the rivet head is removed, drive the remaining portion of the rivet out of the hole with a 1/8 inch diameter punch.

NOTE: *This procedure must be followed to retain the hole size.*

5. Repeat Steps 1–4 for the remaining rivet.
6. Remove the screw in the conventional manner.

Installation

1. Install choke cap gasket.
2. Install the locking and indexing plate.
3. Install the notched gasket.
4. Install choke cap, making certain that bimetal loop is positioned around choke lever tang.
5. While holding cap in place, actuate choke plate to make certain bimetal loop is properly engaged with lever tang. Set retaining clamp over choke cap and orient clamp to match holes in casting (holes are not equally spaced). Make sure retaining clamp is not upside down.
6. Place rivet in rivet gun and trigger lightly to retain rivet (1/8 inch diameter × 1/2 inch long × 1/4 inch diameter head).
7. Press rivet fully into casting after passing through retaining clamp and pop rivet (mandrel breaks off).
8. Repeat this step for the remaining rivet.
9. Install screw in conventional manner. Tighten to (17–20 lb-in.)

FLOAT ADJUSTMENT

1. Invert the air horn assembly and check the clearance from the top of the float to the surface of the air horn with a T-scale. The air horn should be held at eye level when gauging and the float arm should be resting on the needle pin.
2. Do not exert pressure on the needle valve when measuring or adjusting the float. Bend the float arm as necessary to adjust the float level.

CAUTION: *Do not bend the tab at the end of the float arm as it prevents the float from striking the bottom of the fuel bowl when empty and keeps the needle in place.*

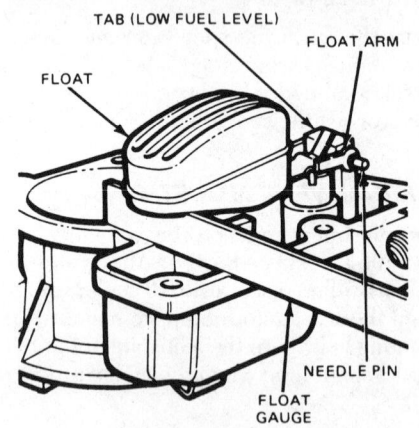

Float level adjustment—Carter YFA

DE-CHOKE ADJUSTMENT

1. Remove the air cleaner assembly.
2. Hold the throttle plate fully open and close the choke plate as far as possible without forcing it. Use a drill of the proper diameter to check the clearance between the choke plate and air horn.
3. If the clearance is not within specification, adjust by bending the arm on the choke lever of the throttle lever. Bending the arm downward will decrease the clearance, and bending it upward will increase the clearance. **Always recheck the clearance after making any adjustment.**

FAST IDLE CAM ADJUSTMENT

1. Put the fast idle screw on the second highest step of the fast idle cam against the shoulder of the high step.
2. Adjust by bending the choke plate connecting rod to obtain the specified clearance

EMISSION CONTROLS AND FUEL SYSTEM

between the lower edge of the choke plate and the air horn wall.

Holley Model 4180—C

The Holley 4180–C 4–V carburetor is a downdraft, two-stage carburetor. It can be considered as two dual carburetors; one supplying a fuel/air mixture throughout the entire range of engine operation (primary stage), and the other functioning only when a greater quantity of fuel/air mixture is required (secondary stage).

The **primary stage** (front section of the carburetor contains a fuel bowl, metering block, and an accelerating pump assembly. The primary barrels each contain a primary and booster venturi, main fuel discharge nozzle, throttle plate, and idle fuel passage. The Model 4180–C uses an electric choke with hot air assist.

The **secondary stage,** (rear section) of the carburetor contains a fuel bowl, metering body, and secondary throttle operating diaphragm assembly. Each secondary barrel contains a primary and booster venturi, idle fuel passages, main secondary fuel discharge nozzle, throttle plate, and a transfer system fuel passage from the primary fuel bowl.

A fuel inlet system for both the primary and the secondary stages for the carburetor provides the fuel metering systems with a constant supply of fuel.

The 4180–C carburetor is used on the 1983 Ford Mustang with the 302 V8 engine.

ACCELERATING PUMP LEVER ADJUSTMENT

1. Using a feeler gauge and with the throttle plates (primary throttle plates) in the wide open position, there should be the specified clearance between the accelerating pump operating lever adjustment screw head and the pump arm when the pump arm is depressed manually.
2. If adjustment is required, loosen and then hold the lock screw and turn the adjusting nut in to increase the clearance and out to decrease the clearance. One half turn of the adjusting nut is equal to approximately 0.015 in. (0.381 mm). When the proper adjustment has been obtained hold the adjustment in position with a wrench and tighten the nut.

FUEL LEVEL FLOAT ADJUSTMENT—DRY

The dry float adjustment is a preliminary fuel level adjustment only. The final adjustment ("Fuel Level Adjustment—Wet") must be performed after the carburetor is installed on the engine.

With the fuel bowls and float assemblies removed, adjust the floats so that the floats are parallel to the fuel bowls, with the top of the fuel bowls inverted.

FUEL LEVEL ADJUSTMENT—WET

The fuel pump pressure and volume must be to specifications prior to performing the following adjustments.

1. Operate the engine to normalize engine temperatures and place the vehicle on a flat surface, as near level as possible. Remove the air cleaner, if it was not previously removed.
2. Run engine at 1000 rpm for about 30 seconds to stabilize the fuel level.
3. Stop engine and remove sight plug on side of primary carburetor bowl.
4. Check fuel level. It should be at bottom of sight plug hole. If fuel spills out when sight plug is removed, lower fuel level. If fuel level is below sight plug hole, raise fuel level.

CAUTION: *Do not loosen lock screw or nut or attempt to adjust fuel level with sight plug removed or engine running because fuel may spray out creating a fire hazard.*

5. Adjust the front level as necessary by loosening the lock screw, and turning the adjusting nut clockwise to **lower** fuel level or counterclockwise to **raise** fuel level. ($\frac{1}{6}$ turn adjusting nut will change fuel level approximately $\frac{1}{32}$ inch). Tighten lock screw and install sight plug, using old gasket. Start engine and run at 1000 rpm for about 30 seconds to stabilize fuel level.
6. Stop engine, remove sight plug and check fuel level. Repeat Step 5 until fuel level is at bottom of sight plug hole. When fuel level is at bottom of sight plug hole, install sight plug using new adjusting plug gasket.
7. Repeat Steps 3–6 for secondary fuel bowl.

NOTE: *The secondary throttle must be used to stabilize the fuel level in the secondary fuel bowl.*

SECONDARY THROTTLE PLATE ADJUSTMENT

1. With carburetor off the engine, hold the secondary throttle plates closed.
2. Turn the secondary throttle shaft lever adjusting screw (stop screw) out (counterclockwise) until the secondary throttle plates seat in the throttle bores.
3. Turn the screw in clockwise until the screw JUST contacts the secondary lever, then turn screw in (clockwise) $\frac{1}{4}$ turn.

CHOKE PULLDOWN ADJUSTMENT

1. Remove the choke thermostat housing, gasket and retainer. See the choke cap removal and installation procedure below.
2. Insert a piece of wire into the choke piston bore to move the piston down against the

EMISSION CONTROLS AND FUEL SYSTEM

stop screw. Maintain light closing pressure on the choke plate and measure the gap between the lower edge of the choke plate and the air horn wall.

3. To adjust, remove the putty covering the adjustment screw and turn the screw clockwise to decrease or counter-clockwise to increase the gap setting. Take care to close the choke plate during screw adjustment. Screw may be turned into side of piston, resulting in damage to piston.

4. Reinstall the choke thermostatic housing, gasket, and retainer.

DECHOKE ADJUSTMENT

1. Hold the throttle in the wide open position.
2. Apply light closing pressure to the choke plate and measure the gap between the lower edge of the choke plate and the air horn wall.
3. To adjust, bend the pawl on the fast idle lever.

CHOKE THERMOSTATIC SPRING HOUSING—(CHOKE CAP)

Removal

1. Remove the carburetor from vehicle.
2. Using a hacksaw carefully cut a slot in the head of the breakaway screw. Using a proper sized straight blade screw driver, remove the breakaway screw in the conventional manner.
3. Repeat Step 2 for the remaining breakaway screw.
4. Remove the remaining standard screw. Remove the retaining ring, choke cap and gasket.

Installation

1. Install the choke cap gasket. Install the choke cap by engaging the bimetal loop on the choke thermostatic lever.
2. Install the retaining ring. Loosely install two new breakaway screws and one standard screw.
3. Align the choke cap to the proper index mark.
4. Tighten the breakaway screws until the heads break off. Tighten the remaining screw to 16–18 inch lbs. (1.8–2.0 Nm).
5. Install carburetor on the vehicle.

FAST IDLE CAM SET

1. Rotate the choke cap 45-degrees counter-clockwise (rich) to close the choke plate. Tighten the attaching screw at the time.
2. Open and close the throttle to place the fast idle screw on the top step of the cam.
3. Place a pulldown gauge between the lower edge of the choke plate and the air horn wall, then open and close the throttle to allow the fast idle cam to drop.
4. Press upward on the fast idle cam. There should be little or no movement indicating that the fast idle screw is on the kickdown (2nd) step of the cam, against the first step.

FUEL INJECTION

Central Fuel Injection

DESCRIPTION

Central Fuel Injection (CFI) is a throttle body injection system in which two fuel injectors are mounted in a common throttle body, spraying fuel down through the throttle valves at the bottom of the body and into the intake manifold.

OPERATION

Fuel is supplied from the fuel tank by a high pressure, in-tank fuel pump. The fuel passes through a filter and is sent to the throttle body where a regulator keeps the fuel delivery pressure at a constant 39 psi. The two fuel injectors are mounted vertically above the throttle plates and are connected in line with the fuel pressure regulator. Excess fuel supplied by the pump, but not needed by the engine, is returned to the fuel tank by a steel fuel return line.

The fuel injection system is linked with and controlled by the Electronic Engine Control (EEC) system.

Air and Fuel Control

The throttle body assembly is comprised of six individual components which perform the job of mixing the air and fuel to the ideal ratio for controlling exhaust emissions and providing performance and economy. The six components are: air control, fuel injector nozzles, fuel pressure regulator, fuel pressure diagnostic valve, cold engine speed control, and throttle position sensor.

Air Control

Air flow to the engine is controlled by two butterfly valves mounted in a two-piece, die-cast aluminum housing called the throttle body. The butterfly valves, or throttle valves, are identical in design to the throttle plates of a conventional carburetor and are actuated by a similar linkage and pedal cable arrangement.

Fuel Injector Nozzles

The fuel injector nozzles are mounted in the throttle body and are electro-mechanical devices which meter and atomize the fuel deliv-

EMISSION CONTROLS AND FUEL SYSTEM 131

ered to the engine. The injector valve bodies consist of a solenoid actuated pintle and needle valve assembly. An electrical control signal from the EED electronic processor activates the solenoid causing the pintle to move inward off its seat and allowing fuel to flow. The fuel flow through the injector is controlled by the amount of time the injector solenoid holds the pintle off its seat.

Fuel Pressure Regulator

The fuel pressure regulator is mounted on the throttle body. The regulator smooths out fuel pressure drops from the fuel pump. It is not sensitive to back pressure in the return line to the tank.

A second function of the pressure regulator is to maintain fuel supply pressure upon engine and fuel pump shut down. The regulator acts as a check valve and traps fuel between itself and the fuel pump. This promotes rapid start ups and helps prevent fuel vapor formation in the lines, or vapor lock. The regulator makes sure that the pressure of the fuel at the injector nozzles stays at a constant 39 psi.

Fuel Pressure Diagnostic Valve

A Schrader-type diagnostic pressure valve is located at the top of the throttle body. This valve can be used by service personnel to monitor fuel pressure, bleed down the system pressure prior to maintenance and to bleed out air which may have been introduced during assembly or filter servicing. A special Ford tool (T80L-9974-A) is used to accomplish these procedures.

CAUTION: *Under no circumstances should compressed air be forced into the fuel system using the diagnostic valve.*

Cold Engine Speed Control

The cold engine speed control serves the same purpose as the fast idle speed device on a carbureted engine, which is to raise engine speed during cold engine idle. A throttle stop cam positioner is used. The cam is positioned by a bimetal spring and an electric heating element. The cold engine speed control is attached to the throttle body. As the engine heats up, the fast idle cam on the cold engine speed control is gradually repositioned by the bimetal spring, heating element and EEC computer until normal idle speed is reached. The EEC computer automatically kicks down the fast idle cam to a lower step (lower engine speed) by supplying vacuum to the automatic kickdown motor which physically moves the high speed cam a predetermined time after the engine starts.

Throttle Position Sensor

This sensor is attached to the throttle body and is used to monitor changes in throttle plate position. The throttle position sensor sends this information to the computer, which uses it to select proper air/fuel mixture, spark timing and EGR control under different engine operating conditions.

Fuel System Inertia Switch

In the event of a collision, the electrical contacts in the inertia switch open and the fuel pump automatically shuts off. The fuel pump will shut off even if the engine does not stop running. The engine, however, will stop a few seconds after the fuel pump stops. It is not possible to restart the engine until the inertia switch is manually reset. The switch is located in the luggage compartment on the left hinge support on all models. To reset, depress both buttons on the switch at the same time.

CAUTION: *Do not reset the inertia switch until the complete fuel system has been inspected for leaks.*

FUEL CHARGING ASSEMBLY REMOVAL AND INSTALLATION

1. Remove the air cleaner.
2. Release the pressure from the fuel system at the diagnostic valve using Tool T80L-9974-A or its equivalent.
3. Disconnect the throttle cable and transmission throttle valve lever.
4. Disconnect the fuel, vacuum and electrical connections. Use care to prevent combustion of spilled fuel.
5. Remove the fuel charging assembly retaining nuts then remove the fuel charging assembly.
6. Remove the mounting gasket from the intake manifold.
7. Installation is the reverse of removal. Tighten the fuel charging assembly nuts to 120 inch lb.

THROTTLE BODY DISASSEMBLY/ASSEMBLY

1. Remove the air cleaner mounting stud in order to separate the upper body from the throttle body.
2. Turn the fuel charging assembly (Throttle Body) over and remove the four screws from the bottom of the throttle body.
3. Separate the throttle body (lower half) from the main body (upper half).
4. Remove the old gasket. If stuck and scraping is necessary, use only a plastic or dull scraper. Take care not to damage gasket surfaces.

5. Remove the three pressure regulator mounting screws. Remove the pressure regulator.

6. Disconnect the electrical connectors at each injector by pulling outward on the connector and not on the wire. Loosen but do not remove the wiring harness retaining screw. Push in on the harness tabs to remove from the upper body.

7. Remove the fuel injector retaining screw. Remove the injection retainer.

8. Pull the injectors, one at a time, from the upper body. Mark the injectors for identification; they must be reinstalled in the same position (choke or throttle side). Each injector is equipped with a small O-ring. If the O-ring does not come out with the injector, carefully pick out of body.

9. Remove the fuel diagnostic valve assembly.

10. Remove the choke cover by drilling the retaining rivets. A ⅛ in. or No. 30 drill is required. A choke mounting kit for reinstallation is available from Ford.

11. Remove the choke cap retaining ring, choke cap and gasket. Remove the thermostat lever screw and lever. Remove the fast idle cam assembly and control rod positioner.

12. Hold the control diaphragm cover in position and remove the two mounting screws. Carefully remove the cover, spring and pull down diaphragm.

13. Remove the fast idle retaining nut, fast idle cam adjuster lever, fast idle lever and E-clip.

14. Remove the potentionmeter (sensor) connector bracket retaining screw. Mark the throttle body and throttle position sensor for correct reinstallation position. Remove the throttle sensor retaining screws and slide the sensor off of the throttle shaft. Remove the throttle positioner retaining screw and remove the throttle positioner.

15. Perform any necessary cleaning or repair.

16. Assemble the upper body by first installing the fuel diagnostic fuel pressure valve assembly.

17. Lubricate the new injector O-rings with a light grade oil. Install the O-rings on each injector. Install the injectors in their appropriate choke or throttle side position. Use a light, twisting, pushing motion to install the injectors.

18. Install the injector retainer and tighten the retaining screw to 30–60 inch lbs.

19. Install the injector wiring harness and snap into position. Tighten the harness retaining screw to 8–10 inch lbs.

20. Snap the electrical connectors into position on the injectors. Lubricate the fuel pressure regulator O-ring with light oil. Install the O-ring and new gasket on the regulator, install the regulator and tighten retaining screws to 27–40 inch lbs.

21. Install the throttle positioner onto the throttle body. Tighten the retaining screw to 32–44 inch lbs.

22. Hold the throttle sensor (potentiometer) with the location identification mark (see step 14) in the 12 o'clock position. The two rotary tangs should be at 3 o'clock and 9 o'clock positions.

23. Slide the sensor onto the throttle shaft with the identification mark still in the 12 o'clock position. Hold the sensor firmly against the throttle body.

24. Rotate the sensor until the identification marks on the sensor and body are aligned. Install the retaining screws and tighten to 13–18 inch lbs.

25. Install the sensor wiring harness bracket retaining screw, tighten to 18–22 inch lbs. Install the E-clip, fast idle lever, fast idle adjustment lever and fast idle retaining nut. Tighten the retaining nut to 16–20 inch lbs.

26. Install the pull down diaphragm, spring and cover. Hold the cover in position and tighten the retaining screws to 13–19 inch lbs.

27. Install the fast idle control rod positioner, fast idle cam and the thermostat lever. Tighten the retaining screw to 13–19 inch lbs.

28. Install the choke cap gasket, bi-metal spring, cap and retaining ring. Install new rivets and snug them with the rivet gun. Do not break rivets, loosely install so choke cover can rotate. Index choke and break rivets to tighten.

29. Install the gasket between the main body and the throttle body. Place the throttle body in position. Install the four retaining screws loosely. Install the air cleaner stud and tighten to 70–95 inch lbs. Tighten the four retaining screws.

30. The rest of the assembly is in the reverse order of disassembly.

ELECTRONIC CONTROL SYSTEM

Electronic Control Assembly (ECA)

The Electronic Control Assembly (ECA) is a solid-state micro-computer consisting of a processor assembly and a calibration assembly. It is located under the instrument panel or passenger's seat and is usually covered by a kick panel. 1981–82 models use an EEC III engine control system, while 1983 and later models use the EEC IV. Although the two systems are similar in appearance and operation, the ECA units are not interchangeable. A multipin connector links the ECA with all system compo-

EMISSION CONTROLS AND FUEL SYSTEM

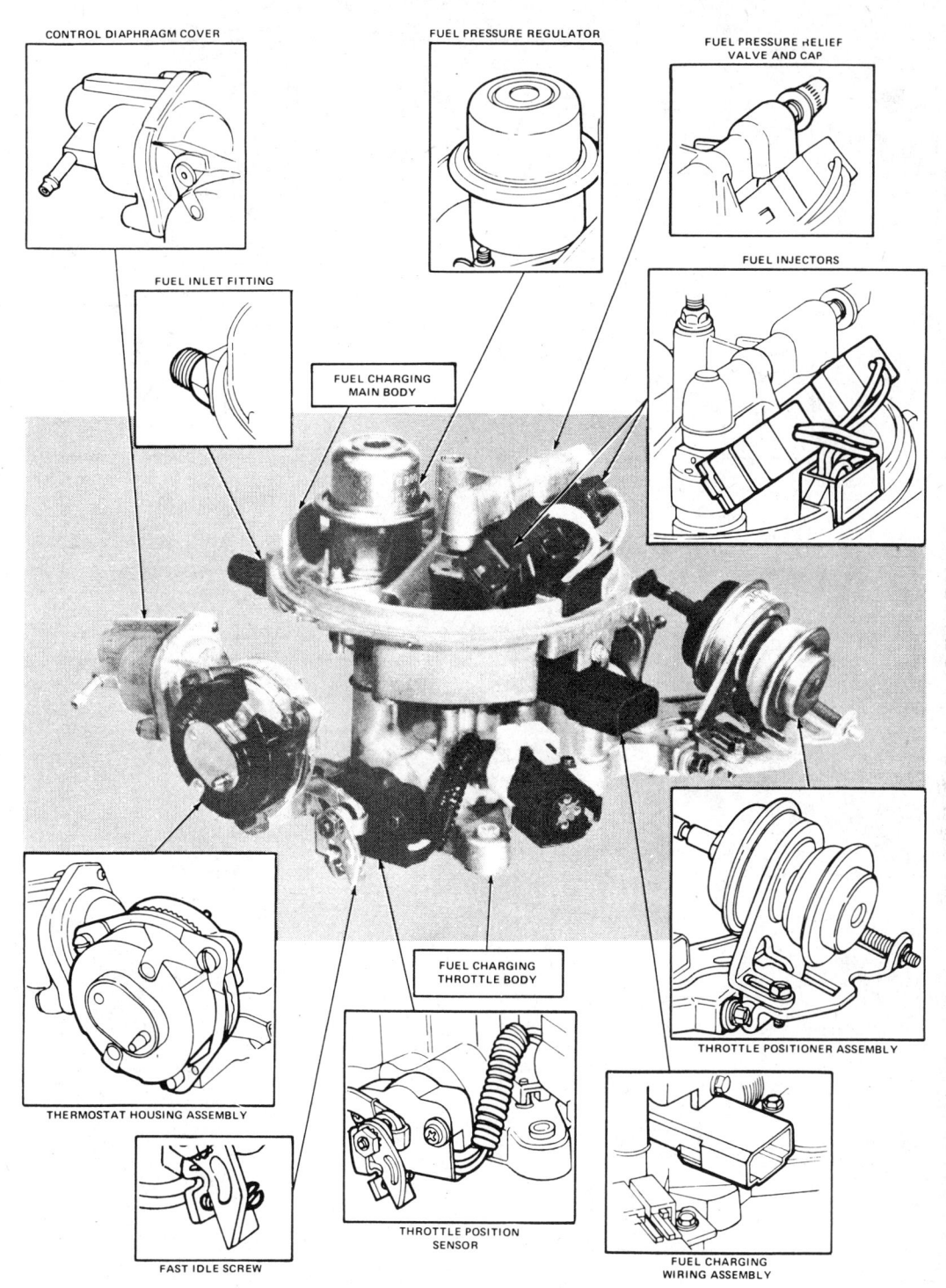

CFI fuel injection 5.0L engine

nents. The processor assembly is housed in an aluminum case. It contains circuits designed to continuously sample input signals from the engine sensors. It then calculates and sends out proper control signals to adjust air/fuel ratio, spark timing and emission system operation. The processor also provides a continuous reference voltage to the B/MAP, EVP and TPS sensors. EEC III reference voltage is 8–10 volts, while EEC IV systems use a 5 bolt reference signal. The calibration assembly is contained in a black plastic housing which plugs into the top of the

134 EMISSION CONTROLS AND FUEL SYSTEM

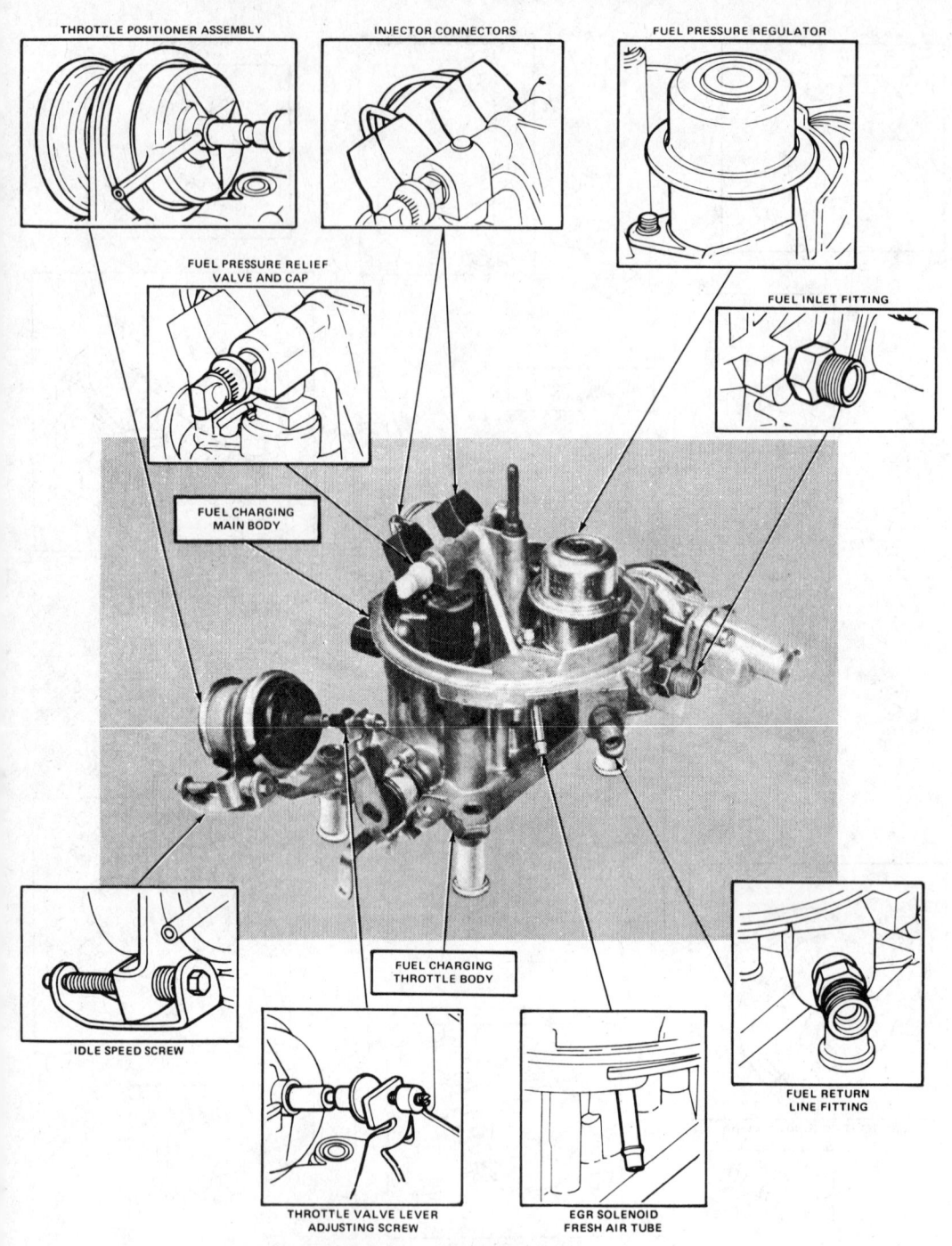

CFI fuel injection 5.0L engine left side view

processor assembly. It contains the memory and programming information used by the processor to determine optimum operating conditions. Different calibration information is used in different vehicle applications, such as California or Federal models. For this reason, careful identification of the engine, year, model and type of electronic control system is essential to insure correct component replacement.

ENGINE SENSORS

Air Charge Temperature Sensor (ACT)

The ACT is threaded into the intake manifold air runner. It is located behind the distributor on V6 engines and directly below the accelerator linkage on V8 engines. The ACT monitors air/fuel charge temperature and sends an appropriate signal to the ECA. This information

EMISSION CONTROLS AND FUEL SYSTEM

is used to correct fuel enrichment for variations in intake air density due to temperature changes.

Barometric & Manifold Absolute Pressure Sensors (B/MAP)

The B/MAP sensor on V8 engines is located on the right fender panel in the engine compartment. The MAP sensor used on V6 engines is separate from the barometric sensor and is located on the left fender panel in the engine compartment. The barometric sensor signals the ECA of changes in atmospheric pressure and density to regulate calculated air flow into the engine. The MAP sensor monitors and signals the ECA of changes in intake manifold pressure which result from engine load, speed and atmospheric pressure changes.

Crankshaft Position (CP) Sensor

The purpose of the CP sensor is to provide the ECA with an accurate ignition timing reference (when the piston reaches 10° BTDC) and injector operation information (twice each crankshaft revolution). The crankshaft vibration damper is fitted with a "pulse ring." As the crankshaft rotates, the pulse ring lobes interrupt the magnetic field at the tip of the CP sensor.

EGR Valve Position Sensor (EVP)

This sensor, mounted on EGR valve, signals the computer of EGR opening so that it may subtract flow from total air flow into the manifold. In this way, EGR flow is excluded from air flow information used to determine mixture requirements.

Engine Coolant Temperature Sensor (ECT)

The ECT is threaded into the intake manifold water jacket directly above the water pump bypass hose. The ECT monitors coolant temperature and signals the ECA, which then uses these signals for mixture enrichment (during cool operation), ignition timing and EGR operation. The resistance value of the ECT increases with temperature, causing a voltage signal drop as the engine warms up.

Exhaust Gas Oxygen Sensor (EGO)

The EGO is mounted in the right side exhaust manifold on V8 engines, in the left and right side exhaust manifolds on V6 models. The EGO monitors oxygen content of exhaust gases and sends a constantly changing voltage signal to the ECA. The ECA analyzes this signal and adjusts the air/fuel mixture to obtain the optimum (stoichiometric) ratio.

Knock Sensor (KS)

This sensor is used on various models equipped with the 3.8L V6 engine. It is attached to the intake manifold in front of the ACT sensor. The KS detects engine vibrations caused by preignition or detonation and provides information to the ECA, which then retards the timing to eliminate detonation.

Thick Film Integrated Module Sensor (TFI)

The TFI module sensor plugs into the distributor just below the distributor cap and replaces the CP sensor on some engines. Its function is to provide the ECA with ignition timing information, similar to what the CP sensor provides.

Throttle Position Sensor (TPS)

The TPS is mounted on the right side of the throttle body, directly connected to the throttle shaft. The TPS senses throttle movement and position and transmits an appropriate electrical signal to the ECA. These signals are used by the ECA to adjust the air/fuel mixture, spark timing and EGR operation according to engine load to idle, part throttle, or full throttle. The TPS is nonadjustable.

ON-CAR SERVICE

NOTE: *Diagnostic and test procedures on the EEC III and EEC IV electronic control systems require special test equipment. Have the testing done by a professional.*

Fuel Pressure Tests

The diagnostic pressure valve (Schrader type) is located at the top of the Fuel charging main body. This valve provides a convenient point for service personnel to monitor fuel pressure, bleed down the system pressure prior to maintenance, and to bleed out air which may become trapped in the system during filter replacement. A pressure gauge with an adapter is required to perform pressure tests.

CAUTION: *Under no circumstances should compressed air be forced into the fuel system using the diagnostic valve. Depressing the pin in the diagnostic valve will relieve system pressure by expelling fuel into the throttle body.*

System Pressure Test

Testing fuel pressure requires the use of a special pressure gauge (T80L-9974-A or equivalent) that attaches to the diagnostic pressure tap on the fuel charging assembly. Depressurize the fuel system before disconnecting any lines.

1. Disconnect fuel return line at throttle body (in-tank high pressure pump) or at fuel rail (in-

EMISSION CONTROLS AND FUEL SYSTEM

line high pressure and in-tank low pressure pumps) and connect the hose to a one-quart calibrated container. Connect pressure gauge.

2. Disconnect the electrical connector to the fuel pump. The connector is located ahead of fuel tank (in-tank high pressure pump) or just forward of pump outlet (in-line high pressure pump). Connect auxiliary wiring harness to connector of fuel pump. Energize the pump for 10 seconds by applying 12 volts to the auxiliary harness connector, allowing the fuel to drain into the calibrated container. Note the fuel volume and pressure gauge reading.

3. Correct fuel pressure should be 35–45 psi (241–310 kPa). Fuel volume should be 10 ozs. in 10 seconds (aluminum) and fuel pressure should maintain minimum 30 psi (206 kPa) immediately after pump cut-off

If pressure condition is met, but fuel flow is not, check for blocked filter(s) and fuel supply lines. After correcting problem, repeat test procedure. If fuel flow is still inadequate, replace high pressure pump. If flow specification is met but pressure is not, check for worn or damaged pressure regulator valve on throttle body. If both pressure and fuel flow specifications are met, but pressure drops excessively after de-energization, check for leaking injector valve(s) and/or pressure regulator valve. If injector valves and pressure regulator valve are okay, replace high pressure pump. If no pressure or flow is seen in fuel system, check for blocked filters and fuel lines. If no trouble is found, replace in-line fuel pump, in-tank fuel pump and the fuel filter inside the tank.

Fuel Injector Pressure Test

1. Connect pressure gauge T80L-9974-A, or equivalent, to fuel pressure test fitting. Disconnect coil connector from coil. Disconnect electrical lead from one injector and pressurize fuel system. Disable fuel pump by disconnecting inertia switch or fuel pump relay and observe pressure gauge reading.

2. Crank engine for 2 seconds. Turn ignition OFF and wait 5 seconds, then observe pressure drop. If pressure drop is 2–16 psi (14–110 kPa), the injector is operating properly. Reconnect injector, activate fuel pump, then repeat the procedure for other injector.

3. If pressure drop is less than 2 psi (14 kPa) or more than 16 psi (110 kPa), switch electrical connectors on injectors and repeat test. If pressure drop is still incorrect, replace disconnected injector with one of the same color code, then reconnect both injectors properly and repeat test.

4. Disconnect and plug vacuum hose to EGR valve. It may be necessary to disconnect the idle speed control (3.8L V6) or throttle kicker solenoid (5.0L V8) and use the throttle body stop screw to set engine speed. Start and run the engine at 1800 RPM (2000 rpm on 1984 and later models). Disconnect left injector electrical connector. Note rpm after engine stabilizes (around 1200 rpm). Reconnect injector and allow engine to return to high idle.

5. Perform same procedure for right injector. Note difference between rpm readings of left and right injectors. If difference is 100 rpm or less, check the oxygen sensor. If difference is more than 100 rpm, replace both injectors.

CFI COMPONENT TESTS

NOTE: *Complete CFI system diagnosis requires the use of special test equipment. Have the system tested professionally.*

Before beginning any component testing, always check the following:

• Check ignition and fuel systems to ensure there is fuel and spark.

• Remove air cleaner assembly and inspect all vacuum and pressure hoses for proper connection to fittings. Check for damaged or pinched hoses.

• Inspect all sub-system wiring harnesses for proper connections to the EGR solenoid valves, injectors, sensors, etc.

• Check for loose or detached connectors and broken or detached wires. Check that all terminals are sealed firmly and are not corroded. Look for partially broken or frayed wires or any shorting between wires.

• Inspect sensors for physical damage. Inspect vehicle electrical system. Check battery for full charge and cable connections for tightness.

• Inspect the relay connector and make sure the ECA power relay is securely attached and making a good ground connection.

High Pressure In-Tank Pump

Disconnect electrical connector just forward of the fuel tank. Connect voltmeter to body wiring harness connector. Turn key ON while watching voltmeter. Voltage should rise to battery voltage, then return to zero after about 1 second. Momentarily turn key to START position. Voltage should rise to about 8 volts while cranking. If voltage is not as specified, check electrical system.

High Pressure In-Line & Low Pressure In-Tank Pumps

Disconnect electrical connector at fuel pumps. Connect voltmeter to body wiring harness connector. Turn key ON while watching voltmeter. Voltage should rise to battery voltage, then return to zero after about 1 second. If voltage is not as specified, check inertia switch and

EMISSION CONTROLS AND FUEL SYSTEM

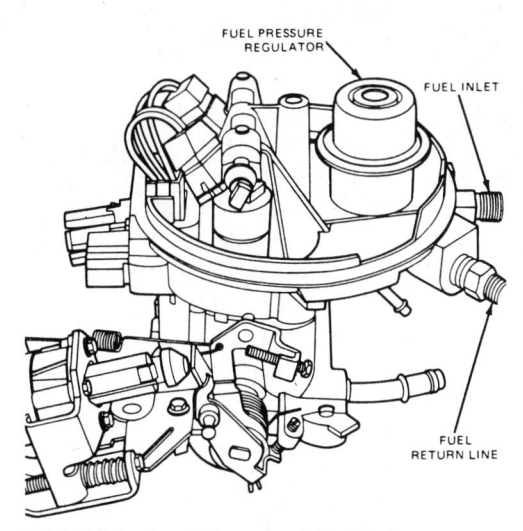

CFI fuel injection 3.8L engine left side view

CFI Resistance Specifications

Component	Resistance (Ohms)
Air Charge Temp (ACT)	
1981–83	1700–60,000
1984	1100–58,000
Coolant (ECT) Sensor	
1981–83	1100–8000
1984—Engine Off	1300–7700
1984—Engine On	1500–4500
Crank Position Sensor	100–640
FGB	30–70
EGR Vent Solenoid	30–70
Fuel Pump Relay	50–100
Throttle Kicker Solenoid	50–100
Throttle Position Sensor	
1981–83 Closed Throttle	3000–5000
1984 Closed Throttle	550–1100
Wide Open Throttle	More than 2100
TAB Solenoid	50–100
TAD Solenoid	50–100

electrical system. Connect ohmmeter to in-line pump wiring harness connector. If no continuity is present, check continuity directly at in-line pump terminals. If no continuity at in-line pump terminals, replace in-line pump. If continuity is present, service or replace wiring harness.

Connect ohmmeter across body wiring harness connector. If continuity is present (about 5 ohms), low pressure pump circuit is OK. If no continuity is present, remove fuel tank and check for continuity at in-tank pump flange terminals on top of tank. If continuity is absent at in-tank pump flange terminals, replace assembly. If continuity is present at in-tank pump but not in harness connector, service or replace wiring harness to in-tank pump.

Solenoid and Sensor Resistance Tests

All CFI components must be disconnected from the circuit before testing resistance with a suitable ohmmeter. Replace any component whose measured resistance does not agree with the specifications chart. Shorting the wiring harness across a solenoid valve can burn out the circuitry in the ECA that controls the solenoid valve actuator. Exercise caution when testing solenoid valves to avoid accidental damage to ECA.

Electronic Multi-Point Injection (EFI)

DESCRIPTION

The Electronic Fuel Injector System (EFI) is classified as a multi-point, pulse time, mass air flow fuel injection system. Fuel is metered into the intake air stream in accordance with engine demand through four injectors mounted on a tuned intake manifold. A blow-through turbocharger system is utilized to reduce fuel delivery time and increase power.

An on board vehicle electronic engine control (EEC) computer accepts inputs from various engine sensors to compute the required fuel flow rate necessary to maintain a pre-

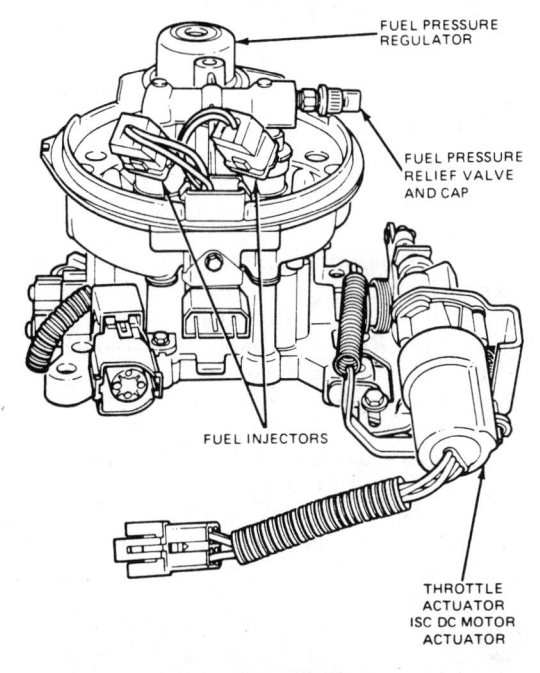

3.8L CFI CHARGING ASSEMBLY WITHOUT 10 PIN CONNECTOR

CFI fuel injection 3.8L engine

138 EMISSION CONTROLS AND FUEL SYSTEM

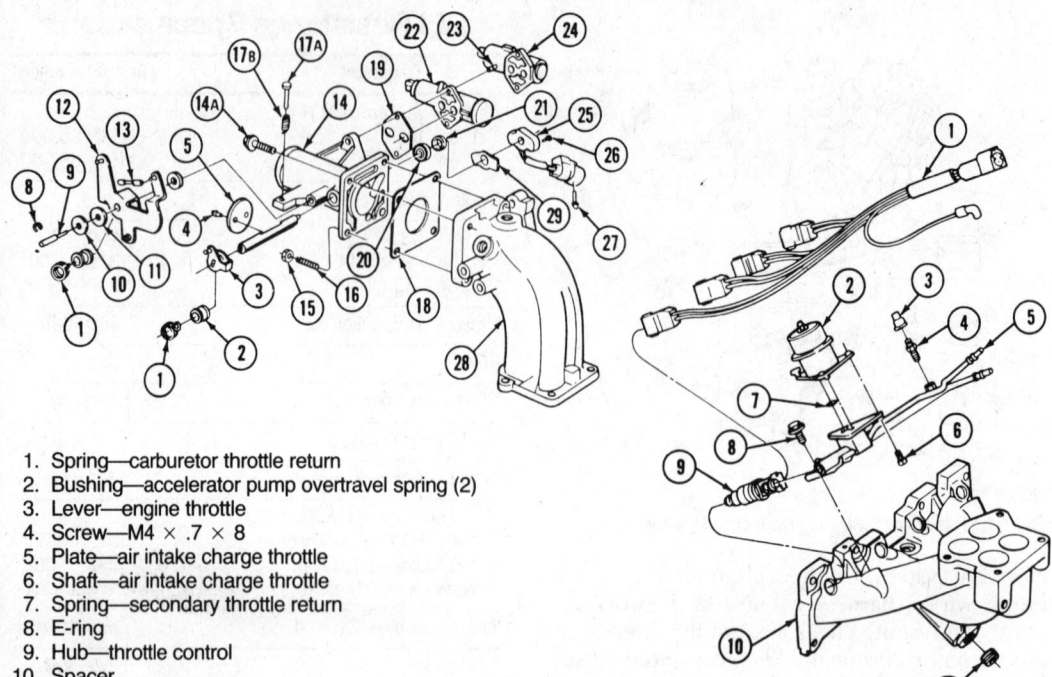

1. Spring—carburetor throttle return
2. Bushing—accelerator pump overtravel spring (2)
3. Lever—engine throttle
4. Screw—M4 × .7 × 8
5. Plate—air intake charge throttle
6. Shaft—air intake charge throttle
7. Spring—secondary throttle return
8. E-ring
9. Hub—throttle control
10. Spacer
11. Washer—nylon (2)
12. Lever—throttle control
13. Rod—engine secondary throttle control
14. Body—air intake charge throttle
14A. Bolt M8 × 1.25 × 30 hex flange head (2 req'd)
15. Nut—M8 (2 req'd)
16. Stud—M8 × 42.5 (2 req'd)
17A. Screw throttle stop
17B. Spring—throttle return control
18. Gasket—air charge control to intake manifold
19. Gasket—air bypass valve
20. Seal—throttle control shaft
21. Bushing—carburetor throttle shaft
22. Valve assembly—throttle air bypass
23. Bolt—M6 × 1.0 × 20 hex head flange
24. Valve assembly—throttle air bypass (alt.)
25. Potentiometer throttle position
26. Screw and washer assembly M4 × 22
27. Screw—M4 × 0.7 × 14.0 hex. washer tap
28. Manifold—intake upper
29. Gasket T.P.S.
1. Wiring harness—fuel charging
2. Regulator assembly—fuel pressure
3. Cap—fuel pressure relief
4. Valve assembly—fuel pressure relief
5. Manifold assembly—fuel injection fuel supply
6. Screw—M5 × 0.8 × 10 socket head (3 req'd)
7. Seal—5/16 × .070 o-ring
8. Bolt (2 req'd)
9. Injector assembly—fuel (4 req'd)
10. Manifold—intake lower
11. Plug

EFI fuel injection 2.3L engine

scribed air/fuel ration throughout the entire engine operational range. The computer than outputs a command to the fuel injectors to meter the approximate quantity of fuel.

OPERATION

The fuel delivery sub-system consists of a high pressure, chassis mounted, electric fuel pump delivering fuel from the fuel tank through a 20 micron fuel filter to a fuel charging manifold assembly.

The fuel charging manifold assembly incorporates electrically actuated fuel injectors directly above each of the engine's four intake ports. The injectors, when energized, spray a metered quantity of fuel into the intake air stream.

A constant fuel pressure drop is maintained across the injector nozzles by a pressure regulator. The regulator is connected in series with the fuel injectors and positioned down stream from them. Excess fuel supplied by the pump, but not required by the engine, passes through the regulator and returns to the fuel tank through a fuel return line.

All injectors are energized simultaneously, once every crankshaft revolution. The period of time that the injectors are energized (injector "on time" or the pulse width) is controlled by the vehicles' Engine Electronic Control (EEC) computer. Air entering the engine is measured by a vane air flow meter located between the air cleaner and the fuel charging manifold assembly. This air flow information and input from various other engine sensors is used to compute the required fuel flow rate neces-

EMISSION CONTROLS AND FUEL SYSTEM

sary to maintain a prescribed air/fuel ratio for the given engine operation. The computer determines the needed injector pulse width and outputs a command to the injector to meter the exact quantity of fuel.

COMPONENT DESCRIPTION

Fuel Injectors

The four fuel injector nozzles are electro-mechanical devices which both meter and atomize fuel delivered to the engine. The injectors are mounted in the lower intake manifold and are positioned so that their tips are directing fuel just ahead of the engine intake valves. The injector bodies consist of a solenoid actuated pintle and needle valve assembly. An electrical control signal from the Electronic Engine Control unit activates the injector solenoid causing the pintle to move inward off the seat, allowing fuel to flow. Since the injector flow orifice is fixed and the fuel pressure drop across the injector tip is constant, fuel flow to the engine is regulated by how long the solenoid is energized. Atomization is obtained by countouring the pintle at the point where the fuel separates.

Fuel Pressure Regulator

The fuel pressure regulator is attached to the fuel supply manifold assembly downstream of the fuel injectors. It regulates the fuel pressure supplied to the injectors. The regulator is a diaphragm operated relief valve in which one side of the diaphragm senses fuel pressure and the other side is subjected to intake manifold pressure. The nominal fuel pressure is established by a spring preload applied to the diaphragm. Balancing one side of the diaphragm with manifold pressure maintains a constant fuel pressure drop across the injectors. Fuel, in excess of that used by the engine, is bypassed through the regulator and returns to the fuel tank.

Air Vane Meter Assembly

The air vane meter assembly is located between the air cleaner and the throttle body and is mounted on a bracket near the LH shock tower. The vane air meter contains two sensors which furnish input to the Electronic Control Assembly—a vane airflow sensor and a vane air temperature. The air vane meter measures the mass of air flow to the engine. Air flow through the body moves a vane mounted on a pivot pin. This vane is connected to a variable resistor (potentiometer) which in turn is connected to a 5 volt reference voltage. The output of this potentiometer varies depending on the volume of air flowing through the sensor. The temperature sensor in the air vane meter measures the incoming air temperature. These two inputs, air volume and temperature, are used by the Electronic Control Assembly to compute the mass air flow. This valve is then used to compute the fuel flow necessary for the optimum air/fuel ratio which is fed to the injectors.

Air Throttle Body Assembly

The throttle body assembly controls air flow to the engine through a single butterfly-type valve. The throttle position is controlled by conventional cable/cam throttle linkage. The body is a single piece die casting made of aluminum. It has a single bore with an air bypass channel around the throttle plate. This bypass channel controls both cold and warm engine idle airflow control as regulated by an air bypass valve assembly mounted directly to the throttle body. The valve assembly is an electromechanical device controlled by the EEC computer. It incorporates a linear actuator which positions a variable area metering valve.

Other features of the air throttle body assembly include:
- An adjustment screw to set the throttle plate at a minimum idle airflow position.
- A preset stop to locate the WOT position.
- A throttle body mounted throttle position sensor.
- A PCV fresh air source located up-stream of the throttle plate.
- Individual ported vacuum taps (as required) for PCV and EVAP control signals.

Fuel Supply Manifold Assembly

The fuel supply manifold assembly is the component that delivers high pressure fuel from the vehicle fuel supply line to the four fuel injectors. The assembly consists of a single preformed tube or stamping with four injector connectors, a mounting flange for the fuel pressure regulator, a pressure relief valve for diagnostic testing or field service fuel system pressure bleed down and mounting attachments which locate the fuel manifold assembly and provide fuel injector retention.

Air Intake Manifold

The air intake manifold is a two piece (upper and lower intake manifold) aluminum casting. Runner lengths are tuned to optimize engine torque and power output. The manifold provides mounting flanges for the air throttle body assembly, fuel supply manifold and accelerator control bracketry and the EGR valve and supply tube. Vacuum taps are provided to support various engine accessories. Pockets for the fuel injectors are machined to prevent both air and fuel leakage. The pockets, in which the injectors are mounted, are placed to direct the in-

140 EMISSION CONTROLS AND FUEL SYSTEM

jector fuel spray immediately in front of each engine intake valve.

COMPONENT REMOVAL AND INSTALLATION

Fuel Charging Assembly

NOTE: *If any of the sub-assemblies are to be serviced and/or removed, with the fuel charging assembly mounted to the engine, the following steps must be taken.*

1. Make sure the ignition key is in the off position.
2. Drain the coolant from the radiator.
3. Disconnect the negative battery cable.
4. Remove the fuel cap to relieve fuel tank pressure.
5. Relieve the pressure from the fuel system at the pressure relief valve. Special tool T80L-9974-A or its equal is needed for this procedure.
6. Disconnect the fuel supply line.
7. Identify and disconnect the fuel return lines and vacuum connections.
8. Disconnect the injector wiring harness by disconnecting the ECT sensor in the heater supply tube, under the lower intake manifold.
9. Disconnect the air by-pass connector from EEC harness.

NOTE: *Not all assemblies may be serviceable while on the engine. In some cases, removal of the fuel charging assembly may facilitate service of the various sub-assemblies. To remove the entire fuel charging assembly, the following should be observed.*

10. Remove the engine air cleaner outlet tube between the vane air meter and air throttle body by loosening two clamps.
11. Disconnect and remove the accelerator and speed control cables (if so equipped) from the accelerator mounting bracket and throttle lever.
12. Disconnect the top manifold vacuum fitting connections by disconnecting:
    a. Rear vacuum line to the dash panel vacuum tree.
    b. Front vacuum line to the air cleaner and fuel pressure regulator.
13. Disconnect the PCV system by removing the following:
    a. Two large forward facing connectors on the throttle body and intake manifold.
    b. Throttle body port hose at the straight plastic connector.
    c. Canister purge line at the straight plastic connector.
    d. PCV hose at the valve cover.
    e. Unbolt the PCV separator support bracket from cylinder head and remove PCV system.
14. Disconnect the EGR vacuum line at the EGR valve.
15. Disconnect the EGR tube from the upper intake manifold by removing the two flange nuts.
16. Remove the dipstick and its tube.
17. Remove the fuel return line.
18. Remove six manifold mounting nuts.
19. Remove the manifold with wiring harness and gasket.
20. Installation is the reverse of removal. Tighten the manifold bolts 12–15 ft. lbs.

Fuel Pressure Regulator

NOTE: *Before attempting this procedure depressurize the fuel system.*

1. Remove the vacuum line at the pressure regulator.
2. Remove the three Allen retaining screws from the regulator housing.
3. Remove the pressure regulator, gasket and O-ring. Discard gasket and inspect O-ring for deterioration.

NOTE: *If scraping is necessary be careful not to damage the gasket surface.*

4. Installation is the reverse of removal. Lubricate the O-ring with light oil prior to installation. Tighten the three screws 27–40 inch lbs.

Fuel Injector Manifold Assembly

1. Remove the fuel tank cap. Release the pressure from the fuel system.
2. Disconnect the fuel supply and return lines.
3. Disconnect the wiring harness from the injectors.
4. Disconnect the vacuum line from the fuel pressure regulator valve.
5. Remove the two fuel injector manifold retaining bolts.
6. Carefully disengage the manifold from the fuel injectors. Remove the manifold.
7. Installation is the reverse of removal. Torque the fuel manifold bolts 15–22 ft. lbs.

Pressure Relief Valve

1. If the fuel charging assembly is mounted to engine, the fuel system must be depressurized.
2. Using an open end wrench or suitable deep well socket, remove the pressure relief valve from the injection manifold.
3. Installation is the reverse of removal. Torque the valve 48–84 inch lbs.

Throttle Position Sensor

1. Disconnect the throttle position sensor from the wiring harness.
2. Remove the two retaining screws.
3. Remove the throttle position sensor.

EMISSION CONTROLS AND FUEL SYSTEM

Ford Electronic Fuel Injection Troubleshooting

Symptom	Possible Problem Areas
Surging, backfire, misfire, runs rough	1. EEC distributor rotor registry ① 2. EGR solenoid(s) defective 3. Distributor, cap, body, rotor, ignition wires, plugs, coil defective 4. Pulse ring behind vibration damper misaligned or damaged 5. Spark plug fouling
Stalls on deceleration	1. EGR solenoid(s) or valve defective 2. EEC distributor rotor registry ①
Stalls at idle	1. Idle speed wrong 2. Throttle kicker not working
Hesitates on acceleration	1. Acceleration enrichment system defective 2. Fuel pump ballast bypass relay not working
Fuel pump noisy	1. Fuel pump ballast bypass relay not working
Engine won't start	1. Fuel pump power relay defective, no spark, EGR system defective, no or low fuel pressure 2. Crankshaft position sensor not sealed, clearance wrong, defective 3. Pulse ring behind vibration damper misaligned, sensor tabs damaged 4. Power and ground wires open or shorted, poor electrical connections 5. Inertia switch tripped
Engine starts and stalls or runs rough	1. Fuel pump ballast wire defective 2. Manifold absolute pressure (MAP) sensor circuit not working 3. Low fuel pressure 4. EGR system problem 5. Microprocessor and calibration assembly faulty
Starts hard when cold	1. Cranking signal circuit faulty

4. Installation is the reverse of removal. Torque the sensor screws 11–16 inch lbs.

NOTE: *This throttle position sensor is not adjustable.*

Air Bypass Valve Assembly

1. Disconnect the air bypass valve assembly connector from the wiring harness.
2. Remove the two air bypass valve retaining screws.
3. Remove the air bypass valve and gasket.

NOTE: *If necessary to remove the gasket by scraping, be careful not to damage the gasket surface.*

4. Installation is the reverse of removal. Torque the air bypass valve assembly 71–102 inch lbs.

Air Intake Throttle Body

1. Remove four throttle body nuts. Make sure that the throttle position sensor connector and air by-pass valve connector have been disconnected from the harness. Disconnect air cleaner outlet tube.
2. Identify and disconnect vacuum hoses.
3. Remove throttle bracket.
4. Carefully separate the throttle body from the upper intake manifold.
5. Remove and discard the gasket between the throttle body and the upper intake manifold.

NOTE: *If scraping is necessary be careful not to damage gasket surfaces, or allow any material to drop into the manifold.*

6. Installation is the reverse of removal. Tighten the throttle body to upper intake manifold nuts 12–15 ft. lbs.

Upper Intake Manifold

1. Disconnect the air cleaner outlet tube from the air intake throttle body.
2. Unplug the throttle position sensor from the wiring harness.
3. Unplug the air by-pass valve connector.
4. Remove three upper manifold retaining bolts.
5. Remove upper manifold assembly.
6. Remove and discard the gasket from the lower manifold assembly.

NOTE: *If scraping is necessary be careful not to damage gasket surfaces, or allow any material to drop into the lower manifold.*

7. Installation is the reverse of removal. Tighten the upper intake manifold bolts 15–22 ft. lbs. Use a new gasket between the manifolds.

142 EMISSION CONTROLS AND FUEL SYSTEM

Fuel Injector

NOTE: *The fuel system must be depressurized prior to starting this procedure.*

1. Disconnect the fuel supply and return lines.
2. Remove the vacuum line from the fuel pressure regulator.
3. Disconnect the wiring harness.
4. Remove the fuel injector manifold assembly.
5. Carefully remove the connectors from the individual injectors.
6. Grasping the injectors body, pull up while gently rocking the injector from side to side.
7. Inspect the injector O-rings (two per injector) for signs of deterioration. Replace as needed.
8. Inspect the injector "plastic hat" (covering the injector pintle) and washer for signs of deterioration. Replace as needed. If a hat is missing, look for it in the intake manifold.
9. Installation is the reverse of removal. Lubricate all O-rings with a light oil. Carefully seat the fuel injector manifold assembly on the four injectors and secure the manifold with the attaching bolts. Torque the bolts 15–22 ft. lbs.

Vane Air Meter

1. Loosen the hose clamp which secures engine air cleaner outlet hose to the vane meter assembly.
2. Remove air intake and outlet tube from the air cleaner.
3. Disengage four spring clamps and remove air cleaner front cover and air cleaner filter panel.
4. Remove the two screw and washer assemblies which secure the air meter to its bracket. Remove the vane air meter assembly.
5. Installation is the reverse of removal.

Fuel Tank

REMOVAL

1. Jack up the car, safely support the rear end with jackstands, and block the front wheels.
2. Drain the fuel from the tank.
3. Disconnect all fuel lines and hoses from the tank assembly.
4. Loosen the retaining straps at the adjusting bolts and remove the fuel tank.

INSTALLATION

1. While an assistant holds the fuel tank in position, install the retaining straps.
2. Check all fuel lines for cracks or splitting and replace as necessary. Connect all fuel lines.
3. Replace the fuel separator if found damaged or inoperable.
4. Tighten the retaining straps securely.

Motorcraft 2150 Specifications

Year	(9510)* Carburetor Identification	Dry Float Level (in.)	Wet Float Level (in.)	Pump Setting Hole # ①	Choke Plate Pulldown (in.)	Fast Idle Cam Linkage Clearance (in.)	Fast Idle (rpm)	Dechoke (in.)	Choke Setting
1979	D9AE-AHA	7/16	13/16	3	0.147	①	②	0.250	3 Rich
	D9AE-AJA	7/16	13/16	3	0.147	①	②	0.250	3 Rich
	D9AE-ANB	7/16	13/16	3	0.129	①	②	—	1 Rich
	D9AE-APB	7/16	13/16	3	0.129	①	②	—	1 Rich
	D9AE-AVB	7/16	13/16	3	0.129	①	②	—	1 Rich
	D9AE-AYA	7/16	13/16	3	0.129	①	②	—	1 Rich
	D9AE-AYB	7/16	13/16	3	0.129	①	②	—	1 Rich
	D9AE-TB	7/16	13/16	3	0.129	①	②	—	2 Rich
	D9AE-UB	7/16	13/16	3	0.129	①	②	—	2 Rich
	D9BE-VB	7/16	13/16	3	0.153	①	②	0.250	2 Rich
	D9BE-YB	7/16	13/16	3	0.153	①	②	—	2 Rich
	D9DE-NB	7/16	13/16	3	0.153	①	②	0.250	2 Rich
	D9DE-RA	7/16	13/16	2	0.125	①	②	0.115	3 Rich
	D9DE-RB	7/16	13/16	2	0.125	①	②	0.115	3 Rich
	D9DE-RD	7/16	13/16	2	0.125	①	②	—	3 Rich

EMISSION CONTROLS AND FUEL SYSTEM

Motorcraft 2150 Specifications (cont.)

Year	(9510) * Carburetor Identification	Dry Float Level (in.)	Wet Float Level (in.)	Pump Setting Hole # ①	Choke Plate Pulldown (in.)	Fast Idle Cam Linkage Clearance (in.)	Fast Idle (rpm)	Dechoke (in.)	Choke Setting
	D9DE-SA	7/16	13/16	2	0.125	①	②	0.250	3 Rich
	D9DE-SC	7/16	13/16	2	0.125	①	②	—	3 Rich
	D9ME-BA	7/16	13/16	2	0.136	①	②	0.115	Index
	D9ME-CA	7/16	13/16	2	0.136	①	②	0.115	Index
	D9OE-CB	7/16	13/16	3	0.132	①	②	0.115	3 Rich
	D9OE-DB	7/16	13/16	3	0.132	①	②	—	3 Rich
	D9OE-EA	7/16	13/16	3	0.132	①	②	0.115	2 Rich
	D9OE-FA	7/16	13/16	3	0.132	①	②	0.115	2 Rich
	D9SE-GA	7/16	13/16	3	0.150	①	②	0.250	2 Rich
	D9VE-LC	7/16	13/16	3	0.145	①	②	0.250	3 Rich
	D9VE-SA	7/16	13/16	3	0.147	①	②	—	3 Rich
	D9VE-UB	7/16	13/16	3	0.155	①	②	0.250	3 Rich
	D9VE-VA	3/8	3/4	3	0.145	①	②	—	3 Rich
	D9VE-YB	3/8	3/4	2	0.145	①	②	0.250	3 Rich
	D9WE-CB	7/16	13/16	3	0.132	①	②	—	3 Rich
	D9WE-DB	7/16	13/16	3	0.132	①	②	—	3 Rich
	D9WE-EB	7/16	13/16	3	0.132	①	②	—	2 Rich
	D9WE-FB	7/16	13/16	3	0.132	①	②	—	2 Rich
	D9WE-JA	7/16	13/16	3	0.150	①	②	0.250	2 Rich
	D9WE-MB	7/16	13/16	3	0.132	①	②	—	1 Rich
	D9WE-NB	7/16	13/16	3	0.132	①	②	—	1 Rich
	D9YE-EA	7/16	13/16	3	0.118	①	②	0.115	1 Rich
	D9YE-FA	7/16	13/16	3	0.118	①	②	0.115	1 Rich
	D9YE-AB	7/16	13/16	3	0.118	①	②	0.115	Index
	D9YE-BB	7/16	13/16	3	0.118	①	②	0.115	Index
	D9YE-CA	7/16	13/16	2	0.118	①	②	0.115	Index
	D9YE-DA	7/16	13/16	2	0.118	①	②	0.115	Index
	D9ZE-AYA	7/16	13/16	3	0.138	①	②	0.115	Index
	D9ZE-BFB	7/16	13/16	2	0.125	①	②	—	3 Rich
	D9ZE-BGB	7/16	13/16	2	0.125	①	②	—	3 Rich
	D9ZE-BHB	7/16	13/16	2	0.125	①	②	0.250	3 Rich
	D9ZE-BJB	7/16	13/16	2	0.125	①	②	—	3 Rich
1980	EO4E-PA, RA	—	13/16	2	0.104	①	②	1/4	③
	EOBE-AUA	—	13/16	3	0.116	①	②	1/4	③
	EODE-SA, TA	—	13/16	2	0.104	①	②	1/4	③
	EOKE-CA, DA	—	13/16	3	0.116	①	②	1/4	③
	EOKE-GA, HA	—	13/16	3	0.116	①	②	1/4	③
	EOKE-JA, KA	—	13/16	3	0.116	①	②	1/4	③
	D84E-TA, UA	—	13/16	2	0.125	①	②	1/4	③

144 EMISSION CONTROLS AND FUEL SYSTEM

Motorcraft 2150 Specifications (cont.)

Year	(9510)* Carburetor Identification	Dry Float Level (in.)	Wet Float Level (in.)	Pump Setting Hole # ①	Choke Plate Pulldown (in.)	Fast Idle Cam Linkage Clearance (in.)	Fast Idle (rpm)	Dechoke (in.)	Choke Setting
	EO4E-ADA, AEA	—	13/16	2	0.104	①	②	1/4	③
	EO4E-CA	—	13/16	2	0.104	①	②	1/4	③
	EO4E-EA, FA	—	13/16	2	0.104	①	②	1/4	③
	EO4E-JA, KA	—	13/16	2	0.137	①	②	1/4	③
	EO4E-SA, TA	—	13/16	2	0.104	①	②	1/4	③
	EO4E-VA, YA	—	13/16	2	0.104	①	②	1/4	③
	EODE-TA, VA	—	13/16	2	0.104	①	②	1/4	③
	EOSE-GA, HA	—	13/16	2	0.104	①	②	1/4	③
	EOSE-LA, MA	—	13/16	2	0.104	①	②	1/4	③
	EOSE-NA	—	13/16	2	0.104	①	②	1/4	③
	EOSE-PA	—	13/16	2	0.137	①	②	1/4	③
	EOVE-FA	—	13/16	2	0.104	①	②	1/4	③
	EOWE-BA, CA	—	13/16	2	0.137	①	②	1/4	③
	D9AE-ANA, APA	—	13/16	3	0.129	①	②	1/4	③
	D9AE-AVA, AYA	—	13/16	3	0.129	①	②	1/4	③
	EOAE-AGA	—	13/16	3	0.159	①	②	1/4	③
1981	EIKE-CA	7/16	0.810	3	0.124	①	②	0.250	③
	EIKE-EA	7/16	0.810	3	0.124	①	②	0.250	③
	EIKE-DA	7/16	0.810	3	0.124	①	②	0.250	③
	EIKE-FA	7/16	0.810	3	0.124	①	②	0.250	③
	EIWE-FA	7/16	0.810	2	0.120	①	②	0.250	③
	EIWE-EA	7/16	0.810	2	0.120	①	②	0.250	③
	EIWE-CA	7/16	0.810	2	0.120	①	②	0.250	③
	EIWE-DA	7/16	0.810	2	0.120	①	②	0.250	③
	EIAE-YA	7/16	0.810	3	0.124	①	②	0.250	③
	EIAE-ZA	7/16	0.810	3	0.124	①	②	0.250	③
	EIAE-ADA	7/16	0.810	3	0.124	①	②	0.250	③
	EIAE-AEA	7/16	0.810	3	0.124	①	②	0.250	③
	EIAE-TA	—	0.810	2	0.104	①	②	0.250	③
	EIAE-UA	—	0.810	2	0.104	①	②	0.250	③
1982	E2ZE-BAA	13/32	0.780	2	0.172	①	1400	0.250	③
	E2ZE-BBA	13/32	0.780	2	0.172	①	1400	0.250	③
	E3CE-LA	7/16	0.810	3	0.103	①	2200	0.250	③
	E3CE-MA	7/16	0.810	3	0.103	①	2200	0.250	③
	E3CE-JA	7/16	0.810	3	0.103	①	2200	0.250	③
	E3CE-KA	7/16	0.810	3	0.103	①	2200	0.250	③
	E3CE-NA	7/16	0.810	3	0.120	①	2100	0.250	③
	E3CE-PA	7/16	0.810	3	0.120	①	2100	0.250	③

① With link in inbound hole of pump lever   ② See underhood sticker   ③ Opposite V notch

EMISSION CONTROLS AND FUEL SYSTEM 145

Carter YFA Specifications

Year	Model ①	Float Level (in.)	Fast Idle Cam (in.)	Choke Plate Pulldown (in.)	Unloader (in.)	Dechoke (in.)	Choke
1983	E3ZE-LA	0.650	0.140	0.260	—	0.220	—
	E3ZE-MA	0.650	0.140	0.260	—	0.220	—
	E3ZE-TB	0.650	0.140	0.240	—	0.220	—
	E3ZE-UA	0.650	0.140	0.240	—	0.220	—
	E3ZE-VA	0.650	0.140	0.260	—	0.220	—
	E3ZE-YA	0.650	0.140	0.260	—	0.220	—
	E3ZE-NB	0.650	0.160	0.260	—	0.220	—
	E3ZE-PB	0.650	0.160	0.260	—	0.220	—
	E3ZE-ASA	0.650	0.160	0.260	—	0.220	—
	E3ZE-APA	0.650	0.140	0.240	—	0.220	—
	E3ZE-ARA	0.650	0.140	0.240	—	0.220	—
	E3ZE-ADA	0.650	0.140	0.260	—	0.220	—
	E3ZE-AEA	0.650	0.140	0.260	—	0.220	—
	E3ZE-ACA	0.650	0.140	0.260	—	0.220	—
	E3ZE-ATA	0.650	0.160	0.260	—	0.220	—
	E3ZE-ABA	0.650	0.140	0.260	—	0.220	—
	E3ZE-UB	0.650	0.140	0.240	—	0.220	—
	E3ZE-TC	0.650	0.140	0.240	—	0.220	—
1984–85	E4ZE-HC, DB	0.650	0.140	0.260	—	0.270	—
	E4ZE-MA, NA	0.650	0.140	0.240	—	0.270	—
	E4ZE-PA, RA	0.650	0.140	0.260	—	0.270	—
	E5ZE-CA	0.650	0.140	0.260	—	0.270	—
	E4ZE-PB, RB	0.650	0.140	0.240	—	0.270	—

① Model number located on the tag or casting

Model 1946

Year	Part Number	Float Level (in.)	Choke Pulldown (in.)	Dechoke (in.)	Fast Idle Cam (in.)	Accelerator Pump Stroke Slot
1980	E0ZE-GA	.69	.110	.150	.05–.09	#2
	E0ZE-BBA	.69	.120	.150	.086	#2
	E0BE-CA	.69	.100	.150	.070	#2
	E0BE-AA	.69	.100	.150	.070	#2
	E0BE-AAA	.69	.115	.150	.090	#1
	E0BE-ZA	.69	.115	.150	.090	#1
	E0ZE-EA	.69	.110	.150	.070	#2
	E0ZE-DA	.69	.110	.150	.070	#2
1981	EIBE-AFA	.69	.113	.150	.082	#2
	EIBE-AKA	.69	.113	.150	.082	#2
	E0BE-CA	.69	.100	.150	.070	#2

146 EMISSION CONTROLS AND FUEL SYSTEM

Model 1946 (cont.)

Year	Part Number	Float Level (in.)	Choke Pulldown (in.)	Dechoke (in.)	Fast Idle Cam (in.)	Accelerator Pump Stroke Slot
	E0BE-AA	.69	.100	.150	.070	#2
1982	E1BE-AGA	.69	.120	.150	.086	#2
	E2BE-CA	.69	.110	.150	.078	#2
	E2BE-BA	.69	.110	.150	.078	#2
	E2BE-JA	.69	.110	.150	.078	#2
	E2BE-HA	.69	.110	.150	.078	#2
	E2BE-TA	.69	.110	.150	.078	#2
	E2BE-SA	.69	.110	.150	.078	#2
1983	E2BE-CA	.69	.110	.150	.078	#2
	E2BE-BA	.69	.110	.150	.078	#2
	E2BE-TA	.69	.110	.150	.078	#2
	E2BE-SA	.69	.110	.150	.078	#2
	E3SE-CA	.69	.105	.150	.078	#2
	E3SE-DA	.69	.105	.150	.078	#2
	E3SE-AA	.69	.095	.150	.078	#2
	E3SE-BA	.69	.095	.150	.078	#2

Holley Model 5200

Year	(9510)* Carburetor Identification	Fast Idle Cam	Acc. Pump Stroke	Dechoke Clearance	Choke Pulldown	Choke Cap Setting (notches)	Float Adjustment
1979	D9BE-AAA/ADA	3.0 mm	No. 2	6.0 mm	6.0 mm	2 Rich	.41–.51
	D9BE-ABA/ACA	3.0 mm	No. 2	6.0 mm	6.0 mm	2 Rich	.41–.51
	D9EE-ANA/APA	3.0 mm	No. 2	6.0 mm	6.0 mm	2 Rich	.41–.51
	D9ZE-BCA/BDA	—	—	—	—	—	—
	D9ZE-MD/ND	3.0 mm	No. 3	6.0 mm	6.0 mm	2 Rich	.41–.51
	D9ZE-SB/TB	—	—	—	—	—	—
1980	D9EE-APA/ANA	2.5–3.5 mm	No. 2	6.0 mm	5.5–6.5 mm	—	.41–.51 in.①
	E0EE-GA/RA	2.0 mm	No. 2	5.0 mm	5.0 mm	—	.46 in.①
	E0EE-JA/TA	2.0 mm	No. 2	5.0 mm	5.0 mm	—	.46 in.①
	E0EE-NA/VA	3.0 mm	No. 2	10.0 mm	6.0 mm	—	.46 in.①
	E0ZE-SB	—	—	—	—	—	—
	E0ZE-AFB	—	—	—	—	—	—
	E0ZE-AAA	4.0 mm	No. 3	6.0 mm	7.0 mm	—	.46 in.①
	E0ZE-ACA	4.0 mm	No. 2	6.0 mm	7.0 mm	—	.46 in.①
1981	E1ZE-YA	.080	No. 2	.200	.200	—	.41–.51
	E0EE-RB	.080	No. 2	.200	.200	—	.41–.51
	E1ZE-VA	.080	No. 2	.200	.200	—	.41–.51

① Dry Setting
*Basic carburetor number for Ford products

EMISSION CONTROLS AND FUEL SYSTEM

Motorcraft Model 2700 VV Specifications

Year	Model	Float Level (in.)	Float Drop (in.)	Fast Idle Cam Setting (notches)	Cold Enrichment Metering Rod (in.)	Control Vacuum (in. H₂O)	Venturi Valve Limiter (in.)	Choke Cap Setting (notches)	Control Vacuum Regulator Setting (in.)
1979	D9ZE-LB	1 3/64	1 15/32	1 Rich/2nd step	.125	①	②	Index	.230
	D84E-KA	1 3/64	1 15/32	1 Rich/3rd step	.125	5.5	61/64	Index	—
1980	All	1 3/64	1 15/32	1 Rich/4th step	.125	③	④	⑤	.075
1981	EIAE-AAA	1.015–1.065	1.435–1.485	—	—	③	④	⑤	—

① Venturi Air Bypass 6.8–7.3
   Venturi Valve Diaphragm 4.6–5.1
② Limiter Setting .38–.42
   Limiter Stop Setting .73–.77
③ See text
④ Opening gap: 0.99–1.01
   Closing gap: 0.94–0.98
⑤ See underhood decal

Holley 4180 Specifications

Year	(9510) * Carburetor Identification	Dry Float Level (in.)	Wet Float Level (in.)	Pump Setting Hole	Choke Plate Pulldown (in.)	Fast Idle Cam Linkage Clearance (in.)	Fast Idle (rpm)	Dechoke (in.)	Choke Setting
'83	E3ZE-AUA	②	①	#1	.195–.215	NA	③	.300	3 Rich
	E3ZE-BGA	②	①	#1	.195–.215	NA	③	.300	3 Rich
'84	E4ZE-SA	②	①	#1	.195–.215	NA	③	.300	1 Lean

① Bottom of sight plug
② See text
③ See Underhood sticker
NA—not available

Chassis Electrical

5

HEATER

Blower Motor
REMOVAL AND INSTALLATION
Except Merkur

MODELS WITHOUT AIR CONDITIONING

The right side ventilator assembly must be removed for access to the blower motor and wheel.

1. Remove the retaining screw for the right register duct mounting bracket.
2. Remove the screws holding the control cable lever assembly to the instrument panel.
3. Remove the glove box liner.
4. Remove the plastic rivets securing the grille to the floor outlet, and remove the grille.
5. Remove the right register duct and register assembly:

    a. Remove the register duct bracket retaining screw on the lower edge of the instrument panel, and disengage the duct from the opening and remove through the glove box opening.

    b. Insert a thin blade under the retaining tab and pry the tab toward the louvers until the retaining tab pivot clears the hole in the register opening. Pull the register assembly end out from the housing only enough to prevent the pivot from going back into the pivot hole. Pry the other retaining tab loose and remove the register assembly from the opening.

6. Remove the retaining screws securing the ventilator assembly to the blower housing. The upper right screw can be reached with a long extension through the register opening; the upper left screw can be reached through the glove box opening. The other two screws are on the bottom of the assembly.
7. Slide the assembly to the right, then down and out from under the instrument panel.
8. Remove the motor lead wire connector from the register and push it back through the hole in the case. Remove the right side cowl trim panel for access, and remove the ground terminal lug retaining screw.
9. Remove the hub clamp spring from the motor shaft and remove the blower wheel.
10. Remove the blower motor bolts from the housing and remove the motor.
11. To install reverse the removal procedure.

MODELS WITH AIR CONDITIONING

The air inlet duct and blower housing assembly must be removed for access to the blower motor.

1. Remove the glove box liner and disconnect the hose from the vacuum motor.
2. Remove the instrument panel lower right side to cowl attaching bolt.
3. Remove the screw attaching the brace to the top of the air inlet duct.

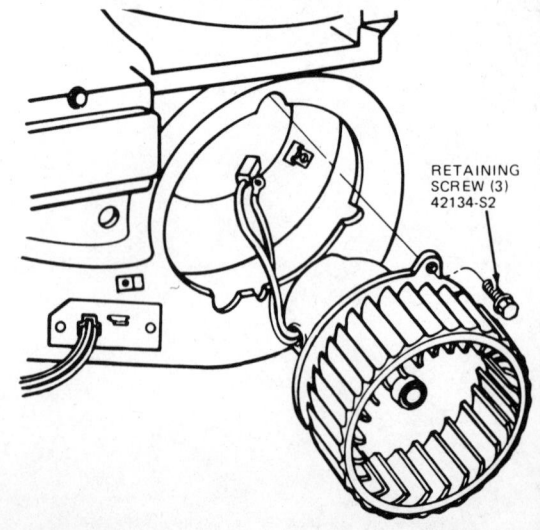

Blower motor and wheel assembly removal—without a/c

CHASSIS ELECTRICAL 149

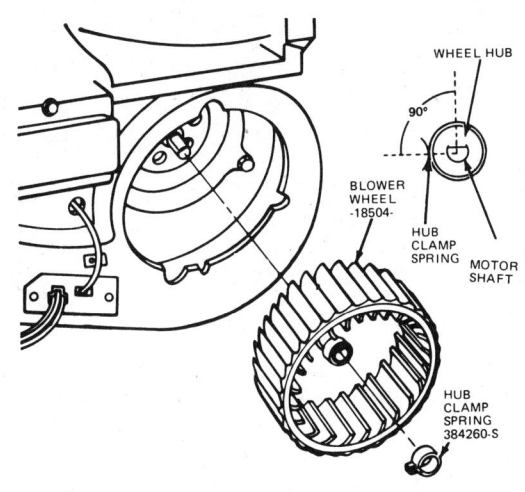

Blower motor wheel removal—without a/c

4. Disconnect the motor wire.
5. Remove the housing lower support bracket to case nut.
6. Remove the side cowl trim panel and remove the ground wire screw.
7. Remove the attaching screw at the top of the air inlet duct.
8. Remove the air inlet duct and housing assembly down and away from the evaporator case.
9. Remove the four blower motor mounting plate screws and remove the blower motor and wheel as an assembly from the housing. Do not remove the mounting plate from the motor.
10. To install reverse the above.

Merkur

NOTE: *Evaporator case removal is required for blower motor replacement.*

1. Remove the evaporator case from the vehicle.
2. Remove the three access cover retaining screws and remove the cover.
3. Remove the screws retaining the scrolls to the lower case assembly. Remove the screws retaining the thermostat.
4. Separate the evaporator case halves after removing the retaining clips.
5. Remove the blower motor mounting screw and the blower motor.
6. Install the blower motor in the reverse order of removal. Be sure to correctly align the thermostat sensor during installation.

EVAPORATOR CASE REMOVAL AND INSTALLATION

CAUTION: *A/C system refrigerant discharge is required. Observe all safety requirements.*

1. Disconnect both the negative and positive cables from the battery (negative cable first).
2. Discharge the A/C system refrigerant at the service access gauge port valve.
3. Remove the engine valve cover.
4. Remove the cowl insulator cover.
5. Pull the water control valve from the retaining clip, remove the retaining clip.
6. Remove the battery shield.
7. Disconnect the vacuum hose from the EGR valve. Disconnect the EGR valve by removing the bolt attaching it to the manifold and move it forward to provide clearance.
8. Remove the two nuts that retain and A/C hose plate and seal to the firewall partition between the engine compartment and evaporator. Remove the plate and seal.
9. Disconnect the wiring harness from the partition. Pull the harness forward to disconnect the tabs connecting the harness to the partition.
10. Remove the Torx bolts that retain the refrigerant lines to the expansion valve. Disconnect the suction line and liquid line at the expansion valve.
11. Remove the weather seal from the upper edge of the partition. Remove the screws that retain the partition to the firewall.
12. Remove the drainage valves from both the right and left side. Remove the partition.
13. Disconnect the deice wiring harness connector. Disconnect the ground wire on the evaporator.
14. Remove the evaporator to firewall attaching bolts.
15. Remove the cowl grille panel. Disconnect the windshield wiper motor arm to gain clearance for evaporator removal.
16. Slide the evaporator case assembly upward and forward out of the engine compartment. Check and replace seals as necessary.
17. Install the evaporator case in the reverse order of removal.

Heater Core

REMOVAL AND INSTALLATION

Except Merkur

MODELS WITHOUT AIR CONDITIONING

It is not necessary to remove the heater case for access to the heater core.

1. Drain enough coolant from the radiator to drain the heater core.
2. Loosen the heater hose clamps on the engine side of the firewall and disconnect the heater hoses. Cap the heater core tubes.
3. Remove the glove box liner.
4. Remove the instrument panel-to-cowl brace retaining screws and remove the brace.
5. Move the temperature lever to warm.

150 CHASSIS ELECTRICAL

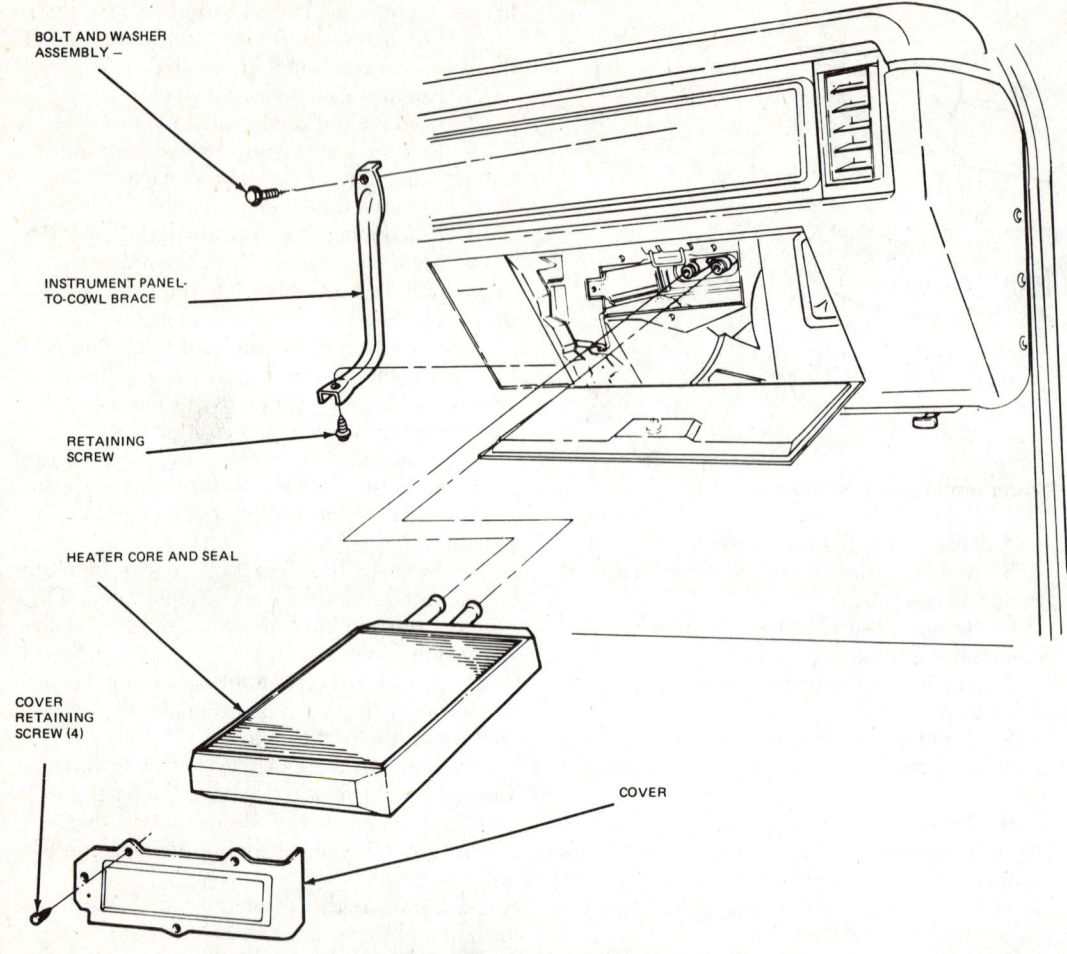

Heater core removal—without a/c

6. Remove the heater core cover screws. Remove the cover through the glove box.
7. Loosen the heater case mounting nuts on the engine side of the firewall.
8. Push the heater core tubes and seal toward the interior of the car to loosen the core.
9. Remove the heater core through the glove box opening.
10. To install reverse the above.

MODELS WITH AIR CONDITIONING

The instrument panel must be removed for access to the heater core.
1. Disconnect the battery ground cable.
2. Remove the instrument panel pad:
   a. Remove the screws attaching the instrument cluster trim panel to the pad.
   b. Remove the screw attaching the pad to the panel at each defroster opening.
   c. Remove the screws attaching the edge of the pad to the panel.
3. Remove the steering column opening cover.
4. Remove the nuts and bracket retaining the steering column to the instrument panel and lay the column against the seat.
5. Remove the instrument panel to brake pedal support screw at the column opening.
6. Remove the screws attaching the lower brace to the panel below the radio, and below the glove box.
7. Disconnect the temperature cable from the door and case bracket.
8. Unplug the 7-port vacuum hose connectors at the evaporator case.
9. Disconnect the resistor wire connector and the blower feed wire.
10. Remove the screws attaching the top of the panel to the cowl. Support the panel while doing this.
11. Remove one screw at each end attaching the panel to the cowl side panels.
12. Move the panel rearward and disconnect the speedometer cable and any wires preventing the panel from lying flat on the seat.
13. Drain the coolant and disconnect the

CHASSIS ELECTRICAL 151

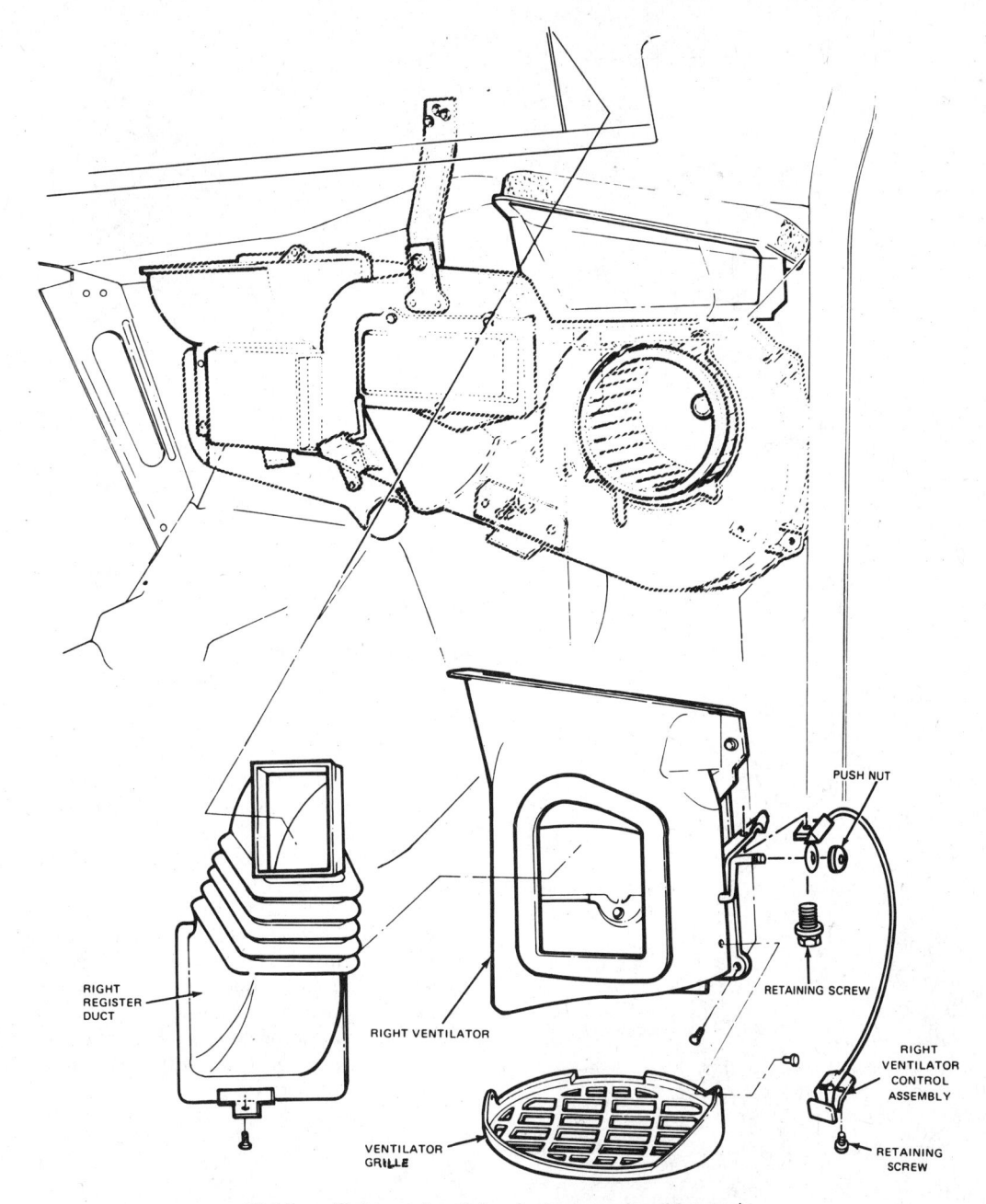

Right ventilator and register duct removal—without a/c

heater hoses from the heater core. Plug the core tubes.

14. Remove the nuts retaining the evaporator case to the firewall in the engine compartment.
15. Remove the case support bracket screws and air inlet duct support bracket.
16. Remove the nut retaining the bracket to the dash panel at the left side of the evaporator case, and the nut retaining the bracket below the case to the dash panel.
17. Pull the case assembly away from the panel to get to the screws retaining the heater core cover to the case.
18. Remove the cover screws and the cover.
19. Lift the heater core and seals from the evaporator case.
20. To install reverse the above.

Merkur

1. Disconnect the negative battery cable.
2. Drain the cooling system. Remove the heater hoses from the heater core tube at the firewall. Plug the core tubes.

CHASSIS ELECTRICAL

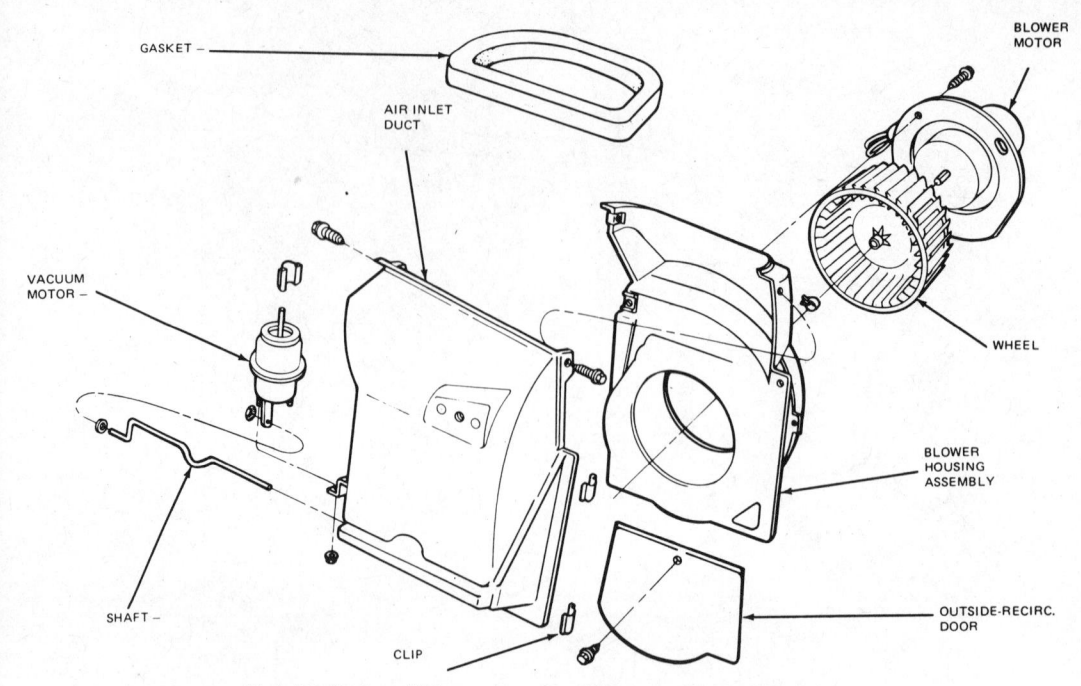

Air inlet duct and blower housing (disassembled)—with a/c

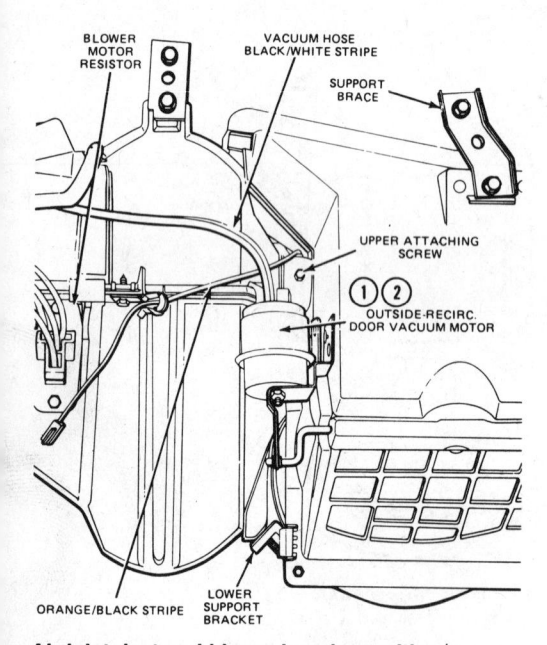

Air inlet duct and blower housing—with a/c

compartment lamp, A/C blower switch and cigarette lighter.

6. Remove the right hand dash panel.
7. Remove all duct hoses from the heater housing.
8. Detach the control cables from the heater housing.
9. Remove the screws that mount the heater housing to the firewall. Pull the heater into the vehicle until the core tubes are clear of the firewall and then pull the housing toward the right side of the vehicle for removal.
10. Remove the heater core from the housing. Install the heater core and housing in the reverse order of removal.

RADIO

REMOVAL AND INSTALLATION
Except Merkur

1. Disconnect the battery ground cable.
2. Disconnect the power lead, speaker leads and antenna lead-in-cable from the radio receiver.
3. Remove the control knobs, discs, control shaft nuts and washers.
4. Remove the ash receptacle and bracket.
5. Remove the radio rear support attaching nut.
6. Remove the instrument panel lower reinforcement.

3. Remove the screws retaining the tube cover and remove the cover and plate from the firewall.
4. From inside the vehicle; remove the center console and move it toward the rear of the vehicle. Remove the right side footwell trim panel.
5. Disconnect the heater control lever. Disconnect the electrical leads from the glove

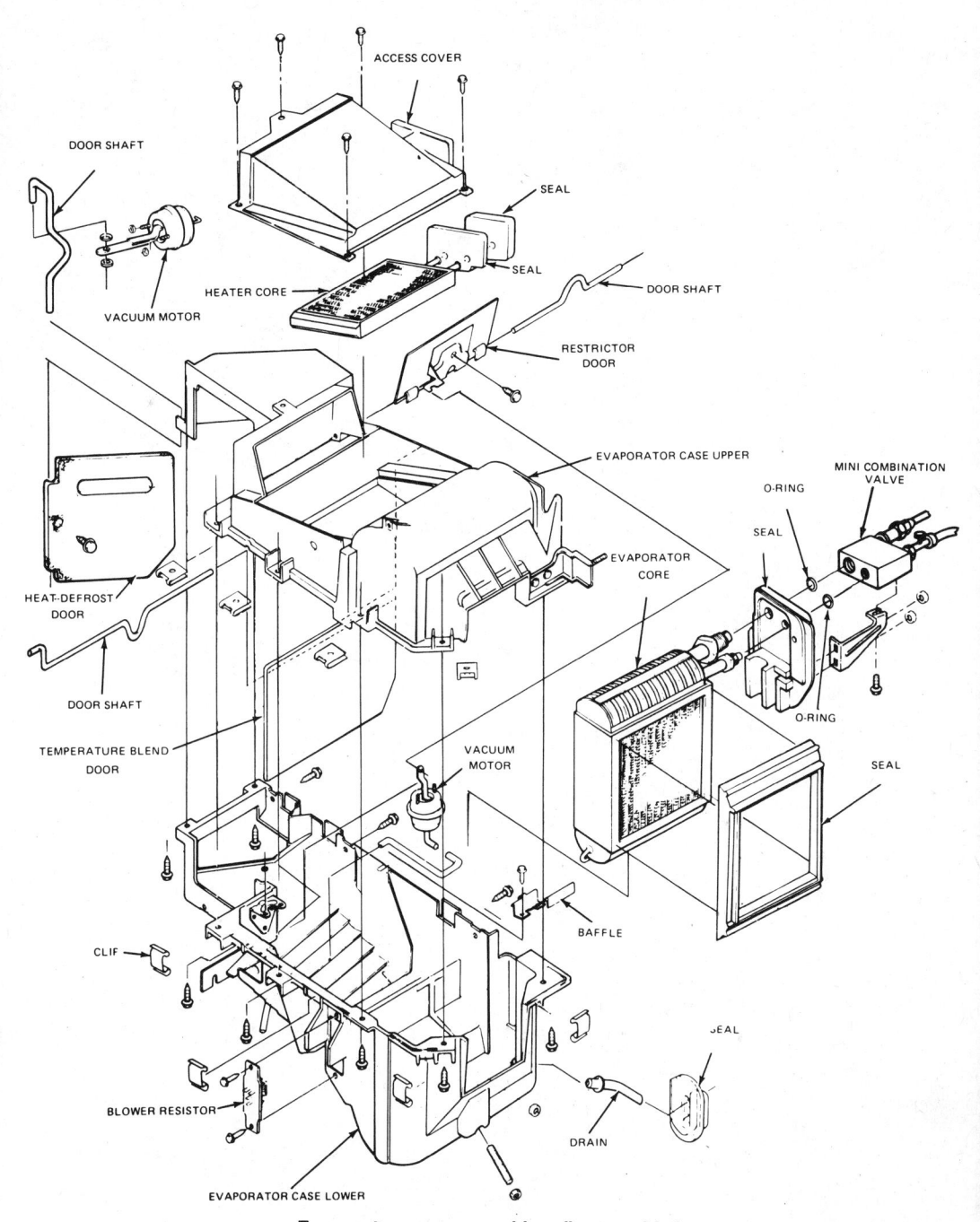

Evaporator case assembly—disassembled

7. Remove the heater or air conditioning floor ducts.

8. Remove the radio receiver from the bezel and the rear support, then lower the radio from the instrument panel.

9. To install reverse the above procedure.

Merkur

1. Remove all of the control knobs including the plastic tone control lever, tuning knob, spacer, balance control and search sensitivity control. Remove the receiver trim panel after removing the securing nuts.

2. Pull the mounting plate securing tangs inward toward the dial and slide the radio forward.

3. Disconnect the power lead, speaker leads and antenna.

4. Install the radio in the reverse order of removal.

154 CHASSIS ELECTRICAL

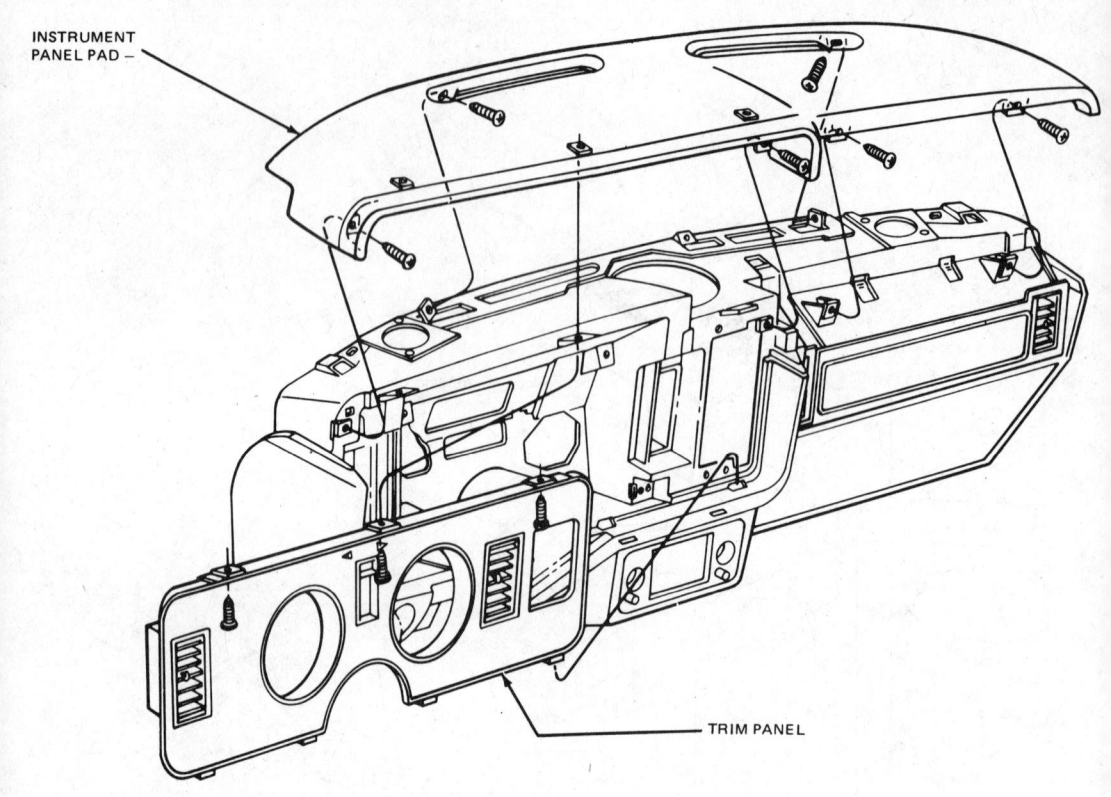

INSTRUMENT PANEL PAD

TRIM PANEL

Instrument panel pad removal

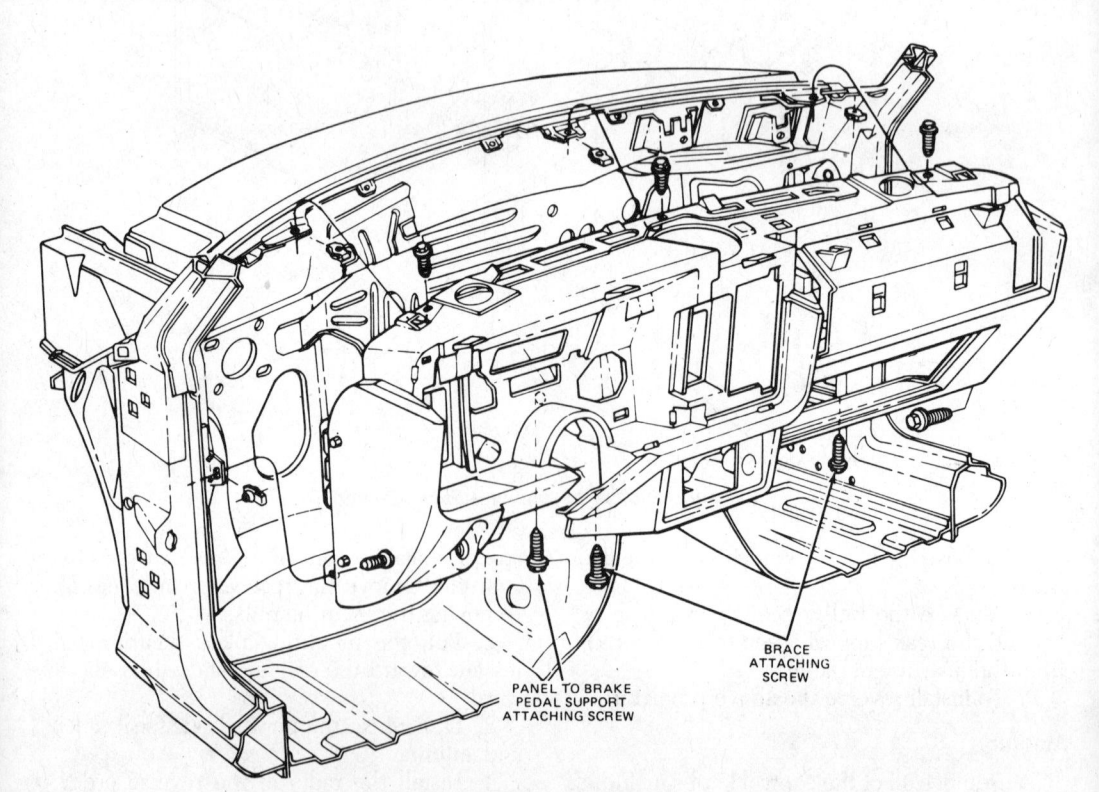

PANEL TO BRAKE PEDAL SUPPORT ATTACHING SCREW

BRACE ATTACHING SCREW

Instrument panel removal

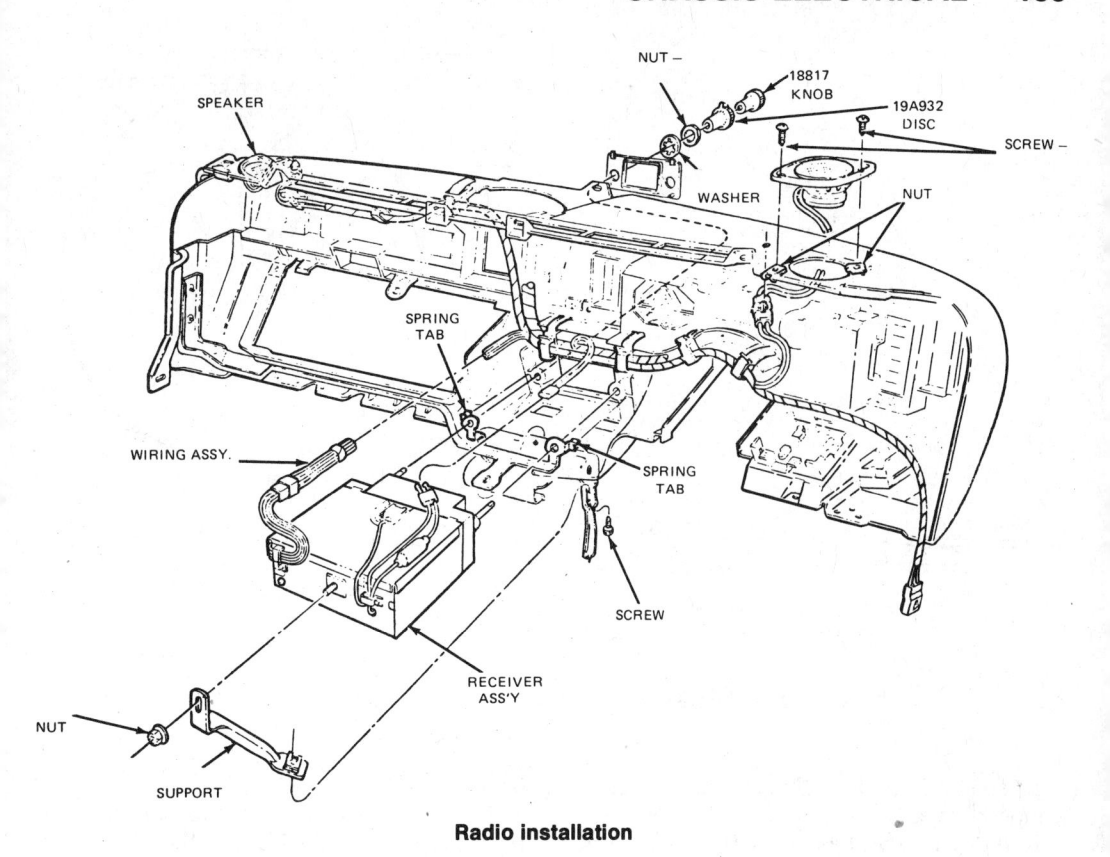

CHASSIS ELECTRICAL 155

Radio installation

Front Speaker (Instrument Panel)
REMOVAL AND INSTALLATION

1. Remove the instrument panel pad.
   a. Remove the three cluster panel retaining screws.
   b. Remove the four instrument panel pad retaining screws at the rear edge of the pad.
   c. Remove the four instrument panel pad retaining screws in the top defroster openings, and remove the pad.
2. Remove the two speaker retaining screws, disconnect the speaker lead and remove the speaker.
3. Installation is the reverse of removal. Make sure the speaker operates properly before installing the instrument panel pad.

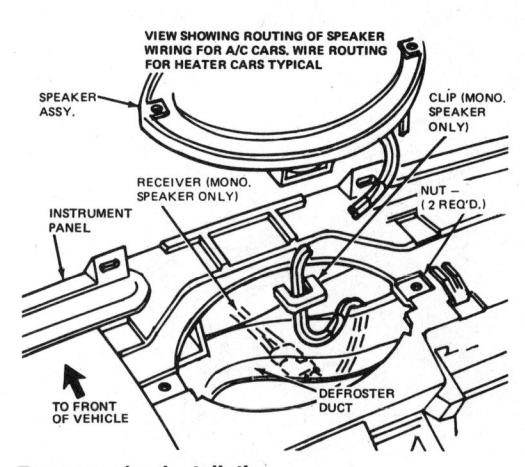

Front speaker installation

WINDSHIELD WIPER SYSTEM

The windshield wipers are actuated by a permanent magnet, rotary type electric motor. The two wiper arms and blades are mounted on a pivot shaft, one at each end of the windshield. The pivot shafts are connected to the motor by linkage arms and attaching clips.

Wiper Arm Assembly
REMOVAL AND INSTALLATION
Except Merkur

1. Raise the blade end of the arm off the windshield and move the slide latch away from the pivot shaft.
2. The wiper arm should now be unlocked and can now be pulled off of the pivot shaft.

156 CHASSIS ELECTRICAL

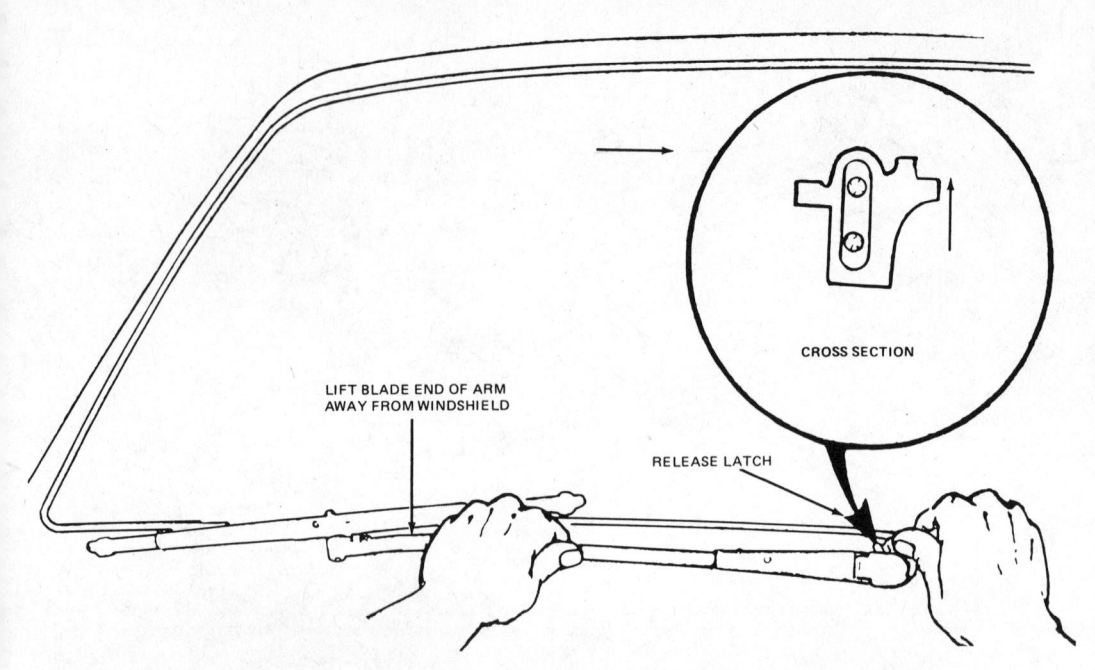

Installation of the wiper arm and blade assembly to the pivot shaft

3. To install, position the auxiliary arm (if so equipped) over the pivot pin, hold it down and push the main arm head over the pivot shaft. Make sure the pivot shaft is in the park position.

4. Hold the main arm head on the pivot shaft while raising the blade end of the wiper arm and push the slide latch into the lock under the pivot shaft. Lower the blade to the windshield.

NOTE: *If the blade does not touch the windshield, the slide latch is not completely in place.*

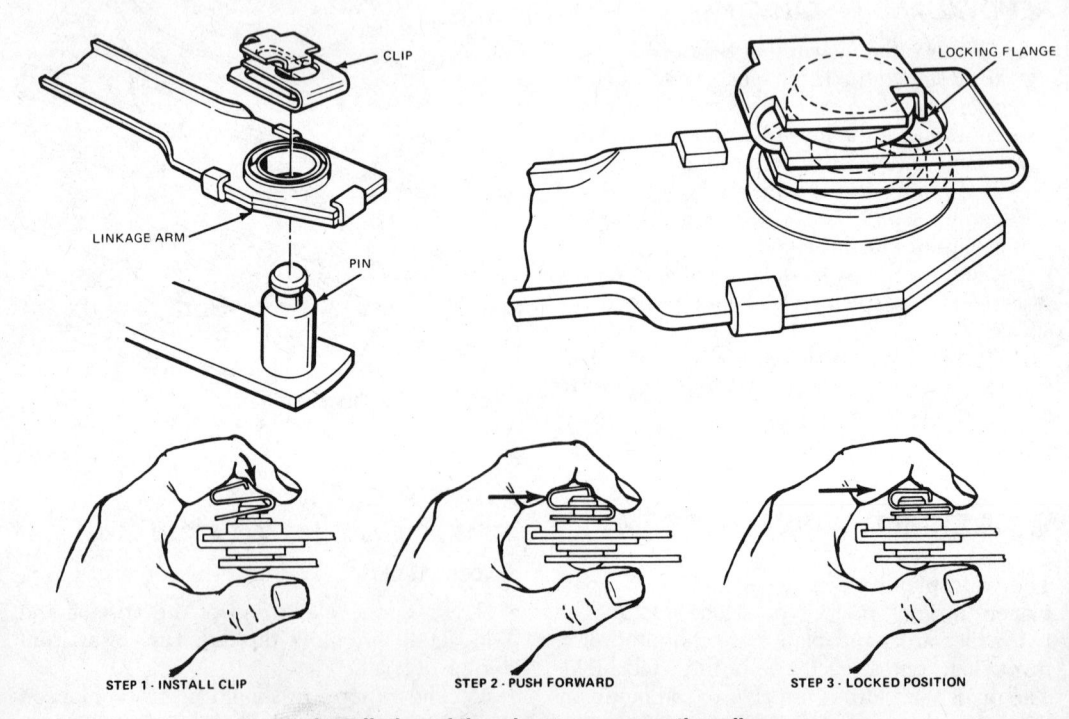

Installation of the wiper arm connecting clips

Wiper Blade (Trico Type)
REPLACEMENT

1. Pull up on the spring lock and pull the blade assembly from the pin.
2. To install, push the blade assembly onto the pin, so that the spring lock engages the pin.

Wiper Element (Tridon)
REPLACEMENT

1. Locate a 7/16" long notch approximately one inch from the end of the plastic backing strip, which is part of the rubber blade element assembly.
2. With the wiper blade removed from the arm place the blade assembly on a firm surface with the notched end of the backing strip visible.
3. Push down on one end of the wiper assembly until the blade is tightly bowed then grasp the tip of the backing strip firmly, pulling and twisting at the same time. The backing strip will then snap out of the retaining tab on the end of the wiper frame.
4. Lift the wiper blade assembly from the surface and slide the backing strip down the frame until the notch lines up with the next retaining tab then twist slightly and the backing strip will snap out. Follow this same procedure with the remaining tabs until the element is removed.
5. To install the blade element reverse the above procedure and make sure all six tabs are locked to the backing strip.

Wiper Motor
REMOVAL AND INSTALLATION
Except Merkur

1. Remove the link retaining clip and disconnect the wiper pivot shaft and link assembly from the motor drive arm.
2. Remove the three motor attaching screws and lower the motor away from the left underside of the instrument panel.
3. Disconnect the motor wiring and remove the motor.
4. Reverse to install.

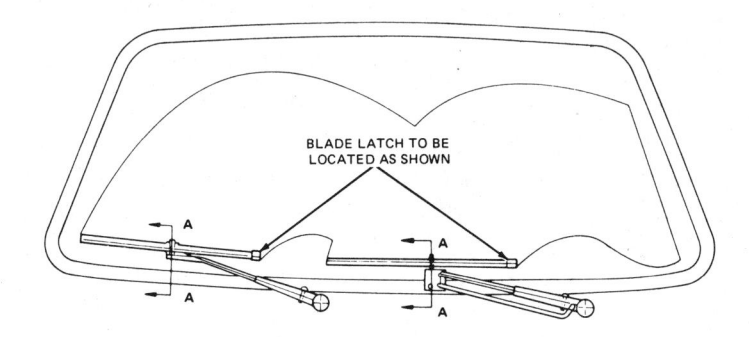

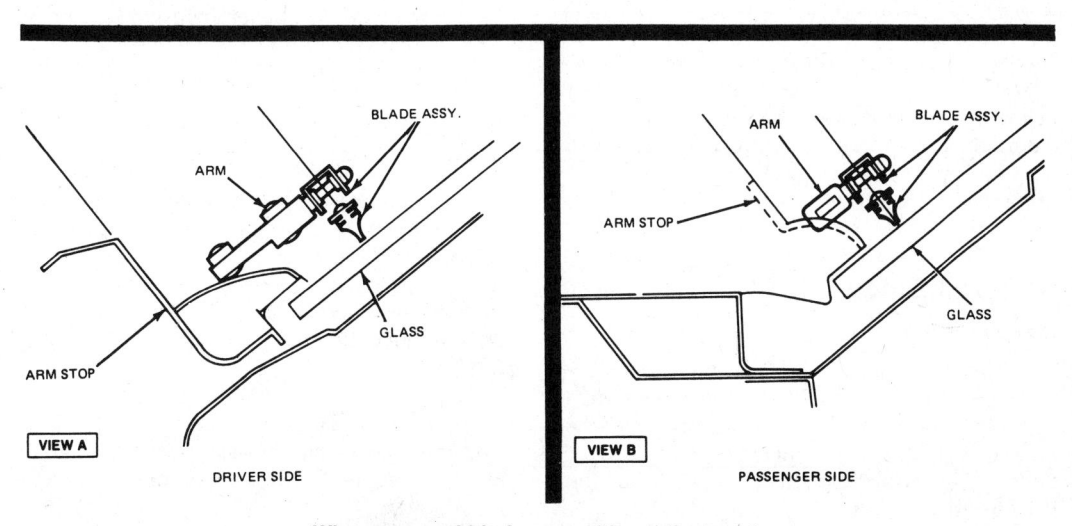

Wiper arm and blade assembly—adjustment

CHASSIS ELECTRICAL

Merkur

FRONT MOTOR

1. Operate the wiper motor and shut off key when the linkage mounting nut is exposed. Disconnect the negative battery cable.
2. Remove the nut that attaches the linkage to the motor. Remove the motor mounting bolts. Remove the motor and disconnect the electrical harness plug.
3. Install the wiper motor in the reverse order of removal.

REAR MOTOR

1. Remove the wiper arm and blade assembly from the pivot shaft.
2. Open the hatch and remove the trim panel carefully.
3. Remove the bolts that attach the wiper motor. Remove the motor and disconnect the wire harness plug.
4. Install the motor in the reverse order of removal.

Pivot Shafts and Wiper Linkage

REMOVAL AND INSTALLATION
Except Merkur

The wiper linkage is mounted below the cowl top grille. The pivot shafts and linkage assemblies are connected together with nonremoveable plastic ball joints. The left and right hand pivot shafts and linkage are serviced as one unit.

1. Disconnect the battery.
2. Remove the cowl top grille attaching screws and the grille.
3. Remove the clip and disconnect the linkage drive arm from the motor crank pin.
4. Remove the two bolts retaining the right pivot shaft to the cowl, and remove the large nut, washer and spacer from the left pivot shaft.
5. To install reverse the removal procedure. Before installing the blade assemblies, make sure the motor is in PARK and the blades are set to the proper dimension. See the Arm and Blade Adjustment procedure.

Arm and Blade

ADJUSTMENT

1. With the arm and blade assemblies removed from pivot shafts turn on the wiper switch and allow the motor to move the pivot shafts three or four cycles, and then turn off the wiper switch. This will place the pivot shafts in the Park position.
2. Install the arm and blade assemblies on the pivot shafts to the correct distance between the windshield lower moulding or weatherstrip and the blade saddle centerline. (Driver's side—1.80–3.0 inches, Passenger's side—2.30–3.50 inches)

INSTRUMENT CLUSTER

REMOVAL
Except Merkur

1. Disconnect the battery ground cable.
2. Remove three upper retaining screws from the instrument cluster trim cover and remove the trim cover.
3. Remove the two upper and two lower screws, retaining the instrument cluster to the instrument panel.
4. Pull the cluster away from the instrument panel and reach behind the instrument cluster to disconnect the speedometer cable by pressing on the flat surface of the plastic connector (quick connect).
5. Pull the cluster further away from the instrument panel, disconnect the two cluster printed circuit connectors from their receptacles in the cluster backplate.
6. Remove the clusters.

INSTALLATION
Except Merkur

1. Apply a 3/16 inch diameter ball of silicone damping grease in the drive hole of the speedometer head.
2. Connect the cluster.
3. Connect the two cluster printed circuit connectors to their receptacles in the cluster backplate.
4. Connect the speedometer cable.
5. Install the two upper and lower screws.
6. Install the three upper retaining screws to the instrument cluster trim cover, and install the trim cover.
7. Connect the battery ground cable.

REMOVAL AND INSTALLATION
Merkur

1. Disconnect the negative battery cable.
2. Remove the screws from the upper steering column shroud and remove the shroud.
3. Remove the rheostat and intermittent wiper control if equipped.
4. Remove the mounting screws and trim panel.
5. Remove the screws that attach the cluster panel to the dash.
6. Pull the cluster forward and disconnect the speedometer cable and harness from the instruments.
7. Install the cluster in the reverse order of removal.

CHASSIS ELECTRICAL 159

Troubleshooting Electrical—Instruments and Accessories

Condition	Possible Cause	Resolution
Cigar lighter—knob pops out before adequate heating	• Defective element • Defective socket	• Replace element • Replace socket
Cigar lighter—element stays in, won't heat up	• Fuse burnt out • Open in wiring • Defective socket • Defective element	• Replace fuse. If fuse blows again, check for short circuit • Service wiring • Replace socket • Replace element
Clock does not work	• Fuse burnt out • Open in wiring • Defective clock	• Replace fuse. If fuse blows again, check for short circuit • Service wiring • Replace clock
Horn sounds continuously—vehicles without speed control	• Short circuit between column disconnect and horn(s) • Short circuit in switch or column wiring	• Service as required • Service as required
Horn sounds continuously—vehicles with speed control	• Short circuit between horn relay disconnect and horn • Grounded circuit between horn switch and horn relay • Open horn switch • Defective horn relay	• Service as required • Service as required • Replace horn switch • Replace horn relay
Horn(s) inoperative	• Fuse or C.B. burnt out • Poor horn ground • Horns out of adjustment • Defective horn • Open in wiring • Defective horn switch • Defective turn signal switch and wiring • Defective horn relay	• Replace fuse or C.B. If fuse or C.B. goes again, check for short circuit • Assure a good ground • Adjust horn • Replace horn • Service wiring • Replace horn switch • Service or replace turn signal switch and wiring • Replace horn relay
Gauge inoperative—(temp., fuel, oil pressure)	• Poor sending unit ground • Defective sending unit • Open in wiring • Open IVR • Defective gauge	• Assure good ground • Replace sending unit • Repair wiring • Replace IVR • Replace gauge
Gauge inaccurate—(temp., fuel, oil pressure)	• Defective sending unit • Defective IVR • Loose wiring	• Replace sending unit • Replace IVR • Service wiring
Oil pressure light does not go out with ignition switch on (engine running)	• Short circuit between bulb and switch • Defective switch • Low oil pressure	• Service as necessary • Replace switch • Refer to engine diagnosis section in Volume II
Oil pressure light does not light with ignition key in start or run position. (engine not running)	• Bulb burnt out • Defective sending unit • Burnt fuse • Open in wiring	• Replace bulb • Check continuity of switch unit. Check ground. Service or replace as required. • Replace fuse. If fuse blows again check for short circuit • Service wiring
Hot temperature warning light does not go out (engine running) • Defective ignition switch	• Defective sending unit • Short circuit	• Replace switch unit • Check circuit to ignition prove out terminal. Service as required • Check continuity of ignition switch prove out circuit. Replace as necessary
Hot temperature warning light does not light with engine cranking	• Fuse burnt out	• Replace fuse. If fuse blows again, check for short circuit

Troubleshooting Electrical—Instruments and Accessories (cont.)

Condition	Possible Cause	Resolution
• Defective ignition switch	• Bulb burnt out • Open in wiring • Engine overheats	• Replace bulb • Check circuit to ignition prove out terminal. Service as required. • Replace ignition switch
"Engine" light does not come on with ignition switch in "run" or "start" (engine not running)	• Fuse burnt out • Defective oil pressure sending unit • Bulb burnt out • Open in wiring	• Replace fuse. If fuse blows again, check for short circuit • Replace switch unit • Replace bulb • Service wiring as required
"Engine" warning light does not go out with ignition switch on (engine running)	• Grounded circuit between bulb and switches • Defective switches • Engine problem	• Service as required • Replace switches • Refer to engine diagnosis section for engine overheating or low oil pressure in Volume II
Key warning buzzer sounds when driver door is opened with key not in ignition lock cylinder	• Short in key warning switch • Short in wiring	• Service or replace key warning switch as necessary • Service as required
Key warning buzzer inoperative	• Fuse burnt out • Drivers door courtesy light switch defective • Defective buzzer • Open in wiring • Defective key warning switch	• Replace fuse. If fuse blows again, check for short circuit • Replace switch • Replace buzzer • Service wiring • Replace key warning switch
"Headlights on" buzzer inoperative	• Improperly installed relay and wiring connections • Open circuit, short circuit or faulty connection • Improper relay ground • Defective relay	• Check and service as required • Service as required • Assure relay ground • Replace relay
Speedometer noisy	• Improper cable connection or routing • Binding sensor • Cable core kinked, burred or bent • Damaged driven gear • Defective speedometer	• Check for proper cable connections at head. Check cable for kinks or bends. Service or replace as required. • Check sensor for binding, erratic or noisy operation. Lube or replace sensor • Lube and replace as required • Replace driven gear • Replace speedometer head
Speedometer/odometer inoperative	• Cable disconnected • Cable broken • Binding in sensor and/or speedometer	• Connect cable • Replace cable • Replace sensor or speedometer
Speedometer/odometer inaccurate	• Incorrect driven gear • Incorrect drive gear • Faulty speedometer	• Check speedometer and odometer over a measured mile. Check proper cable driven gear to match axle ratio and tire size. Replace gear. • Check for proper drive gear for axle ratio and tire size. Replace gear. • Replace speedometer
Ignition switch—improper operation	• Binding lock cylinder • Binding ignition switch • Ignition slide switch out of adjustment • Open in wiring • Inoperative ignition switch	• Service or replace lock cylinder • Replace switch • Adjust slide switch • Service wiring • Replace switch (see Chapter 8)

CHASSIS ELECTRICAL

Instrument Panel

REMOVAL AND INSTALLATION

1983 and Later—Mustang and Capri (Manual A/C)

1. Disconnect the ground cable from the battery.
2. Remove the instrument panel pad.
3. Remove the two screws attaching the steering column lower cover to the instrument panel and remove the cover.
4. Remove the steering column trim shrouds by removing the screws on the underside of the shroud.
5. Remove the four nuts attaching the steering column to the brake pedal support and carefully lower the steering column only enough for access to the transmission gear shift selector lever and cable assembly (automatic transmission vehicles only).

NOTE: *Care must be used to assure that the column is not lowered too far to prevent damage to the selector lever and/or cable.*

6. Reach between the steering column and the instrument panel and gently lift the selector lever cable off the shift selector lever. Then, remove the cable clamp from the steering column tube.
7. Lay the steering column to rest on the front seat.
8. Remove the one screw attaching the instrument panel to the brake pedal support at the steering column opening.
9. Remove the one screw attaching the lower brace to the lower edge of the instrument panel below the radio.
10. Remove the one screw attaching the brace to the lower edge of the instrument panel below the glovebox.
11. Disconnect the temperature control cable from the temperature blend door and the evaporator case bracket.
12. Disconnect the 7-port vacuum hose connector at the evaporator case.
13. Disconnect the blower resistor wire connector from the resistor on the evaporator housing, and the blower motor feed wire at the in-line connector near the blower resistor wire connector.
14. Support the instrument panel and, with an angle phillips screwdriver, remove three screws attaching the top of the instrument panel to the cowl.
15. Remove the screws attaching each end of the instrument panel to the cowl side panels.
16. Move the instrument panel rearward and disconnect the speedometer cable from the speedometer and any wires that will not allow the instrument panel to lay on the front seat.

Use care not to scratch the instrument panel or the steering column.

17. Place the instrument panel near the installed position and connect any wires or connectors that were disconnected during removal.
18. Connect the speedometer cable to the speedometer.
19. Place the instrument panel in position and install one screw at each end of the instrument panel.
20. Install the three screws along the top front edge of the instrument panel with an angle phillips screwdriver.
21. Connect the two support braces to the lower edge of the instrument panel with one screw each.
22. Connect the temperature control cable to the temperature blend door crank arm and the bracket.
23. Connect the vacuum hoses at the 7-port connector and the blower motor wires at the resistor and in-line connector near the resistor.
24. Install the screw attaching the instrument panel to the brake pedal support.
25. Position the steering column near the brake panel support.
26. Connect the transmission gear shift selector lever cable to the shift selector lever. Then, connect the cable clamp to the steering column tube.
27. Position the steering column against the brake pedal support and install the four attaching nuts.
28. Adjust the transmission selector indicator.
29. Install the steering column shroud.
30. Position the steering column opening cover to the instrument panel and install the two attaching screws.
31. Install the instrument panel pad and connect the ground cable to the battery.
32. Connect the temperature control cable to the temperature blend door crank arm and adjust as necessary.

Speedometer Cable

REPLACEMENT

1. Reach up behind the speedometer and depress the flat, quick disconnect tab (thumb latch), while pulling back on the cable.
2. If just the inner core is to be replaced pull the core from the casing. If the inner core is broken, raise and support the car and remove the cable-to-transmission clamp and pull the cable core from the transmission.
3. If both the cable and casing need to be replaced disconnect the cable from the speedometer head and push through the opening in

CHASSIS ELECTRICAL

Speedometer cable and casing routing

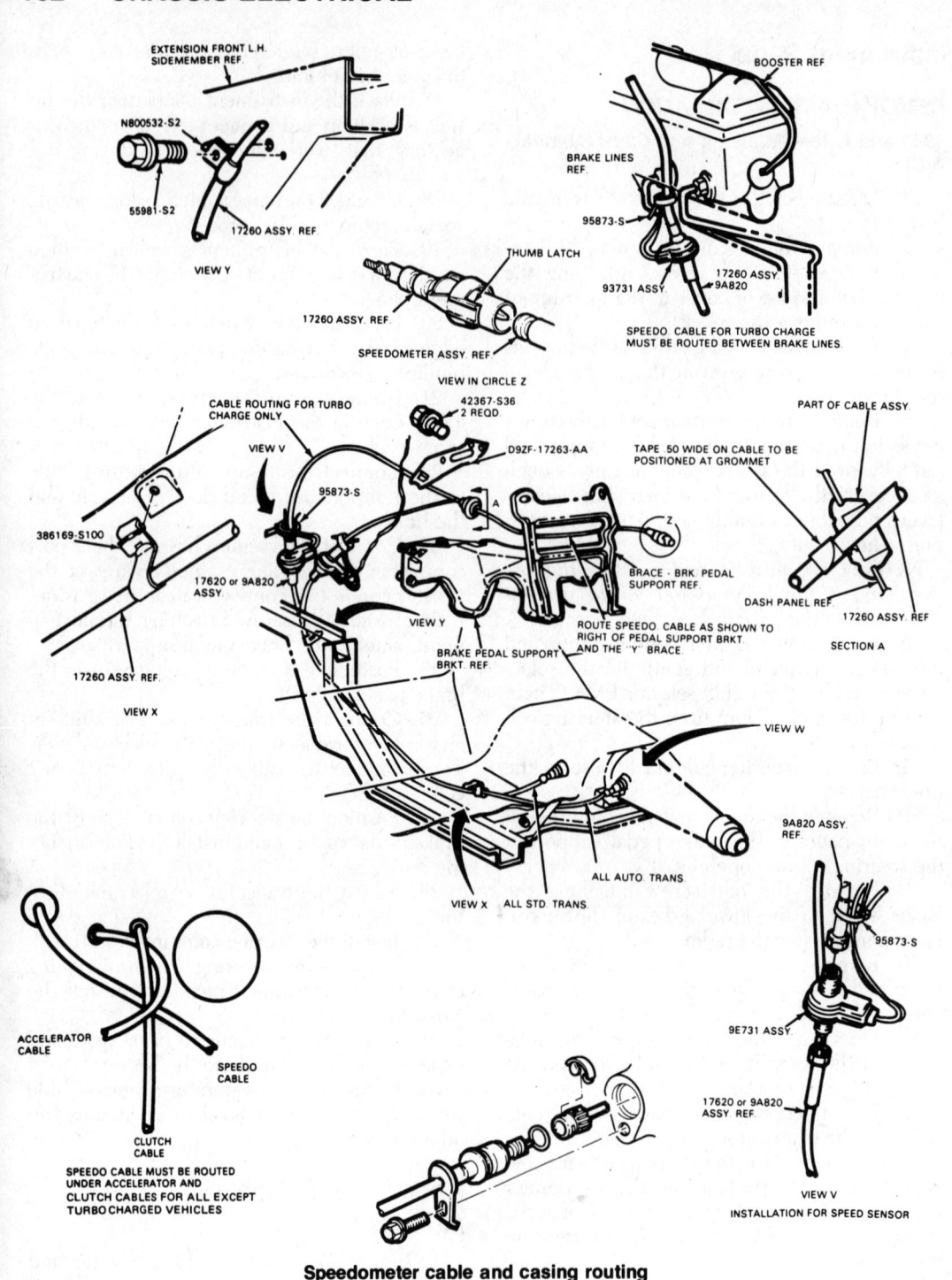

the dash panel or floor pan. Raise the car on a hoist and disconnect the cable from the transmission and the retaining clips. To prevent kinking reroute the cable assembly properly. See the illustration.

Ignition Switch

Removal and Installation procedures for the ignition switch is found in Chapter 8.

CHASSIS ELECTRICAL 163

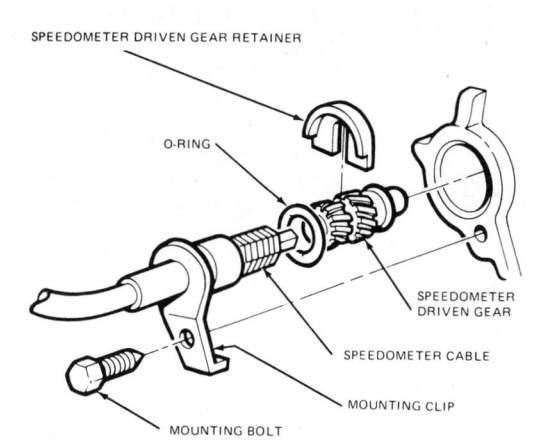

Speedometer cable to transmission mounting

LIGHTING

Headlamps

All 1980 and later models use halogen sealed beams. The halogen sealed beams provide a whiter light while reducing the electrical load. Although the halogen sealed beams are fully interchangeable with the conventional sealed beams it is recommended that all of the sealed beams be of the same type.

CAUTION: *Halogen bulbs contain gas under pressure. The bulb may shatter if the glass envelope is scratched or the bulb is dropped. Handle the bulb carefully and only by its plastic base. Keep bulb away from children.*

REMOVAL AND INSTALLATION

Except Merkur

1. Remove the headlamp door mounting screws and remove the headlamp door.
2. Remove the four retainer ring screws and remove the retainer ring from the headlamp. Pull the headlamp bulb forward and disconnect the wiring assembly plug.
3. To install, connect the wiring plug to the new headlamp bulb and position the bulb so that the bulb tabs are in the slots.
4. Attach the bulb retaining ring to the assembly and install the screws.
5. Place the headlamp door into position and install the mounting screws.

Merkur

1. Make sure the headlight switch is off. The bulb is unplugged from the rear of the grille assembly.
2. Remove the electrical connector from the bulb by pulling the connector rearward.
3. Remove the bulb retaining ring by rotating it counterclockwise about 1/8 of a turn and sliding it rearward off the headlamp body. Keep the ring to mount the new bulb.
4. Carefully remove the headlamp bulb from its socket in the reflector by gently pulling it straight out. Dispose of the burned out bulb.
5. Install the new bulb in the reverse order of removal.

CIRCUIT PROTECTION

Fusible Links

In addition to fuses and circuit breakers some wiring harnesses incorporate fusible links to protect the wiring.

NOTE: *Refer to the Circuit Protection Chart to find out what circuits use fusible links.*

The fusible link is a short length of special Hypalon (high temperature) insulated wire, integral with the engine compartment wiring harness and should not be confused with standard wire. It is several wire gauges smaller than the circuit which it protects. Under no circumstances should a fuse link replacement repair be made using a length of standard wire cut from bulk stock or from another wiring harness.

To repair any blown fuse link use the following procedure:

1. Determine which circuit is damaged, its location and the cause of the open fuse link. If the damaged fuse link is one of three fed by a common No. 10 or 12 gauge feed wire, determine the specific affected circuit.
2. Disconnect the negative battery cable.
3. Cut the damaged fuse link from the wiring harness and discard it. If the fuse link is one of the three circuits fed by a single feed wire, cut it out of the harness at each splice end and discard it.
4. Identify and procure the proper fuse link and butt connectors for attaching the fuse link to the harness.
5. To repair any fuse link in a 3-link group with one feed:
   a. After cutting the open link out of the harness, cut each of the remaining undamaged fuse links close to the feed wire weld.
   b. Strip approximately ½ inch of insulation from the detached ends of the two good fuse links. Then insert two wire ends into one end of a butt connector and carefully push one stripped end of the replacement fuse link into the same end of the butt connector and crimp all three firmly together.

NOTE: *Care must be taken when fitting the three fuse links into the butt connector as the internal diameter is a snug fit for three wires. Make sure to use a proper crimping*

164 CHASSIS ELECTRICAL

REMOVE EXISTING VINYL TUBE SHIELDING REINSTALL OVER FUSE LINK BEFORE CRIMPING FUSE LINK TO WIRE ENDS

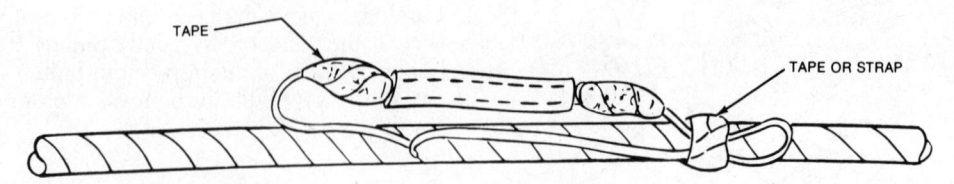

TAPE

TAPE OR STRAP

TYPICAL REPAIR USING THE SPECIAL #17 GA. (9.00" LONG-YELLOW) FUSE LINK REQUIRED FOR THE AIR/COND. CIRCUITS (2) #687E and #261A LOCATED IN THE ENGINE COMPARTMENT

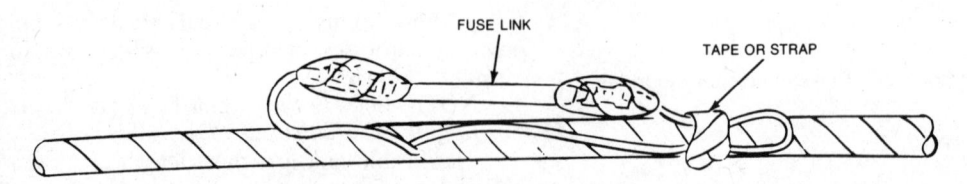

FUSE LINK

TAPE OR STRAP

TYPICAL REPAIR FOR ANY IN-LINE FUSE LINK USING THE SPECIFIED GAUGE FUSE LINK FOR THE SPECIFIC CIRCUIT

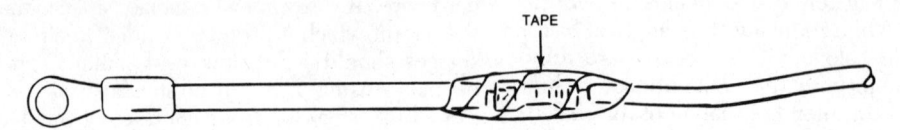

TAPE

TYPICAL REPAIR USING THE EYELET TERMINAL FUSE LINK OF THE SPECIFIED GAUGE FOR ATTACHMENT TO A CIRCUIT WIRE END

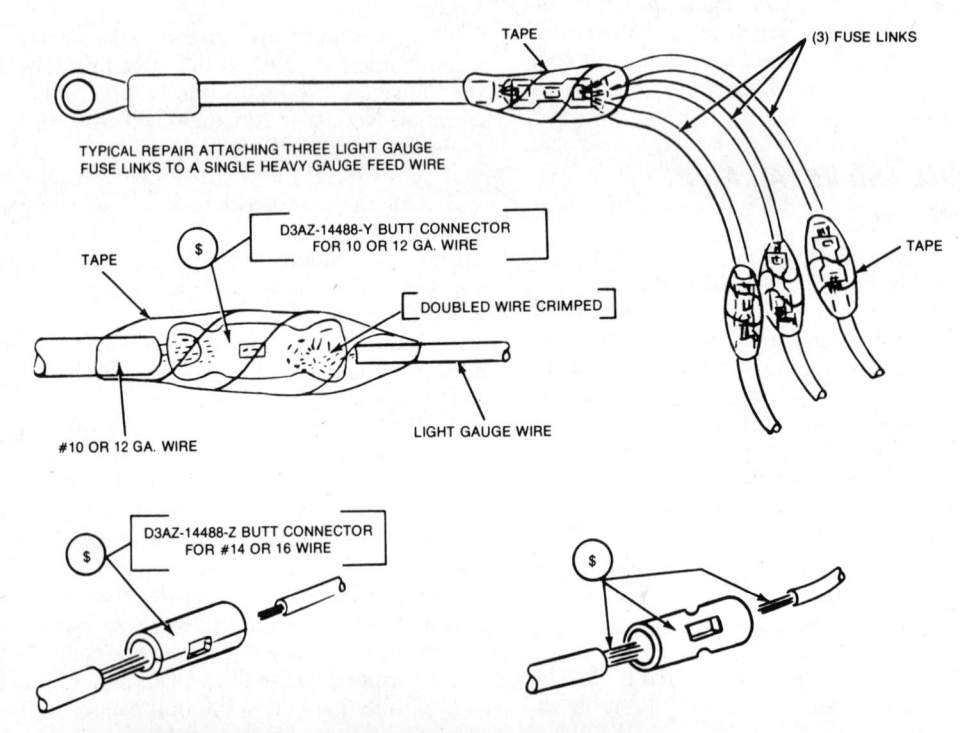

TAPE

(3) FUSE LINKS

TYPICAL REPAIR ATTACHING THREE LIGHT GAUGE FUSE LINKS TO A SINGLE HEAVY GAUGE FEED WIRE

D3AZ-14488-Y BUTT CONNECTOR FOR 10 OR 12 GA. WIRE

TAPE

DOUBLED WIRE CRIMPED

TAPE

#10 OR 12 GA. WIRE

LIGHT GAUGE WIRE

D3AZ-14488-Z BUTT CONNECTOR FOR #14 OR 16 WIRE

FUSIBLE LINK REPAIR PROCEDURE

General fusible link repair procedure

Light Bulb Specifications

Function	Trade Number
Exterior illumination	
Headlamps	H4656 Low Beam
	H4651 High Beam
Front park/Turn lamps	1157
Front side marker lamps	194
Rear tail/Stop lamps & turn	1157
License plate lamp	168
Back-up lamp	1156
Interior illumination	
Turn signal indicator	194
Electric de-ice nomenclature (opt.)	**
Heater control nomenclature	161
A/C control nomenclature (opt.)	161
Glove compartment lamp (opt.)	1816
Courtesy lamp—under instrument panel (opt.)	N.A.
Ash tray lamp (opt.)	1892
Digital clock lamp (Opt.)	194
High beam indicator	194
Warning lamps	194
Gauge illumination—all	
Dome lamp (standard)	906
Dome/Map lamp (opt.): dome	906
map	1816
Trunk compartment lamp (opt.)	89
Engine compartment lamp (opt.)	89
Automatic transmission "PRND21" indicator (floor)	1893
Radio lamps	
Dial illumination	1893
AM, AM/FM	
AM/FM/MPX/Tape	
Premium sound indicator	
Stereo indicator lamp	

tool. Pliers, side cutters, etc. will not apply the proper crimp to retain the wires and withstand a pull test.

c. After crimping the butt connector to the three fuse links, cut the weld portion from the feed wire and strip approximately ½ inch of insulation from the cut end. Insert the stripped end into the open end of the butt connector and crimp very firmly.

d. To attach the remaining end of the replacement fuse link strip approximately ½ inch of insulation from the wire end of the circuit from which the blown fuse link was removed, and firmly crimp a butt connector or equivalent to the stripped wire. Then, insert the end of the replacement link into the other end of the butt connector and crimp firmly.

e. Using rosin core solder with a consistency of 60 percent tin and 40 percent lead, solder the connectors and the wires at the repairs and insulate with electrical tape.

6. To replace any fuse link on a single circuit in a harness, cut out the damaged portion, strip approximately ½ inch of insulation from the two wire ends and attach the appropriate replacement fuse link to the stripped wire ends with two proper size butt connectors. Solder the connectors and wires and insulate with tape.

7. To repair any fuse link which has an eyelet terminal on one end such as the charging circuit, cut off the open fuse link behind the weld, strip approximately ½ inch of insulation from the cut end and attach the appropriate new eyelet fuse link to the cut stripped wire with an appropriate size butt connector. Solder the connectors and wires at the repair and insulate with tape.

8. Connect the negative battery cable to the battery and test the system for proper operation.

NOTE: *Do not mistake a resistor wire for a fuse link. The resistor wire is generally longer and has print stating "Resistor don't cut or splice."*

NOTE: *When attaching a single No. 16, 17, 18 or 20 gauge fuse link to a heavy gauge wire, always double the stripped wire end of the fuse link before inserting and crimping it into the butt connector for positive wire retention.*

Fusible Link Location

Fuse Link	GA	Location
Lamp feed	16	Near voltage regulator
Ignition feed	16	Near voltage regulator
Charging circuit	14	Near starter motor relay
Heated backlite and power door locks	16	Near starter motor relay
Engine compartment lamp	20	Near starter motor relay

Circuit Breaker

A circuit breaker is an electrical switch which breaks the circuit in case of an overload. The circuit breaker is located at the top of the fuse panel.

Circuit Breaker Location

Location	Size	Circuit Protected
Part of headlight switch	22 amp.	Headlights, high-beam indicator
Fuse panel	6 amp.	Windshield wiper-washer system

Fuse Panel

The fuse panel is located in the lower left portion of the instrument panel, behind a trim cover. A circuit breaker and a turn signal flasher

CHASSIS ELECTRICAL

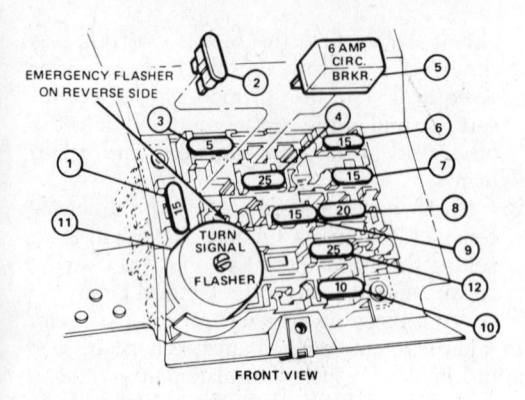

FRONT VIEW

1. Turn signal back-up lamps
   15 amp. fuse
2. Heater (std.) 15 amp. fuse
   air conditioning 30 amp. fuse
3. Instrument panel lamps 5 amp. fuse
4. Accessory-A/C clutch 25 amp. fuse
5. Windshield wiper/washer 6 amp.
   circuit breaker
6. Stop lamps-emergency warning
   amp. fuse
7. Courtesy lamps
   15 amp. fuse
8. Cigar lighter-horn
   20 amp. fuse
9. Radio 15 amp. fuse
10. Warning lamps
    10 amp. fuse
11. Turn signal flasher
12. Electric choke
    25 amp. fuse

Fuse and circuit breaker panel

are also located in the fuse panel. To check out or replace a fuse or circuit breaker proceed as follows:

1. Remove the two screws and remove the fuse panel trim cover.
2. Locate the blown fuse or malfunctioning circuit breaker and remove it by pulling it out of the cavity.
3. Using the same amp rating push the fuse or circuit breaker into the panel until it seats fully.

Warning Buzzer Locations
Key Warning and Seat Belt Timer Buzzer

The key warning buzzer and the seat belt timer buzzer are combined into one unit on the Mustang/Capri. The buzzer assembly is mounted on the extreme right end of the relay panel above the glove box.

WIRING DIAGRAMS

Wiring diagrams have been left out of this book. As cars have become more complex, and available with longer and longer option lists wiring diagrams have grown in size and complexity also. It has been virtually impossible to provide a readable reproduction in a reasonable number of pages. Information on ordering wiring diagrams from the vehicle manufacturer can be found in the owners manual.

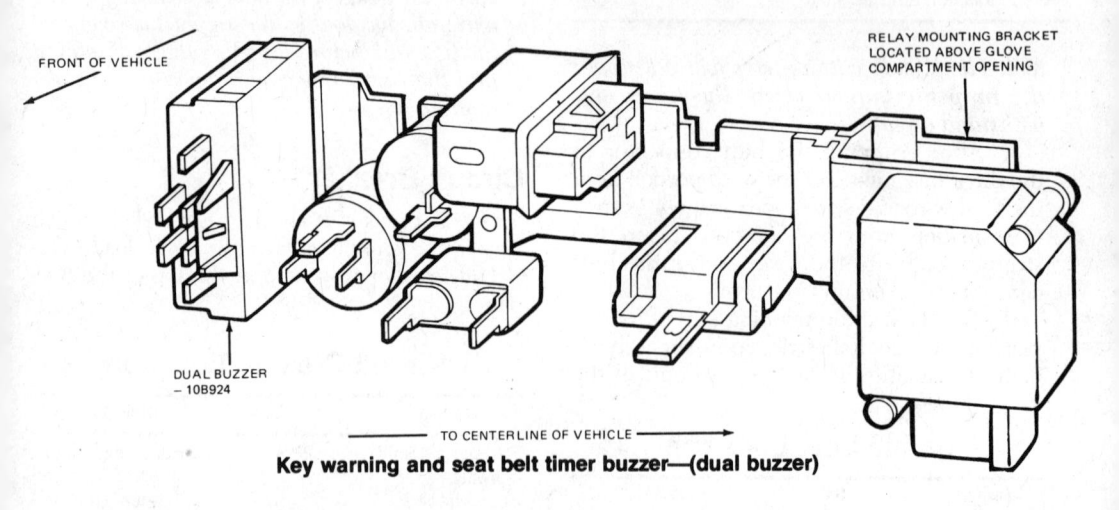

Key warning and seat belt timer buzzer—(dual buzzer)

Clutch and Transmission
6

MANUAL TRANSMISSION

Model RAD Four Speed
REMOVAL AND INSTALLATION

1. Raise the vehicle on a hoist.
2. Mark the driveshaft so that it may be reinstalled in the same relative position to the rear axle companion flange. Remove the driveshaft and install Tool T71P-7095-A or equivalent in the extension housing to prevent lubricant leakage.
3. Disconnect backup lamp switch wires.
4. Remove the speedometer cable attaching screw, lift the cable from the extension housing, and plug the hole to prevent oil spillage.
5. Support the transmission with a jack and remove the bolts that attach the crossmember to the body.
6. Remove the two bolts that attach crossmember-to-extension housing, and remove the crossmember.
7. Lower the transmission as required to permit access tm the shift lever bolts.
8. Remove the three shift lever attaching bolts. Lift the shift lever out of the transmission extension housing.
9. Remove the bolts that attach the transmission assembly to the flywheel housing. Slide the transmission away from the flywheel housing and from under the vehicle.
10. Install the clutch release lever and bearing.
11. Apply a film of chassis lube to the input shaft front bearing retainer. Position the transmission assembly into the flywheel housing and install and tighten attaching bolts to specifica-

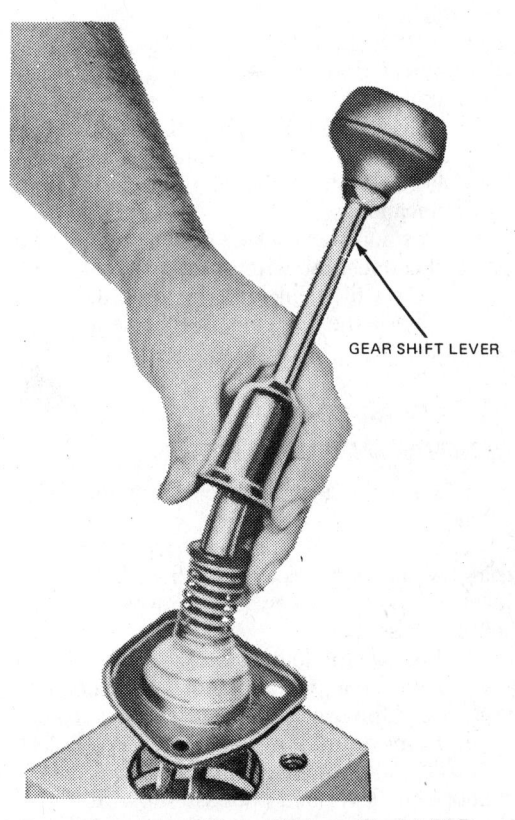

Shift lever boot removal—Model RAD

Removing or installing shift lever-Model RAD

168 CLUTCH AND TRANSMISSION

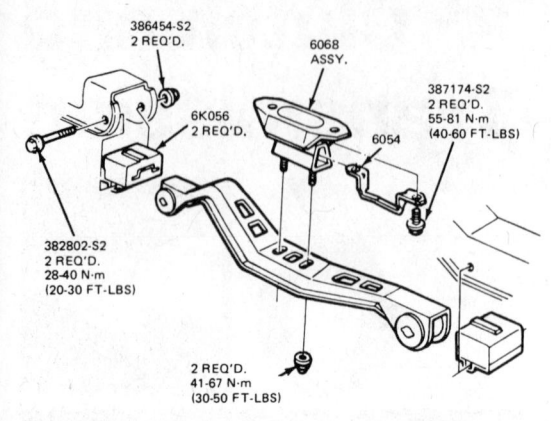

Transmission crossmember—All four speeds

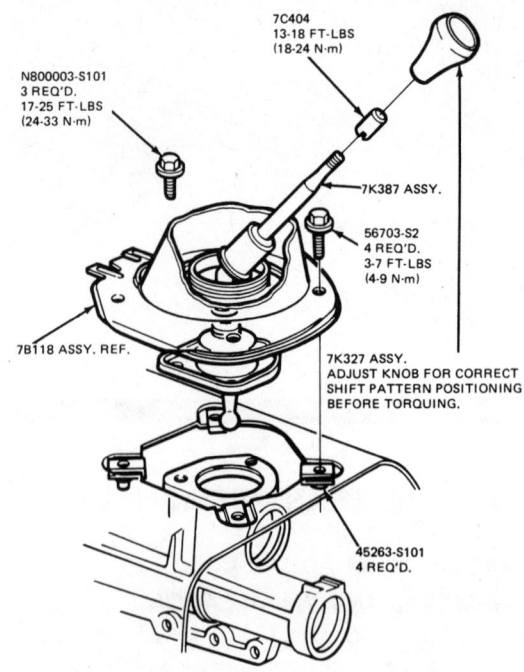

Gearshift lever installation—Model 79ET, 80ET

tion. It may be necessary to place the transmission in gear and rotate the output shaft to align the input shaft and clutch splines.

12. Raise the transmission to install the shift lever in the extension housing. Install the three metric attaching bolts.
13. Raise the transmission until it is in its normal position. Install and secure the crossmember to the body with the attaching bolts, and tighten to specification. Install the two bolts that attach the crossmember to the extension housing, and tighten to specification.
14. Install the speedometer cable and tighten the attaching screw to specification.
15. Install the driveshaft, making sure that it is connected to the pinion flange in its original position.
16. Fill the transmission with the specified lubricant until it appears at the bottom of the filler plug hole. Install the filler plug and tighten to specification.
17. Position the backup switch wire in the clip and connect the wire to the switch.
18. Lower the vehicle to the ground.
19. Check the transmission for proper operation.

ET Four Speed

REMOVAL AND INSTALLATION

1. Place the gear shift lever in Neutral position.
2. Remove the attaching screws at rear of coin tray and lift to release from front hold down notch on boot retainer. Lift it over the gear shift lever boot.
3. Remove the four capscrews attaching the boot to the floor pan and move the boot upward out of the way.
4. Remove the three lever attaching bolts. NOTE: *The attaching bolts are Metric (M8).* Remove the lever and boot assembly from the extension housing.
5. Remove the gear shift knob and locknut and slide the boot off the lever.
6. Working from under the hood, remove upper bolts (or stud nuts) that attach flywheel housing to engine.
7. Raise the vehicle on a hoist.
8. Mark the position of the driveshaft relative to the axle companion flange. Remove the driveshaft and install Toll T71P-7095-A or equivalent in the extension housing to prevent lubricant leakage.
9. Remove the clutch release lever dust cover.
10. Disconnect the clutch release cable from the release lever.
11. Remove the started motor attaching bolts and place the starter to one side.
12. Remove the speedometer cable attaching screw and lift the cable from the extension housing.
13. Support the rear of the engine with a jack and remove the bolts that attach the crossmember to the body.
14. Remove the bolt (or bolts) that attaches crossmember to extension housing, and remove the crossmember.
15. Lower the engine as required to permit removal of bolts that attach the flywheel housing to the engine. Slide the transmission away from the engine and from under the vehicle.

NOTE: *It may be necessary to slide the mounting bracket forward from the catalytic converter heat shield in order to move the*

CLUTCH AND TRANSMISSION

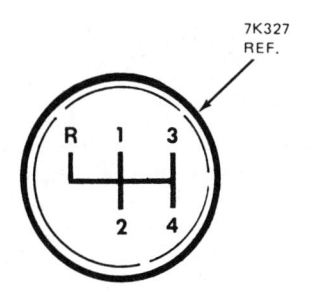

WITH LEVER IN NEUTRAL POSITION, INSTALL LOCKING NUT 7C404 UNTIL HAND TIGHT. THEN INSTALL KNOB 7K327 UNTIL HAND TIGHT. BACK KNOB OFF UNTIL SHIFT PATTERN ALIGNS WITH THE ℄ OF DRIVE LINE. TIGHTEN LOCKING NUT 13-18 FT-LBS (18-24 N·m) NO THREADS SHALL BE VISIBLE AFTER NUT HAS BEEN TIGHTENED. SHIFT PATTERN ALIGNMENT MUST BE WITHIN ±15° OF ℄ OF DRIVE LINE.

Shift knob installation—Model 79ET, 80ET

transmission rearward far enough to remove it.

16. Remove the cover attaching bolts and drain the lubricant into a container.
17. Remove the bolts that attach flywheel housing to transmission case and remove the housing.
18. Install a new shift rod seal in the flywheel housing (if the old seal is damaged).
19. Position flywheel housing on transmission case, and install and tighten the attaching bolts to 35–45 ft. lb.
20. Install the clutch release lever and bearing.
21. Make certain that machined surfaces of flywheel housing and engine are free of dirt and foreign material.
22. Apply a film of C4AZ-19584-A lubricant or equivalent to the input shaft bearing retainer. Position the flywheel housing and transmission assembly on the engine block.

NOTE: *It may be necessary to place the transmission in gear and rotate the output shaft to align the input shaft and clutch splines.*

23. Slide the flywheel housing firmly and squarely onto the locating dowels, to be sure of a positive engagement. Then, holding the flywheel housing firmly in position on the dowels, thread the attaching bolts through the hollow portion of the dowels and into the housing. Tighten the bolts to 38–55 ft. lb.
24. Install and tighten the center attaching bolts.
25. Lower the vehicle and install the two upper attaching bolts or stud nuts. Tighten to 38–55 ft. lb.
26. Make sure the shift lever insulator is in a straight downward position on the shift rail.
27. Position the shift lever in the extension housing so that the forked ends engage in the insulator properly.
28. Install the three metric attaching bolts (M8) and tighten to specifications.
29. Slide the boot over the lever and install the attaching bolts. Tighten the bolts to specifications.
30. Install the gear shift knob and adjust as shown in the illustrations.
31. Position the coin tray over the shift lever boot.
32. Secure the tray to front notch on boot retaining ring and attach at rear with screws.
33. Raise the vehicle. Raise the engine until the transmission reaches its normal position. Secure the crossmember to the body with the attaching bolts, and tighten to 28–40 ft. lb. Install the bolt that attaches crossmember to extension housing, and tighten to 50–70 ft. lb.
34. Position the catalytic converter heat shield mounting bracket to the transmission mount.
35. Remove Tool T71P-7095-A or equivalent, install the speedometer cable and tighten the attaching screw to specification.
36. Position the starter, install the attaching bolts, and tighten to specification.
37. Apply grease to the ball end of the clutch release lever. Install the clutch release fork dust cover.
38. Install the driveshaft, making sure that it is connected to the pinion flange in its original position.
39. Fill the transmission with the specified lubricant until it appears at the bottom of the filler plug hole. Install the filler plug and tighten to specification.
40. Install the backup lamp switch and connect the wire to the switch.
41. Lower the vehicle to the ground.
42. Check the transmission for proper operation.

5 Speed O/D Transmission

REMOVAL AND INSTALLATION

Shift Lever and Boot Assembly

1. Remove the four bolts attaching shift boot to floor pan.
2. Remove the two bolts attaching the shift lever to transmission.
3. Install the two bolts attaching the shift lever to transmission. Tighten to 23–32 ft. lbs.

NOTE: *Shift lever bolts must only be installed in one direction (from left side of shift lever).*

4. Install the four bolts attaching the shift boot to floor pan. Tighten to 3–7 ft. lbs.

CLUTCH AND TRANSMISSION

Transmission

1. Raise and safely support the vehicle.
2. Mark the driveshaft so that it may be installed in the same relative position. Disconnect the driveshaft from the rear U-joint flange. Slide the driveshaft off the transmission output shaft and install the extension housing seal installation tool into the extension housing to prevent lubricant leakage.
3. Remove the four bolts attaching the catalytic converter. Remove converter.
4. Remove the two nuts attaching the rear transmission support to the crossmember. Remove bolts.
   On turbocharged engines, remove the catalytic converter and inlet pipe.
5. Support the engine and transmission with a transmission jack.
6. Remove the two nuts from the crossmember bolts. Remove bolts, raise jack slightly and remove crossmember.
7. Lower transmissin to expose the two bolts securing the shift handle to the shift tower. Using a socket, remove the two nuts and bolts. Remove shift handle.
8. Disconnect the wiring harness from the backup lamp switch. On 5.0L engine, disconnect top gear sensing switch.
9. Remove the bolt from the speedometer cable retainer and remove speedometer driven gear from the transmission.
10. Remove the four bolts that secure the transmission to the flywheel housing.
11. Move the transmission and jack rearward until the transmission input shaft clears the flywheel housing. If necessary, lower the engine enough to obtain clearance for transmission removal. Do not depress the clutch pedal while the transmission is removed.
12. Make sure that the mounting surface of the transmission and the flywheel housing are free of dirt, paint, and burrs. Install two guide pins in the flywheel housing lower mounting bolt holes. Raise the transmission and move forward on the guide pins until the input shaft splines enter the clutch hub splines and the case is positioned against the flywheel housing.
13. Install the two upper transmission to flywheel housing mounting bolts snug, and then remove the two guide pins. Install the two lower mounting bolts. Tighten all mounting bolts to 35–55 ft. lbs.
14. Using a transmission jack, raise the transmission until the shift handle can be secured to the shift tower. Install and tighten the attaching bolts and washers to 23–32 ft. lbs.
15. Connect the speedometer cable to the extension housing. Tighten the attaching screw to 36–54 ft. lbs.
16. Using a transmission jack, raise the rear of the transmission and install the transmission support. Install and tighten attaching bolts to 36–50 ft. lbs.
17. With the transmission extension housing resting on the engine rear support, install the transmission extension housing attaching bolts. Tighten the bolts to 25–35 ft. lbs.
18. Connect the backup lamp switch wiring harness. On 5.0L engine, connect top gear sensing switch.
19. Install the catalytic converter and tighten the attaching bolts to 20–30 ft. lbs.
20. Remove the extension housing installation tool and slide the forward end of the driveshaft over the transmission output shaft. Connect the driveshaft to the rear U-joint flange. Make sure driveshaft index marks align. Tighten U-bolt nuts to 42–57 ft. lbs.
21. Fill the transmission to the proper level with the specified lubricant (ESP-M2C83-C Dexron II or equivalent).
22. Lower the vehicle. Check the shift and crossover motion for full shift engagement and smooth crossover operation.

CLUTCH

The 1979–80 Mustang and Capri models require only a pedal height adjustment. Beginning with the 1981 models, a self-adjusting clutch is standard. This automatic clutch system allows the clutch pedal to be adjusted by the driver during normal vehicle operation. All that is required in this adjustment is that the driver, by either using his hand or by placing his toe under the clutch pedal, pull the pedal up until it stops. The movement requires very little effort (about 10 lbs.).

To complete the adjustment, depress the clutch pedal with a relatively slow movement. During this movement, a "clock" may be heard which means an adjustment was necessary and has been accomplished. You should make this self-adjustment about every 5,000 miles or less.

Pedal Adjustment
Except 6-200 Engine

1. Working under the car, remove the dust shield.
2. Loosen the clutch cable locknut. To raise the pedal, turn the adjusting nut clockwise; to lower the pedal, turn it counterclockwise.
3. On the four cylinder engine, adjust the pedal height to 5.3 in.; on the 255 and 302-V8 adjust the height to 6.5 in.
4. Tighten the locknut. When the pedal is adjusted properly, the pedal can be raised about

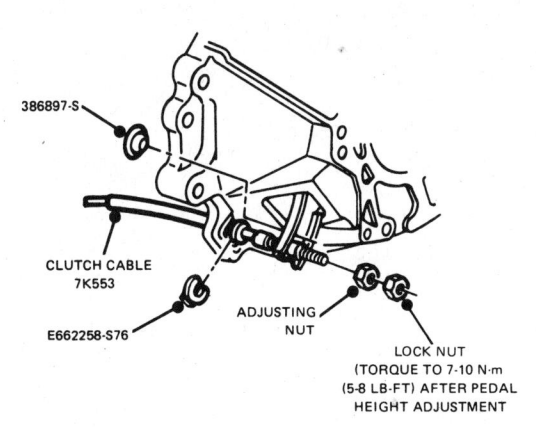

CLUTCH AND TRANSMISSION 171

Clutch pedal adjustment—4 cyl. V8 engines

Clutch pedal adjustment—6 cyl. 200 engine

2¾ in. on the four cylinder model and about 1½ in. on the V8 to reach the pedal stop.
5. Install the dust shield.

Six Cyl. 200 Cu In. Engine

1. Pull the clutch cable toward the front of the car until the adjusting nut can be rotated. In order to free the nut from the rubber insulator, it may be necessary to block the clutch release forward so the clutch is partially disengaged.
2. Rotate the adjusting nut to obtain a 5.3 in. pedal height. Depress the pedal a few times and recheck the adjustment. When the pedal is properly adjusted, it can be raised about 2¾ in. to reach the pedal stop.

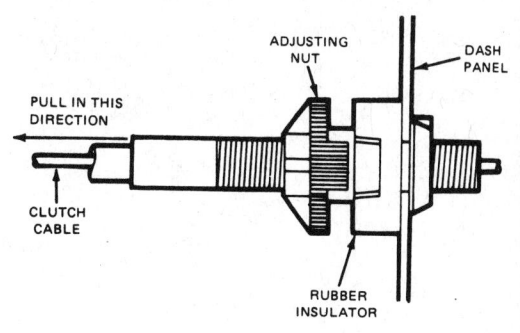

Clutch Assembly

REMOVAL AND INSTALLATION

Four Cyl—140 Cu In. Engine (Except Turbocharged)

1. Raise and safely support the vehicle.
2. Remove the dust shield.
3. Loosen the clutch cable lock and adjusting nut. Remove rubber cable plug and disconnect the cable from the release lever.
4. Remove the retaining clip and remove the clutch cable from the flywheel housing.
5. Remove the starter electrical cable and the starter motor from the flywheel housing.
6. Remove the bolts that secure the engine rear plate to the front lower part of the flywheel housing.
7. Remove the transmission and flywheel housing.

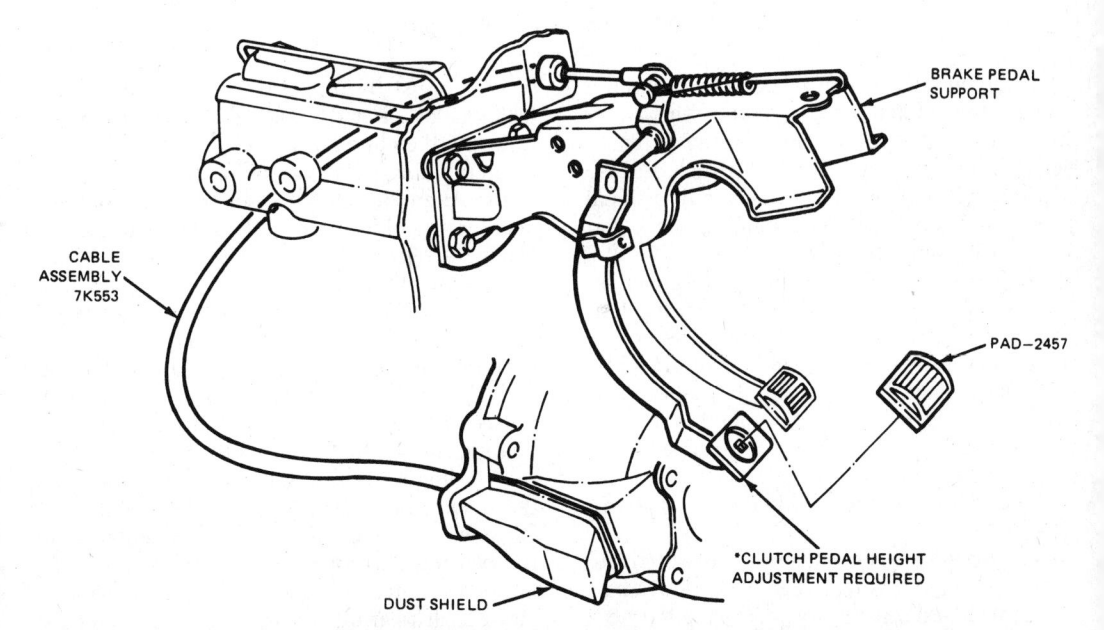

Clutch pedal and cable assembly—all engines

172 CLUTCH AND TRANSMISSION

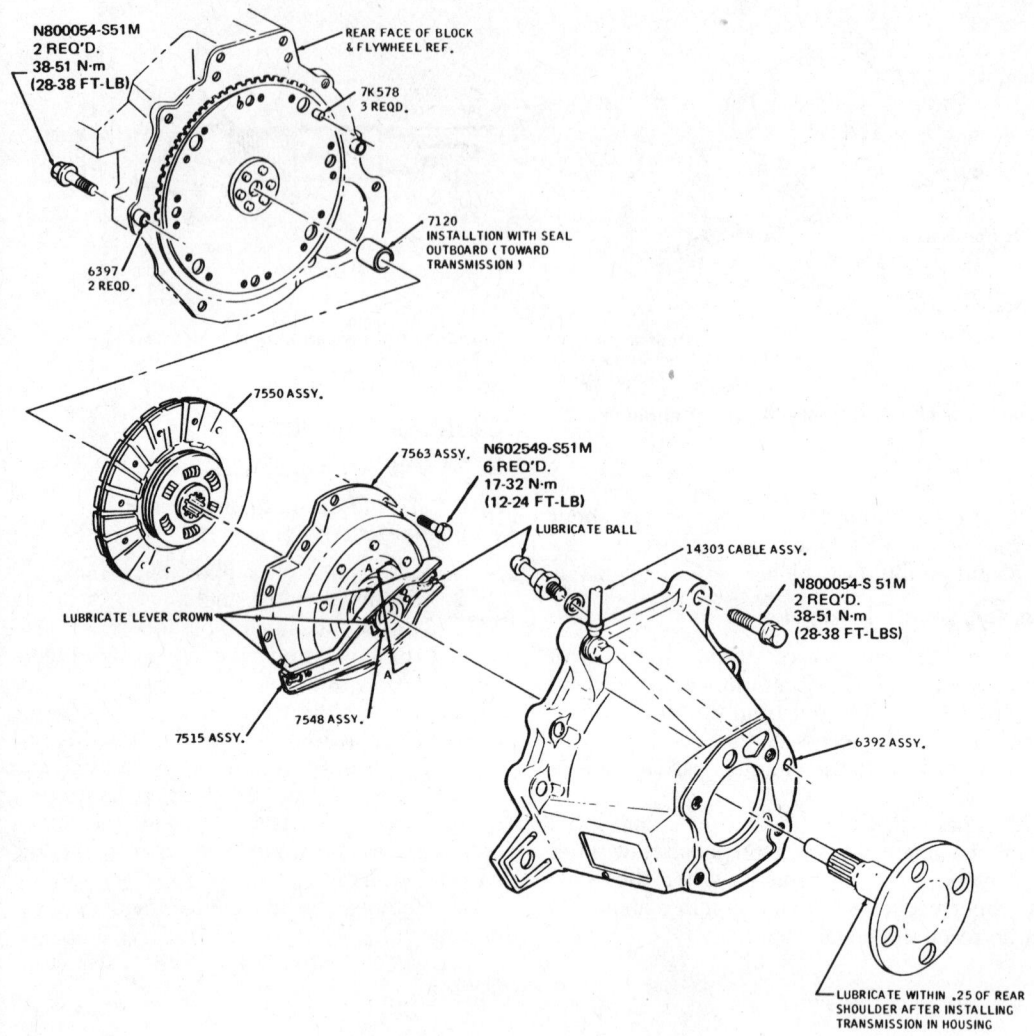

Clutch installation—4 cyl. engine

8. Remove the clutch release lever from the housing by pulling it through the window in the housing until the retainer spring is disengaged from the pivot. Inspect clutch release bearing and replace if required. If original bearing is reused, note orientation, mark, and install in the same position.

9. Loosen the six pressure plate cover attaching bolts evenly to release the spring tension gradually and avoid distorting the cover. If the same pressure plate and cover are to be reinstalled, mark the cover and flywheel so that the pressure plate can be reinstalled in its original position. Remove the pressure plate and clutch disc from the flywheel.

10. Install the clutch release lever if it was removed.

11. Position the clutch disc and pressure plate assembly on the flywheel. The three dowel pins on the flywheel must be properly aligned with the pressure plate. Bent, damaged or missing dowels, must be replaced. Start the cover attaching bolts but do not tighten them. Avoid touching the clutch disc face, dropping parts or contaminating parts with oil or grease.

12. Align the clutch disc using the proper alignment tool inserted in the pilot bearing. Alternately tighten the cover bolts to 12–14 ft. lb. Remove the alignment tool.

13. Apply a light film of lithium base grease to (1) the outside diameter of the transmission front bearing retainer, (2) the release lever fork and anti-rattle spring where they contact the release bearing hub, and (3) to the release bearing surface that contacts the pressure plate release fingers. Then, fill the grease groove of the release bearing hub with the same grease. Clean all excess grease from inside the bore of the bearing hub, otherwise, excess grease will be forced onto the spline by the transmission input shaft bearing retainer, and will contaminate the clutch disc.

CLUTCH AND TRANSMISSION 173

14. Attach the clutch release bearing to the release lever.

15. Attach the release lever and release bearing to the flywheel housing.

16. Inspect the flywheel housing dowel holes for misalignment and wear.

17. Make certain that the flywheel housing and cylinder block mounting surfaces are clean and that the dowels are in good condition.

18. Install the flywheel housing and transmission.

19. Install the bolts that secure the engine rear plate to the front lower part of the flywheel housing.

20. Connect the clutch cable to the flywheel housing and connect the retaining clip.

21. Install the starter motor and starter electrical cable.

22. Connect the clutch cable and return spring to the release lever and reinstall the dust shield and return spring to the rear crossmember.

23. Adjust the clutch pedal height adjustment.

Six Syl. 200 Cu In., Four Cyl. 140 Cu In. (Turbocharged), V8 Engines

1. Raise and safely support the vehicle.
2. Remove the transmission. (Refer to the procedure outlined earlier.)
3. Remove the dust shield.
4. Loosen the clutch adjusting nut to provide slack in the clutch cable and disengage the clutch cable from the release lever.
5. Disengage the clutch cable from the flywheel housing.

6. Remove the starter electrical cable, then the starter motor from the flywheel housing.

7. Remove the bolts that secure the engine rear plate to the front lower part of the flywheel housing.

8. Remove the bolts that attach the housing to the cylinder block.

9. Move the housing back just far enough to clear the pressure plate, and remove.

10. Remove the clutch release lever from the housing by pulling it through the window in the housing until the retainer spring is disengaged from the pivot.

11. Loosen the six pressure plate cover attaching bolts evenly to release the spring tension without distorting the cover. If the same pressure plate and cover assembly is to be installed after the clutch is removed, mark the cover and flywheel so that the pressure plate can be reinstalled in the same position.

12. Remove the pressure plate and clutch disc from the flywheel.

13. Install the clutch release lever.

14. Place the clutch disc and pressure plate assembly in position on the flywheel. Start the cover attaching bolts to hold the pieces in place, but do not tighten them. Avoid touching the clutch disc facing, dropping the parts or contaminating them with oil or grease as clutch chatter may result.

15. Align the clutch disc using an alignment tool. To avoid distorting the pressure plate cover, alternately tighten the bolts, a few turns at a time, until they are all snug. Then, tighten the six pressure plate cover bolts to specification. Remove the alignment tool.

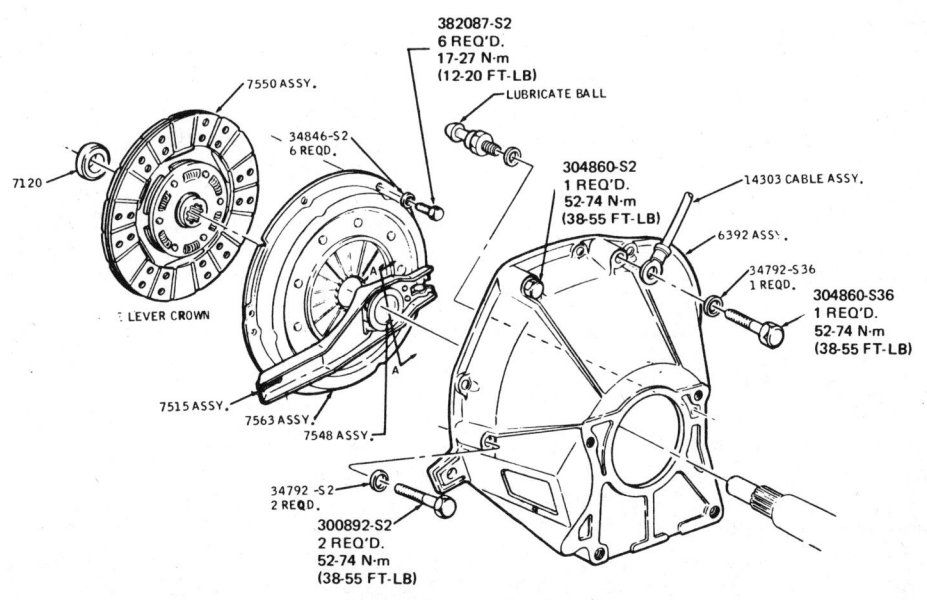

Clutch installation—6 cyl. engine

174 CLUTCH AND TRANSMISSION

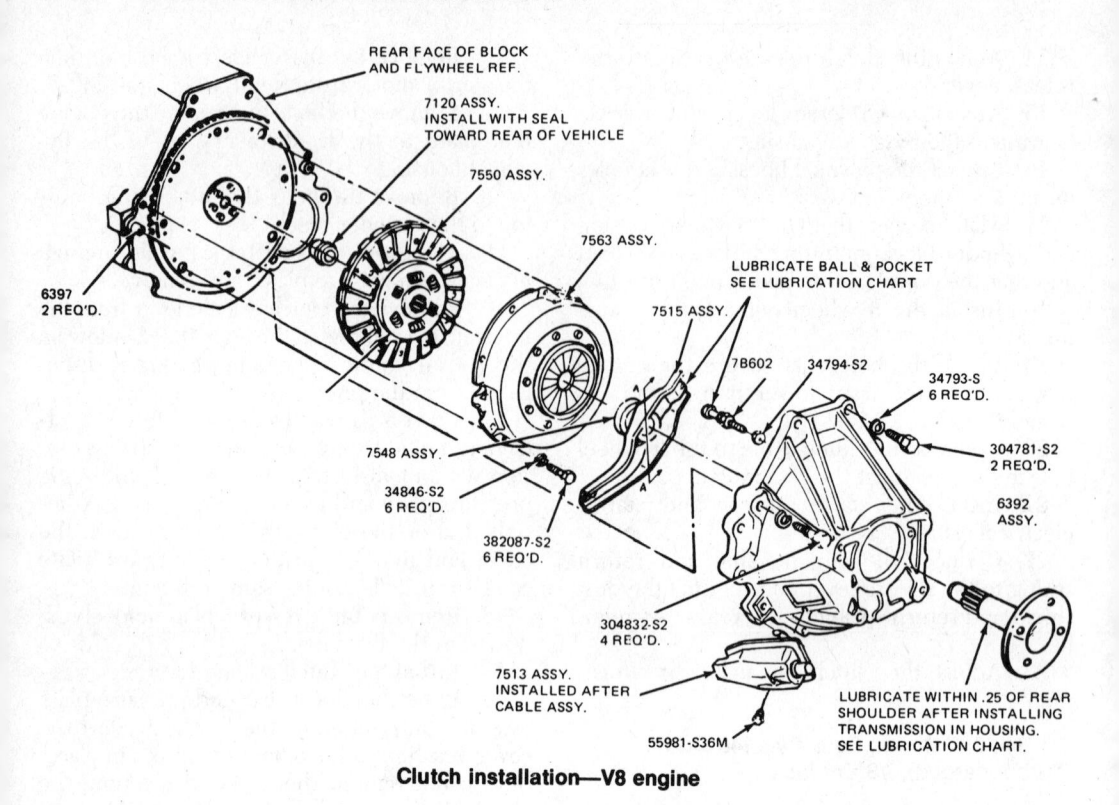

Clutch installation—V8 engine

16. Apply a light film of lithium base grease to (1) the outside diameter of the transmission front bearing retainer, (2) both sides of the release lever fork where it contacts the release bearing spring clips and (3) to the release bearing surface that contacts the pressure plate release fingers. Then, fill the grease groove of the release bearing hub with the same lithium base grease. Clean all excess grease from inside the bore of the bearing hub, otherwise, excess grease will be forced onto the spline by the transmission input shaft bearing retainer, and will contaminate the clutch disc. Place the release bearing on the release lever and make certain that the flywheel housing and the cylinder block mounting surfaces are clean. Check to see that the dowels are in good condition. Position the housing on the dowels in the cylinder block. Install and alternately tighten the attaching bolts to 28–38 ft. lb. (4-140) and 38–55 ft. lb. on all others.
17. Connect the clutch cable to the flywheel housing.
18. Install the starter motor and starter electrical cable.
18. Connect the clutch cable to the release lever and reinstall the dust shield.
20. Install the transmission.
21. Adjust the clutch pedal height and adjustment.

AUTOMATIC TRANSMISSION

NOTE: *C3, C4 and AOD transmission use Dexron® II fluid, the C5 transmission uses Type H fluid.*

PAN REPLACEMENT, FLUID AND FILTER CHANGE

1. Raise the car on a hoist or jack stands.
2. Some models require that the transmission fluid filler tube be disconnected to drain the pan; all others can be drained by loosening the pan bolts and letting the fluid drain out when the pan is lowered.
3. When the fluid has stopped draining to the level of the pan flange, remove the pan bolts starting at the rear and along both sides of the pan, allowing it to drop and drain gradually. Remove the pan and gasket.
4. Remove the bolts holding the filter in place, remove the filter, clean, and replace it. The filter may be reused after cleaning it in a nondetergent solution, such as new transmission fluid.

NOTE: *The C4 filter and gasket retain the throttle pressure limit valve within the lower control valve body. The valve and its spring will drop out when the filter is removed. The valve is installed large end first into the valve body; the spring fits over the valve shaft.*

CLUTCH AND TRANSMISSION 175

Fluid pan removal, automatic transmissions (shown upside down)

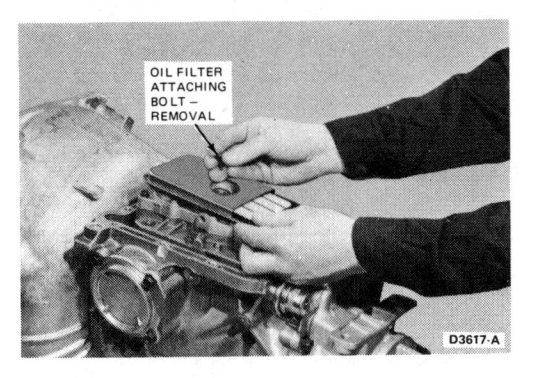

Filter element removal, automatics (shown upside down)

5. After completing any repairs or adjustments, install the fluid filter screen, new pan gasket, and the pan on the transmission. Tighten the pan attaching bolts to 12–16 ft. lbs.

6. Install three quarts of transmission fluid through the filler tube. If the filler tube was removed to drain the transmission, install the filler tube using a new O-ring.

7. Start and run the engine for a few minutes at low idle speed, and then at the fast idle speed (about 1,200 rpm) until the normal operating temperature is reached. Do not race the engine.

8. Move the selector lever through all gear positions, then place it in the Park position. Check the fluid level and add fluid until the level is between the ADD and FULL marks on the dipstick. Do not overfill.

NOTE: *The level should be at FULL after the engine is completely warmed up. Do not overfill.*

INTERMEDIATE BAND ADJUSTMENT

C3 Transmission

NOTE: *The torque values and number of turns given in these procedures must be exactly correct to prevent transmission damage.*

1. Wipe clean the area around the adjusting screw on the side of the transmission, near the left front corner of the transmission.
2. Remove the adjusting screw locknut and discard it.
3. Install a new locknut on the adjusting screw but do not tighten it.
4. Tighten the adjusting screw to *exactly* 10 ft. lbs.
5. Back off the adjusting screw *exactly* 1½ turns for 1979 models, 2 turns, 1980 and later.
6. Hold the adjusting screw so that it *does not turn* and tighten the adjusting screw locknut to 35–45 ft. lbs.

C4 and C5 Transmission

1. Wipe clean the area around the adjusting screw on the side of the transmission.
2. Remove the adjusting screw locknut and discard it.
3. Install a new locknut on the adjusting screw but do not tighten it yet.
4. Tighten the adjusting screw to *exactly* 10 ft. lbs.
5. Back off the adjusting screw *exactly* 1¾ turns on the C4 and 4¼ turns on the C5.
6. Hold the adjusting screw so that it *does not turn* and tighten the adjusting screw locknut to 35–45 ft. lbs.

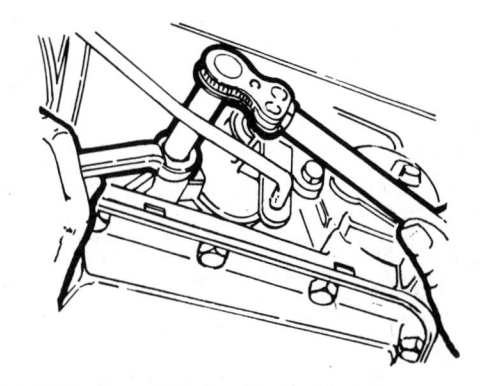

C-4, C-5 intermediate band adjustment

LOW-REVERSE BAND ADJUSTMENT

C4 and C5 Transmission

1. Wipe clean the area around the adjusting screw on the side of the transmission, near the right-rear corner.
2. Remove the adjusting screw locknut and discard it.
3. Install a new locknut on the adjusting screw but do not tighten it.
4. Tighten the adjusting screw to *exactly* 10 ft. lbs.

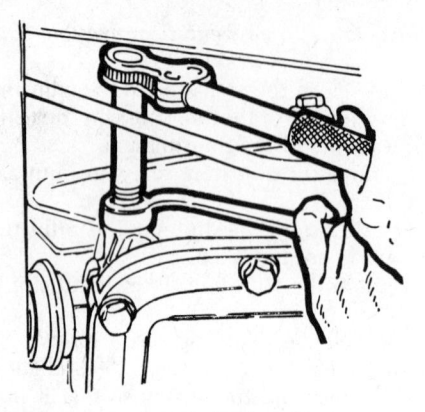

176 CLUTCH AND TRANSMISSION

C-4, C-5 reverse band adjustment

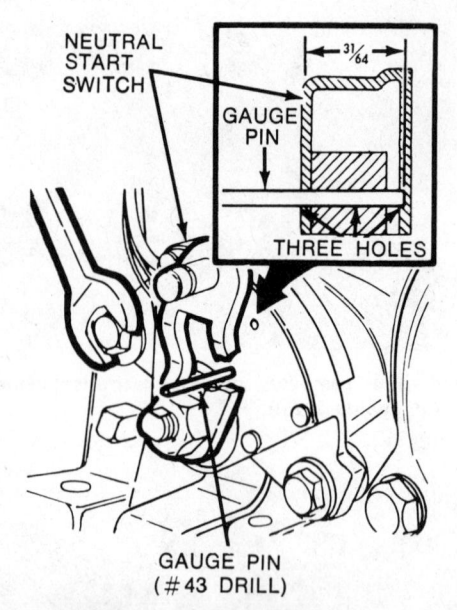

5. Back off the adjusting screw *exactly 3 full turns*.
6. Hold the adjusting screw so that it *does not turn* and tighten the adjusting screw to 35–45 ft. lbs.

NEUTRAL START SWITCH ADJUSTMENT

NOTE: *No adjustment is possible on the C3 transmission.*

C4 and C5 Transmission

1. Place the transmission selector lever in the Neutral position.
2. Raise the vehicle on a hoist and loosen the two bolts that attach the neutral switch to the transmission.
3. Rotate the switch until a gauge pin (shank end of a no. 43 drill bit) can be inserted through the gauge pin holes in the switch. The gauge pin must be inserted a full $31/64$ in. into the switch, through all three holes in the switch.
4. Tighten the switch retaining bolts and remove the pin.

C-4 neutral start switch adjustment

SHIFT LINKAGE ADJUSTMENT

1. Place transmission shift lever in D.
2. Raise vehicle and loosen manual lever shift rod retaining nut. Move transmission lever to D position. D is second from rear.

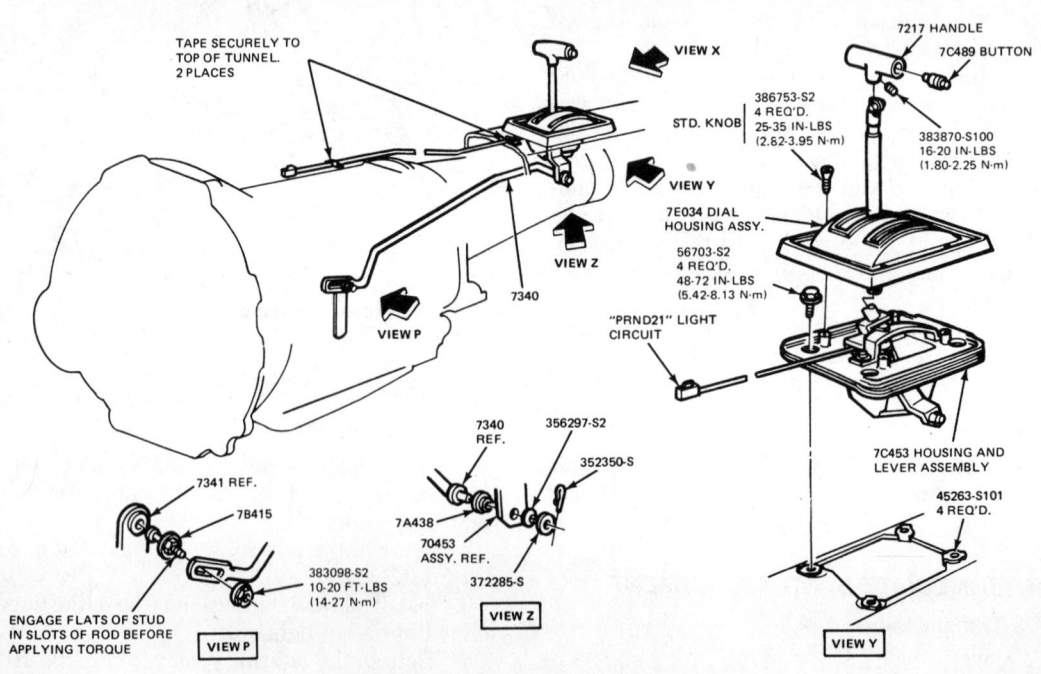

Shift linkage, all automatic models

CLUTCH AND TRANSMISSION

3. With transmission shift lever and transmission manual lever in position, tighten nut.
4. Check transmission operation for all selector lever detent positions.

DOWNSHIFT (THROTTLE) LINKAGE ADJUSTMENT

1. With the engine off, disconnect the throttle and downshift return springs, if equipped.
2. Hold the carburetor throttle lever in the wide open position against the stop.
3. Hold the transmission downshift linkage in the full downshift position against the internal stop.
4. Turn the adjustment screw on the carburetor downshift lever to obtain 0.010–0.080 in. clearance between the screw tip and the throttle shaft lever tab.
5. Release the transmission and carburetor to their normal free position.

AOD IDLE SPEED ADJUSTMENT

Whenever it is necessary to adjust the idle speed by more than 50 rpm either above or below the factory specifications, the adjustment screw on the linkage lever at the carburetor should also be adjusted to the following specifications:

Idle Speed Change (rpm)	Adjustment Screw Turns
50–100 increase	1½ turns out
50–100 decrease	1½ turns in
100–150 increase	2½ turns out
100–150 decrease	2½ turns in

After making any idle speed adjustments, make sure the linkage lever and throttlelever are in contact with the throttle lever at its idle stop and verify that the shift lever is in N (neutral).

REMOVAL AND INSTALLATION

1. Raise and safely support the vehicle.
2. Drain transmission fluid.
3. Remove the converter drain plug access cover and adapter plate bolts from the lower end of the converter housing.
4. Remove the four flywheel to converter attaching nuts. Crank the engine to turn the converter to gain access to the nuts, using a wrench on the crankshaft pulley attaching bolt. **On belt driven overhead camshaft engines, never turn the engine backwards.**
5. Crank the engine until the converter drain plug is accessible and remove the plug. Place a drain pan under the converter to catch the fluid. After all the fluid has been drained from the converter, reinstall the plug and tighten to specification.
6. Remove the driveshaft and install the extension housing seal replacer tool in the extension housing.
7. Remove the speedometer cable from the extension housing.
8. Disconnect the shift rod at the transmission manual lever. Disconnect the downshift rod at the transmission downshift lever.
9. Remove the starter-to-converter housing attaching bolts and position the starter out of the way.
10. Disconnect the neutral start switch wires from the switch.
11. Remove the vacuum line from the transmission vacuum unit.
12. Position a transmission jack under the transmission and raise it slightly.
13. Remove the engine rear support-to-crossmember nut.
14. Remove the crossmember-to-frame side support attaching bolts and remove the crossmember.
15. Remove the inlet pipe steady rest from the inlet pipe and rear engine support; then disconnect the muffler inlet pipe at the exhaust manifold and secure it.
16. Lower the jack under the transmission and allow the transmission to hang.
17. Position a jack to the front of the engine and raise the engine to gain access to the two upper converter housing-to-engine attaching bolts.
18. Disconnect the oil cooler lines at the transmission. Plug all openings to keep out dirt.
19. Remove the lower converter housing-to-engine attaching bolts.
20. Remove the transmission filler tube, if not already removed.
21. Secure the transmission to the jack with a safety chain.
22. Remove the two upper converter housing-to-engine attaching bolts. Move the transmission to the rear and down to remove it from under the vehicle.
23. Tighten the converter drain plug to 20–30 ft. lb. if not previously done.
24. Position the converter to the transmission making sure the converter hub is fully engaged in the pump gear. The dimension given in the illustration is for guidance only. It does not indicate engagement.
25. With the converter properly installed, place the transmission on the jack and secure with safety chain.
26. Rotate the converter so the drive studs and drain plug are in alignment with their holes in the flywheel.
27. With the transmission mounted on a transmission jack, move the converter and transmission assembly forward into position

CLUTCH AND TRANSMISSION

being careful not to damage the flywheel and the converter pilot.

During this move, to avoid damage, do not allow the transmission to get into a nosed down position as this will cause the converter to move forward and disengage from the pump gear. The converter must rest squarely against the flywheel. This indicates that the converter pilot is not binding in the engine crankshaft.

28. Install the two upper converter housing-to-engine attaching bolts and tighten to 28–38 ft. lb.

29. Remove the safety chain from the transmission.

30. Insert the filler tube in the stub tube and secure it to the cylinder block with the attaching bolt. Tighten the bolt to 28–38 ft. lb. If the stub tube is loosened or dislodged, it should be replaced.

31. Install the oil cooler lines in the retaining clip at the cylinder block. Connect the lines to the transmission case.

32. Remove the jack supporting the front of the engine.

33. Position the muffler inlet pipe support bracket to the converter housing and install the four lower converter housing-to-engine attaching bolts. Tighten the bolts to 28–38 ft. lb.

34. Raise the transmission. Position the crossmember to the frame side supports and install the attaching bolts. Tighten the bolts to 30–40 ft. lb.

35. Lower the transmission and install the rear engine support-to-crossmember nut. Tighten the nut to 30–40 ft. lb.

36. Remove the transmission jack.

37. Install the vacuum hose on the transmission vacuum unit. Install the vacuum line into the retaining clip.

38. Connect the neutral start switch plug to the switch.

39. Install the starter and tighten the attaching bolts.

40. Install the four flywheel-to-converter attaching nuts.

When assembling the flywheel to the converter, first install the attaching nuts and tighten to 20–34 ft. lb.

41. Install the converter drain plug access cover and adaptor plate bolts. Tighten the bolts to 15–20 ft. lb.

42. Connect the muffler inlet pipe to the exhaust manifold.

43. Connect the transmission shift rod to the manual lever.

44. Connect the downshift rod to the downshift lever.

45. Connect the speedometer cable to the extension housing.

46. Install the driveshaft. Tighten the companion flange U-bolt attaching nuts to 30 ft. lb.

47. Adjust the manual and downshift linkage as required.

48. Lower the vehicle. Fill the transmission to the proper level with Dexron® II. Type H for AOD transmissions.

Pour in five quarts of fluid; then run the engine and add fluid as required.

49. Check the transmission, converter assembly and oil cooler lines for leaks.

Drive Train

7

DRIVESHAFT AND UNIVERSAL JOINTS

The driveshaft is the means by which the power from the engine and transmission (in the front of the car) is transferred to the differential and rear axles, and finally to the rear wheels.

The driveshaft assembly incorporates two universal joints—one at each end—and a slip yoke at the front end of the assembly, which fits into the back of the transmission. Or, in the case of the Merkur, a two piece driveshaft and a cushioned center support.

All driveshafts are balanced when installed in a car. It is, therefore, imperative that before applying undercoating to the chassis, the driveshaft and universal joint assembly be completely covered to prevent the accidental application of undercoating to their surfaces, and the subsequent loss of balance.

DRIVESHAFT REMOVAL

1. Mark the relationship of the rear driveshaft yoke and the drive pinion flange of the axle. If the original, yellow alignment marks are visible, there is no need for new marks. The purpose of this marking is to facilitate installation of the assembly in its exact original position, thereby maintaining proper balance of the driveshaft assembly.

2. Remove the four bolts which hold the rear universal joint to the pinion flange. Wrap tape around the loose bearing caps in order to prevent them from falling off the spider. Remove the center support (if equipped) mounting bolts.

3. Pull the driveshaft toward the rear of the

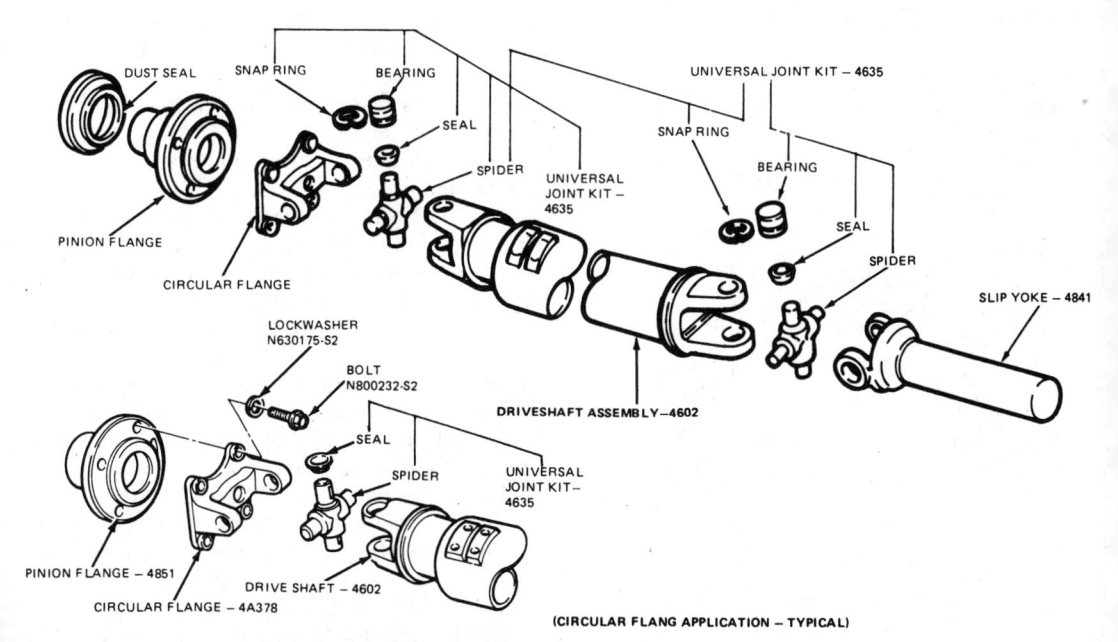

Driveshaft and U-joints disassembled

DRIVE TRAIN

Troubleshooting the Driveline

The Problem	Is Caused By	What to Do
Shudder as car accelerates from stop or low speed	• Loose U-joint • Defective center bearing	• Tighten U-joint or have it replaced • Have center bearing replaced
Loud clunk in driveshaft when shifting gears	• Worn U-joint	• Have U-joints replaced
Roughness or vibration at any speed	• Out-of-balance, bent or dented driveshaft • Worn U-joints • U-joint clamp bolts loose	• Have driveshaft serviced • Have U-joints serviced • Tighten U-joint clamp bolts
Squeaking noise at low speeds	• Lack of U-joint lubrication	• Lubricate U-joint; if problem persists, have U-joint serviced
Knock or clicking noise	• U-joint or driveshaft hitting frame tunnel • Worn CV joint	• Correct overloaded condition • Have CV joint replaced

vehicle until the slip yoke clears the transmission housing and the seal. Plug the hole at the rear of the transmission housing or place a container under the opening to catch any fluid which might leak out.

UNIVERSAL JOINT OVERHAUL

1. Position the driveshaft assembly in a sturdy vise.
2. Remove the snap-rings which retain the bearing caps in the slip yoke (front only) and in the driveshaft (front and rear).
3. Using a large punch or an arbor press, drive one of the bearing caps in toward the center of the universal joint, which will force the opposite bearing cap out.
4. As each bearing cap is pressed or punched far enough out of the universal joint assembly so that it is accessible, grip it with a pair of pliers, and pull it from the driveshaft yoke. Then drive or press the spider in the opposite direction in order to make the opposite bearing cap accessible and pull it free with a pair of pliers. Use this procedure to remove all bearings from both universal joints.
5. After removing the bearings, lift the spider from the yoke.
6. Thoroughly clean all dirt and foreign matter from the yoke area on both ends of the driveshaft.

NOTE: *When installing new bearings within the yokes, it is advisable to use an arbor press. However, if this tool is not available, the bearings should be driven into position with extreme care, as a heavy jolt on the needle bearings can easily damage or misalign them, greatly shortening their life and hampering their efficiency.*

7. Start a new bearing into the rear yoke at the rear of the driveshaft.
8. Position a new spider in the rear yoke and press (or drive) the new bearing cap 1/4 in. below the outer surface of the yoke.
9. With the bearing cap in position, install a new snap-ring.
10. Start a new bearing cap into the opposite side of the yoke.
11. Press (or drive) the bearing cap until the opposite bearing—which you have just installed—contacts the inner surface of the snap-ring.
12. Install a new snap-ring on the second bearing cap. It may be necessary to grind the surface of this second snap-ring to facilitate easy entry into its proper position.
13. Reposition the driveshaft in the vise to facilitate work on the front universal joint.
14. Install the new bearing caps, new spider, and new snap-rings in the same manner as you did for the rear universal joint.
15. Position the slip yoke on the spider. Install new bearings and snap-rings.

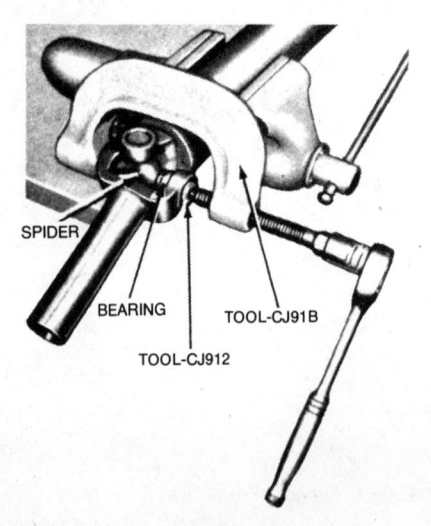

Removing U-joint bearing cap

DRIVE TRAIN

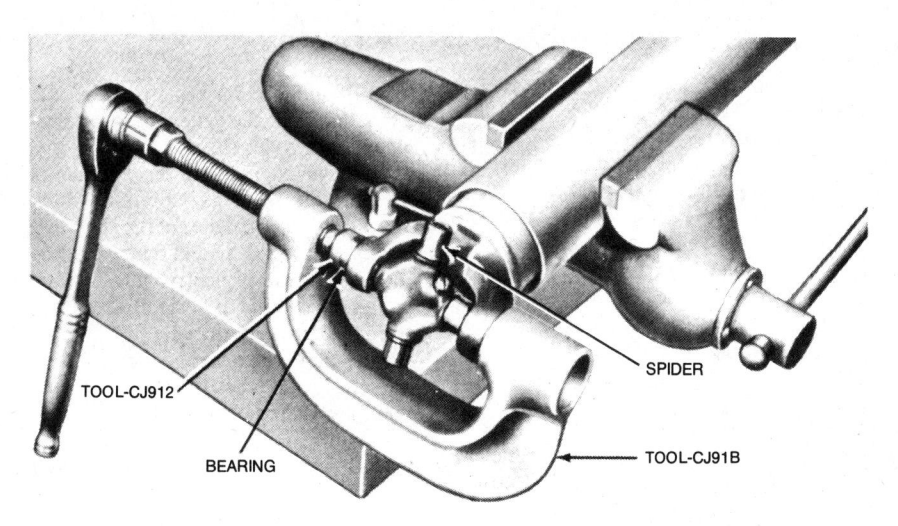

Installing bearing cap

16. Check both reassembled joints for freedom of movement. If misalignment of any part is causing a blind, a sharp rap on the side of the yoke with a brass hammer should seat the bearing needles, and provide the desired freedom of movement. Care should be exercised to firmly support the shaft end during this operation, as well as to prevent blows to the bearings themselves. Under no circumstances should a driveshaft be installed in a car if there is any bind in the universal joints.

DRIVESHAFT INSTALLATION

1. Carefully inspect the rubber seal in the end of the transmission extension housing. Replace it if it is damaged.
2. Examine the lugs on the axle pinion flange and replace the flange if the lugs are shaved or distorted.
3. Coat the yoke spline with lubricant.
4. Remove the plug which you inserted into the rear of the transmission housing.
5. Insert the yoke into the transmission housing and onto the transmission output shaft. Make sure that the yoke assembly does not bottom on the output shaft with excessive force.
6. Locate the marks which you made on the rear driveshaft yoke and the pinion flange prior to removal of the driveshaft assembly. Install the driveshaft assembly with the marks properly aligned. Install center support mounting.
7. Install the U-bolts and nuts that attach the universal joint to the pinion flange. Torque the U-bolt nuts to 8–15 ft. lbs.

DRIVE AXLE

Understanding Rear Axles

The rear axle is a special type of transmission that reduces the speed of the drive from the engine and transmission and divides the power to the rear wheels. Power enters the rear axle from the driveshaft via the companion flange. The flange is mounted on the drive pinion shaft. The drive pinion shaft and gear which carry the power into the differential turn at engine speed. The gear on the end of the pinion shaft drives a large ring gear the axis of rotation of which is 90° away from that of the pinion. The pinion and gear reduce the speed and multiply the power by the gear ratio of the axle, and change the direction of rotation to turn the axle shafts which drive both wheels. The rear axle gear ratio is found by dividing the number of pinion gear teeth into the number of ring gear teeth.

The ring gear drives the differential case. The case provides the two mounting points for the ends of a pinion shaft on which are mounted two pinion gears. The pinion gears drive the two side gears, one of which is located on the inner end of each axle shaft.

By driving the axle shafts through this arrangement, the differential allows the outer

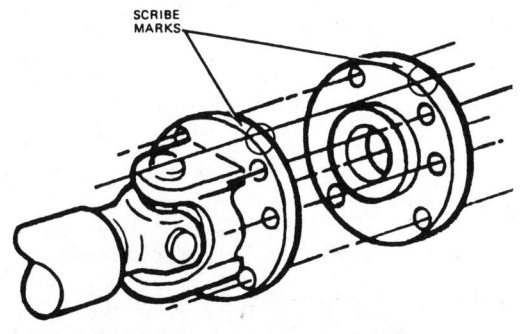

Driveshaft to axle U-joint connection, showing scribe marking

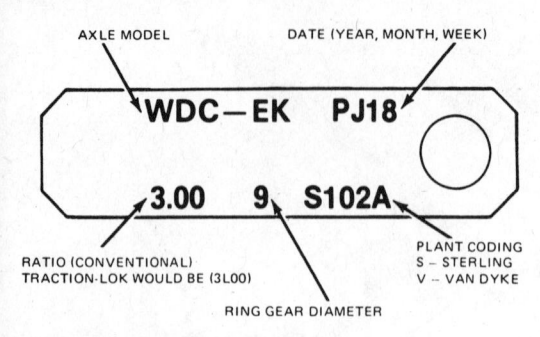

DRIVE TRAIN

Rear axle identification tag

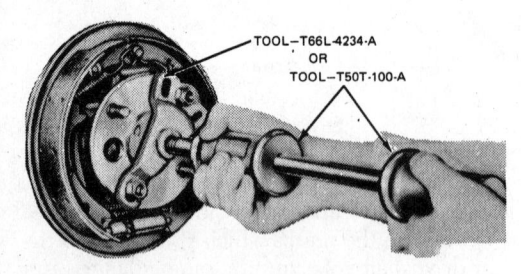

- AXLE MODEL: WDC—EK
- DATE (YEAR, MONTH, WEEK): PJ18
- RATIO (CONVENTIONAL) TRACTION-LOK WOULD BE (3L00): 3.00
- RING GEAR DIAMETER: 9
- PLANT CODING S – STERLING V – VAN DYKE: S102A

Axle shaft removal—all models
TOOL–T66L-4234-A OR TOOL–T50T-100-A

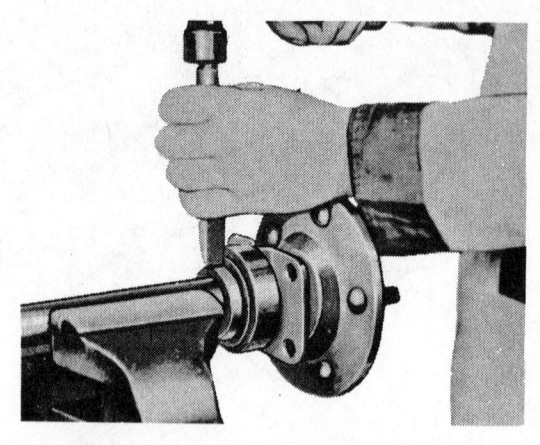

Loosening the inner retaining ring—6¾ in. axle

drive wheel to turn faster than the inner drive wheel in a turn.

The main drive pinion and the side bearings, which bear the weight of the differential case, are shimmed to provide proper bearing preload, and to position the pinion and ring gears properly.

NOTE: *The proper adjustment of a relationship of the ring and pinion gears is critical. It should be attempted only by those with extensive equipment and/or experience.*

The rear wheels are connected to the differential assembly by axle shafts. The axle shafts are supported in the rear axle housing by bearings and are retained in the housing by bearing retainer plates which bolt to the rear brake mounting plates.

The differential assembly is mounted on two tapered bearings. These bearings are retained in the axle housing by removable bearing caps.

The drive pinion is mounted in the axle on two roller bearings.

An identification tag is attached to one of the inspection plate attaching bolts. The information on this tag must be used when ordering replacement parts.

AXLE SHAFT AND/OR BEARING REPLACEMENT

NOTE: *Bearings must be pressed on and off the shaft with an arbor press. Unless you have access to one, it is inadvisable to attempt to perform any repair work on the axle shaft and bearing assemblies.*

6¾ Ring Gear Axle

1. Remove the wheel, tire, and brake drum.
2. Remove the nuts holding the axle retainer plate to the backing plate.
3. Remove the retainer and install the nuts, fingertight, to prevent the brake backing plate from being dislodged.
4. Pull out the axle shaft and bearing assembly, using a slide hammer.

NOTE: *If a slide hammer is not available, the axle can sometimes be pried out using pry bars on opposing sides of the hub.*

If end-play is found to be excessive, the bearing should be replaced. Shimming the bearing is not recommended as this ignores end-play of the bearing itself and could result in improper seating of the bearing.

5. Using a chisel, nick the bearing retainer in three or four places. The retainer does not have to be cut, merely collapsed sufficiently, to allow the bearing retainer to be slid from the shaft.
6. Press off the bearing and install the new one by pressing it into position.
7. Press on the new retainer.

NOTE: *Do not attempt to press the bearing and the retainer on at the same time.*

8. Assemble the shaft and bearing in the housing, being sure that the bearing is seated properly in the housing.
9. Install the retainer, drum, wheel, and tire.

7½" Ring Gear Axle

1. Jack up and support the rear of the car.
2. Remove the wheels and tires from the brake drums.
3. Place a drain pan under the housing and drain the lubricant by loosening the housing cover.
4. Remove the nuts securing the brake drums to the axle shaft flanges and remove the drums.

DRIVE TRAIN

Axle shaft bearing removal and installation, using press

5. Remove the housing cover and gasket, if used.
6. Position jackstands under the rear frame member and lower the axle housing. This is done to give easy access to the inside of the differential.
7. Working through the opening in the differential case, remove the side gear pinion shaft lockbolt and the side gear pinion shaft.
8. Push the axle shafts inward and remove the C-locks from the inner end of the axle shafts. Temporarily replace the shaft and lockbolt to retain the differential gears in position.
9. Remove the axle shafts with a slide hammer. Be sure the seal is not damaged by the splines on the axle shaft.
10. Remove the bearing and oil seal from the housing. Both the seal and bearing can be removed with a slide hammer. Two types of bearings are used on some axles, one requiring a press fit and the other a loose fit. A loose fitting bearing does not necessarily indicate excessive wear.
11. Inspect the axle shaft housing and axle shafts for burrs or other irregularities. Replace any worn or damaged parts. A light yellow color on the bearing journal of the axle shaft is normal, and does not require replacement of the axle shaft. Slight pitting and wear is also normal.
12. Lightly coat the wheel bearing rollers with axle lubricant. Install the bearings in the axle housing until the bearing seats firmly against the shoulder.
13. Wipe all lubricant from the oil seal bore, before installing the seal.
14. Inspecting the original seals for wear. If necessary, these may be replaced with new seals, which are prepacked with lubricant and do not require soaking.
15. Install the oil seal.
NOTE: *Installation of the seal without the proper tool can cause distortion and seal leakage. Oil seals for the right-side are marked with green stripes and the word RIGHT. Seals for the left-side are marked yellow with the word LEFT. Do not interchange seals from side to side.*
16. Remove the lockbolt and pinion shaft. Carefully slide the axle shafts into place. Be careful that you do not damage the seal with the splined end of the axle shaft. Engage the splined end of the shaft with the differential side gears.
17. Install the axle shaft C-locks on the inner end of the axle shafts and seat the C-locks in the counterbore of the differential side gears.
18. Rotate the differential pinion gears until the differential pinion shaft can be installed. Install the differential pinion shaft lockbolt. Tighten to 15–22 ft. lbs.
19. Install the brake drum on the axle shaft flange.
20. Install the wheel and tire on the brake drum and tighten the attaching nuts.
21. Clean the gasket surface of the rear housing and apply a bead of silicone sealer on the gasket surface. The bead should run inside of the bolt holes. Install the cover.
22. Raise the rear axle so that it is in the runnion position. Add the amount of specified lubricant to bring the lubricant level to 1¼" below the filler hole.

AXLE SHAFT SEAL REPLACEMENT

1. Remove the axle shaft from the rear axle. See the previous procedure for details.
2. Using a two-fingered seal puller (slide hammer), remove the seal from the axle housing.
3. Clean the recess in the rear axle housing from which the seal was removed.
4. Position a new seal on the housing and drive it into the housing with a seal installation tool.

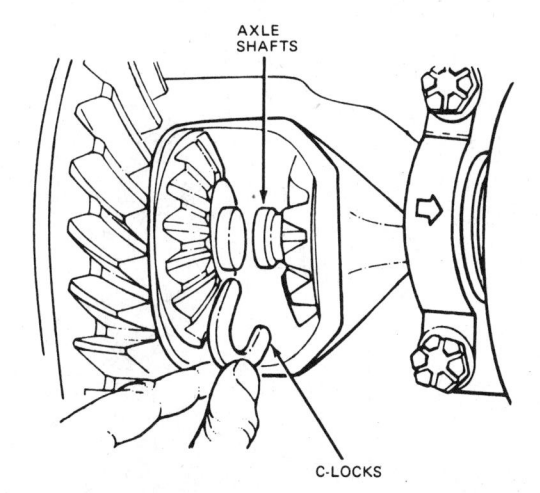

Removal and installation of C-locks and axle shafts—7½ in. ring gear

184 DRIVE TRAIN

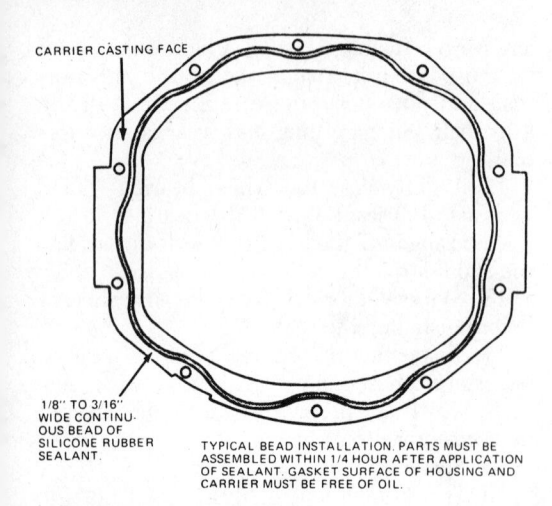

Installing sealer—all models

NOTE: *The right and left axle shaft seals are different and not interchangeable. If the wrong seal is installed on the wrong side of the axle, it will leak.*

5. Install the axle shaft.

HalfShafts-Merkur

The half-shafts are the connecting link between the rear axle and the rear wheels. The inboard end of each half-shaft is attached to the axle stub shafts. The outboard ends of the half-shafts are attached to the rear wheel flange stub shafts. The half-shafts rotate and drive the rear wheels when engine torque flowing through the driveshaft to the rear axle causes rotation of the differential side gears.

Since the Merkur is equipped with independent rear suspension, the half-shafts must have built-in flexibility. As the suspension moves up and down in response to road conditions, the half-shafts continously rotate through changing angles. Constant velocity (CV) joints at each end of the half-shaft provide the flexibilty needed to compensate for suspension movement.

The CV joint consists of an inner race, cage and six ball bearings inside a housing which also forms the outer bearing race.

The half-shafts are of unequal length. The right side is longer than the left. Do not interchange half-shafts.

REMOVAL AND INSTALLATION

1. Be sure the vehicle is in Neutral and that the parking brake is fully released.
2. Raise and support the rear of the vehicle with the rear wheels hanging free.
3. Remove the bolts attaching the half-shaft to the wheel stub shaft. Turn the driveshaft as necessary to gain access to the bolts.

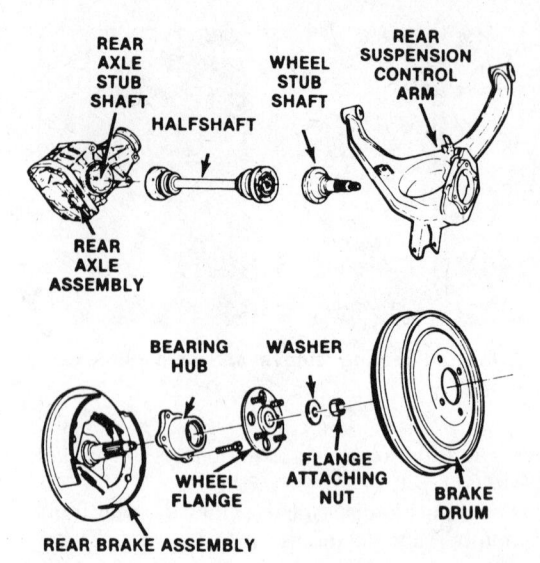

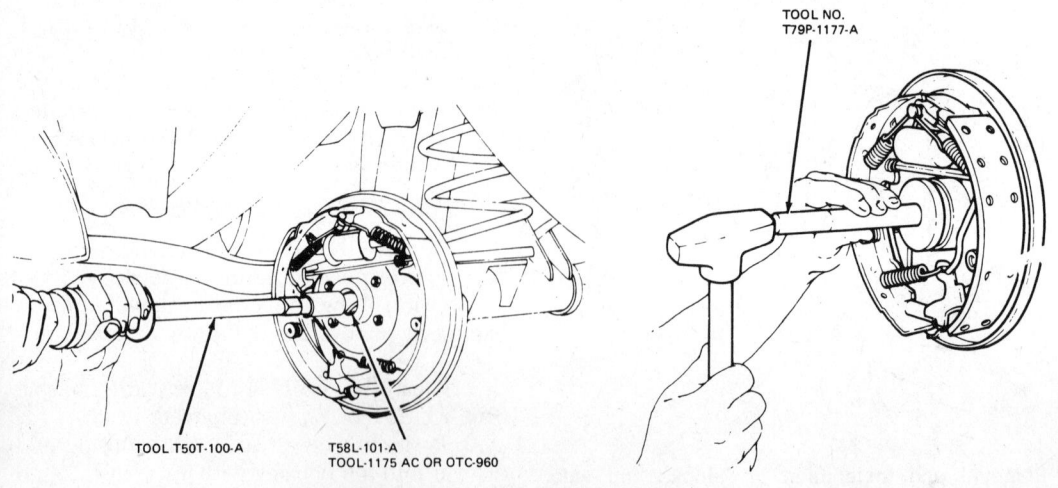

Merkur halfshafts/wheel hub assemblies

Axle seal replacement—all models

DRIVE TRAIN

4. Secure the free end of the half-shaft with wire and remove the mounting bolts from the axle stub shaft. Remove the half-shaft.
5. Service as required. Install the half-shaft in the reverse order of removal. Tighten the attaching bolts to 28–31 ft. lbs.

Wheel Stub Shaft
REMOVAL AND INSTALLATION

1. With vehicle raised and support with the rear suspension hanging.
2. Remove the brake drum and wheel flange.
3. Remove the bolts attaching the half-shaft to the wheel stub axle. Suspend the half-shaft with wire, do not permit it to hang free.
4. From under the vehicle, pull the stub axle from the wheel retainer.
5. Service as necessary. Install in the reverse order of removal.

CV Joint
SERVICE

1. Remove the half-shaft and secure in a soft jawed vise.
2. Break and remove the boot clamps. Peel the boot away from the joint and slide it along the axle.
3. Remove the snap ring from the end of the shaft. Remove the CV joint from the shaft with a suitable two-jawed puller.
4. Clamp the CV joint in a vise equipped with protective jaws. Use a small flat tipped pry bar and roll the inner race and ball cage out of the outer race.
5. The balls can now be removed by prying them out of the cage.
6. Remove the inner race by aligning one of the bearing races with the cage and then rolling the race out of the cage.
7. Inspect all parts after cleaning. Replace as necessary.
8. Assemble the inner race, cage and ball bearings.
9. Install the assembly in the housing with two of the ball bearings entering two races. Pull upward on the inner race and roll the assembly into position.

NOTE: *The narrow ends of the inner races must be aligned with the wide ends of the housing races before the race, cage and ball assembly can enter the housing.*

10. Pack the CV joint with lubricant CLAZ-19590-B,C,D or E or the equivalent.
11. Install the CV joint on the half-shaft and install the snap-ring. A hammer and socket can be used to mount the joint.
12. Install a new boot and secure with clamps.

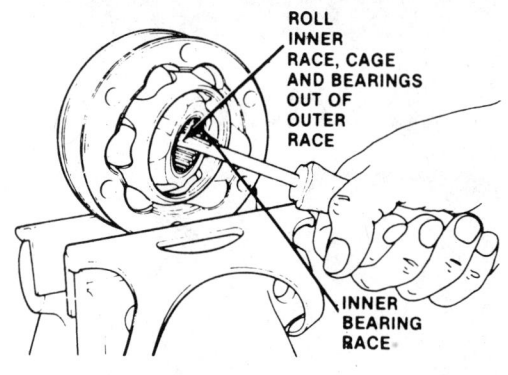

Merkur CV joints

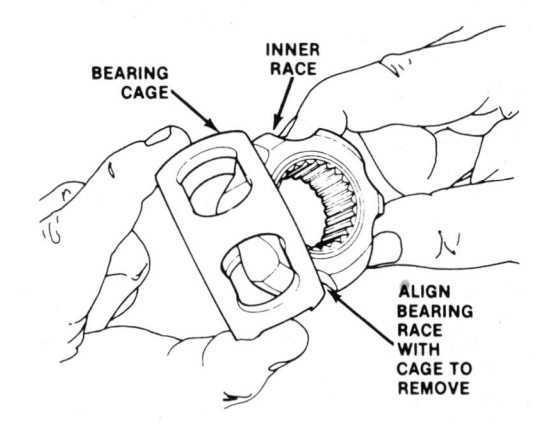

Merkur CV joint component alignment

Suspension and Steering

8

FRONT SUSPENSION

Mustang/Capri models use a modified version of the MacPherson strut front suspension. The design utilizes shock struts with coil springs mounted between the lower arm and a spring pocket in the No. 2 crossmember. The shock struts are non-repairable, and must be replaced as a unit. The ball joints lower suspension arm bushings are not separately serviced, and they also must be replaced by replacing the suspension arm assembly. The ball joint seal can be replaced separately.

The Merkur uses a true McPherson strut suspension, with the coil spring mounted on the strut.

Springs—Except Merkur

NOTE: *Always use extreme caution when working with coil springs. Make sure the vehicle is supported sufficiently.*

REMOVAL AND INSTALLATION

1. Raise the front of the vehicle and place safety stands under both sides of the jack pads just back of the lower arms.
2. Remove the wheel and tire assembly.
3. Disconnect the stabilizer bar link from the lower arm.

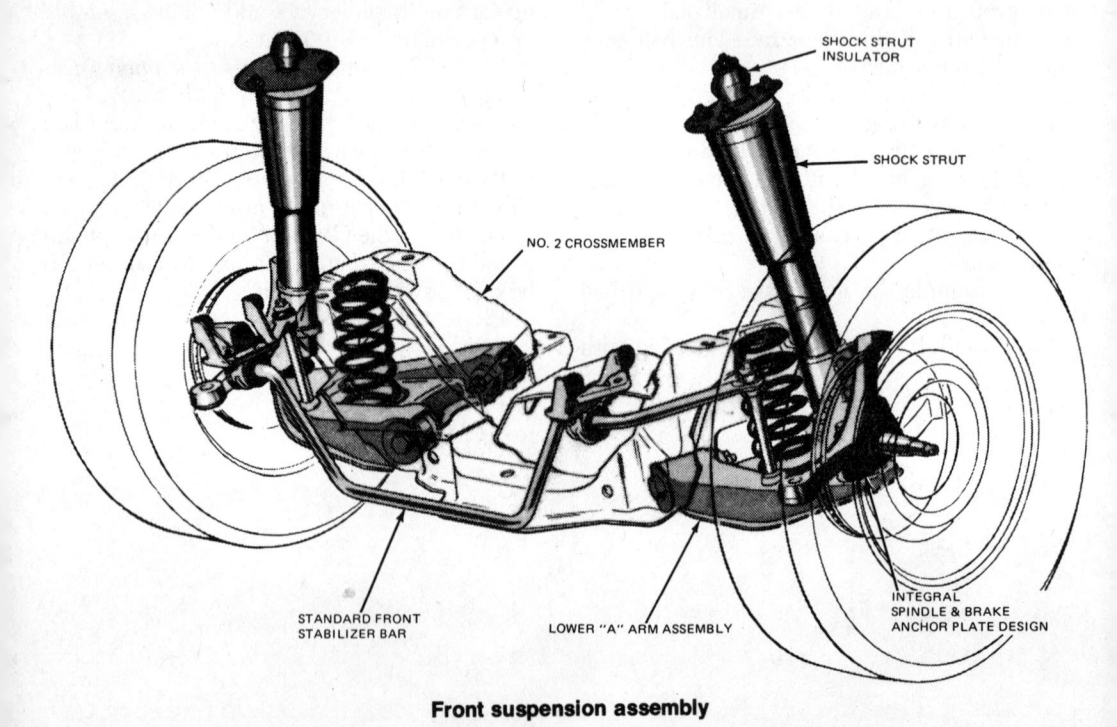

Front suspension assembly

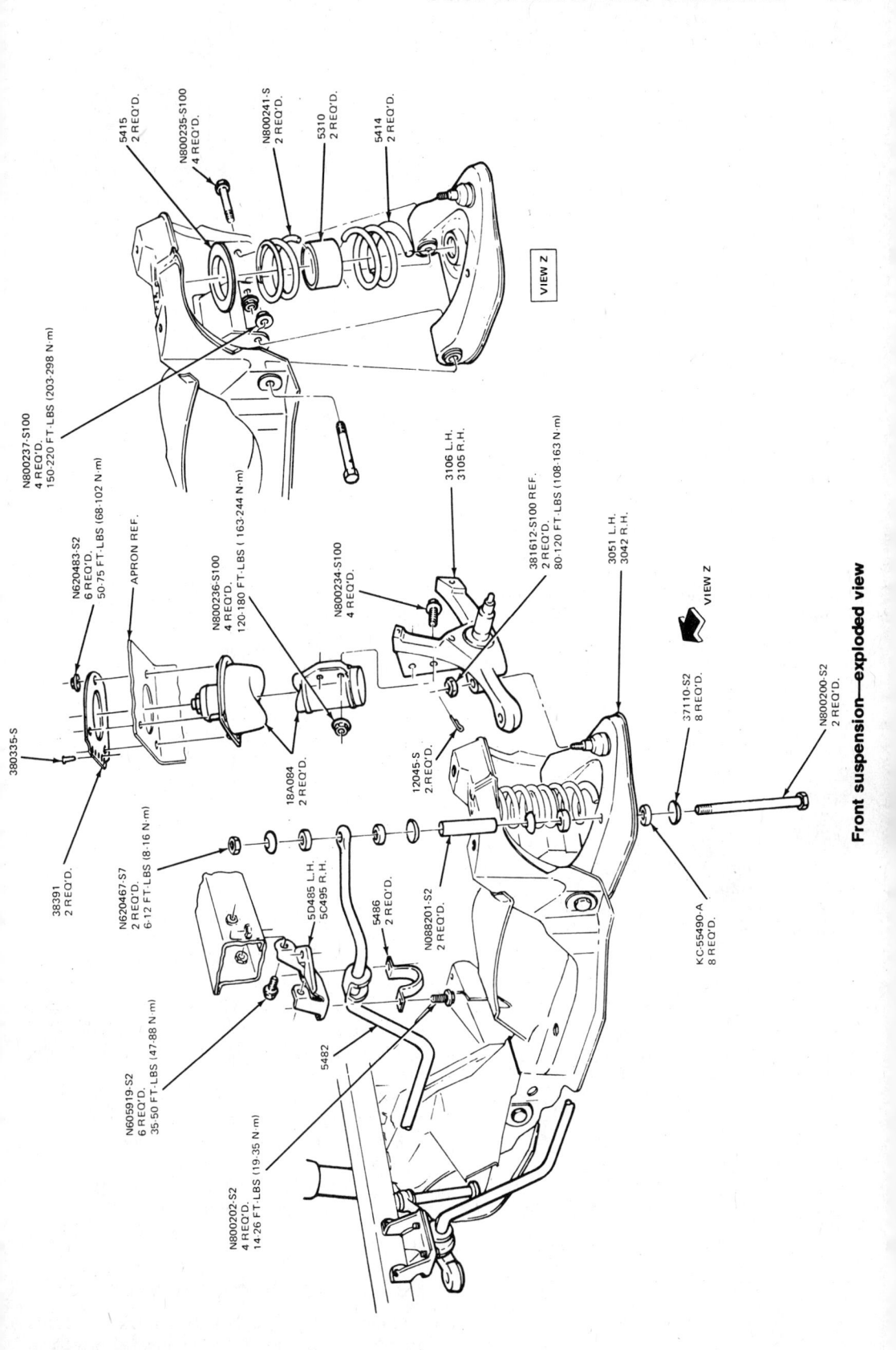

SUSPENSION AND STEERING

Front suspension—exploded view

SUSPENSION AND STEERING

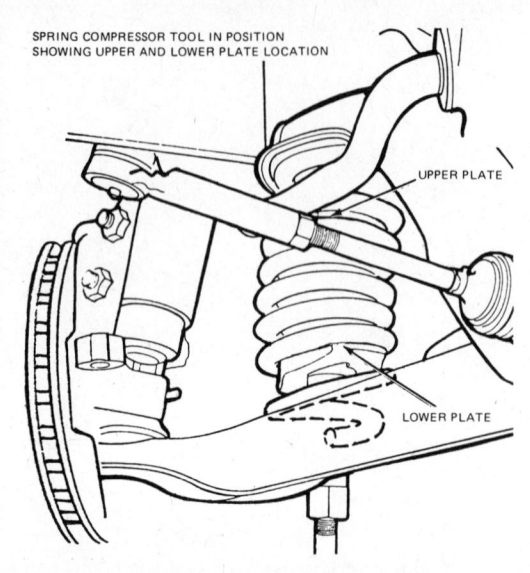

Spring compressor tool in position showing upper and lower plate location

Spring compressed and removed from the vehicle

4. Remove the steering gear bolts, and move the steering gear out of the way.
5. Disconnect the tie rod from the steering spindle.
6. Using a spring compressor, install one plate with the pivot ball seat down into the coils of the spring. Rotate the plate, so that it is fully seated into the lower suspension arm spring seat.
7. Install the other plate with the pivot ball seat up into the coils of the spring. Insert the ball nut through the coils of the spring, so it rests in the upper plate.
8. Insert the compression rod into the opening in the lower arm through the lower and upper plate. Install the upper ball nut on the rod, and return the securing pin.

NOTE: *This pin can be inserted only one way into the upper ball nut because of a stepped hole design.*

9. With the upper ball nut secured, turn the upper plate so it walks up the coil until it contacts the upper spring seat.
10. Install the lower ball nut, thrust bearing and forcing nut on the compression rod.
11. Rotate the nut until the spring is compressed enough so that it is free in its seat.
12. Remove the two lower control arm pivot bolts and nuts, and disengage the lower arm from the frame crossmember and remove the spring assembly.
13. If a new spring is to be installed, mark the position of the upper and lower plates on the spring with chalk. Measure the compressed length of the spring as well as the amount of the spring curvature to assist in the compressing and installation of a new spring.
14. Loosen the nut to relieve spring tension, and remove the tools from the spring.
15. Assemble the spring compressor tool, and locate it in the same position as indicated in step 13 of the removal procedure.

NOTE: *Before compressing the coil spring, be sure the upper ball nut securing pin is inserted properly.*

16. Compress the coil spring until the spring height reaches the dimension in step 13.
17. Position the coil spring assembly into the lower arm.

NOTE: *Make sure that the lower end of the spring is properly positioned between the two holes in the lower arm spring pocket depression.*

18. To finish installing the coil spring reverse the removal procedure.

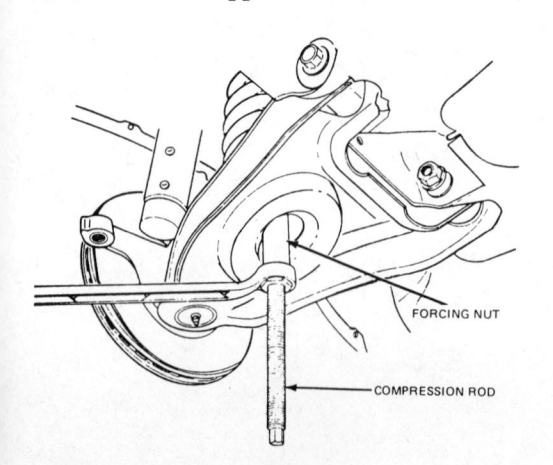

Spring compressed for removal

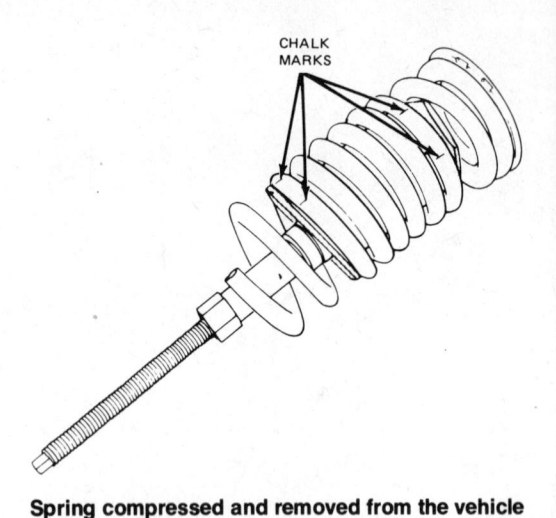

Ball Joints—Except Merkur

Ball joints are not replaceable. If the ball joints are found to be defective the lower control arm assembly must be replaced.

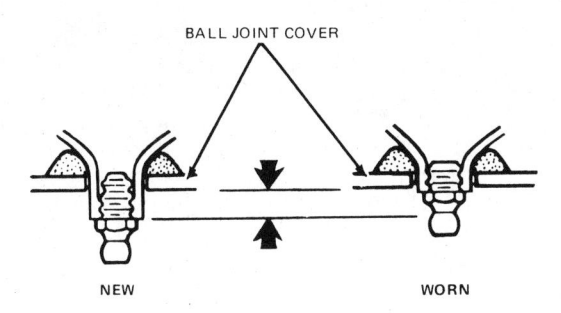

SUSPENSION AND STEERING

Inspection of lower ball joint

INSPECTION

1. Support the vehicle in normal driving position with bolt ball joints loaded.
2. Wipe the grease fitting and checking surface, so they are free of dirt and grease. The checking surface is the round boss into which the grease fitting is threaded.
3. The checking surface should project outside the cover. If the checking surface is inside the cover, replace the lower arm assembly.

Shock Strut—Except Merkur

REMOVAL AND INSTALLATION

1. Place the ignition key in the unlocked position to permit free movement of the front wheels.
2. Working from the engine compartment remove the nut (16 mm) that attaches the strut to the upper mount. A screwdriver in the slot will hold the rod stationary while removing the nut.

NOTE: *The vehicle should not be driven while the nut is removed so make sure the car is in position for hoisting purposes.*

3. Raise the front of the vehicle by the lower control arms, and place safety stands under the frame jacking pads, rearward of the wheels.
4. Remove the tire and wheel assembly.
5. Remove the brake caliper, rotor assembly, and dust shield.
6. Remove the two lower nuts and bolts attaching the strut to the spindle.
7. Lift the strut up from the spindle to compress the rod, then pull down and remove the strut.
8. With the rod half extended, place the rod through the upper mount and hand start the mount as soon as possible.
9. Extend the strut and position into the spindle.
10. Install the two lower mounting bolts and hand start the nuts.
11. Tighten the nut that attaches the strut to the upper body mount to 60–75 ft. lbs. This can be done from inside the engine compartment.

NOTE: *Position a screwdriver in the slot to hold the rod stationary while the nut is being tightened.*

12. Remove the suspension load from the lower control arms by lowering the hoist and tighten the lower mounting nuts to 150 ft. lbs.
13. Raise the suspension control arms and install the brake caliper, rotor assembly and dust shield.
14. Install the tire and wheel assembly.
15. Remove the safety stands and lower the vehicle.

Lower Control Arm—Except Merkur

REMOVAL AND INSTALLATION

1. Raise the front of the vehicle and position safety stands under both sides of the jack pads, just to the rear of the lower arms.
2. Remove the wheel and tire assembly.
3. Disconnect the stabilizer bar link from the lower arm.
4. Remove the disc brake caliper, rotor and dust shield.
5. Remove the steering gear bolts and position out of the way.
6. Remove the cotter pin from the ball joint stud nut, and loosen the ball joint nut one or two turns.
7. Tap the spindle sharply to relieve the stud pressure.
8. Remove the tie-rod end from the spindle. Place a floor jack under the lower arm, supporting the arm at both bushings. Remove both lower arm bolts, lower the jack and remove the coil spring as outlined earlier in the chapter.
9. Remove the ball nut and remove the arm assembly.
10. Place the new arm assembly into the spindle and tighten the ball joint nut to 100 ft. lbs. Install the cotter pin.
11. Position the coil spring in the upper spring pocket. Make sure the insulator is on top of the spring and the lower end is properly positioned between the two holes in the depression of the lower arm.
12. Carefully raise the lower arm with the floor jack until the bushings are properly positioned in the crossmember.
13. Install the lower arm bolts and nuts, finger tight only.
14. Install and tighten the steering gear bolts.
15. Connect the tie-rod end and tighten the nut to 35–47 ft. lbs.
16. Connect the stabilizer link bolt and nut and tighten to 10 ft. lbs.

190 SUSPENSION AND STEERING

17. Install the brake dust shield, rotor and caliper.
18. Install the wheel and tire assembly.
19. Remove the safety stands and lower the vehicle. After the vehicle has been lowered to the floor and at curb height, tighten the lower arm nuts to 210 ft. lbs.

Strut-Merkur

REMOVAL AND INSTALLATION

1. Raise and support the front of the vehicle on jackstands after loosening the front wheel lug nuts.
2. Remove the wheel and tire assembly. Position a floor jack under the lower control arm, raise the jack until it is slightly lower than the control arm.
3. Remove the pinch bolt that secures the strut to the lower control arm. Use a small pry bar to spread the mounting flange ears and push down on the lower control arm to separate the arm and strut. Lower the jack if necessary, but do not allow the brake hose to stretch. When separated, rest the control arm on the jack.
4. Hold the top of the strut by inserting a 6 mm hex wrench in the slot provided and remove the locknut.
5. Remove the strut assembly from the vehicle.
6. Install replacement strut in the reverse order of removal.

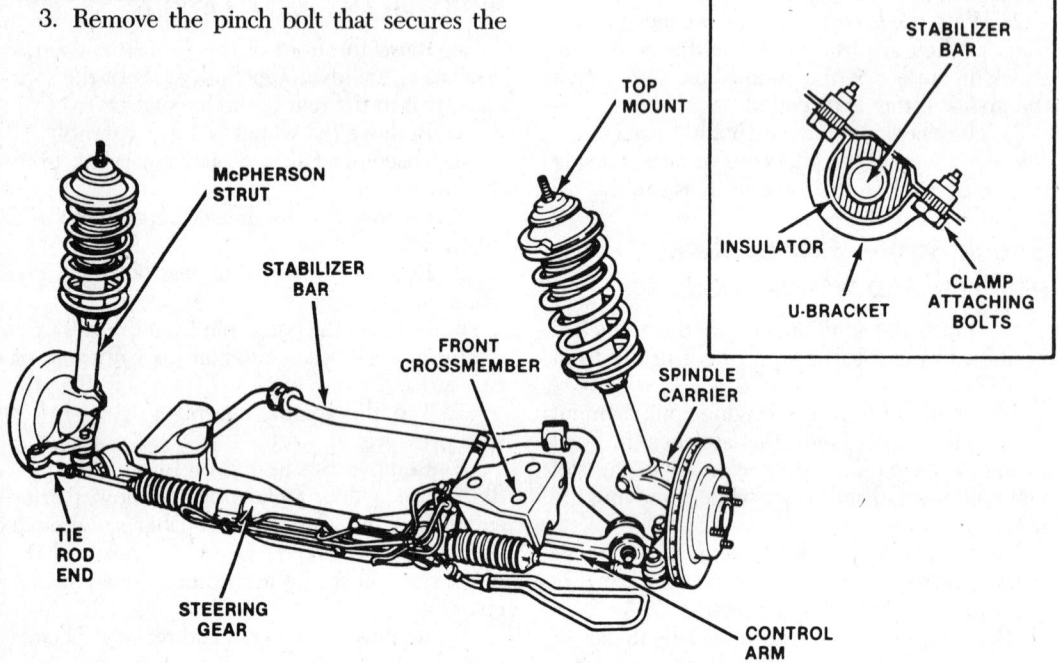

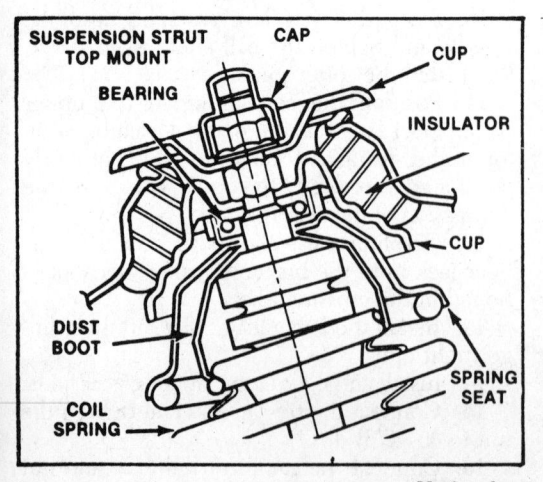

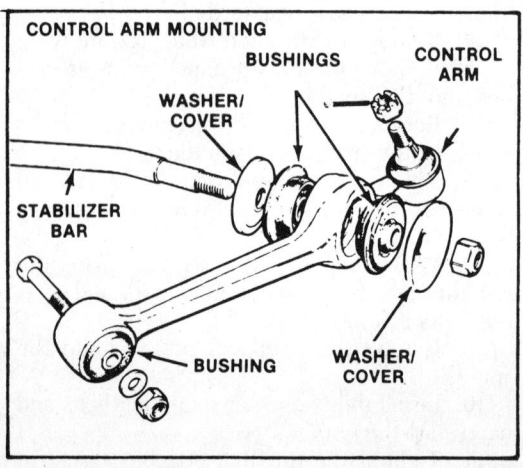

Merkur front suspension

SUSPENSION AND STEERING 191

Control Arm/Stabilizer Bar Bushings-Merkur

REMOVAL AND INSTALLATION

1. Raise and support the front of the vehicle. Remove the front wheels.
2. Remove the cotter pin and attaching nut and separate the control arm from the spindle carrier.
3. Remove the pivot bolt attaching the control arm to the crossmember.
4. Remove the nut attaching the stabilizer bar to the control arm. Remove the front washer/plastic cover from the end of the stabilizer bar.
5. Remove the control arm and bushings as an assembly.
6. Remove the rear washer/plastic cover from the end of the stabilizer bar. Service bushings as necessary, they are pressed into the bar.
7. Install in the reverse order of removal. Tighten all mounting bolts snugly and lower the vehicle so full weight is on the suspension. Tighten the bolts as follows: Control Arm Pivot Bolt- 11 ft. lbs. + 90° Stabilizer Nut- 52–81 ft. lbs.

Stabilizer Bar—Merkur

REMOVAL AND INSTALLATION

1. Raise and support the vehicle safely. Remove the attaching nuts and front washer covers from the ends of the stabilizer bar.
2. Remove the four bolts securing the two U-brackets and torque brace to the body.
3. Detach one control arm pivot bolt and pull the control arm out of the crossmember. Pull the stabilizer out of the lower control arms and remove it from the vehicle.
4. Service as required and install in the reverse order. Refer to Control Arm procedure for torque specifications.

Steering Knuckle and Wheel Bearings—Merkur

REMOVAL AND INSTALLATION

The front wheels on the Merkur are attached to spindle shafts which are supported on opposed, tapered roller bearings. The spindle hub casting forms a housing for the bearings and shaft while providing the necessary suspension and steering connection points. Self-setting wheel bearings are used that never require adjustment and are lubricated with high temperature, long life grease.

1. Raise and safely support the vehicle. Remove the front wheels and brake calipers. Suspend the calipers on wire to prevent brake hose damage.

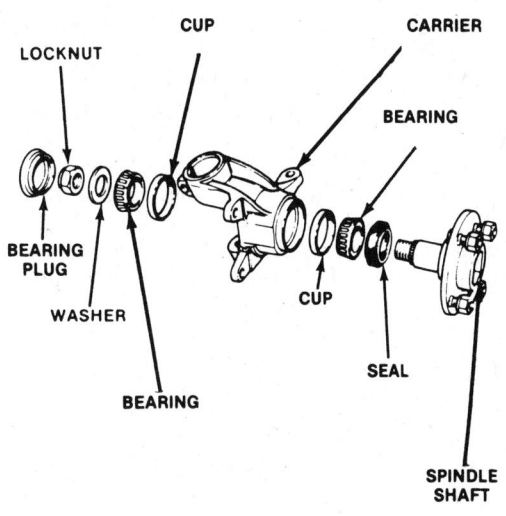

Merkur spindle/knuckle exploded view

2. Matchmark the rotor and wheel stud. The unit is balanced by the factory and must be installed in the same position to maintain balance.
3. Remove the cotter pin and the tie-rod end attaching nut. Remove the tie-rod from the spindle.
4. Remove the cotter pin and control arm attaching nut and remove the control arm from the knuckle.
5. Remove the strut mounting to knuckle pinch bolt. Spread the ears and remove the knuckle from the strut assembly.
6. Place the spindle and hub in a vise, wheel studs pointing downward and clamped between two pieces of wood and the vise jaws.
7. Remove the bearing plug from the rear of the knuckle using a flat drift.
8. Use a 27mm socket to remove the spindle bearing locknut.

CAUTION: *Spindles from the right side of the vehicle are equipped with left handed threads and are loosened by turning clockwise. Spindles from the left side of the vehicle are equipped with right handed threads which are loosened by turning counterclockwise. The spindles are marked with an R or L on the large hexagonal recess.*

9. Lift the spindle carrier and inner bearing off the (hub) spindle shaft. Remove the inner bearing and splined washer. If the bearing is to be reused, tag for location identification.
10. Clamp the spindle carrier (knuckle) in a vise and remove the grease seal using a flat prybar. Remove the outer bearing and tag for location identification.
11. Remove bearing cups from the spindle, if necessary, using a bearing puller jaws on a slide hammer.
12. Clean and inspect all parts. Press new

SUSPENSION AND STEERING

bearing cups into the spindle. Pack the wheel bearing with high temperature grease.

13. Install the outer bearing and grease seal in the spindle (knuckle). Install the spindle shaft (hub).
14. Install the inner bearing and splined washer. Install the spindle bearing locknut and tighten to 202–232 ft. lbs. Install the bearing cover plug.

CAUTION: *Be sure the spindle is mounted secure in the vise but do not damage the studs. The amount of torque required for the locknut is extremely important. If a higher or lower torque is applied bearing failure is likely to occur.*

15. Install the spindle (knuckle) in the reverse order of removal. Torque the attaching parts as follows:
    - Strut to Spindle Pinch Bolt- 59–66 ft. lbs.
    - Lower Control Arm Nut- 48–63 ft. lbs.
    - Tie Rod End Nut- 15–23 ft. lbs.

Front End Alignment

On the Mustang and Capri the caster and camber are set at the factory and cannot be changed. Only the toe is adjustable.

TOE-IN ADJUSTMENT

Toe is the difference in distance between the front and the rear of the front wheels.

1. Start the engine and move the steering wheel back and forth several times until it is in the straight ahead position.
2. Turn the engine off, and lock the steering wheel in place using a steering wheel holder.
3. Loosen the jam nuts and adjust the left and right spindle connecting rod sleeves until each wheel has one half of the desired total toe-in specification.
4. After the adjustment is made tighten the jam nuts to 35–50 ft. lbs.

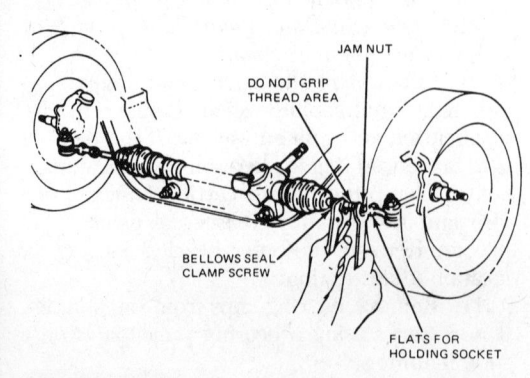

Toe-in adjustment

REAR SUSPENSION

The rear suspension (except Merkur) is a four link coil spring design. The rear axle is suspended from the body by two upper arms which control side to side movement and two lower arms which control forward and rearward movement. Shock absorbers are located on each side. Each coil spring is mounted between an upper seat which is welded to the body and a lower seat which is part of the lower arm assembly. The shock absorbers are attached to an upper shock bracket which is welded to the rear axle tubes. The Merkur is equipped with full independent rear suspension, consisting of semi-trailing control arms, shock absorbers and coil springs.

Springs—Except Merkur

NOTE: *Always use extreme caution when working with coil springs. Make sure the vehicle is supported sufficiently.*

REMOVAL AND INSTALLATION

NOTE: *Ford recommends that if one spring requires replacement the other spring should be replaced also.*

1. Raise the vehicle and support the body at the rear body crossmember.
2. Lower the hoist until the rear shocks are fully suspended.

NOTE: *The axle must be supported by the hoist, or a transmission jack, or jack stands.*

3. Place a transmission jack under the lower

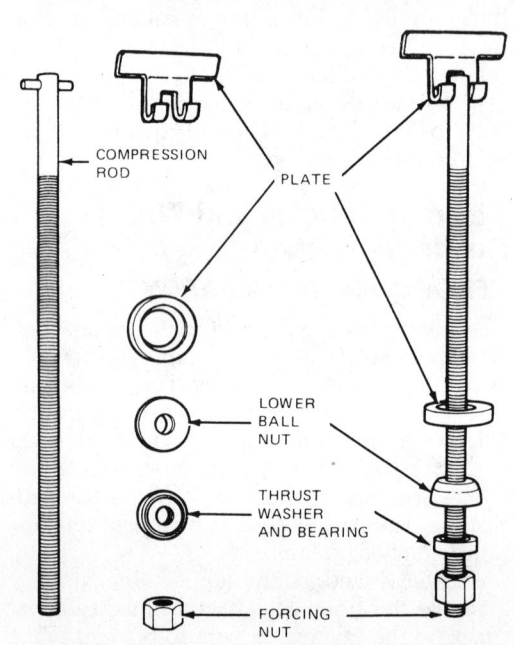

Spring compressor tool for MacPherson struts

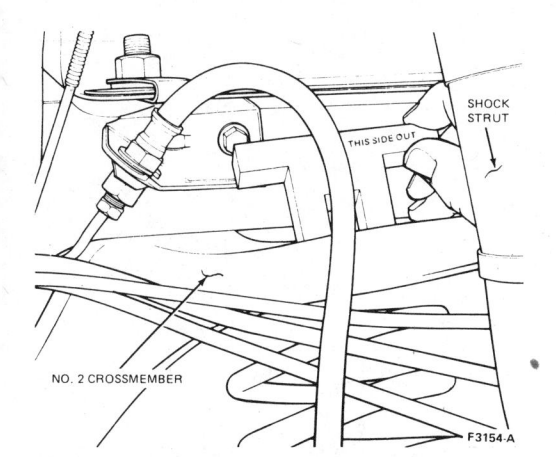

SUSPENSION AND STEERING

pivot bolt and nut, with the nut facing outwards. Do not torque at this time.

9. Lower the transmission jack. Raise the axle to curb height. Torque the lower arm pivot bolt to 85 ft. lbs.

10. If the vehicle is equipped with a rear stablizer bar, install it at this time. Torque the horizontal mount bolts to 35 ft. lbs. and the verticle mount bolts to 20 ft. lbs.

11. Remove the crossmember supports and lower the vehicle.

Shock Absorbers-Except Merkur
BOUNCE TEST

Each shock absorber can be tested by bouncing the corner of the vehicle until maximum up and down movement is obtained. Release the car. It should stop bouncing in one or two bounces. Compare both front corners or both rear corners but do not compare the front to the rear. If one corner bounces longer than the other it sould be inspected for damage and possibly be replaced.

REMOVAL AND INSTALLATION

1. Open the trunk on the two door models or remove the side panel trim covers on the three door models to gain access to the upper shock attachment.

2. On the two door models remove the rubber cap from the shock absorber stud.

3. Remove the shock absorber attaching nut, washer and insulator.

4. Raise the vehicle on a hoist supporting the rear axle.

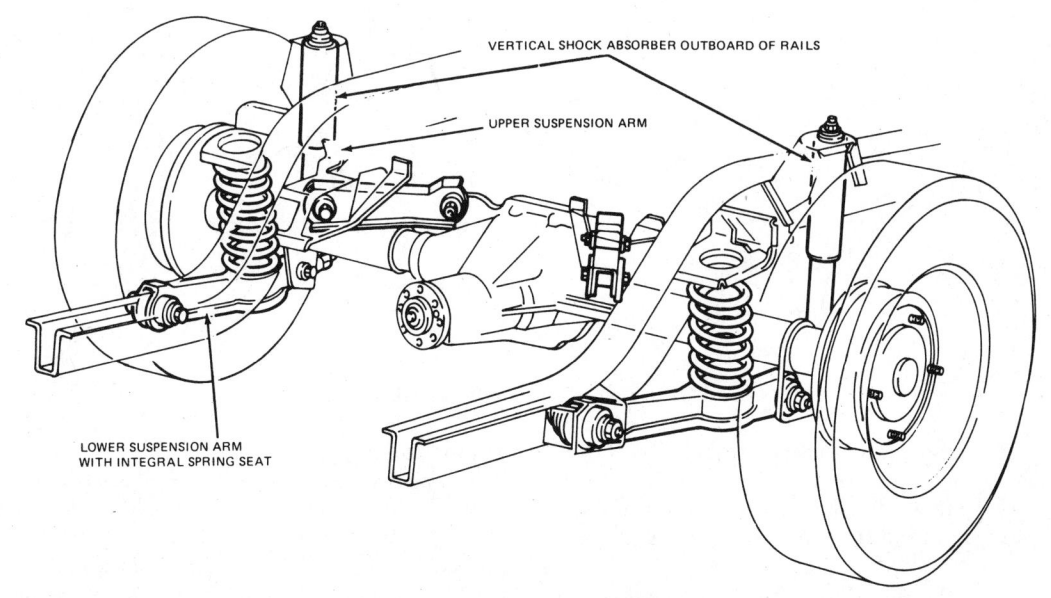

Spring compressor tool—upper plate being placed into spring pocket cavity on the No. 2 crossmember

arm pivot bolt and remove the bolt and nut. Lower the transmission jack slowly until the coil spring load is relieved.

4. If the vehicle is equipped with a rear stabilizer bar remove the four retaining bolts and remove the stabilizer bar.

5. Remove the coil spring and insulators from the vehicle.

6. Place the upper spring insulator into the spring seat in the body. Tape in place if necessary.

7. Place the lower spring insulator on the lower arm. Install the internal damper into the spring.

8. Position the coil spring on the lower arm spring seat. Slowly raise the transmission jack until the arm is in position. Insert a new rear

Rear suspension assembly

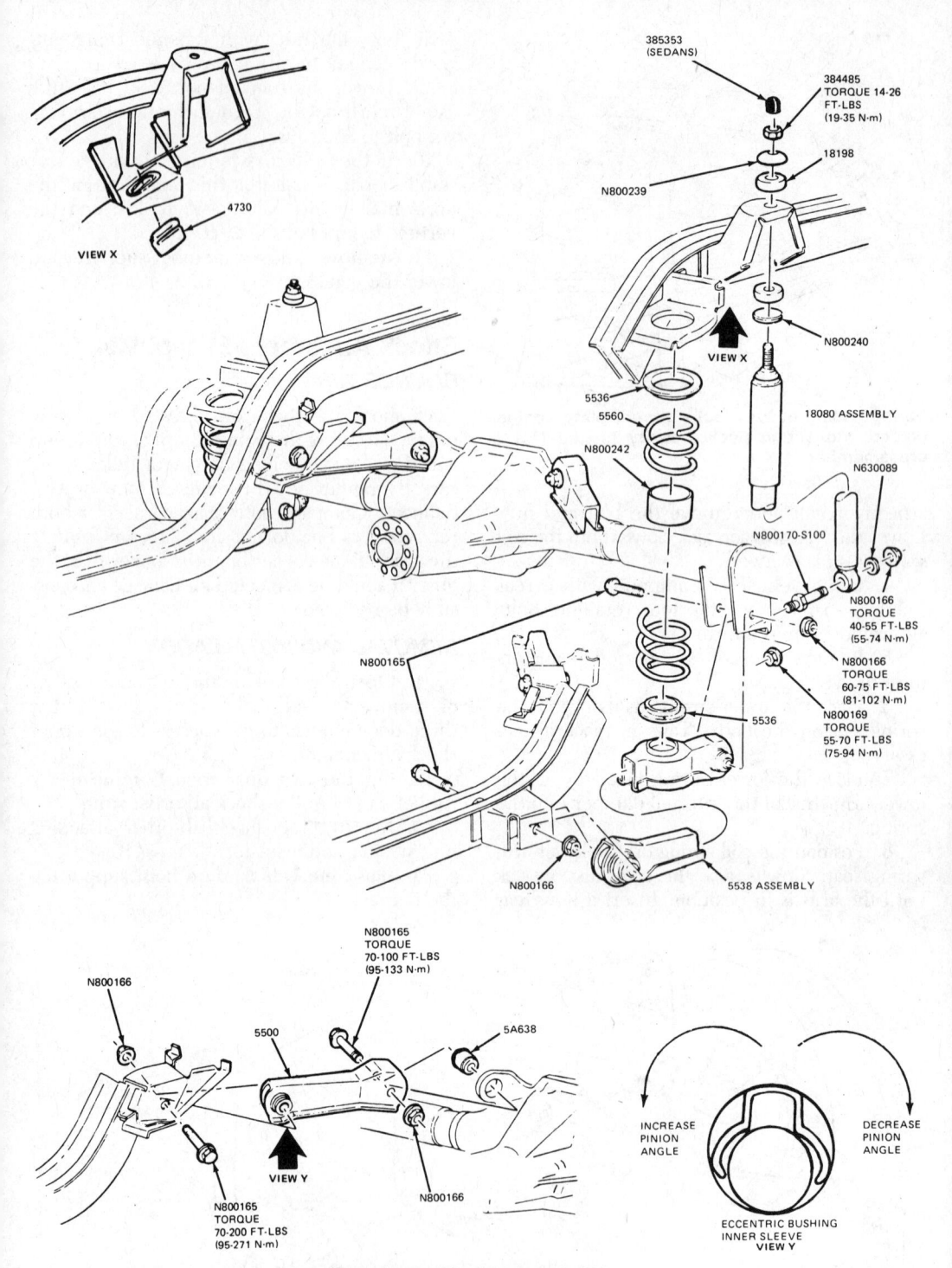

194 SUSPENSION AND STEERING

Rear suspension-exploded view

5. Compress the shock absorber to clear the hole in the upper shock tower.
6. Remove the lower shock absorber nut and washer from the shock mounting stud, and remove the shock abosrber.
7. Expel all air from the new shock absorber by extending the shock absorber fully at its right side up position, then turning it upside down and fully compressing it. Follow this procedure at least three times to expel the air.
8. With the shock absorber in the compressed position place the lower shock mounting eye over the stud in the lower mounting bracket and install the washer and new self

SUSPENSION AND STEERING 195

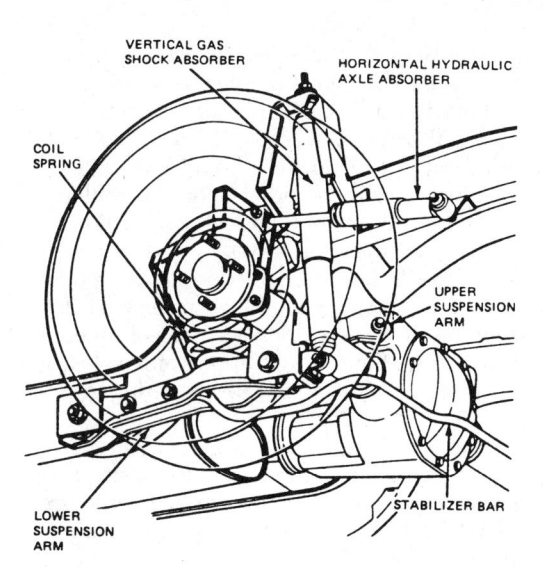

Performance handling rear suspension shock mounting

locking attaching nut. Do not torque at this time.

9. Place the inner washer and insulator on the upper attaching stud.
10. Extend the shock absorber and position the upper stud into the hole in the upper shock.
11. While holding the shock in this position, torque the lower attaching nut to 45 ft. lbs.
12. Lower the vehicle and install the insulator, outer washer and nut to the upper shock stud. Torque the nut to 20 ft. lbs.
13. Install the side panel trim covers on the three door models and the rubber cap on the two door models.

Shock Absorber-Merkur
REMOVAL AND INSTALLATION

1. Remove the rear parcel shelf. Remove the shock absorber trim cover from the rear wheel housing.
2. Raise and support the rear of the vehicle on jackstands. Position a floorjack under the control arm. Raise it enough to relieve coil spring tension from the shock. Remove the upper shock end mounting nut and bolt.
3. Remove the cap cover from the lower shock mount. Remove the nut and bolt mounting the lower shock eye. Remove the shock.
4. Install the shock absorber in the reverse order of removal. Tighten the mounting nuts and bolts to 30–40 ft. lbs.

Coil Spring—Merkur
REMOVAL AND INSTALLATION

1. Raise and support the rear of the vehicle on jackstands, allowing the rear suspension to hang free.

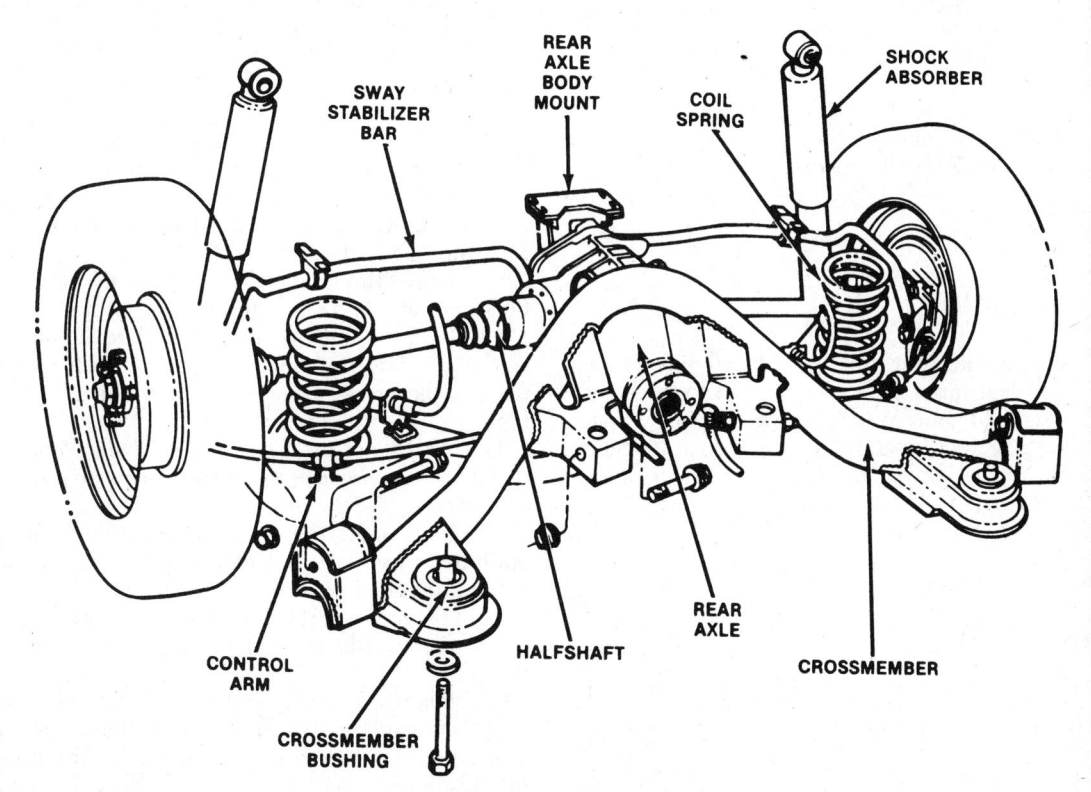

Merkur rear suspension

SUSPENSION AND STEERING

2. Remove the half-shaft to outer wheel stub mounting bolts and secure the shaft with wire so it does not hang unsupported.

3. Remove the clip attaching the rear brake hose to the routing bracket on the control arm.

4. Disconnect the brake hose from the line using flare wrenches.

5. Raise the control arm slightly with a floor jack and disconnect the lower end of the shock absorber.

6. Slowly lower and remove the floor jack. Position the floor jack under the axle housing and support it lightly.

7. Remove the bolts that attach the rear axle mount to the body and disconnect the rear axle vent tube.

8. Slowly and carefully lower the floor jack until the coil spring can be removed.

9. Install the coil spring in the reverse order of removal. Tighten the attaching parts to the following torque specifications:
- Axle to Body Bolts- 14–18 ft. lbs. Loctite® applied.
- Shock Bolt and Nut- 30–40 ft. lbs.
- Half-Shaft Bolts- 28–31 ft. lbs.
- Stabilizer Bar- Merkur

REMOVAL AND INSTALLATION

1. Loosen the rear wheel lugs. Raise and support the rear of the vehicle on jackstands. Remove the wheels.

2. Disconnect the stabilizer from the control arm by prying the links from the control arm.

3. Remove the U-bracket mounting bolts and remove the stabilizer bar.

4. Install in the reverse order of removal. Tighten the body bracket mounting bolts to 15–18 ft. lbs.

STEERING

The steering gear is of the rack and pinion type. The gear input shaft is connected to the steering shaft by means of a flexible coupling. A pinion gear, machined on the input shaft, engages the rack and rotation of the input shaft pinion causes the rack to move laterally.

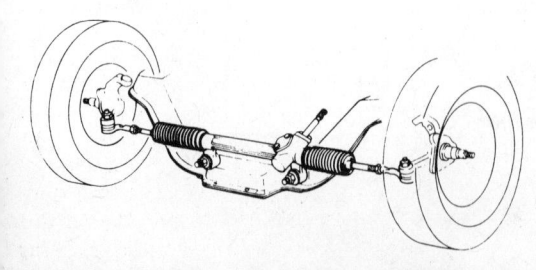

Typical rack and pinion steering gear linkage

The tie-rod is attached at each end of the rack joint. This allows the tie-rods to move with the front suspension. The gear is sealed at each end with rubber bellows. The steering gear is filled with approximately 5 oz of SAE-90 EP oil at initial assembly, and checking or refilling is not required unless fluid leakage is evident or repairs become necessary.

Couplings attaching the tie-rods are retained on the rack, are pinned, and cannot be disassembled in service. Replacement of inner tie-rods, rack, housing, or upper pinion bearing requires installation of a new steering gear assembly.

If the steering linkage, front suspension, and steering column components are in good condition, there should be no more than 3/8 in. freeplay in the steering wheel when measured at the rim of the wheel.

If a loud knock is heard when turning the steering wheel from lock-to-lock, the pinion bearing preload should be checked. A faint knock from the steering wheel when driving on very rough roads is normal and not an indication of a steering defect.

CAUTION: *When the front wheels of the vehicle are suspended completely off the ground, do not turn the wheels quickly or forcefully from lock to lock. This could cause a buildup of hydraulic pressure within the steering gear with could damage or blow out the bellows.*

Steering Gear

REMOVAL AND INSTALLATION

1. Disconnect the negative battery cable from the battery.

2. Remove the one bolt retaining the flexible coupling to the input shaft.

3. Leave the ignition key in the ON position, and raise and safely support the vehicle.

4. Remove the two tie rod end retaining cotter pins and nuts. Separate the studs from the spindle arms, using a ball joint separator tool.

NOTE: *Do not use a hammer or similar tool as this may damage the spindle arms or rod studs.*

5. Disconnect the power steering lines (if equipped). Support the steering gear, and remove the nuts, insulator washers, and bolts retaining the steering gear to the crossmember.

6. Remove the steering gear assembly from the vehicle.

7. Insert the imput shaft into the flexible coupling aligning the flats and position the steering gear to the No. 2 crossmember. Install the two bolts.

8. Connect the tie rod ends to the spindle

SUSPENSION AND STEERING

arms and install the two retaining nuts. Tighten to 40 ft. lbs. Install the two cotter pins.

9. Lower the vehicle and install the one bolt retaining the flexible coupling to the input shaft. Tighten the bolt to 30 ft. lbs.
10. Turn the ignition key to the off position.
11. Reconnect the negative battery cable.
12. Check the front end alignment (toe) and adjust if necessary.

ADJUSTMENTS

There are two adjustments which can be performed on the rack and pinion steering gear: support yoke-to-rack adjustment and pinion bearing preload adjustment. The steering gear assembly must be removed from the car to perform either adjustment.

Support Yoke-to-Rack

1. Remove the steering gear from the car.
2. Mount the steering gear in a soft-jawed vise with the yoke cover up. Clean the exterior of the gear.
3. Remove the yoke cover, gasket, shims, and yoke spring. Clean the yoke cover and support thoroughly.
4. Reinstall the yoke cover on the support yoke.
5. Tighten the yoke cover until the cover just touches the yoke support.
6. Measure the clearance between the cover and support yoke flange.
7. To the clearance figure measured in Step 6, add 0.006 in.
8. Measure the thickness of the shims and gasket that were removed from under the yoke cover in Step 3.
9. Subtract the figure obtained in Step 8 from the figure obtained in Step 7. The remainder from this subtraction is the thickness of the shim that must be added under the yoke cover to obtain the correct support yoke-to-rack adjustment.

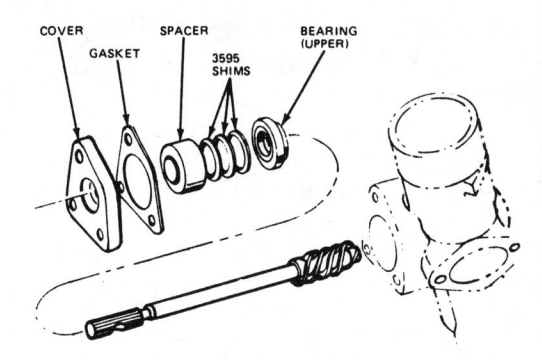

Pinion bearing cover and shim arrangement

10. Remove the yoke cover and install the yoke spring, shims, and gasket removed in Step 3, plus a shim of the correct thickness.
11. Apply sealer to the yoke cover bolts and install the yoke cover.
12. Turn the pinion shaft to ensure proper operation of the gear.

NOTE: *Return the pinion shaft to its centered position before installing it in the car.*

Pinion Bearing Preload

1. Remove the steering gear assembly from the car.
2. Mount the steering gear in a soft-jawed vise and clean the exterior of the gear.
3. Remove the pinion cover.
4. Clean the pinion flange area and remove the gasket and shims.
5. Install a new gasket and install shims until the shim pack is flush with the gasket. Check by placing a straightedge on top of the gasket and applying light pressure.
6. Remove the gasket and shims and reinstall the shims in the following order: the thinnest of the select fit shims first, followed by the other select fit shims and the 0.093 in. shim next to the cover.
7. To the above shim pack, add a 0.005 in. shim to preload the bearing. Place it in the correct order in the shim pack.
8. Apply sealer to the cover attaching bolts and install the cover and gasket.

Tie Rod Articulation Effort

1. Install the hook end of a pull scale through the hole in the tie rod end stud. The effort to move the tie rod should be 1–5 pounds.
   NOTE: *Do not damage the tie rod neck.*
2. Replace the ball joint/tie rod assembly if the effort falls outside this range. Save the tie rod end for use on the new tie rod assembly.

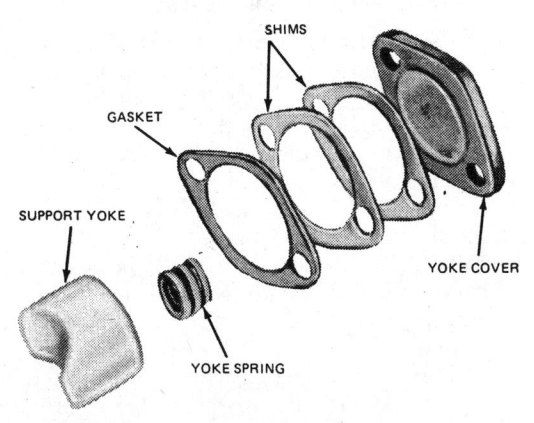

Support yoke arrangement

198 SUSPENSION AND STEERING

Tie Rod Ends, Bellows and Tie Rod Ball Joint Sockets—Except Merkur

1. Remove the steering gear assembly.
2. Clean the exterior of the gear thoroughly, and mount the steering gear in a soft jawed vise.
3. Loosen the jam nuts on the outer ends of the tie rods adjacent to the tie rod ends.
4. Remove the tie rod ends and jam nuts.
5. Remove the four clamps, retaining the bellows to the gear housing and the tie rods. Drain the lubricant and remove the bellows.
6. Remove the spiral pin from the ball housing with Tool T78P-3504-N or equivalent.
7. Using a ball housing torque adapter, Tool T78P-3504-AA or equivalent, locate the point of the locking screw in the large hole midway along the length of the housing and tighten firmly.
8. Attach a standard ½-inch drive rachet handle to the tool. Expose enough jack teeth to install an adjustable wrench over the flat formed by the tops of the rack teeth. Loosen the ball housing tie rod assembly by holding the adjustable wrench and turning the ball housing torque adapter tool.

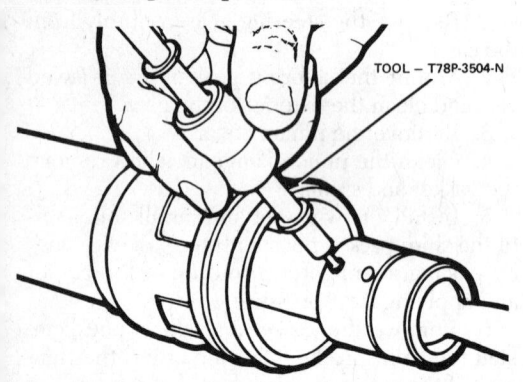

Removing the spiral pin from the ball housing

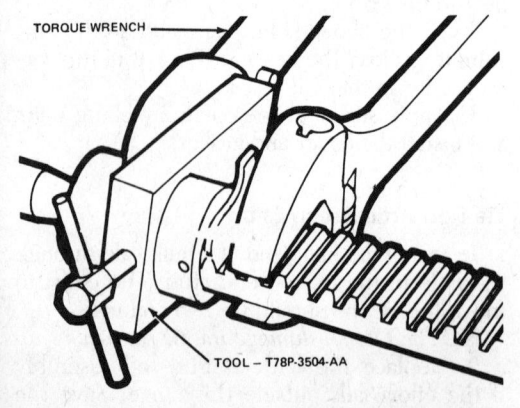

Removing or installing the tie rod ball housing assembly

NOTE: *If the rack is not restrained by the adjustable wrench, the pinion will be damaged.*

9. Thread the tie rod assembly onto the end of the rack.
10. Install the ball housing torque adapter tool on the ball housing. Locate the point of the locking screw in the large hole midway along the length of the housing and tighten firmly.
11. Hold the rack with an adjustable wrench on the flat of the rack and as near the end of the rack as possible. Holding the rack with an adjustable wrench tighten the ball housing to 50 ft. lbs. by turning the torque adapter tool with the ½-inch drive torque wrench.
12. Rotate the tie rod at least ten times (do not force the tie rod against limits of articulation travel) before measuring the articulation effort. If articulation effort is not to specification, replace the tie rod. Refer to Tie Rod Articulation Effort under Adjustments outlined earlier.
13. Insert the spiral retaining pin into the small hole in the ball housing, and tap lightly with a hammer until seated.
14. Apply some lubricant to the tie rods in the undercut where the bellows will be clamped. This will prevent the bellows from twisting during toe adjustment. Install the small bellows clamps. Install the large bellows clamp on the right side only (opposite end from the pinion).
15. Place the gear in the vertical position with the pinion end of the gear up. Fill the housing with 5 ounces of Ford D8AZ-19578-A or equivalent (fluid grease).
16. Install the left large bellows clamp, fastening the bellows to the gear housing.
17. Install the jam nuts and tie rod ends on the tie rods.

Steering Wheel

REMOVAL AND INSTALLATION

1. On the two and three spoke wheels remove the wheel hub cover by pulling outward. On the four spoke wheels push out the emblem from the backside of the steering wheel.
2. Remove and discard the steering wheel attaching nut.
3. Install a steering wheel puller on the end of the shaft and remove the wheel.

NOTE: *The use of a knock-off type steering wheel puller or the use of a hammer on the steering shaft will damage the collapsible column.*

4. Position the steering wheel on the end of the shaft and align the marks on the steering wheel with the marks on the shaft.

SUSPENSION AND STEERING 199

1. Emblem assy.
2. Nut 5/8-18 hex
3. Wheel assy-stng
4. Lock cyl-(body)
5. Key-(body)
6. Ring
7. Bearing
8. Gear-stng col lock
9. Shroud-upper

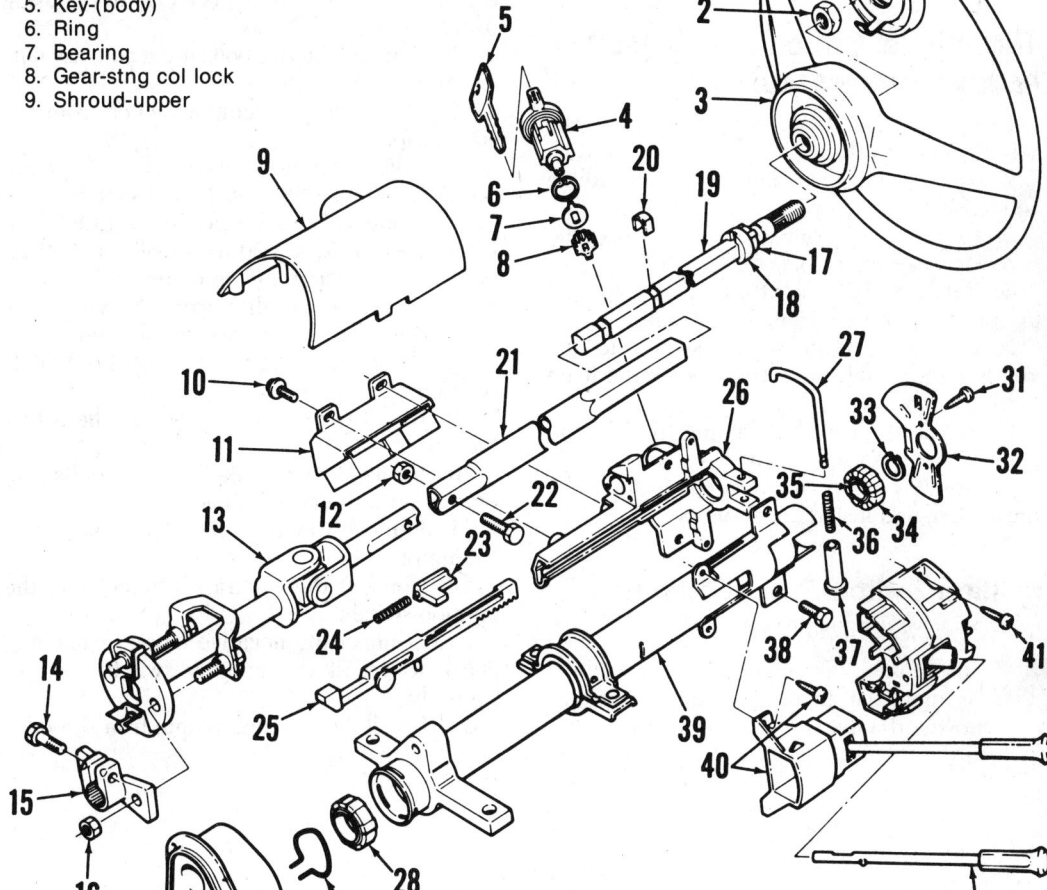

10. Bolt (break off head) (2 req'd)
11. Switch assy.-ignition
12. Nut 3/8-16 hex lock
13. Shaft assy-stng col lower
14. Bolt-3/8-24 x 1.22
15. Flange-stng shaft lower
16. Nut 3/8-16 hex lock
17. Cam-turn sig turn off
18. Lock-stng col position
19. Shaft-stng gear upper
20. Anti-rattle clips
21. Shaft-stng gear lower
22. Bolt 3/8-16 x 1 3/8 hex
23. Pawl-stng col lock
24. Spring-stng col lock
25. Actuator assy-stng col lock
26. Housing-stng col lock cyl
27. Lever-stng col lock actuator
28. Bearing assy-stng gear shaft lower
29. Ring-stng gear shaft lower bearing retainer
30. Boot assy-stng col

31. Screw no. 8-18 x .62 pan hd. tap (2 req'd)
32. Retainer-stng col upper bearing
33. Retainer-stng col upper bearing
34. Sleeve-stng col upper bearing
35. Bearing assy-stng col upper
36. Spring-stng col lock
37. Knob-stng col lock actuator
38. Bolt-M8 x 1.25 hex hd (2 req'd)
39. Tube assy col outer
40. Wash/wipe switch & screws (body)
41. Screw no. 8-18 x .62 pan hd tap (2 req'd)
42. Handle & shank assy-turn sig switch
43. Shroud-stng col lower
44. Screw no. 8-18 x 1.50 pan hd tap (4 req'd)
45. Foam cover
46. Screw (4 req'd)

Standard (non-tilt) steering column assembly showing ignition switch placement

SUSPENSION AND STEERING

5. Install a new wheel nut and torque to 35 ft. lbs.
6. Install the hub cover to the steering wheel.

Turn Signal Switch-Except Merkur
REMOVAL AND INSTALLATION

1. Remove the four screws retaining the steering column shroud.
2. Remove the turn signal lever by pulling and twisting straight out.
3. Peel back the foam shield. Disconnect the two electrical connectors.
4. Remove the two attaching screws and disengage the switch from the housing.
5. To install, position the switch to the housing and install the screws. Stick the foam to the switch.
6. Install the lever by aligning the key and pushing the lever fully home.
7. Install the two electrical connectors, test the switch, and install the shroud.

Ignition Switch-Except Merkur
REMOVAL AND INSTALLATION

1. Disconnect the negative battery cable.
2. Remove the steering column trim shroud by removing the five self-tapping screws.
3. Disconnect the ignition switch electrical connector.
4. Drill out the "break-off head" bolts that connect the switch to the lock cylinder housing using a $\frac{1}{8}$ inch drill.
5. Remove the two bolts using an "easy out" tool or equivalent.
6. Disengage the ignition switch from the actuator pin.
7. Adjust the ignition switch to the lock position. When adjusting the old switch to the lock position slide the carrier to the LOCK position then insert a .050 inch drill bit through the switch housing and into the carrier, preventing movement of the carrier. New switches are held in place by plastic shipping pins.
8. Rotate the ignition key to the LOCK position.
9. Install the ignition switch on the actuator pin.
10. Install new "break-off head" bolts and tighten until the heads break off.
11. Remove the adjustment drill bit by adjusting pin.
12. Connect the electrical connector to the ignition switch.
13. Connect the negative battery cable and check to see if the ignition switch operates properly.
14. Install the steering column trim shrouds.

Brakes 9

HYDRAULIC SYSTEM

The hydraulic system is composed of the master cylinder, the brake lines, the brake pressure differential valve, and the wheel cylinders (drum brakes) and/or calipers (disc brakes).

The master cylinder serves as a brake fluid reservoir and as a hydraulic pump. Brake fluid is stored in the two sections of the master cylinder. The front half of the master cylinder holds the fluid that is used to activate the rear brakes. The rear half of the master cylinder holds the fluid that activates the front brakes. Tandem master cylinder is required by federal law as a safety device. Since the front hydraulic system is independent of the rear system, a fluid leak in one system would only cause that system to fail, allowing the other system to stop the car.

When the brake pedal is depressed, it moves a piston mounted in the bottom of the master cylinder. The movement of this piston creates hydraulic pressure in the master cylinder. This pressure is carried to the wheel cylinders or calipers by the brake lines.

On the way to the wheels, the brake fluid passes through the control valve assembly.

The brake control valve assembly may consist of a pressure differential valve, a metering valve, and a proportioning valve. These valves are housed within a single cast-iron or aluminum valve body (housing). The pressure differential and metering valves are located in the central bore of the valve body. The proportioning valve is located in a separate angular or vertical bore.

The metering valve is located in the front end of the control valve central bore between the front brake system inlet port and the front brake outlet ports. Its function is to regulate the hydraulic pressure to the front disc brakes. The metering valve location at the front end of the housing center bore provides easy accessibility to the valve bleeder rod during bleeding of the front brake system.

The brake warning light switch is mounted at the center of the valve body with the spring-loaded plunger fitting into a tapered shoulder groove in the center of the piston. With the piston in a centralized position the switch contacts remain open.

Should there be a loss of pressure in either the front or rear brake system, when the brake pedal is applied, the piston will move off center, closing the switch contacts and turning on the warning light.

After repairs are made and the brake system bled, the piston will center itself upon brake application and the switch contacts will open, turning off the warning light.

NOTE: *The brake warning/low fluid switch is contained in the master cylinder reservoir cover assembly on Merkur models.*

The proportioning valve regulates the rear brake system hydraulic pressure and is located between the rear brake system inlet and outlet ports.

When the brake pedal is applied, the full rear brake fluid pressure passes through the proportioning valve to the rear brake hydraulic system until the valve split point is attained. Above the split point, the proportioning valve reduces hydraulic pressure to the rear brakes for balanced braking.

When the hydraulic pressure reaches the wheels, after the pedal has been depressed, it enters the wheel cylinders or calipers. Here it comes into contact with a piston or pistons. The hydraulic pressure causes the piston(s) to move, which moves the brake shoes or pads (disc brakes), causing them to come into contact with the drums or rotors (disc brakes). Friction between the brake shoes and the drums causes the car to slow down. There is a relationship between the amount of pressure that is applied to the brake pedal and the amount of force which

202 BRAKES

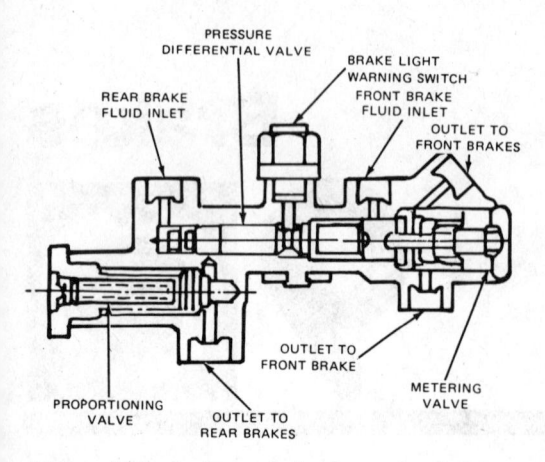

1980 and later brake control valve—aluminum

moves the brake shoes against the drums. Therefore, the harder the brake pedal is depressed, the quicker the car will stop.

Since a hydraulic system is one which operates on fluids, air is a natural enemy of the brake system. Air in the hydraulic system retards the passage of hydraulic pressure from the master cylinder to the wheels. Anytime a hydraulic component below the master cylinder is opened or removed, the system must be bled of air to ensure proper operation. Air trapped in the hydraulic system can also cause the brake warning light to come on, even though the system has not failed. This is especially true after repairs have been performed on the system.

The wheel cylinders used with drum brakes are composed of a cylinder with a polished inside bore, which is mounted on the brake shoe backing plate, two boots, two pistons, two cups, a spring, and a bleeder screw. When hydraulic pressure enters the wheel cylinder, it contacts the two cylinder cups. The cups seal the cylinder and prevent fluid from leaking out. The hydraulic pressure forces the cups outward. The cups in turn force the pistons outward. The pistons contact the brake shoes and the hydraulic pressure in the wheel cylinders overcomes the pressure of the brake springs, causing the shoes to contact the brake drum. When the brake pedal is released, the brake shoe return springs pull the brake shoes away from the drum. This forces the pistons back toward the center of the wheel cylinder. Wheel cylinders can fail in two ways; they can leak or lock up. Leaking wheel cylinders are caused either by defective cups or irregularities in the wheel cylinder bore. Frozen wheel cylinders are caused by foreign matter getting into the cylinders and preventing the pistons from sliding freely.

The calipers used with disc brakes contain a piston, piston seal, piston dust boot, and bleeder screw. When hydraulic pressure enters the caliper, the piston is forced outward causing the disc brake pad to come into contact with the rotor. When the brakes are applied, the piston seal, mounted on the caliper housing, becomes slightly distorted in the direction of the rotor. When the brakes are released, the piston seal moves back to its normal position and, at the same time, pulls the piston back away from the brake pad. This allows the brake pads to move away from the rotor. Calipers can fail in three ways, two of these being caused by defective piston seals. When a piston seal becomes worn, it can allow brake fluid to leak out to contaminate the pad and rotor. If a piston seal becomes weak, it can fail to pull the piston away from the brake shoe when the brakes are released, allowing the brake pad to drag on the rotor when the car is being driven. If foreign material enters the caliper housing, it can prevent the piston from sliding freely, causing the brakes to stick on the rotor.

Clean, high-quality brake fluid is essential to the proper operation of the brake system. Al-

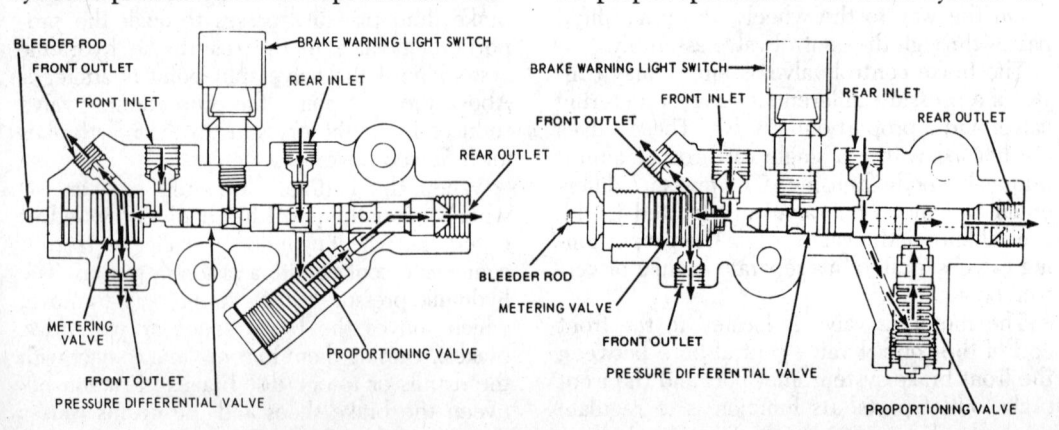

Brake control valve—1979 with cast iron housing

WAGNER ELECTRIC DESIGN   KELSEY-HAYES DESIGN

BRAKES

Brake Specifications
All measurements given are (in.) unless noted

Year	Model	Lug Nut Torque (ft. lbs.)	Master Cylinder Bore	Brake Disc Minimum Thickness	Brake Disc Maximum Run-Out	Brake Drum Max Machine O/S	Brake Drum Max Wear Limit	Minimum Lining Thickness Front	Minimum Lining Thickness Rear
1979	All	70–115	0.938	0.810	0.003	9.060	0.007	②	③
1980	All	70–115	0.875 ④	0.810	0.003	9.060	0.007	②	③
1981–82	All	80–105	0.875 ④	0.810	0.003	9.060	0.007	②	③
1983–85	Exc. Merkur	80–105	0.827 ⑤	0.810	0.003	9.060	0.007	②	③
1985	Merkur	75–101	0.940	0.950	0.003	10.040	0.007	②	③

NOTE: *Minimum lining thickness is as recommended by the manufacturer. Because of variations in state inspection regulations, the minimum allowable thickness may be different than recommended by the manufacturer.*
① DISC—9.3 in. outside, 6.24 in. inside
② Lining Measures ⅛ in. above metal shoe
③ Lining Measures 1/16" in. above rivets
④ 0.750 in. with power brakes
⑤ SVO—1.125

ways buy the highest quality brake fluid available. If the brake fluid should become contaminated, it should be drained and flushed, and the master cylinder filled with new fluid. Never reuse brake fluid. Any brake fluid that is removed from the brake system should be discarded.

Since the hydraulic system is sealed, there must be a leak somewhere in the system if the master cylinder is repeatedly low on fluid.

Master Cylinder

REMOVAL—EXCEPT MERKUR

1. Disconnect the negative battery cable.
2. Disconnect the stoplamp switch wries at the connector.
3. Remove the spring retainer and slide the stop lamp switch off the brake pedal pin just far enough to clear the end of the pin.
4. Loosen the master cylinder attaching nuts or bolts from the inside of the engine compartment and slide the master cylinder push rod, nylon washers, and bushings off the brake pedal pin.
5. Remove the brake lines from the master cylinder.
6. Remove the master cylinder attaching bolts and remove the master cylinder from the car.

OVERHAUL—EXCEPT MERKUR

1. Clean the outside of the master cylinder, and remove the cap and rubber gasket. Drain and discard the fluid that is in the master cylinder.
2. Remove the secondary piston stop bolt from the bottom of the cylinder.
3. Remove the bleeder screw from the cylinder.
4. Depress the primary piston and remove the snap-ring from the groove in the rear of the master cylinder bore.
5. Remove the primary piston and push rod from the master cylinder bore. Do not attempt to service the primary piston in any other way than removing the push rod from it. The primary piston must be replaced as an assembly.
6. Remove the secondary piston from the master cylinder.

NOTE: *Do not disassemble the master cylinder any further than this as no other parts for the master cylinder are serviced.*

7. Clean all parts in isopropyl alcohol.
8. Thoroughly inspect all parts for wear. If the primary or secondary pistons are defective, they should be replaced as an assembly. Check the master cylinder bore for scoring. The cylinder can be honed to remove surface blemishes, but no more than 0.003 in. can be removed from the cylinder walls. If in doubt, replace the master cylinder.

NOTE: *Before installing any part in the master cylinder, dip it in clean brake fluid.*

9. Install the secondary piston assembly in the master cylinder.
10. Install the primary piston assembly in the master cylinder.
11. Install the push rod, retainer, and boot, depress the piston, and install the snapring.
12. Install the secondary piston stop bolt and O-ring in the bottom of the master cylinder.
13. Install the bleeder screw.

204 BRAKES

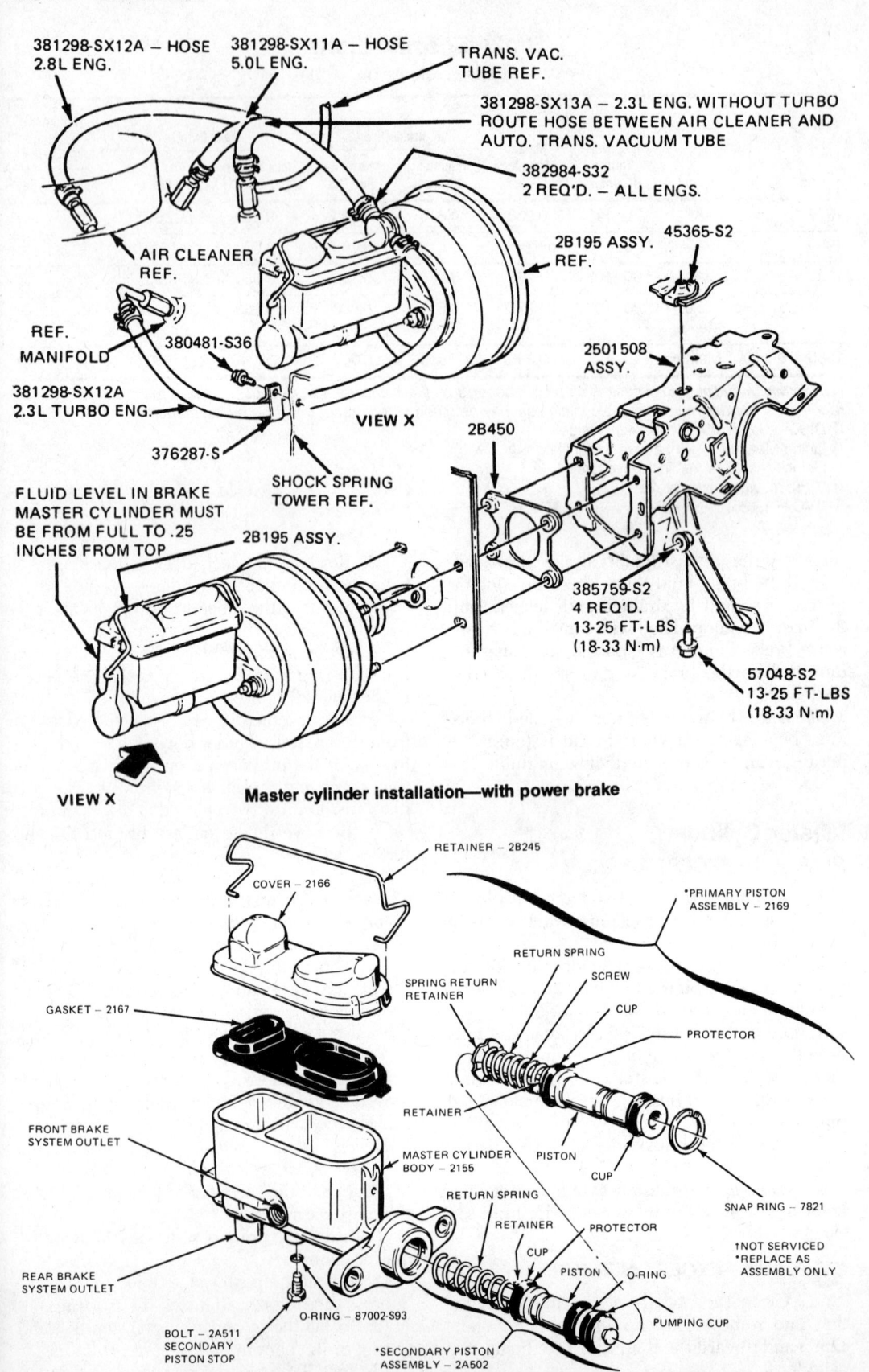

Master cylinder installation—with power brake

- 381298-SX12A – HOSE 2.8L ENG.
- 381298-SX11A – HOSE 5.0L ENG.
- TRANS. VAC. TUBE REF.
- 381298-SX13A – 2.3L ENG. WITHOUT TURBO ROUTE HOSE BETWEEN AIR CLEANER AND AUTO. TRANS. VACUUM TUBE
- 382984-S32 2 REQ'D. – ALL ENGS.
- 2B195 ASSY. REF.
- 45365-S2
- 2501508 ASSY.
- AIR CLEANER REF.
- REF. MANIFOLD
- 380481-S36
- 381298-SX12A 2.3L TURBO ENG.
- 376287-S
- VIEW X
- SHOCK SPRING TOWER REF.
- 2B450
- FLUID LEVEL IN BRAKE MASTER CYLINDER MUST BE FROM FULL TO .25 INCHES FROM TOP
- 2B195 ASSY.
- 385759-S2 4 REQ'D. 13-25 FT-LBS (18-33 N·m)
- 57048-S2 13-25 FT-LBS (18-33 N·m)
- VIEW X

Master cylinder—disassembled view

- RETAINER – 2B245
- COVER – 2166
- *PRIMARY PISTON ASSEMBLY – 2169
- RETURN SPRING
- SCREW
- CUP
- GASKET – 2167
- PROTECTOR
- RETAINER
- PISTON
- FRONT BRAKE SYSTEM OUTLET
- MASTER CYLINDER BODY – 2155
- CUP
- SNAP RING – 7821
- RETURN SPRING
- RETAINER
- PROTECTOR
- CUP
- PISTON
- REAR BRAKE SYSTEM OUTLET
- O-RING
- †NOT SERVICED *REPLACE AS ASSEMBLY ONLY
- O-RING – 87002-S93
- PUMPING CUP
- BOLT – 2A511 SECONDARY PISTON STOP
- *SECONDARY PISTON ASSEMBLY – 2A502

BRAKES 205

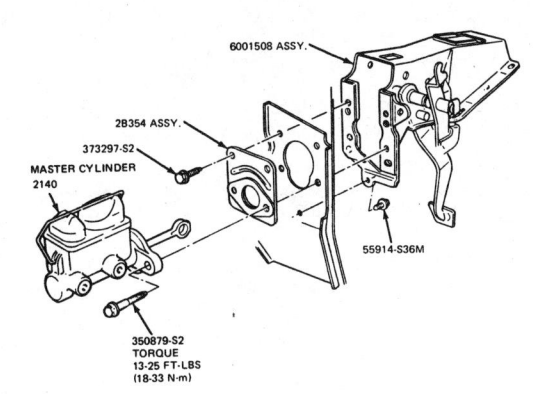

Master cylinder installation—without power brake

14. Fill the master cylinder with new fluid, depress the push rod, and open the bleeder to remove most of the air from the master cylinder.

INSTALLATION—EXCEPT MERKUR

1. Insert the push rod and boot through the dash panel opening, and position the master cylinder on the panel.
2. Install the master cylinder retaining bolts or nuts but do not tighten them.
3. Coat the nylon bushings with light engine oil. Install the nylon washer and bushing on the brake pedal pin.
4. Position the stoplamp switch and master cylinder push rod on the brake pedal pin. Install the nylon bushing and washer and secure them with the spring retainer.
5. Connect the wires at the stoplamp switch connector.
6. Tighten the master cylinder attaching nuts or bolts and connect the brake lines to the master cylinder.
7. Fill the master cylinder with new brake fluid.
8. Bleed the dual master cylinder and the primary and secondary brake systems.
9. Centralize the pressure differential valve.

REMOVAL AND INSTALLATION—MERKUR

1. Disconnect the low fluid level sensor wiring at the master cylinder reservoir cap.
2. Disconnect the brake lines from the master cylinder. Cap the lines and plug the master cylinder outlets.
3. Remove the nuts that retain the master cylinder to the brake booster and remove the master cylinder.
4. Install the master cylinder over the booster mounting studs. Loosely install the mounting nuts so that the master cylinder can be moved slightly (on the mounting studs).
5. Connect the brake lines to the master cylinder. Tighten the master cylinder mounting nuts to 16–20 ft. lbs.

6. Fill the master cylinder with fluid. Bleed the brake system.

OVERHAUL—MERKUR

1. Remove the master cylinder from the vehicle. Remove the reservoir cap and drain the brake fluid.
2. Clamp the master cylinder in a vise that is equipped with soft jaw covers.
3. Carefully pry the reservoir out of the mounting seals on the top of the master cylinder. Remove the reservoir seals from the top of the master cylinder.
4. Remove the O-ring from the front of the master cylinder bore. Push inward on the primary piston and remove the snap ring retainer from the master cylinder bore.
5. Remove the washer from the front of the primary piston. Remove the primary piston assembly. Remove the master cylinder from the vise and tap the cylinder with a piece of wood to remove the secondary piston assembly.
6. Clean the master cylinder bore and inspect it for pitting or scores that would indicate replacement instead of rebuilding.

NOTE: *Some aftermarket rebuilding kits contain seals only, while others contain primary and secondary piston assemblies.*

7. If using a seals only rebuilding kit; remove the seals from the primary and secondary piston assemblies. Clean the piston assemblies.
8. Install new seals on the piston assemblies. Lubricate the master cylinder bore and piston assemblies with clean brake fluid.
9. Install the secondary piston. Install the primary piston. To prevent damage to the seal lips, ease the piston and seal assemblies into the master cylinder bore while slowly rotating and pushing.
10. Install the washer and snap ring in the master cylinder bore. Install the O-ring in the front of the master cylinder and new reservoir seals in the top.
11. Install the reservoir, with the filler cap in position to prevent the entry of dirt.

Brake Control Valve Assembly

The brake control valve assemblies may consist of a pressure differential valve, metering valve, and a proportioning valve or pressure differential and proportioning valve assembly. These valves are housed in a signal aluminum or cast iron housing.

REMOVAL AND INSTALLATION

NOTE: *The pressure control valve on Merkur models is located under the brake booster and retained by one bolt. Disconnect the brake lines and remove the mounting bolt.*

206 BRAKES

Install the valve in reverse order. Bleed the brake system after installation.

1. Disconnect the brake warning light switch wire harness connector from the warning light switch.
2. Disconnect the front brake system inlet tube and the rear system inlet tube from the brake control valve assembly.
3. Disconnect the rear system outlet tube from the brake control valve assembly.
4. Remove the control valve retaining nuts or bolts and remove the control valve.
5. To install reverse the removal procedure. Bleed the brake system and centralize the pressure differential valve.

Centralizing the Pressure Differential Valve

Except Merkur

After any repair or bleeding of the brake system the dual brake warning light switch should be centralized.

1. Turn the ignition switch to ACC or ON position.
2. Depress the brake pedal and the piston will center itself, causing the brake warning light to go out if it was already lit.
3. Turn the ignition switch to the OFF position.
4. Check the operation of the brakes before driving.

Bleeding the Hydraulic System

NOTE: *If it is known that only one system has air in it, only that system has to be bled since the front and rear hydraulic systems are independent.*

1. Fill the master cylinder with brake fluid.
2. Install a 3/8 in. box-end wrench on the bleeder screw on the right rear wheel.
3. Push a piece of small-diameter rubber tubing over the bleeder screw until it is flush against the wrench. Submerge the other end of the rubber tubing in a glass jar partially filled with clean brake fluid. Make sure the rubber tire fits on the bleeder screw snugly or you may get zapped with brake fluid when the bleeder screw is opened.
4. Have a friend apply pressure to the brake pedal. Open the bleeder screw and observe the bottle of brake fluid. If bubbles appear in the glass jar, it means there is air in the system. When your friend has pushed the pedal to the floor, immediately close the bleeder screw *before he releases the pedal.*
5. Repeat this procedure until no bubbles appear in the jar. Refill the master cylinder.

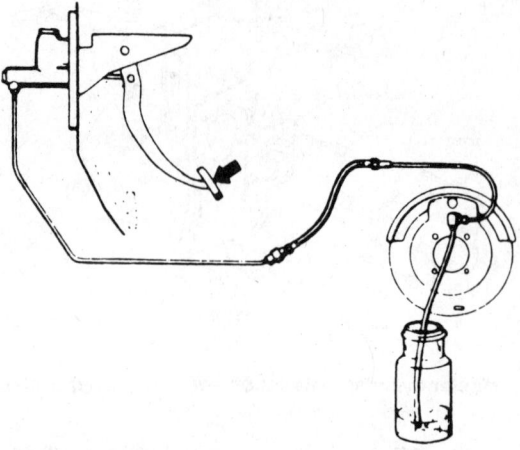

Bleeding the hydraulic brake system

6. Repeat this procedure on the left rear, right front, and left front wheels, in that order. Periodically refill the master cylinder so it does not run dry.
7. If the brake warning light is on, depress the brake pedal firmly. If there is no air in the system, the light will go out.

FRONT DISC BRAKES

The major components of the disc brake system are the brake pads, the caliper, and the rotor (disc). The caliper is similar in function to the wheel cylinder used with drum brakes, and the rotor is similar to the brake drum used in drum brakes.

The major difference between drum brakes and disc brakes is that with drum brakes, the wheel cylinder forces the brake shoes *out* against the brake drum to stop the car, while with disc brakes, the caliper forces the brake pads *inward* to squeeze the rotor and stop the car. The biggest advantage of disc brakes over drum brakes is that the caliper and brake pads enclose only a small portion of the rotor, leaving the rest of it exposed to outside air. This aids in rapid heat dissipation, reducing brake fade.

The disc brake system style used is known as sliding caliper disc brakes. The name of this system is derived from the sliding action of the brake caliper on the anchor plate during braking. The platelike brake rotor is attached to and mounted on the car by the front wheel hub. A brake caliper anchor plate, attached to the front wheel spindle, mounts over the top of, but does not touch, the rotor. The caliper is mounted in the middle of the large opening in the anchor plate. When the brake pedal is depressed, and hydraulic force is generated, the piston in the caliper forces the inboard brake pad inward and into contact with the brake rotor. The caliper

BRAKES

Caliper assembly—disassembled view

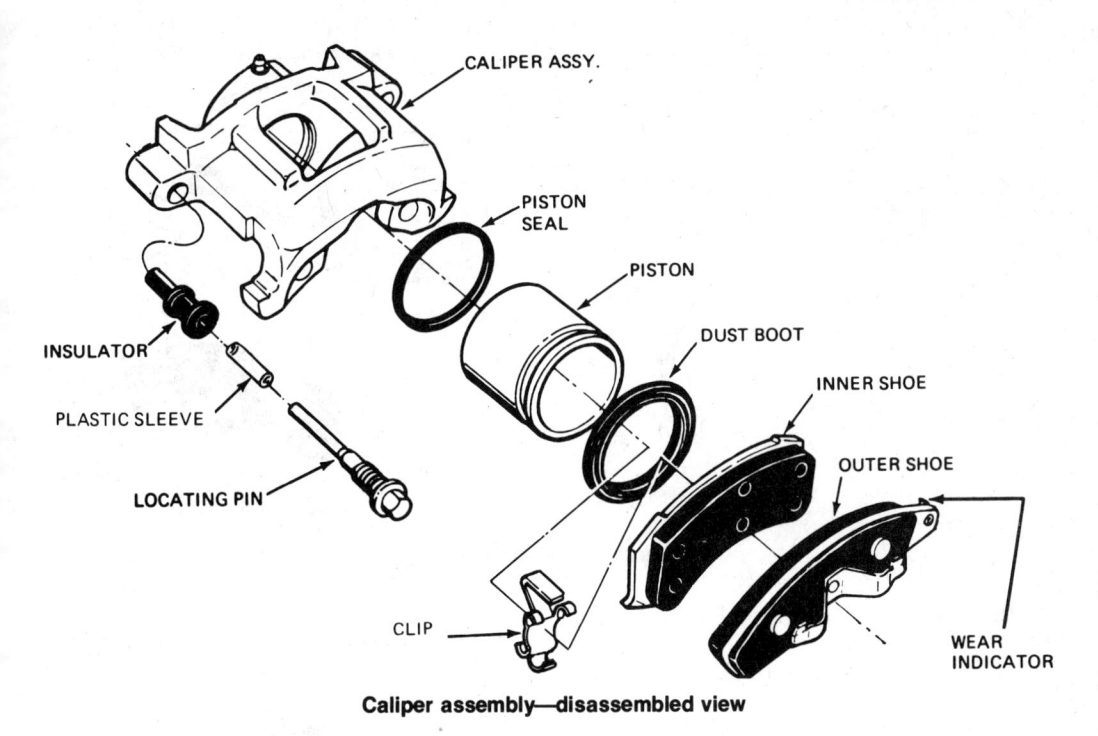

now begins to act like a C-clamp, with the inboard shoe and the piston acting as the adjustable screw. Since there is only a small amount of clearance between the brake pads and the rotor, the inboard shoe contacts the rotor almost as soon as the brake pedal is depressed. As the brake pedal is depressed further, it increases the amount of hydraulic pressure sent to the piston in the caliper. Since the inboard shoe is already in contact with the brake rotor, it cannot be moved. As the caliper pushes on the inboard brake shoe, the increased hydraulic pressure forces the back of the caliper housing away from the back of the piston. This causes the caliper to slide inward on the anchor plate and force the outboard brake pad into contact with the rotor. Thus the name sliding caliper. This happens very quickly, so both pads contact the rotor at about the same time.

When the brakes are released, the piston seal in the caliper housing (which was stretched during brake application) returns to its normal position and, in so doing, pulls the piston back away from the brake pad. A very slight wobble in the rotor as the car begins to move pushes the brake pads back so they are not in contact with the rotor. The clearance between the pads and the rotor is very slight, but it is sufficient to prevent brake drag. The same clearance is maintained even when the brake pads wear as the car accumulates mileage and, because of this, disc brakes do not have to be adjusted.

Disc Brake Pads

NOTE: *Merkur models are equipped with an electronic sensor that will cause a dash mounted warning light to come on when an inboard brake pad has worn to a thickness of 1.5mm. When the light comes on, remove the wheel and inspect the pads. Worn pads must be replaced.*

INSPECTION

1. Remove the wheel and tire assembly.
2. Visually inspect the lining. If the lining is worn to within ⅛ inch of the metal shoe all four shoe and lining assemblies must be replaced.
3. Visually check the caliper and hoses for leakage. If a seal is leaking, the caliper must be disassembled and new seals installed.

REMOVAL AND INSTALLATION
Except Merkur

1. Remove about half of the fluid from the master cylinder reservoir.
2. Loosen the lug nuts and raise and support the vehicle.
3. Remove the front wheel. Be careful to avoid damage to the caliper splash shield or bleed screw.
4. Remove the caliper locating pins. Remove the caliper assembly from the integral spindle anchor plate and rotor. Remove the outer shoe from the caliper.

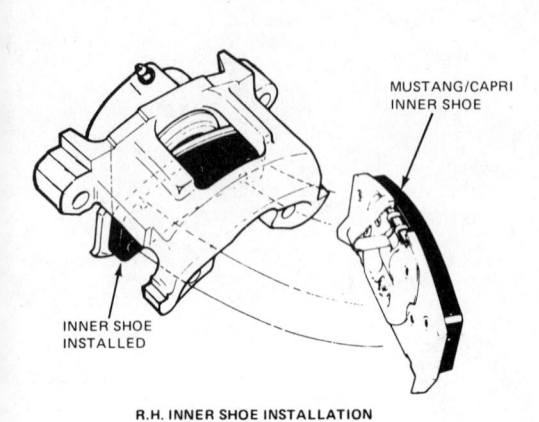

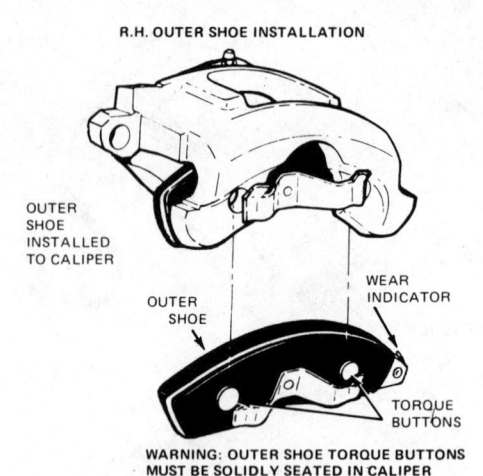

208 BRAKES

Disc brake shoe installation

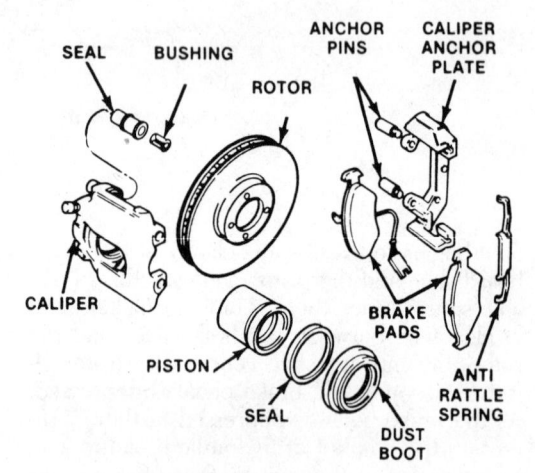

Merkur front disc brakes

5. Remove the inner shoe and inspect the rotor surfaces.
6. Secure the caliper assembly with a length of wire.
7. Remove and discard the plastic bushings inside the caliper locating pin insulators.
8. Remove and discard the locating insulators.
9. Using a 4 inch C-clamp and a 2¾ × 1 × ¼ in. piece of wood, seat the piston in its bore.
10. Install new insulators and sleeves in the caliper housing. Both insulator flanges must straddle the housing holes and the sleeves must bottom in the insulators as well as under the upper lip.
11. Inner shoes are marked left and right. Install the proper inner shoe in the caliper. Do not bend the clips too far or they will become distorted.
12. Outer shoes are marked left and right. Install the proper outer shoe making sure that the clip and buttons are properly seated.
13. Refill the master cylinder.
14. Install the wheel, lower the car and test the brakes.

Merkur

1. Remove about ⅓ of the brake fluid from the master cylinder.
2. Loosen the wheel lugs. Raise and support the vehicle on jackstands.
3. Remove the wheels.
4. Disconnect the wear indicator harness connector.
5. Remove the caliper to anchor plate attaching pins and lift the caliper assembly off of the rotor without disconnecting the brake hose. The anti-rattle spring will fall off when the caliper is removed.
6. Remove the inboard and outboard brake pads from the caliper. The inboard pad is retained in the caliper piston with a retaining clip.
7. Use a C-clamp and push the caliper piston carefully back into the caliper bore. Take care not to damage the piston boot.
8. Remove the backing paper from the outboard pad before installation. Install the inboard and outboard pads on the caliper.
9. Place the caliper in position over the rotor. Make sure the brake pads are properly engaged on the anchor plate.
NOTE: *Be sure the sensor wire is positioned correctly between the caliper and anchor before installing the anchor bolts.*
CAUTION: *When the caliper is installed, make sure the brake hose has not been kinked by twisting the caliper during servicing. A kinked hose condition will create a loop in the hose which tightens during vehicle operation and will rub against itself possibly causing a hydraulic leak.*

BRAKES 209

10. Install the anchor mounting bolts. Tighten the bolts evenly to 18–23 ft. lbs.

11. Install the anti-rattle spring. Connect the wear sensor harness. Make sure the harness sealing ring is in position before installation.

12. Position the wear sensor wiring connector in the routing clip. Install the wheel. Add brake fluid, as necessary, to the master cylinder after pumping the brakes several times to position the brake pads.

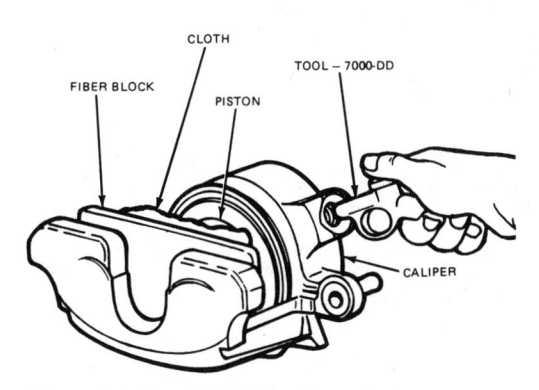

Caliper
OVERHAUL

1. Loosen the front wheel lug nuts.
2. Raise and support the car.
3. Remove the front wheel taking care to avoid damage to the splash shield and bleeder screw.
4. Loosen the flexible brake hose-to-brake tube fitting at the frame and remove the horseshoe type retaining clip from the hose and bracket and unscrew it from the caliper. Plug the hose to avoid contaminants from entering the brake fluid.

NOTE: *If both calipers are being removed, mark them left and right.*

5. Remove the caliper locating pins.
6. Lift the caliper from the rotor.
7. Place a wadded cloth in front of the piston and apply compressed air at the hose hole.

CAUTION: *Never attempt to stop the piston with your hand. The piston can emerge from its bore with considerable force due to built-up air pressure.*

8. Remove the dust boot and piston seal.

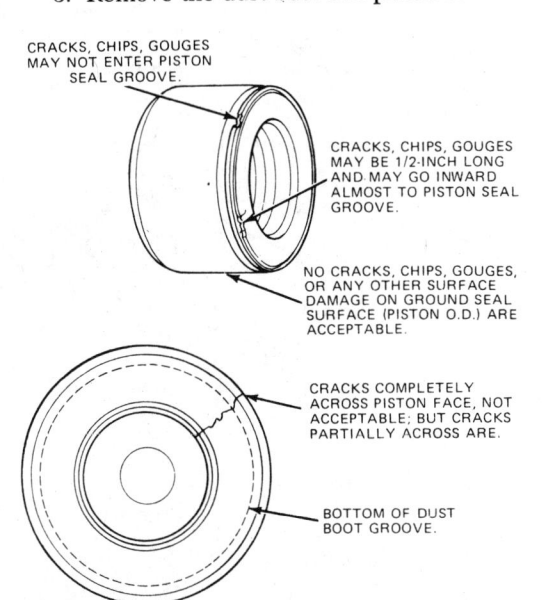

Removing the piston from the caliper

9. Clean all metal parts in isopropyl alcohol. Dry all parts with compressed air.
10. Coat all parts with clean brake fluid before installing. Make certain that the seal does not become twisted, and that it is firmly seated in its groove.
11. Install a new dust boot and insert the piston in its bore. Spread the dust boot over the piston as it's installed.
12. Position the caliper over the rotor with the outer shoe against the rotor braking surface to prevent pinching the boot.
13. Connect the locating pins to the anchor plate and insulators. Be sure the locating pins are free of dirt, grease or oil.
14. Torque the locating pins to 30–40 ft. lbs.
15. Unplug the hose and install it into the caliper and torque it to 20–30 ft. lbs.

NOTE: *It is not necessary for the hose to be flush with the caliper when tightened; two or three threads may be visible when properly torqued. Do not over-torque.*

16. Connect the upper end of the hose. Tighten the fitting nut to 10–18 ft. lbs.
17. Bleed the system and center the differential valve. Fill the master cylinder to within ¼ in. of the top of the reservoir.

Outer Bearing and Hub and Rotor
REMOVAL AND INSTALLATION
Except Merkur

1. Remove the caliper assembly and temporarily secure it to the upper suspension with a piece of wire.
2. Remove the grease cap from the hub.
3. Remove the cotter key, nut retainer and adjusting nut.
4. Pull outward on the hub and rotor assembly enough to loosen the washer and outer wheel bearing.
5. Push the hub and rotor back onto the spindle and remove the washer and outer wheel bearing.

Piston surface irregularities, disc brake

210 BRAKES

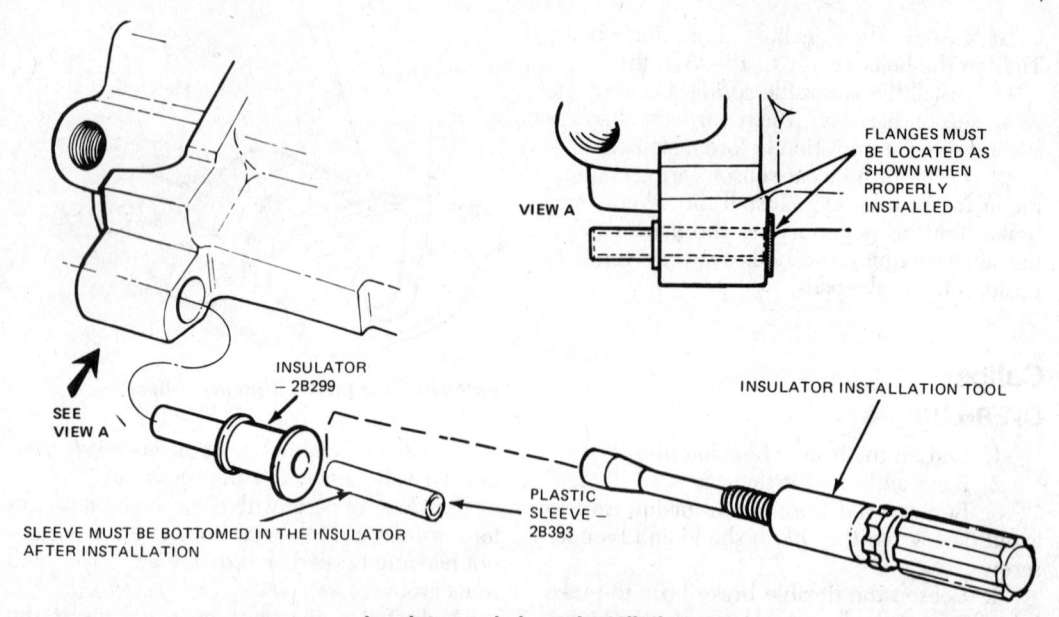

Insulator and sleeve installation

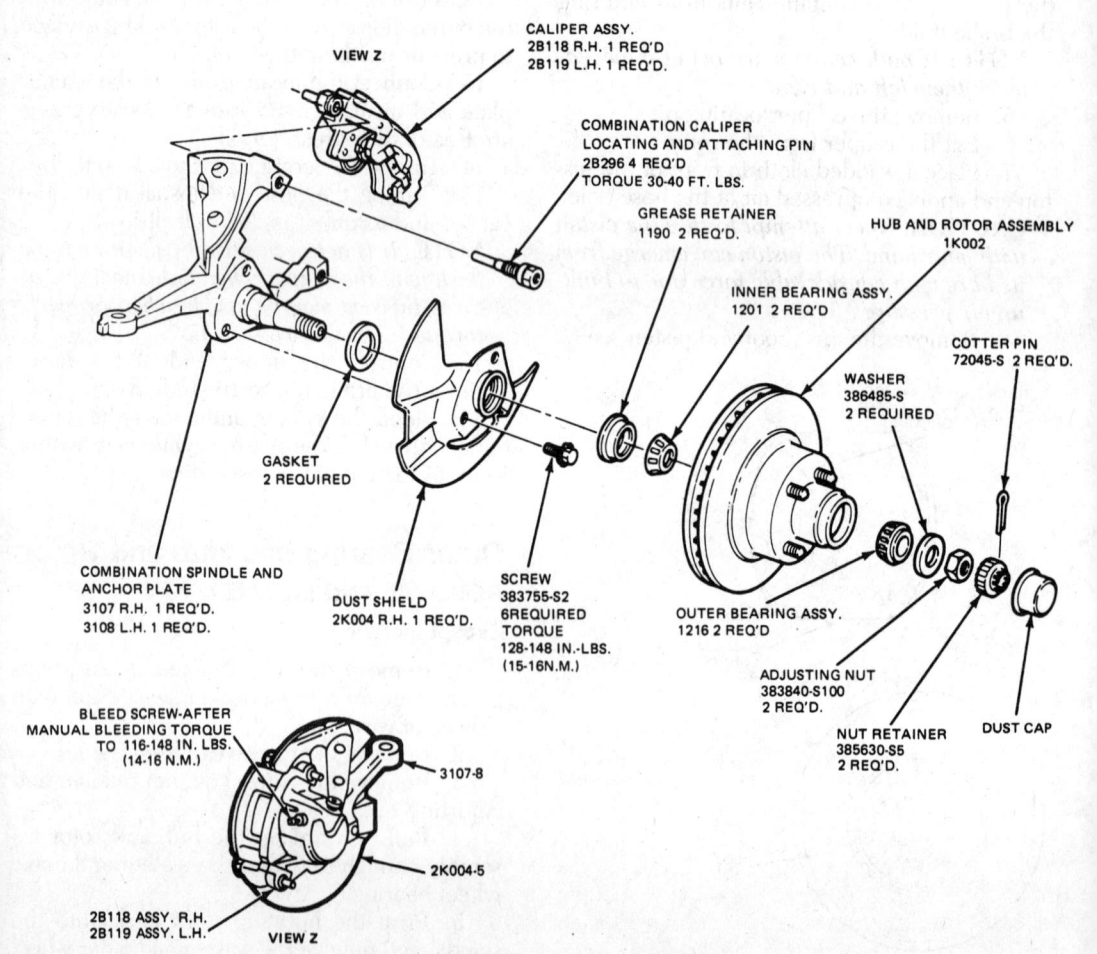

- INSULATOR – 2B299
- PLASTIC SLEEVE – 2B393
- INSULATOR INSTALLATION TOOL
- SLEEVE MUST BE BOTTOMED IN THE INSULATOR AFTER INSTALLATION
- SEE VIEW A
- VIEW A — FLANGES MUST BE LOCATED AS SHOWN WHEN PROPERLY INSTALLED

Caliper, shield and rotor assembly

- VIEW Z
- CALIPER ASSY. 2B118 R.H. 1 REQ'D 2B119 L.H. 1 REQ'D.
- COMBINATION CALIPER LOCATING AND ATTACHING PIN 2B296 4 REQ'D TORQUE 30-40 FT. LBS.
- GREASE RETAINER 1190 2 REQ'D.
- HUB AND ROTOR ASSEMBLY 1K002
- INNER BEARING ASSY. 1201 2 REQ'D
- WASHER 386485-S 2 REQUIRED
- COTTER PIN 72045-S 2 REQ'D.
- OUTER BEARING ASSY. 1216 2 REQ'D
- ADJUSTING NUT 383840-S100 2 REQ'D.
- NUT RETAINER 385630-S5 2 REQ'D.
- DUST CAP
- GASKET 2 REQUIRED
- COMBINATION SPINDLE AND ANCHOR PLATE 3107 R.H. 1 REQ'D. 3108 L.H. 1 REQ'D.
- DUST SHIELD 2K004 R.H. 1 REQ'D.
- SCREW 383755-S2 6 REQUIRED TORQUE 128-148 IN.-LBS. (15-16 N.M.)
- BLEED SCREW-AFTER MANUAL BLEEDING TORQUE TO 116-148 IN. LBS. (14-16 N.M.)
- 3107-8
- 2K004-5
- 2B118 ASSY. R.H. 2B119 ASSY. L.H.
- VIEW Z

BRAKES

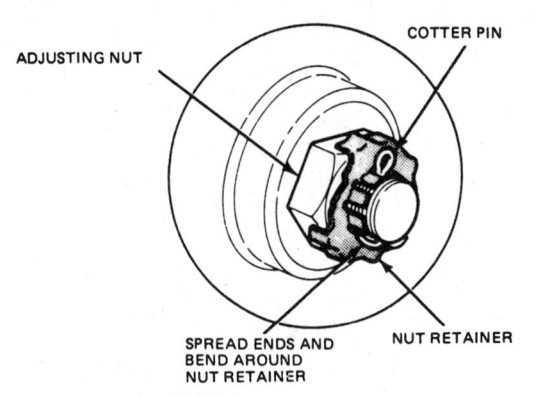

Adjusting outer wheel bearing

6. Slide the wheel hub and rotor assembly off the wheel spindle.

7. If the rotor is being replaced with a new one clean the surface of the rotor with carburetor degreaser.

8. If the original rotor is being installed place it on a clean, paper covered surface with the wheel studs facing upwards.

9. Working through the hole in the center of the wheel hub, tap the grease seal out of the rear of the hub with a screwdriver or drift.

NOTE: *Be careful not to damage the inner bearing while knocking out the grease seal.*

10. Remove the grease and bearing from under the rotor, and discard the grease seal.

11. Clean the inner and outer bearings and the wheel hub with a suitable solvent. Remove all old grease.

12. Thoroughly dry and wipe clean all components.

13. Clean all old grease from the spindle on the car.

14. Carefully check the bearings for any sign of scoring or other damage. If the roller bearings or bearing cages are damaged, the bearing and the corresponding bearing cup in the rotor hub must be replaced. The bearing cups must be driven out of the rotor hub to be removed. The outer bearing cup is driven out of the front of the rotor from the rear and vice versa for the inner bearing cup.

15. Whether you are reinstalling the old bearings or installing new ones, the bearings must be packed with wheel bearing grease. To do this, place a glob of grease in your left palm, then, holding one of the bearings in your right hand, drag the edge of the bearing heavily through the grease. This must be done to work as much grease as possible through the roller bearings and cage. Turn the bearing and continue to pull it through the grease until the grease is packed between the bearings and the cage all the way around the circumference of the bearing. Repeat this operation until all of the bearings are packed with grease.

16. Pack the inside of the rotor hub with a moderate amount of grease, between the bearing cups. Do not overload the hub with grease.

17. Apply a small amount of grease to the spindle.

18. Place the rotor, face down, on a protected surface and install the inner bearing.

19. Coat the lip of a new grease seal with a small amount of grease and position it on the rotor.

20. Place a block of wood on top of the grease seal and tap on the block with a hammer to install the seal. Turn the block of wood to different positions to seat it squarely in the hub.

21. Position the rotor on the spindle.

22. Install the outer bearing and washer on the spindle, inside the rotor hub.

23. Install the bearing adjustment nut and tighten it to 17–25 ft. lbs. while spinning the rotor. This will seat the bearing.

24. Back off the adjusting nut one half turn.

25. Tighten the adjusting nut to 10–15 in. lbs.

26. Install the nut lock on the adjusting nut so two of the slots align with the holes in the spindle.

27. Install a new cotter pin and bend the ends back so that they will not interfere with the dust cap.

28. Install the dust cap.

Merkur

NOTE: *For front wheel bearing service procedures, refer to Chapter 8, Steering Knuckle Service.*

1. Loosen the wheel lugs. Raise and support the front of the vehicle on jackstands.

2. Remove the front wheel.

3. Remove the disc brake caliper. Suspend the caliper out of the way with a piece of wire. Do not allow the caliper to be supported by the brake hose.

4. Mark the tip of a wheel lug and corresponding point on the rotor with paint or scribe a reference mark so that the rotor maybe installed in the same position to maintain factory balancing.

5. Remove the retaining clip from the wheel lug and remove the rotor.

6. Install the rotor in the reverse order of removal after aligning the balance reference marks.

REAR DISC BRAKES

Caliper, Rotor, Brake Pads
REMOVAL AND INSTALLATION

1. Raise and support the rear of the vehicle on jackstands.

212 BRAKES

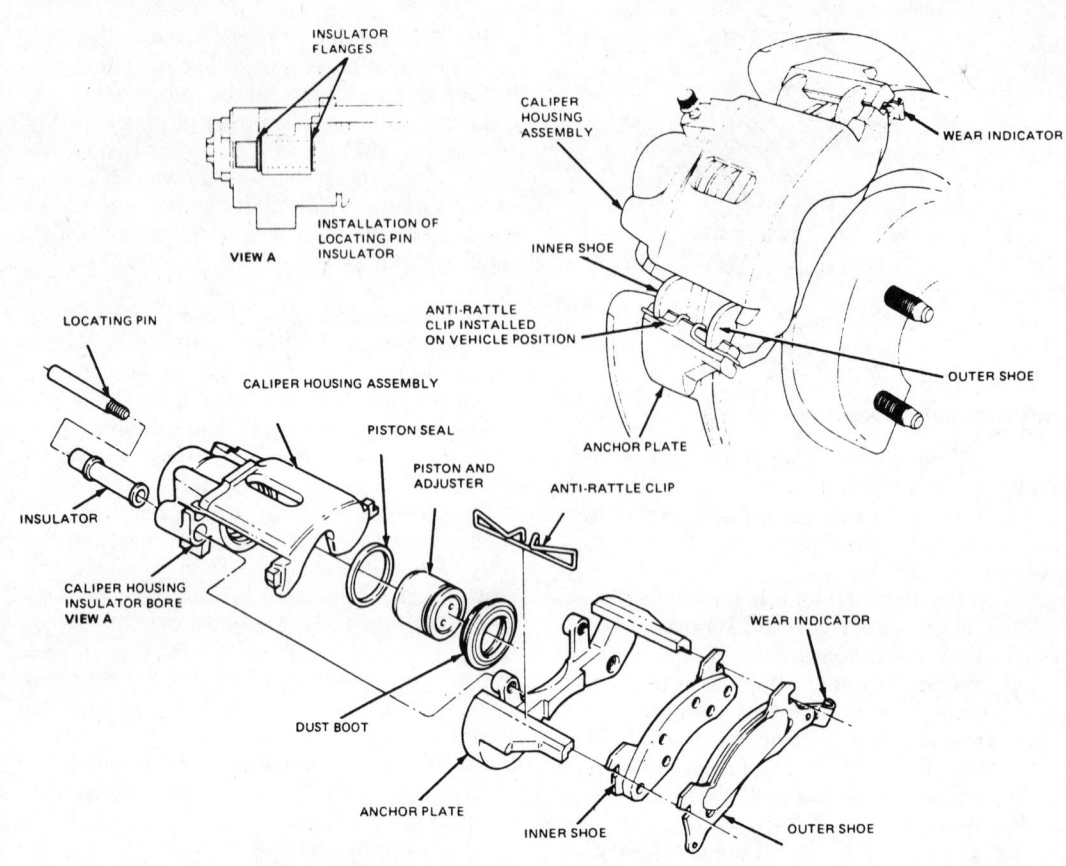

Rear disc brake caliper and anchor plate

2. Remove the wheels. Disconnect the parking brake cable from the caliper lever and bracket using care to avoid kinking or cutting the return spring or cable.

3. Remove the caliper mounting pins. Lift the caliper assembly away from the anchor plate by pushing the caliper upward toward the anchor plate while rotating the lower end out of the anchor plate.

4. If insufficient clearance between the brake pads, caliper and rotor prevent caliper removal, it will be necessary to loosen the caliper end retainer ½ turn (maximum) to allow the piston to be pushed back into its bore.

5. To loosen the end retainer, remove the parking brake lever, then mark or scribe the end retainer and caliper housing to be sure that the end retainer is not loosened more than ½ turn.

CAUTION: *If the retainer must be loosened more than ½ turn, the seal between the thrust screw and caliper housing maybe broken causing brake fluid to leak into the parking brake mechanism chamber. If fluid is leaking into the chamber, the end retainer must be removed and internal parts cleaned and lubricated.*

6. Push the caliper piston back slightly into its bore and remove the caliper. Do not use excessive force on the piston, or damage to the parking brake assembly may occur.

7. Remove the outer brake pad from the anchor plate. Mark the brake pad for position identification if it is to be reinstalled.

8. Remove the rotor retainer clips and the rotor. Remove the inner brake pad from the anchor. Mark the pad for reinstallation position. Remove the anti-rattle spring from the anchor plate.

9. Remove the hollow brake bolt and brake hose from the caliper.

10. Clean the caliper, anchor plate and rotor assemblies. Inspect for signs of brake fluid leakage, excessive wear or damage. The caliper must be inspected for leakage both in the piston boot area and at the parking brake operating shaft seal area. Rebuild or replace parts as necessary.

11. If the end retainer has been loosened only ½ turn, install the caliper in the anchor plate without the brake pads installed. Tighten the end retainer to 75–96 ft. lbs.

12. Install the parking brake lever on its splined shaft, the lever arm must point down and to the rear. Tighten the retainer to 16–22 ft. lbs. Check to make sure the parking brake

lever rotates freely after tightening the retainer. Remove the caliper from the anchor plate.

13. If new brake pads are to be installed, the caliper piston must be screwed back into its bore. A special tool, Ford number T75P-2588-B or the equivalent must be used. If the service tool use is of old design, modification is required. An illustration is provided for tool modification purposes.

14. The piston is screwed back into the caliper bore with the caliper mounted on the anchor plate without the rotor and brake pads installed.

15. Position the service tool, hold the shaft and turn the handle counterclockwise until the tool is firmly seated against the piston.

16. Loosen the handle about ¼ turn. Hold the handle in position and rotate the tool until the piston is fully bottomed in the caliper bore. The piston is bottomed when there is no further inward movement and the tool handle meets turning resistance.

17. Make sure the anchor plate and caliper sliding surfaces are clean and free of rust and dirt. Lubricate the sliding surfaces of the anchor plate with high temperature grease. Install the anti-rattle spring on the lower rail of the anchor plate.

18. Install the inner brake pad in position on the anchor plate.

NOTE: *Different rotors are used on the right and left hand side of the vehicle. The center cooling fins must point towards the rear of the vehicle when the rotor is installed.*

19. Install the brake rotor and secure the retainer clips.

20. Install the outer brake pad (wear indicator toward the upper end of brake assembly).

21. Connect the brake hose, using a new washer, to the caliper. Tighten the attaching bolt to 20–30 ft. lbs.

22. Position the upper part of the caliper in position on the anchor plate and rotate the caliper until it is completely over the rotor. Take care so that the piston boot is not damaged.

23. Pull the caliper outward so that the inboard brake pad is firmly against the brake rotor. Measure the clearance between the outer pad and the rotor. Clearance should be 1/32–3/32 inch. If the clearance is not within specifications caliper piston readjustment is required. Refer to Steps 13–16. Rotating the tool shaft counterclockwise will narrow the clearance, clockwise rotation will increase the clearance. ¼ inch turn of the tool moves the caliper piston about 1/16 inch.

CAUTION: *A clearance greater than 3/32 inch may allow the parking brake adjuster to pull out of the caliper piston when the service brake is applied. This will cause the parking brake mechanism to fail to adjust. It is then necessary to replace the piston/adjuster.*

24. After clearance adjustment or check is completed, lubricate the anchor plate attaching pins and the inside of the caliper locator with silicone grease. Add one drop of Loctite[RG] or equivalent to the pin threads, hand start and tighten the pins to 29–37 ft. lbs.

25. Connect the parking brake cable to the bracket and lever on the caliper.

26. Bleed the entire brake system. Be sure the master cylinder is filled to within ⅛ inch from the top.

27. With the engine running (transmission in Park and wheel blocked), pump the service brake lightly about 40 times. Allow at least one second between brake applications. Check the parking brake for excessive travel or light effort. Continue pumping and checking parking brake adjustment until correct. Be sure that the parking brake caliper levers are returning to the "off" position when the parking brake is released.

28. Install the wheels, raise the vehicle and remove the jackstands. Be sure a firm brake pedal is present and road test the vehicle.

Caliper
OVERHAUL

1. Remove the caliper assembly.
2. Remove the parking brake cable bracket and caliper end retainer.
3. Lift out the operating shaft, thrust bearing and balls. Remove the thrust screw anti-rotating pin with a magnet or tweezers.
4. Remove the thrust screw by rotating it counterclockwise with a ¼ inch allen wrench.
5. Remove the piston and adjuster assembly by installing Tool T75P-2588-A or equivalent through the back of the caliper housing and pushing the piston out.

CAUTION: *Use care, when pushing the piston out of its bore, not to damage the polished surface in the thrust screw bore. Do not attempt to remove the adjuster can from the piston, it is press fitted.*

6. Remove the piston seal, boot, thrust screw C-ring seal, end retainer O-ring seal, end retainer lip seal and pin insulator from the caliper and piston/adjuster assembly.
7. Clean all of the metal parts with isopropyl alcohol. Use clean, dry compressed air to clean out and dry the grooves and passages. Be sure the caliper bore and all components are completely clean and free of any foreign material. Inspect the caliper bore for damage or excessive wear. The thrust screw bore must be smooth and free of pitting. If the piston is pit-

BRAKES

ted or scored, or if the chrome plating is wearing off, replace the piston/adjuster assembly.

8. If the adjuster can is loose or appears high in the piston and not seated correctly or is damaged, replace the piston/adjuster assembly.

9. Check the adjuster operation by assembling the adjuster screw into the piston. Pull in opposite directions on the piston and adjuster (about ¼ inch). Release the adjuster. When pulling the two pieces apart, the brass drive ring should remain stationary, causing the nut to rotate. When releasing the two parts, the nut must remain stationary and the drive ring must rotate. If the actions described do not occur, replace the piston/adjuster assembly.

10. Inspect the ball pockets, threads, grooves and bearing surfaces of the thrust screw and operating shaft for wear, pitting or damage. Replace any part that shows wear. Inspect the thrust bearing for rust, pitting or wear. Inspect the bearing surface of the end retainer for wear. Inspect the parking brake lever and shaft for wear. Replace parts as necessary.

11. Apply a coat of clean brake fluid to the new caliper piston seal and install it in the caliper bore. Be sure the seal is not twisted and that it is fully seated.

12. Install the dust boot by seating the flange squarely in the outer groove of the caliper. Coat the piston/adjuster assembly with clean brake fluid and install it in the caliper bore. Spread the dust boot over the piston and install the dust boot flange in the piston groove.

13. Secure the caliper in a vise with the adjuster end up. Fill the piston/adjuster assembly with clean brake fluid up to the bottom edge of the thrust screw bore.

14. Coat a new thrust screw O-ring with clean brake fluid. Install the O-ring in the thrust screw groove. Install the thrust screw by turning it into the piston/adjuster assembly with a ¼ inch allen wrench until the top surface of the thrust screw is flush with the bottom of the threaded bore. Use care to avoid cutting the O-ring seal. Index the screw so that the notches of the thrust screw and caliper housing are aligned and insert the anti-rotation pin.

NOTE: *The thrust screw and operating shaft are not interchangable from side to side becaused of the direction ramp in the ball pockets. The pocket surface of the operating shaft and the thrust screw are stamped for side of operation (R or L).*

15. Place a ball in each of the three pockets. Apply a liberal amount of silicone grease on all components of the parking brake mechanism. Install the operating shaft on the balls.

16. Coat the thrust bearing with silicone grease and install it on the operating shaft. Install a new lip seal and O-ring on the end retainer. Coat the lip seal and O-ring with silicone grease and install the end retainer on the caliper. Hold the operating shaft firmly seated

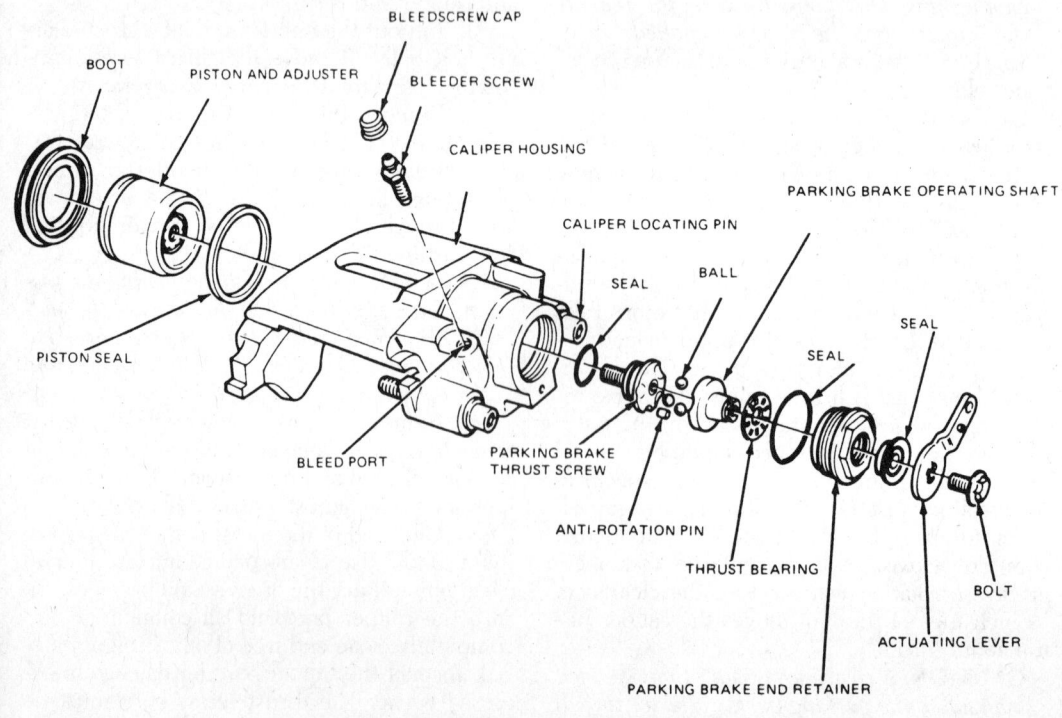

Rear caliper exploded view

BRAKES 215

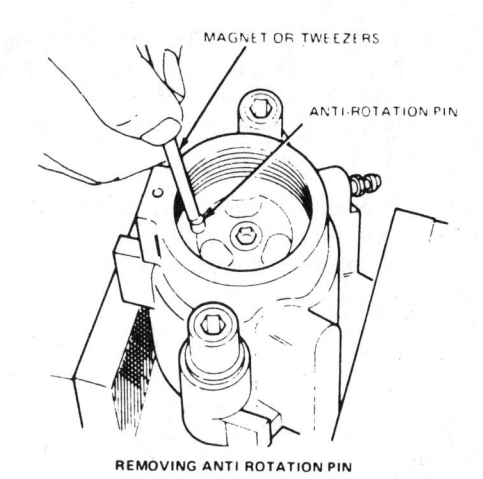

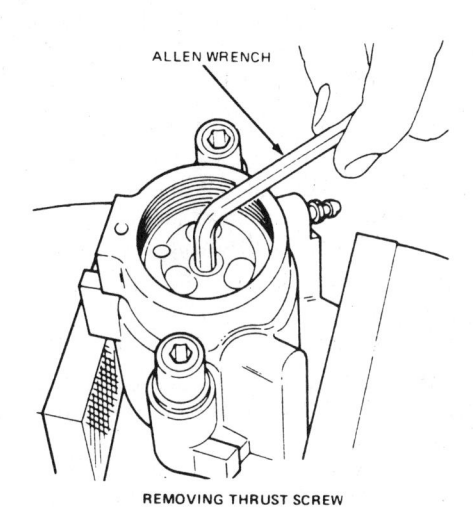

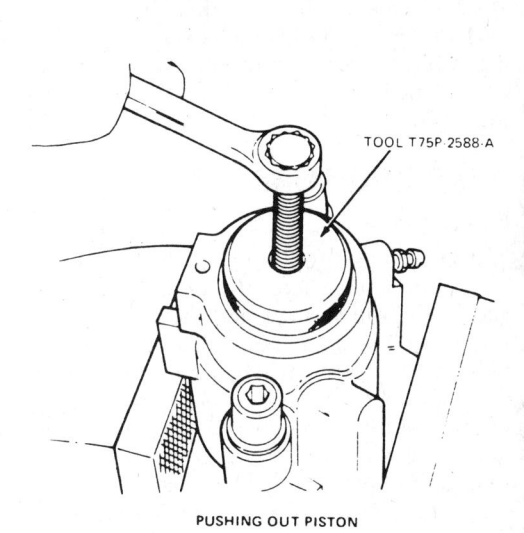

Rear caliper service

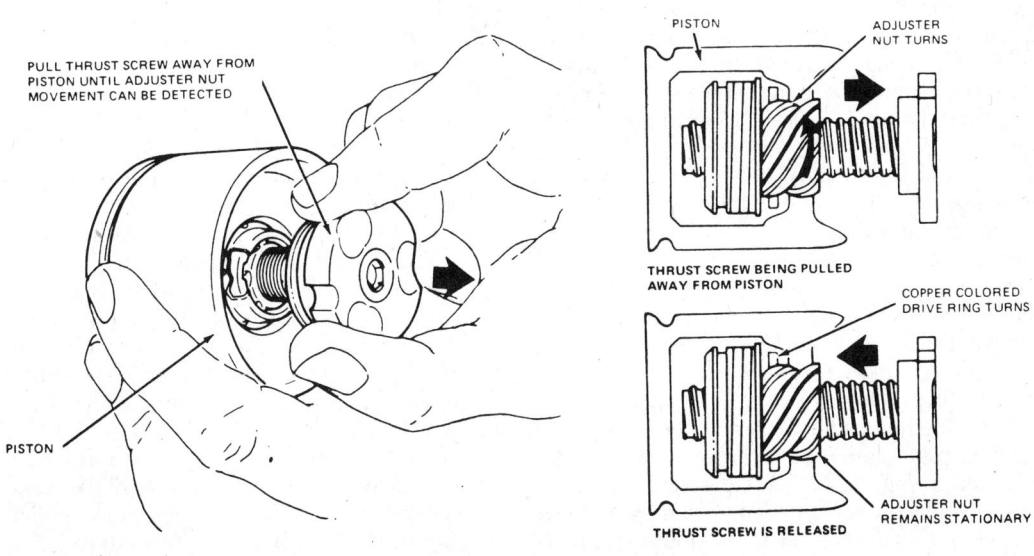

Rear caliper adjuster operation

against the internal mechanism while installing the end retainer to prevent mislocation of the balls. If the lip seal is pushed out of position, reseat the seal. Tighten the end retainer to 75–95 ft. lbs.

17. Install the parking brake lever. The lever must point down and rearward and must rotate freely after tightening the retainer.

18. Mount the caliper in a vise and bottom the caliper piston by screwing it clockwise with Tool T75P-2588-B.

19. Refer to the previous section on Caliper, Rotor and Brake Pad servicing. Install the caliper and adjust as necessary.

20. When install the parking brake cable brackets on the caliper housing, apply the service brake and rotate the parking brake bracket until the bracket lever stop contacts the actuating lever. Hold the bracket in position and tighten the bolts to 30–44 ft. lbs. Complete caliper installation.

REAR DRUM BRAKES
Except Merkur

The major components of the system are the drum, the brake shoes, the brake shoe return and hold-down springs, and the automatic adjuster assembly. The rear brakes also incorporate a parking brake mechanism.

When the brake pedal is depressed, and hydraulic pressure is delivered to the wheel cylinder, the wheel cylinder expands to force the shoes against the drum. The primary shoe moves first, contacting the drum and pivoting slightly on its hold-down spring mounting pin. As the top of the primary (front) shoe contacts the drum, the bottom of the shoe moves slightly away from the drum. This movement is transferred through the adjusting screw to the secondary brake shoe, where it aids the wheel cylinder in bringing the secondary shoe in contact with the drum. Friction between the brake shoes and the drum causes the car to slow down and stop. When the brake pedal is released, the brake shoe return springs move the brakes away from the drum. If the lining on the brakes becomes contaminated or if the lining or drum becomes grooved, the engagement of the brakes and the drum will become very harsh causing the brakes to lock up and/or squeal. If the brake shoes on one wheel contact the drum before the same action occurs in the other wheels, the brakes will pull to one side when applied.

The automatic adjuster assembly consists of a cable, cable guide, adjuster lever, automatic adjuster spring, and adjusting screw. The automatic adjuster operates only when the brakes are applied while the car is backing up. When the brakes are applied with the car moving rearward, the movement of the secondary (rear) brake shoe (the automatic adjuster is attached to this shoe) causes the adjuster cable to pull the adjusting lever upward. When the brakes are released, the automatic adjuster spring pulls the adjusting lever downward. As the lever moves downward, it contacts the star wheel on the adjusting screw and pushes it downward. This causes the adjusting screw to unscrew slightly (expand) and move the brake shoes closer to the drum. The adjusting lever then rests on the star wheel of the adjusting screw until the brakes are applied the next time the car backs up. If the brake adjustment is OK, the secondary shoe will not have to move very far to contact the drum. This limited shoe movement will not lift the adjusting lever off the star wheel, thus the brakes will not be adjusted.

The parking brake mechanism in the wheel consists of a parking brake link and lever. The link fits between the two brake shoes. The lever is attached to the parking brake cable and the secondary brake shoe. When the parking brake is applied, the rear brake shoes are moved into contact with the brake drums.

INSPECTION

1. Raise the rear of the car and support the car with safety stands. Make sure the parking brake is not on.

2. To check the rear brakes, remove the lug nuts that attach the wheels to the axle shaft and remove the tires and wheels from the car. Pull the brake drum off the axle shaft. If the brakes are adjusted too tightly to remove the drum, see step three. If you can remove the drum, see step four.

3. If the brakes are too tight to remove the drum, get under the car (make sure you have safety stands under the car to support it) and remove the rubber plug from the bottom of the brake backing plate. Shine a flashlight into the slot in the plate. You will see the top of the adjusting screw star wheel and the adjusting lever for the automatic brake adjusting mechanism. To back off the adjusting screw, you must first insert a small, thin screwdriver or a piece of firm wire (coat hanger wire) into the adjusting slot and push the adjusting lever away from the adjusting screw. Insert a brake adjusting spoon into the slot and engage the top of the star wheel. Lift the bottom of the adjusting spoon to force the adjusting screw star wheel downward. Repeat this operation until the brake drum is free of the brake shoes and can be pulled off. See the brake adjustment procedure for an illustration.

BRAKES

4. Clean the brake shoes and the inside of the brake drum. There must be at least 1/32 in. of brake lining above the heads of the brake shoe attaching rivets. The lining should not be cracked or contaminated with grease or brake fluid. If there is grease or brake fluid on the lining, it must be replaced and the source of the leak must be found and corrected. Brake fluid on the lining means leaking wheel cylinders. Grease on the brake lining means a leaking grease retainer (front wheels) or axle seal (rear brakes). If the lining is slightly glazed but otherwise in good condition, it can be cleaned with medium sandpaper. Lift the bottom of the wheel cylinder boots and inspect the ends of the wheel cylinders. A small amount of fluid in the end of the cylinders should be considered normal. If fluid runs out of the cylinder when the boots are lifted, however, the wheel cylinder must be rebuilt or replaced. Examine the inside of the brake drum. It should have a smooth, dull finish. If excessive brake shoe wear has caused grooves to wear in the drum, it must be machined or replaced. If the inside of the drum is slightly glazed, but otherwise in good condition, it can be cleaned with medium sandpaper.

5. If no repairs are required, install the drum and wheel. If the brake adjustment was changed to remove the drum, adjust the brakes until the drum will just fit over the brakes. After the wheel is installed it will be necessary to complete the adjustment. See the brake adjustment procedure in this chapter. If a front wheel was removed, tighten the wheel bearing adjusting nut to 17–25 ft. lbs. while spinning the wheel. This will seat the bearing. Loosen the adjusting nut 1/2 turn, then retighten it to 10–15 in. lbs.

Brake Shoe
REMOVAL

NOTE: *If you are not thoroughly familiar with the procedures involved in brake replacement, disassemble and assemble only one side at a time, leaving the other wheel intact as a reference.*

1. Remove the brake drum. See the above "Inspection" procedure.
2. Place the hollow end of a brake spring service tool (available at auto parts stores) on the brake shoe anchor pin and twist it to disengage one of the brake retracting springs. Repeat this operation to remove the other spring.

   CAUTION: *Be careful the springs do not slip off the tool during removal, as they could cause personal injury.*

Drum brake retracting spring removal

3. Reach behind the brake backing plate and place a finger on the end of one of the brake hold-down spring mounting pins. Using a pair of pliers grasp the washer on the top of the hold-down spring that corresponds to the pin that you are holding. Push down on the pliers and turn them 90° to align the slot in the washer with the head on the spring mounting pin. Remove the spring and washer and repeat this operation on the holddown spring on the other brake shoe.

4. Place the tip of the screwdriver on the top of the brake adjusting screw and move the screwdriver upward to lift up on the brake adjusting lever. When there is enough slack in the automatic adjuster cable, disconnect the loop on the top of the cable from the anchor pin. Grasp the top of each brake shoe and move it outward to disengage it from the wheel cylinder (and parking brake link on the rear wheels). When the brake shoes are clear, lift them from the backing plate. Twist the shoes slightly and the automatic adjuster assembly will disassemble itself.

5. Grasp the end of the brake cable spring with a pair of pliers and, using the brake lever as a fulcrum, pull the end of the spring away from the lever. Disengage the cable from the brake lever.

Wheel Cylinder
OVERHAUL

Since the travel of the pistons in the wheel cylinder changes when new brake shoes are installed, it is possible for previously good wheel cylinders to start leaking after new brakes are installed. Therefore, to save yourself the expense of having to replace new brakes that become saturated with brake fluid and the aggravation of having to take everything apart again, it is strongly recommended that wheel cylin-

218 BRAKES

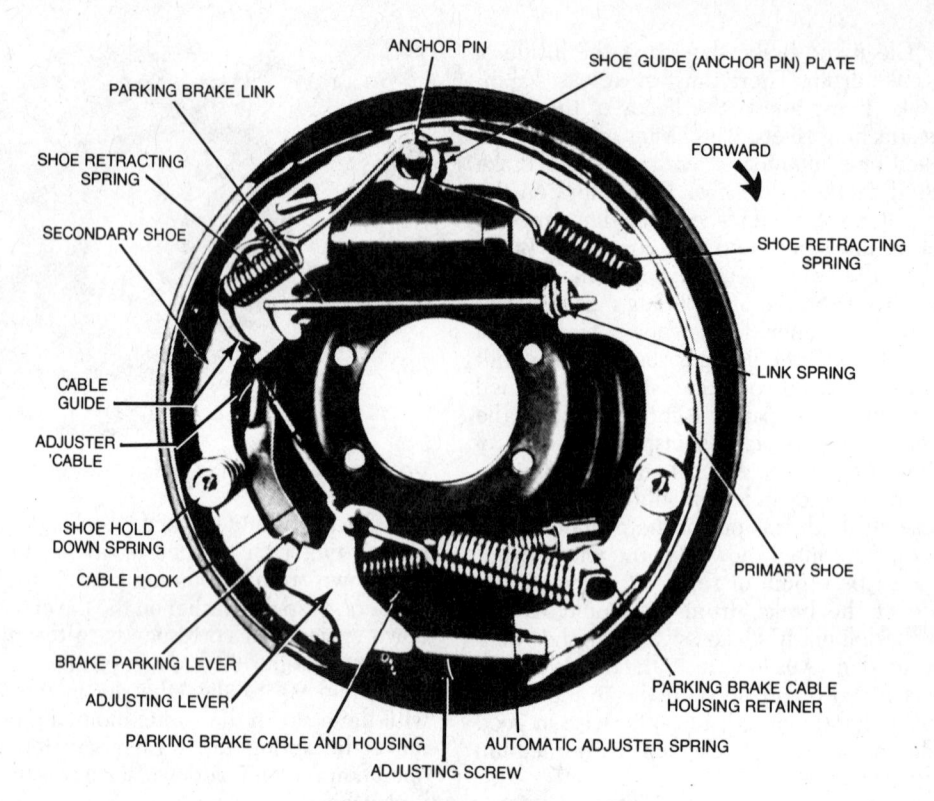

Rear brake assembly

ders be rebuilt every time new brake shoes are installed. This is especially true for cars with high mileage.

1. Remove the brakes.
2. Place a bucket or some old newspapers under the brake backing plate to catch the brake fluid that will run out of the wheel cylinder.
3. Remove the boots from the ends of the wheel cylinders.
4. Push one piston toward the center of the cylinder to force the opposite piston and cup out the other end of the cylinder. Reach in the open end of the cylinder and push the spring, cup, and piston out of the cylinder.
5. Remove the bleeder screw from the rear of the cylinder, on the back of the backing plate.
6. Inspect the inside of the wheel cylinder. If it is scored in any way, the cylinder must be honed with a wheel cylinder hone or fine emery paper, and finished with crocus cloth if emery paper is used. If the inside of the cylinder is excessively worn, the cylinder will have to be replaced, as only 0.003 in. of material can be removed from the cylinder walls. Whenever honing or cleaning wheel cylinders, keep a small amount of brake fluid in the cylinder to serve as a lubricant.

7. Clean any foreign matter from the pistons. The sides of the pistons must be smooth for the wheel cylinders to operate properly.
8. Clean the cylinder bore with alcohol and a lint-free rag. Pull the rag through the bore several times to remove all foreign matter and dry the cylinder.
9. Install the bleeder screw and the return spring in the cylinder.

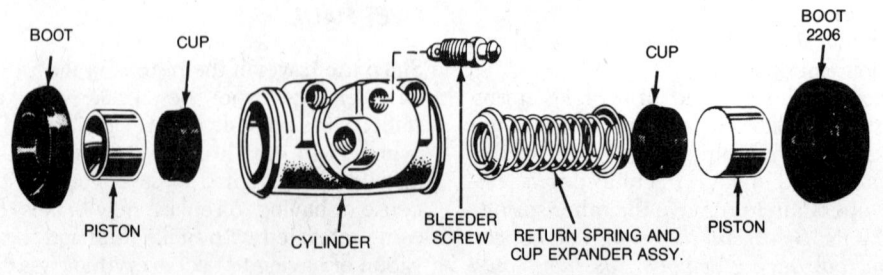

Exploded view of wheel cylinder

BRAKES 219

10. Coat new cylinder cups with new brake fluid and install them in the cylinder. Make sure they are square in the bore or they will leak.
11. Install the pistons in the cylinder after coating them with new brake fluid.
12. Coat the insides of the boots with new brake fluid and install them on the cylinder. Install and bleed the brakes.

REPLACEMENT

1. Remove the brake shoes.
2. Loosen the brake line on the rear of the cylinder, but do not pull the line away from the cylinder or it may bend.
3. Remove the bolts and lockwashers that attach the wheel cylinder to the backing plate and remove the cylinder.
4. Position the new wheel cylinder on the backing plate and install the cylinder attaching bolts and lockwashers.
5. Attach the metal brake line.
6. Install the brakes and bleed the brake system.

Brake Shoe
INSTALLATION

1. The brake cable must be connected to the secondary brake shoe before the shoe is installed on the backing plate. To do this, first transfer the parking brake lever from the old secondary shoe to the new one. This is accomplished by spreading the bottom of the horseshoe clip and disengaging the lever. Position the lever on the new secondary shoe and install the spring washer and the horseshoe clip. Close the bottom of the clip after installing it. Grasp the metal tip of the parking brake cable with a pair of pliers. Position a pair of side cutters on the end of the cable coil spring and, using the pliers as a fulcrum, pull the coil spring back with the side cutters. Position the cable in the parking brake lever.
2. Apply a *light* coating of high-temperature grease to the brake shoe contact points on the backing plate. Position the primary brake shoe on the front of the backing plate and install the hold-down spring and washer over the mounting pin. Install the secondary shoe on the rear of the backing plate.
3. Install the parking brake link between the notch in the primary brake shoe and the notch in the parking brake lever.
4. Install the automatic adjuster cable loop end on the anchor pin. Make sure the crimped side of the loop faces the backing plate.
5. Install the return spring in the primary brake shoe and, using the tapered end of a brake spring service tool, slide the top of the spring onto the anchor pin.
CAUTION: *Be careful the spring does not slip off the tool during installation, as it could cause personal injury.*
6. Install the automatic adjuster cable guide in the secondary brake shoe, making sure the flared hole in the cable guide is inside the hole in the brake shoe. Fit the cable into the groove in the top of the cable guide.
7. Install the secondary shoe return spring through the hole in the cable guide and the brake shoe. Using the brake spring tool, slide the top of the spring onto the anchor pin.
8. Clean the threads on the adjusting screw and apply a light coating of high-temperature grease to the threads. Screw the adjuster closed, then open it one-half turn.
9. Install the adjusting screw between the brake shoes with the star wheel nearest to the secondary shoe. Make sure the star wheel is in a position that is accessible from the adjusting slot in the backing plate.
10. Install the short hooked end of the automatic adjuster spring in the proper hole in the primary brake shoe.
11. Connect the hooked end of the automatic adjuster cable and the free end of the automatic adjuster spring in the slot in the top of the automatic adjuster lever.
12. Pull the automatic adjuster lever (the lever will pull the cable and spring with it) downward and to the left and engage the pivot hook of the lever in the hole in the secondary brake shoe.
13. Check the entire brake assembly to make sure everything is installed properly. Make sure the shoes engage the wheel cylinder properly and are flush on the anchor pin. Make sure the automatic adjuster cable is flush on the anchor pin and in the slot on the back of cable guide. Make sure the adjusting lever rests on the adjusting screw star wheel. Pull upward on the adjusting cable until the adjusting lever is free of the star wheel, then release the cable. The adjusting lever should snap back into place on the adjusting screw star wheel and turn the wheel one tooth.
14. Expand the brake adjusting screw until the brake drum will just fit over the brake shoes.
15. Install the wheel and drum and adjust the brakes. See "Brake Adjustment."

Brake
ADJUSTMENT

1. Raise the car and support it with safety stands.
2. Remove the rubber plug from the adjusting slot on the backing plate.

220 BRAKES

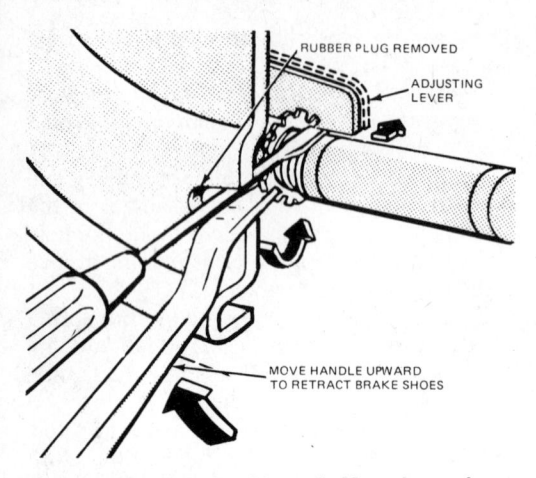

Brake adjustment, backing off; Move lever downward to tighten

3. Insert a brake adjusting spoon into the slot and engage the lowest tooth on the star wheel possible. Move the end of the brake spoon downward to move the star wheel upward and expand the adjusting screw. Repeat this operation until the brakes lock the wheel.

4. Insert a small screwdriver or piece of firm wire (coat hanger wire) into the adjusting slot and push the automatic adjuster lever out and free of the star wheel on the adjusting screw.

5. Holding the adjusting lever out of the way, engage the topmost tooth possible on the star wheel with a brake adjusting spoon. Move the end of the adjusting spoon upward to move the adjusting screw downward and contact the adjusting screw. Back the adjustment off until the wheel spins freely with a minimum of drag. Keep track of the number of turns the star wheel is backed off.

6. Repeat this operation on the other side of the car of the set (front or rear) of brakes that you are adjusting. When backing off the brakes on the other side, the star wheel must be backed off the same number of turns to prevent side-to-side brake pull.

7. Repeat this operation on the other set of brakes.

Merkur Rear Brakes

DESCRIPTION

Rear brakes are of the non-servo design. The brakes are applied by a double-acting wheel cylinder attached to the top of the brake backing plate. The brake shoes are attached to the backing plate with a holddown spring, pin and washer. The rear brakes are fitted with a self-adjusting mechanism which maintains low brake pedal condition by maintaining constant drum to lining clearance. As the linings wear, the self-adjuster automatically repositions the brake shoes outward toward the drums.

The self-adjuster is mounted on the parking brake strut and consists of a cam, wheel and spring. The cam fits into a slot in the primary shoe. The cam linings. The stationary wheel is riveted to the strut. The wheel locks against the cam after the cam has rotated to a new position. The cam is held against the wheel by spring tension with prevents slippage between the serrated edges of the components.

Before the cam can rotate, the brake pedal must be pushed and the linings must move outward against the brake drum. As the primary shoe moves, the gap between the shoe and self adjuster closes. If the gap closes just as the shoes contact the drum, the adjustment is correct. If the gap has closed, but the shoes have not contacted the drum, further outward movement of the shoe will cause the cam to rotate to a new position relative to the fixed wheel. As the shoe returns inward, the adjuster cam spring will immediately pull the cam into contact with the fixed wheel holding the cam and spring in the new adjusted position.

REMOVAL AND INSTALLATION

Brake Drum

1. Loosen the wheel lugs slightly. Raise and support the rear of the vehicle on jackstands. Remove the wheels.

2. Make sure the parking brake is released. Remove the retaining clips from the wheel studs and slide the brake drum off.

3. Should difficulty be experienced in removing the drum due to tight brake shoe adjustment, the self adjuster must be released.

4. Disconnect the brake line from the wheel cylinder. Remove the wheel cylinder mounting bolts.

5. Push the wheel cylinder away from the backing plate to provide an access opening in the backing plate.

6. Insert a thin bladed tool through the backing plate and rotate the self adjuster cam to the released position.

7. Remove the brake drum.

8. Position the wheel cylinder and install the mounting bolts loosely. Attach the brake line to the wheel cylinder. Tighten the mounting bolts to 5–7 ft. lbs. Bleed the brake system upon after finishing servicing.

9. Service as required. Install the brake drum in the reverse order of removal.

Brake Shoes

1. Remove the brake drum.

2. Remove both brake holddown springs. To prevent rotation during removal, hold each

BRAKES 221

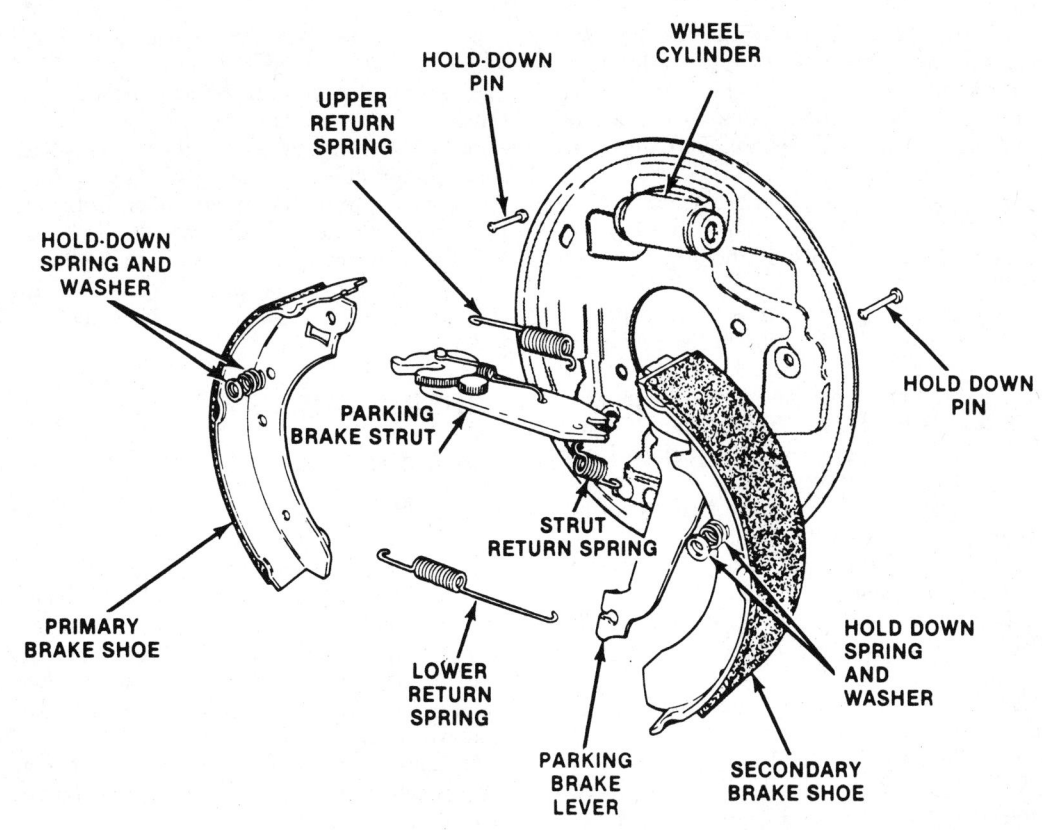

Merkur rear drum brakes

holddown pin head with a finger behind the backing plate.

3. Pry the lower edge of the primary shoe away from its position against the bottom anchor.

4. Remove the lower return spring.

5. Remove the brake shoes and adjuster assembly by passing the strut under the wheel cylinder and over the axle hub.

6. Pull the top of the primary shoe away from the secondary shoe to disconnect the strut from the secondary shoe.

8. Disconnect the parking brake cable from the secondary shoe lever. Remove the strut return spring from the secondary shoe.

8. Remove the adjuster cam spring. Pull the primary shoe away from the strut while rotating the cam to the fully released position.

9. Remove the primary shoe spring. Remove the primary shoe from the strut.

10. Inspect the self adjuster for free movement of the cam. Check the strut for bends or distortion. Make sure that the parking brake lever slot is not elongated or twisted. Check the rivet that holds the adjusting wheel, it must be tight and the wheel must not rotate.

11. Check the backing plate for deep grooves that would restrict shoe movement. Check the lower anchor plate, it must be tight. Check the bearing hub mounting bolts for tightness. Torque is 45–48 ft. lbs.

12. Check all springs for separated or twisted coils or twisted or damaged shanks. If the springs show discoloration they are overheated and must be replaced.

13. Check the wheel cylinders for signs of leakage. Carefully pull the lower edges of the cylinder boots away from the cylinders to see if the interior of the boot and end of the cylinder are wet with brake fluid. A small amount of wetness is nearly always present and acts as a lubricant for the cylinder pistons. An excessive amount of fluid indicates seal leakage and the cylinder should be removed, disassembled and inspected then rebuilt or replaced.

14. Clean the brake drums and check them for scoring or deep grooves. If grooves/scoring is visible have the drums machined. If the drums are visually alright and a drum gauge is on hand, check the drum at various locations to determine wear. Replace or machine as required.

15. Apply a light coating of high temperature grease on the backing plate brake shoe support ledges.

16. Connect the parking lever and cable to the secondary shoe. To connect the cable, position the cable end through the lever and grip it with a pair of locking pliers. Push the lever

against the spring until it can be rotated over the cable into position. The plastic washer must be between the spring and the lever.

17. Place the secondary shoe in position on the backing plate and secure with the holddown pin and spring.

18. Install the strut and cam assembly on the primary shoe. Rotate the cam to the fully released position and install the adjuster cam spring.

19. Install the primary shoe to strut spring.

20. Install the strut spring in the secondary shoe and then into the strut. Place the strut on the parking brake lever and move the primary shoe toward the backing plate. The strut will then "click" into place over the parking brake lever and secondary shoe web.

21. Install the lower return spring with the longest leg on the secondary shoe.

22. Pry the lowest end of the primary shoe into position against the anchor plate while holding the top of the shoe against the backing plate in contact with the wheel cylinder piston end.

23. Install the primary shoe holddown pin and spring.

24. Make sure the heel of each brake shoe is located behind the anchor plate. Check each shoe component for proper installation. If necessary push the adjuster cam to the released position.

25. Install both brake drums. Push the brake pedal hard twice to set the self adjuster cam position. The cam will make a ratcheting sound as it sets. Adjust the parking brake as necessary.

Wheel Cylinder

1. Remove the wheel and brake drum.
2. Disconnect the brake hose line from the cylinder and plug the line.
3. Pull the primary shoe away from the wheel cylinder. The self adjuster cam will rotate outward to hold the brake shoes away from the wheel cylinder.
4. Remove the wheel cylinder mounting bolts, the wheel cylinder and mounting O-ring from the backing plate.
5. Install in the reverse order of removal. Tighten the wheel cylinder mounting bolts to 5–7 ft. lbs. Bleed the brake system.

Cylinder Rebuilding

1. Remove the wheel cylinder.
2. Remove the dust boots, pistons, seals and spring. Remove the bleeder screw.
3. Remove the seals from the pistons.
4. Wash all metal parts with clean denatured alcohol and dry with compressed air or a lint free cloth.

5. Make sure that the bleeder screw and wheel cylinder bleeder hole are clean and opened. Inspect the cylinder bore for scratches, scoring or other damage. Light scores or scratches can be cleaned with crocus cloth. Wash the cylinder after cleaning up scores etc.

6. Install the seals on the pistons. Lubricate the seals with clean fresh brake fluid. Lubricate the wheel cylinder bore with brake fluid.

7. Install the spring, pistons and boots. Install the bleeder screw. Install the wheel cylinder.

PARKING BRAKE

CABLE ADJUSTMENT
Except Merkur

1. Fully release the parking brake.
2. Place the transmission in Neutral and raise the rear axle until the rear wheels clear the floor. The weight of the car must be on the springs.
3. Pry the handle cover up inside the car. The rear of the cover is held by two screws. Tighten the adjusting nut until the rear brakes drag when the rear wheels are turned.
4. Loosen the adjusting nut until the rear wheels can be turned without the rear brakes dragging.
5. Lower the rear of the vehicle and check the operation of the parking brake.

Merkur

NOTE: *Parking brake stop plungers are installed in both rear brake backing plates. These plungers are used to determine correct parking brake adjustment.*

1. Be sure the parking brake lever is in the released position. Pump the brake pedal several times to insure proper self adjuster setting.
2. Raise the support the rear of the vehicle.
3. Loosen the parking brake adjuster locknut and rotate the adjuster sleeve along the cable casing until in and out movement can be felt at both parking brake stop plungers.
4. Tighten the adjuster against the retaining bracket until a slight movement is felt at the stop plunger. Tighten the locknut by hand against the sleeve as much as possible. Tighten an additional two "clicks" with a pair of pliers.
5. Turn the rear wheels by hand to be sure the brake linings are not dragging against the drum. Readjust if necessary.

REMOVAL AND INSTALLATION
Except Merkur

1. Release the parking brake and loosen the lock and adjusting nut.

BRAKES 223

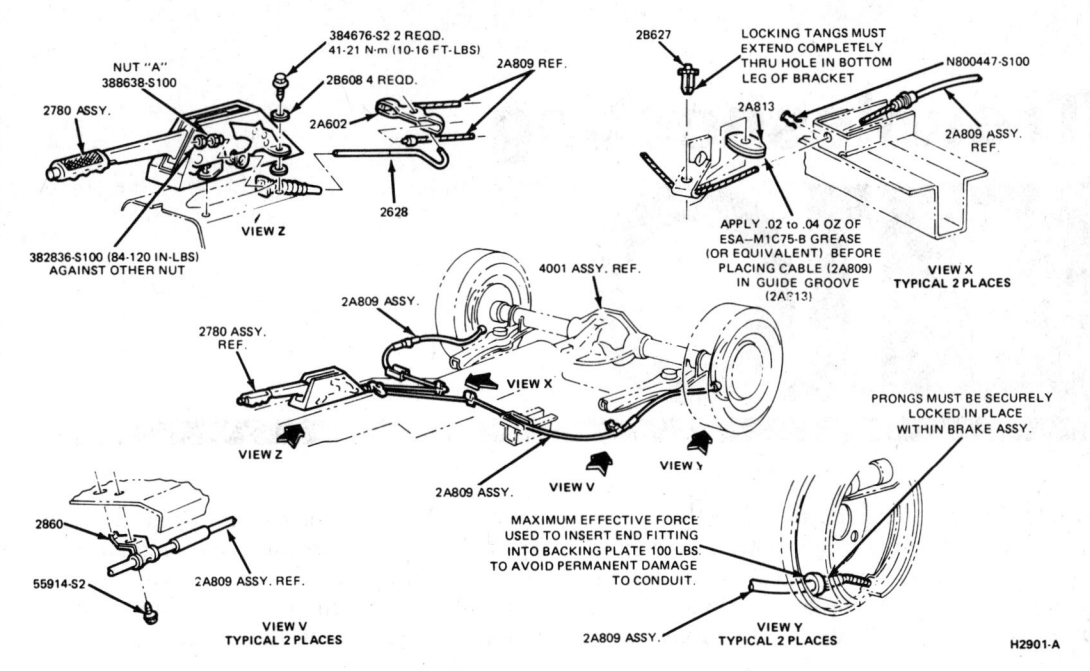

Parking brake system

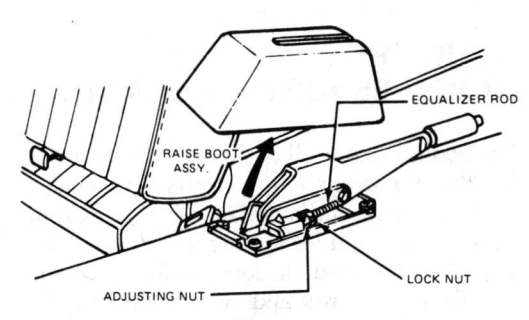

Parking brake control assembly

2. Raise the vehicle and support it properly.
3. Remove the rear wheel parking brake cable from the equalizer.
4. Remove the hairpin clip that attaches the conduit to the conduit bracket, and remove the retaining clip that attaches the cable to the underbody.
5. Remove the rear wheels and tires then remove the brake drums.
6. Remove the self adjuster springs, and remove the adjuster springs from the backing plates.
7. Disconnect the ends of the cables from the parking brake levers on the secondary brake shoes.
8. Compress the cable retainer prongs, and pull the cable ends from the backing plates.
9. To install reverse the above procedure and adjust the parking brake as previously described.

Merkur

1. Raise and support the rear of the vehicle.
2. Loosen the parking brake adjuster locknut.
3. Remove the brake drums and brake shoes. Disconnect the parking brake cable from the secondary brake shoe lever.
4. Spread the retaining clip on the cable casing and pull the cable from the backing plate.
5. Remvoe the clip and clevis pin attaching the cable equalizer to the parking brake lever rod.
6. Open the routing clamps and disengage the cable from both control arms. Thread the cable through both body brackets and remove it from the vehicle.
7. Install the new parking brake cable in the reverse order of removal. Adjust as necessary.

Troubleshooting 10

This section is designed to aid in the quick, accurate diagnosis of automotive problems. While automotive repairs can be made by many people, accurate troubleshooting is a rare skill for the amateur and professional alike.

In its simplest state, troubleshooting is an exercise in logic. It is essential to realize that an automobile is really composed of a series of systems. Some of these systems are interrelated; others are not. Automobiles operate within a framework of logical rules and physical laws, and the key to troubleshooting is a good understanding of all the automotive systems.

This section breaks the car or truck down into its component systems, allowing the problem to be isolated. The charts and diagnostic road maps list the most common problems and the most probable causes of trouble. Obviously it would be impossible to list every possible problem that could happen along with every possible cause, but it will locate MOST problems and eliminate a lot of unnecessary guesswork. The systematic format will locate problems within a given system, but, because many automotive systems are interrelated, the solution to your particular problem may be found in a number of systems on the car or truck.

USING THE TROUBLESHOOTING CHARTS

This book contains all of the specific information that the average do-it-yourself mechanic needs to repair and maintain his or her car or truck. The troubleshooting charts are designed to be used in conjunction with the specific procedures and information in the text. For instance, troubleshooting a point-type ignition system is fairly standard for all models, but you may be directed to the text to find procedures for troubleshooting an individual type of electronic ignition. You will also have to refer to the specification charts throughout the book for specifications applicable to your car or truck.

TOOLS AND EQUIPMENT

The tools illustrated in Chapter 1 (plus two more diagnostic pieces) will be adequate to troubleshoot most problems. The two other tools needed are a voltmeter and an ohmmeter. These can be purchased separately or in combination, known as a VOM meter.

In the event that other tools are required, they will be noted in the procedures.

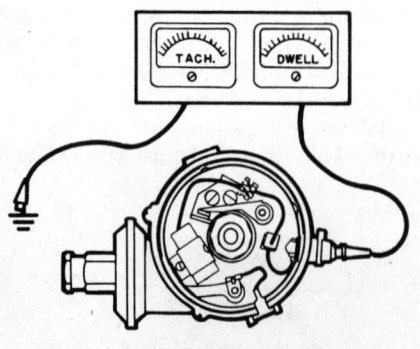

Tach-dwell hooked-up to distributor

TROUBLESHOOTING

Troubleshooting Engine Problems

See Chapters 2, 3, 4 for more information and service procedures.

Index to Systems

System	To Test	Group
Battery	Engine need not be running	1
Starting system	Engine need not be running	2
Primary electrical system	Engine need not be running	3
Secondary electrical system	Engine need not be running	4
Fuel system	Engine need not be running	5
Engine compression	Engine need not be running	6
Engine vacuum	Engine must be running	7
Secondary electrical system	Engine must be running	8
Valve train	Engine must be running	9
Exhaust system	Engine must be running	10
Cooling system	Engine must be running	11
Engine lubrication	Engine must be running	12

Index to Problems

Problem: Symptom	Begin at Specific Diagnosis, Number
Engine Won't Start:	
Starter doesn't turn	1.1, 2.1
Starter turns, engine doesn't	2.1
Starter turns engine very slowly	1.1, 2.4
Starter turns engine normally	3.1, 4.1
Starter turns engine very quickly	6.1
Engine fires intermittently	4.1
Engine fires consistently	5.1, 6.1
Engine Runs Poorly:	
Hard starting	3.1, 4.1, 5.1, 8.1
Rough idle	4.1, 5.1, 8.1
Stalling	3.1, 4.1, 5.1, 8.1
Engine dies at high speeds	4.1, 5.1
Hesitation (on acceleration from standing stop)	5.1, 8.1
Poor pickup	4.1, 5.1, 8.1
Lack of power	3.1, 4.1, 5.1, 8.1
Backfire through the carburetor	4.1, 8.1, 9.1
Backfire through the exhaust	4.1, 8.1, 9.1
Blue exhaust gases	6.1, 7.1
Black exhaust gases	5.1
Running on (after the ignition is shut off)	3.1, 8.1
Susceptible to moisture	4.1
Engine misfires under load	4.1, 7.1, 8.4, 9.1
Engine misfires at speed	4.1, 8.4
Engine misfires at idle	3.1, 4.1, 5.1, 7.1, 8.4

Sample Section

Test and Procedure	Results and Indications	Proceed to
4.1—Check for spark: Hold each spark plug wire approximately ¼" from ground with gloves or a heavy, dry rag. Crank the engine and observe the spark.	If no spark is evident:	4.2
	If spark is good in some cases:	4.3
	If spark is good in all cases:	4.6

TROUBLESHOOTING

Specific Diagnosis

This section is arranged so that following each test, instructions are given to proceed to another, until a problem is diagnosed.

Section 1—Battery

Test and Procedure	Results and Indications	Proceed to
1.1—Inspect the battery visually for case condition (corrosion, cracks) and water level.	If case is cracked, replace battery:	1.4
	If the case is intact, remove corrosion with a solution of baking soda and water (**CAUTION**: *do not get the solution into the battery*), and fill with water:	1.2
1.2—Check the battery cable connections: Insert a screwdriver between the battery post and the cable clamp. Turn the headlights on high beam, and observe them as the screwdriver is gently twisted to ensure good metal to metal contact.	If the lights brighten, remove and clean the clamp and post; coat the post with petroleum jelly, install and tighten the clamp:	1.4
	If no improvement is noted:	1.3
1.3—Test the state of charge of the battery using an individual cell tester or hydrometer.	If indicated, charge the battery. **NOTE:** *If no obvious reason exists for the low state of charge (i.e., battery age, prolonged storage), proceed to:*	1.4

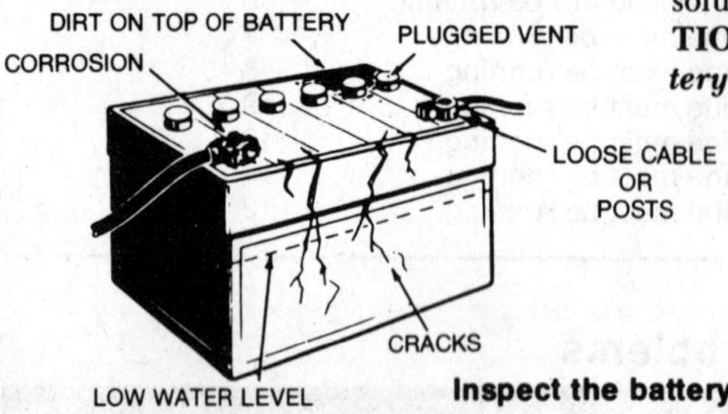

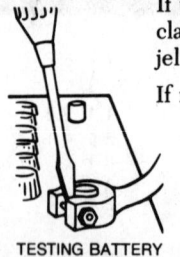

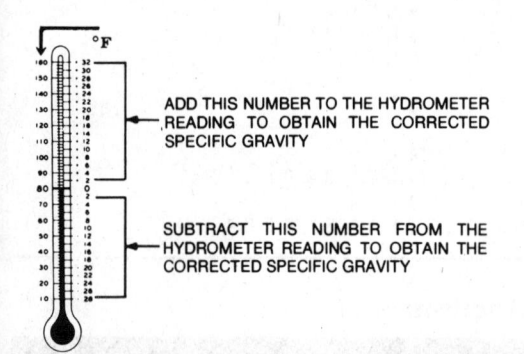

Specific Gravity (@ 80° F.)

Minimum	Battery Charge
1.260	100% Charged
1.230	75% Charged
1.200	50% Charged
1.170	25% Charged
1.140	Very Little Power Left
1.110	Completely Discharged

The effects of temperature on battery specific gravity (left) and amount of battery charge in relation to specific gravity (right)

1.4—Visually inspect battery cables for cracking, bad connection to ground, or bad connection to starter.	If necessary, tighten connections or replace the cables:	2.1

TROUBLESHOOTING 227

Section 2—Starting System
See Chapter 3 for service procedures

Test and Procedure	Results and Indications	Proceed to
Note: Tests in Group 2 are performed with coil high tension lead disconnected to prevent accidental starting.		
2.1—Test the starter motor and solenoid: Connect a jumper from the battery post of the solenoid (or relay) to the starter post of the solenoid (or relay).	If starter turns the engine normally:	2.2
	If the starter buzzes, or turns the engine very slowly:	2.4
	If no response, replace the solenoid (or relay).	3.1
	If the starter turns, but the engine doesn't, ensure that the flywheel ring gear is intact. If the gear is undamaged, replace the starter drive.	3.1
2.2—Determine whether ignition override switches are functioning properly (clutch start switch, neutral safety switch), by connecting a jumper across the switch(es), and turning the ignition switch to "start".	If starter operates, adjust or replace switch:	3.1
	If the starter doesn't operate:	2.3
2.3—Check the ignition switch "start" position: Connect a 12V test lamp or voltmeter between the starter post of the solenoid (or relay) and ground. Turn the ignition switch to the "start" position, and jiggle the key.	If the lamp doesn't light or the meter needle doesn't move when the switch is turned, check the ignition switch for loose connections, cracked insulation, or broken wires. Repair or replace as necessary:	3.1
	If the lamp flickers or needle moves when the key is jiggled, replace the ignition switch.	3.3

Checking the ignition switch "start" position

STARTER RELAY (IF EQUIPPED)

2.4—Remove and bench test the starter, according to specifications in the engine electrical section.	If the starter does not meet specifications, repair or replace as needed:	3.1
	If the starter is operating properly:	2.5
2.5—Determine whether the engine can turn freely: Remove the spark plugs, and check for water in the cylinders. Check for water on the dipstick, or oil in the radiator. Attempt to turn the engine using an 18" flex drive and socket on the crankshaft pulley nut or bolt.	If the engine will turn freely only with the spark plugs out, and hydrostatic lock (water in the cylinders) is ruled out, check valve timing:	9.2
	If engine will not turn freely, and it is known that the clutch and transmission are free, the engine must be disassembled for further evaluation:	Chapter 3

228 TROUBLESHOOTING

Section 3—Primary Electrical System

Test and Procedure	Results and Indications	Proceed to
3.1—Check the ignition switch "on" position: Connect a jumper wire between the distributor side of the coil and ground, and a 12V test lamp between the switch side of the coil and ground. Remove the high tension lead from the coil. Turn the ignition switch on and jiggle the key.	If the lamp lights:	3.2
	If the lamp flickers when the key is jiggled, replace the ignition switch:	3.3
	If the lamp doesn't light, check for loose or open connections. If none are found, remove the ignition switch and check for continuity. If the switch is faulty, replace it:	3.3

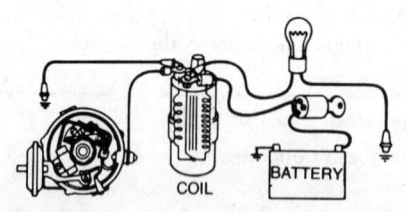

Checking the ignition switch "on" position

3.2—Check the ballast resistor or resistance wire for an open circuit, using an ohmmeter. See Chapter 3 for specific tests.	Replace the resistor or resistance wire if the resistance is zero. **NOTE:** *Some ignition systems have no ballast resistor.*	3.3

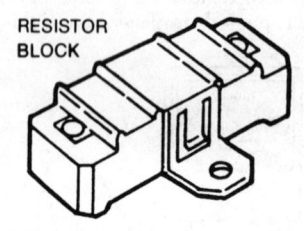

Two types of resistors

3.3—On point-type ignition systems, visually inspect the breaker points for burning, pitting or excessive wear. Gray coloring of the point contact surfaces is normal. Rotate the crankshaft until the contact heel rests on a high point of the distributor cam and adjust the point gap to specifications. On electronic ignition models, remove the distributor cap and visually inspect the armature. Ensure that the armature pin is in place, and that the armature is on tight and rotates when the engine is cranked. Make sure there are no cracks, chips or rounded edges on the armature.	If the breaker points are intact, clean the contact surfaces with fine emery cloth, and adjust the point gap to specifications. If the points are worn, replace them. On electronic systems, replace any parts which appear defective. If condition persists:	3.4

TROUBLESHOOTING 229

Test and Procedure	Results and Indications	Proceed to
3.4—On point-type ignition systems, connect a dwell-meter between the distributor primary lead and ground. Crank the engine and observe the point dwell angle. On electronic ignition systems, conduct a stator (magnetic pickup assembly) test. See Chapter 3.	On point-type systems, adjust the dwell angle if necessary. **NOTE:** *Increasing the point gap decreases the dwell angle and vice-versa.*	**3.6**
	If the dwell meter shows little or no reading;	**3.5**
	On electronic ignition systems, if the stator is bad, replace the stator. If the stator is good, proceed to the other tests in Chapter 3.	

Dwell is a function of point gap

3.5—On the point-type ignition systems, check the condenser for short: connect an ohmeter across the condenser body and the pigtail lead.	If any reading other than infinite is noted, replace the condenser	**3.6**

Checking the condenser for short

3.6—Test the coil primary resistance: On point-type ignition systems, connect an ohmmeter across the coil primary terminals, and read the resistance on the low scale. Note whether an external ballast resistor or resistance wire is used. On electronic ignition systems, test the coil primary resistance as in Chapter 3.	Point-type ignition coils utilizing ballast resistors or resistance wires should have approximately 1.0 ohms resistance. Coils with internal resistors should have approximately 4.0 ohms resistance. If values far from the above are noted, replace the coil.	**4.1**

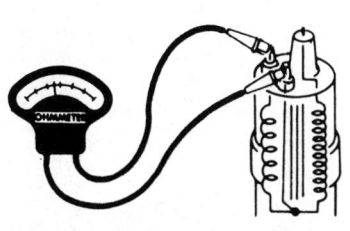

Check the coil primary resistance

230 TROUBLESHOOTING

Section 4—Secondary Electrical System
See Chapters 2–3 for service procedures

Test and Procedure	Results and Indications	Proceed to
4.1—Check for spark: Hold each spark plug wire approximately ¼" from ground with gloves or a heavy, dry rag. Crank the engine, and observe the spark.	If no spark is evident:	4.2
	If spark is good in some cylinders:	4.3
	If spark is good in all cylinders:	4.6

Check for spark at the plugs

4.2—Check for spark at the coil high tension lead: Remove the coil high tension lead from the distributor and position it approximately ¼" from ground. Crank the engine and observe spark. **CAUTION:** *This test should not be performed on engines equipped with electronic ignition.*	If the spark is good and consistent:	4.3
	If the spark is good but intermittent, test the primary electrical system starting at 3.3:	3.3
	If the spark is weak or non-existent, replace the coil high tension lead, clean and tighten all connections and retest. If no improvement is noted:	4.4
4.3—Visually inspect the distributor cap and rotor for burned or corroded contacts, cracks, carbon tracks, or moisture. Also check the fit of the rotor on the distributor shaft (where applicable).	If moisture is present, dry thoroughly, and retest per 4.1:	4.1
	If burned or excessively corroded contacts, cracks, or carbon tracks are noted, replace the defective part(s) and retest per 4.1:	4.1
	If the rotor and cap appear intact, or are only slightly corroded, clean the contacts thoroughly (including the cap towers and spark plug wire ends) and retest per 4.1:	
	If the spark is good in all cases:	4.6
	If the spark is poor in all cases:	4.5

Inspect the distributor cap and rotor

TROUBLESHOOTING

Test and Procedure	Results and Indications	Proceed to
4.4—Check the coil secondary resistance: On point-type systems connect an ohmmeter across the distributor side of the coil and the coil tower. Read the resistance on the high scale of the ohmmeter. On electronic ignition systems, see Chapter 3 for specific tests.	The resistance of a satisfactory coil should be between 4,000 and 10,000 ohms. If resistance is considerably higher (i.e., 40,000 ohms) replace the coil and retest per 4.1. **NOTE:** *This does not apply to high performance coils.*	

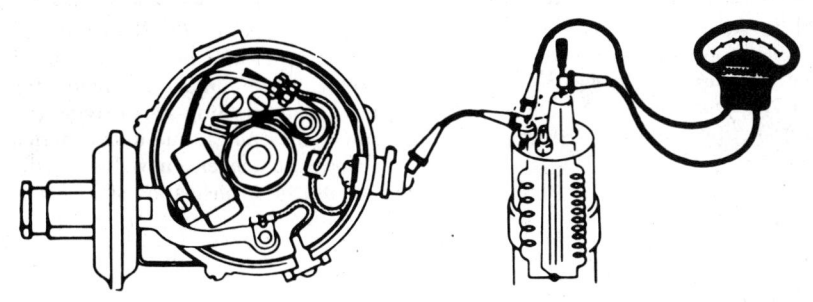

Testing the coil secondary resistance

4.5—Visually inspect the spark plug wires for cracking or brittleness. Ensure that no two wires are positioned so as to cause induction firing (adjacent and parallel). Remove each wire, one by one, and check resistance with an ohmmeter.	Replace any cracked or brittle wires. If any of the wires are defective, replace the entire set. Replace any wires with excessive resistance (over 8000 Ω per foot for suppression wire), and separate any wires that might cause induction firing.	4.6

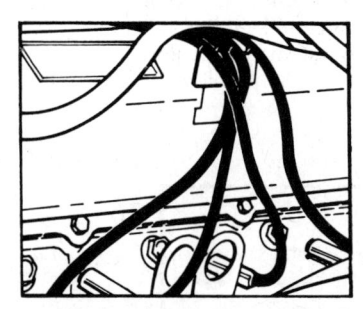

Misfiring can be the result of spark plug leads to adjacent, consecutively firing cylinders running parallel and too close together

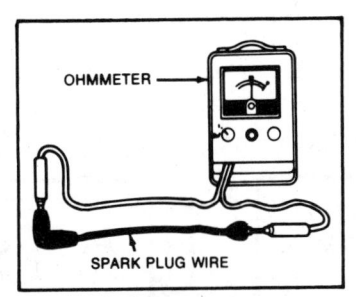

On point-type ignition systems, check the spark plug wires as shown. On electronic ignitions, do not remove the wire from the distributor cap terminal; instead, test through the cap

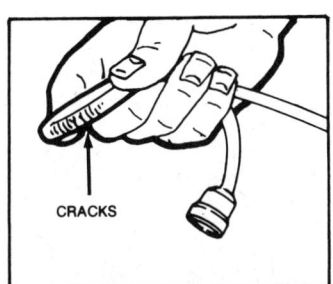

Spark plug wires can be checked visually by bending them in a loop over your finger. This will reveal any cracks, burned or broken insulation. Any wire with cracked insulation should be replaced

4.6—Remove the spark plugs, noting the cylinders from which they were removed, and evaluate according to the color photos in the middle of this book.	See following.	See following.

232 TROUBLESHOOTING

Test and Procedure	Results and Indications	Proceed to
4.7—Examine the location of all the plugs.	The following diagrams illustrate some of the conditions that the location of plugs will reveal.	4.8

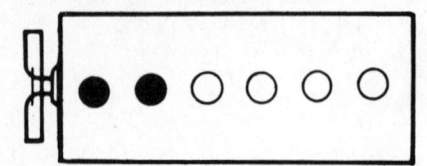

Two adjacent plugs are fouled in a 6-cylinder engine, 4-cylinder engine or either bank of a V-8. This is probably due to a blown head gasket between the two cylinders

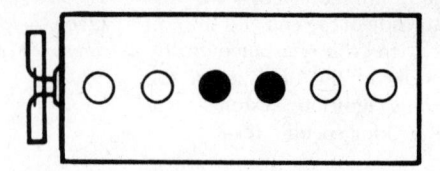

The two center plugs in a 6-cylinder engine are fouled. Raw fuel may be "boiled" out of the carburetor into the intake manifold after the engine is shut-off. Stop-start driving can also foul the center plugs, due to overly rich mixture. Proper float level, a new float needle and seat or use of an insulating spacer may help this problem

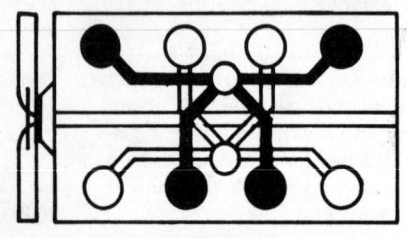

An unbalanced carburetor is indicated. Following the fuel flow on this particular design shows that the cylinders fed by the right-hand barrel are fouled from overly rich mixture, while the cylinders fed by the left-hand barrel are normal

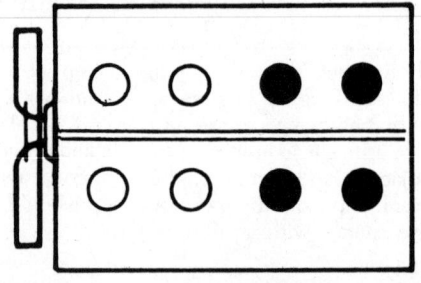

If the four rear plugs are overheated, a cooling system problem is suggested. A thorough cleaning of the cooling system may restore coolant circulation and cure the problem

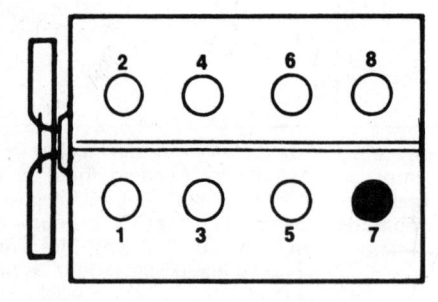

Finding one plug overheated may indicate an intake manifold leak near the affected cylinder. If the overheated plug is the second of two adjacent, consecutively firing plugs, it could be the result of ignition cross-firing. Separating the leads to these two plugs will eliminate cross-fire

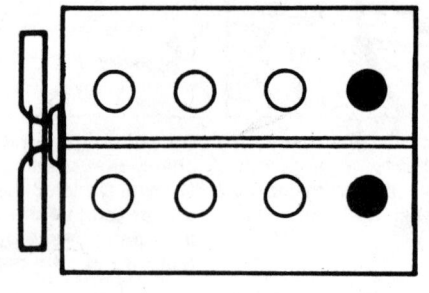

Occasionally, the two rear plugs in large, lightly used V-8's will become oil fouled. High oil consumption and smoky exhaust may also be noticed. It is probably due to plugged oil drain holes in the rear of the cylinder head, causing oil to be sucked in around the valve stems. This usually occurs in the rear cylinders first, because the engine slants that way

TROUBLESHOOTING 233

Test and Procedure	Results and Indications	Proceed to
4.8—Determine the static ignition timing. Using the crankshaft pulley timing marks as a guide, locate top dead center on the compression stroke of the number one cylinder.	The rotor should be pointing toward the No. 1 tower in the distributor cap, and, on electronic ignitions, the armature spoke for that cylinder should be lined up with the stator.	4.8
4.9—Check coil polarity: Connect a voltmeter negative lead to the coil high tension lead, and the positive lead to ground (**NOTE:** *Reverse the hook-up for positive ground systems*). Crank the engine momentarily.	If the voltmeter reads up-scale, the polarity is correct:	5.1
	If the voltmeter reads down-scale, reverse the coil polarity (switch the primary leads):	5.1

Checking coil polarity

Section 5—Fuel System
See Chapter 4 for service procedures

Test and Procedure	Results and Indications	Proceed to
5.1—Determine that the air filter is functioning efficiently: Hold paper elements up to a strong light, and attempt to see light through the filter.	Clean permanent air filters in solvent (or manufacturer's recommendation), and allow to dry. Replace paper elements through which light cannot be seen:	5.2
5.2—Determine whether a flooding condition exists: Flooding is identified by a strong gasoline odor, and excessive gasoline present in the throttle bore(s) of the carburetor.	If flooding is not evident:	5.3
	If flooding is evident, permit the gasoline to dry for a few moments and restart.	
	If flooding doesn't recur:	5.7
	If flooding is persistent:	5.5

If the engine floods repeatedly, check the choke butterfly flap

5.3—Check that fuel is reaching the carburetor: Detach the fuel line at the carburetor inlet. Hold the end of the line in a cup (not styrofoam), and crank the engine.	If fuel flows smoothly:	5.7
	If fuel doesn't flow (**NOTE:** *Make sure that there is fuel in the tank*), or flows erratically:	5.4

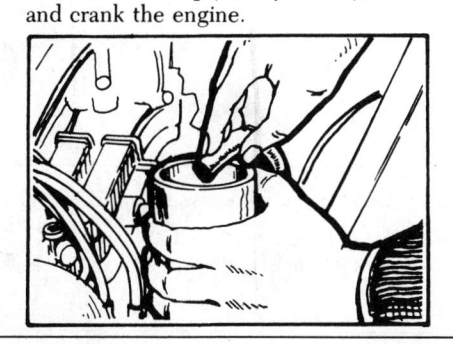

Check the fuel pump by disconnecting the output line (fuel pump-to-carburetor) at the carburetor and operating the starter briefly

TROUBLESHOOTING

Test and Procedure	Results and Indications	Proceed to
5.4—Test the fuel pump: Disconnect all fuel lines from the fuel pump. Hold a finger over the input fitting, crank the engine (with electric pump, turn the ignition or pump on); and feel for suction.	If suction is evident, blow out the fuel line to the tank with low pressure compressed air until bubbling is heard from the fuel filler neck. Also blow out the carburetor fuel line (both ends disconnected):	5.7
	If no suction is evident, replace or repair the fuel pump: **NOTE:** *Repeated oil fouling of the spark plugs, or a no-start condition, could be the result of a ruptured vacuum booster pump diaphragm, through which oil or gasoline is being drawn into the intake manifold (where applicable).*	5.7
5.5—Occasionally, small specks of dirt will clog the small jets and orifices in the carburetor. With the engine cold, hold a flat piece of wood or similar material over the carburetor, where possible, and crank the engine.	If the engine starts, but runs roughly the engine is probably not run enough. If the engine won't start:	5.9
5.6—Check the needle and seat: Tap the carburetor in the area of the needle and seat.	If flooding stops, a gasoline additive (e.g., Gumout) will often cure the problem:	5.7
	If flooding continues, check the fuel pump for excessive pressure at the carburetor (according to specifications). If the pressure is normal, the needle and seat must be removed and checked, and/or the float level adjusted:	5.7
5.7—Test the accelerator pump by looking into the throttle bores while operating the throttle.	If the accelerator pump appears to be operating normally:	5.8
	If the accelerator pump is not operating, the pump must be reconditioned. Where possible, service the pump with the carburetor(s) installed on the engine. If necessary, remove the carburetor. Prior to removal:	5.8

Check for gas at the carburetor by looking down the carburetor throat while someone moves the accelerator

5.8—Determine whether the carburetor main fuel system is functioning: Spray a commercial starting fluid into the carburetor while attempting to start the engine.	If the engine starts, runs for a few seconds, and dies:	5.9
	If the engine doesn't start:	6.1

TROUBLESHOOTING

Test and Procedure	Results and Indications	Proceed to
5.9—Uncommon fuel system malfunctions: See below:	If the problem is solved: If the problem remains, remove and recondition the carburetor.	6.1

Condition	Indication	Test	Prevailing Weather Conditions	Remedy
Vapor lock	Engine will not restart shortly after running.	Cool the components of the fuel system until the engine starts. Vapor lock can be cured faster by draping a wet cloth over a mechanical fuel pump.	Hot to very hot	Ensure that the exhaust manifold heat control valve is operating. Check with the vehicle manufacturer for the recommended solution to vapor lock on the model in question.
Carburetor icing	Engine will not idle, stalls at low speeds.	Visually inspect the throttle plate area of the throttle bores for frost.	High humidity, 32–40° F.	Ensure that the exhaust manifold heat control valve is operating, and that the intake manifold heat riser is not blocked.
Water in the fuel	Engine sputters and stalls; may not start.	Pump a small amount of fuel into a glass jar. Allow to stand, and inspect for droplets or a layer of water.	High humidity, extreme temperature changes.	For droplets, use one or two cans of commercial gas line anti-freeze. For a layer of water, the tank must be drained, and the fuel lines blown out with compressed air.

Section 6—Engine Compression
See Chapter 3 for service procedures

Test and Procedure	Results and Indications	Proceed to
6.1—Test engine compression: Remove all spark plugs. Block the throttle wide open. Insert a compression gauge into a spark plug port, crank the engine to obtain the maximum reading, and record.	If compression is within limits on all cylinders:	7.1
	If gauge reading is extremely low on all cylinders:	6.2
	If gauge reading is low on one or two cylinders: (If gauge readings are identical and low on two or more adjacent cylinders, the head gasket must be replaced.)	6.2

Checking compression

6.2—Test engine compression (wet): Squirt approximately 30 cc. of engine oil into each cylinder, and retest per 6.1.	If the readings improve, worn or cracked rings or broken pistons are indicated:	See Chapter 3
	If the readings do not improve, burned or excessively carboned valves or a jumped timing chain are indicated: NOTE: *A jumped timing chain is often indicated by difficult cranking.*	7.1

236 TROUBLESHOOTING

Section 7—Engine Vacuum
See Chapter 3 for service procedures

Test and Procedure	Results and Indications	Proceed to
7.1—Attach a vacuum gauge to the intake manifold beyond the throttle plate. Start the engine, and observe the action of the needle over the range of engine speeds.	See below.	See below

Normal engine
INDICATION: normal engine in good condition
Proceed to: 8.1
Gauge reading: steady, from 17–22 in./Hg.

Sticking valves
INDICATION: sticking valves or ignition miss
Proceed to: 9.1, 8.3
Gauge reading: intermittent fluctuation at idle

Incorrect valve timing
INDICATION: late ignition or valve timing, low compression, stuck throttle valve, leaking carburetor or manifold gasket
Proceed to: 6.1
Gauge reading: low (10–15 in./Hg) but steady

Carburetor requires adjustment
INDICATION: improper carburetor adjustment or minor intake leak.
Proceed to: 7.2
Gauge reading: drifting needle

Blown head gasket
INDICATION: ignition miss, blown cylinder head gasket, leaking valve or weak valve spring
Proceed to: 8.3, 6.1
Gauge reading: needle fluctuates as engine speed increases

Burnt or leaking valves
INDICATION: burnt valve or faulty valve clearance. Needle will fall when defective valve operates
Proceed to: 9.1
Gauge reading: steady needle, but drops regularly

Clogged exhaust system
INDICATION: choked muffler, excessive back pressure in system
Proceed to: 10.1
Gauge reading: gradual drop in reading at idle

Worn valve guides
INDICATION: worn valve guides
Proceed to: 9.1
Gauge reading: needle vibrates excessively at idle, but steadies as engine speed increases

White pointer = steady gauge hand   Black pointer = fluctuating gauge hand

CHILTON'S
AUTO BODY REPAIR TIPS

**Tools and Materials • Step-by-Step Illustrated Procedures
How To Repair Dents, Scratches and Rust Holes
Spray Painting and Refinishing Tips**

EASY STEP-BY-STEP TIPS FROM PROS

With a little practice, basic body repair procedures can be mastered by any do-it-yourself mechanic. The step-by-step repairs shown here can be applied to almost any type of auto body repair.

TOOLS & MATERIALS

You may already have basic tools, such as hammers and electric drills. Other tools unique to body repair — body hammers, grinding attachments, sanding blocks, dent puller, half-round plastic file and plastic spreaders — are relatively inexpensive and can be obtained wherever auto parts or auto body repair parts are sold. Portable air compressors and paint spray guns can be purchased or rented.

Auto Body Repair Kits

The best and most often used products are available to the do-it-yourselfer in kit form, from major manufacturers of auto body repair products. The same manufacturers also merchandise the individual products for use by pros.

Kits are available to make a wide variety of repairs, including holes, dents and scratches and fiberglass, and offer the advantage of buying the materials you'll need for the job. There is little waste or chance of materials going bad from not being used. Many kits may also contain basic body-working tools such as body files, sanding blocks and spreaders. Check the contents of the kit before buying your tools.

BODY REPAIR TIPS

Safety

Many of the products associated with auto body repair and refinishing contain toxic chemicals. Read all labels before opening containers and store them in a safe place and manner.

• Wear eye protection (safety goggles) when using power tools or when performing any operation that involves the removal of any type of material.

• Wear lung protection (disposable mask or respirator) when grinding, sanding or painting.

Sanding

1 Sand off paint before using a dent puller. When using a non-adhesive sanding disc, cover the back of the disc with an overlapping layer or two of masking tape and trim the edges. The disc will last considerably longer.

2 Use the circular motion of the sanding disc to grind *into* the edge of the repair. Grinding or sanding away from the jagged edge will only tear the sandpaper.

3 Use the palm of your hand flat on the panel to detect high and low spots. Do not use your fingertips. Slide your hand slowly back and forth.

WORKING WITH BODY FILLER

Mixing The Filler

Cleanliness and proper mixing and application are extremely important. Use a clean piece of plastic or glass or a disposable artist's palette to mix body filler.

1 Allow plenty of time and follow directions. No useful purpose will be served by adding more hardener to make it cure (set-up) faster. Less hardener means more curing time, but the mixture dries harder; more hardener means less curing time but a softer mixture.

2 Both the hardener and the filler should be thoroughly kneaded or stirred before mixing. Hardener should be a solid paste and dispense like thin toothpaste. Body filler should be smooth, and free of lumps or thick spots.

Getting the proper amount of hardener in the filler is the trickiest part of preparing the filler. Use the same amount of hardener in cold or warm weather. For contour filler (thick coats), a bead of hardener twice the diameter of the filler is about right. There's about a 15% margin on either side, but, if in doubt use less hardener.

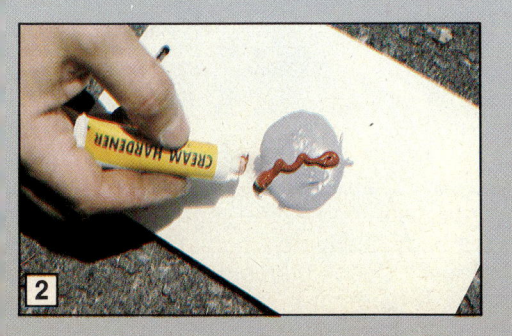

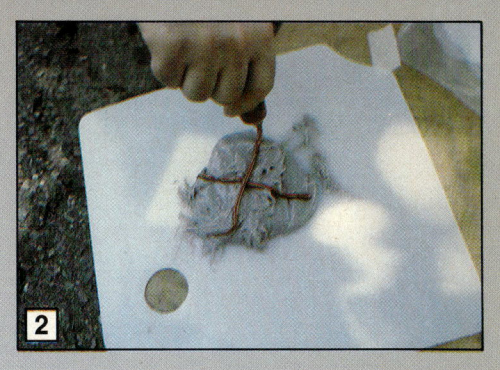

3 Mix the body filler and hardener by wiping across the mixing surface, picking the mixture up and wiping it again. Colder weather requires longer mixing times. Do not mix in a circular motion; this will trap air bubbles which will become holes in the cured filler.

Applying The Filler

1 For best results, filler should not be applied over 1/4" thick.

Apply the filler in several coats. Build it up to above the level of the repair surface so that it can be sanded or grated down.

The first coat of filler must be pressed on with a firm wiping motion.

Apply the filler in one direction only. Working the filler back and forth will either pull it off the metal or trap air bubbles.

REPAIRING DENTS

Before you start, take a few minutes to study the damaged area. Try to visualize the shape of the panel before it was damaged. If the damage is on the left fender, look at the right fender and use it as a guide. If there is access to the panel from behind, you can reshape it with a body hammer. If not, you'll have to use a dent puller. Go slowly and work the metal a little at a time. Get the panel as straight as possible before applying filler.

1 This dent is typical of one that can be pulled out or hammered out from behind. Remove the headlight cover, headlight assembly and turn signal housing.

2 Drill a series of holes ½ the size of the end of the dent puller along the stress line. Make some trial pulls and assess the results. If necessary, drill more holes and try again. Do not hurry.

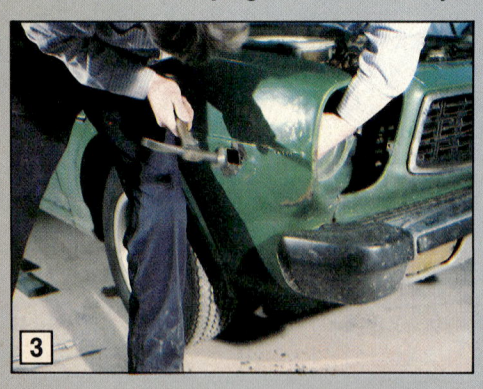

3 If possible, use a body hammer and block to shape the metal back to its original contours. Get the metal back as close to its original shape as possible. Don't depend on body filler to fill dents.

4 Using an 80-grit grinding disc on an electric drill, grind the paint from the surrounding area down to bare metal. Use a new grinding pad to prevent heat buildup that will warp metal.

5 The area should look like this when you're finished grinding. Knock the drill holes in and tape over small openings to keep plastic filler out.

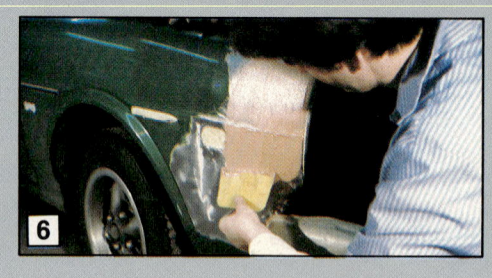

6 Mix the body filler (see Body Repair Tips). Spread the body filler evenly over the entire area (see Body Repair Tips). Be sure to cover the area completely.

7 Let the body filler dry until the surface can just be scratched with your fingernail. Knock the high spots from the body filler with a body file ("Cheesegrater"). Check frequently with the palm of your hand for high and low spots.

8 Check to be sure that trim pieces that will be installed later will fit exactly. Sand the area with 40-grit paper.

9 If you wind up with low spots, you may have to apply another layer of filler.

10 Knock the high spots off with 40-grit paper. When you are satisfied with the contours of the repair, apply a thin coat of filler to cover pin holes and scratches.

11 Block sand the area with 40-grit paper to a smooth finish. Pay particular attention to body lines and ridges that must be well-defined.

12 Sand the area with 400 paper and then finish with a scuff pad. The finished repair is ready for priming and painting (see Painting Tips).

Materials and photos courtesy of Ritt Jones Auto Body, Prospect Park, PA.

REPAIRING RUST HOLES

There are many ways to repair rust holes. The fiberglass cloth kit shown here is one of the most cost efficient for the owner because it provides a strong repair that resists cracking and moisture and is relatively easy to use. It can be used on large and small holes (with or without backing) and can be applied over contoured areas. Remember, however, that short of replacing an entire panel, no repair is a guarantee that the rust will not return.

1 Remove any trim that will be in the way. Clean away all loose debris. Cut away all the rusted metal. But be sure to leave enough metal to retain the contour or body shape.

2 Grind away all traces of rust with a 24-grit grinding disc. Be sure to grind back 3-4 inches from the edge of the hole down to bare metal and be sure all traces of paint, primer and rust are removed.

3 Block sand the area with 80 or 100 grit sandpaper to get a clear, shiny surface and feathered paint edge. Tap the edges of the hole inward with a ball peen hammer.

4 If you are going to use release film, cut a piece about 2-3" larger than the area you have sanded. Place the film over the repair and mark the sanded area on the film. Avoid any unnecessary wrinkling of the film.

5 Cut 2 pieces of fiberglass matte to match the shape of the repair. One piece should be about 1" smaller than the sanded area and the second piece should be 1" smaller than the first. Mix enough filler and hardener to saturate the fiberglass material (see Body Repair Tips).

6 Lay the release sheet on a flat surface and spread an even layer of filler, large enough to cover the repair. Lay the smaller piece of fiberglass cloth in the center of the sheet and spread another layer of filler over the fiberglass cloth. Repeat the operation for the larger piece of cloth.

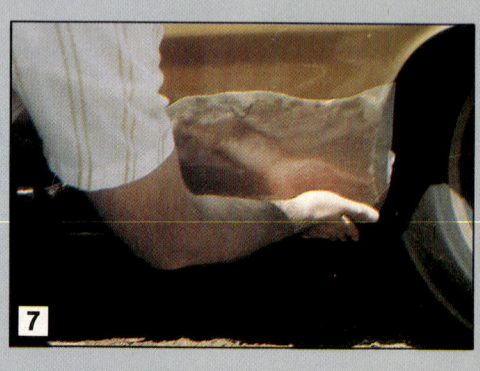

7 Place the repair material over the repair area, with the release film facing outward. Use a spreader and work from the center outward to smooth the material, following the body contours. Be sure to remove all air bubbles.

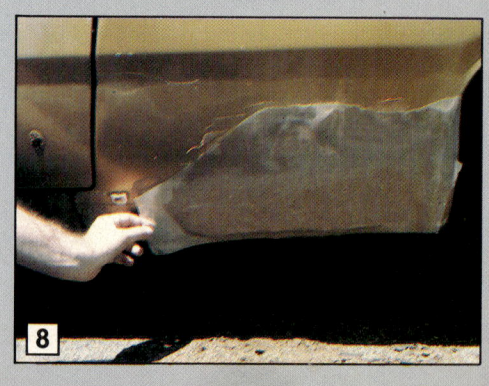

8 Wait until the repair has dried tack-free and peel off the release sheet. The ideal working temperature is 60°-90° F. Cooler or warmer temperatures or high humidity may require additional curing time. Wait longer, if in doubt.

9 Sand and feather-edge the entire area. The initial sanding can be done with a sanding disc on an electric drill if care is used. Finish the sanding with a block sander. Low spots can be filled with body filler; this may require several applications.

10 When the filler can just be scratched with a fingernail, knock the high spots down with a body file and smooth the entire area with 80-grit. Feather the filled areas into the surrounding areas.

11 When the area is sanded smooth, mix some topcoat and hardener and apply it directly with a spreader. This will give a smooth finish and prevent the glass matte from showing through the paint.

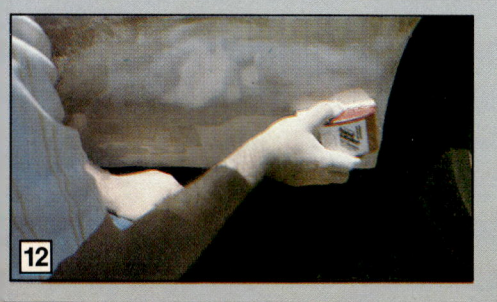

12 Block sand the topcoat smooth with finishing sandpaper (200 grit), and 400 grit. The repair is ready for masking, priming and painting (see Painting Tips).

Materials and photos courtesy Marson Corporation, Chelsea, Massachusetts

PAINTING TIPS

Preparation

1 SANDING — Use a 400 or 600 grit wet or dry sandpaper. Wet-sand the area with a 1/4 sheet of sandpaper soaked in clean water. Keep the paper wet while sanding. Sand the area until the repaired areatapers into the original finish.

2 CLEANING — Wash the area to be painted thoroughly with water and a clean rag. Rinse it thoroughly and wipe the surface dry until you're sure it's completely free of dirt, dust, fingerprints, wax, detergent or other foreign matter.

3 MASKING — Protect any areas you don't want to overspray by covering them with masking tape and newspaper. Be careful not get fingerprints on the area to be painted.

4 PRIMING — All exposed metal should be primed before painting. Primer protects the metal and provides an excellent surface for paint adhesion. When the primer is dry, wet-sand the area again with 600 grit wet-sandpaper. Clean the area again after sanding.

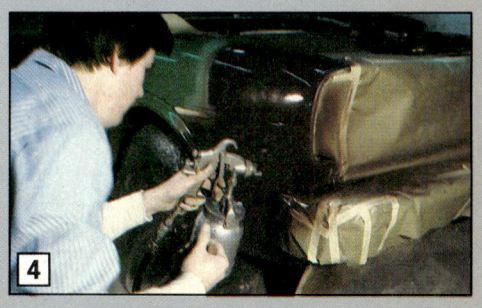

Painting Techniques

Paint applied from either a spray gun or a spray can (for small areas) will provide good results. Experiment on an old piece of metal to get the right combination before you begin painting.

SPRAYING VISCOSITY (SPRAY GUN ONLY) — Paint should be thinned to spraying viscosity according to the directions on the can. Use only the recommended thinner or reducer and the same amount of reduction regardless of temperature.

AIR PRESSURE (SPRAY GUN ONLY) — This is extremely important. Be sure you are using the proper recommended pressure.

TEMPERATURE — The surface to be painted should be approximately the same temperature as the surrounding air. Applying warm paint to a cold surface, or vice versa, will completely upset the paint characteristics.

THICKNESS — Spray with smooth strokes. In general, the thicker the coat of paint, the longer the drying time. Apply several thin coats about 30 seconds apart. The paint should remain wet long enough to flow out and no longer; heavier coats will only produce sags or wrinkles. Spray a light (fog) coat, followed by heavier color coats.

DISTANCE — The ideal spraying distance is 8"-12" from the gun or can to the surface. Shorter distances will produce ripples, while greater distances will result in orange peel, dry film and poor color match and loss of material due to overspray.

OVERLAPPING — The gun or can should be kept at right angles to the surface at all times. Work to a wet edge at an even speed, using a 50% overlap and direct the center of the spray at the lower or nearest edge of the previous stroke.

RUBBING OUT (BLENDING) FRESH PAINT — Let the paint dry thoroughly. Runs or imperfections can be sanded out, primed and repainted.

Don't be in too big a hurry to remove the masking. This only produces paint ridges. When the finish has dried for at least a week, apply a small amount of fine grade rubbing compound with a clean, wet cloth. Use lots of water and blend the new paint with the surrounding area.

WRONG	CORRECT	WRONG
Thin coat. Stroke too fast, not enough overlap, gun too far away.	Medium coat. Proper distance, good stroke, proper overlap.	Heavy coat. Stroke too slow, too much overlap, gun too close.

Test and Procedure	Results and Indications	Proceed to
7.2—Attach a vacuum gauge per 7.1, and test for an intake manifold leak. Squirt a small amount of oil around the intake manifold gaskets, carburetor gaskets, plugs and fittings. Observe the action of the vacuum gauge.	If the reading improves, replace the indicated gasket, or seal the indicated fitting or plug: If the reading remains low:	8.1 7.3
7.3—Test all vacuum hoses and accessories for leaks as described in 7.2. Also check the carburetor body (dashpots, automatic choke mechanism, throttle shafts) for leaks in the same manner.	If the reading improves, service or replace the offending part(s): If the reading remains low:	8.1 6.1

Section 8—Secondary Electrical System
See Chapter 2 for service procedures

Test and Procedure	Results and Indications	Proceed to
8.1—Remove the distributor cap and check to make sure that the rotor turns when the engine is cranked. Visually inspect the distributor components.	Clean, tighten or replace any components which appear defective.	8.2
8.2—Connect a timing light (per manufacturer's recommendation) and check the dynamic ignition timing. Disconnect and plug the vacuum hose(s) to the distributor if specified, start the engine, and observe the timing marks at the specified engine speed.	If the timing is not correct, adjust to specifications by rotating the distributor in the engine: (Advance timing by rotating distributor opposite normal direction of rotor rotation, retard timing by rotating distributor in same direction as rotor rotation.)	8.3
8.3—Check the operation of the distributor advance mechanism(s): To test the mechanical advance, disconnect the vacuum lines from the distributor advance unit and observe the timing marks with a timing light as the engine speed is increased from idle. If the mark moves smoothly, without hesitation, it may be assumed that the mechanical advance is functioning properly. To test vacuum advance and/or retard systems, alternately crimp and release the vacuum line, and observe the timing mark for movement. If movement is noted, the system is operating.	If the systems are functioning: If the systems are not functioning, remove the distributor, and test on a distributor tester:	8.4 8.4
8.4—Locate an ignition miss: With the engine running, remove each spark plug wire, one at a time, until one is found that doesn't cause the engine to roughen and slow down.	When the missing cylinder is identified:	4.1

TROUBLESHOOTING

Section 9—Valve Train
See Chapter 3 for service procedures

Test and Procedure	Results and Indications	Proceed to
9.1—Evaluate the valve train: Remove the valve cover, and ensure that the valves are adjusted to specifications. A mechanic's stethoscope may be used to aid in the diagnosis of the valve train. By pushing the probe on or near push rods or rockers, valve noise often can be isolated. A timing light also may be used to diagnose valve problems. Connect the light according to manufacturer's recommendations, and start the engine. Vary the firing moment of the light by increasing the engine speed (and therefore the ignition advance), and moving the trigger from cylinder to cylinder. Observe the movement of each valve.	Sticking valves or erratic valve train motion can be observed with the timing light. The cylinder head must be disassembled for repairs.	See Chapter 3
9.2—Check the valve timing: Locate top dead center of the No. 1 piston, and install a degree wheel or tape on the crankshaft pulley or damper with zero corresponding to an index mark on the engine. Rotate the crankshaft in its direction of rotation, and observe the opening of the No. 1 cylinder intake valve. The opening should correspond with the correct mark on the degree wheel according to specifications.	If the timing is not correct, the timing cover must be removed for further investigation.	See Chapter 3

Section 10—Exhaust System

Test and Procedure	Results and Indications	Proceed to
10.1—Determine whether the exhaust manifold heat control valve is operating: Operate the valve by hand to determine whether it is free to move. If the valve is free, run the engine to operating temperature and observe the action of the valve, to ensure that it is opening.	If the valve sticks, spray it with a suitable solvent, open and close the valve to free it, and retest. If the valve functions properly: If the valve does not free, or does not operate, replace the valve:	10.2 10.2
10.2—Ensure that there are no exhaust restrictions: Visually inspect the exhaust system for kinks, dents, or crushing. Also note that gases are flowing freely from the tailpipe at all engine speeds, indicating no restriction in the muffler or resonator.	Replace any damaged portion of the system:	11.1

TROUBLESHOOTING

Section 11—Cooling System
See Chapter 3 for service procedures

Test and Procedure	Results and Indications	Proceed to
11.1—Visually inspect the fan belt for glazing, cracks, and fraying, and replace if necessary. Tighten the belt so that the longest span has approximately ½" play at its midpoint under thumb pressure (see Chapter 1).	Replace or tighten the fan belt as necessary: *Checking belt tension*	11.2
11.2—Check the fluid level of the cooling system.	If full or slightly low, fill as necessary: If extremely low:	11.5 11.3
11.3—Visually inspect the external portions of the cooling system (radiator, radiator hoses, thermostat elbow, water pump seals, heater hoses, etc.) for leaks. If none are found, pressurize the cooling system to 14–15 psi.	If cooling system holds the pressure: If cooling system loses pressure rapidly, reinspect external parts of the system for leaks under pressure. If none are found, check dipstick for coolant in crankcase. If no coolant is present, but pressure loss continues: If coolant is evident in crankcase, remove cylinder head(s), and check gasket(s). If gaskets are intact, block and cylinder head(s) should be checked for cracks or holes. If the gasket(s) is blown, replace, and purge the crankcase of coolant: NOTE: *Occasionally, due to atmospheric and driving conditions, condensation of water can occur in the crankcase. This causes the oil to appear milky white. To remedy, run the engine until hot, and change the oil and oil filter.*	11.5 11.4 12.6
11.4—Check for combustion leaks into the cooling system: Pressurize the cooling system as above. Start the engine, and observe the pressure gauge. If the needle fluctuates, remove each spark plug wire, one at a time, noting which cylinder(s) reduce or eliminate the fluctuation.	Cylinders which reduce or eliminate the fluctuation, when the spark plug wire is removed, are leaking into the cooling system. Replace the head gasket on the affected cylinder bank(s). *Pressurizing the cooling system*	

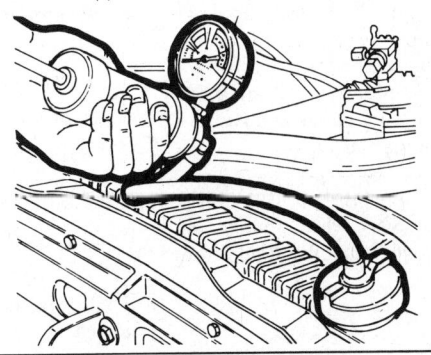

TROUBLESHOOTING

Test and Procedure	Results and Indications	Proceed to
11.5—Check the radiator pressure cap: Attach a radiator pressure tester to the radiator cap (wet the seal prior to installation). Quickly pump up the pressure, noting the point at which the cap releases.	If the cap releases within ± 1 psi of the specified rating, it is operating properly:	11.6
	If the cap releases at more than ± 1 psi of the specified rating, it should be replaced:	11.6
11.6—Test the thermostat: Start the engine cold, remove the radiator cap, and insert a thermometer into the radiator. Allow the engine to idle. After a short while, there will be a sudden, rapid increase in coolant temperature. The temperature at which this sharp rise stops is the thermostat opening temperature.	If the thermostat opens at or about the specified temperature:	11.7
	If the temperature doesn't increase: (If the temperature increases slowly and gradually, replace the thermostat.)	11.7
11.7—Check the water pump: Remove the thermostat elbow and the thermostat, disconnect the coil high tension lead (to prevent starting), and crank the engine momentarily.	If coolant flows, replace the thermostat and retest per 11.6:	11.6
	If coolant doesn't flow, reverse flush the cooling system to alleviate any blockage that might exist. If system is not blocked, and coolant will not flow, replace the water pump.	

Checking radiator pressure cap

Section 12—Lubrication
See Chapter 3 for service procedures

Test and Procedure	Results and Indications	Proceed to
12.1—Check the oil pressure gauge or warning light: If the gauge shows low pressure, or the light is on for no obvious reason, remove the oil pressure sender. Install an accurate oil pressure gauge and run the engine momentarily.	If oil pressure builds normally, run engine for a few moments to determine that it is functioning normally, and replace the sender.	—
	If the pressure remains low:	12.2
	If the pressure surges:	12.3
	If the oil pressure is zero:	12.3
12.2—Visually inspect the oil: If the oil is watery or very thin, milky, or foamy, replace the oil and oil filter.	If the oil is normal:	12.3
	If after replacing oil the pressure remains low:	12.3
	If after replacing oil the pressure becomes normal:	—

Test and Procedure	Results and Indications	Proceed to
12.3—Inspect the oil pressure relief valve and spring, to ensure that it is not sticking or stuck. Remove and thoroughly clean the valve, spring, and the valve body.	If the oil pressure improves: If no improvement is noted:	— 12.4
12.4—Check to ensure that the oil pump is not cavitating (sucking air instead of oil): See that the crankcase is neither over nor underfull, and that the pickup in the sump is in the proper position and free from sludge.	Fill or drain the crankcase to the proper capacity, and clean the pickup screen in solvent if necessary. If no improvement is noted:	12.5
12.5—Inspect the oil pump drive and the oil pump:	If the pump drive or the oil pump appear to be defective, service as necessary and retest per 12.1:	12.1
	If the pump drive and pump appear to be operating normally, the engine should be disassembled to determine where blockage exists:	See Chapter 3
12.6—Purge the engine of ethylene glycol coolant: Completely drain the crankcase and the oil filter. Obtain a commercial butyl cellosolve base solvent, designated for this purpose, and follow the instructions precisely. Following this, install a new oil filter and refill the crankcase with the proper weight oil. The next oil and filter change should follow shortly thereafter (1000 miles).		

TROUBLESHOOTING EMISSION CONTROL SYSTEMS

See Chapter 4 for procedures applicable to individual emission control systems used on specific combinations of engine/transmission/model.

TROUBLESHOOTING THE CARBURETOR
See Chapter 4 for service procedures

Carburetor problems cannot be effectively isolated unless all other engine systems (particularly ignition and emission) are functioning properly and the engine is properly tuned.

TROUBLESHOOTING

Condition	Possible Cause
Engine cranks, but does not start	1. Improper starting procedure 2. No fuel in tank 3. Clogged fuel line or filter 4. Defective fuel pump 5. Choke valve not closing properly 6. Engine flooded 7. Choke valve not unloading 8. Throttle linkage not making full travel 9. Stuck needle or float 10. Leaking float needle or seat 11. Improper float adjustment
Engine stalls	1. Improperly adjusted idle speed or mixture **Engine hot** 2. Improperly adjusted dashpot 3. Defective or improperly adjusted solenoid 4. Incorrect fuel level in fuel bowl 5. Fuel pump pressure too high 6. Leaking float needle seat 7. Secondary throttle valve stuck open 8. Air or fuel leaks 9. Idle air bleeds plugged or missing 10. Idle passages plugged **Engine Cold** 11. Incorrectly adjusted choke 12. Improperly adjusted fast idle speed 13. Air leaks 14. Plugged idle or idle air passages 15. Stuck choke valve or binding linkage 16. Stuck secondary throttle valves 17. Engine flooding—high fuel level 18. Leaking or misaligned float
Engine hesitates on acceleration	1. Clogged fuel filter 2. Leaking fuel pump diaphragm 3. Low fuel pump pressure 4. Secondary throttle valves stuck, bent or misadjusted 5. Sticking or binding air valve 6. Defective accelerator pump 7. Vacuum leaks 8. Clogged air filter 9. Incorrect choke adjustment (engine cold)
Engine feels sluggish or flat on acceleration	1. Improperly adjusted idle speed or mixture 2. Clogged fuel filter 3. Defective accelerator pump 4. Dirty, plugged or incorrect main metering jets 5. Bent or sticking main metering rods 6. Sticking throttle valves 7. Stuck heat riser 8. Binding or stuck air valve 9. Dirty, plugged or incorrect secondary jets 10. Bent or sticking secondary metering rods. 11. Throttle body or manifold heat passages plugged 12. Improperly adjusted choke or choke vacuum break.
Carburetor floods	1. Defective fuel pump. Pressure too high. 2. Stuck choke valve 3. Dirty, worn or damaged float or needle valve/seat 4. Incorrect float/fuel level 5. Leaking float bowl

TROUBLESHOOTING

Condition	Possible Cause
Engine idles roughly and stalls	1. Incorrect idle speed 2. Clogged fuel filter 3. Dirt in fuel system or carburetor 4. Loose carburetor screws or attaching bolts 5. Broken carburetor gaskets 6. Air leaks 7. Dirty carburetor 8. Worn idle mixture needles 9. Throttle valves stuck open 10. Incorrectly adjusted float or fuel level 11. Clogged air filter
Engine runs unevenly or surges	1. Defective fuel pump 2. Dirty or clogged fuel filter 3. Plugged, loose or incorrect main metering jets or rods 4. Air leaks 5. Bent or sticking main metering rods 6. Stuck power piston 7. Incorrect float adjustment 8. Incorrect idle speed or mixture 9. Dirty or plugged idle system passages 10. Hard, brittle or broken gaskets 11. Loose attaching or mounting screws 12. Stuck or misaligned secondary throttle valves
Poor fuel economy	1. Poor driving habits 2. Stuck choke valve 3. Binding choke linkage 4. Stuck heat riser 5. Incorrect idle mixture 6. Defective accelerator pump 7. Air leaks 8. Plugged, loose or incorrect main metering jets 9. Improperly adjusted float or fuel level 10. Bent, misaligned or fuel-clogged float 11. Leaking float needle seat 12. Fuel leak 13. Accelerator pump discharge ball not seating properly 14. Incorrect main jets
Engine lacks high speed performance or power	1. Incorrect throttle linkage adjustment 2. Stuck or binding power piston 3. Defective accelerator pump 4. Air leaks 5. Incorrect float setting or fuel level 6. Dirty, plugged, worn or incorrect main metering jets or rods 7. Binding or sticking air valve 8. Brittle or cracked gaskets 9. Bent, incorrect or improperly adjusted secondary metering rods 10. Clogged fuel filter 11. Clogged air filter 12. Defective fuel pump

TROUBLESHOOTING FUEL INJECTION PROBLEMS

Each fuel injection system has its own unique components and test procedures, for which it is impossible to generalize. Refer to Chapter 4 of this Repair & Tune-Up Guide for specific test and repair procedures, if the vehicle is equipped with fuel injection.

TROUBLESHOOTING ELECTRICAL PROBLEMS

See Chapter 5 for service procedures

For any electrical system to operate, it must make a complete circuit. This simply means that the power flow from the battery must make a complete circle. When an electrical component is operating, power flows from the battery to the component, passes through the component causing it to perform its function (lighting a light bulb), and then returns to the battery through the ground of the circuit. This ground is usually (but not always) the metal part of the car or truck on which the electrical component is mounted.

Perhaps the easiest way to visualize this is to think of connecting a light bulb with two wires attached to it to the battery. If one of the two wires attached to the light bulb were attached to the negative post of the battery and the other were attached to the positive post of the battery, you would have a complete circuit. Current from the battery would flow to the light bulb, causing it to light, and return to the negative post of the battery.

The normal automotive circuit differs from this simple example in two ways. First, instead of having a return wire from the bulb to the battery, the light bulb returns the current to the battery through the chassis of the vehicle. Since the negative battery cable is attached to the chassis and the chassis is made of electrically conductive metal, the chassis of the vehicle can serve as a ground wire to complete the circuit. Secondly, most automotive circuits contain switches to turn components on and off as required.

Every complete circuit from a power source must include a component which is using the power from the power source. If you were to disconnect the light bulb from the wires and touch the two wires together (don't do this) the power supply wire to the component would be grounded before the normal ground connection for the circuit.

Because grounding a wire from a power source makes a complete circuit—less the required component to use the power—this phenomenon is called a short circuit. Common causes are: broken insulation (exposing the metal wire to a metal part of the car or truck), or a shorted switch.

Some electrical components which require a large amount of current to operate also have a relay in their circuit. Since these circuits carry a large amount of current, the thickness of the wire in the circuit (gauge size) is also greater. If this large wire were connected from the component to the control switch on the instrument panel, and then back to the component, a voltage drop would occur in the circuit. To prevent this potential drop in voltage, an electromagnetic switch (relay) is used. The large wires in the circuit are connected from the battery to one side of the relay, and from the opposite side of the relay to the component. The relay is normally open, preventing current from passing through the circuit. An additional, smaller, wire is connected from the relay to the control switch for the circuit. When the control switch is turned on, it grounds the smaller wire from the relay and completes the circuit. This closes the relay and allows current to flow from the battery to the component. The horn, headlight, and starter circuits are three which use relays.

It is possible for larger surges of current to pass through the electrical system of your car or truck. If this surge of current were to reach an electrical component, it could burn it out. To prevent this, fuses, circuit breakers or fusible links are connected into the current supply wires of most of the major electrical systems. When an electrical current of excessive power passes through the component's fuse, the fuse blows out and breaks the circuit, saving the component from destruction.

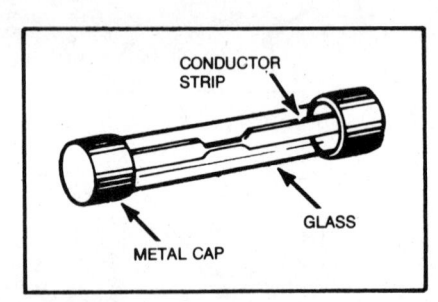

Typical automotive fuse

A circuit breaker is basically a self-repairing fuse. The circuit breaker opens the circuit the same way a fuse does. However, when either the short is removed from the circuit or the surge subsides, the circuit breaker resets itself and does not have to be replaced as a fuse does.

A fuse link is a wire that acts as a fuse. It is normally connected between the starter relay and the main wiring harness. This connection is usually under the hood. The fuse link (if installed) protects all the

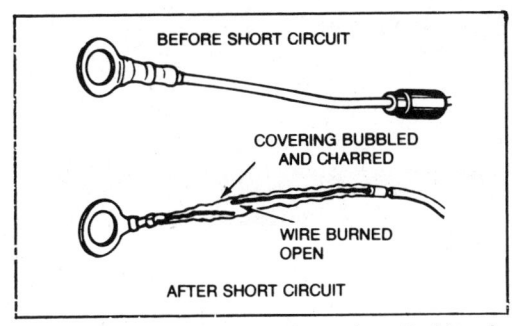

Most fusible links show a charred, melted insulation when they burn out

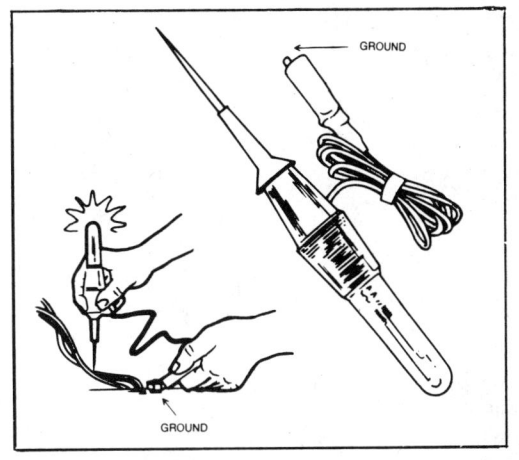

The test light will show the presence of current when touched to a hot wire and grounded at the other end

chassis electrical components, and is the probable cause of trouble when none of the electrical components function, unless the battery is disconnected or dead.

Electrical problems generally fall into one of three areas:

1. The component that is not functioning is not receiving current.
2. The component itself is not functioning.
3. The component is not properly grounded.

The electrical system can be checked with a test light and a jumper wire. A test light is a device that looks like a pointed screwdriver with a wire attached to it and has a light bulb in its handle. A jumper wire is a piece of insulated wire with an alligator clip attached to each end.

If a component is not working, you must follow a systematic plan to determine which of the three causes is the villain.

1. Turn on the switch that controls the inoperable component.
2. Disconnect the power supply wire from the component.
3. Attach the ground wire on the test light to a good metal ground.
4. Touch the probe end of the test light to the end of the power supply wire that was disconnected from the component. If the component is receiving current, the test light will go on.

NOTE: *Some components work only when the ignition switch is turned on.*

If the test light does not go on, then the problem is in the circuit between the battery and the component. This includes all the switches, fuses, and relays in the system. Follow the wire that runs back to the battery. The problem is an open circuit between the battery and the component. If the fuse is blown and, when replaced, immediately blows again, there is a short circuit in the system which must be located and repaired. If there is a switch in the system, bypass it with a jumper wire. This is done by connecting one end of the jumper wire to the power supply wire into the switch and the other end of the jumper wire to the wire coming out of the switch. If the test light lights with the jumper wire installed, the switch or whatever was bypassed is defective.

NOTE: *Never substitute the jumper wire for the component, since it is required to use the power from the power source.*

5. If the bulb in the test light goes on, then the current is getting to the component that is not working. This eliminates the first of the three possible causes. Connect the power supply wire and connect a jumper wire from the component to a good metal ground. Do this with the switch which controls the component turned on, and also the ignition switch turned on if it is required for the component to work. If the component works with the jumper wire installed, then it has a bad ground. This is usually caused by the metal area on which the component mounts to the chassis being coated with some type of foreign matter.

6. If neither test located the source of the trouble, then the component itself is defective. Remember that for any electrical system to work, all connections must be clean and tight.

TROUBLESHOOTING

Troubleshooting Basic Turn Signal and Flasher Problems
See Chapter 5 for service procedures

Most problems in the turn signals or flasher system can be reduced to defective flashers or bulbs, which are easily replaced. Occasionally, the turn signal switch will prove defective.

F = Front   R = Rear   ● = Lights off   ○ = Lights on

Condition		Possible Cause
Turn signals light, but do not flash	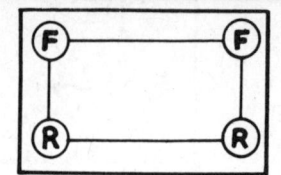	Defective flasher
No turn signals light on either side	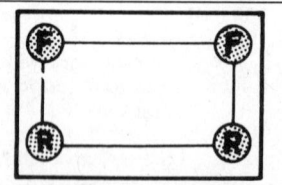	Blown fuse. Replace if defective. Defective flasher. Check by substitution. Open circuit, short circuit or poor ground.
Both turn signals on one side don't work	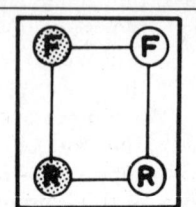	Bad bulbs. Bad ground in both (or either) housings.
One turn signal light on one side doesn't work	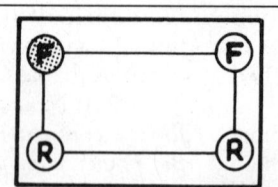	Defective bulb. Corrosion in socket. Clean contacts. Poor ground at socket.
Turn signal flashes too fast or too slowly	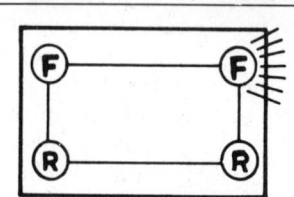	Check any bulb on the side flashing too fast. A heavy-duty bulb is probably installed in place of a regular bulb. Check the bulb flashing too slowly. A standard bulb was probably installed in place of a heavy-duty bulb. Loose connections or corrosion at the bulb socket.
Indicator lights don't work in either direction		Check if the turn signals are working. Check the dash indicator lights. Check the flasher by substitution.
One indicator light doesn't light		On systems with one dash indicator: See if the lights work on the same side. Often the filaments have been reversed in systems combining stoplights with tail-lights and turn signals. Check the flasher by substitution. On systems with two indicators: Check the bulbs on the same side. Check the indicator light bulb. Check the flasher by substitution.

TROUBLESHOOTING

Troubleshooting Lighting Problems
See Chapter 5 for service procedures

Condition	Possible Cause
One or more lights don't work, but others do	1. Defective bulb(s) 2. Blown fuse(s) 3. Dirty fuse clips or light sockets 4. Poor ground circuit
Lights burn out quickly	1. Incorrect voltage regulator setting or defective regulator 2. Poor battery/alternator connections
Lights go dim	1. Low/discharged battery 2. Alternator not charging 3. Corroded sockets or connections 4. Low voltage output
Lights flicker	1. Loose connection 2. Poor ground. (Run ground wire from light housing to frame) 3. Circuit breaker operating (short circuit)
Lights "flare"—Some flare is normal on acceleration—If excessive, see "Lights Burn Out Quickly"	High voltage setting
Lights glare—approaching drivers are blinded	1. Lights adjusted too high 2. Rear springs or shocks sagging 3. Rear tires soft

Troubleshooting Dash Gauge Problems

Most problems can be traced to a defective sending unit or faulty wiring. Occasionally, the gauge itself is at fault. See Chapter 5 for service procedures.

Condition	Possible Cause

COOLANT TEMPERATURE GAUGE

Gauge reads erratically or not at all	1. Loose or dirty connections 2. Defective sending unit. 3. Defective gauge. To test a bi-metal gauge, remove the wire from the sending unit. Ground the wire for an instant. If the gauge registers, replace the sending unit. To test a magnetic gauge, disconnect the wire at the sending unit. With ignition ON gauge should register COLD. Ground the wire; gauge should register HOT.

AMMETER GAUGE—TURN HEADLIGHTS ON (DO NOT START ENGINE). NOTE REACTION

Ammeter shows charge Ammeter shows discharge Ammeter does not move	1. Connections reversed on gauge 2. Ammeter is OK 3. Loose connections or faulty wiring 4. Defective gauge

248 TROUBLESHOOTING

Condition	Possible Cause
OIL PRESSURE GAUGE	
Gauge does not register or is inaccurate	1. On mechanical gauge, Bourdon tube may be bent or kinked. 2. Low oil pressure. Remove sending unit. Idle the engine briefly. If no oil flows from sending unit hole, problem is in engine. 3. Defective gauge. Remove the wire from the sending unit and ground it for an instant with the ignition ON. A good gauge will go to the top of the scale. 4. Defective wiring. Check the wiring to the gauge. If it's OK and the gauge doesn't register when grounded, replace the gauge. 5. Defective sending unit.
ALL GAUGES	
All gauges do not operate All gauges read low or erratically All gauges pegged	1. Blown fuse 2. Defective instrument regulator 3. Defective or dirty instrument voltage regulator 4. Loss of ground between instrument voltage regulator and frame 5. Defective instrument regulator
WARNING LIGHTS	
Light(s) do not come on when ignition is ON, but engine is not started Light comes on with engine running	1. Defective bulb 2. Defective wire 3. Defective sending unit. Disconnect the wire from the sending unit and ground it. Replace the sending unit if the light comes on with the ignition ON. 4. Problem in individual system 5. Defective sending unit

Troubleshooting Clutch Problems

It is false economy to replace individual clutch components. The pressure plate, clutch plate and throwout bearing should be replaced as a set, and the flywheel face inspected, whenever the clutch is overhauled. See Chapter 6 for service procedures.

Condition	Possible Cause
Clutch chatter	1. Grease on driven plate (disc) facing 2. Binding clutch linkage or cable 3. Loose, damaged facings on driven plate (disc) 4. Engine mounts loose 5. Incorrect height adjustment of pressure plate release levers 6. Clutch housing or housing to transmission adapter misalignment 7. Loose driven plate hub
Clutch grabbing	1. Oil, grease on driven plate (disc) facing 2. Broken pressure plate 3. Warped or binding driven plate. Driven plate binding on clutch shaft
Clutch slips	1. Lack of lubrication in clutch linkage or cable (linkage or cable binds, causes incomplete engagement) 2. Incorrect pedal, or linkage adjustment 3. Broken pressure plate springs 4. Weak pressure plate springs 5. Grease on driven plate facings (disc)

TROUBLESHOOTING

Troubleshooting Clutch Problems (cont.)

Condition	Possible Cause
Incomplete clutch release	1. Incorrect pedal or linkage adjustment or linkage or cable binding 2. Incorrect height adjustment on pressure plate release levers 3. Loose, broken facings on driven plate (disc) 4. Bent, dished, warped driven plate caused by overheating
Grinding, whirring grating noise when pedal is depressed	1. Worn or defective throwout bearing 2. Starter drive teeth contacting flywheel ring gear teeth. Look for milled or polished teeth on ring gear.
Squeal, howl, trumpeting noise when pedal is being released (occurs during first inch to inch and one-half of pedal travel)	Pilot bushing worn or lack of lubricant. If bushing appears OK, polish bushing with emery cloth, soak lube wick in oil, lube bushing with oil, apply film of chassis grease to clutch shaft pilot hub, reassemble. NOTE: Bushing wear may be due to misalignment of clutch housing or housing to transmission adapter
Vibration or clutch pedal pulsation with clutch disengaged (pedal fully depressed)	1. Worn or defective engine transmission mounts 2. Flywheel run out. (Flywheel run out at face not to exceed 0.005") 3. Damaged or defective clutch components

Troubleshooting Manual Transmission Problems
See Chapter 6 for service procedures

Condition	Possible Cause
Transmission jumps out of gear	1. Misalignment of transmission case or clutch housing. 2. Worn pilot bearing in crankshaft. 3. Bent transmission shaft. 4. Worn high speed sliding gear. 5. Worn teeth or end-play in clutch shaft. 6. Insufficient spring tension on shifter rail plunger. 7. Bent or loose shifter fork. 8. Gears not engaging completely. 9. Loose or worn bearings on clutch shaft or mainshaft. 10. Worn gear teeth. 11. Worn or damaged detent balls.
Transmission sticks in gear	1. Clutch not releasing fully. 2. Burred or battered teeth on clutch shaft, or sliding sleeve. 3. Burred or battered transmission mainshaft. 4. Frozen synchronizing clutch. 5. Stuck shifter rail plunger. 6. Gearshift lever twisting and binding shifter rail. 7. Battered teeth on high speed sliding gear or on sleeve. 8. Improper lubrication, or lack of lubrication. 9. Corroded transmission parts. 10. Defective mainshaft pilot bearing. 11. Locked gear bearings will give same effect as stuck in gear.
Transmission gears will not synchronize	1. Binding pilot bearing on mainshaft, will synchronize in high gear only. 2. Clutch not releasing fully. 3. Detent spring weak or broken. 4. Weak or broken springs under balls in sliding gear sleeve. 5. Binding bearing on clutch shaft, or binding countershaft. 6. Binding pilot bearing in crankshaft. 7. Badly worn gear teeth. 8. Improper lubrication. 9. Constant mesh gear not turning freely on transmission mainshaft. Will synchronize in that gear only.

TROUBLESHOOTING

Condition	Possible Cause
Gears spinning when shifting into gear from neutral	1. Clutch not releasing fully. 2. In some cases an extremely light lubricant in transmission will cause gears to continue to spin for a short time after clutch is released. 3. Binding pilot bearing in crankshaft.
Transmission noisy in all gears	1. Insufficient lubricant, or improper lubricant. 2. Worn countergear bearings. 3. Worn or damaged main drive gear or countergear. 4. Damaged main drive gear or mainshaft bearings. 5. Worn or damaged countergear anti-lash plate.
Transmission noisy in neutral only	1. Damaged main drive gear bearing. 2. Damaged or loose mainshaft pilot bearing. 3. Worn or damaged countergear anti-lash plate. 4. Worn countergear bearings.
Transmission noisy in one gear only	1. Damaged or worn constant mesh gears. 2. Worn or damaged countergear bearings. 3. Damaged or worn synchronizer.
Transmission noisy in reverse only	1. Worn or damaged reverse idler gear or idler bushing. 2. Worn or damaged mainshaft reverse gear. 3. Worn or damaged reverse countergear. 4. Damaged shift mechanism.

TROUBLESHOOTING AUTOMATIC TRANSMISSION PROBLEMS

Keeping alert to changes in the operating characteristics of the transmission (changing shift points, noises, etc.) can prevent small problems from becoming large ones. If the problem cannot be traced to loose bolts, fluid level, misadjusted linkage, clogged filters or similar problems, you should probably seek professional service.

Transmission Fluid Indications

The appearance and odor of the transmission fluid can give valuable clues to the overall condition of the transmission. Always note the appearance of the fluid when you check the fluid level or change the fluid. Rub a small amount of fluid between your fingers to feel for grit and smell the fluid on the dipstick.

If the fluid appears:	It indicates:
Clear and red colored	Normal operation
Discolored (extremely dark red or brownish) or smells burned	Band or clutch pack failure, usually caused by an overheated transmission. Hauling very heavy loads with insufficient power or failure to change the fluid often result in overheating. Do not confuse this appearance with newer fluids that have a darker red color and a strong odor (though not a burned odor).
Foamy or aerated (light in color and full of bubbles)	1. The level is too high (gear train is churning oil) 2. An internal air leak (air is mixing with the fluid). Have the transmission checked professionally.
Solid residue in the fluid	Defective bands, clutch pack or bearings. Bits of band material or metal abrasives are clinging to the dipstick. Have the transmission checked professionally.
Varnish coating on the dipstick	The transmission fluid is overheating

TROUBLESHOOTING DRIVE AXLE PROBLEMS

First, determine when the noise is most noticeable.

Drive Noise: Produced under vehicle acceleration.

Coast Noise: Produced while coasting with a closed throttle.

Float Noise: Occurs while maintaining constant speed (just enough to keep speed constant) on a level road.

External Noise Elimination

It is advisable to make a thorough road test to determine whether the noise originates in the rear axle or whether it originates from the tires, engine, transmission, wheel bearings or road surface. Noise originating from other places cannot be corrected by servicing the rear axle.

ROAD NOISE

Brick or rough surfaced concrete roads produce noises that seem to come from the rear axle. Road noise is usually identical in Drive or Coast and driving on a different type of road will tell whether the road is the problem.

TIRE NOISE

Tire noise can be mistaken as rear axle noise, even though the tires on the front are at fault. Snow tread and mud tread tires or tires worn unevenly will frequently cause vibrations which seem to originate elsewhere; *temporarily, and for test purposes only,* inflate the tires to 40–50 lbs. This will significantly alter the noise produced by the tires, but will not alter noise from the rear axle. Noises from the rear axle will normally cease at speeds below 30 mph on coast, while tire noise will continue at lower tone as speed is decreased. The rear axle noise will usually change from drive conditions to coast conditions, while tire noise will not. Do not forget to lower the tire pressure to normal after the test is complete.

ENGINE/TRANSMISSION NOISE

Determine at what speed the noise is most pronounced, then stop in a quiet place. With the transmission in Neutral, run the engine through speeds corresponding to road speeds where the noise was noticed. Noises produced with the vehicle standing still are coming from the engine or transmission.

FRONT WHEEL BEARINGS

Front wheel bearing noises, sometimes confused with rear axle noises, will not change when comparing drive and coast conditions. While holding the speed steady, lightly apply the footbrake. This will often cause wheel bearing noise to lessen, as some of the weight is taken off the bearing. Front wheel bearings are easily checked by jacking up the wheels and spinning the wheels. Shaking the wheels will also determine if the wheel bearings are excessively loose.

REAR AXLE NOISES

Eliminating other possible sources can narrow the cause to the rear axle, which normally produces noise from worn gears or bearings. Gear noises tend to peak in a narrow speed range, while bearing noises will usually vary in pitch with engine speeds.

Noise Diagnosis

The Noise Is:	Most Probably Produced By:
1. Identical under Drive or Coast	Road surface, tires or front wheel bearings
2. Different depending on road surface	Road surface or tires
3. Lower as speed is lowered	Tires
4. Similar when standing or moving	Engine or transmission
5. A vibration	Unbalanced tires, rear wheel bearing, unbalanced driveshaft or worn U-joint
6. A knock or click about every two tire revolutions	Rear wheel bearing
7. Most pronounced on turns	Damaged differential gears
8. A steady low-pitched whirring or scraping, starting at low speeds	Damaged or worn pinion bearing
9. A chattering vibration on turns	Wrong differential lubricant or worn clutch plates (limited slip rear axle)
10. Noticed only in Drive, Coast or Float conditions	Worn ring gear and/or pinion gear

TROUBLESHOOTING

Troubleshooting Steering & Suspension Problems

Condition	Possible Cause
Hard steering (wheel is hard to turn)	1. Improper tire pressure 2. Loose or glazed pump drive belt 3. Low or incorrect fluid 4. Loose, bent or poorly lubricated front end parts 5. Improper front end alignment (excessive caster) 6. Bind in steering column or linkage 7. Kinked hydraulic hose 8. Air in hydraulic system 9. Low pump output or leaks in system 10. Obstruction in lines 11. Pump valves sticking or out of adjustment 12. Incorrect wheel alignment
Loose steering (too much play in steering wheel)	1. Loose wheel bearings 2. Faulty shocks 3. Worn linkage or suspension components 4. Loose steering gear mounting or linkage points 5. Steering mechanism worn or improperly adjusted 6. Valve spool improperly adjusted 7. Worn ball joints, tie-rod ends, etc.
Veers or wanders (pulls to one side with hands off steering wheel)	1. Improper tire pressure 2. Improper front end alignment 3. Dragging or improperly adjusted brakes 4. Bent frame 5. Improper rear end alignment 6. Faulty shocks or springs 7. Loose or bent front end components 8. Play in Pitman arm 9. Steering gear mountings loose 10. Loose wheel bearings 11. Binding Pitman arm 12. Spool valve sticking or improperly adjusted 13. Worn ball joints
Wheel oscillation or vibration transmitted through steering wheel	1. Low or uneven tire pressure 2. Loose wheel bearings 3. Improper front end alignment 4. Bent spindle 5. Worn, bent or broken front end components 6. Tires out of round or out of balance 7. Excessive lateral runout in disc brake rotor 8. Loose or bent shock absorber or strut
Noises (see also "Troubleshooting Drive Axle Problems")	1. Loose belts 2. Low fluid, air in system 3. Foreign matter in system 4. Improper lubrication 5. Interference or chafing in linkage 6. Steering gear mountings loose 7. Incorrect adjustment or wear in gear box 8. Faulty valves or wear in pump 9. Kinked hydraulic lines 10. Worn wheel bearings
Poor return of steering	1. Over-inflated tires 2. Improperly aligned front end (excessive caster) 3. Binding in steering column 4. No lubrication in front end 5. Steering gear adjusted too tight
Uneven tire wear (see "How To Read Tire Wear")	1. Incorrect tire pressure 2. Improperly aligned front end 3. Tires out-of-balance 4. Bent or worn suspension parts

TROUBLESHOOTING

HOW TO READ TIRE WEAR

The way your tires wear is a good indicator of other parts of the suspension. Abnormal wear patterns are often caused by the need for simple tire maintenance, or for front end alignment.

Excessive wear at the center of the tread indicates that the air pressure in the tire is consistently too high. The tire is riding on the center of the tread and wearing it prematurely. Occasionally, this wear pattern can result from outrageously wide tires on narrow rims. The cure for this is to replace either the tires or the wheels.

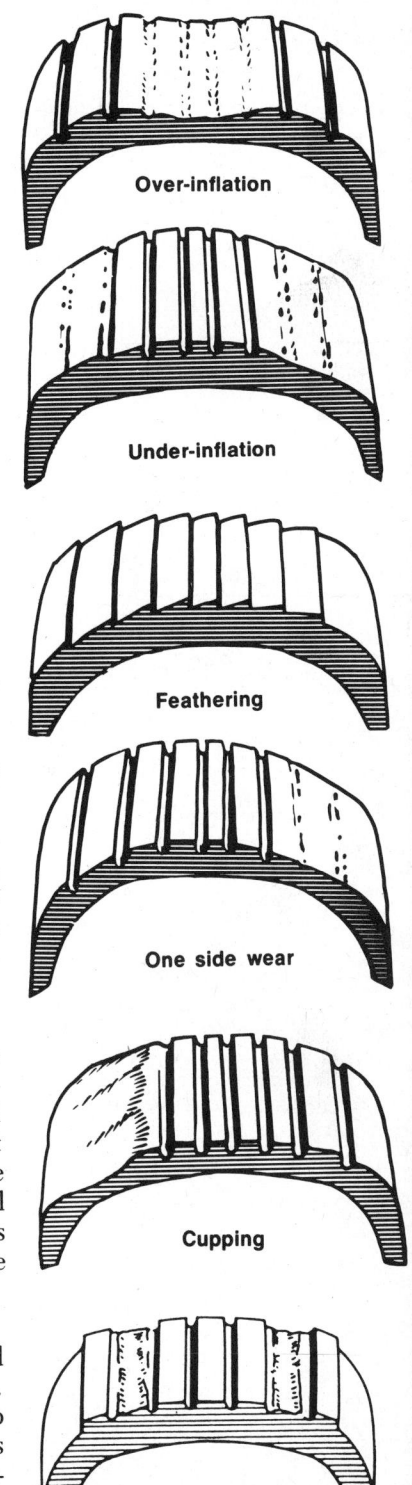

Over-inflation

This type of wear usually results from consistent under-inflation. When a tire is under-inflated, there is too much contact with the road by the outer treads, which wear prematurely. When this type of wear occurs, and the tire pressure is known to be consistently correct, a bent or worn steering component or the need for wheel alignment could be indicated.

Under-inflation

Feathering is a condition when the edge of each tread rib develops a slightly rounded edge on one side and a sharp edge on the other. By running your hand over the tire, you can usually feel the sharper edges before you'll be able to see them. The most common causes of feathering are incorrect toe-in setting or deteriorated bushings in the front suspension.

Feathering

When an inner or outer rib wears faster than the rest of the tire, the need for wheel alignment is indicated. There is excessive camber in the front suspension, causing the wheel to lean too much putting excessive load on one side of the tire. Misalignment could also be due to sagging springs, worn ball joints, or worn control arm bushings. Be sure the vehicle is loaded the way it's normally driven when you have the wheels aligned.

One side wear

Cups or scalloped dips appearing around the edge of the tread almost always indicate worn (sometimes bent) suspension parts. Adjustment of wheel alignment alone will seldom cure the problem. Any worn component that connects the wheel to the suspension can cause this type of wear. Occasionally, wheels that are out of balance will wear like this, but wheel imbalance usually shows up as bald spots between the outside edges and center of the tread.

Cupping

Second-rib wear is usually found only in radial tires, and appears where the steel belts end in relation to the tread. It can be kept to a minimum by paying careful attention to tire pressure and frequently rotating the tires. This is often considered normal wear but excessive amounts indicate that the tires are too wide for the wheels.

Second-rib wear

TROUBLESHOOTING

Troubleshooting Disc Brake Problems

Condition	Possible Cause
Noise—groan—brake noise emanating when slowly releasing brakes (creep-groan)	Not detrimental to function of disc brakes—no corrective action required. (This noise may be eliminated by slightly increasing or decreasing brake pedal efforts.)
Rattle—brake noise or rattle emanating at low speeds on rough roads, (front wheels only).	1. Shoe anti-rattle spring missing or not properly positioned. 2. Excessive clearance between shoe and caliper. 3. Soft or broken caliper seals. 4. Deformed or misaligned disc. 5. Loose caliper.
Scraping	1. Mounting bolts too long. 2. Loose wheel bearings. 3. Bent, loose, or misaligned splash shield.
Front brakes heat up during driving and fail to release	1. Operator riding brake pedal. 2. Stop light switch improperly adjusted. 3. Sticking pedal linkage. 4. Frozen or seized piston. 5. Residual pressure valve in master cylinder. 6. Power brake malfunction. 7. Proportioning valve malfunction.
Leaky brake caliper	1. Damaged or worn caliper piston seal. 2. Scores or corrosion on surface of cylinder bore.
Grabbing or uneven brake action—Brakes pull to one side	1. Causes listed under "Brakes Pull". 2. Power brake malfunction. 3. Low fluid level in master cylinder. 4. Air in hydraulic system. 5. Brake fluid, oil or grease on linings. 6. Unmatched linings. 7. Distorted brake pads. 8. Frozen or seized pistons. 9. Incorrect tire pressure. 10. Front end out of alignment. 11. Broken rear spring. 12. Brake caliper pistons sticking. 13. Restricted hose or line. 14. Caliper not in proper alignment to braking disc. 15. Stuck or malfunctioning metering valve. 16. Soft or broken caliper seals. 17. Loose caliper.
Brake pedal can be depressed without braking effect	1. Air in hydraulic system or improper bleeding procedure. 2. Leak past primary cup in master cylinder. 3. Leak in system. 4. Rear brakes out of adjustment. 5. Bleeder screw open.
Excessive pedal travel	1. Air, leak, or insufficient fluid in system or caliper. 2. Warped or excessively tapered shoe and lining assembly. 3. Excessive disc runout. 4. Rear brake adjustment required. 5. Loose wheel bearing adjustment. 6. Damaged caliper piston seal. 7. Improper brake fluid (boil). 8. Power brake malfunction. 9. Weak or soft hoses.

Troubleshooting Disc Brake Problems (cont.)

Condition	Possible Cause
Brake roughness or chatter (pedal pumping)	1. Excessive thickness variation of braking disc. 2. Excessive lateral runout of braking disc. 3. Rear brake drums out-of-round. 4. Excessive front bearing clearance.
Excessive pedal effort	1. Brake fluid, oil or grease on linings. 2. Incorrect lining. 3. Frozen or seized pistons. 4. Power brake malfunction. 5. Kinked or collapsed hose or line. 6. Stuck metering valve. 7. Scored caliper or master cylinder bore. 8. Seized caliper pistons.
Brake pedal fades (pedal travel increases with foot on brake)	1. Rough master cylinder or caliper bore. 2. Loose or broken hydraulic lines/connections. 3. Air in hydraulic system. 4. Fluid level low. 5. Weak or soft hoses. 6. Inferior quality brake shoes or fluid. 7. Worn master cylinder piston cups or seals.

Troubleshooting Drum Brakes

Condition	Possible Cause
Pedal goes to floor	1. Fluid low in reservoir. 2. Air in hydraulic system. 3. Improperly adjusted brake. 4. Leaking wheel cylinders. 5. Loose or broken brake lines. 6. Leaking or worn master cylinder. 7. Excessively worn brake lining.
Spongy brake pedal	1. Air in hydraulic system. 2. Improper brake fluid (low boiling point). 3. Excessively worn or cracked brake drums. 4. Broken pedal pivot bushing.
Brakes pulling	1. Contaminated lining. 2. Front end out of alignment. 3. Incorrect brake adjustment. 4. Unmatched brake lining. 5. Brake drums out of round. 6. Brake shoes distorted. 7. Restricted brake hose or line. 8. Broken rear spring. 9. Worn brake linings. 10. Uneven lining wear. 11. Glazed brake lining. 12. Excessive brake lining dust. 13. Heat spotted brake drums. 14. Weak brake return springs. 15. Faulty automatic adjusters. 16. Low or incorrect tire pressure.

TROUBLESHOOTING

Condition	Possible Cause
Squealing brakes	1. Glazed brake lining. 2. Saturated brake lining. 3. Weak or broken brake shoe retaining spring. 4. Broken or weak brake shoe return spring. 5. Incorrect brake lining. 6. Distorted brake shoes. 7. Bent support plate. 8. Dust in brakes or scored brake drums. 9. Linings worn below limit. 10. Uneven brake lining wear. 11. Heat spotted brake drums.
Chirping brakes	1. Out of round drum or eccentric axle flange pilot.
Dragging brakes	1. Incorrect wheel or parking brake adjustment. 2. Parking brakes engaged or improperly adjusted. 3. Weak or broken brake shoe return spring. 4. Brake pedal binding. 5. Master cylinder cup sticking. 6. Obstructed master cylinder relief port. 7. Saturated brake lining. 8. Bent or out of round brake drum. 9. Contaminated or improper brake fluid. 10. Sticking wheel cylinder pistons. 11. Driver riding brake pedal. 12. Defective proportioning valve. 13. Insufficient brake shoe lubricant.
Hard pedal	1. Brake booster inoperative. 2. Incorrect brake lining. 3. Restricted brake line or hose. 4. Frozen brake pedal linkage. 5. Stuck wheel cylinder. 6. Binding pedal linkage. 7. Faulty proportioning valve.
Wheel locks	1. Contaminated brake lining. 2. Loose or torn brake lining. 3. Wheel cylinder cups sticking. 4. Incorrect wheel bearing adjustment. 5. Faulty proportioning valve.
Brakes fade (high speed)	1. Incorrect lining. 2. Overheated brake drums. 3. Incorrect brake fluid (low boiling temperature). 4. Saturated brake lining. 5. Leak in hydraulic system. 6. Faulty automatic adjusters.
Pedal pulsates	1. Bent or out of round brake drum.
Brake chatter and shoe knock	1. Out of round brake drum. 2. Loose support plate. 3. Bent support plate. 4. Distorted brake shoes. 5. Machine grooves in contact face of brake drum (Shoe Knock). 6. Contaminated brake lining. 7. Missing or loose components. 8. Incorrect lining material. 9. Out-of-round brake drums. 10. Heat spotted or scored brake drums. 11. Out-of-balance wheels.

TROUBLESHOOTING

Troubleshooting Drum Brakes (cont.)

Condition	Possible Cause
Brakes do not self adjust	1. Adjuster screw frozen in thread. 2. Adjuster screw corroded at thrust washer. 3. Adjuster lever does not engage star wheel. 4. Adjuster installed on wrong wheel.
Brake light glows	1. Leak in the hydraulic system. 2. Air in the system. 3. Improperly adjusted master cylinder pushrod. 4. Uneven lining wear. 5. Failure to center combination valve or proportioning valve.

Mechanic's Data

General Conversion Table

Multiply By	To Convert	To	
	LENGTH		
2.54	Inches	Centimeters	.3937
25.4	Inches	Millimeters	.03937
30.48	Feet	Centimeters	.0328
.304	Feet	Meters	3.28
.914	Yards	Meters	1.094
1.609	Miles	Kilometers	.621
	VOLUME		
.473	Pints	Liters	2.11
.946	Quarts	Liters	1.06
3.785	Gallons	Liters	.264
.016	Cubic inches	Liters	61.02
16.39	Cubic inches	Cubic cms.	.061
28.3	Cubic feet	Liters	.0353
	MASS (Weight)		
28.35	Ounces	Grams	.035
.4536	Pounds	Kilograms	2.20
—	To obtain	From	Multiply by

Multiply By	To Convert	To	
	AREA		
.645	Square inches	Square cms.	.155
.836	Square yds.	Square meters	1.196
	FORCE		
4.448	Pounds	Newtons	.225
.138	Ft./lbs.	Kilogram/meters	7.23
1.36	Ft./lbs.	Newton-meters	.737
.112	In./lbs.	Newton-meters	8.844
	PRESSURE		
.068	Psi	Atmospheres	14.7
6.89	Psi	Kilopascals	.145
	OTHER		
1.104	Horsepower (DIN)	Horsepower (SAE)	.9861
.746	Horsepower (SAE)	Kilowatts (KW)	1.34
1.60	Mph	Km/h	.625
.425	Mpg	Km/1	2.35
—	To obtain	From	Multiply by

Tap Drill Sizes

National Coarse or U.S.S.

Screw & Tap Size	Threads Per Inch	Use Drill Number
No. 5	40	39
No. 6	32	36
No. 8	32	29
No. 10	24	25
No. 12	24	17
1/4	20	8
5/16	18	F
3/8	16	5/16
7/16	14	U
1/2	13	27/64
9/16	12	31/64
5/8	11	17/32
3/4	10	21/32
7/8	9	49/64

National Coarse or U.S.S.

Screw & Tap Size	Threads Per Inch	Use Drill Number
1	8	7/8
1 1/8	7	63/64
1 1/4	7	1 7/64
1 1/2	6	1 11/32

National Fine or S.A.E.

Screw & Tap Size	Threads Per Inch	Use Drill Number
No. 5	44	37
No. 6	40	33
No. 8	36	29
No. 10	32	21

National Fine or S.A.E.

Screw & Tap Size	Threads Per Inch	Use Drill Number
No. 12	28	15
1/4	28	3
6/16	24	1
3/8	24	Q
7/16	20	W
1/2	20	29/64
9/16	18	33/64
5/8	18	37/64
3/4	16	11/16
7/8	14	13/16
1 1/8	12	1 3/64
1 1/4	12	1 11/64
1 1/2	12	1 27/64

MECHANIC'S DATA 259

Drill Sizes In Decimal Equivalents

Inch	Decimal	Wire	mm	Inch	Decimal	Wire	mm	Inch	Decimal	Wire & Letter	mm	Inch	Decimal	Letter	mm	Inch	Decimal	mm
1/64	.0156		.39		.0730	49			.1614		4.1		.2717		6.9		.4331	11.0
	.0157		.4		.0748		1.9		.1654		4.2		.2720	I		7/16	.4375	11.11
	.0160	78			.0760	48			.1660	19			.2756		7.0		.4528	11.5
	.0165		.42		.0768		1.95		.1673		4.25		.2770	J		29/64	.4531	11.51
	.0173		.44	5/64	.0781		1.98		.1693		4.3		.2795		7.1	15/32	.4688	11.90
	.0177		.45		.0785	47			.1695	18			.2810	K			.4724	12.0
	.0180	77			.0787		2.0	11/64	.1719		4.36	9/32	.2812		7.14	31/64	.4844	12.30
	.0181		.46		.0807		2.05		.1730	17			.2835		7.2		.4921	12.5
	.0189		.48		.0810	46			.1732		4.4		.2854		7.25	1/2	.5000	12.70
	.0197		.5		.0820	45			.1770	16			.2874		7.3		.5118	13.0
	.0200	76			.0827		2.1		.1772		4.5		.2900	L		33/64	.5156	13.09
	.0210	75			.0846		2.15		.1800	15			.2913		7.4	17/32	.5312	13.49
	.0217		.55		.0860	44			.1811		4.6		.2950	M			.5315	13.5
	.0225	74			.0866		2.2		.1820	14			.2953		7.5	35/64	.5469	13.89
	.0236	73			.0886		2.25		.1850	13		19/64	.2969		7.54		.5512	14.0
	.0240	73	.6		.0890	43			.1850		4.7		.2992		7.6	9/16	.5625	14.28
	.0250	72			.0906		2.3		.1870		4.75		.3020	N			.5709	14.5
	.0256		.65		.0925		2.35	3/16	.1875		4.76		.3031		7.7	37/64	.5781	14.68
	.0260	71			.0935	42			.1890		4.8		.3051		7.75		.5906	15.0
	.0276		.7	3/32	.0938		2.38		.1890	12			.3071		7.8	19/32	.5938	15.08
	.0280	70			.0945		2.4		.1910	11			.3110		7.9	39/64	.6094	15.47
	.0292	69			.0960	41			.1929		4.9	5/16	.3125		7.93		.6102	15.5
	.0295		.75		.0965		2.45		.1935	10			.3150		8.0	5/8	.6250	15.87
	.0310	68			.0980	40			.1960	9			.3160	O			.6299	16.0
1/32	.0312		.79		.0981		2.5		.1969		5.0		.3189		8.1	41/64	.6406	16.27
	.0315		.8		.0995	39			.1990	8			.3228		8.2		.6496	16.5
	.0320	67			.1015	38			.2008		5.1		.3230	P		21/32	.6562	16.66
	.0330	66			.1024		2.6		.2010	7			.3248		8.25		.6693	17.0
	.0335		.85		.1040	37		13/64	.2031		5.16		.3268		8.3	43/64	.6719	17.06
	.0350	65			.1063		2.7		.2040	6		21/64	.3281		8.33	11/16	.6875	17.46
	.0354		.9		.1065	36			.2047		5.2		.3307		8.4		.6890	17.5
	.0360	64			.1083		2.75		.2055	5			.3320	Q		45/64	.7031	17.85
	.0370	63		7/64	.1094		2.77		.2067		5.25		.3346		8.5		.7087	18.0
	.0374		.95		.1100	35			.2087		5.3		.3386		8.6	23/32	.7188	18.25
	.0380	62			.1102		2.8		.2090	4			.3390	R			.7283	18.5
	.0390	61			.1110	34			.2126		5.4		.3425		8.7	47/64	.7344	18.65
	.0394		1.0		.1130	33			.2130	3		11/32	.3438		8.73		.7480	19.0
	.0400	60			.1142		2.9		.2165		5.5		.3445		8.75	3/4	.7500	19.05
	.0410	59			.1160	32			.2188	7/32	5.55		.3465		8.8	49/64	.7656	19.44
	.0413		1.05		.1181		3.0		.2205		5.6		.3480	S			.7677	19.5
	.0420	58			.1200	31			.2210	2			.3504		8.9	25/32	.7812	19.84
	.0430	57			.1220		3.1		.2244		5.7		.3543		9.0		.7874	20.0
	.0433		1.1	1/8	.1250		3.17		.2264		5.75		.3580	T		51/64	.7969	20.24
	.0453		1.15		.1260		3.2		.2280	1			.3583		9.1		.8071	20.5
	.0465	56			.1280		3.25		.2283		5.8	23/64	.3594		9.12	13/16	.8125	20.63
3/64	.0469		1.19		.1285	30			.2323		5.9		.3622		9.2		.8268	21.0
	.0472		1.2		.1299		3.3		.2340	A			.3642		9.25	53/64	.8281	21.03
	.0492		1.25		.1339		3.4	15/64	.2344		5.95		.3661		9.3	27/32	.8438	21.43
	.0512		1.3		.1360	29			.2362		6.0		.3680	U			.8465	21.5
	.0520	55			.1378		3.5		.2380	B			.3701		9.4	55/64	.8594	21.82
	.0531		1.35		.1405	28			.2402		6.1		.3740		9.5		.8661	22.0
	.0550	54		9/64	.1406		3.57		.2420	C		3/8	.3750		9.52	7/8	.8750	22.22
	.0551		1.4		.1417		3.6		.2441		6.2		.3770	V			.8858	22.5
	.0571		1.45		.1440	27			.2460	D			.3780		9.6	57/64	.8906	22.62
	.0591		1.5		.1457		3.7		.2461		6.25		.3819		9.7		.9055	23.0
	.0595	53			.1470	26			.2480		6.3		.3839		9.75	29/32	.9062	23.01
	.0610		1.55		.1476		3.75	1/4	.2500	E	6.35		.3858		9.8	59/64	.9219	23.41
1/16	.0625		1.59		.1495	25			.2520		6.		.3860	W			.9252	23.5
	.0630		1.6		.1496		3.8		.2559		6.5		.3898		9.9	15/16	.9375	23.81
	.0635	52			.1520	24			.2570	F		25/64	.3906		9.92		.9449	24.0
	.0650		1.65		.1535		3.9		.2598		6.6		.3937		10.0	61/64	.9531	24.2
	.0669		1.7		.1540	23			.2610	G			.3970	X			.9646	24.5
	.0670	51		5/32	.1562		3.96		.2638		6.7		.4040	Y		31/32	.9688	24.6
	.0689		1.75		.1570	22		17/64	.2656		6.74	13/32	.4062		10.31		.9843	25.0
	.0700	50			.1575		4.0		.2657		6.75		.4130	Z		63/64	.9844	25.0
	.0709		1.8		.1590	21			.2660	H			.4134		10.5	1	1.0000	25.4
	.0728		1.85		.1610	20			.2677		6.8	27/64	.4219		10.71			

Index

A

Air cleaner, 7
Air conditioning inspection, 18
Air pump, 102
Alternator, 49
Antifreeze, 25
Automatic transmission, 174
    Adjustments, 175
    Filter change, 174
    Pan removal, 174
    Removal and installation, 177
Axle
    Axle shaft, bearings and seals, 182
    Fluid recommendations, 24
    Lubricant level, 24

B

Ball joints, 188
Battery
    Fluid level, 11
    Jump starting, 29
    Removal and installation, 53
Belts, 11
Brakes
    Adjustment, 219
    Bleeding, 206
    Disc brakes, 206
        Caliper, 209, 211
        Pads, 207, 211
        Rotor, 209
    Drum brakes, 216
        Drum, 216
        Shoes, 217
        Wheel cylinder, 217
    Fluid level, 26
    Master cylinder, 203
    Parking brake, 222
    Proportioning valve, 205

C

Calipers, 209, 211
Camber, 192
Camshaft and bearings, 84
Capacities, 22
Carburetor
    Adjustments, 116
    Overhaul, 116
    Replacement, 115
    Specifications, 142
Caster, 192
Chassis lubrication, 27
Charging system, 49
Choke, 114
Circuit breakers, 163
Clutch, 170
Coil (ignition), 41
Compression testing, 69

Connecting rods and bearings, 92
Constant velocity (CV) joints, 185
Control arm
    Lower, 189
Cooling system, 99
Crankcase ventilation valve, 9
Crankshaft, 92
Cylinder head
    Inspection, 74
    Rebuilding, 74
    Removal and installation, 64
Cylinders
    Inspection, 90
    Reboring, 90
    Refinishing, 90

D

Differential
    Fluid level, 24
Disc brakes, 206, 211
Distributor
    Removal and installation, 48
Drive axle, 181
Driveshaft, 179
Drum brakes, 216

E

EGR valve, 105
Electrical
    Chassis, 148
    Engine, 48
Electronic Ignition, 33
Emission controls, 102
Engine
    Camshaft, 84
    Cylinder head, 64
    Cylinders, 90
    Exhaust manifold, 62
    Fluids and lubricants, 21
    Front (timing) cover, 79
    Front seal, 79
    Identification, 5
    Intake manifold, 60
    Main bearings, 92
    Oil pump, 98
    Pistons, 87
    Rear main seal, 97
    Removal and installation, 53
    Rings, 87
    Rocker arms and/or shafts, 59
    Specifications, 54
    Timing belt, 83
    Timing chains, 79
    Timing gears, 79
    Turbocharger, 63
    Valve guides, 75
    Valves, 75
    Valve springs, 75

INDEX

Evaporative canister, 9
Exhaust manifold, 62

F

Firing orders, 43
Flashers, 163
Fluids and lubricants, 21
    Automatic transmission, 24
    Battery, 11
    Chassis greasing, 27
    Coolant, 25
    Drive axle, 24
    Engine oil, 22
    Manual transmission, 24
    Master cylinder, 26
    Power steering pump, 27
Front brakes, 206
Front hubs, 191
Front Suspension
    Ball joints, 188
    Lower control arm, 189
    Shock absorbers, 189
    Springs, 186
    Struts, 190
    Wheel alignment, 192
Front wheel bearings, 191
Fuel injection, 45, 130
Fuel filter, 20
Fuel pump, 110
Fuel system, 110
Fuel tank, 142
Fuses and circuit breakers, 163
Fusible links, 163

G

Gearshift linkage adjustment
    Automatic, 176

H

Halfshafts, 184
Headlights, 163
Heater
    Blower, 148
    Core, 149

I

Identification
    Engine, 5
    Transmission, 6
    Vehicle, 5
Idle speed and mixture adjustment, 44
Ignition switch, 200
Ignition timing, 41
Instrument cluster, 158
Instrument panel, 161
Intake manifold, 60

J

Jacking points, 28
Jump starting, 29

K

Knuckles, 191

L

Lower control arm, 189
Lubrication
    Chassis, 27
    Differential, 24
    Engine, 22
    Transmission, 24

M

Main bearings, 92
Maintenance intervals, 30
Manifolds
    Intake, 60
    Exhaust, 62
Manual transmission, 167
Master cylinder, 203
Mechanic's data, 259
Model identification, 5

N

Neutral safety switch, 176

O

Oil and fuel recommendations, 21
Oil and filter change (engine), 23
Oil level check, 22
Oil pan, 94
Oil pump, 98

P

Parking brake, 222
Pistons, 87
PCV valve, 9
Pushing, 28

R

Radiator, 99
Radio, 152
Rear axle, 182, 185
Rear brakes
Rear main oil seal, 97
Rear suspension
    Shock absorbers, 193
    Springs, 195
Rear wheel bearings, 182
Regulator, 51
Rings, 87

262 INDEX

Rocker arms or shat, 59
Routine maintenance, 7

S

Safety notice ii, 4
Serial number location, 5
Shock absorbers
  Front, 189
  Rear, 193
Spark plugs, 31
Special tools, ii
Specifications
  Brakes, 203
  Camshaft, 57
  Capacities, 22
  Carburetorr, 142
  Crankshaft and connecting rod, 56
  General engine, 54
  Piston and ring, 57
  Torque, 55
  Tune-up, 32
  Valves, 55
Speedometer cable, 161
Springs
  Front, 186
  Rear, 192
Starter, 51
Steering gear, 196
Steering knuckles, 191
Steering linkage, 198
Steering wheel, 198
Stripped threads, 67

T

Thermostat, 100
Tie rod ends, 198
Timing (ignition), 41
Timing belt, 83

Timing chain, 79
Timing gears, 79
Tires, 20
Tools, 2
Transmission
  Automatic, 174
  Manual, 167
Troubleshooting, 224
Turbocharger, 63
Tune-up
  Procedures, 31
  Specifications, 32
Turn signal switch, 200

U

U-joints, 180

V

Valve guides, 77
Valves
  Adjustment, 46, 74
  Service, 75
  Specifications, 55
Valve springs, 75
Vehicle identification, 5

W

Water pump, 100
Wheel alignment, 192
Wheel bearings, 191, 209
Wheel cylinders, 217
Windshield wipers
  Arm, 155
  Blade, 19
  Linkage, 158
  Motor, 157
  Rear window wiper, 158

Chilton's Repair & Tune-Up Guides

The Complete line covers domestic cars, imports, trucks, vans, RV's and 4-wheel drive vehicles.

RTUG Title	Part No.
AMC 1975-82	7199
Covers all U.S. and Canadian models	
Aspen/Volare 1976-80	6637
Covers all U.S. and Canadian models	
Audi 1970-73	5902
Covers all U.S. and Canadian models.	
Audi 4000/5000 1978-81	7028
Covers all U.S. and Canadian models including turbocharged and diesel engines	
Barracuda/Challenger 1965-72	5807
Covers all U.S. and Canadian models	
Blazer/Jimmy 1969-82	6931
Covers all U.S. and Canadian 2- and 4-wheel drive models, including diesel engines	
BMW 1970-82	6844
Covers U.S. and Canadian models	
Buick/Olds/Pontiac 1975-85	7308
Covers all U.S. and Canadian full size rear wheel drive models	
Cadillac 1967-84	7462
Covers all U.S. and Canadian rear wheel drive models	
Camaro 1967-81	6735
Covers all U.S. and Canadian models	
Camaro 1982-85	7317
Covers all U.S. and Canadian models	
Capri 1970-77	6695
Covers all U.S. and Canadian models	
Caravan/Voyager 1984-85	7482
Covers all U.S. and Canadian models	
Century/Regal 1975-85	7307
Covers all U.S. and Canadian rear wheel drive models, including turbocharged engines	
Champ/Arrow/Sapporo 1978-83	7041
Covers all U.S. and Canadian models	
Chevette/1000 1976-86	6836
Covers all U.S. and Canadian models	
Chevrolet 1968-85	7135
Covers all U.S. and Canadian models	
Chevrolet 1968-79 Spanish	7082
Chevrolet/GMC Pick-Ups 1970-82 Spanish	7468
Chevrolet/GMC Pick-Ups and Suburban 1970-86	6936
Covers all U.S. and Canadian $1/2$, $3/4$ and 1 ton models, including 4-wheel drive and diesel engines	
Chevrolet LUV 1972-81	6815
Covers all U.S. and Canadian models	
Chevrolet Mid-Size 1964-86	6840
Covers all U.S. and Canadian models of 1964-77 Chevelle, Malibu and Malibu SS; 1974-77 Laguna; 1978-85 Malibu; 1970-86 Monte Carlo; 1964-84 El Camino, including diesel engines	
Chevrolet Nova 1986	7658
Covers all U.S. and Canadian models	
Chevy/GMC Vans 1967-84	6930
Covers all U.S. and Canadian models of $1/2$, $3/4$, and 1 ton vans, cutaways, and motor home chassis, including diesel engines	
Chevy S-10 Blazer/GMC S-15 Jimmy 1982-85	7383
Covers all U.S. and Canadian models	
Chevy S-10/GMC S-15 Pick-Ups 1982-85	7310
Covers all U.S. and Canadian models	
Chevy II/Nova 1962-79	6841
Covers all U.S. and Canadian models	
Chrysler K- and E-Car 1981-85	7163
Covers all U.S. and Canadian front wheel drive models	
Colt/Challenger/Vista/Conquest 1971-85	7037
Covers all U.S. and Canadian models	
Corolla/Carina/Tercel/Starlet 1970-85	7036
Covers all U.S. and Canadian models	
Corona/Cressida/Crown/Mk.II/Camry/Van 1970-84	7044
Covers all U.S. and Canadian models	

RTUG Title	Part No.
Corvair 1960-69	6691
Covers all U.S. and Canadian models	
Corvette 1953-62	6576
Covers all U.S. and Canadian models	
Corvette 1963-84	6843
Covers all U.S. and Canadian models	
Cutlass 1970-85	6933
Covers all U.S. and Canadian models	
Dart/Demon 1968-76	6324
Covers all U.S. and Canadian models	
Datsun 1961-72	5790
Covers all U.S. and Canadian models of Nissan Patrol; 1500, 1600 and 2000 sports cars; Pick-Ups; 410, 411, 510, 1200 and 240Z	
Datsun 1973-80 Spanish	7083
Datsun/Nissan F-10, 310, Stanza, Pulsar 1977-86	7196
Covers all U.S. and Canadian models	
Datsun/Nissan Pick-Ups 1970-84	6816
Covers all U.S and Canadian models	
Datsun/Nissan Z & ZX 1970-86	6932
Covers all U.S. and Canadian models	
Datsun/Nissan 1200, 210, Sentra 1973-86	7197
Covers all U.S. and Canadian models	
Datsun/Nissan 200SX, 510, 610, 710, 810, Maxima 1973-84	7170
Covers all U.S. and Canadian models	
Dodge 1968-77	6554
Covers all U.S. and Canadian models	
Dodge Charger 1967-70	6486
Covers all U.S. and Canadian models	
Dodge/Plymouth Trucks 1967-84	7459
Covers all $1/2$, $3/4$, and 1 ton 2- and 4-wheel drive U.S. and Canadian models, including diesel engines	
Dodge/Plymouth Vans 1967-84	6934
Covers all $1/2$, $3/4$, and 1 ton U.S. and Canadian models of vans, cutaways and motor home chassis	
D-50/Arrow Pick-Up 1979-81	7032
Covers all U.S. and Canadian models	
Fairlane/Torino 1962-75	6320
Covers all U.S. and Canadian models	
Fairmont/Zephyr 1978-83	6965
Covers all U.S. and Canadian models	
Fiat 1969-81	7042
Covers all U.S. and Canadian models	
Fiesta 1978-80	6846
Covers all U.S. and Canadian models	
Firebird 1967-81	5996
Covers all U.S. and Canadian models	
Firebird 1982-85	7345
Covers all U.S. and Canadian models	
Ford 1968-79 Spanish	7084
Ford Bronco 1966-83	7140
Covers all U.S. and Canadian models	
Ford Bronco II 1984	7408
Covers all U.S. and Canadian models	
Ford Courier 1972-82	6983
Covers all U.S. and Canadian models	
Ford/Mercury Front Wheel Drive 1981-85	7055
Covers all U.S. and Canadian models Escort, EXP, Tempo, Lynx, LN-7 and Topaz	
Ford/Mercury/Lincoln 1968-85	6842
Covers all U.S. and Canadian models of FORD Country Sedan, Country Squire, Crown Victoria, Custom, Custom 500, Galaxie 500, LTD through 1982, Ranch Wagon, and XL; MERCURY Colony Park, Commuter, Marquis through 1982, Gran Marquis, Monterey and Park Lane; LINCOLN Continental and Towne Car	
Ford/Mercury/Lincoln Mid-Size 1971-85	6696
Covers all U.S. and Canadian models of FORD Elite, 1983-85 LTD, 1977-79 LTD II, Ranchero, Torino, Gran Torino, 1977-85 Thunderbird; MERCURY 1972-85 Cougar,	

continued on next page

RTUG Title	Part No.	RTUG Title	Part No.
1983-85 Marquis, Montego, 1980-85 XR-7; LINCOLN 1982-85 Continental, 1984-85 Mark VII, 1978-80 Versailles		**Mercedes-Benz 1974-84** Covers all U.S. and Canadian models	6809
Ford Pick-Ups 1965-86 Covers all ½, ¾ and 1 ton, 2- and 4-wheel drive U.S. and Canadian pick-up, chassis cab and camper models, including diesel engines	6913	**Mitsubishi, Cordia, Tredia, Starion, Galant 1983-85** Covers all U.S. and Canadian models	7583
		MG 1961-81 Covers all U.S. and Canadian models	6780
Ford Pick-Ups 1965-82 Spanish	7469	**Mustang/Capri/Merkur 1979-85** Covers all U.S. and Canadian models	6963
Ford Ranger 1983-84 Covers all U.S. and Canadian models	7338	**Mustang/Cougar 1965-73** Covers all U.S. and Canadian models	6542
Ford Vans 1961-86 Covers all U.S. and Canadian ½, ¾ and 1 ton van and cutaway chassis models, including diesel engines	6849	**Mustang II 1974-78** Covers all U.S. and Canadian models	6812
		Omni/Horizon/Rampage 1978-84 Covers all U.S. and Canadian models of DODGE omni, Miser, 024, Charger 2.2; PLYMOUTH Horizon, Miser, TC3, TC3 Tourismo; Rampage	6845
GM A-Body 1982-85 Covers all front wheel drive U.S. and Canadian models of BUICK Century, CHEVROLET Celebrity, OLDSMOBILE Cutlass Ciera and PONTIAC 6000	7309		
		Opel 1971-75 Covers all U.S. and Canadian models	6575
GM C-Body 1985 Covers all front wheel drive U.S. and Canadian models of BUICK Electra Park Avenue and Electra T-Type, CADILLAC Fleetwood and deVille, OLDSMOBILE 98 Regency and Regency Brougham	7587	**Peugeot 1970-74** Covers all U.S. and Canadian models	5982
		Pinto/Bobcat 1971-80 Covers all U.S. and Canadian models	7027
		Plymouth 1968-76 Covers all U.S. and Canadian models	6552
		Pontiac Fiero 1984-85 Covers all U.S. and Canadian models	7571
GM J-Car 1982-85 Covers all U.S. and Canadian models of BUICK Skyhawk, CHEVROLET Cavalier, CADILLAC Cimarron, OLDSMOBILE Firenza and PONTIAC 2000 and Sunbird	7059	**Pontiac Mid-Size 1974-83** Covers all U.S. and Canadian models of Ventura, Grand Am, LeMans, Grand LeMans, GTO, Phoenix, and Grand Prix	7346
		Porsche 924/928 1976-81 Covers all U.S. and Canadian models	7048
GM N-Body 1985-86 Covers all U.S. and Canadian models of front wheel drive BUICK Somerset and Skylark, OLDSMOBILE Calais, and PONTIAC Grand Am	7657	**Renault 1975-85** Covers all U.S. and Canadian models	7165
		Roadrunner/Satellite/Belvedere/GTX 1968-73 Covers all U.S. and Canadian models	5821
GM X-Body 1980-85 Covers all U.S. and Canadian models of BUICK Skylark, CHEVROLET Citation, OLDSMOBILE Omega and PONTIAC Phoenix	7049	**RX-7 1979-81** Covers all U.S. and Canadian models	7031
		SAAB 99 1969-75 Covers all U.S. and Canadian models	5988
GM Subcompact 1971-80 Covers all U.S. and Canadian models of BUICK Skyhawk (1975-80), CHEVROLET Vega and Monza, OLDSMOBILE Starfire, and PONTIAC Astre and 1975-80 Sunbird	6935	**SAAB 900 1979-85** Covers all U.S. and Canadian models	7572
		Snowmobiles 1976-80 Covers Arctic Cat, John Deere, Kawasaki, Polaris, Ski-Doo and Yamaha	6978
Granada/Monarch 1975-82 Covers all U.S. and Canadian models	6937	**Subaru 1970-84** Covers all U.S. and Canadian models	6982
Honda 1973-84 Covers all U.S. and Canadian models	6980	**Tempest/GTO/LeMans 1968-73** Covers all U.S. and Canadian models	5905
International Scout 1967-73 Covers all U.S. and Canadian models	5912	**Toyota 1966-70** Covers all U.S. and Canadian models of Corona, MkII, Corolla, Crown, Land Cruiser, Stout and Hi-Lux	5795
Jeep 1945-87 Covers all U.S. and Canadian CJ-2A, CJ-3A, CJ-3B, CJ-5, CJ-6, CJ-7, Scrambler and Wrangler models	6817		
		Toyota 1970-79 Spanish	7467
		Toyota Celica/Supra 1971-85 Covers all U.S. and Canadian models	7043
Jeep Wagoneer, Commando, Cherokee, Truck 1957-86 Covers all U.S. and Canadian models of Wagoneer, Cherokee, Grand Wagoneer, Jeepster, Jeepster Commando, J-100, J-200, J-300, J-10, J20, FC-150 and FC-170	6739	**Toyota Trucks 1970-85** Covers all U.S. and Canadian models of pick-ups, Land Cruiser and 4Runner	7035
		Valiant/Duster 1968-76	6326
		Volvo 1956-69 Covers all U.S. and Canadian models	6529
Laser/Daytona 1984-85 Covers all U.S. and Canadian models	7563	**Volvo 1970-83** Covers all U.S. and Canadian models	7040
Maverick/Comet 1970-77 Covers all U.S. and Canadian models	6634	**VW Front Wheel Drive 1974-85** Covers all U.S. and Canadian models	6962
Mazda 1971-84 Covers all U.S. and Canadian models of RX-2, RX-3, RX-4, 808, 1300, 1600, Cosmo, GLC and 626	6981	**VW 1949-71** Covers all U.S. and Canadian models	5796
		VW 1970-79 Spanish	7081
Mazda Pick-Ups 1972-86 Covers all U.S. and Canadian models	7659	**VW 1970-81** Covers all U.S. and Canadian Beetles, Karmann Ghia, Fastback, Squareback, Vans, 411 and 412	6837
Mercedes-Benz 1959-70 Covers all U.S. and Canadian models	6065		
Merecedes-Benz 1968-73 Covers all U.S. and Canadian models	5907		

Chilton's Repair & Tune-Up Guides are available at your local retailer or by mailing a check or money order for **$12.50** plus **$2.25** to cover postage and handling to:

731 205

A 73 88 1

Chilton Book Company
Dept. DM
Radnor, PA 19089

NOTE: When ordering be sure to include your name & address, book part No. & title.